Classic 1000 Slow Cooker Recipes

SUE SPITLER

foulsham
LONDON • NEW YORK • TORONTO • SYDNEY

foulsham

Capital Point, 33 Bath Road, Slough, Berkshire, SL1 3UF, England

Foulsham books can be found in all good bookshops and direct from www.foulsham.com

ISBN: 978-0-572-03596-9

With additional recipes by Catherine Atkinson and Carolyn Humphries

A CIP record for this book is available from the British Library.

Many thanks to Perrin Davis, the dedicated editor of the US edition of this book. It would not have been possible without my first Surrey publisher, Susan Schwartz. Current publisher Doug Seibold's continued enthusiasm is greatly appreciated. Thanks also to the creative team that was invaluable in testing the recipes that went into this book: Susan Barnes, Jane Ellis, Jean Ann Morton, Carol Roessler, Chef Kevin Stantz and Fran Wagner. And to Pat Molden for her help in editing.

Printed in Denmark by Nørhaven, Viborg

Contents

Introduction

The first slow cookers appeared on the market in the early '70s and their popularity has never stopped growing. The original slow cooker was called a crock pot, because of the ceramic 'casserole' inside the cooker, and the name 'crock pot' is now often used generically. Today, the numbers of slow-cooker enthusiasts are growing, as they learn from their friends how useful a slow cooker can be. From students to business people, slow-cooker users can't praise enough the joy of being able to get a meal together with the minimal amount of preparation and then to come home after a busy day to a hot meal that's ready to eat. These days, too, as people aim to save on fuel for cooking – for economic as well as environmental reasons – the slow cooker has earned its place in the modern kitchen. Because on average it saves about 80 per cent of the energy of normal cooking, you couldn't ask for a better way to produce a nourishing and healthy hot meal that's eco-friendly.

The attraction goes further than this. Cheaper cuts of meat that need longer cooking are transformed into meltingly tender and flavourful meals. Food keeps moist, and the flavours and nutrients are trapped in, because the gentle heat creates less evaporation, and as the steam condenses on the lid it drips back into the casserole taking the flavours with it. The flavours of soups, casseroles and stocks blend and meld beautifully, meats cook to be rich and tender with little shrinkage, and because food is not turned during cooking, it doesn't break up, so softer ingredients such as fish and fruit cook perfectly and remain whole.

With the steam sealed in, you will also notice that there is less in the kitchen than when you cook with a conventional cooker.

Because slow cookers have at least two settings, you can choose to cook on Low – so your dish cooks all day while you are out at work – or on High – taking half the time. The perfect option for our busy lifestyles.

Another advantage is being able to keep your meal warm once cooked. Today's busy families often need to eat at different times. The Low setting means that food will keep warm for several hours without spoiling so that everyone can enjoy a freshly cooked meal even if they eat it later than the rest of the family.

All in all, the slow-cooker experience is one that is appealing to more and more people. This book contains a selection of the tastiest and quickest dishes to appeal to veteran slow-cooker users and those who have just discovered this wonderful piece of kitchen equipment.
We hope you will enjoy them.

The benefits of a slow cooker

Those who are already fans will know the many benefits of using a slow cooker but if you are new to slow cooking, there may be more advantages than you thought.

- All-in-one-pot convenience.

- Easy clean-up and no other pans needed.

- Versatile for many kinds of foods, from appetisers to desserts.

- Meets multiple cooking needs, such as poaching, stewing, braising, roasting and baking.

- Saves cooking time and energy

- Safe to leave plugged in all day so you can leave your meal cooking while you are out at work.

- A choice of settings so you can choose how long your cooking time will be for maximum convenience.

- The warm setting keeps food ready for family members' varying dinner times.

- It's portable, so it can be taken with you for use in campers or if you want to cook away from home.

All these advantages – and more that you can think of – make this a great piece of equipment to help improve your busy lifestyle.

Choosing your slow cooker

You can now find a huge selection of slow cookers – from the basic and functional to stylish designs for serving at the table – but the most important factor is to make sure the cooker has the BEAB safety symbol. The pot, or crock, should be removable and may be of ceramic or heat-resistant glass. The lid should fit tightly and will be either glass or ceramic. There is no advantage to having a glass lid, however, as the condensation will obscure your view of the cooking food anyway. The main heat settings are High and Low, which are the ones used in this book, although some slow cookers also have a Medium setting.

The cooker size you choose will depend on the size of your family, whether you often entertain and what kinds of dishes you want to prepare. In this book the 3.25–3.5 litre /5¾–6 pint size slow cooker is the most frequently used and is considered to be an average family size; however, if you have a larger family, or you like to entertain, the 5.5 litre/9½ pint size would be more suitable. In this size you will also be able to cook roasts and make a larger selection of the cakes, which need to be cooked in a cake tin for best results. Another advantage of having a larger cooker is that you can cook in bulk for freezing. A cooker with a wide crock will be useful for cooking whole peppers, fruit and fish.

Bear in mind that the cooker must be at least a third full to operate properly. A tightly packed pot will not work correctly; similarly, one item, such as a pork chop, in the crock will overcook unless it is filled to at least a third with liquid. If cooking for one, you would be better to choose a smaller slow cooker, or you can double up the liquid to be on the safe side.

If you entertain a lot, a 1 litre/1¾ pint slow cooker is a perfect addition for making and serving dips, snack mixes, meatballs and so on.

Using your slow cooker

Always refer to your manufacturer's instructions as slow cookers do vary slightly between models and manufacturers. However, you should find these general principles helpful when using your slow cooker. You can also look at the FAQ pages for more useful tips.

- Assume a 3.25–3.5 litre/5¾–6 pint slow cooker is being used unless a specific size is stated in the recipe.

- Preheat your slow cooker, if necessary, with the lid on while you prepare the ingredients.

- In general, the order in which ingredients go into the slow cooker makes little difference. If a certain order is required, it will be stated in the recipe.

- Most manufacturers do not recommend cooking frozen foods. For food safety, thaw meat, fish and vegetables completely before adding to the slow cooker. Add thawed frozen vegetables during the last 15–20 minutes of cooking time so that they will not overcook.

- When cooking soups and casseroles, this book assumes the slow cooker will be at least half full. If less than half full, the cooking time will be less, so check that the food is cooked sooner than stated in the recipe.

- Never fill a slow cooker to the top. Leave at least a 5 cm/2 in space between the top of the crock pot and the lid to allow space for simmering.

- If you are cooking a large joint or bird, cut it in half before cooking. It will then cook quicker.

- Stirring while cooking is not necessary in a slow cooker unless specified in the recipe. In fact, each time the lid is removed to stir there is a loss of heat, thus increasing the cooking time.

- If cooking cakes or breads, do not lift the lid during the first 1½–2 hours of cooking time.

- Leave the slow cooker undisturbed during the cooking period and keep the lid on, otherwise the water seal around the rim will be broken and it will take a considerable time to regain the lost heat.

- Cooked food will remain hot in the slow cooker for 30 minutes after the cooker is switched off. If you want to keep food hot for longer, set the slow cooker to Low, but note that this isn't suitable for egg-based or rice dishes. (Rice should not be kept warm as it encourages the growth of harmful bacteria.)

- Most foods can be cooked on High or Low, depending on your preferred cooking time, but fish, rice and egg-based dishes must be cooked on Low.

- If you are going to be out all day, it is best to cook on Low. That way the food will not spoil if you are delayed returning home. (This is particularly important if you don't have a programmable slow cooker.

Foil handles

If you make foil handles, you can easily remove whole roasts and chicken from the slow cooker. Cut two long strips of heavy-duty foil that will fit into the slow cooker, going across the bottom and extending to the top of the sides of the crock. Fold the strips in half two or three times to increase their strength. Fit the strips into the slow cooker and then add the roast or chicken.

Frequently asked questions

Here are answers to the questions most commonly posed by new slow-cooker users.

Do I need to stir the ingredients while cooking?

No. Valuable heat is lost every time the lid is lifted, requiring an increase in cooking time.

Can slow cookers be left unattended?

Yes. One of the main benefits of a slow cooker is that you can put in your ingredients, leave home and come back to a delicious meal. Slow cookers operate on a low wattage.

Can I use my slow cooker to prepare roasts, whole chickens and other meats so that they can be sliced, rather than cooked until they are very tender and falling apart?

Yes. To cook meat perfectly for slicing and serving, use a meat thermometer and cook to the temperature recommended for the type of meat. See the chapters for poultry, beef, pork and lamb for recipes of this type.

Sometimes my recipe has finished cooking but the sauce is too watery. How can I thicken the juices?

If you want to thicken the juices, turn the slow cooker to High and cook, covered, for 10 minutes. Stir in 1 tbsp cornflour or 2 tbsp flour with 50 ml/2 fl oz cold water for every 250 ml/8 fl oz of liquid. Stir for 2–3 minutes until thickened. Or the dish can be uncovered and cooked on High for 20–30 minutes to the desired consistency.

*What if I don't have all day to cook food – can I still use my
slow cooker?*

Higher cooking temperatures can be used to cook foods
more quickly. The following conversion chart compares
cooking times for High and Low settings:

High	Low
3 hours	7 hours
4 hours	8 hours
5 hours	9 hours
6 hours	10 hours
7 hours	11 hours
8 hours	12 hours

Manufacturers' recommendations on times can vary and
should be checked in the instruction manual.

Tips for using specific foods

Foods do not always cook in the slow cooker in the same way that they would if cooked conventionally. The obvious example is that vegetables generally take longer to cook than meat. These tips will help you learn about any differences from conventional cooking.

Beans and pulses

Dried beans will cook in soups and stews with ample liquid in 7–8 hours on Low. They do not need to be pre-soaked, with the exception of red kidney beans. These need to be pre-soaked overnight and then fast boiled for 10 minutes before they are added to the slow cooker because they contain toxins that need to be boiled off. Acid ingredients, such as tomatoes and vinegar, prevent beans from becoming tender, so add these near to the end of cooking time when the beans are already tender. Dried lentils and split peas do not require soaking and can be added to the recipe at the beginning of cooking time.

Convenience foods

The emphasis in this book is recipes that are simple and convenient, so we have occasionally suggested adding a ready-made sauce or a can of soup to enrich the cooking liquid, or other convenience foods for speed. You can use tomato sauce from a jar, or if you prefer to make your own you will find a recipe for a slow-cooker Tomato Sauce on page 354. It's a well-flavoured sauce that is suitable for making in bulk and freezing.

Dairy products

Full-fat dairy products are more stable and don't curdle as easily as lower-fat milk products. In this book, milk products are added near the end of cooking time and combined with cornflour to increase stability. Therefore, these recipes are suitable for low-fat products if you prefer. Evaporated

13

milk and canned cream soups can be added to the slow cooker at the beginning of cooking time.

Frozen vegetables

Thaw and add to the slow cooker during the last 15–20 minutes of cooking time to retain the best texture.

Herbs and spices

Add fresh herbs at the end for optimum colour and flavour. Add ground spices and dried herbs at the beginning.

Liquids

Liquid (stock, water or wine) aids heat transfer and facilitates even cooking. When doubling recipes for casseroles, if you increase the liquid by one and a half times this is usually sufficient.

Meats

Less tender cuts of meat, such as pork shoulder, braising or stewing steak are perfect for long, slow cooking. Minced meats need to be browned and crumbled with a fork before adding to the slow cooker, otherwise they will cook into a clump. Other cuts do not need to be browned. The difference in appearance and flavour is minimal and not browning saves time and dirty pans.

Pasta

Dried pasta should be cooked al dente and added to the slow cooker during the last 15–20 minutes of cooking time (on High). Small soup pasta, such as stellette or orzo, can be added, uncooked, during the last 20–30 minutes of cooking (on High). Fresh pastas can be added, uncooked, during the last 15–20 minutes of cooking (on High).

Rice

Easy-cook long-grain rice is the best for cooking in the slow cooker, although medium-grain risotto rice also works. Be sure that the recipe has plenty of liquid and add the uncooked rice during the last 1½–2 hours of cooking time (on High). Other types of rice – such as jasmine, basmati or brown – should be cooked and added near to the end of cooking time.

Seafood

Add shellfish and pieces of fish during the last 30 minutes of cooking time (on Low), depending upon the quantity and thickness of the fish.

Thickening agents

Cornflour and flour can be used for thickening soups, casseroles and gravies. Not every slow cooker achieves boiling in a reasonable amount of time, so cornflour is used to thicken the recipes in this book. It thickens more quickly than flour at lower than boiling temperature and it leaves no aftertaste.

> ### Thickening
>
> If you want to thicken the cooking juices once your meal is almost ready, turn the slow cooker to High and cook, covered, for 10 minutes. Stir in 1 tbsp cornflour or 2 tbsp flour with 50 ml/2 fl oz cold water for every 250 ml/8 fl oz of liquid. Stir for 2–3 minutes until thickened. Or the dish can be uncovered and cooked on High for 20–30 minutes to the desired consistency.

Vegetables

High-moisture vegetables, such as butternut squash or courgettes, cook more quickly than root vegetables, so cut into larger pieces or add during the last hour of cooking time (on Low).

Tips for making desserts and breads in the slow cooker

Your slow cooker is not only good for casseroles. A variety of delicious desserts and breads can be made in the slow cooker: perfect creamy cheesecakes, cakes, breads, biscuits, bread puddings, custards and poached fruit are some examples.

- Making most breads and desserts requires a 5.5 litre/9½ pint slow cooker to accommodate the various sizes of pans and dishes used, although some can be cooked directly in the crock (see below). You may need to experiment with recipe times a little, as various slow cookers cook a little differently. The shape and dimensions of the crock do influence cooking times. Recipes will indicate a range of possible cooking times.

- Cakes and other baked goods may be a little sticky on top, but they can be frosted, glazed or sprinkled with icing sugar or cocoa.

- Test that cakes and breads are cooked by using a cocktail stick. Do this as quickly as possible so that the lid of the slow cooker can be replaced to prevent the loss of heat. If the lid is removed often, the cooking time will be increased.

- Baked goods are best eaten the day they are made. They can be 'refreshed' the next day with minimal microwave heating before serving.

- Most cake recipes can be cooked directly in a greased and floured crock in a 2.75 litre/4¾ pint slow cooker. The cooking time will be less than if cooked in a pan, the edges may be a little dry, and if the slow cooker heats unevenly, one side of the cake may be browner. You'll need to experiment a little!

• Many desserts are baked in a 18 cm/7 in springform cake tin. Before using, fill the tin with water to make sure it doesn't leak, or wrap the outside of the tin in foil.

• Place baking pans, casseroles and soufflé dishes on a small rack for best heat circulation and more even cooking. A tuna can, with both ends cut off, can be used as a rack.

• Some cakes and cheesecakes are cooked with three layers of kitchen paper put under the lid, which absorbs unneeded moisture and assures the best quality.

• There are no general rules for adapting conventional cakes, cheesecakes or breads to slow-cooker cooking. Each item cooks differently, so it's best to use recipes that have been developed for the slow cooker.

Healthy cooking

We all like to eat tasty food – and that doesn't have to mean that it's not good for you, too! Try to make sure you get your five fruit and veg a day, keep sweet things as treats now and then, and get a good balance of complex carbohydrates and protein.

Fat

We do need some fat in our diet but, in general, we eat too much – in proportion to everything else – and we tend to eat too much saturated fat. In keeping with today's trend of healthy eating, many of the recipes are low in fat. Others contain yoghurt, buttermilk, soured cream, or hard or soft cheeses, and you may prefer to use a lower-fat version of these (see Cream Cheese on page 20 about using low-fat soft cheeses). Rather than using a low-fat hard cheese, such as Cheddar that may not have much flavour, you may find the recipe would work as well using a smaller amount of a mature Cheddar. This would give you the flavour without the fat. For most other cheeses you can now find healthy-choice versions, which would work well in these recipes.

Other ways to reduce the fat in your food is to choose lean cuts of meat and always to trim meat and poultry of all fat before cooking, unless it is being roasted, when the fat will drain away. Minced meats can be very fatty, so choose lean mince. You will see the difference in the colour, which will be red rather than pale pink. Although a little more expensive, the flavour will be better and you'll have more meat for your money. Minced meats are first fried in a pan in the recipes; if you use a slotted spoon to transfer the meat to the slow cooker you will leave the fat behind in the frying pan and can discard it.

Salt

Because convenience foods and snacks are routinely high in salt, our taste buds have become accustomed to it, but salt is very unhealthy and it is best to reduce it in our home-cooked food. Salt is added at the end of cooking time in these recipes; try to gradually lower the amount you add to dishes and perhaps try a low-salt alternative instead.

Cooking for vegetarians

The book includes chapters for vegetarian soups and vegetarian main meals. Vegetarian recipes also appear in other chapters and all are coded with a Ⓥ.

When making vegetable dishes for vegetarians, remember to use alternative ingredients such as vegetarian Worcestershire sauce – or use a mushroom sauce – and vegetarian cheeses. Many cheeses are now marked 'suitable for vegetarians' on the packets. Always check before buying, because a traditional Cheddar or Parmesan cheese, for example, contains animal rennet and is therefore not suitable. Also, if cooking for strict vegetarians you would need to use a vegetarian wine, if called for in the recipe, as most wines are fined (or cleared) with animal products.

Recipes marked Ⓥ that contain Worcestershire sauce, cheese or wine assume you will buy a vegetarian version if you are cooking for people who do not eat meat.

Specific ingredients

The ingredients in this book are readily available in supermarkets and health food shops. The following is some helpful information on some of the ingredients we've used.

Butter   This is generally suggested in preference to margarine or spreads for its lack of trans-fats and improved flavour.

Cooking sprays   Vegetable and olive oil cooking sprays are used to reduce the amounts of oil or fat needed in the recipes. These are a healthy and convenient way to use oils and mean that you can enjoy home-made croûtons and garlic bread, for example, without them being heavy with fat. As an alternative you could brush oil on very thinly.

Cream cheese   The block type of soft cheese is usually specified in the recipes in this book. The tub type is much softer in texture and does not always work the same in recipes. If you are substituting low-fat soft cheese in your favourite recipes for dips, use the block type and add any liquid ingredients gradually, as the soft cheese thins much more quickly than full-fat or reduced-fat soft cheese. Low-fat soft cheese can be used to make cake glaze but not icing, as it thins with the addition of icing sugar and cannot be thickened.

Herbs   In most recipes, dried herbs are called for. As a general rule, fresh herbs may be substituted for dried by using two to three times as much as indicated for the dried version.

Margarine or spread   If you prefer to use margarine instead of butter, use an all-vegetable product that is trans-fat free. Use block rather than diet or 'soft' margarine, as they do not perform well in baking.

White vegetable fat   The manufacturing process of white vegetable fat usually creates trans-fats, so shop carefully for one of the new trans-fat-free brands.

Slow cooker tips

- Never leave uncooked food in a slow cooker that isn't turned on.

- Steamed dishes, recipes that include a raising agent and recipes with large pieces of meat should always be cooked on High.

- Never put the crock pot in the fridge. Prepared ingredients can be stored in the fridge in a sealed container.

- Mix the ingredients together when you first put them into the slow cooker and stir again before serving.

- Do not remove the lid during cooking unless you are adding ingredients. Add them quickly and replace the lid quickly and firmly afterwards.

- If you wish to freeze any slow-cooked food, remove it from the slow cooker and leave it to cool quickly, then refrigerate and freeze.

- Do not place the slow cooker in a direct draught. If using it in a room with a low temperature, allow longer cooking times, especially when cooking on Low.

- If your recipe is not ready by the stated cooking time, increase the heat to High and cook for another hour.

- Remember that the High heat on a slow cooker is still lower than the lowest heat on a conventional oven.

Notes on the Recipes

- Do not mix metric and imperial measures. Follow one set only.

- The ingredients are listed in the order in which they are used in the recipe.

- All spoon measurements are level: 1 tsp = 5 ml, 1 tbsp = 15 ml.

- Eggs are medium unless otherwise stated. If you use a different size, adjust the amount of liquid added to obtain the right consistency.

- All vegetables are medium unless otherwise stated.

- Always wash, peel, core and seed, if necessary, fresh foods before use. Ensure that all produce is as fresh as possible and in good condition.

- Always wash meat, poultry and fish before cooking.

- Seasoning and the use of strongly flavoured ingredients, such as onions and garlic, are very much a matter of personal taste. Taste the food and adjust the seasoning to suit your own taste, but also see Salt on page 22.

- Chillies are used in many recipes and some recipes call for a particularly hot combination of fresh chillies and chilli powder. If you prefer your chilli dishes to be milder, omit the chilli powder, or adjust to your preference. Always deseed chillies if you are not keen on fiery chilli heat. After preparing fresh chillies, scrub your hands well with soap and water to remove any remains of capsaicin, the substance that creates the heat in chillies. Just a small amount can badly irritate your eyes, if you rub them with your fingers. If you prefer, wear rubber gloves when preparing chillies.

- Use dried or fresh herbs as indicated. If you substitute dried for fresh, use half the quantity stated – or vice versa. There is no substitute for fresh parsley and coriander.

- A fresh bouquet garni is traditionally made up of sprigs of thyme, parsley and a bay leaf tied together with string or wrapped in muslin. Sachets of bouquet garni are readily available in supermarkets or you can use dried mixed herbs instead.

- Can sizes are approximate and will depend on the particular brand.

- Use your own discretion in substituting ingredients and personalising the recipes. Make notes of particular successes as you go along.

- Use whichever kitchen gadgets you like to speed up preparation and cooking times: mixers for whisking; food processors for grating, slicing, mixing or kneading; blenders for liquidising.

Basic Stocks

Making stocks in the slow cooker couldn't be easier. You can simply prepare the ingredients, then leave them gently cooking on Low all day. No steamy kitchen, no checking that it's boiling too hard! Then you have beautifully flavoured stocks to use in your cooking. Make sure you freeze your stocks in suitable quantities – in 300 ml/½ pint containers is usually a good size.

Simple Chicken Stock

A super basic stock.

MAKES ABOUT 1.5 LITRES/2½ PINTS

1 litre/1¾ pints water
1 cooked or raw chicken carcass, broken into pieces
2 celery sticks, thickly sliced
3 small onions, thickly sliced,
3 carrots, thickly sliced
1 small turnip, quartered
5 garlic cloves
2 bay leaves
½ tsp whole peppercorns
1 tsp dried sage leaves
salt and freshly ground black pepper, to taste

Combine all the ingredients, except the salt and pepper, in the slow cooker. Cover and cook on Low for 6–8 hours. Strain, discarding the meat, vegetables and seasonings. Season to taste with salt and pepper. Refrigerate the stock overnight. Skim the fat from the surface of the stock.

Fresh Chicken Stock

Soups and casseroles are transformed with a good home-made stock, and chicken is the most popular to make and use. Cook this version if you need to make a good stock from scratch.

MAKES ABOUT 1.5 LITRES/2½ PINTS

1 litre/1¾ pints water
1.5 kg/3 lb chicken pieces
2 celery sticks, thickly sliced
3 small onions, thickly sliced,
3 carrots, thickly sliced
1 small turnip, quartered
5 garlic cloves
2 bay leaves
½ tsp whole peppercorns
1 tsp dried sage leaves
salt and freshly ground black pepper, to taste

Combine all the ingredients, except the salt and pepper, in the slow cooker. Cover and cook on Low for 6–8 hours. Strain, discarding the meat, vegetables and seasonings. Season to taste with salt and pepper. Refrigerate the stock overnight. Skim the fat from the surface of the stock.

Rich Chicken Stock

A veal knuckle is added here to make a richer stock. It's an ideal recipe to make when you're entertaining and need a stock that's especially full-flavoured to bring the very best out of the dish you are preparing.

3.5 litres/6 pints water
250 ml/8 fl oz dry white wine or water
1 chicken (about 1.5 kg/3 lb), cut into pieces, fat trimmed
1 veal knuckle, cracked (optional)
2 onions, thickly sliced
2 leeks (white parts only), thickly sliced
4 medium carrots, thickly sliced
4 celery sticks, thickly sliced
1 garlic clove, peeled
½ tsp dried basil
½ tsp dried thyme
½ tsp dried tarragon
10 black peppercorns
4 whole cloves
salt and freshly ground black pepper, to taste

Combine all the ingredients, except the salt and pepper, in a 5.5 litre/9¼ pint slow cooker. Cover and cook on Low for 6–8 hours. Strain the stock through a double layer of muslin, discarding the solids. Season to taste with salt and pepper. Refrigerate until chilled. Remove the fat from the surface of the stock.

Turkey Stock

The perfect ending for a Christmas turkey, this stock can be used for Turkey Noodle Soup (see page 82) or as a substitute in recipes calling for chicken stock.

3.5 litres/6 pints water
250 ml/8 fl oz dry white wine or water
1 turkey carcass, cut up
2 medium onions, thickly sliced
2 leeks (white parts only), thickly sliced
4 medium carrots, thickly sliced
4 celery sticks, thickly sliced
1 tsp dried thyme
10 black peppercorns
6 sprigs of fresh parsley
salt and freshly ground black pepper, to taste

Combine all the ingredients, except the salt and pepper, in a 5.5 litre/9½ pint slow cooker. Cover and cook on Low for 6–8 hours. Strain the stock through a double layer of muslin, discarding the solids. Season to taste with salt and pepper. Refrigerate until chilled. Remove the fat from the surface of the stock.

Beef Stock

A good beef stock is perfect for meat dishes and soups that require a stronger flavour. Although a home-made beef stock is not usually prepared for everyday meals, it will make all the difference when cooking something special.

MAKES ABOUT 2.25 LITRES/4 PINTS

2.25 litres/4 pints water
2 ribs from cooked beef rib roast, fat trimmed
4 large onions, thickly sliced
4 medium carrots, thickly sliced
4 celery sticks, thickly sliced
1 parsnip, halved
2 bay leaves
8 black peppercorns
5 sage leaves
salt, to taste

Combine all the ingredients, except the salt, in a 5.5 litre/9½ pint slow cooker. Cover and cook on Low for 6–8 hours. Strain the stock through a double layer of muslin, discarding the solids. Season to taste with salt. Refrigerate until chilled. Remove the fat from the surface of the stock.

Fragrant Beef Stock

Dried mushrooms, red wine and herbs give a rich flavour to this stock. Brown the beef before adding it to the crock pot, if you like, for an even richer stock.

MAKES ABOUT 3.25 LITRES/5¾ PINTS

2.75 litres/4¾ pints water
250 ml/8 fl oz dry red wine (optional)
900 g/2 lb short ribs of beef, fat trimmed
900 g/2 lb beef marrow bones
450 g/1 lb cubed chuck steak, fat trimmed
1 large onion, chopped
3 medium carrots, thickly sliced
3 celery sticks, thickly sliced
25 g/1 oz dried mushrooms
1 garlic clove, halved
10 black peppercorns
1 bay leaf
1 tsp dried basil
1 tsp thyme leaves
1 tbsp soy sauce
salt, to taste

Combine all the ingredients, except the salt, in a 5.5 litre/9½ pint slow cooker. Cover and cook on Low for 6–8 hours. Strain the stock through a double layer of muslin, discarding the solids. Season to taste with salt. Refrigerate until chilled. Remove the fat from the surface of the stock.

Veal Stock

Because veal bones can be difficult to find it's worth making this delicately flavoured stock when you can find the ingredients and then freezing it. Brown the veal for a richer flavour.

MAKES ABOUT 2.25 LITRES/4 PINTS

2.25 litres/4 pints water
700 g/1½ lb veal cubes for stewing
1 onion, chopped
1 small carrot, chopped
1 small celery stick, chopped
1 veal knuckle or about 750 g/1¾ lb veal bones
2 bay leaves
6 black peppercorns
3 whole cloves
salt and freshly ground black pepper, to taste

Combine all the ingredients, except the salt and pepper, in a 5.5 litre/9½ pint slow cooker. Cover and cook on Low for 6–8 hours. Strain through a double layer of muslin, discarding the solids. Season to taste with salt and pepper. Refrigerate until chilled. Remove the fat from the surface of the stock.

Fish Stock

Ask your fishmonger or at the fish counter of your supermarket for bones to make this stock. If you use the fish heads, remove the gills first, as they can make the stock bitter.

MAKES ABOUT 1.5 LITRES/2½ PINTS

1.5 litres/2½ pints water
900 g–1.5 kg/2–3 lb fish bones
(from non-oily fish)
1 large onion, chopped
1 celery stick, chopped
2 bay leaves
7–8 black peppercorns
½ tsp sea salt
½ tsp white pepper

Combine all the ingredients in the slow cooker. Cook on Low for 4–6 hours. Strain through a double layer of muslin, discarding the solids.

Easy Fish Stock

Any mildly flavoured fish will make a delicious stock. Avoid strongly flavoured fish, such as salmon or tuna. Fish stock is best used on the day it is made, but it can also be frozen for up to 2 months.

MAKES ABOUT 1 LITRE/1¾ PINTS

900 ml/1½ pints water
175 ml/6 fl oz dry white wine or water
700 g/1½ lb fresh or frozen fish steaks,
cubed (2.5 cm/1 in)
1 onion, finely chopped
1 carrot, finely chopped
3 celery sticks with leaves, halved
3 sprigs of fresh parsley
3 lemon slices
8 black peppercorns
salt, to taste

Combine all the ingredients, except the salt, in the slow cooker. Cover and cook on Low for 4–6 hours. Strain the stock through a double layer of muslin, discarding the solids. Season to taste with salt.

Basic Vegetable Stock Ⓥ

Perfect for vegetarian recipes, a good home-made stock gives a much rounder flavour than using a stock cube. As vegetables used in stocks are later discarded, they should be scrubbed but do not need to be peeled.

MAKES ABOUT 2 LITRES/3½ PINTS

2 litres/3½ pints water
250 ml/8 fl oz dry white wine or water
1 large onion, thickly sliced
1 leek (white part only), thickly sliced
1 carrot, thickly sliced
1 celery stick, thickly sliced
450 g/1 lb mixed chopped vegetables
(broccoli, French beans, cabbage,
potatoes, tomatoes, courgettes or
squash, peppers, mushrooms, etc.)
6–8 sprigs of fresh parsley
1 bay leaf
4 whole allspice
1 tbsp black peppercorns
2 tsp dried mixed herbs
or 1 sachet of bouquet garni
salt, to taste

Combine all the ingredients, except the salt, in a 5.5 litre/9½ pint slow cooker. Cover and cook on Low for 6–8 hours. Strain the stock, discarding the solids. Season to taste with salt.

Roasted Vegetable Stock ⓥ

Roasting vegetables intensifies their flavours, adding richness to the stock. The beetroot adds a subtle sweetness to the stock, but only use it if you don't object to the pink colour it creates!

MAKES ABOUT 2 LITRES/3½ PINTS

2 litres/3½ pints water
250 ml/8 fl oz dry white wine or water
1 medium onion, coarsely chopped
1 leek (white part only),
   coarsely chopped
1 carrot, coarsely chopped
1 courgette, coarsely chopped
1 turnip, coarsely chopped
1 beetroot, coarsely chopped
1 tomato, coarsely chopped
½ small butternut or acorn squash,
   cubed (5 cm/2 in)
1 garlic bulb, cut in half crosswise
175 g/6 oz kale, coarsely chopped
6 sprigs of fresh parsley
1 bay leaf
1–2 tsp dried mixed herbs or 1 sachet
   of bouquet garni
1 tsp black peppercorns
4 whole allspice
salt and freshly ground black
   pepper, to taste

Arrange the vegetables, except the kale, in a single layer on a greased, foil-lined Swiss roll tin. Bake at 220°C/ gas 7/fan oven 200°C until tender and browned, 35–40 minutes.

Transfer the vegetables to a 5.5 litre/ 9½pint slow cooker and add the remaining ingredients, except the salt and pepper. Cover and cook on Low for 4–6 hours. Strain, discarding the solids. Season to taste with salt and pepper.

Mediterranean Stock ⓥ

A lovely stock, scented with orange and fennel. This is an unusual stock that will add richness to fresh soups and casseroles containing Mediterranean ingredients.

MAKES ABOUT 2 LITRES/3½ PINTS

2 litres/3½ pints water
250 ml/8 fl oz dry white wine or water
juice of 1 orange
1 large onion, thickly sliced
1 leek (white part only), thickly sliced
1 carrot, thickly sliced
1 sweet potato, thickly sliced
1 courgette, thickly sliced
1 celery stick, thickly sliced
½ small fennel bulb, sliced
½ red pepper, sliced
2 medium tomatoes, quartered
1 medium garlic bulb, cut in
   half crosswise
225 g/8 oz coarsely chopped
   spinach or cos lettuce
6 sprigs of fresh parsley
1 strip of orange zest
   (7.5 cm/3 in x 2.5 cm/1 in)
1 bay leaf
1–2 tsp mixed herbs
1 tsp black peppercorns
4 whole allspice
salt, to taste

Combine all the ingredients, except the salt, in a 5.5 litre/9½ pint slow cooker. Cover and cook on Low for 4 6 hours. Strain, discarding the solids. Season to taste with salt.

Oriental Stock ⓥ

A light stock – fragrant with fresh coriander, ginger and five-spice powder – will bring Asian soups and entrées alive. Tamari is similar to soy sauce but with a smoother, richer taste.

MAKES ABOUT 2 LITRES/3½ PINTS

2 litres/3½ pints water
350 g/12 oz pak choi or Chinese cabbage, shredded
65 g/2½ oz fresh coriander, coarsely chopped
1 large onion, sliced
1 carrot, sliced
1 small red pepper, sliced
5 cm/2 in fresh root ginger, sliced
3 large garlic cloves, crushed
3 dried shiitake mushrooms
4 tsp tamari
2 star anise
2 tsp Chinese five-spice powder
1½ tsp Szechuan peppercorns, toasted
salt and freshly ground black pepper, to taste

Combine all the ingredients, except the salt and pepper, in a 5.5 litre/9½ pint slow cooker. Cover and cook on Low for 4–6 hours. Strain, discarding the solids. Season to taste with salt and pepper.

Rich Mushroom Stock ⓥ

Dried shiitake mushrooms add richness and an unmistakeable depth of flavour to this stock.

MAKES ABOUT 2 LITRES/3½ PINTS

1 litre/1¾ pints water
175 ml/6 fl oz dry white wine (optional)
1 large onion, sliced
1 leek (white part only), sliced
1 celery stick, sliced
350 g/12 oz button mushrooms
3 large garlic cloves, crushed
40–50 g/1½– 2 oz dried shiitake mushrooms
6 sprigs of fresh parsley
¾ tsp dried sage
¾ tsp dried thyme
1½ tsp black peppercorns
salt, to taste

Combine all the ingredients, except the salt, in a 5.5 litre/9½ pint slow cooker. Cover and cook on Low for 6–8 hours. Strain, discarding the solids. Season to taste with salt and pepper.

First-course Soups

Soups are a perfect way to enjoy the benefits of healthy vegetables. This collection includes a range of flavours, mainly of delicious vegetable soups that are ideal to start a meal or as a light lunch or supper dish with your favourite rolls or crusty bread. This chapter also has some tasty accompaniments such as Crispy Croûtons and Spiced Soured Cream.

Cream of Asparagus Soup ⓥ

A deliciously sophisticated dish for the asparagus season.

SERVES 6

900 g/2 lb asparagus, cut into chunks
750 ml/1¼ pints vegetable stock
2 onions, chopped
3 garlic cloves, crushed
1 tsp dried marjoram
1 tsp grated lemon zest
a pinch of freshly grated nutmeg
120 ml/4 fl oz semi-skimmed milk
salt and white pepper, to taste
90 ml/6 tbsp soured cream

Reserve a few asparagus tips for garnish, then combine all the ingredients, except the milk, salt, white pepper and soured cream, in the slow cooker. Cover and cook on Low for 6–8 hours. Process the soup and milk in a food processor or blender until smooth. Season to taste with salt and white pepper. Serve warm or refrigerate and serve chilled. Top each bowl of soup with a dollop of soured cream.

Cream of Broccoli Soup ⓥ

Broccoli is a wonder food – high in antioxidants and packed with nutrients – and it has a lovely fresh taste too.

SERVES 6

750 ml/1¼ pints vegetable stock
900 g/2 lb broccoli, cut into pieces (2.5 cm/1 in)
2 onions, chopped
3 garlic cloves, crushed
½ tsp dried thyme
a pinch of freshly grated nutmeg
120 ml/4 fl oz semi-skimmed milk
salt and white pepper, to taste
90 ml/6 tbsp soured cream
Crispy Croûtons (see below)

Combine all the ingredients, except the milk, salt, white pepper, soured cream and croûtons, in the slow cooker. Cover and cook on Low for 6–8 hours. Process the soup and milk in a food processor or blender until smooth. Season to taste with salt and white pepper. Serve warm or refrigerate and serve chilled. Top each bowl of soup with a dollop of soured cream and sprinkle with croûtons.

Crispy Croûtons ⓥ

The classic extra ideal for sprinkling on any soup.

SERVES 6 AS AN ACCOMPANIMENT

3 slices firm or day-old French or Italian bread, cubed (1–2 cm/½–¾ in)
vegetable cooking spray

Spray the bread cubes with cooking spray. Arrange in a single layer on a baking tray. Bake at 190°C/gas 5/fan oven 170°C until browned, 8–10 minutes, stirring occasionally. Cool. Store in an airtight container for up to 2 weeks.

Broccoli and Dill Soup Ⓥ

A great flavour combination – and a beautifully soft green colour.

SERVES 6

750 ml/1¼ pints vegetable stock
900 g/2 lb broccoli, cut into pieces (2.5 cm/1 in)
2 onions, chopped
3 garlic cloves, crushed
30 ml/2 tbsp chopped fresh dill
120 ml/4 fl oz semi-skimmed milk
salt and white pepper, to taste
90 ml/6 tbsp soured cream

Combine the stock, broccoli, onions and garlic in the slow cooker. Cover and cook on Low for 6–8 hours. Add the fresh dill and milk and process the soup in a food processor or blender until smooth. Season to taste with salt and white pepper. Serve warm or refrigerate and serve chilled. Top each bowl of soup with a dollop of soured cream.

Broccoli and Kale Soup Ⓥ

Kale is a slightly less common vegetable but you can buy it in most supermarkets.

SERVES 6

750 ml/1¼ pints vegetable stock
900 g/2 lb broccoli, cut into pieces (2.5 cm/1 in)
2 onions, chopped
3 garlic cloves, crushed
½ tsp dried thyme
100 g/4 oz kale
salt and white pepper, to taste
90 ml/6 tbsp soured cream

Combine all the ingredients, except the kale, salt, white pepper and soured cream, in the slow cooker. Cover and cook on Low for 6–8 hours. Add the kale and cook for a further 15 minutes. Process the soup in a food processor or blender until smooth. Season to taste with salt and white pepper. Serve warm or refrigerate and serve chilled. Top each bowl of soup with a dollop of soured cream.

Broccoli and Cucumber Soup Ⓥ

Most people don't think to cook with cucumber but you should give it a try.

SERVES 6

750 ml/1¼ pints vegetable stock
900 g/2 lb broccoli, cut into pieces (2.5 cm/1 in)
1 cucumber, thickly sliced
2 onions, chopped
3 garlic cloves, crushed
25 g/1 oz fresh coriander, chopped
120 ml/4 fl oz semi-skimmed milk
salt and white pepper, to taste
90 ml/6 tbsp soured cream

Combine all the ingredients, except the milk, salt, white pepper and soured cream, in the slow cooker. Cover and cook on Low for 6–8 hours. Add the coriander and cook for a further 15 minutes. Process the soup and milk in a food processor or blender until smooth. Season to taste with salt and white pepper. Serve warm or refrigerate and serve chilled. Top each bowl of soup with a dollop of soured cream.

Creamy Broccoli and Potato Soup ⓥ

Leeks add roundness to the flavour of this creamy soup. For a colourful touch, garnish each bowl of soup with a lemon slice.

SERVES 6

750 ml/1¼ pints vegetable stock
2 broccoli heads, chopped
600 g/1 lb 6 oz potatoes, peeled and diced
4 medium leeks (white parts only), sliced
250 ml/8 fl oz milk
2 tbsp cornflour
salt and white pepper, to taste

Combine all the ingredients, except the milk, cornflour, salt and pepper, in the slow cooker and cook on Low for 6–8 hours. Stir in the combined milk and cornflour, stirring until thickened, 2–3 minutes. Process the soup in a food processor or blender until smooth. Season to taste with salt and white pepper.

Herbed Broccoli and Cauliflower Bisque ⓥ

The unmistakeable taste of basil goes surprisingly well with broccoli and cauliflower.

SERVES 6

750 ml/1¼ pints vegetable stock
2 heads of broccoli, coarsely chopped
½ small head of cauliflower, coarsely chopped
250 g/9 oz potatoes, peeled and coarsely chopped
8 spring onions, thinly sliced
1 tbsp dried basil
250 ml/8 fl oz milk
salt and freshly ground black pepper, to taste

Combine all the ingredients, except the milk, salt and pepper, in the slow cooker. Cover and cook on High for 4–5 hours. Process the soup and milk in a food processor or blender until smooth. Season to taste with salt and pepper.

Hot-and-sour Cabbage Soup ⓥ

Oriental chilli oil adds to the authentic flavour of this soup, a slow-cooker version of the classic Chinese dish.

SERVES 4

1.2 litres/3 pints vegetable stock
75 g/3 oz green cabbage, shredded
1 small carrot, chopped
¼ red pepper, finely chopped
2 spring onions, thinly sliced
1 small garlic clove, crushed
1 tsp finely grated fresh root ginger
1½ tbsp soy sauce
2 tsp cider vinegar
a dash of oriental hot chilli oil
1 tbsp cornflour
½ tbsp light brown sugar

Combine the stock, vegetables, garlic and ginger in the slow cooker. Cover and cook on Low for 6–8 hours. Stir in the combined remaining ingredients during the last 2–3 minutes.

Dilled Carrot Soup Ⓥ

Carrot soup is always a favourite, whether hot or chilled. Here carrots are teamed with dill for a fresh, clean flavour.

SERVES 6

750 ml/1¼ pints vegetable stock
400 g/14 oz can chopped tomatoes
450 g/1 lb carrots, thickly sliced
3 onions, chopped
1 medium floury potato, peeled and cubed
2 garlic cloves, crushed
1–1½ tsp dried dill
2–3 tbsp lemon juice
salt and white pepper, to taste
90 ml/6 tbsp plain yoghurt

Combine all the ingredients, except the lemon juice, salt, white pepper and yoghurt, in the slow cooker. Cover and cook on Low 6–8 hours. Process the soup in a food processor or blender until smooth. Season to taste with lemon juice, salt and white pepper. Serve the soup warm or refrigerate and serve chilled. Garnish each bowl of soup with a dollop of yoghurt.

Cream of Cauliflower Soup with Cheese Ⓥ

The family favourite, cauliflower cheese, but in a bowl! This puréed soup has a velvety texture and is perfect for lunch or a first course.

SERVES 6

900 ml/1½ pints vegetable stock
350 g/12 oz cauliflower, cut into florets
1 large floury potato, peeled and cubed
1 onion, chopped
2 garlic cloves, crushed
120 ml/4 fl oz semi-skimmed milk
1 tbsp cornflour
75 g/3 oz Cheddar cheese, grated

salt and white pepper, to taste
ground mace or freshly grated nutmeg, to garnish

Combine the stock, cauliflower, potato, onion and garlic in the slow cooker. Cover and cook on Low for 6–8 hours. Remove about half the vegetables from the soup with a slotted spoon and reserve. Purée the remaining soup in a food processor or blender until smooth. Return to the slow cooker. Add the reserved vegetables. Cover and cook on High for 10 minutes. Stir in the combined milk and cornflour, stirring for 2–3 minutes. Add the cheese, stirring until melted. Season to taste with salt and white pepper. Sprinkle each bowl of soup with mace or nutmeg.

Chilled Cauliflower Soup Ⓥ

The addition of fragrant, fresh-flavoured dill makes this a lovely soup for a summer lunch.

SERVES 6

900 ml/1½ pints vegetable stock
350 g/12 oz cauliflower, cut into florets
1 large floury potato, peeled and cubed
1 onion, chopped
2 garlic cloves, crushed
120 ml/4 fl oz semi-skimmed milk
1 tbsp dried dill
salt and white pepper, to taste
chopped fresh dill or parsley, to garnish

Combine the stock, cauliflower, potato, onion and garlic in the slow cooker. Cover and cook on Low for 6–8 hours. Purée the soup with the milk and dried dill in a food processor or blender until smooth. Season to taste with salt and white pepper. Serve chilled, garnished with fresh dill or parsley.

Courgette Soup Ⓥ

A perfect soup for that summer glut of courgettes. It can also be made with marrow or patty pan squash.

SERVES 6

750 ml/1¼ pints vegetable stock
4 medium courgettes, chopped
275 g/10 oz floury potato, peeled and cubed
75 g/3 oz chopped shallots
3 spring onions, chopped
2 garlic cloves, crushed
1½ tsp dried tarragon
50 g/2 oz chopped kale or spinach
120 ml/4 fl oz semi-skimmed milk
1 tbsp cornflour
salt and white pepper, to taste
cayenne pepper, to garnish
Garlic Croûtons (see right)

Combine the stock, courgettes, potato, shallots, onions, garlic and tarragon in the slow cooker. Cover and cook on High for 4–5 hours, adding the kale and combined milk and cornflour during the last 15 minutes. Process the soup in a food processor or blender until smooth. Season to taste with salt and white pepper. Serve warm or chilled. Sprinkle each bowl of soup with cayenne pepper and top with Garlic Croûtons.

Garlic Croûtons Ⓥ

Delicious and crunchy with a hint of garlic – or more if you like!

SERVES 6 AS AN ACCOMPANIMENT

3 slices firm or day-old French bread, cubed (1 cm/½ in)
vegetable cooking spray
1 tsp garlic powder

Spray the bread cubes with cooking spray. Sprinkle with garlic powder and toss. Arrange in single layer on a baking tray. Bake at 190°C/gas 5/ fan oven 170°C until browned, 8–10 minutes, stirring occasionally.

Courgette Soup with Garlic and Curry Ⓥ

Lots of garlic, and a hint of curry and marjoram enliven courgettes in this wonderful summer soup.

SERVES 8

1 litre/1¾ pints vegetable stock
500 g/18 oz courgettes, sliced
4 onions, chopped
4 garlic cloves, crushed
2 tbsp tarragon vinegar
2 tsp curry powder
1 tsp dried marjoram
¼ tsp celery seeds
120 ml/4 fl oz plain yoghurt
salt and cayenne pepper, to taste
paprika, to garnish

Combine all the ingredients, except the yoghurt, salt, cayenne pepper and paprika, in the slow cooker. Cover and cook on Low for 6–8 hours. Process the soup and yoghurt in a food processor or blender until smooth. Season to taste with salt and cayenne pepper. Serve warm or refrigerate and serve chilled. Sprinkle each bowl of soup with paprika.

Fennel Bisque with Walnuts Ⓥ

The delicate aniseed flavour of fennel makes a delicious soup.

SERVES 6

900 ml/1½ pints vegetable stock
350 g/12 oz fennel bulbs, sliced
1 large floury potato, peeled and cubed
1 large leek, sliced
2 garlic cloves, crushed
120 ml/4 fl oz semi-skimmed milk
salt and white pepper, to taste
50 g/2 oz blue cheese, crumbled
50 g/2 oz walnuts, toasted and
  chopped

Combine the stock, fennel, potato, leek and garlic in the slow cooker. Cover and cook on Low for 6–8 hours. Purée the soup and milk in a food processor or blender until smooth. Return to the slow cooker. Season to taste with salt and white pepper. Sprinkle each bowl of soup with blue cheese and walnuts to serve.

Garlic Soup with Toasted Bread Ⓥ

Long, slow cooking mellows the pungency of garlic, making it gorgeously rich. A beaten egg can be stirred into the soup before serving.

SERVES 4

1 litre/1¾ pints vegetable stock
6–8 garlic cloves, finely chopped
½ tsp ground cumin
½ tsp dried oregano
salt and cayenne pepper, to taste
4 slices French or sourdough bread
vegetable cooking spray
chopped fresh coriander, to garnish

Combine the stock, garlic, cumin and oregano in the slow cooker. Cover and cook on High for 4 hours. Season to taste with salt and cayenne pepper.

Spray both sides of the bread slices generously with cooking spray. Cook in a frying pan over medium heat until golden, about 2 minutes on each side. Place a slice of bread in each soup bowl. Ladle the soup over and sprinkle with coriander.

Fragrant Mushroom Soup

An important element of this soup's success is the Fragrant Beef Stock, which really makes it something special.

SERVES 4

550 g/1¼ lb mushrooms
750 ml/1¼ pints Fragrant Beef Stock
  (see page 26) or beef stock
1 tbsp light soy sauce
2 tbsp cornflour
50 ml/2 fl oz water
2 tbsp dry sherry (optional)
½ tsp lemon juice
salt and freshly ground black pepper,
  to taste

Slice 100 g/4 oz of the mushrooms and reserve. Coarsely chop the remaining mushrooms and stalks. Combine the chopped mushrooms, stock and soy sauce in the slow cooker. Cover and cook on Low for 4–6 hours. Process the soup in a food processor or blender until smooth. Return to the slow cooker. Add the sliced mushrooms. Cover and cook on High for 30 minutes. Stir in the combined cornflour and water, stirring for 2–3 minutes. Stir in the sherry and lemon juice. Season to taste with salt and pepper.

Lemon Mushroom Soup

Fresh and dried mushrooms combine in this richly flavoured, lemon-accented soup.

SERVES 6

375 ml/13 fl oz hot water
25 g/1 oz dried porcini or other dried mushrooms
750 ml/1¼ pints Rich Chicken Stock (see page 31) or chicken or vegetable stock
50 ml/2 fl oz dry white wine (optional)
225 g/8 oz brown cap mushrooms, quartered
1 onion, thinly sliced
4 large garlic cloves, crushed
1 tsp dried rosemary leaves
flesh of ½ lemon, chopped
15 g/½ oz parsley, chopped
50 ml/2 fl oz water
2 tbsp cornflour
salt and freshly ground black pepper, to taste
Bruschetta (see right)

Pour the hot water over the porcini mushrooms in a bowl. Leave to stand until softened, about 20 minutes. Remove the mushrooms with a slotted spoon. Strain the liquid through a double layer of muslin and reserve. Inspect the mushrooms carefully, rinsing if necessary, to remove any grit. Chop coarsely. Combine the porcini mushrooms and reserved liquid with the remaining ingredients, except the lemon, parsley, water, cornflour, salt, pepper and Bruschetta, in the slow cooker. Cover and cook on Low for 6–8 hours, adding the lemon and parsley during the last 5 minutes. Stir in the combined water and cornflour for 2–3 minutes. Season to taste with salt and pepper. Place a Bruschetta in each soup bowl and ladle the soup over.

Bruschetta ⓥ

Delicious with so many recipes, this is particularly happy with Mediterranean-style flavours.

MAKES 6

6 slices French bread (2 cm/¾ in)
olive oil cooking spray
1 garlic clove, halved

Spray both sides of the bread lightly with cooking spray. Grill on a baking sheet 3 cm/1¼ in from the heat source, until browned, 2–3 minutes on each side. Rub the top sides of the bread with the cut sides of the garlic.

White Onion Soup ⓥ

The mild sweetness of white onions makes this soup different, but try it with other onion varieties too. For a richer flavour, brown the onions in a frying pan before adding to the slow cooker.

SERVES 8

1.5 litres/2½ pints vegetable stock
6 large white onions, thinly sliced
2 garlic cloves, crushed
1 tsp sugar
1½ tsp dried sage
2 bay leaves
2–3 tbsp cornflour
50 ml/2 fl oz water
salt and white pepper, to taste
snipped chives or sliced spring onions, to garnish

Combine all the ingredients, except the cornflour, water, salt and white pepper in a 5.5 litre/9½ pint slow cooker. Cover and cook on High for 5–6 hours. Discard the bay leaves. Stir in the combined cornflour and water, stirring for 2–3 minutes. Process the soup in a food processor or blender until smooth. Season to taste with salt and white pepper. Serve warm or chilled. Sprinkle each bowl of soup with chives or spring onion.

Three-onion Soup with Mushrooms 🟊

For a soup with a richer flavour, sprinkle the onions, leeks and shallots with 1 tsp sugar and cook in 1 tbsp butter in a large frying pan over medium-low heat until the onions are golden, about 15 minutes.

SERVES 6

1.5 litres/2½ pints vegetable stock
6 onions, thinly sliced
2 small leeks, thinly sliced
150 g/5 oz shallots or spring onions, chopped
175 g/6 oz mushrooms, sliced
1 tsp sugar
salt and freshly ground black pepper, to taste

Combine all the ingredients, except the salt and pepper, in the slow cooker. Cover and cook on Low for 6–8 hours. Season to taste with salt and pepper.

Red Onion and Apple Soup with Curry

Slow cooking brings out the sweetness of red onions, lending a well-rounded flavour to this autumn soup.

SERVES 6

1.5 litres/2½ pints Rich Chicken Stock (see page 25) or chicken or vegetable stock
550 g/1¼ lb red onions, thinly sliced
4 tart cooking apples, peeled and coarsely grated
1 carrot, cubed (1 cm/½ in)
1 large bay leaf
1 tsp curry powder
1 tsp chilli powder
¼ tsp dried thyme
¼ tsp ground allspice
salt and freshly ground black pepper, to taste
mango chutney, to garnish

Combine all the ingredients, except the salt and pepper, in the slow cooker. Cover and cook on High for 4–5 hours. Discard the bay leaf. Season to taste with salt and pepper. Serve with chutney to stir into the soup.

Onion and Leek Soup with Pasta 🟊

All the flavour and health-giving properties of these vegetables from the allium family are found in a bowl of this soup. You're spoilt for choice when it comes to suitable pasta shapes to use. Soup pasta, farfalle or conchiglie are all good.

SERVES 6

1.75 litres/3 pints vegetable stock
8 onions, sliced
2 medium leeks (white parts only), sliced
6 garlic cloves, crushed
1 tsp sugar
100 g/4 oz pasta, cooked
salt and white pepper, to taste
6 tsp freshly grated Parmesan cheese

Combine all the ingredients, except the pasta, salt, white pepper and Parmesan cheese, in the slow cooker. Cover and cook on High for 4–5 hours, adding the pasta during the last 20 minutes. Season to taste with salt and white pepper. Sprinkle each bowl of soup with 1 tsp Parmesan cheese.

Canadian Pea Soup

A delicious version of this well-known classic.

SERVES 4

1.2 litres/2 pints water
225 g/8 oz dried yellow split peas
50 g /2 oz diced lean salt pork
1 small onion, quartered
1 leek (white part only), sliced
1 carrot, sliced
1 small parsnip, cubed
1 large tomato, chopped
1 garlic cloves, crushed
2 whole cloves
1 tsp dried thyme
1 bay leaf
salt and freshly ground black pepper,
** to taste**

Combine all the ingredients, except the salt and pepper, in the slow cooker. Cover and cook on Low for 6–8 hours. Discard the bay leaf. Season to taste with salt and pepper.

Hot Chilli Vichyssoise Ⓥ

Potato soup will never be boring if served Tex-Mex style. This version, prepared with chillies, certainly packs a punch!

SERVES 6

1 litre/1¾ pints vegetable stock
450 g/1 lb new red potatoes,
** unpeeled, halved**
1 medium leek (white part only), sliced
1 poblano chilli, very finely chopped
1 jalapeño or other medium-hot chilli,
** very finely chopped**
6 garlic cloves, peeled
1½ tsp ground cumin
½ tsp chilli powder
½ tsp dried oregano
175 ml/6 fl oz semi-skimmed milk
1 tbsp cornflour
10 g/¼ oz chopped fresh coriander
salt, to taste

Combine all the ingredients, except the milk, cornflour, coriander and salt, in a 5.5 litre/9½ pint slow cooker. Cover and cook on High for 4–5 hours. Stir in the combined milk and cornflour, stirring for 2–3 minutes. Process the soup in a food processor or blender until smooth. Stir in the coriander. Season with salt. Serve warm or chilled.

Ginger Pumpkin Soup Ⓥ

Bright pumpkin with a hint of ginger – lovely! Yellow winter squash, such as butternut or onion, can be substituted for the pumpkin.

SERVES 6

750 ml/1¼ pints vegetable stock
1 small pumpkin (about 900 g/2 lb),
** peeled, seeded and cubed**
2 onions, chopped
1 tbsp chopped fresh root ginger
1 tsp crushed garlic
120 ml/4 fl oz dry white wine, or
** vegetable stock**
½ tsp ground cloves
salt and freshly ground black pepper,
** to taste**

Combine all the ingredients, except the salt and pepper, in the slow cooker. Cover and cook on High for 4–5 hours. Process the soup in a food processor or blender until smooth. Season to taste with salt and pepper.

Spinach and Pasta Soup with Basil Ⓥ

Chickpeas and spinach are comfortable Mediterranean partners. Here they are served in a soup flavoured with basil. Serve with garlic bread or focaccia.

SERVES 4

1.5 litres/2½ pints vegetable stock
1 small onion, finely chopped
1 crushed garlic clove
1–1½ tsp dried basil leaves
75 g/3 oz chopped plum tomatoes, fresh or canned
150 g/5 oz drained canned chickpeas, rinsed
275 g/10 oz frozen chopped spinach, thawed
75 g/3 oz vermicelli, broken and cooked
salt and freshly ground black pepper, to taste
2 tbsp freshly grated Parmesan cheese, to garnish

Combine all the ingredients, except the spinach, pasta, salt and pepper, in the slow cooker. Cover and cook on High for 4–6 hours, adding the spinach and pasta during the last 30 minutes. Season to taste with salt and pepper. Sprinkle each bowl of soup with Parmesan cheese.

Spinach and Pasta Soup with Ham and Beans

This makes a substantial first-course soup, so team with a light main course.

SERVES 4

1.5 litres/2½ pints vegetable or chicken stock
225–350 g/8–12 oz boneless pork loin, cubed
1 small onion, finely chopped
1 crushed garlic clove
1–1½ tsp dried basil leaves
75 g/3 oz chopped plum tomatoes, fresh or canned
150 g/5 oz drained canned haricot or cannellini beans, rinsed
275 g/10 oz frozen chopped spinach, thawed
75 g/3 oz vermicelli, broken and cooked
salt and freshly ground black pepper, to taste
2 tbsp freshly grated Parmesan cheese, to garnish

Combine all the ingredients, except the spinach, pasta, salt and pepper, in the slow cooker. Cover and cook on High for 4–6 hours, adding the spinach and pasta during the last 30 minutes. Season to taste with salt and pepper. Sprinkle each bowl of soup with Parmesan cheese.

Acorn Squash Soup Ⓥ

Sweet spices complement this autumn soup, making it especially warming. It will also work well with any winter squash or pumpkin.

SERVES 6

450 ml/¾ pint vegetable stock
2 medium acorn squash, peeled and cubed
1 onion, chopped
½ tsp ground cinnamon
¼ tsp ground coriander
¼ tsp cumin
120 ml/4 fl oz semi-skimmed milk
1 tbsp cider vinegar
salt and freshly ground black pepper, to taste

Combine all the ingredients, except the milk, vinegar, salt and pepper, in the slow cooker. Cover and cook on Low for 6–8 hours. Process the soup, milk and vinegar in a food processor or blender until smooth. Season to taste with salt and pepper.

Apple Squash Soup Ⓥ

This soup is the perfect autumn offering, combining the newly ripened squashes with the bright flavour of cider, and enlivened with spices.

SERVES 8

750 ml/1¼ pints vegetable stock
350 ml/12 fl oz cider
1 large butternut squash (about 1.25 kg/2½ lb), peeled, seeded and cubed
2 tart cooking apples, peeled, cored and chopped
3 onions, chopped
2 tsp ground cinnamon
¼ tsp ground ginger,
¼ tsp ground cloves
a pinch of freshly grated nutmeg
salt and freshly ground black pepper, to taste
Spiced Soured Cream (see below)

Combine all the ingredients, except the salt, pepper and Spiced Soured Cream, in the slow cooker. Cover and cook on High for 4–5 hours. Process the soup in a food processor or blender until smooth. Season to taste with salt and pepper. Serve with Spiced Soured Cream.

Spiced Soured Cream Ⓥ

This gently spicy cream goes particularly well with oriental soups.

SERVES 8 AS AN ACCOMPANIMENT

120 ml/4 fl oz soured cream
1 tsp sugar
½ tsp ground cinnamon
a pinch of ground ginger
1–2 tsp lemon juice

Combine all the ingredients.

Squash and Fennel Bisque Ⓥ

A delicious soup – you can thin with additional stock if necessary.

SERVES 6

750 ml/1¼ pints vegetable stock
1 fennel bulb, sliced
1 celery stick, sliced
275 g/10 oz floury potato, peeled and cubed
75 g/3 oz chopped shallots
3 spring onions, chopped
2 garlic cloves, crushed
50 g/2 oz chopped spinach
120 ml/4 fl oz semi-skimmed milk
1 tbsp cornflour
salt and white pepper, to taste
cayenne pepper, to garnish
Garlic Croûtons (see page 34)

Combine the stock, fennel, celery, potato, shallots, onions and garlic in the slow cooker. Cover and cook on High for 4–5 hours, adding the kale and blended milk and flour during the last 15 minutes. Process the soup in a food processor or blender until smooth. Season to taste with salt and white pepper. Serve warm or chilled. Sprinkle each bowl of soup with cayenne pepper and top with Garlic Croûtons.

Cream of Tomato Soup

A soup similar to the favourite brand-name canned tomato soup we all remember eating as kids. Canned tomatoes are necessary for the flavour, so don't substitute fresh.

SERVES 4

450 ml/¾ pint full-fat milk
400 g/14 oz can chopped tomatoes
1–2 tsp beef bouillon granules, or a beef stock cube
3 tbsp cornflour
a pinch of bicarbonate of soda
2 tsp sugar
25 g/1 oz butter or margarine
salt and freshly ground black pepper, to taste

Combine 250 ml/8 fl oz milk, the tomatoes and bouillon granules in the slow cooker. Cover and cook on Low for 3–4 hours. Process in a food processor or blender until smooth, then return to the slow cooker. Cover and cook on High for 10 minutes. Stir in the combined remaining milk and the cornflour, stirring for 2–3 minutes. Stir in the bicarbonate of soda, sugar and butter or margarine. Season to taste with salt and pepper.

Winter Gazpacho

This hot version of gazpacho brings vegetable-garden flavours and a bright assortment of garnishes to the winter dinner table.

SERVES 6

1 litre/1¾ pints tomato juice
1 carrot, chopped
1 celery stick, chopped
½ green pepper, chopped
2 tsp Worcestershire sauce
1 tsp beef bouillon granules, or a beef stock cube
¼ tsp dried tarragon
75 g/3 oz spinach
salt and cayenne pepper, to taste
1 small onion, chopped
1 hard-boiled egg
1 small avocado, cubed
Garlic Croûtons (see page 34)

Combine the tomato juice, carrot, celery, pepper, Worcestershire sauce, bouillon granules and tarragon in the slow cooker. Cover and cook on High for 4–5 hours, adding the spinach during the last 15 minutes. Process the soup in a food processor or blender until smooth. Season to taste with salt and cayenne pepper. Serve in shallow bowls. Sprinkle with chopped onion, egg, avocado and Garlic Croûtons.

Baked Two-tomato Soup Ⓥ

This makes a very impressive starter for a dinner party.

SERVES 6

**1 quantity Two-tomato Soup
(see below right)
375 g/13 oz ready-rolled puff pastry
1 egg, beaten
2 tbsp freshly grated Parmesan cheese**

Make the soup as above and ladle into ovenproof bowls. Cut the pastry into 6 rounds just a little larger than the size of the tops of the bowls. Moisten the edges of the pastry with egg and place on top of the bowls, pressing gently over the rims. Brush with egg and sprinkle each with 1–2 tsp freshly grated Parmesan cheese. Bake at 190°C/ gas 5/fan oven 170°C until the pastry is puffed and golden, about 20 minutes.

Smoky Tomato Bisque

Smoked pork hocks and a wide range of vegetables, herbs and spices give a rich and full flavour to this tomato soup.

SERVES 8

**600 ml/1 pint beef stock
2 x 400 g/14 oz cans chopped
tomatoes
175 g/6 oz tomato purée
2 small smoked pork hocks
1 large onion, chopped
1 potato, peeled and cubed
1 carrot, sliced
1 small red pepper
2 celery sticks, sliced
2 garlic cloves, crushed
1 tsp dried thyme
½ tsp ground allspice
½ tsp curry powder
375 ml/13 fl oz full-fat milk
2 tbsp cornflour**

**1 tsp sugar
salt and freshly ground black pepper,
to taste**

Combine all the ingredients, except the milk, cornflour, sugar, salt and pepper, in the slow cooker. Cover and cook on High for 4–5 hours. Discard the pork hocks. Process the soup and 250 ml/8 fl oz milk in a food processor or blender until smooth. Return to the slow cooker. Cover and cook on High for 10 minutes. Stir in the combined remaining milk, the cornflour and sugar, stirring for 2–3 minutes. Season to taste with salt and pepper.

Two-tomato Soup Ⓥ

The concentrated flavour of sun-dried tomatoes enhances the taste of garden-ripe tomato soup.

SERVES 6

**1 litre/1¾ pints vegetable stock
700 g/1½ lb chopped ripe or canned
tomatoes
2 onions, chopped
1 celery stick, chopped
1 carrot, chopped
2 tsp crushed garlic cloves
1 large floury potato, peeled and
cubed
25 g/1 oz sun-dried tomatoes (not in
oil), at room temperature
½ tsp dried basil leaves
120 ml/4 fl oz semi-skimmed milk
2–3 tsp sugar
salt and freshly ground black pepper,
to taste**

Combine all the ingredients, except the milk, sugar, salt and pepper, in the slow cooker. Cover and cook on High for 4–5 hours. Process the soup and milk in a food processor or blender until smooth. Season to taste with sugar, salt and pepper.

Zesty Tomato and Vegetable Soup

Italian tomatoes make this flavourful vegetable soup with a hint of chilli especially good.

SERVES 6

450 ml/¾ pint beef stock
2 x 400 g/14 oz cans Italian plum tomatoes
50 ml/2 fl oz dry white wine
1 tsp lemon juice
1 onion, chopped
1 large celery stick, chopped
1 carrot, chopped
1 red pepper, chopped
¾ tsp celery salt
a pinch of crushed chilli flakes
salt and freshly ground black pepper, to taste

Combine all the ingredients, except the salt and pepper, in the slow cooker. Cover and cook on High for 4–5 hours. Process the soup in a food processor or blender until smooth. Season to taste with salt and pepper. Serve warm or refrigerate and serve chilled.

Cream of Turnip Soup Ⓥ

A much underrated vegetable, this recipe really brings out the flavour.

SERVES 6

900 ml/1½ pints vegetable stock
350 g/12 oz turnips, chopped
1 large floury potato, peeled and cubed
1 onion, chopped
2 garlic cloves, crushed
120 ml/4 fl oz semi-skimmed milk
1 tbsp cornflour
75 g/3 oz Swiss cheese, grated
½ tsp dried thyme
salt and white pepper, to taste
ground mace or freshly grated nutmeg, to garnish

Combine the stock, turnips, potato, onion and garlic in the slow cooker. Cover and cook on Low for 6–8 hours. Purée the soup, milk, cornflour, cheese and thyme in a food processor or blender until smooth. Season to taste with salt and white pepper. Sprinkle each bowl of soup with mace or nutmeg.

Garden Soup Ⓥ

A light, colourful soup, which showcases an appealing blend of vegetables.

SERVES 6

1 litre/1¾ pints vegetable stock
2 onions, chopped
150 g/5 oz drained, canned cannellini beans, rinsed
½ red pepper, diced
1 celery stick, diced
1 carrot, diced
2 garlic cloves, crushed
1 bay leaf
1½ tsp dried Italian herb seasoning
65 g/2½ oz diced yellow summer squash, such as patty pan
65 g/2½ oz courgettes
2 medium tomatoes, diced
salt and freshly ground black pepper, to taste

Combine all the ingredients, except the squash, courgettes, tomatoes, salt and pepper, in the slow cooker. Cover and cook on Low for 6–8 hours, adding the squash, courgettes and tomatoes during the last 30 minutes. Discard the bay leaf. Season to taste with salt and pepper.

43

Many-vegetable Soup Ⓥ

Asparagus, mushrooms and broccoli team with traditional soup vegetables to make an unusual and delightful combination. You can use any vegetables you like, so It's an ideal soup to make when you need to use up leftovers in the fridge.

SERVES 4

450 ml/¾ pint vegetable stock
½ tsp dried tarragon
1 carrot, coarsely chopped
1 celery stick, coarsely chopped
1 onion, coarsely chopped
50 g/2 oz mushrooms, coarsely chopped
100 g/4 oz small broccoli florets, coarsely chopped
175 g/6 oz asparagus, sliced (2.5 cm/1 in)
250 ml/8 fl oz plain yoghurt
2 tbsp cornflour
salt and freshly ground black pepper, to taste

Combine the stock, tarragon and vegetables, except the asparagus, in the slow cooker. Cover and cook on Low for 6–8 hours, adding the asparagus during the last 20 minutes. Stir in the combined yoghurt and cornflour, stirring for 2–3 minutes. Season to taste with salt and pepper.

Stracciatelle with Mini-meatballs

Turkey Meatballs are a real treat when served mini-size with a tasty soup. When you stir the egg whites into the hot soup they look like threads or, in Italian, stracciatelle – 'torn rags'.

SERVES 4

1 litre/1¾ pints chicken stock
100 g/4 oz spinach, sliced
Turkey Meatballs (see below)
1 celery stick, chopped
1 onion, chopped
1 carrot, sliced
50 g/2 oz pastina or other small soup pasta
1 egg white, lightly beaten
salt and freshly ground black pepper, to taste
shaved Parmesan cheese, to garnish

Combine all the ingredients, except the pasta, egg white, salt and pepper, in the slow cooker. Cover and cook on Low for 6–8 hours, adding the pasta during the last 30 minutes. Slowly stir the egg white into the soup. Season to taste with salt and pepper. Garnish each bowl of soup with Parmesan cheese.

Turkey Meatballs

These tasty little meatballs can be added to any number of soups but particularly suit fairly substantial ones.

MAKES 24 MEATBALLS

225 g/8 oz lean minced turkey
½ small onion, very finely chopped
2 tbsp seasoned dry breadcrumbs
1 tbsp freshly grated Parmesan cheese
2 tbsp tomato purée

Combine all the ingredients in a bowl. Shape the mixture into 24 small meatballs and add to the soup before cooking.

Vegetable and Barley Soup

Pearl barley is a traditional addition to soups, and here it enhances a tomato-based soup of beans, potatoes and cabbage. Any vegetables you like can be substituted for those listed.

SERVES 8

2.25 litres/4 pints beef stock
400 g/14 oz ready-made tomato sauce
350 g/12 oz potatoes, peeled and cubed
275 g/10 oz French beans, cut into short lengths
225 g/8 oz cabbage, thinly sliced
25 g/1 oz finely chopped parsley
1 tbsp dried Italian herb seasoning
1–2 tsp chilli powder
65 g/2½ oz pearl barley
salt and freshly ground black pepper, to taste

Combine all the ingredients, except the barley, salt and pepper, in a 5.5 litre/9½ pint slow cooker. Cover and cook on High for 2 hours. Add the barley and cook for 2 hours. Season to taste with salt and pepper.

Bean and Barley Soup with Kale

This nutritious soup with a gentle spike of chilli is a great start to any meal.

SERVES 8

1.75 litres/3 pints Fragrant Beef Stock (see page 26) or beef stock
2 x 400 g/14 oz cans cannellini beans, rinsed and drained
3 onions, chopped
1 large carrot, chopped
225 g/8 oz mushrooms, sliced
1 tsp crushed garlic
¼ tsp crushed chilli flakes, to taste
2 tsp dried thyme
90 g/3½ oz pearl barley

225 g/8 oz sliced kale
1 tbsp lemon juice
salt and freshly ground black pepper, to taste

Combine all the ingredients, except the barley, kale, lemon juice, salt and pepper, in a 5.5 litre/9½ pint slow cooker. Cover and cook on High for 2–3 hours. Add the barley and cook for 2 hours, adding the kale during the last 30 minutes. Stir in the lemon juice. Season to taste with salt and pepper.

Haricot Bean and Spinach Soup

A delicious, hearty soup with the meaty taste of smoked pork and a wholesome flavour created by lots of vegetables.

SERVES 6

2.25 litres/4 pints chicken stock
1 smoked pork hock (optional)
275g/10 oz dried haricot beans, rinsed
1 large chopped onion
2 garlic cloves, crushed
2 large carrots, sliced
2 celery sticks, sliced
2 bay leaves
¾ tsp dried marjoram
¾ tsp dried thyme
¾ tsp dried basil
50 g/2 oz pearl barley
400 g/14 oz can tomatoes
275 g/10 oz frozen chopped spinach, thawed
salt and cayenne pepper, to taste

Combine all the ingredients, except the barley, tomatoes, spinach, salt and cayenne pepper, in a 5.5 litre/9½ pint slow cooker. Cover and cook on Low until the beans are tender, 6–8 hours. Add the barley and cook for 2 hours, adding the tomatoes and spinach during the last 30 minutes. Discard the pork hock and bay leaves. Season to taste with salt and cayenne pepper.

Lentil Soup

This satisfying soup is good on a cold day – and it's quick to prepare. Lentils have a good savoury flavour and work exceptionally well cooked this way.

SERVES 6

2.25 litres/4 pints water
1 large smoked pork hock
450 g/1 lb dried brown lentils
2 onions, finely chopped
1 celery stick, finely chopped
1 carrot, finely chopped
2 tsp sugar,
2 tsp beef bouillon granules, or a beef
  stock cube
¼ tsp dry mustard powder
½ tsp dried thyme
salt and cayenne pepper, to taste

Combine all the ingredients, except the salt and cayenne pepper, in a 5.5 litre/9½ pint slow cooker. Cover and cook on Low for 6–8 hours. Discard the pork hock. Season to taste with salt and cayenne pepper.

Lentil Soup with Orzo

The rice-shaped pasta called orzo makes a simple soup exciting. For a hearty vegetarian meal, make this soup with Roasted Vegetable Stock (see page 28).

SERVES 6

450 ml/¾ pint beef stock
2 x 400 g/14 oz cans plum tomatoes
250 ml/8 fl oz water
225 g/8 oz dried lentils
4 onions, minced or very finely
  chopped
1 large carrot, chopped
1 large celery stick, chopped
3 large garlic cloves, crushed
1 tsp dried oregano leaves
¼ tsp crushed chilli flakes
100 g/4 oz orzo or other small soup
  pasta

175 g/6 oz spinach, sliced
salt and freshly ground black pepper,
  to taste

Combine all the ingredients, except the orzo, spinach, salt and pepper, in a 5.5 litre/9½ pint slow cooker. Cover and cook on High for 4–5 hours, adding the orzo and spinach during the last 30 minutes. Season to taste with salt and pepper.

Sausage and Lentil Soup

A thick and hearty soup accented with the robust taste of sausage. Use any sausages you like. You could even try some game sausages for a more pronounced flavour.

SERVES 4

175 g/6 oz good-quality pork or beef
  sausage, casings removed
1.5 litres/2½ pints beef stock
200 g/7 oz chopped tomatoes
225 g/8 oz red lentils
2 onions, chopped
1 medium carrot, chopped
½ tsp dried thyme
1 small bay leaf
1 tsp lemon juice
salt and freshly ground black pepper,
  to taste

Cook the sausage in a frying pan over medium heat, crumbling with a fork, until browned, about 8 minutes. Combine the sausage and the remaining ingredients, except the lemon juice, salt and pepper, in a 5.5 litre/9½ pint slow cooker. Cover and cook on Low for 6–8 hours. Discard the bay leaf. Season to taste with lemon juice, salt and pepper.

Lentil Soup with Fennel

Use vegetable stock instead of beef if you want to make a vegetarian version of this tasty, lentil-based soup.

SERVES 4

1 small fennel bulb, sliced
1.5 litres/2½ pints beef stock
200 g/7 oz chopped tomatoes
225 g/8 oz red lentils
2 onions, chopped
1 medium carrot, chopped
½ tsp crushed fennel seeds
1 small bay leaf
1 tsp lemon juice
salt and freshly ground black pepper, to taste

Reserve a few fennel fronds and chop them coarsely. Combine the ingredients, except the lemon juice, salt and pepper, in the slow cooker. Cover and cook on Low for 6–8 hours. Discard the bay leaf. Season to taste with lemon juice, salt and pepper. Garnish with the reserved fennel tops.

Dutch Split Pea Soup

A rich and delicious treat.

SERVES 4

1.2 litres/2 pints water
225 g/8 oz dried split green peas
100 g/4 oz smoked sausage
1 leek (white parts only), sliced
1 celery stick, sliced
1 carrot, sliced
50 g/2 oz celeriac, cubed
1 large tomato, chopped
1 garlic clove, crushed
1 tsp dried thyme
1 bay leaf
salt and freshly ground black pepper, to taste

Combine all the ingredients, except the salt and pepper, in the slow cooker. Cover and cook on Low for 6–8 hours. Remove the sausage. Process the soup in a food processor or blender until smooth. Slice the sausage and stir it into the soup. Season to taste with salt and pepper.

Split-pea Soup Jardinière

This 'gardener's style' split-pea soup is flavoured the old-fashioned way with a ham bone, leek, turnip and carrot.

SERVES 4

1.2 litres/2 pints water
225 g/8 oz dried split green peas
1 meaty ham bone
1 small onion, quartered
1 leek (white parts only), sliced
1 celery stick, sliced
1 carrot, sliced
1 small turnip, cubed
1 large tomato, chopped
1 garlic clove, crushed
2 whole cloves
1 tsp dried thyme
1 bay leaf
salt and freshly ground black pepper, to taste

Combine all the ingredients, except the salt and pepper, in the slow cooker. Cover and cook on Low for 6–8 hours. Remove the ham bone. Remove and shred the meat. Return the shredded meat to the soup. Discard the bones and bay leaf. Season to taste with salt and pepper.

Snacks and Starters

We don't always need an appetiser for a meal, but this collection gives you starters, dishes that are good served as snacks, or as a mezze-style collection of dishes, plus loads of party-style nibbles. We've given these in party quantities so you can either make them and store in an airtight container, reduce the quantities by half, and the times by just less than half – or invite more guests!

Garlic and Rosemary Cashew Nuts Ⓥ

This recipe is delicious made with any type of nut and stores well so it's worth making a large quantity. Store in an airtight container.

SERVES 24

700 g/1½ lb cashew nuts
40 g/1½ oz butter or margarine, melted
1 tbsp sugar
3 tbsp dried rosemary leaves, crushed
¾ tsp cayenne pepper
½ tsp garlic powder

Heat the slow cooker on High for 15 minutes. Add the cashew nuts. Drizzle the butter or margarine over the cashew nuts and toss. Sprinkle with the combined remaining ingredients and toss. Cover and cook on Low for 2 hours, stirring every hour. Turn the heat to High. Uncover and cook for 30 minutes, stirring after 15 minutes. Turn the heat to Low to keep warm for serving or remove from the slow cooker and cool.

Garlic and Pepper Almonds Ⓥ

Buttery almonds with garlic and pepper go well with drinks. Try a mixture of coarsely ground black, red and green peppercorns for a gourmet touch! Make a quantity and store in an airtight container.

SERVES 24

700 g/1½ lb whole unblanched almonds
50 g/2 oz butter or margarine, melted
3 garlic cloves, crushed
2–3 tsp coarsely ground pepper

Heat the slow cooker on High for 15 minutes. Add the almonds. Drizzle the butter or margarine over the almonds and toss. Sprinkle with garlic and pepper, and toss. Cover and cook on Low for 2 hours, stirring every 30 minutes. Turn the heat to High. Uncover and cook for 30 minutes, stirring after 15 minutes. Turn the heat to Low to keep warm for serving or remove from the slow cooker and cool.

Spicy-glazed Nuts Ⓥ

You can use any nuts for this recipe. Make a quantity and store in an airtight container.

SERVES 24

130 g/4½ oz butter or margarine, melted
50 g/2 oz icing sugar
1 tsp ground cinnamon
1 tsp mixed spice
700 g/1½ lb mixed nuts

Heat the slow cooker on High for 15 minutes. Mix the butter or margarine, sugar and spices. Pour over the nuts in a large bowl and toss. Transfer the mixture to the slow cooker. Cover and cook on High for 30 minutes.

Uncover and cook until the nuts are crisply glazed, 45–60 minutes, stirring every 20 minutes. Pour the nuts in a single layer on baking trays and cool.

Sweet Curried Soy Nuts Ⓥ

Soy nuts make an unusual change, but the recipe would also work well with peanuts, walnuts, blanched almonds or pecan nuts.

SERVES 24

50 g/2 oz butter or margarine, melted
700 g/1½ lb roasted soy nuts
1½ tbsp sugar
1 tbsp curry powder
salt, to taste

Heat the slow cooker on High for 15 minutes. Drizzle the butter or margarine over the soy nuts in a large bowl and toss. Sprinkle with the combined sugar and curry powder, and toss. Transfer to the slow cooker. Cover and cook on Low for 2 hours, stirring every 15 minutes. Turn the heat to High. Remove the lid and cook for 30 minutes, stirring after 15 minutes. Season to taste with salt. Turn the heat to Low to keep warm for serving or remove from the slow cooker and cool.

Sugar-glazed Five-spice Pecan Nuts Ⓥ

Pecan nuts are spiced and sweetened up to make an unusual and very tasty appetiser. Make a quantity and store in an airtight container.

SERVES 24

130 g/4½ oz butter or margarine, melted
50 g/2 oz icing sugar
1 tsp ground cinnamon
¾ tsp Chinese five-spice powder
700 g/1½ lb pecan nut halves

Heat the slow cooker on High for 15 minutes. Mix the butter or margarine, sugar and spices. Pour over the pecans in a large bowl and toss. Transfer the mixture to the slow cooker. Cover and cook on High for 30 minutes. Uncover and cook until the nuts are crisply glazed, 45–60 minutes, stirring every 20 minutes. Pour the pecan nuts in a single layer on baking trays and cool.

Cranberry and Nut Mix Ⓥ

Nutritious nuts and dried cranberries star in this savoury-sweet snack mix. Try using blueberries instead of cranberries for a change.

SERVES 8

200 g/7 oz roasted almonds
40 g/1½ oz wheat squares cereal, such as Shreddies
40 g/1½ oz mini pretzel twists
175 g/6 oz dried cranberriess
vegetable cooking spray
¾ tsp crushed dried rosemary
¾ tsp thyme leaves
garlic salt, to taste

Heat the slow cooker on High for 15 minutes. Add the almonds, cereal, pretzels and cranberries. Spray the mixture generously with cooking spray and toss. Sprinkle with the herbs and toss again. Cover and cook on Low for 2 hours, stirring every 20 minutes. Turn the heat to High. Uncover and cook for 30 minutes, stirring after 15 minutes. Season to taste with garlic salt. Turn the heat to Low to keep warm for serving or remove from the slow cooker and cool.

Snack Mix Ⓥ

A great snack mix for nibbling or for sharing with a gathering of friends.

SERVES 16

3 cups low-fat granola
175 g/6 oz mini pretzels
6 sesame sticks, broken into halves
500 g/18 oz mixed dried fruit, coarsely chopped
butter-flavoured cooking spray
1 tsp ground cinnamon
½ tsp freshly grated nutmeg

Heat the slow cooker on High for 15 minutes. Add the granola, pretzels, sesame sticks and dried fruit. Spray the mixture generously with cooking spray and toss. Sprinkle with the combined spices and toss. Cook, uncovered, on High for 1½ hours, stirring every 30 minutes. Keep warm on Low for serving or remove from the slow cooker and cool.

Herb Party Mix Ⓥ

A colourful snack mix, with lots of variety!

SERVES 16

100 g/4 oz small square cheese biscuits
130 g/4½ oz mini pretzels
1½ cups potato sticks
175 g/6 oz peanuts
100 g/4 oz butter or margarine, melted
½ tsp Tabasco sauce
1 tbsp dried Italian herb seasoning
½–1 tsp garlic salt

Heat the slow cooker on High for 15 minutes. Add the cheese biscuits, pretzels, potato sticks and peanuts. Drizzle with the combined remaining ingredients and toss. Cook, uncovered, on High for 1½ hours, stirring every 30 minutes. Keep warm on Low for serving or remove from the slow cooker and cool.

Chutney Cheese Dip Ⓥ

Fruity, spicy flavours with cheese make a fun dip for crudités or pitta bread pieces.

SERVES 16

450 g/1 lb soft cheese, at room temperature
225 g/8 oz Cheddar cheese, grated
150 g/5 oz chopped mango chutney
½ onion, finely chopped
40 g/1½ oz chopped raisins
2–4 tsp finely chopped fresh root ginger
2–4 garlic cloves, crushed
1–2 tsp curry powder
dippers: baked pitta bread pieces, assorted vegetables

Put the cheeses in a a 1.5 litre/2½ pint slow cooker. Cover and cook on Low until the cheese has melted, about 30 minutes. Mix in the remaining ingredients, except the dippers. Cover and cook until hot, 1–1½ hours. Serve with dippers.

Pepperoni Cheese Dip

Salami, ham, or smoked turkey can be substituted for the pepperoni in this piquant creamy dip.

SERVES 10

225 g/8 oz soft cheese with onions and chives
175 g/6 oz Emmental or Gruyère cheese, grated
90 g/3½ oz sliced pepperoni, chopped
½ green pepper, chopped
¼ tsp cayenne pepper
120–150 ml/4–5 fl oz full-fat milk
dippers: assorted vegetables, crackers, breadsticks

Put the cheeses in a the slow cooker. Cover and cook on Low until the cheeses have melted, about 30 minutes. Mix in the remaining ingredients, except the dippers. Cover and cook until hot, about 1½ hours. Serve with dippers.

Hot Artichoke Dip Ⓥ

A lovely creamy artichoke mixture that's given a little kick with cayenne.

SERVES 16

100 g/4 oz soft cheese, at room temperature
400 g/14 oz artichoke hearts, drained and finely chopped
40 g/1½ oz freshly grated Parmesan cheese
120 ml/4 fl oz mayonnaise
120 ml/4 fl oz soured cream
1–2 tsp lemon juice
1 spring onion, thinly sliced
2 garlic cloves, crushed
salt and cayenne pepper, to taste

dippers: assorted vegetables, breadsticks, crackers

Put the soft cheese in a 1.5 litre/2½ pint slow cooker. Cover and cook on Low until the cheese has melted, about 30 minutes. Mix in the remaining ingredients, except the salt, cayenne pepper and dippers. Cover and cook until hot, 1–1½ hours. Season to taste with salt and cayenne pepper. Serve with dippers.

Curry-spiced Mixed Nuts Ⓥ

This very simple blend of sweet, savoury and buttery flavours is a popular spicy nibble. Make a quantity and store in an airtight container.

SERVES 24

700 g/1½ lb mixed nuts
50 g/2 oz butter or margarine, melted
2 tbsp sugar
1½ tsp curry powder
1 tsp garlic powder
1 tsp ground cinnamon

Heat the slow cooker on High for 15 minutes. Add the nuts. Drizzle the butter or margarine over the nuts and toss. Sprinkle with the combined remaining ingredients and toss. Cover and cook on Low for 2 hours, stirring every 20 minutes. Turn the heat to High. Uncover and cook for 30 minutes, stirring after 15 minutes. Turn the heat to Low to keep warm for serving or remove from the slow cooker and cool.

Spinach and Artichoke Dip Ⓥ

Colourful and creamy – a great dip for parties.

SERVES 16

100 g/4 oz soft cheese, at room temperature
400 g/14 oz artichoke hearts, drained and finely chopped
130 g/4½ oz well drained, thawed, frozen chopped spinach
½ roasted red pepper, chopped
40 g/1½ oz freshly grated Parmesan cheese
120 ml/4 fl oz mayonnaise
120 ml/4 fl oz soured cream
1–2 tsp lemon juice
1 spring onion, thinly sliced
2 garlic cloves, crushed
salt and cayenne pepper, to taste

dippers: assorted vegetables, breadsticks, crackers

Put the soft cheese in a 1.5 litre/2½ pint slow cooker. Cover and cook on Low until the cheese has melted, about 30 minutes. Mix in the remaining ingredients, except the salt, cayenne pepper and dippers. Cover and cook until hot, 1–1½ hours. Season to taste with salt and cayenne pepper. Serve with dippers.

Artichoke and Prawn Dip

Make sure you thaw the prawns, if frozen.

SERVES 16

100 g/4 oz soft cheese, at room
  temperature
400 g/14 oz artichoke hearts, drained
  and finely chopped
130 g/4½ oz well drained, thawed,
  frozen chopped spinach
90 g/3½ oz chopped prawns
1–2 tbsp drained capers
½ roasted red pepper, chopped
40 g/1½ oz freshly grated Parmesan
  cheese
120 ml/4 fl oz mayonnaise
120 ml/4 fl oz soured cream
1–2 tsp lemon juice
1 spring onion, thinly sliced
2 garlic cloves, crushed
salt and cayenne pepper, to taste

**dippers: assorted vegetables,
  breadsticks, crackers**

Put the soft cheese in a 1.5 litre/2½ pint
slow cooker. Cover and cook on Low
until the cheese has melted, about 30
minutes. Mix in the remaining ingredients,
except the salt, cayenne pepper and
dippers. Cover and cook until hot, 1–1½
hours. Season to taste with salt and
cayenne pepper. Serve with dippers.

Hot Crab and Artichoke Dip

Smooth and delicious – with a hint of spice.

SERVES 16

100 g/4 oz soft cheese, at room
  temperature
400 g/14 oz artichoke hearts, drained
  and finely chopped
130 g/4½ oz well drained, thawed,
  frozen chopped spinach
350 g/12 oz coarsely chopped white
  crab meat
2 tbsp chopped pickled jalapeño, or
  medium-hot, chilli
½ roasted red pepper, chopped
40 g/1½ oz freshly grated Parmesan
  cheese
120 ml/4 fl oz mayonnaise
120 ml/4 fl oz soured cream
1–2 tsp lemon juice
1 spring onion, thinly sliced
2 garlic cloves, crushed
salt and cayenne pepper, to taste

**dippers: assorted vegetables,
  breadsticks, crackers**

Put the soft cheese in a a 1.5 litre/2½
pint slow cooker. Cover and cook on Low
until the cheese has melted, about 30
minutes. Mix in the remaining ingredients,
except the salt, cayenne pepper and
dippers. Cover and cook until hot, 1–1½
hours. Season to taste with salt and
cayenne pepper. Serve with dippers.

Beef and Thousand Island Dip

This is like a combination of all the favourite sandwich fillings, but in a dip!

SERVES 12

175 g/6 oz soft cheese, at room temperature
100 g/4 oz Emmental or Gruyère cheese, grated
100 g/4 oz sauerkraut, rinsed and drained
50 g/2 oz cooked beef, chopped
2 tbsp thousand island salad dressing
1 tbsp snipped fresh chives
1 tsp caraway seeds, lightly crushed

dippers: halved rye bread slices, assorted vegetables

Put the cheeses in the slow cooker. Cover and cook on Low until the cheeses have melted, about 30 minutes. Mix in the remaining ingredients, except the dippers. Cover and cook until hot, 1–1½ hours. Serve with dippers.

Dried Beef and Onion Dip

This warm, creamy dip can also be served cold – just beat soft cheese and soured cream until smooth and mix in the remaining ingredients. You can buy beef jerky in specialist outlets, but you could also make the dip with cold roast beef.

SERVES 16

350 g/12 oz soft cheese, at room temperature
175 ml/6 fl oz mayonnaise
130 g/4½ oz dried beef jerky, chopped
2 spring onions, thinly sliced
2 tbsp dried onion flakes
1 tsp garlic salt

dippers: crackers, assorted vegetables, breadsticks

Put the soft cheese in the slow cooker. Cover and cook on Low until the cheese has melted, about 30 minutes. Mix in the remaining ingredients, except the dippers. Cover and cook until hot, 1–1½ hours. Serve with dippers.

Toasted Onion Dip

The flavour secret here is toasting the dried onion flakes. The dip is served hot or can be cooled to room temperature.

SERVES 12

6–8 tbsp dried onion flakes
450 g/1 lb soft cheese, at room temperature
150 ml/¼ pint plain yoghurt
150 ml/¼ pint mayonnaise
4 small spring onions, chopped
3 garlic cloves, crushed
½ tsp beef bouillon granules
120–175 ml/4–6 fl oz semi-skimmed milk
1–2 tsp lemon juice
4–6 drops red pepper sauce
salt and white pepper, to taste

dippers: assorted vegetables, breadsticks

Cook the onion flakes in a small frying pan over medium to medium-low heat until toasted, 3–4 minutes, stirring frequently. Remove from the heat. Put the soft cheese in a 1.5 litre/2½ pint slow cooker. Cover and cook on Low until the cheese has melted, about 30 minutes. Mix in the yoghurt, mayonnaise, spring onions, garlic, bouillon, onion flakes and 120 ml/4 fl oz milk. Cover and cook until hot, 1–1½ hours. Season to taste with lemon juice, pepper sauce, salt and white pepper. Stir in the remaining milk, if desired for consistency. Serve with dippers.

Garlic and Three-cheese Dip Ⓥ

If you like, use minced garlic from a jar to make this recipe extra-easy. You will need 2–3 tbsp. This dip can also be a spread. Beat the cheeses until blended and mix in the garlic, pepper and milk.

SERVES 12

225 g/8 oz soft cheese, at room temperature
50 g/2 oz goats' cheese
25 g/1 oz freshly grated Parmesan cheese
1–2 large garlic cloves, preferably roasted, crushed
a pinch of white pepper
150 ml/¼ pt semi-skimmed milk

dippers: assorted vegetables and crackers

Put the soft cheese and goats' cheese in a 1.5 litre/2½ pint slow cooker. Cover and cook on Low until the cheese has melted, about 30 minutes. Mix in the Parmesan cheese, garlic, white pepper and 120 ml/4 fl oz milk. Cover and cook until hot, 1–1½ hours. Stir in the remaining milk, if desired for consistency. Serve with dippers.

Chilli con Queso Ⓥ

If you prefer a dip with less heat, substitute green peppers and 2–3 tsp minced jalapeño chillies for the poblano chillies.

SERVES 12

2 small poblano or other mild chillies, halved
225 g/8 oz processed cheese slices, chopped
100 g/4 oz mature Cheddar cheese, grated
1 small onion, finely chopped
2 small tomatoes, finely chopped
½ tsp dried oregano

2–4 tbsp semi-skimmed milk
tortilla chips

Put the chillies, skin sides up, on a baking tray. Bake at 220°C/gas 7/fan oven 200°C until the chillies are browned and soft, about 20 minutes. Cool. Discard the seeds and stems, and chop coarsely. Put the cheeses in a 1.5 litre/2½ pint slow cooker. Cover and cook on Low until the cheeses have melted, about 30 minutes. Add the chillies and the remaining ingredients, except the tortilla chips. Cover and cook until hot, 1–1½ hours. Serve with tortilla chips.

Black Bean and Green Chilli with Cheese Ⓥ

This dip is fiery! Reduce the amount of crushed chilli flakes and/or omit the red pepper sauce for a milder dip.

SERVES 16

225 g/8 oz Monterey Jack or Cheddar cheese, cubed
225 g/8 oz soft cheese, at room temperature
250 ml/8 fl oz mayonnaise
50 g/2 oz freshly grated Parmesan cheese
90 g/3½ oz drained, canned black or red kidney beans, rinsed
100 g/4 oz green chillies from a jar, diced
2 garlic cloves, crushed
2 tsp crushed chilli flakes
½–1 tsp red pepper sauce

dippers: tortilla chips, assorted vegetables

Put the Monterey Jack or Cheddar cheese and soft cheese in a 1.5 litre/2½ pint slow cooker. Cover and cook on Low until the cheeses have melted, about 30 minutes. Mix in the remaining ingredients, except the dippers. Cover and cook until hot, 1–1½ hours. Serve with dippers.

Black Bean and Chorizo with Cheese

Milder but still really tasty.

SERVES 16

225 g/8 oz Monterey Jack or Cheddar cheese, cubed
225 g/8 oz soft cheese, at room temperature
¼ recipe Mexican Chorizo (see page 205)
250 ml/8 fl oz mayonnaise
1–2 tsp pickled jalapeño or other medium-hot chillies
50 g/2 oz freshly grated Parmesan cheese
90 g/3½ oz drained, canned black or red kidney beans, rinsed
2 garlic cloves, crushed

dippers: tortilla chips, assorted vegetables

Put the Monterey Jack or Cheddar cheese and soft cheese in a 1.5 litre/2½ pint slow cooker. Cover and cook on Low until the cheeses have melted, about 30 minutes. Mix in the remaining ingredients, except the dippers. Cover and cook until hot, 1–1½ hours. Serve with dippers.

Queso Wraps

The Mexican Chorizo can be used in many Mexican recipes. For the best flavour, make it several hours in advance and refrigerate, so that the flavours meld.

SERVES 16

175 g/6 oz Cheddar cheese, grated
100 g/4 oz processed cheese, cubed
½ roasted red pepper from a jar, chopped
120–175 ml/4–6 fl oz semi-skimmed milk

¼ quantity Mexican Chorizo (see page 205)
16 flour or corn tortilla wraps (15 cm/6 in), warmed
thinly sliced spring onion and chopped fresh coriander, to garnish

Put the cheeses in a 1.5 litre/2½ pint slow cooker. Cover and cook on Low until the cheeses have melted, about 30 minutes. Mix in the remaining ingredients, except the tortillas and garnishes. Cover and cook until hot, 1–1½ hours. Spoon about 3 tbsp of the cheese mixture into the centre of each wrap. Sprinkle with spring onion and fresh coriander, and roll up.

Refried Bean Dip ⓥ

Refried black beans can also be used in this Mexican dip.

SERVES 16

225 g/8 oz processed cheese, cubed
2 x 400 g/14 oz cans refried beans
50 ml/2 fl oz taco sauce or salsa
3 spring onions, chopped
1–2 tbsp chopped pickled jalapeño or other medium-hot chillies

dippers: tortilla chips, assorted vegetables

Put the cheese in a 1.5 litre/2½ pint slow cooker. Cover and cook on Low until the cheese has melted, about 30 minutes. Mix in the remaining ingredients, except the dippers. Cover and cook until hot, 1–1½ hours. Serve with dippers.

Spicy Cheese and Seafood Dip

Plenty of ground pepper adds a definite hot accent to this very easy dip of cheese, prawns and crab meat.

SERVES 8

225 g/8 oz Monterey Jack or mature Cheddar cheese, cubed
225 g/8 oz soft cheese, at room temperature
freshly grated black pepper
175 ml/6 fl oz full-fat milk
175 g/6 oz cooked prawns, thawed if frozen, chopped
175 g/6 oz white crab meat
50 g/2 oz pitted green olives, chopped

dippers: assorted vegetables, crackers, breadsticks

Put the cheeses in a 1.5 litre/2½ pint slow cooker. Cover and cook on Low until the cheese has melted, about 30 minutes. Add plenty of black pepper. Mix in the remaining ingredients, except the dippers. Cover and cook until hot, 1–1½ hours. Serve with dippers.

Easy Monterey Jack Prawn Dip

Use half Cheddar and half Monterey Jack, if you like.

SERVES 8

450 g/1 lb Monterey Jack or mature Cheddar cheese, cubed
225 g/8 oz soft cheese, at room temperature
freshly grated black pepper
175 ml/6 fl oz full-fat milk
350 g/12 oz cooked prawns, thawed if frozen, chopped
50 g/2 oz pitted black olives, chopped

dippers: assorted vegetables, crackers, breadsticks

Put the cheeses in a 1.5 litre/2½ pint slow cooker. Cover and cook on Low until the cheese has melted, about 30 minutes. Add plenty of black pepper. Mix in the remaining ingredients, except the dippers. Cover and cook until hot, 1–1½ hours. Serve with dippers.

Smoked Salmon Dip

Not just any smoked salmon dip, this version has artichoke hearts, capers and garlic for a dip with zip! Any smoked fish can be substituted for the salmon, if you like.

SERVES 16

225 g/8 oz reduced-fat soft cheese, at room temperature
375 ml/13 fl oz mayonnaise
400 g/14 oz can artichoke hearts, drained and chopped
350 g/12 oz smoked salmon
50 g/2 oz freshly grated Parmesan cheese
40 g/1½ oz drained capers
3 large garlic cloves, crushed
3–4 dashes Tabasco sauce

dippers: assorted vegetables, crackers

Put the soft cheese in a 1.5 litre/2½ pint slow cooker. Cover and cook on Low until the cheese has melted, about 30 minutes. Mix in the remaining ingredients, except the dippers. Cover and cook until hot, 1–1½ hours. Serve with dippers.

Smoked Mackerel Dip

A simple and tasty option.

SERVES 16

225 g/8 oz reduced-fat goats' cheese
175 ml/6 fl oz soured cream
175 ml/6 fl oz mayonnaise
350 g/12 oz smoked mackerel
50 g/2 oz freshly grated Parmesan
cheese
40 g/1½ oz drained capers
3 large garlic cloves, crushed
3–4 dashes Tabasco sauce

dippers: assorted vegetables, crackers

Put the soft cheese in a 1.5 litre/2½ pint slow cooker. Cover and cook on Low until the cheese has melted, about 30 minutes. Mix in the remaining ingredients, except the dippers. Cover and cook until hot, 1–1½ hours. Serve with dippers.

Aubergine Caviar Ⓥ

Tenderly cooked aubergine makes a lovely smooth base for a dip with garlic, yoghurt and oregano.

SERVES 6

1 large aubergine (about 700 g/1½ lb)
2 tomatoes, finely chopped
½ onion, finely chopped
50 ml/2 fl oz yoghurt
3 garlic cloves, crushed
2 tbsp olive oil
½ tsp dried oregano
1–2 tbsp lemon juice
salt and freshly ground black pepper,
to taste

dippers: pitta bread wedges

Pierce the aubergine in several places with a fork and put in the slow cooker. Cover and cook on Low until tender, 4–5 hours. Cool to room temperature. Cut the aubergine in half. Scoop out the pulp with a spoon. Mash the aubergine and mix with the remaining ingredients,

seasoning to taste with lemon juice, salt and pepper. Serve with dippers.

Cheese Fondue Ⓥ

The fondue is back from the 1970s by popular demand! Substitute other cheeses for the Emmental or Gruyère, if you prefer.

SERVES 12

225 g/8 oz Emmental or Gruyère
cheese, grated
1 tbsp plain flour
225 g/8 oz soft cheese, at room
temperature
about 175 ml/6 fl oz dry white wine
or apple juice
1 garlic clove, crushed
cayenne pepper, to taste

dippers: cubed French bread, assorted
vegetables

Toss the Emmental or Gruyère cheese in the flour. Combine the cheeses, wine or apple juice and garlic in a 1.5 litre/2½ pint slow cooker. Cover and cook on Low until the cheeses have melted and the fondue is hot, 1–1½ hours. Season to taste with cayenne pepper. Serve with dippers. If the fondue becomes too thick, stir in additional wine or apple juice or a little milk

Bacon and Chipotle Fondue

A very satisfying and rich fondue – but with a bit of a kick!

SERVES 12

225 g/8 oz Emmental or Gruyère cheese, grated
1 tbsp plain flour
225 g/8 oz soft cheese, at room temperature
about 175 ml/6 fl oz dry white wine or apple juice
1 garlic clove, crushed
1–2 tsp finely chopped chipotle chillies in adobo sauce
100–175 g/4–6 oz crisply cooked, crumbled bacon
cayenne pepper, to taste

dippers: cubed French bread, assorted vegetables

Toss the Emmental or Gruyére cheese with the flour. Combine the cheeses, wine or apple juice, garlic and chillies in a 1.5 litre/2½ pint slow cooker. Cover and cook on Low until the cheeses have melted and the fondue is hot, 1–1½ hours. Stir in the bacon and season with cayenne pepper to taste. Serve with dippers. If the fondue becomes too thick, stir in additional wine or apple juice or a little milk.

Tomato Cheddar Fondue Ⓥ

A lovely mild, but tasty, fondue. For extra spiciness, add a chopped hot chilli from a jar.

SERVES 16

450 g/1 lb mild Cheddar cheese, cubed
400 g/14 oz can chopped tomatoes

75 g/3 oz black or green olives, sliced
1 large garlic clove, crushed

dippers: tortilla chips, assorted vegetables

Put the cheese in a 1.5 litre/2½ pint slow cooker. Cover and cook on Low until the cheese has melted, about 30 minutes. Mix in the remaining ingredients, except the dippers. Cover and cook until hot, about 1½ hours. Serve with dippers.

Blue Cheese Fondue Ⓥ

Just about any variety of blue cheese would be good in this fondue, but blue Stilton woud work particularly well.

SERVES 12

225 g/8 oz Emmental or Gruyère cheese, grated
1 tbsp plain flour
150 g/5 oz soft cheese, at room temperature
75 g/3 oz blue cheese, crumbled
about 175 ml/6 fl oz dry white wine or apple juice
2 garlic cloves, crushed
2 spring onions, thinly sliced
cayenne pepper, to taste

dippers: cubed French bread, assorted vegetables

Toss the Emmental or Gruyère cheese with the flour. Combine the cheeses, wine or apple juice, garlic and spring onion in a 1.5 litre/2½ pint slow cooker. Cover and cook on Low until the cheeses have melted and the fondue is hot, 1–1½ hours. Season to taste with cayenne pepper. Serve with dippers. If the fondue becomes too thick, stir in additional wine or apple juice or a little milk.

Prawn Fondue

Remember to allow the prawns to thaw, if using frozen, before adding them to the slow cooker.

SERVES 12

100 g/4 oz Emmental or Gruyère cheese, grated
100 g/4 oz Cheddar cheese, grated
1 tbsp plain flour
225 g/8 oz soft cheese, at room temperature
about 175 ml/6 fl oz dry white wine or apple juice
1 garlic clove, crushed
225 g/8 oz cooked, peeled prawns, chopped
cayenne pepper, to taste

dippers: cubed French bread, assorted vegetables

Toss the Emmental or Gruyère cheese and Cheddar cheese with the flour. Combine the cheeses, wine or apple juice and garlic in a 1.5 litre/2½ pint slow cooker. Cover and cook on Low until the cheeses have melted and the fondue is hot, 1–1½ hours, adding the prawns for the last 15 minutes of cooking. Season to taste with cayenne pepper. Serve with dippers. If the fondue becomes too thick, stir in additional wine or apple juice or a little milk.

Black Bean Cheesecake with Salsa Ⓥ

This fabulous appetiser can also be served in larger pieces for brunch or supper – sauté wedges of cheesecake in a lightly greased large frying pan over medium-low heat until warm and browned on both sides.

SERVES 24

oil, for greasing
dry breadcrumbs, for coating
550 g/1¼ lb soft cheese, at room temperature
6 eggs
400 g/14 oz can black beans, rinsed and drained
½ jalapeño, or medium-hot, chilli, finely chopped
2 tbsp finely chopped onion
2 garlic cloves, crushed
2 tsp dried cumin
½ tsp dried oregano
½ tsp chilli powder
½ tsp salt
½ tsp cayenne pepper
250 ml/8 fl oz tomato salsa

Grease an 18 cm/7 in springform cake tin and coat with breadcrumbs. Beat the soft cheese in large bowl until fluffy. Beat in the eggs. Mix in the remaining ingredients, except the salsa. Pour into the prepared tin and put on the rack of a 5.5 litre/9½ pint slow cooker. Put three layers of kitchen paper over the top of the slow cooker. Cover and cook on High until the cheesecake is set and a sharp knife inserted halfway between the centre and the edge of the cheesecake comes out almost clean, about 4 hours. Transfer the tin to a wire rack and cool for 1 hour. Remove the cheesecake from the tin and cool completely on the wire rack. Refrigerate for 8 hours or overnight. Serve with the salsa.

Chicken Liver Pâté

This superb pâté has a velvety texture and a hint of sweetness from the apple.

SERVES 16

450 g/1 lb chicken livers
½ onion, finely chopped
1 small apple, peeled and finely chopped
2–4 tbsp brandy (optional)
100 g/4 oz unsalted butter or margarine, at room temperature
salt and cayenne pepper, to taste

Combine the chicken livers, onion and apple in the slow cooker. Cover and cook on High until the livers are no longer pink in the centre, about 3 hours. Process the liver mixture and brandy in a food processor or blender until very smooth, adding the butter or margarine 2 tbsp at a time. Season to taste with salt and cayenne pepper. Spoon into a serving dish and refrigerate until chilled.

Ginger-soy Chicken Wings

Chinese five-spice powder, soy sauce, maple syrup and fresh root ginger combine for a spectacular flavour.

SERVES 8 AS A STARTER

1.5 kg/3 lb (about 16) chicken wings with the wing tips removed
75 ml/5 tbsp soy sauce
1 tbsp maple syrup
1 tbsp fresh root ginger, finely grated
3 garlic cloves, crushed
1½ tsp Chinese five-spice powder
3 spring onions, sliced
1 tbsp sesame seeds, toasted

Combine all the ingredients, except the spring onions and sesame seeds, in the slow cooker. Cover and cook on High for 3–4 hours, draining off the fat after 2 hours. Arrange the chicken wings on a platter. Garnish with spring onions and sesame seeds.

Teriyaki Chicken Wings

A few Japanese flavourings transform simple chicken wings into a moreish nibble. The wings can be grilled briefly after cooking if you want them to be browned.

SERVES 8 AS A STARTER

1.5 kg/3 lb (about 16) chicken wings with the wing tips removed, halved
350 g/12 oz light brown sugar
250 ml/8 fl oz soy sauce
2 tbsp hoisin sauce
1 tsp ground ginger
½ tsp garlic powder
1 tbsp chopped fresh parsley
1 tbsp toasted sesame seeds

Put the chicken wings in the slow cooker. Pour the combined remaining ingredients, except the parsley and sesame seeds, over the chicken wings. Cover and cook on High for 3–4 hours. Sprinkle with parsley and sesame seeds.

Buffalo Chicken Wings

Hot and spicy chicken wings are served with a cooling creamy Blue Cheese Dressing.

SERVES 8 AS A STARTER

50 g/2 oz butter or margarine
4 tbsp Tabasco sauce
1 tbsp white distilled vinegar
1.5 kg/3 lb (about 16) chicken wings with the wing tips removed, halved
salt and freshly ground black pepper, to taste
Blue Cheese Dressing (see page 65)

Combine the butter or margarine, Tabasco sauce and vinegar in the slow cooker. Turn the heat to High and cook until the butter or margarine has melted, about 15 minutes. Sprinkle the chicken wings with salt and pepper. Grill until lightly browned, about 5 minutes on each side. Add to the slow cooker and toss with the butter mixture. Cover and cook on High for 3–4 hours. Serve with the Blue Cheese Dressing.

Blue Cheese Dressing Ⓥ

A tasty dressing for soups and salads.

SERVES 8

**175 ml/6 fl oz mayonnaise or salad
  dressing
40 g/1½ oz blue cheese, crumbled
1½ tbsp red wine vinegar
1 tsp celery seeds
½ tsp salt
a pinch of cayenne pepper
a pinch of black pepper**

Mix all the ingredients.

Meatballs in Tomato Pasilla Chilli Sauce

Spicy meatballs are served with an even hotter sauce. Use three chillies only if you enjoy a truly hot sauce! The meatballs can be made in advance and frozen. Thaw before using.

SERVES 12 AS A STARTER

**2–3 pasilla or other hot chillies
oil, for greasing
2 x 400 g/14 oz cans chopped
  tomatoes
salt, to taste
Jalapeño Meatballs (see right)**

Cook the chillies in a large lightly greased pan over medium heat until softened. Discard the stems, seeds and veins. Process the chillies and tomatoes in a blender until smooth. Season to taste with salt. Combine the tomato mixture and meatballs in the slow cooker. Cover and cook on High until the meatballs are cooked, about 4 hours. Turn the heat to Low to keep warm for serving.

Jalapeño Meatballs

You can vary the mince you use.

SERVES 12 AS A STARTER

**225 g/8 oz pork tenderloin or other
  lean pork, minced
225 g/8 oz lean minced beef
1 egg
15 g/½ oz dry breadcrumbs
½ onion, finely chopped
2 garlic cloves, crushed
1 tsp very finely chopped jalapeño or
  other medium-hot chilli
1 tsp dried oregano
salt and freshly ground black pepper,
  to taste**

Combine all the ingredients in a bowl. Shape the mixture into 24 meatballs.

Sweet-and-sour Meatballs

A simple sweet chilli and mustard sauce tastes good with meatballs. This recipe can be made substituting 450 g/1 lb smoked sausage or hot dogs for the Party Meatballs.

SERVES 12 AS A STARTER

**Party Meatballs (see page 62)
450 ml/¾ pint chilli sauce from a jar
275 g/10 oz apricot jam
1 tbsp Dijon mustard
1 tbsp lemon juice**

Place the meatballs in the slow cooker with the remaining ingredients. Cover and cook on High until the meatballs are cooked, about 4 hours. Turn the heat to Low to keep warm for serving.

Party Meatballs

Make these with pork for a change.

SERVES 12 AS A STARTER

450 g/1 lb lean minced beef
20 g/¾ oz dry breadcrumbs
1 egg
2 tbsp dried minced onion
1 tsp garlic powder
½ tsp salt
½ tsp pepper

Combine all the ingredients in a bowl. Shape the mixture into 24 meatballs.

Island Barbecue Meatballs

Use your favourite barbecue sauce in this orange-and-pineapple accented appetiser.

SERVES 12 AS A STARTER

Party Meatballs (see above)
450 ml/¾ pint barbecue sauce
425 g/15 oz orange marmalade
¾ tsp ground allspice
225 g/8 oz can pineapple pieces,
   drained

Place the meatballs in the slow cooker with the remaining ingredients. Cover and cook on High until the meatballs are cooked, about 4 hours. Turn the heat to Low to keep warm for serving.

Eggs Rarebit

This makes an ideal light lunch or supper dish, with plenty of protein to keep your energy levels up.

SERVES 6

225 g/8 oz grated Cheddar cheese
225 g/8 oz soft cheese, at room
   temperature
250 ml/8 fl oz beer
½ tsp dry mustard powder
½ tsp Worcestershire or mushroom
   sauce
cayenne pepper, to taste
6 slices multigrain bread, toasted
175 g/6 oz sliced ham, warmed
6 eggs, poached
crisp cooked bacon, crumbled, paprika
   and chopped chives, to garnish

Combine the cheeses, beer, mustard powder and Worcestershire or mushroom sauce in the slow cooker. Cover and cook on low until the cheeses have melted, about 2 hours, stirring twice during cooking. Season to taste with cayenne pepper. Put the toasted bread on serving plates. Top each with some ham and a poached egg and spoon the rarebit mixture over. Sprinkle with bacon crumbs, paprika and chives.

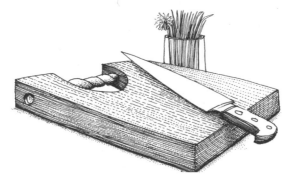

Main-course Soups

In this chapter you'll find some heartier fare – great for making into main meals with crusty bread or a crisp, fresh side salad. Of course, there's nothing to stop you using them to precede a main meal if you have the appetite.

Asparagus and Tomato Soup with Cheese Ⓥ

The flavours of asparagus, tomatoes and Cheddar cheese, accented with mustard, taste great in this soup.

SERVES 6

750 ml/1¼ pints vegetable stock
400 g/14 oz can chopped tomatoes
1 onion, chopped
1 carrot, chopped
½ tsp dried marjoram
¼ tsp dry mustard powder
¼ tsp white pepper
100 g/4 oz easy-cook long-grain rice
550 g/1¼ lb asparagus spears, sliced and cooked
100 g/4 oz Cheddar cheese, grated
salt, to taste

Combine all the ingredients, except the rice, asparagus, cheese and salt, in the slow cooker. Cover and cook on Low for 8–10 hours, stirring in the rice during the last 4 hours and the asparagus during the last 40 minutes. Add the cheese and stir until melted. Season to taste with salt.

Aubergine Soup with Roasted Red Pepper Sauce Ⓥ

For speed, 350 g/12 oz roasted red peppers from a jar, drained, can be substituted for the peppers in the recipe.

SERVES 4

1.2 litres/2 pints vegetable stock
2 medium aubergines, peeled and cubed (2 cm/¾ in)
2 small onions, chopped
¼ green pepper, chopped
2 garlic cloves, crushed
salt and white pepper, to taste
Roasted Red Pepper Sauce (see below)

Combine all the ingredients, except the salt, white pepper and Roasted Red Pepper Sauce, in the slow cooker. Cover and cook on High for 4–5 hours. Process the soup in a food processor or blender until smooth. Season to taste with salt and white pepper. Serve warm or refrigerate and serve chilled. Swirl a large tablespoon of Roasted Red Pepper Sauce into each bowl of soup before serving.

Roasted Red Pepper Sauce Ⓥ

This recipe can also be cooked in a 2.75 litre/4¾ pint slow cooker, without using a casserole. Cooking time will be 3–3½ hours.

SERVES 4

2 large red peppers, halved
1 tsp sugar

Put the peppers, skin sides up, on a grill pan. Grill until the skins are blistered and blackened. Put the peppers in a plastic bag for 5 minutes. Remove from the bag and peel off the skins. Process the peppers and sugar in a food processor or blender until smooth.

63

Sweet-and-sour Cabbage Soup

This rich, tangy cabbage soup is made with both beef and turkey.

SERVES 8

225 g/8 oz minced beef
225 g/8 oz minced or finely chopped turkey breast
oil, for greasing
2.25 litres/4 pints Fragrant Beef Stock (see page 26)
425 g/15 oz ready-made tomato sauce
225 g/8 oz thinly sliced green cabbage
1 large onion, chopped
1 carrot, sliced
2 garlic cloves, crushed
2 tbsp cider vinegar
2 tbsp brown sugar
1 bay leaf
1 tsp dried thyme
a pinch of ground cinnamon
90 g/3½ oz raisins
100 g/4 oz easy-cook long-grain rice
salt and freshly ground black pepper, to taste

Cook the minced beef and turkey in a lightly greased large frying pan over medium heat until browned, about 5 minutes, crumbling the meat with a fork. Combine the meats and remaining ingredients, except the rice, salt and pepper, in a 5.5 litre/9½ pint slow cooker. Cover and cook on Low for 6–8 hours, adding the rice during the last 2 hours. Discard the bay leaf. Season to taste with salt and pepper.

Creamy Carrot Soup Ⓥ

Orange and ginger flavour this delicious soup. It is also excellent served chilled.

SERVES 8

500 ml/17 fl oz vegetable stock
4 large carrots, sliced
120 ml/4 fl oz frozen orange juice concentrate
1 cm/½ in piece fresh root ginger, chopped
½ tsp dried tarragon
½ tsp dried thyme
375 ml/13 fl oz semi-skimmed milk
1 tbsp cornflour
salt and freshly ground black pepper, to taste
soured cream, to garnish

Combine the stock, carrots, orange juice concentrate, ginger and herbs in the slow cooker. Cover and cook on Low for 4–6 hours, adding 250 ml/8 fl oz milk during the last 30 minutes. Turn the slow cooker to High and cook for 10 minutes. Stir in the combined remaining milk and the cornflour, stirring for 2–3 minutes. Process the soup in a food processor or blender until smooth. Season to taste with salt and pepper. Garnish each bowl of soup with a dollop of soured cream.

Cauliflower Soup Ⓥ

This velvety soup is flavoured with curry powder and crushed chilli flakes for spicy highlights.

SERVES 4–6

750 ml/1¼ pints vegetable stock
1 large cauliflower, in florets
2 small carrots, diced
1 onion, chopped
1 celery stick, sliced
1 tsp curry powder
¼ tsp crushed chilli flakes
250 ml/8 fl oz semi-skimmed milk
juice of ½ lemon
salt and freshly ground black pepper, to taste
paprika, to garnish

Combine all the ingredients, except the milk, lemon juice, salt and pepper, in the slow cooker. Cover and cook on High for 4–6 hours. Process the soup and milk in a food processor or blender until smooth. Season to taste with lemon juice, salt and pepper. Sprinkle each bowl of soup with paprika.

Creamy Cauliflower Soup

If you are lucky enough to grow your own vegetables, this is certainly one to try.

SERVES 6

450 ml/¾ pint chicken stock
150 g/5 oz floury potatoes, peeled and cubed
½ cauliflower, coarsely chopped
1 onion, chopped
50 g/2 oz leek, chopped
450 ml/¾ pint semi-skimmed milk
50 g/2 oz freshly grated Parmesan cheese
2 tbsp cornflour
salt and freshly ground black pepper, to taste
freshly grated nutmeg, to garnish

Combine the stock, potatoes, cauliflower, onion and leek in the slow cooker. Cover and cook on Low for 6–8 hours, stirring in 375 ml/13 fl oz milk and the cheese during the last 30 minutes. Turn the slow cooker to High and cook for 10 minutes. Stir in the combined remaining milk and the cornflour, stirring for 2–3 minutes. Season to taste with salt and pepper. Process the soup in a food processor or blender until smooth. Serve hot, or refrigerate and serve chilled. Sprinkle with grated nutmeg to serve.

Cheddar, Broccoli and Potato Soup

For variation, cauliflower can be substituted for part or all of the broccoli.

SERVES 6

1 litre/1¾ pints chicken or beef stock
2 onions, chopped
1 celery stick, finely chopped
1 carrot, finely chopped
350 g/12 oz floury potatoes, unpeeled and cubed
½ tsp celery seeds
½ tsp dried thyme
350 g/12 oz small broccoli florets
250 ml/8 fl oz semi-skimmed milk
2 tbsp cornflour
225 g/8 oz mild Cheddar cheese, grated
salt and freshly ground black pepper, to taste

Combine all the ingredients, except the broccoli, milk, cornflour, cheese, salt and pepper, in the slow cooker. Cover and cook on Low for 6–8 hours, adding the broccoli during the last 30 minutes. Turn the heat to High and cook for 10 minutes. Stir in the combined milk and cornflour, stirring for 2–3 minutes. Add the cheese, stirring for 2–3 minutes until melted. Season to taste with salt and pepper.

Curried Sweetcorn Soup Ⓥ

A variety of spices and coconut milk make this soup an exotic treat.

SERVES 6

450 ml/¾ pint vegetable stock
350 g/12 oz sweetcorn, thawed if
frozen
3 onions, chopped
1 jalapeño or other medium-hot chilli,
finely chopped
3 large garlic cloves, crushed
2.5 cm/1 in piece fresh root ginger,
finely grated
½ tsp ground cumin
½ tsp ground cinnamon
250 ml/8 fl oz semi-skimmed milk
400 g/14 oz can light coconut milk
2 tbsp cornflour
salt and freshly ground black pepper,
to taste
chopped fresh coriander, to garnish

Combine the stock, sweetcorn, onions, chilli, garlic, ginger and spices in the slow cooker. Cover and cook on Low for 6–8 hours, stirring in the milk during the last 30 minutes. Turn the heat to High and cook for 10 minutes. Add the combined coconut milk and cornflour, stirring for 2–3 minutes. Season to taste with salt and pepper. Sprinkle each bowl of soup with fresh coriander.

Cream of Mushroom Soup Ⓥ

This mushroom soup works well with any kind of mushroom. For a richer taste, use full-fat milk or single cream instead of semi-skimmed milk.

SERVES 4

750 ml/1¼ pints vegetable stock
450 g/1 lb mushrooms, sliced
2 onions, chopped
375 ml/13 fl oz semi-skimmed milk
2 tbsp cornflour
salt and freshly ground black pepper,
to taste

Combine all the ingredients, except the milk, cornflour, salt and pepper, in the slow cooker. Cover and cook on Low for 5–6 hours, stirring in 250 ml/8 fl oz milk during the last 30 minutes. Turn the heat to High and cook for 10 minutes. Stir in the combined remaining milk and the cornflour, stirring for 2–3 minutes. Season to taste with salt and pepper.

Brandied Onion Soup

This soup is wonderful because slow cooking melds the flavours. If you like, cook the onions in 1 tbsp butter or margarine in a large frying pan over medium-low heat until golden before assembling the ingredients in the slow cooker.

SERVES 8

8 onions, thinly sliced
2.25 litres/4 pints Fragrant Beef Stock
(see page 26), or beef stock
2–4 tbsp brandy (optional)
salt and freshly ground black pepper,
to taste

Combine the onions and stock in a 5.5 litre/9½ pint slow cooker. Cover and cook on Low for 6–8 hours. Add the brandy. Season to taste with salt and pepper.

Onion and Potato Soup

Use floury potatoes for good results.

SERVES 8

8 onions, thinly sliced
2.25 litres/4 pints Fragrant Beef Stock (see page 26), or beef stock
500 g/18 oz peeled and cubed potatoes
¼ tsp dried marjoram
¼ tsp dried thyme
2–4 tbsp brandy (optional)
salt and freshly ground black pepper, to taste
2 tbsp grated Emmental or Gruyère cheese

Combine all the ingredients, except the brandy, salt, pepper and cheese, in the slow cooker. Cover and cook on Low for 6–8 hours. Add the brandy. Season to taste with salt and pepper and serve sprinkled with cheese.

Curried Onion and Potato Soup

Enjoy this spicy soup warm in the winter. Sip it chilled from soup cups in the summer.

SERVES 4

1 litre/1¾ pints vegetable stock
6 onions, coarsely chopped
350 g/12 oz potatoes, peeled and diced
1 garlic clove, crushed
1¼ tsp ground cumin
1¼ tsp ground turmeric
1¼ tsp curry powder
175 ml/6 fl oz semi-skimmed milk
salt and freshly ground black pepper, to taste

Combine all the ingredients, except the milk and salt and pepper, in the slow cooker. Cover and cook on Low for 6–8 hours. Process the soup and milk in a food processor or blender until smooth. Season to taste with salt and pepper. Serve warm or refrigerate and serve chilled.

Easy Curried Potato Soup

Very simple ingredients that you'll probably already have in stock are used here to produce a wonderful soup.

SERVES 4

1 litre/1¾ pints vegetable stock
700 g/1½ lb baking potatoes, peeled and cubed
1 large onion, chopped
1 apple, peeled and diced
2 cm/¾ in piece fresh root ginger, finely grated
2 large garlic cloves, crushed
½ tsp caraway seeds
2–3 tsp curry powder
400 g/14 oz can tomatoes
salt and freshly ground black pepper, to taste

Combine all the ingredients, except the tomatoes, salt and pepper, in the slow cooker. Cover and cook on Low until the potatoes are tender, about 8 hours. Process half the potato mixture in a food processor or blender until smooth. Return to the slow cooker and add the tomatoes. Cover and cook on High for 15 minutes. Season to taste with salt and pepper.

67

Smoky Cheese and Potato Soup Ⓥ

I suggest using smoked Gouda but you could use another smoked cheese or just plain Cheddar if you prefer.

SERVES 4

1 litre/1¾ pints vegetable stock
700 g/1 ½ lb baking potatoes, peeled and cubed
1 large onion, chopped·
1 apple, peeled and diced
2 large garlic cloves, crushed
400 g/14 oz can tomatoes
175 ml/6 fl oz soured cream
1 tbsp cornflour
salt and freshly ground black pepper, to taste
100 g/4 oz grated smoked Gouda cheese

Combine the stock, potatoes, onion, apple and garlic in the slow cooker. Cover and cook on Low until the potatoes are tender, about 8 hours. Process half the potato mixture in a food processor or blender until smooth. Return to the slow cooker and add the tomatoes. Blend the soured cream and cornflour and add to the slow cooker, stirring for 2 minutes. Cover and cook on High for 15 minutes. Season to taste with salt and pepper and serve sprinkled with cheese.

Velvet Vichyssoise

Although typically served chilled, this soup of leek and potatoes is also wonderful served warm.

SERVES 6

450 ml/¾ pint chicken stock
600 g/1 lb 6 oz floury potatoes, peeled and cubed
1 onion, chopped
50 g/2 oz leek, chopped
450 ml/¾ pint semi-skimmed milk
2 tbsp cornflour
salt and freshly ground black pepper, to taste
snipped chives, to garnish

Combine the stock, potatoes, onion and leek in the slow cooker. Cover and cook on Low for 6–8 hours, stirring in 375 ml/13 fl oz milk during the last 30 minutes. Turn the slow cooker to High and cook for 10 minutes. Stir in the combined remaining milk and the cornflour, stirring for 2–3 minutes. Season to taste with salt and pepper. Process the soup in a food processor or blender until smooth. Serve hot, or refrigerate and serve chilled. Sprinkle each bowl of soup with chives.

Ripe Tomato and Leek Soup Ⓥ

Here's a perfect soup for summer's ripest tomatoes. Choose vine-ripened ones for the best flavour.

SERVES 6

1 litre/1¾ pints vegetable stock
6 large tomatoes, chopped
2 leeks (white parts only), sliced
3 garlic cloves, crushed
1 tsp dried basil
salt and white pepper, to taste
6 tbsp soured cream
6 fresh basil sprigs, to garnish

Combine all the ingredients, except the salt, pepper, soured cream and basil, in the slow cooker. Cover and cook on Low for 6–8 hours. Process the soup in a food processor or blender until smooth. Season to taste with salt and white pepper. Serve warm or refrigerate and serve chilled. Garnish each bowl of soup with a dollop of soured cream and a basil sprig.

Sweet Potato Vichyssoise

A superb variation on traditional vichyssoisse.

SERVES 6

450 ml/¾ pint chicken stock
600 g/1 lb 6 oz sweet potatoes, peeled and cubed
1 onion, chopped
6 spring onions, chopped
300 ml/½ pint orange juice
4 tbsp milk
2 tbsp cornflour
½ tsp ground cinnamon
½ tsp ground mace
salt and freshly ground black pepper, to taste
grated orange zest, to garnish

Combine the stock, potatoes, onion and spring onions in the slow cooker. Cover and cook on Low for 6–8 hours, stirring in the orange juice during the last 30 minutes. Turn the slow cooker to High and cook for 10 minutes. Stir in the combined milk and the cornflour, stirring for 2–3 minutes. Add the cinnamon and mace and season to taste with salt and pepper. Process the soup in a food processor or blender until smooth. Serve hot, or refrigerate and serve chilled. Sprinkle each bowl of soup with grated orange zest.

Two-season Squash Soup

Winter butternut squash and summer garden courgettes are combined in this perfect soup.

SERVES 6

750 ml/1¼ pints beef stock
2 × 400 g/14 oz cans chopped tomatoes
400 g/14 oz can cannellini beans, drained and rinsed
1 butternut squash, peeled, seeded and cubed
2 courgettes, sliced
2 onions, chopped
2 garlic cloves, crushed
1 tsp Worcestershire sauce
1 tsp dried marjoram
½ tsp dried rosemary
salt and freshly ground black pepper, to taste

Combine all the ingredients, except the salt and pepper, in a 5.5 litre/9½ pint slow cooker. Cover and cook on High for 4–6 hours. Season to taste with salt and pepper.

Creamy Tomato Soup with Chunky Vegetables Ⓥ

A grown-up version of that comforting soup we know so well, plus chunky pieces of vegetables.

SERVES 4

1 litre/1¾ pints vegetable stock
225 g/8 oz ready-made tomato sauce
175 g/6 oz cauliflower, cut into small florets
1 courgette, diced
1 green pepper, diced
2 onions, diced
175 g/6 oz new potatoes, unpeeled and cubed
1 large garlic clove, crushed
¾ tsp dried basil
¼ tsp dried thyme
¼ tsp dried marjoram
a pinch of dry mustard powder
175 ml/6 fl oz semi-skimmed milk
1 tbsp cornflour
2 tbsp dry sherry (optional)
salt and freshly ground black pepper, to taste

Combine all the ingredients, except the milk, cornflour, sherry, salt and pepper, in the slow cooker. Cover and cook on High for 4–6 hours. Stir in the combined milk and cornflour, stirring for 2–3 minutes. Stir in the sherry. Season to taste with salt and pepper.

Tomato Soup with Pasta

Nothing matches sweet, sun-ripened tomatoes so well as the summer flavours of basil and oregano. Freeze ripe tomatoes from your garden for making this soup in the winter, too.

SERVES 6

750 ml/1¼ pints Rich Chicken Stock (see page 25), or chicken or vegetable stock
1.5 kg/3 lb tomatoes, coarsely chopped
1 onion, chopped
1 carrot, chopped
½ celery stick, chopped
1 garlic clove, crushed
1 tsp dried basil
1 tsp dried oregano
½ tsp anise seeds, lightly crushed
100 g/4 oz small soup pasta, such as stelline, orzo or rings
salt and freshly ground black pepper, to taste
freshly grated Parmesan cheese, to garnish

Combine all the ingredients, except the pasta, salt, pepper and cheese, in a 5.5 litre/9½ pint slow cooker. Cover and cook on Low for 6–8 hours. Process the soup in a food processor or blender until smooth. Return the soup to the slow cooker. Cover and cook on High for 10 minutes. Stir in the pasta and cook until al dente, about 20 minutes. Season to taste with salt and pepper. Sprinkle each bowl of soup with Parmesan cheese.

Garden Harvest Soup ⓥ

Here is perfect summer fare, but you can also vary the vegetables according to what is in season in your garden or from your greengrocer.

SERVES 6

1.2 litres/2 pints vegetable stock
150 g/5 oz French beans, cut into
   short lengths
2 onions, sliced
1 courgette, sliced
175 g/6 oz yellow summer squash,
   such as courgette or patty pan,
   sliced
2 small carrots, sliced
1 small red pepper, sliced
1 small yellow pepper, sliced
75 g/3 oz sweetcorn
2 garlic cloves, crushed
½ tsp dried basil
½ tsp dried oregano
75 ml/2½ fl oz semi-skimmed milk
salt and freshly ground black pepper,
   to taste

Combine all the ingredients, except the milk, salt and pepper, in a 5.5 litre/9½ pint slow cooker. Cover and cook on Low for 8–10 hours, adding the milk during the last 10 minutes. Season to taste with salt and pepper.

Light Minestrone

Minestrone does not always contain pasta, nor is it always a heavy, hearty soup. Enjoy this light version of an old favourite.

SERVES 8

1.2 litres/2 pints beef stock
175 g/6 oz sugarsnap peas
175 g/6 oz broccoli florets
1 courgette, sliced
1 large carrot, sliced
150 g/5 oz cherry tomatoes, halved
1 onion, chopped
1 celery stick, chopped
½ fennel bulb, sliced
2 garlic cloves, crushed
1 tsp dried basil
1 tsp dried oregano
salt and freshly ground black pepper,
   to taste
Parmesan Croûtons (see below)

Combine all the ingredients, except the salt, pepper and Parmesan Croûtons, in a 5.5 litre/9½ pint slow cooker. Cover and cook on Low for 6–8 hours. Season to taste with salt and pepper. Sprinkle each bowl of soup with Parmesan Croûtons.

Parmesan Croûtons ⓥ

These delicious crispy croûtons go well with Mediterranean flavours.

SERVES 8 AS AN ACCOMPANIMENT

3 slices firm or day-old Italian bread,
   cubed (1–2 cm/½–¾ in)
vegetable cooking spray
2 tbsp freshly grated Parmesan cheese

Spray the bread cubes with cooking spray. Sprinkle with Parmesan cheese and toss. Arrange in a single layer on a baking tray. Bake at 190°C/gas 5/ fan oven 170°C until browned, 8–10 minutes, stirring occasionally.

Minestrone with Basil Pesto Ⓥ

In the basil-loving town of Genoa, the addition of aromatic Basil Pesto distinguishes the local version of minestrone.

SERVES 6

1.5 litres/2 ½ pints vegetable stock
400 g/14 oz can cannellini beans, drained and rinsed
1 small leek (white part only), chopped
1 small carrot, chopped
½ celery stick, chopped
1 small yellow pepper, chopped
1 large garlic clove, crushed
225 g/8 oz yellow summer squash, such as courgette or patty pan, cubed
50 g/2 oz frozen peas, thawed
100 g/4 oz elbow macaroni, cooked
Basil Pesto (see right)
salt and freshly ground black pepper, to taste
freshly grated Parmesan cheese, to garnish

Combine the stock, beans, leek, carrot, celery, pepper and garlic in a 5.5 litre/9½ pint slow cooker. Cover and cook on High for 4–5 hours, adding the squash during the last hour. Add the peas, macaroni and Basil Pesto to the slow cooker and cook for a further 20 minutes. Season to taste with salt and pepper. Sprinkle each bowl of soup with Parmesan cheese.

Basil Pesto Ⓥ

Basil pesto is something you will use over and over again. Try stirring it into cooked pasta for a quick supper dish or spread on rolled-out puff pastry, then folded or twisted before baking as an alternative to cheese straws.

SERVES 6 AS AN ACCOMPANIMENT

15 g/½ oz fresh basil
1 garlic clove
1½ tbsp freshly grated Parmesan cheese
1½ tbsp pine nuts or flaked almonds
1–2 tbsp olive oil
1 tsp lemon juice
salt and freshly ground black pepper, to taste

Process the basil, garlic, Parmesan cheese and pine nuts or almonds in a food processor or blender, adding the oil and lemon juice gradually, until the mixture is very finely chopped. Season to taste with salt and pepper.

Summer Soup with Tomato Relish ⓥ

Sweetcorn and courgettes make an interesting and colourful soup topped with a fresh tomato relish.

SERVES 4

1 litre/1¾ pints vegetable stock
450 g/1 lb yellow summer squash, such
   as courgette or patty pan, chopped
2 large onions, coarsely chopped
250 g/9 oz sweetcorn
75 g/3 oz potato, peeled and diced
1 large garlic clove, chopped
¼ tsp dry mustard powder
120 ml/4 fl oz semi-skimmed milk
1–2 tsp lemon juice
salt and freshly ground black pepper,
   to taste
chopped fresh coriander, to garnish
Fresh Tomato Relish (see right)

Combine the stock, squash, onions, 100 g/4 oz sweetcorn, potato, garlic and mustard in the slow cooker. Cover and cook on High for 4–6 hours. Process the soup and milk in a food processor or blender until smooth. Return to the slow cooker and add the remaining sweetcorn. Cover and cook on High for 10 minutes. Season the soup to taste with lemon juice, salt and pepper. Sprinkle each bowl of soup with fresh coriander. Serve with the Fresh Tomato Relish to stir into the soup.

Fresh Tomato Relish ⓥ

A handy relish to go with all kinds of dishes.

SERVES 4

1 large, ripe tomato, peeled and
   finely diced
4 tbsp chopped fresh coriander
1 tbsp red wine vinegar
¼ tsp salt

Combine all the ingredients and use as directed in the recipe.

Easy Tortilla Soup ⓥ

This simple tortilla soup uses many convenience ingredients to speed preparation. The flavours are hot, so reduce the quantities of chillies or omit the chilli flakes if you prefer a milder chilli flavour.

SERVES 6

900 ml/1½ pints vegetable stock
400 g/14 oz can chopped tomatoes
400 g/14 oz can spicy chilli beans,
   undrained
100 g/4 oz green chillies from a jar,
   drained and chopped
2 small onions, chopped
1 garlic clove, crushed
2 tsp red wine vinegar
¼ tsp crushed chilli flakes, to taste
15 g/½ oz fresh coriander, chopped
salt, to taste
6 corn tortillas (15 cm/6 in), cut into
   1 cm/½ in strips
vegetable cooking spray
½ small avocado, peeled and cubed

Combine all the ingredients, except the coriander, salt, tortillas, cooking spray and avocado, in a 5.5 litre/9½ pint slow cooker. Cover and cook on Low for 6–8 hours. Stir in the coriander and season to taste with salt. Put the tortilla strips on a baking sheet. Spray with cooking spray and toss. Bake at 190°C/gas 5/fan oven 170°C until crisp, about 5 minutes. Put the tortilla strips and avocado in each soup bowl. Ladle the soup over.

Old-fashioned Chicken and Vegetable Soup

This homely, heartwarming soup, bursting with vegetables, is just like Grandma used to make.

SERVES 6

1.2 litres/2 pints chicken stock
450 g/1 lb skinless chicken breast
    fillet, cubed (2 cm/¾ in)
275 g/10 oz waxy potatoes, peeled
    and diced
100 g/4 oz cabbage, thinly sliced
2 small carrots, sliced
130 g/4½ oz swede or parsnip, cubed
½ celery stick, sliced
3 spring onions, sliced
½ cauliflower head, in small florets
50 g/2 oz medium egg noodles,
    cooked
salt and freshly ground black pepper,
    to taste

Combine all the ingredients, except the cauliflower, noodles, salt and pepper, in the slow cooker. Cover and cook on Low for 6–8 hours, adding the cauliflower and noodles during the last 30 minutes. Season to taste with salt and pepper.

Classic Chicken Noodle Soup

Here is comfort food at its best – and it's so quick to make too.

SERVES 4

900 ml/1½ pints chicken stock
100 g/4 oz skinless chicken breast
    fillet, cubed (2 cm/¾ in)
100 g/4 oz boneless chicken thighs,
    cubed (2 cm/¾ in)
1 large celery stick, sliced
1 large carrot, sliced
2 onions, chopped
1 tsp dried marjoram
1 bay leaf
150 g/5 oz cooked wide noodles
salt and freshly ground black pepper,
    to taste

Combine all the ingredients, except the noodles, salt and pepper, in the slow cooker. Cover and cook on High for 4–6 hours, adding the noodles during the last 20 minutes. Discard the bay leaf. Season to taste with salt and pepper.

Chicken and Vegetable Noodle Soup

This chicken noodle soup is loaded with vegetables for extra goodness and nutrition. Balsamic vinegar adds a unique depth of flavour.

SERVES 6

2.25 litres/4 pints Rich Chicken Stock
    (see page 25) or chicken stock
225 g/8 oz skinless chicken breast
    fillet, cubed (1 cm/½ in)
2 onions, chopped
1 large celery stick, chopped
1 large carrot, chopped
1 parsnip, chopped
150 g/5 oz French beans, cut into
    short lengths
¾ tsp dried thyme
¾ tsp dried rosemary
1–2 tsp balsamic vinegar
175 g/6 oz small broccoli florets
50 g/2 oz frozen peas, thawed
100 g/4 oz noodles, cooked
salt and freshly ground black pepper,
    to taste

Combine all the ingredients, except the broccoli, peas, noodles, salt and pepper, in the slow cooker. Cover and cook on High for 4–6 hours, stirring in the broccoli, peas and noodles during the last 20–30 minutes. Season to taste with salt and pepper.

Country Chicken Noodle Soup

Made with stewing chicken and home-made egg noodles, this soup is bursting with traditional flavour.

SERVES 6

1 small chicken (about 900 g/2 lb), cut into pieces
1.5 litres/2½ pints water
1 large carrot, sliced
175 g/6 oz sweetcorn
1 small onion, chopped
½ tsp dried marjoram
Country Noodles (see below)
50 g/2 oz frozen peas, thawed
1 tbsp chopped fresh parsley
salt and freshly ground black pepper, to taste

Combine the chicken, water, carrots, sweetcorn, onion and marjoram in the slow cooker. Cover and cook on Low for 6–8 hours. Remove the chicken from the slow cooker. Cut the meat into small pieces and return to the slow cooker Cover and cook on High for 30 minutes. Bring a pan of water to the boil. Unroll the noodles, add to the pan and boil for 3 minutes, then drain. Add the noodles to the slow cooker with the peas and parsley and cook for a further 5 minutes. Season to taste with salt and pepper.

Country Noodles Ⓥ

It's so easy to make your own noodles for soup, and you can cut them to the size you and your family like best.

SERVES 6 AS AN ACCOMPANIMENT

100 g/4 oz plain flour, plus extra for dusting
1 egg
1 tbsp water
¼ tsp salt

Put the flour on the work surface. Make a well in the centre and add the egg, water and salt. Gradually mix the flour into the egg with a fork until a dough is formed. Knead the dough on a floured surface until smooth, kneading in additional flour if the dough is sticky. Leave the dough to stand, covered, at room temperature for 1 hour. Roll out the dough on a lightly floured surface to 3 mm thickness. Loosely roll up the dough and cut into 5 mm/¼ in slices. Use as directed in the recipe.

Alphabet Chicken Soup

Kids like the alphabet letters in this traditional chicken soup – and you couldn't get a better way of serving them nutritious food that they will enjoy.

SERVES 4

2.25 litres/4 pints chicken stock
450 g/1 lb skinless chicken breast fillet, cubed (1 cm/½ in)
1 onion, chopped
1 carrot, chopped
1 celery stick, chopped
1 large garlic clove, crushed
1 large bay leaf
½ tsp dried thyme
a pinch of celery seeds
50 g/2 oz alphabet pasta
salt and freshly ground black pepper, to taste

Combine all the ingredients, except the pasta, salt and pepper, in the slow cooker. Cover and cook on Low for 6–8 hours, adding the pasta during the last 20 minutes. Discard the bay leaf. Season to taste with salt and pepper.

Chunky Chicken and Pasta Soup

It's worth keeping some soup pasta in the storecupboard. It tastes good because it absorbs the soup flavours as it cooks, it looks attractive and it makes a soup more substantial.

SERVES 4

900 ml/1½ pints chicken stock
400 g/14 oz can chopped tomatoes
225 g/8 oz skinless chicken breast
**   fillet, cubed**
2 onions, chopped
½ green pepper, diced
½ red pepper, diced
1 garlic clove, crushed
¾ tsp dried basil
¾ tsp dried oregano
100 g/4 oz ditalini
15 g/½ oz chopped fresh parsley
salt and freshly ground black pepper,
**   to taste**

Combine all the ingredients, except the pasta, parsley, salt and pepper, in the slow cooker. Cover and cook on High for 4–6 hours, stirring in the pasta and parsley during the last 20–30 minutes. Season to taste with salt and pepper.

Chicken and Rice Soup

The combination of tarragon, turnip and parsnip gives this soup its great flavour.

SERVES 6

2.25 litres/4 pints chicken stock
450 g/1 lb skinless chicken breast
**   fillet, cubed (1 cm/½ in)**
2 onions, finely chopped
65 g/2½ oz parsnip, coarsely chopped
65 g/2½ oz turnip, coarsely chopped
1 carrot, coarsely chopped
1 celery stick, coarsely chopped
1 garlic clove, chopped
2 bay leaves

½ tsp dried thyme
½ tsp dried tarragon
100 g/4 oz easy-cook long-grain rice
salt and freshly ground black pepper,
**   to taste**

Combine all the ingredients, except the rice, salt and pepper, in a 5.5 litre/9½ pint slow cooker. Cover and cook on Low for 6–8 hours, adding the rice during the last 2 hours. Discard the bay leaves. Season to taste with salt and pepper.

Chicken and Barley Soup

Pearl barley is an old favourite in soups because it adds a pleasing texture as well as flavour.

SERVES 6

1 litre/1¾ pints chicken stock
250 ml/8 fl oz water
350 g/12 oz skinless chicken breast
**   fillet, cubed (2 cm/¾ in)**
2 onions, chopped
1 small carrot, coarsely chopped
1 small celery stick, coarsely chopped
1 garlic clove, crushed
15 g/½ oz chopped fresh parsley
½ tsp dried thyme
1 bay leaf
65 g/2½ oz pearl barley
salt and freshly ground black pepper,
**   to taste**

Combine all the ingredients, except the salt and pepper, in the slow cooker. Cover and cook on High for 4–6 hours. Discard the bay leaf. Season to taste with salt and pepper.

Chunky Chicken Soup

Rice makes this a substantial soup, but you can try other grains – millet, wheat berries or bulghar would be delicious.

SERVES 6

1.5 litres/2½ pints chicken stock
400 g/14 oz can tomatoes
450 g/1 lb skinless chicken breast
fillet, cubed (2.5 cm/1 in)
275 g/10 oz drained canned
chickpeas, rinsed
½ cauliflower, coarsely chopped
1 large onion, chopped
1 small celery stick, thinly sliced
1 small carrot, thinly sliced
1 tsp dried basil
1 tsp dried thyme
1 tsp dried marjoram
100 g/4 oz easy-cook long-grain rice
salt and freshly ground black pepper,
to taste

Combine all the ingredients, except the rice, salt and pepper, in the slow cooker. Cover and cook on Low for 6–8 hours, adding the rice during the last 2 hours. Season to taste with salt and pepper.

Chicken and Vegetable Soup with Lettuce

Quickly cooked frisée lettuce tastes good in this soup. Kale, Swiss chard, watercress or spinach can be used instead, if you prefer.

SERVES 6

1.5 litres/2½ pints chicken stock
700 g/1½ lb skinless chicken breast
fillet, cubed (2 cm/¾ in)
400 g/14 oz can chopped tomatoes
2 medium waxy potatoes, peeled and
diced
1 large onion, chopped
1 celery stick, chopped
1 carrot, chopped
2 large garlic cloves, crushed
1½ tsp dried marjoram
½ tsp dried basil
50 g/2 oz uncooked orzo
½ frisée lettuce, coarsely chopped
salt and freshly ground black pepper,
to taste

Combine all the ingredients, except the orzo, lettuce, salt and pepper, in a 5.5 litre/9½ pint slow cooker. Cover and cook on Low for 6–8 hours, adding the orzo and lettuce during the last 20 minutes. Season to taste with salt and pepper.

Chicken and Chilli Soup

The green chillies add a spicy Mexican flavour. Keep a jar of chillies in the cupboard for when you feel in the mood for something very hot!

SERVES 6

1 litre/1¾ pints chicken stock
225 g/8 oz skinless chicken breast fillet, cubed (2 cm/¾ in)
100 g/4 oz green chillies from a jar, drained and chopped
150 g/5 oz drained canned kidney beans, rinsed
175 g/6 oz cauliflower, in small florets
1 onion, finely chopped
1 celery stick, finely chopped
1 large garlic clove, crushed
2 tbsp cornflour
50 ml/2 fl oz cold water
100 g/4 oz Cheddar cheese, grated
salt and freshly ground black pepper, to taste

Combine all the ingredients, except the cornflour, water, cheese, salt and pepper, in the slow cooker. Cover and cook on Low for 6–8 hours. Add the combined cornflour and water, stirring for 2–3 minutes. Add the cheese, stirring until melted. Season to taste with salt and pepper.

Herbed Chicken Soup with Split Peas

This easy variation of split pea soup uses chicken instead of the more traditional ham.

SERVES 8

2.25 litres/4 pints chicken stock
450 g/1 lb dried green split peas
350 g/12 oz skinless chicken breast fillet, cubed (2 cm/¾ in)
2 spring onions, sliced
½ carrot, sliced
½ celery stick, sliced
1 tsp dried marjoram
salt and freshly ground black pepper, to taste

Combine all the ingredients, except the salt and pepper, in the slow cooker. Cover and cook on High for 4–6 hours. Season to taste with salt and pepper.

Chicken and Sweetcorn Soup

This soup makes an easy meal to prepare quickly on a workday – and it tastes excellent too!

SERVES 6

375 ml/13 fl oz fat-free chicken stock
425 g/15 oz can cream-style
sweetcorn
225 g/8 oz skinless chicken breast
fillet, cubed
350 g/12 oz potatoes, peeled and diced
2 small onions, chopped
375 ml/13 fl oz semi-skimmed milk
2 tbsp cornflour
salt and freshly ground black pepper,
to taste

Combine all the ingredients, except the milk, cornflour, salt and pepper, in the slow cooker. Cover and cook on High for 4–6 hours, stirring in 250 ml/8 fl oz milk during the last 30 minutes. Stir in the combined remaining milk and the cornflour, stirring for 2–3 minutes. Season to taste with salt and pepper.

Hearty Meatballs

Great in soups or with pastas, you can also make these with pork.

MAKES 18 MEATBALLS

700 g/1½ lb lean minced beef
1 small onion, finely chopped
1 egg
40 g/1½ oz dry breadcrumbs
2 garlic cloves, crushed
1–2 tsp beef bouillon granules, or a
beef stock cube
½ tsp salt
¼ tsp pepper

Combine all the ingredients in a bowl. Shape the mixture into 18 meatballs.

Hearty Meatball and Vegetable Soup

Minced beef meatballs are quick to prepare and make this a substantial meal. If the meatballs are browned in a lightly greased frying pan, or baked at 180°C/gas 4/fan oven 160° until browned, they will be less fragile and more attractive. Add the meatballs to the slow cooker carefully, so that they don't break apart.

SERVES 6

250 ml/8 fl oz beef stock
2 x 400 g/14 oz cans chopped
tomatoes
3 carrots, thickly sliced
1 tsp dried basil
Hearty Meatballs (see left)
2 small courgettes, sliced
50 g/2 oz frozen peas, thawed
2 tbsp cornflour
50 ml/2 fl oz cold water
salt and freshly ground black pepper,
to taste
350 g/12 oz noodles or fettuccine,
cooked, warm

Combine the stock, tomatoes, carrots, basil and meatballs in the slow cooker, making sure the meatballs are submerged. Cover and cook on Low for 6–8 hours, adding the courgettes and peas during the last 20 minutes. Turn the heat to High and cook for 10 minutes. Stir in the combined cornflour and water, stirring for 2–3 minutes. Season to taste with salt and pepper. Serve over noodles.

Italian-style Meatball Stew

A delicious Mediterranean-style option.

SERVES 6

250 ml/8 fl oz beef stock
2 × 400 g/14 oz cans chopped
  tomatoes
3 carrots, thickly sliced
100 g/4 oz small mushrooms, halved
1 tsp dried Italian herb seasoning
Turkey Meatballs (see below)
2 small courgettes, sliced
50 g/2 oz frozen peas, thawed
2 tbsp cornflour
50 ml/2 fl oz cold water
salt and freshly ground black pepper,
  to taste
350 g/12 oz noodles or fettuccine,
  cooked, warm

Combine the stock, tomatoes, carrots, mushrooms, herb seasoning and meatballs in the slow cooker, making sure the meatballs are submerged. Cover and cook on Low for 6–8 hours, adding the courgettes and peas during the last 20 minutes. Turn the heat to High and cook for 10 minutes. Stir in the combined cornflour and water, stirring for 2–3 minutes. Season to taste with salt and pepper. Serve over noodles.

Turkey Meatballs

Turkey mince is both tasty and economical.

MAKES 18 MEATBALLS

350 g/12 oz minced turkey
1 small egg
1 tbsp seasoned dry breadcrumbs
1 garlic clove, crushed
2 tsp dried Italian herb seasoning
salt and freshly ground black pepper,
  to taste

Combine all the ingredients in a bowl. Shape the mixture into 18 meatballs.

Chicken Meatball Soup

The Chicken Meatballs can be prepared in advance, covered and refrigerated, several hours before making the soup.

SERVES 8

2.25 litres/4 pints chicken stock
2 onions, chopped,
1 large carrot, thickly sliced
1 courgette, thickly sliced
Chicken Meatballs (see below)
salt and freshly ground black pepper,
  to taste

Combine all the ingredients, except the salt and pepper, in the slow cooker, making sure the meatballs are submerged. Cover and cook on Low for 6–8 hours. Season to taste with salt and pepper.

Chicken Meatballs

Light, tasty meatballs to add to soups or to snack on.

MAKES 24 MEATBALLS

450 g/1 lb chicken breast, minced
40 g/1½ oz fresh wholemeal
  breadcrumbs
15 g/½ oz freshly grated Parmesan
  cheese
1 small egg
1 garlic clove, crushed
1 tsp dried Italian herb seasoning

Combine all the ingredients in a bowl. Shape the mixture into 24 meatballs.

Garden Meatball Soup

A tasty and filling soup.

SERVES 8

2.25 litres/4 pints beef stock
2 onions, chopped,
1 large carrot, thickly sliced
1 courgette, thickly sliced
100 g/4 oz sliced cabbage
400 g/14 oz can kidney beans, drained
    and rinsed
400 g/14 oz can tomatoes
Minced Beef Meatballs (see below)
salt and freshly ground black pepper,
    to taste

Combine all the ingredients, except
the salt and pepper, in the slow
cooker, making sure the meatballs
are submerged. Cover and cook
on Low for 6–8 hours. Season to
taste with salt and pepper.

Minced Beef Meatballs

*Mini beef meatballs to bring an Italian
boost to your soup.*

MAKES 24 MEATBALLS

450 g/1 lb minced beef
40 g/1½ oz fresh wholemeal
    breadcrumbs
15 g/½ oz freshly grated Parmesan
    cheese
1 small egg
1 garlic clove, crushed
1 tsp dried Italian herb seasoning
salt and freshly ground black pepper,
    to taste

Combine all the ingredients in a bowl.
Shape the mixture into 24 meatballs.

Home-style Turkey and Vegetable Soup

*Here's the perfect soup to feed a crowd
economically, using turkey wings,
cannellini beans and well-flavoured
vegetables.*

SERVES 12

1.6 litres/2¾ pints chicken stock
750 ml/1¼ pints water
1.75 kg/4 lb turkey wings
4 onions, coarsely chopped
¼ tsp dried marjoram
¼ tsp dried thyme
400 g/14 oz can chopped tomatoes
400 g/14 oz can cannellini beans,
    drained and rinsed
150 g/5 oz swede or turnip, chopped
1 large celery stick, chopped
100 g/4 oz cabbage, chopped
1 large carrot, chopped
250 g/9 oz sweetcorn
50 g/2 oz pearl barley
25 g/1 oz uncooked ditalini
salt and freshly ground black pepper,
    to taste

Combine the stock, water, turkey, onions
and herbs in a 5.5 litre/9½ pint slow
cooker. Cover and cook on High for
4–5 hours. Remove the turkey wings.
Remove and shred the meat and reserve.
Discard the bones. Skim the fat from the
soup. Add the remaining ingredients,
except the pasta, salt and pepper, to the
slow cooker. Cover and cook on High for
3–4 hours, adding the reserved turkey
and pasta during the last 20 minutes.
Season to taste with salt and pepper.

Turkey Noodle Soup

Use some of that leftover Christmas turkey to make a substantial soup with vegetables and noodles.

SERVES 6

2.4 litres/4¼ pints Turkey Stock (see page 25) or chicken stock
1 large carrot, chopped
1 large celery stick, chopped
2 onions, chopped
75 g/3 oz mushrooms, sliced
3 large garlic cloves, crushed
¾ tsp dried marjoram
¾ tsp dried thyme
100 g/4 oz egg noodles, cooked
550 g/1¼ lb cooked turkey, diced
100 g/4 oz frozen peas, thawed
salt and freshly ground black pepper, to taste

Combine all the ingredients, except the noodles, turkey, peas, salt and pepper, in a 5.5 litre/9½ pint slow cooker. Cover and cook on Low for 6–8 hours, adding the noodles, turkey and peas during the last 15 minutes. Season to taste with salt and pepper.

Turkey and Wild Rice Soup

You can vary the herbs and vegetables according to what is available.

SERVES 6

2.4 litres/4¼ pints Turkey Stock (see page 25) or chicken stock
1 large carrot, chopped
1 large celery stick, chopped
150 g/5 oz turnip or parsnip, cubed
2 onions, chopped
75 g/3 oz mushrooms, sliced
3 large garlic cloves, crushed
¾ tsp dried marjoram
¾ tsp dried thyme
550 g/1¼ lb cooked turkey, diced

225 g/8 oz cooked wild rice
salt and freshly ground black pepper, to taste

Combine all the ingredients, except the turkey, rice, salt and pepper, in the slow cooker. Cover and cook on Low for 6–8 hours, adding the turkey and rice during the last 20 minutes. Season to taste with salt and pepper.

Turkey Soup with Tarragon

This chunky, mustard-spiked soup makes a great one-dish meal.

SERVES 4

1 litre/1¾ pints chicken stock
450 g/1 lb skinless turkey breast fillet, cubed (2 cm/¾ in)
2 large potatoes, peeled and cubed
2 onions, coarsely chopped
1 celery stick, thinly sliced
1 small carrot, thinly sliced
1 tbsp dried tarragon
1–1½ tbsp Dijon mustard
salt and freshly ground black pepper, to taste

Combine all the ingredients, except the salt and pepper, in the slow cooker. Cover and cook on Low for 8–12 hours. Season to taste with salt and pepper.

Beef Soup with Red Wine

The robust flavour of this soup is reminiscent of the classic Burgundy Beef.

SERVES 6

1 litre/1¾ pints beef stock
450 g/1 lb lean stewing beef, cubed
175 g/6 oz bacon, diced
225 g/8 oz ready-made tomato sauce
120 ml/4 fl oz dry red wine
700 g/1½ lb waxy potatoes, peeled and cubed
2 onions, chopped
75 g/3 oz mushrooms, sliced
1 carrot, sliced
1 celery stick, sliced
1 garlic clove, crushed
1½ tsp dried thyme
2 bay leaves
salt and freshly ground black pepper

Combine all the ingredients, except the salt and pepper, in a 5.5 litre/9½ pint slow cooker. Cover and cook on Low for 6–8 hours. Discard the bay leaves. Season to taste with salt and pepper.

Smoky Bean and Spinach Soup

Smoked bacon lends a subtle flavour to this soup. You can use your own home-made tomato sauce if you prefer.

SERVES 6

1.5 litres/2½ pints chicken stock
400 g/14 oz ready-made tomato sauce
400 g/14 oz can cannellini beans, rinsed and drained
175 g/6 oz smoked bacon, thinly sliced
1 garlic clove, crushed
1 tbsp dried Italian herb seasoning
275 g/10 oz frozen chopped spinach, thawed and drained
50 g/2 oz uncooked orzo
salt and freshly ground black pepper

Combine all the ingredients, except the spinach, orzo, salt and pepper, in the slow cooker. Cover and cook on Low for 6–8 hours, adding the spinach and orzo during the last 20 minutes. Season to taste with salt and pepper.

Beefy Bean Soup

Shin of beef flavours this bean soup. You can substitute 450 g/1 lb cubed lean beef for the shin of beef to turn it into a stew, if you like.

SERVES 8

2.25 litres/4 pints water
450 g/1 lb shin of beef
2 x 400 g/14 oz cans kidney beans, drained and rinsed
400 g/14 oz can tomatoes
2 carrots, sliced
2 onions, sliced
150 g/5 oz turnips, diced
150 g/5 oz French beans, cut into short lengths
1 celery stick, chopped
1 tsp dried oregano
1 tsp dried thyme
1 bay leaf
salt and freshly ground black pepper, to taste

Combine all the ingredients, except the salt and pepper, in a 5.5 litre/9½ pint slow cooker. Cover and cook on Low for 6–8 hours. Remove the beef. Shred the meat and return to the soup. Discard the bay leaf. Season to taste with salt and pepper.

Haricot Bean Soup with Ham

Beans can be cooked in the slow cooker without soaking as long as the recipe cooks for 8–10 hours. For a shorter cooking time, soak the beans overnight.

SERVES 6

1.5 litres/2½ pints chicken stock
225 g/8 oz dried haricot or cannellini beans, rinsed
250 g/9 oz lean smoked ham, cubed
1 onion, chopped
2 small carrots, chopped
1 celery stick, chopped
1 garlic clove, crushed
¼ tsp dried thyme
1 bay leaf
salt and freshly ground black pepper, to taste

Combine all the ingredients, except the salt and pepper, in the slow cooker. Cover and cook on Low until the beans are tender, 8–10 hours. Discard the bay leaf. Season to taste with salt and pepper.

Workday Bean Soup

This economical soup requires very little chopping, so it is useful to fit into a busy work schedule. Dried herbs and spices give it plenty of flavour.

SERVES 6

1.5 litres/2½ pints beef stock
175 g/6 oz dried pinto beans
175 g/6 oz dried cannellini beans, rinsed
½ red or green pepper, finely diced
1 onion, sliced
1 celery stick celery, sliced
1 bay leaf
2 tbsp sugar
1–2 tsp chilli powder
¼ tsp dried thyme
¼ tsp dry mustard powder
¼ tsp ground allspice
¼ tsp freshly ground black pepper
225 g/8 oz tomato purée
1 tbsp cider vinegar
salt and freshly ground black pepper, to taste

Combine all the ingredients, except the tomato purée, vinegar, salt and pepper, in the slow cooker. Cover and cook on Low until the beans are tender, 8–10 hours, adding the tomato purée and vinegar during the last 30 minutes. Discard the bay leaf. Season to taste with salt and pepper.

Beef and Barley Soup

This hearty, rib-sticking soup is even better if made a day or so in advance, when the flavours can mature and blend even more.

SERVES 8

500 ml/17 fl oz water
400 ml/14 fl oz beef stock
400 g/14 oz can chopped tomatoes
450 g/1 lb lean stewing beef, cubed
150 g/5 oz French beans, cut into short lengths
175 g/6 oz parsnips or potatoes, peeled and cubed
2 onions, chopped
1 large celery stick, chopped
1 large carrot, chopped
1 garlic clove, crushed
½ tsp dried marjoram
½ tsp dried thyme
1 bay leaf
50 g/2 oz pearl barley
50 g/2 oz frozen peas, thawed
salt and freshly ground black pepper, to taste

Combine all the ingredients, except the peas, salt and pepper, in a 5.5 litre/ 9½ pint slow cooker. Cover and cook on Low for 6–8 hours, adding the peas during the last 20 minutes. Discard the bay leaf. Season to taste with salt and pepper.

Beef, Vegetable and Barley Soup

Thick and hearty, this soup will particularly appeal to the family on a cold winter's day.

SERVES 6

350 g/12 oz minced beef
oil, for greasing
1.5 litres/2½ pints Fragrant Beef Stock (see page 26)
400 g/14 oz can tomatoes
175 g/6 oz cabbage, coarsely shredded
175 g/6 oz potato, peeled and cubed
2 onions, chopped
1 celery stick, sliced
1 carrot, sliced
2 large garlic cloves, crushed
1 tsp dried thyme
1 tsp dried basil
1 tsp chilli powder
1 tsp paprika
½ tsp dry mustard powder
2 bay leaves
50 g/2 oz pearl barley
salt and freshly ground black pepper, to taste

Cook the beef in a lightly greased frying pan over medium heat until browned, about 5 minutes, crumbling with a fork. Combine the beef and the remaining ingredients, except the salt and pepper, in a 5.5 litre/9½ pint slow cooker. Cover and cook on Low for 6–8 hours. Discard the bay leaves. Season to taste with salt and pepper.

Stuffed Green Pepper Soup

This zesty soup has the flavour of baked stuffed green peppers.

SERVES 6

450 g/1 lb lean minced beef, browned and crumbled
1 litre/1¾ pints tomato juice
2 x 400 g/14 oz cans chopped tomatoes
2 medium onions, chopped
2 green peppers, chopped
150 g/5 oz easy-cook long-grain rice
salt and freshly ground black pepper, to taste

Combine all the ingredients, except the rice, salt and pepper, in the slow cooker. Cover and cook on Low for 6–8 hours, stirring in the rice during the last 2 hours. Season to taste with salt and pepper.

Hamburger Goulash Soup

This is a great main-course soup, richly flavoured with paprika, tomato, herbs and Worcestershire sauce.

SERVES 6

350–450 g/12–16 oz lean minced beef
oil, for greasing
750 ml/1¼ pints beef stock
225 g/8 oz canned tomatoes
500 g/18 oz potatoes, peeled and cubed
1 onion, chopped
½ large red or green pepper, chopped
3 tbsp paprika
¾ tsp chilli powder
¾ tsp garlic powder
½ tsp caraway seeds
½ tsp dried thyme
1 tbsp Worcestershire sauce
50 ml/2 fl oz tomato ketchup
salt and freshly ground black pepper, to taste

Cook the beef in a large, lightly greased pan over medium heat until browned, about 5 minutes, crumbling with a fork. Add the beef and the remaining ingredients, except the salt and pepper, to the slow cooker. Cover and cook on Low for 6–8 hours. Season to taste with salt and pepper.

Hamburger and Vegetable Soup

Add hamburger ingredients to a soup of vegetables and barley in a tomato sauce and then add sweet–sour flavourings for a definite hit with the family.

SERVES 4-6

350 g/12 oz lean minced beef
1 large onion, finely chopped
2 large garlic cloves, crushed
oil, for greasing
1.2 litres/2 pints beef stock
400 g/14 oz ready-made tomato sauce
175 g/6 oz potato, peeled and diced
1 large carrot, thinly sliced
175 g/6 oz sweetcorn
150 g/5 oz canned baby butter beans
1½ celery sticks, sliced
2 tbsp pearl barley
2 tbsp light brown sugar
2 tbsp apple cider vinegar
¾ tsp dry mustard powder
¾ tsp dried thyme
1 large bay leaf
salt and freshly ground black pepper, to taste

Cook the beef, onion and garlic in the oil in a large, lightly greased frying pan over medium heat until the beef is browned, about 5 minutes, crumbling the beef with a fork. Combine the beef mixture and remaining ingredients, except the salt and pepper, in a 5.5 litre/9½ pint slow cooker. Cover and cook on Low for 6–8 hours. Discard the bay leaf. Season to taste with salt and pepper.

Vegetable Soup with Chilli Meatballs

Lightly spiced meatballs add the perfect touch to this simple vegetable soup.

SERVES 8

2.25 litres/4 pints chicken stock
2 onions, thinly sliced
175 g/6 oz canned sweetcorn with peppers
2 small carrots, thinly sliced
Chilli Meatballs (see below)
275 g/10 oz frozen chopped spinach, thawed and drained
2–4 tbsp dry sherry (optional)
salt and freshly ground black pepper, to taste

Combine all the ingredients, except the spinach, sherry, salt and pepper, in a 5.5 litre/9½ pint slow cooker. Cover and cook on Low for 6–8 hours, adding the spinach and sherry during the last 20 minutes. Season to taste with salt and pepper.

Chilli Meatballs

Make these as hot as you like.

MAKES 32 MEATBALLS

700 g/1½ lb lean minced beef
1 small onion, finely chopped
20 g/¾ oz dry breadcrumbs
1 garlic clove, crushed
½–1 tbsp chilli powder
2 tsp ground cumin
1 egg
½ tsp salt

Combine all the ingredients in a bowl. Shape the mixture into 32 meatballs.

Vegetable Soup with Cabbage Rolls

For something different, stuff cabbage leaves with minced veal and cook them in a mixed vegetable soup.

SERVES 4

Cabbage Rolls (see below)
1.2 litres/2 pints chicken stock
4 celery sticks, sliced
1 large potato, peeled and cubed
1 onion, chopped
1 carrot, chopped
1 tomato, chopped
175 g/6 oz sweetcorn
salt and freshly ground black pepper, to taste
50 g/2 oz Emmental or Gruyère cheese, grated

Put the Cabbage Rolls, seam sides down, in a 5.5 litre/9½ pint slow cooker. Add the remaining ingredients, except the salt, pepper and cheese. Cover and cook on Low for 8–10 hours. Season to taste with salt and pepper. Spoon the Cabbage Rolls into shallow soup bowls. Ladle the soup over and sprinkle with cheese.

Cabbage Rolls

Try using minced lamb instead of veal as an alternative.

SERVES 4

12 cabbage leaves
350 g/12 oz minced veal
25 g/1 oz fresh breadcrumbs
2 eggs
¾–1 tsp dried marjoram
¾–1 tsp dried thyme
½ tsp salt

Put the cabbage leaves in boiling water until softened, about 1 minute. Drain well. Trim the thick veins from the leaves so that they lay flat. Mix the remaining ingredients and divide into eight equal parts. Put on to the cabbage leaves and fold the sides and ends in to make packets.

Salt Beef and Cabbage Soup

This soup duplicates the flavour of a traditional New England 'boiled dinner' made with salt, or 'corned', beef.

SERVES 6

2 litres/3½ pints/8½ cups chicken stock
225 g/8 oz salt beef or brisket, fat trimmed, cubed (1 cm/½ in)
700 g/1½ lb waxy potatoes, peeled and cubed
225 g/8 oz cabbage, thinly sliced
12 baby carrots, halved
1 large onion, chopped
2 large garlic cloves, crushed
2 bay leaves
1 tbsp cider vinegar
2 tsp Dijon mustard
2 tsp caraway seeds
salt and freshly ground black pepper, to taste

Combine all the ingredients, except the salt and pepper, in a 5.5 litre/9½ pint slow cooker. Cover and cook on Low for 6–8 hours. Discard the bay leaves. Season to taste with salt and pepper.

Vegetable Oxtail Soup

Slow cooking brings out the rich flavour of oxtails, making this vegetable soup especially good. The oxtails can be browned first, if you prefer.

SERVES 6

1.5 litres/2½ pints beef stock
450 g/1 lb oxtails, sliced (5 cm/2 in)
2 large tomatoes, chopped
1 large celery stick, sliced
2 small onions, sliced
2 small carrots, sliced
100 g/4 oz parsnip, diced
1 potato, peeled and diced
1 tsp dried thyme
1 bay leaf
65 g/2½ oz pearl barley
salt and freshly ground black pepper, to taste

Combine all the ingredients, except the salt and pepper, in a 5.5 litre/9½ pint slow cooker. Cover and cook on High for 6–8 hours. Remove the oxtails from the soup. Remove the meat from the bones and return to the soup. Discard the bones and bay leaf. Season to taste with salt and pepper.

Lamb and White Bean Soup

If you enjoy bean soup, try this well-flavoured version that is cooked with lamb shanks.

SERVES 6

2.25 litres/4 pints beef stock
250 g/9 oz dried cannellini or haricot beans, rinsed
2 lamb shanks (about 750 g/1¾ lb)
175 g/6 oz cabbage, thinly sliced
2 large carrots, sliced
2 celery sticks, sliced
2 garlic cloves, crushed
1 large onion, finely chopped
3 bay leaves
1½ tsp dried thyme
1½ tsp dried marjoram
½ tsp crushed celery seeds
½ tsp dry mustard powder
salt and freshly ground black pepper, to taste

Combine all the ingredients, except the salt and pepper, in a 5.5 litre/9½ pint slow cooker. Cover and cook on Low until the beans are tender, 7–8 hours. Remove the lamb shanks. Cut the meat into bite-sized pieces and return to the soup. Discard the bones and bay leaves. Season to taste with salt and pepper.

Lamb Soup with Barley

Lean lamb, with traditional stewing vegetables and barley, is cooked with herbs and wine for plenty of big flavours. The soup can also be made with lean pork or beef.

SERVES 8

1.5 litres/2½ pints chicken stock
700 g/1½ lb lean stewing lamb, cubed
1 litre/1¾ pints water
3 onions, sliced
2 carrots, sliced
200 g/7 oz turnips, sliced
1 large celery stick, sliced
3 large garlic cloves, crushed
1 tsp dried oregano
1 tsp dried rosemary
1 bay leaf
120 ml/4 fl oz dry white wine (optional)
90 g/3½ oz pearl barley
salt and freshly ground black pepper, to taste

Combine all the ingredients, except the salt and pepper, in a 5.5 litre/9½ pint slow cooker. Cover and cook on Low for 6–8 hours. Discard the bay leaf. Season to taste with salt and pepper.

Lamb, Split Pea, Bean and Barley Soup

Split peas go very well with the rich flavour of lamb in this country-style soup.

SERVES 8

2 litres/3½ pints water
2–4 beef stock cubes
900 g/2 lb lamb shanks
400 g/14 oz dried green split peas
130 g/4½ oz dried haricot or cannellini beans, rinsed
50 g/2 oz pearl barley
2 onions, chopped
1 small carrot, sliced
½ celery stick, sliced
1 garlic clove, crushed
1 tsp dried thyme
1 tsp dried basil
½ tsp celery seeds, crushed
3 bay leaves
salt and freshly ground black pepper, to taste

Combine all the ingredients, except the salt and pepper, in a 5.5 litre/9½ pint slow cooker. Cover and cook on Low until the beans are tender, 8–10 hours. Remove the lamb shanks. Remove the meat, cut into bite-sized pieces and return to the soup. Discard the bones and bay leaves. Season to taste with salt and pepper.

Four-bean Soup with Sausage

This hearty soup has a Mexican accent and spicy flavour without being too hot. Adjust the quantity of chilli to your own taste.

SERVES 8

225 g/8 oz smoked sausage, sliced
400 g/14 oz can tomatoes
400 ml/14 fl oz reduced-fat chicken stock
400 g/14 oz can chickpeas, drained and rinsed
400 g/14 oz can pinto beans, drained and rinsed
400 g/14 oz can black beans, drained and rinsed
225 g/8 oz mild salsa from a jar
175 ml/6 fl oz vegetable juice
225 g/8 oz French beans, halved
2 onions, chopped
½ green pepper, chopped
1 celery stick, chopped
1 garlic clove, crushed
1 small jalapeño or other medium-hot chilli, chopped
1–3 tsp chilli powder
1 tsp dried oregano
salt and Tabasco sauce, to taste

Combine all the ingredients, except the salt and Tabasco sauce, in a 5.5 litre/9½ pint slow cooker. Cover and cook on Low for 8–12 hours. Season to taste with salt and Tabasco sauce.

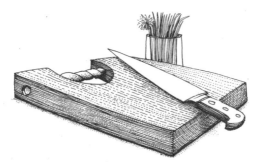

Rice and Aduki Bean Soup with Vegetables Ⓥ

In this easy soup – an Indian-style rice-and-bean stew – slightly sweet aduki beans replace the usual dhal or legume.

SERVES 6

900 ml/1½ pints vegetable stock
400 g/14 oz can aduki beans, drained and rinsed
2 large carrots, sliced
350 g/12 oz canned butter beans
400 g/14 oz chopped plum tomatoes
1 small jalapeño or other medium-hot chilli, finely chopped
1 tsp ground cumin
1 tsp ground turmeric
1 cm/½ in piece fresh root ginger, finely grated
100 g/4 oz easy-cook long-grain rice
salt and freshly ground black pepper, to taste
40 g/1½ oz toasted sunflower seeds

Combine all the ingredients, except the rice, salt, pepper and sunflower seeds, in a 5.5 litre/9½ pint slow cooker. Cover and cook on High for 4–6 hours, adding the rice during the last 2 hours. Season to taste with salt and pepper. Sprinkle each bowl of soup with sunflower seeds.

Roasted Red Pepper, Sweetcorn and Black Bean Soup Ⓥ

A jar of roasted red peppers and a can of black beans are great storecupboard time-savers for this hearty, colourful soup.

SERVES 4

1 litre/1¾ pints vegetable stock
400 g/14 oz can black beans, drained and rinsed
350 g/12 oz roasted red peppers from a jar, drained and diced
175 g/6 oz sweetcorn
4 onions, chopped
¾ tsp dried thyme
a pinch of crushed chilli flakes
a pinch of ground allspice
75 g/3 oz lean ham, diced
150 g/5 oz easy-cook long-grain rice
salt and freshly ground black pepper, to taste

Combine all the ingredients, except the rice, salt and pepper, in the slow cooker, cover and cook on High for 4–6 hours, adding the rice during the last 2 hours. Season to taste with salt and pepper.

Black Bean Soup with Rice and Ham

Try serving this spicy and flavourful soup with a cooling salsa, soured cream and tortilla chips.

SERVES 6

1.2 litres/2 pints chicken stock
400 g/14 oz can black beans, drained and rinsed
1 onion, chopped
3 garlic cloves, crushed
2 sliced carrots
2 celery sticks
1 small green pepper, sliced
350 g/12 oz lean smoked ham, diced
1 tsp ground cumin
½ tsp crushed chilli flakes
65 g/2½ oz easy-cook long-grain rice
20 g/¾ oz fresh coriander, chopped
salt and pepper to taste

Combine all the ingredients, except the rice, coriander, salt and pepper, in a 5.5 litre/9½ pint slow cooker. Cover and cook on Low for 6–8 hours, adding the rice during the last 2 hours. Stir in the coriander. Season to taste with salt and pepper.

Sausage and Black Bean Soup

Smoked sausage and a glug of Worcestershire sauce flavour this piquant black bean soup.

SERVES 6

2.5 litres/4¼ pints chicken stock
450 g/1 lb dried black beans, rinsed
225 g/8 oz smoked pork or turkey
   sausage, sliced
1 large carrot, sliced
2 onions, chopped
1 celery stick, chopped
2 tbsp Worcestershire sauce
2 tsp dried marjoram
1 bay leaf
salt and freshly ground black pepper,
   to taste
lemon wedges

Combine all the ingredients, except the salt, pepper and lemon wedges, in a 5.5 litre/9½ pint slow cooker. Cover and cook on Low until the beans are tender, 7–8 hours. Discard the bay leaf. Season to taste with salt and pepper. Serve with lemon wedges.

Sherried Black Bean Soup

The sugar and sherry give this a delicious flavour.

SERVES 6

2.5 litres/4¼ pints chicken stock
450 g/1 lb dried black beans, rinsed
225 g/8 oz smoked pork or turkey
   sausage, sliced
1 large carrot, sliced
2 onions, chopped
1 celery stick, chopped
2 tbsp Worcestershire sauce
2 tsp crushed cumin seeds
1 tsp dried oregano

1 bay leaf
1–2 tsp brown sugar
1–2 tbsp dry sherry
salt and freshly ground black pepper,
   to taste
lemon wedges

Combine all the ingredients, except the sherry, salt, pepper and lemon wedges, in a 5.5 litre/9½ pint slow cooker. Cover and cook on Low until the beans are tender, 7–8 hours. Discard the bay leaf. Season to taste with sherry, salt and pepper. Serve with lemon wedges.

Chickpea and Pasta Soup ⓥ

This soup makes an ideal lunch dish – not too filling for the middle of the day.

SERVES 4

1 litre/1¾ pints vegetable stock
400 g/14 oz can chickpeas, drained
   and rinsed
225 g/8 oz ready-made tomato sauce
1 onion, chopped
1 garlic clove, crushed
1 celery stick, finely chopped
1 carrot, finely chopped
1 bay leaf
½ tsp dried thyme
½ tsp dried basil
1 small courgette, chopped
75 g/3 oz ditalini or orzo
salt and freshly ground black pepper,
   to taste

Combine all the ingredients, except the courgettes, pasta, salt and pepper, in the slow cooker. Cover and cook on High for 4–6 hours, adding the courgettes and pasta during the last 20 minutes. Discard the bay leaf. Season to taste with salt and pepper.

Storecupboard Soup ⓥ

Use up what's in the cupboard today with this economical soup – pay day's tomorrow!

SERVES 8

1.5 litres/2½ pints vegetable stock
400 g/14 oz can chickpeas, drained and rinsed
350 g/12 oz potatoes, peeled and cubed
2 onions, chopped
2 garlic cloves, crushed
65 g/2½ oz easy-cook long-grain rice
2 tbsp freshly grated Parmesan cheese
salt and freshly ground black pepper, to taste

Combine all the ingredients, except the rice, cheese, salt and pepper, in a 5.5 litre/9½ pint slow cooker. Cover and cook on High for 4–5 hours, adding the rice during the last 2 hours. Stir in the Parmesan cheese. Season to taste with salt and pepper.

Curried Bean Soup ⓥ

You can also use any other white bean, such as haricot, soya or butter, or use chickpeas, in this creamy, rich soup.

SERVES 6

900 ml/1½ pints vegetable stock
2 x 400 g/14 oz cans cannellini beans, drained and rinsed
2 onions, chopped
1 small sliced leek, chopped
3 large garlic cloves, crushed
1 tbsp curry powder
120 ml/4 fl oz semi-skimmed milk
salt and freshly ground black pepper, to taste
6 tbsp soured cream
chopped fresh coriander, to garnish

Combine all the ingredients, except the milk, salt, pepper, soured cream and coriander, in the slow cooker. Cover and cook on High for 4–6 hours. Process the soup and milk in a food processor or blender until smooth. Season to taste with salt and pepper. Top each bowl of soup with a tablespoon of soured cream and sprinkle with fresh coriander.

Soya Bean and Barley Soup

An excellent winter soup with robust seasonings. Frozen soya beans make a tasty and nourishing addition to soups and casseroles.

SERVES 4

1.5 litres/2½ pints vegetable or chicken stock
400 g/14 oz can chopped tomatoes
2 onions, chopped,
175 g/6 oz frozen soya beans, thawed
1 celery stick, thinly sliced
65 g/2½ oz turnip, cubed
1 ham hock
¾ tsp dried thyme
¾ tsp dried marjoram
1 bay leaf
50 g/2 oz pearl barley
½–1 tsp sugar
salt and freshly ground black pepper, to taste

Combine all the ingredients, except the sugar, salt and pepper, in the slow cooker. Cover and cook on High for 4–6 hours. Discard the ham hock and bay leaf. Skim the fat from the soup. Season to taste with sugar, salt and pepper.

White Bean Soup Ⓥ

Canned beans add quick-and-easy protein and flavour to dishes. Haricot beans can be substituted for the cannellini beans, if you like, in this delicately flavoured soup.

SERVES 4

450 ml/¾ pint vegetable stock
2 × 400 g/14 oz cans cannellini beans, drained and rinsed
2 large celery sticks, chopped
1 medium onion, chopped
3 spring onions, sliced
1–2 garlic cloves, crushed
½ tsp dried dill
½ tsp dried thyme
a pinch of ground allspice
juice of 1 lemon
salt and cayenne pepper, to taste

Combine all the ingredients, except the salt and cayenne pepper, in the slow cooker. Cover and cook on Low for 3–4 hours. Process the soup in a food processor or blender until smooth. Season to taste with salt and pepper.

White Bean and Pasta Soup Ⓥ

Enjoy the combination of beans and pasta in this Italian-seasoned soup.

SERVES 6

2 x 400 g/14 oz cans cannellini beans, drained and rinsed
2.25 litres/4 pints vegetable stock
225 g/8 oz ready-made tomato sauce
1 large onion, chopped
1 carrot, sliced
1 celery stick, sliced
25 g/1 oz fresh parsley, chopped
2 garlic cloves, chopped
1 tbsp dried Italian herb seasoning

175 g/6 oz angel hair pasta, broken into 7.5 cm/3 in pieces
salt and freshly ground black pepper, to taste

Combine all the ingredients, except the pasta, salt and pepper, in a 5.5 litre/9½ pint slow cooker. Cover and cook on Low for 6–8 hours, adding the pasta during the last 15 minutes. Season to taste with salt and pepper.

White Bean Soup with Spinach Ⓥ

This soup is a meal in a bowl. Serve with warm crusty bread and a crisp green salad.

SERVES 8

2.25 litres/4 pints vegetable stock
250 g/9 oz dried cannellini beans, rinsed
50 g/2 oz pearl barley
1 large onion, chopped
1 small carrot, sliced
½ celery stick, sliced
2 garlic cloves, crushed
2 bay leaves
1 tsp dried marjoram
1 tsp dried basil
½ tsp dried thyme
400 g/14 oz can chopped tomatoes
275 g/10 oz frozen chopped spinach, thawed and drained
salt and freshly ground black pepper, to taste

Combine all the ingredients, except the tomatoes, spinach, salt and pepper, in a 5.5 litre/9½ pint slow cooker. Cover and cook on Low until the beans are tender, 7–8 hours, adding the tomatoes with the liquid and the spinach during the last 30 minutes. Discard the bay leaves. Season to taste with salt and pepper.

Hearty Bean and Barley Soup

Bean and barley soup makes a good family meal for a chilly evening.

SERVES 8

2.5 litres/4¼ pints beef stock
350 g/12 oz dried cannellini beans, rinsed
50 g/2 oz pearl barley
1 meaty ham bone
175 g/6 oz cabbage, thinly sliced
4 onions, chopped
1 small carrot, sliced
½ celery stick, sliced
2 garlic cloves, crushed
3 bay leaves
1½ tsp dried thyme
225 g/8 oz ready-made tomato sauce
salt and freshly ground black pepper, to taste

Combine all the ingredients, except the tomato sauce, salt and pepper, in a 5.5 litre/9½ pint slow cooker. Cover and cook on Low until the beans are tender, 8–10 hours, adding the tomato sauce during the last 30 minutes. Discard the bay leaves. Season to taste with salt and pepper.

Ham, Spinach and Pasta Soup

Be sure to add leafy greens, like spinach, and small pasta, such as orzo, near the end of the cooking time, as they cook quickly.

SERVES 4

1.2 litres/2 pints chicken stock
400 g/14 oz ready-made tomato sauce
175 g/6 oz lean ham, cubed
1 onion, chopped
2 tsp dried Italian herb seasoning
100 g/4 oz orzo or other small soup pasta
225 g/8 oz spinach, sliced
salt and freshly ground black pepper, to taste

Combine all the ingredients, except the pasta, spinach, salt and pepper, in the slow cooker. Cover and cook on High for 4–6 hours, stirring in the orzo and spinach during the last 20–30 minutes. Season to taste with salt and pepper.

Vegetable Soup with Country Ham

Country ham, beef stock and chicken taste particularly good with asparagus in this delicious soup.

SERVES 6

2.25 litres/4 pints beef stock
400 g/14 oz can butter or haricot beans, drained and rinsed
350 g/12 oz skinless chicken breast fillet, cubed
225 g/8 oz country ham, fat trimmed, diced
175 g/6 oz waxy potatoes, peeled and cubed
150 g/5 oz French beans, cut into short lengths
1 onion, chopped
50 g/2 oz leek, chopped
1 carrot, sliced
1 celery stick, sliced
2 large garlic cloves, crushed
1 tsp dried thyme
130 g/4½ oz asparagus spears, cut into short lengths
salt and freshly ground black pepper, to taste

Combine all the ingredients, except the asparagus, salt and pepper, in a 5.5 litre/9½ pint slow cooker. Cover and cook on Low for 6–8 hours, adding the asparagus during the last 30 minutes. Season to taste with salt and pepper.

95

Split Pea Soup with Ham

Serve this hearty soup with thick slices of garlic bread for a pleasing weekday meal.

SERVES 8

1.5 litres/2½ pints water
400 g/14 oz can chicken stock
450 g/1 lb dried split peas
250 g/9 oz lean ham, cubed
3 onions, chopped
1 large carrot, chopped
1 celery stick, sliced
1–2 tsp beef bouillon granules, or a
    beef stock cube
1 tsp dried marjoram
salt and freshly ground black pepper,
    to taste

Combine all the ingredients, except the salt and pepper, in a 5.5 litre/9½ pint slow cooker. Cover and cook on High for 4–6 hours. Season to taste with salt and pepper.

Split Pea Soup with Barley

Rich and filling.

SERVES 8

2 litres/3½ pints water
400 g/14 oz can chicken stock
450 g/1 lb dried split peas
90 g/3½ oz pearl barley
3 onions, chopped
1 large carrot, chopped
1 celery stick, sliced
1–2 tsp beef bouillon granules, or a
    beef stock cube
1 tsp dried marjoram
salt and freshly ground black pepper,
    to taste

Combine all the ingredients, except the salt and pepper, in a 5.5 litre/9½ pint slow cooker. Cover and cook on High for 4–6 hours. Season to taste with salt and pepper.

Savoury Pea Soup with Smoked Sausage

Crusty rolls make a good accompaniment.

SERVES 8

1.5 litres/2½ pints water
400 g/14 oz can chicken stock
450 g/1 lb dried split peas
225 g/8 oz smoked pork or turkey
    sausage, halved lengthways and
    sliced
3 onions, chopped
1 large carrot, chopped
1 celery stick, sliced
350 g/12 oz diced potato
1 tsp dried thyme
1 bay leaf
1–2 tsp beef bouillon granules, or a
    beef stock cube
1 tsp dried marjoram
Tabasco sauce, to taste
salt and freshly ground black pepper,
    to taste

Combine all the ingredients, except the Tabasco, salt and pepper, in a 5.5 litre/9½ pint slow cooker. Cover and cook on High for 4–6 hours. Discard the bay leaf. Season to taste with salt and pepper.

Hearty Split Pea, Bean and Barley Soup

Pulses always make a hearty soup – and they're very nutritious too.

SERVES 6

1.75 litres/3 pints water
1 meaty ham bone
175 g/6 oz dried green split peas
50 g/2 oz pearl barley
25 g/1 oz dried black-eyed peas, rinsed
75 g/3 oz haricot beans
1–2 beef stock cubes
1 onion, roughly chopped
1 small carrot, thinly sliced
1 small celery stick, thinly sliced
1 garlic clove, crushed
¼ tsp dried thyme
¼ tsp celery seeds, crushed
1–2 bay leaves
salt and freshly ground black pepper, to taste

Combine all the ingredients, except the salt and pepper, in the slow cooker. Cover and cook on Low for 6–8 hours. Remove the ham bone, cut the meat into bite-sized pieces and return to the soup. Discard the bone and the bay leaves. Season to taste with salt and pepper.

Farmhouse Soup

Ham hock, black-eyed peas and barley combine to give this soup a homely flavour and richness.

SERVES 6

2.25 litres/4 pints chicken stock
75 g/3 oz dried black-eyed peas, rinsed
50 g/2 oz pearl barley
2 small ham hocks
350 g/12 oz French beans, cut into short lengths
2 onions, chopped
½ carrot, sliced
½ celery stick, chopped
1 garlic clove, crushed
2 tsp dried basil
½ tsp dried thyme
1 bay leaf
400 g/14 oz can chopped tomatoes
a pinch of crushed chilli flakes
salt and freshly ground black pepper, to taste

Combine all the ingredients, except the tomatoes, crushed chilli flakes, salt and pepper, in a 5.5 litre/9½ pint slow cooker. Cover and cook on Low for 6–8 hours, adding the tomatoes and the chilli flakes during the last 45 minutes. Discard the bay leaf and ham hocks. Season to taste with salt and pepper.

Black-eyed Pea and Lentil Soup

This soup is flavourful, economical and full of protein. Black-eyed peas have a distinctive nutty taste that goes very well with the smoked ham and lentils.

SERVES 4–6

1.2 litres/2 pints beef stock
100 g/4 oz red lentils
75 g/3 oz dried black-eyed peas, rinsed
100 g/4 oz lean smoked ham, cubed
1 small carrot, chopped
1 small celery stick, chopped
1 small onion, chopped
1 garlic clove, crushed
¼ tsp dried thyme
¼ tsp dried rosemary
200 g/7 oz can chopped tomatoes
salt and freshly ground black pepper, to taste

Combine all the ingredients, except the tomatoes, salt and pepper, in the slow cooker. Cover and cook on Low for 6–8 hours, adding the tomatoes during the last 45 minutes. Season to taste with salt and pepper.

Lentil and Vegetable Soup with Ham

Lentils lend a wonderful homely flavour and heartiness to this simple soup.

SERVES 4

1 litre/1¾ pints Rich Chicken Stock (see page 31) or chicken stock
1 small ham hock
100 g/4 oz dried red lentils
1 onion, chopped
1 carrot, chopped
1 celery stick, chopped
75 g/3 oz ham, diced
¼ tsp crushed chilli flakes
400 g/14 oz can tomatoes
salt and freshly ground black pepper, to taste

Combine all the ingredients, except the tomatoes, salt and pepper, in the slow cooker. Cover and cook on High for 4–6 hours, adding the tomatoes during the last 45 minutes. Discard the ham hock. Season to taste with salt and pepper.

Beef and Lentil Soup

Beef and lentils flavoured with traditional savoury ingredients make a satisfying and robust soup that could well become a family favourite.

SERVES 4

1.5 litres/2½ pints beef stock
2 tbsp dry white wine (optional)
225 g/8 oz lean stewing beef, cubed
225 g/8 oz dried red lentils
2 onions, finely chopped
25 g/1 oz leeks, finely chopped
1 small carrot, finely chopped
1 small celery stick, finely chopped
salt and freshly ground black pepper, to taste

Combine all the ingredients, except the salt and pepper, in the slow cooker. Cover and cook on Low for 4–6 hours. Season to taste with salt and pepper.

Spicy Lentil and Tomato Soup With Ham

This easy, spicy lentil soup is seasoned with ham, tomatoes and a lively blend of herbs.

SERVES 6

1.5 litres/2½ pints chicken stock
2 × 400 g/14 oz cans Italian plum tomatoes, coarsely chopped, undrained
75 g/3 oz lean ham, finely diced
75 g/3 oz dried red or brown lentils
4 onions, chopped
100 g/4 oz green cabbage, shredded
1 large celery stick, finely chopped
1 large carrot, finely chopped
150 g/5 oz drained canned chickpeas, rinsed
2 large garlic cloves, crushed
1 tbsp dried basil
½ tsp dried oregano
½ tsp dried thyme
salt and cayenne pepper, to taste

Combine all the ingredients, except the salt and cayenne pepper, in the slow cooker. Cover and cook on High for 4–6 hours. Season to taste with salt and cayenne pepper.

Easy Barley and Chickpea Soup

Mustard and thyme combine to give a great flavour to this tomato-based soup of chickpeas, barley and French beans.

SERVES 6

1.5 litres/2½ pints beef stock
400 g/14 oz can chickpeas, rinsed and drained
400 g/14 oz ready-made tomato sauce
½ onion, finely chopped
½ celery stick, finely chopped
½ carrot, finely chopped
½ onion, finely chopped
2 tsp sugar
⅓ tsp dry mustard powder
½ tsp dried thyme
65 g/2½ oz pearl barley
400 g/14 oz can French beans, drained and cut into short lengths
salt and freshly ground black pepper, to taste

Combine all the ingredients, except the French beans, salt and pepper, in a 5.5 litre/9½ pint slow cooker. Cover and cook on High for 4–5 hours, adding the French beans during the last 30 minutes. Season to taste with salt and pepper.

Fish and Seafood Soups

Fish cooks well in the slow cooker, though it can cook very quickly so some recipes call for adding the fish towards the end. Remember that you can vary the cooking times by choosing Low or High – see details on page 12. If you do want to leave your sauce cooking, use Low for 6–8 hours, then turn to High for the final phase of cooking. Alternatively, simply cook on High for the first 3–4 hours and add your final ingredients to finish. Vary the fish you use depending on what is available – most white fish, for example, will work in recipes that specify cod.

Fish Soup with Vegetables

Mushrooms and a medley of vegetables in a tomato base surround a selection of fish in this sustaining soup. It just needs warm bread to serve.

SERVES 8

3 x 400 g/14 oz cans chopped
   tomatoes
450 ml/¾ pint tomato juice
175 ml/6 fl oz fish stock
175 ml/6 fl oz dry white wine or
   water
2 onions, chopped
3 potatoes, peeled and diced
1 celery stick, chopped
½ sliced pepper, chopped
1 carrot, chopped
50 g/2 oz mushrooms, chopped
4 garlic cloves, crushed
1 tsp dried oregano
225 g/8 oz skinless halibut, cubed
225 g/8 oz skinless sole, cubed
225 g/8 oz skinless snapper, cubed
salt and freshly ground black pepper,
   to taste

Combine all the ingredients, except the fish, salt and pepper, in a 5.5 litre/9½ pint slow cooker. Cover and cook on Low for 6–8 hours, adding the fish during the last 15–20 minutes. Season to taste with salt and pepper.

Hearty Seafood Soup

Scallops add a luxurious touch to this superb soup. Serve with a tossed green salad and warm garlic bread.

SERVES 6

3 x 400 g/14 oz cans chopped
   tomatoes
250 ml/8 fl oz fish stock
120 ml/4 fl oz dry white wine
   or fish stock
3 medium potatoes, peeled and diced
100 g/4 oz sweetcorn, thawed if frozen
1 small onion, finely chopped
1 small carrot, finely chopped
½ green pepper, finely chopped
2 tsp dried basil
1 tsp dried oregano
225 g/8 oz skinless cod, cubed
225 g/8 oz skinless lemon sole, flounder
   or other flatfish fillets, diced
225 g/8 oz scallops, diced
salt and freshly ground black pepper,
   to taste

Combine all the ingredients, except the fish, salt and pepper, in the slow cooker. Cover and cook on Low for 6–8 hours, adding the fish during the last 15–20 minutes. Season to taste with salt and pepper.

Shortcut Fish Soup

This easy soup uses a base of prepared pasta sauce. To make it extra quick, choose fish sold in pieces for fish pie fillings at the supermarket.

SERVES 6

500 g/18 oz jar tomato and herb
    pasta sauce
250 ml/8 fl oz fish stock
250 ml/8 fl oz water
120 ml/4 fl oz dry white wine or water
1 onion, thinly sliced
2 garlic cloves, crushed
¼ tsp crushed chilli flakes
450 g/1 lb assorted skinless fish fillets
    such as cod or haddock, monkfish,
    hake, whiting, pollack, snapper or
    plaice
175 g/6 oz whole clams from a jar or
    can, or rinsed, drained cockles
salt and freshly ground black pepper,
    to taste

Combine all the ingredients, except the fish, clams, salt and pepper, in the slow cooker. Cover and cook on Low for 6–8 hours. Turn the slow cooker to High, add the fish and clams or cockles with their liquor and cook for 15–20 minutes. Season to taste with salt and pepper.

Fisherman's Catch

Choose two or three kinds of fish for this soup, selecting from cod, flounder, lemon sole, red snapper, salmon, hake, halibut or haddock.

SERVES 6

400 g/14 oz can chopped tomatoes
250 ml/8 fl oz fish stock
250 ml/8 fl oz dry white wine
    or fish stock
1 onion, chopped
1 celery stick, chopped
1 carrot, chopped
1 tsp dried rosemary
700 g/1½ lb skinless fish fillets, cubed
20 g/¾ oz fresh parsley, chopped
75 ml/2½ fl oz semi-skimmed milk
1 tbsp cornflour
salt and freshly ground black pepper
6 ciabatta slices, toasted

Combine the tomatoes with the liquid, fish stock, wine, vegetables and rosemary in the slow cooker. Cover and cook on Low for 8–9 hours. Turn the slow cooker to High, add the fish and parsley and cook for 15 minutes. Stir in the combined milk and cornflour, stirring for 2–3 minutes. Season to taste with salt and pepper. Put the bread in the soup bowls. Ladle the soup over.

Pesto Fish Soup

A Mediterranean touch in this tasty combination.

SERVES 6

400 g/14 oz can chopped tomatoes
250 ml/8 fl oz fish stock
250 ml/8 fl oz dry white wine
    or fish stock
1 onion, chopped
1 celery stick, chopped
1 carrot, chopped
150 g/5 oz cooked cannellini or
    haricot beans
1 tsp dried rosemary
700 g/1½ lb skinless fish fillets, cubed
20 g/¾ oz fresh parsley, chopped
1 tbsp cornflour
salt and freshly ground black pepper,
    to taste
50 ml/2 fl oz Basil Pesto (see page 72)
6 ciabatta slices, toasted.

Combine the tomatoes with the liquid, fish stock, wine, vegetables, beans and rosemary in the slow cooker. Cover and cook on Low for 8–9 hours. Turn the slow cooker, add the fish and parsley and cook for 15 minutes. Stir in the combined milk and cornflour, stirring for 2–3 minutes. Season to taste with salt and pepper and stir in the pesto. Put the bread in the soup bowls. Ladle the soup over.

Light Salmon Bisque with Dill

Dill complements the flavour of fresh salmon in this light, tempting bisque.

SERVES 4

750 ml/1¼ pints fish stock
250 g/9 oz potatoes, peeled and chopped
2 onions, chopped
1 celery stick, finely chopped
1 carrot, finely chopped
1 tbsp tomato purée
1½ tsp dried dill
¼–½ tsp dry mustard powder
225–350 g/8–12 oz salmon fillet, skinned
300 ml/½ pint full-fat milk
2 tbsp cornflour
2–3 tsp lemon juice
salt and white pepper, to taste

Combine the stock, vegetables, tomato purée, dill and mustard powder in the slow cooker. Cover and cook on Low for 6–8 hours, add the salmon fillet and 250 ml/8 fl oz of the milk during the last 15 minutes. Remove the salmon and reserve. Process the soup in a food processor or blender until smooth. Return to the slow cooker.

Flake the reserved salmon into small pieces using a fork. Add to the slow cooker. Cover and cook on High for 10 minutes. Stir in the combined remaining milk and the cornflour, stirring for 2–3 minutes. Season to taste with lemon juice, salt and white pepper.

Salmon and Wild Rice Soup

A very special soup. The rich flavours of salmon and wild rice perfectly complement one another.

SERVES 6

750 ml/1¼ pints fish or chicken stock
130 g/4½ oz mushrooms, sliced
2 small onions, chopped
1 celery stick, sliced
1 garlic clove, crushed
½ tsp dry mustard powder
½ tsp dried rosemary
25 g/1 oz wild rice, cooked
250 ml/8 fl oz semi-skimmed milk
450 g/1 lb thick salmon fillet, skinned and cubed
1 tbsp cornflour
salt and cayenne pepper, to taste
2 bacon rashers, cooked until crisp, crumbled

Combine the stock, vegetables, garlic, mustard powder and rosemary in the slow cooker. Cover and cook on Low for 6–8 hours, adding the wild rice and 120 ml/4 fl oz of the milk during the last 20 minutes. Add the salmon. Cover and cook on High for 10–15 minutes. Stir in the combined remaining milk and the cornflour, stirring for 2–3 minutes. Season to taste with salt and cayenne pepper. Sprinkle each bowl of soup with the bacon.

Courgette and Tuna Soup

This easy and convenient soup is made with canned tuna, and it's also delicious made with canned salmon.

SERVES 4

1.2 litres/2 pints chicken stock
2 courgettes, chopped
2 onions, finely chopped
1 large celery stick, finely chopped
3 large garlic cloves, crushed
2 x 185 g/6½ oz cans tuna in water, drained
450 ml/¾ pint full-fat milk
2 tbsp cornflour
1–2 tsp lemon juice
100–175 g/4–6 oz Cheddar cheese, grated
salt and freshly ground black pepper, to taste
Tabasco sauce

Combine the stock, vegetables and garlic in the slow cooker. Cover and cook on Low for 7–8 hours. Then turn the slow cooker to High, add the tuna and 250 ml/8 fl oz of the milk and cook for a further 30 minutes. Stir in the combined remaining milk and the cornflour, stirring for 2–3 minutes. Season to taste with lemon juice. Add the cheese, stirring until melted. Season to taste with salt, pepper and Tabasco sauce.

Maryland Crab Soup

Old Bay seasoning, available from specialist suppliers, is the key ingredient for a traditional Maryland soup, but paprika can be used instead. Prawns can be substituted for crabmeat for a delicious variation.

SERVES 6

1.5 litres/2½ pints beef stock
600 ml/1 pint fish stock
550 g/1¼ lb canned plum tomatoes, coarsely chopped, with their juice
500 g/18 oz waxy potatoes, peeled and diced
100 g/4 oz sweetcorn, thawed if frozen
2 large onions, finely chopped
2 carrots, finely chopped
2 celery sticks, finely chopped
2 bay leaves
½ tsp dry mustard powder
1–2 tbsp Old Bay seasoning, or 1 tbsp paprika
350 g/12 oz fresh crabmeat, cut into small pieces
2 bacon rashers, cooked until crisp, crumbled
25 g/1 oz fresh parsley, finely chopped
salt and freshly ground black pepper, to taste

Combine all the ingredients, except the crabmeat, bacon, parsley, salt and pepper, in a 5.5 litre/9½ pint slow cooker. Cover and cook on Low for 6–8 hours, adding the crab, bacon and parsley during the last 20 minutes. Discard the bay leaves. Season to taste with salt and pepper.

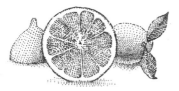

103

Tuna and Rice Soup

A soup with subtle and delicious flavours.

SERVES 6

**750 ml/1¼ pints fish or chicken stock
130 g/4½ oz mushrooms, sliced
2 small onions, chopped
1 celery stick, sliced
1 garlic clove, crushed
½ tsp dried tarragon
25 g/1 oz long-grain rice, cooked
250 ml/8 fl oz semi-skimmed milk
450 g/1 lb thick tuna steak, skinned
and cubed
1 tbsp cornflour
lemon juice, to taste
salt and cayenne pepper, to taste
2 bacon rashers, cooked until crisp,
crumbled**

Combine the stock, vegetables, garlic, and tarragon in the slow cooker. Cover and cook on Low for 6–8 hours, adding the rice and 120 ml/4 fl oz of the milk during the last 20 minutes. Add the tuna. Cover and cook on High for 10–15 minutes. Stir in the combined remaining milk and the cornflour, stirring for 2–3 minutes. Season to taste with lemon juice, salt and cayenne pepper. Sprinkle each bowl of soup with the bacon.

Georgia Fish Soup

Peanut butter is the surprise ingredient in this unusual and piquant fish soup.

SERVES 6

**375 ml/13 fl oz fish stock
375 ml/13 fl oz water
2 x 400 g/14 oz cans chopped
tomatoes
2 onions, thinly sliced
½ green pepper, chopped
2 garlic cloves, crushed,
1–2 tsp chilli powder
½ tsp dried thyme
75–100 g/3–4 oz peanut butter
275 g/10 oz thawed frozen or fresh
okra, sliced (blanch fresh for 1
minute in boiling water)
450 g/1 lb skinless cod or haddock
fillets, cubed
salt and freshly ground black pepper,
to taste
Tabasco sauce**

Combine all the ingredients, except the peanut butter, okra, cod, salt, pepper and Tabasco sauce, in the slow cooker. Cover and cook on Low for 7–8 hours. Turn the slow cooker to High, add the peanut butter and okra and cook for 15 minutes, then add the cod and cook for a further 15 minutes. Season to taste with salt and pepper. Serve with Tabasco sauce.

Cioppino

This version of a soup originally from San Francisco that uses the 'catch of the day' is made with shellfish.

SERVES 6

400 g/14 oz can chopped tomatoes
250 ml/8 fl oz fish stock
250 ml/8 fl oz water
120 ml/4 fl oz dry white wine or fish stock
2 onions, thinly sliced
4 spring onions, thinly sliced
1 green pepper, thinly sliced
3 large garlic cloves, crushed
1 tbsp olive oil
½ tsp dried tarragon
½ tsp dried thyme
½ tsp dried rosemary
1 bay leaf
450 g/1 lb crabmeat or firm white fish, cubed
350 g/12 oz large raw prawns, peeled and deveined, thawed if frozen
18 clams, scrubbed (discard any that remain open when tapped)
salt and freshly ground black pepper, to taste

Combine all the ingredients, except the seafood, salt and pepper, in the slow cooker. Cover and cook on Low for 6–8 hours, adding the seafood during the last 15–20 minutes. Discard the bay leaf and any clams that have not opened. Season to taste with salt and pepper.

Mediterranean Cioppino

Oregano and basil meld with red wine and tomatoes to produce a full Italian flavour for this soup.

SERVES 6

2 x 400 g/14 oz cans chopped tomatoes
175 g/6 oz tomato purée
250 ml/8 fl oz fish stock or water
120 ml/4 fl oz dry red wine or fish stock
¼ green pepper, chopped
½ onion, chopped
1 garlic clove, crushed
1 tsp dried oregano
1 tsp dried basil
375 g/13 oz clams from a jar or can, finely chopped, with liquor, or cockles
225 g/8 oz skinless sole or monkfish fillet, cubed
225 g/8 oz cooked peeled prawns, thawed if frozen
salt and freshly ground black pepper, to taste

Combine all the ingredients, except the seafood, salt and pepper, in the slow cooker. Cover and cook on Low for 6–8 hours, adding the clams and liquor during the last hour and the remaining seafood, including the cockles, if using, during the last 15–20 minutes. Season to taste with salt and pepper.

Prawn Bisque

This creamy bisque with a hint of spiciness tastes good with Garlic Croûtons (see page 34) scattered over the top.

SERVES 4

1.5 litres/2½ pints fish or chicken stock
50 ml/2 fl oz tomato purée
3 onions, chopped
3–4 tsp curry powder
½ tsp paprika
250 ml/8 fl oz semi-skimmed milk
2 tbsp cornflour
700 g/1½ lb large, raw prawns, peeled and deveined, thawed if frozen
300 g/11 oz tomatoes, finely chopped
salt and cayenne pepper, to taste

Combine all the ingredients, except the prawns, tomatoes, salt, milk, cornflour and cayenne pepper, in the slow cooker. Cover and cook on High for 4 hours. Stir in the combined milk and cornflour, stirring for 2–3 minutes. Add the prawns and cook for 10 minutes. Process the soup in a food processor or blender until smooth. Return to the slow cooker and add the tomatoes. Cover and cook on High for 10 minutes. Season to taste with salt and pepper.

Okra with Prawns

Okra and tomato are given a kick with chilli and make a tasty base for red snapper and prawns.

SERVES 6

1 litre/1¾ pints fish or chicken stock
600 g/1 lb 6 oz tomatoes, finely chopped
225 g/8 oz okra, trimmed and sliced
1 small onion, sliced
1 small green pepper, sliced
1 bay leaf
¼ tsp crushed chilli flakes
350 g/12 oz skinless red snapper fillets, cubed
350 g/12 oz large, raw prawns, peeled and deveined, thawed if frozen
salt and freshly ground black pepper, to taste
50 g/2 oz rice, cooked, hot

Combine the stock, vegetables, bay leaf and chilli flakes in a 5.5 litre/9½ pint slow cooker. Cover and cook on Low for 8 hours, adding the seafood during the last 20 minutes. Discard the bay leaf. Season to taste with salt and pepper. Serve over rice in bowls.

Mexican Sweetcorn and Prawn Soup

This fiery soup is finished off with a swirl of Roasted Red Pepper Sauce.

SERVES 4

450 ml/¾ pint vegetable stock
500 g/18 oz sweetcorn, thawed if frozen
2 small onions chopped
1 jalapeño or other hot chilli, finely chopped
1 garlic clove, crushed
1 tbsp chopped fresh coriander
1 tbsp chopped fresh oregano
350 g/12 oz cooked peeled prawns, thawed if frozen
salt and cayenne pepper, to taste
Roasted Red Pepper Sauce (see page 63)

Combine the stock, sweetcorn, onions, chilli and garlic in the slow cooker. Cover and cook on High for 4–5 hours. Process the soup with the herbs in a food processor or blender until smooth. Return to the slow cooker. Add the prawns. Cover and cook on High for 10 minutes. Season to taste with salt and cayenne pepper. Serve warm or refrigerate and serve chilled. Swirl about 3 tbsp of Roasted Red Pepper Sauce into each bowl of soup.

Caribbean-style Fish Soup

Annatto seeds are available from specialist outlets and ethnic supermarkets. They are often used in Caribbean and Mexican cooking, where they impart a subtle flavour and a deep yellow colour. This dish still tastes good without them, however.

SERVES 4

2 tsp vegetable oil
1 tbsp annatto seeds (optional)
1 onion, thinly sliced
450 ml/¾ pint chicken stock
400 g/14 oz can chopped tomatoes
1 sweet potato, peeled and cubed
1 tsp dried thyme
100 g/4 oz frozen peas, thawed
450 g/1 lb skinless lemon sole or
    flounder fillets, cubed (2 cm/¾ in)
3–4 tsp lemon juice
salt and freshly ground black pepper,
    to taste

Heat the oil in large pan over medium-high heat. Add the annatto seeds, if using, and cook until the oil is bright yellow, about 3 minutes. Remove the seeds with a slotted spoon and discard. Add the onion to the pan. Sauté for 2 minutes. Combine the onion mixture, stock, tomatoes, sweet potato and thyme in the slow cooker. Cover and cook on Low for 8–9 hours. Turn the slow cooker to High, add the peas and sole and cook for 15 minutes. Season to taste with lemon juice, salt and pepper.

Niçoise Fish Soup

Fennel seeds and turmeric add a special flavour dimension to this great soup.

SERVES 8

750 ml/1¼ pints water
250 ml/8 fl oz fish stock
400 g/14 oz tomatoes, chopped
2 onions, chopped
3 large garlic cloves, crushed
½ tsp dried thyme
½ tsp crushed fennel seeds
½ tsp ground turmeric
1 bay leaf
900 g/2 lb assorted skinless fish fillets
    such as cod, halibut, haddock,
    whiting, red snapper, cubed
salt and cayenne pepper, to taste
Bruschetta (see page 36)

Combine all the ingredients, except the fish, salt, cayenne pepper and Bruschetta, in the slow cooker. Cover and cook on High for 4–5 hours, adding the fish during the last 15–20 minutes. Discard the bay leaf. Season to taste with salt and cayenne pepper. Serve with Bruschetta

Tuscan Fish Soup

Along the Tuscan coast, each town boasts its own incomparable fish soup. Here is one version.

SERVES 6

1 litre/1¾ pints chicken stock
120 ml/4 fl oz dry red wine or chicken stock
1.5 kg/3 lb tomatoes, peeled, seeded and chopped
2 onions, chopped
3 garlic cloves, crushed
1 tsp dried oregano,
1 tsp dried sage
1 tsp dried rosemary
¼ tsp crushed chilli flakes
550 g/1¼ lb assorted skinless fish fillets or steaks, such as haddock, sole, salmon, hake, red snapper, tuna or halibut, cubed
175 g/6 oz cooked peeled prawns, thawed if frozen
salt and freshly ground black pepper, to taste
6 ciabatta slices, toasted
2 garlic cloves, halved

Combine all the ingredients, except the seafood, salt, pepper, bread and garlic, in the slow cooker. Cover and cook on High for 4–5 hours, adding the seafood during the last 15 minutes. Season to taste with salt and pepper. Rub the bread with the garlic cloves. Put in soup bowls and ladle the soup over.

Mediterranean-style Prawn and Vegetable Soup

Orange zest and fennel seeds add a fragrant edge to this tasty soup.

SERVES 6

400 g/14 oz can chopped tomatoes
225 g/8 oz ready-made tomato sauce
450 ml/¾ pint vegetable stock
120 ml/4 fl oz dry white wine or orange juice
175 g/6 oz sliced mushrooms
1 onion, chopped
½ green pepper, chopped
3 garlic cloves, crushed
2 strips orange zest
2 bay leaves
¾ tsp dried marjoram
¾ tsp dried basil
½ tsp crushed fennel seeds
450 g/1 lb large, raw prawns, peeled and deveined, thawed if frozen
salt and freshly ground black pepper, to taste

Combine all the ingredients, except the prawns, salt and pepper, in the slow cooker. Cover and cook on Low for 6–8 hours. Turn the slow cooker to High, add the prawns and cook for 15 minutes. Discard the bay leaves. Season to taste with salt and pepper.

Kakavia

This is the Greek version of the French bouillabaisse, a lovely combination of fish and shellfish in a rich vegetable soup.

SERVES 12

2 x 400 g/14 oz cans chopped tomatoes
1 litre/1¾ pints fish stock
120 ml/4 fl oz dry white wine or fish stock
4 onions chopped
2 celery sticks, chopped
3 large garlic cloves, crushed
2 leeks (white parts only), sliced
3 large carrots, chopped
3 bay leaves
1 tsp dried thyme
3–4 tbsp lemon juice
900 g/2 lb skinless fish fillets, such as halibut, salmon, cod, hake, whiting or red snapper, cubed
12 clams, scrubbed (discard any that remain open when tapped)
12 mussels, scrubbed and beards removed (discard any that remain open when tapped)
350 g/12 oz large, raw prawns, peeled and deveined, thawed if frozen
salt and freshly ground black pepper, to taste

Combine all the ingredients, except the seafood, salt and pepper, in a 5.5 litre/9½ pint slow cooker. Cover and cook on Low for 6–8 hours, adding the seafood during the last 15–20 minutes. Discard the bay leaves and any clams or mussels that have not opened. Season to taste with salt and pepper.

Spanish Fish Soup

This unique soup is flavoured with ground almonds and thickened with breadcrumbs.

SERVES 8

1 litre/1¾ pints fish stock
120 ml/4 fl oz dry white wine or fish stock
2 onions, chopped
1 tsp paprika
½ tsp crushed cumin seeds
40 g/1½ oz fresh breadcrumbs
75 g/3 oz ground almonds
900 g/2 lb skinless cod or monkfish fillet, cubed
2 hard-boiled egg yolks, finely chopped
250 ml/8 fl oz semi-skimmed milk
2 tbsp cornflour
salt and cayenne pepper, to taste
8 thin lemon slices
fresh chopped parsley, to garnish

Combine the fish stock, wine, onions, paprika, cumin seeds, breadcrumbs and almonds in the slow cooker. Cover and cook on Low for 6–8 hours. Turn the slow cooker to High, add the fish and egg yolks and cook for 10 minutes. Stir in the combined milk and cornflour, stirring for 2–3 minutes. Season to taste with salt and cayenne pepper. Garnish each bowl of soup with a lemon slice and sprinkle with parsley.

Portuguese-style Fisherman's Soup

An attractive and robust medley of vegetables and fish seasoned with chilli, saffron and paprika.

SERVES 6

2 x 400 g/14 oz cans chopped
  tomatoes
375 ml/13 fl oz chicken stock
175 ml/6 fl oz dry white wine or
  water
2 large onions, finely chopped
1 small carrot, chopped
½ celery stick, chopped
½ red pepper, chopped
1 large garlic clove, crushed
3–4 waxy potatoes, unpeeled and cubed
1 bay leaf
1–2 tsp chilli powder
2 tsp paprika
a pinch of saffron threads, crumbled
  (optional)
½ tsp celery seeds
½ tsp dried thyme
a pinch of crushed chilli flakes
24 fresh mussels, scrubbed and beards
  removed (discard any that remain
  open when tapped)
700 g/1½ lb skinless white fish
  fillets, such as hake, cod, monkfish,
  haddock or whiting, cubed
225 g/8 oz cooked peeled prawns,
  thawed if frozen
salt and cayenne pepper, to taste

Combine all the ingredients, except the seafood, salt and cayenne pepper, in a 5.5 litre/9½ pint slow cooker. Cover and cook on Low for 6–8 hours, adding the seafood during the last 15–20 minutes. Discard the bay leaf and any mussels that remain closed. Season to taste with salt and cayenne pepper.

Caldo de Pescado

This South American fish soup includes a mixed bag of vegetables and seafood, with a flavour accent of orange.

SERVES 10

1 litre/1¾ pints Easy Fish Stock (see
  page 33) or 450 ml/¾ pint each fish
  stock and water
2 x 400 g/14 oz cans chopped
  tomatoes
4 onions, chopped
350 g/12 oz potatoes, peeled and sliced
1 large red pepper, chopped
2 large sweetcorn cobs, cut into
  2.5 cm/1 in pieces
3 garlic cloves, crushed
1 tsp grated orange zest
1 tsp ground turmeric
450 g/1 lb skinless red snapper fillets,
  cubed
350 g/12 oz large, raw prawns, peeled
  and deveined, thawed if frozen
salt and cayenne pepper, to taste

Combine all the ingredients, except the seafood, salt and cayenne pepper, in a 5.5 litre/9½ pint slow cooker. Cover and cook on Low for 6–8 hours, adding the seafood during the last 15 minutes. Season to taste with salt and cayenne pepper.

Fish Soup Marseilles

Fresh fennel gives this soup its authentic 'south of France' flavour.

SERVES 6

900 ml/1½ pints Mediterranean Stock (see page 28) or vegetable stock
400 g/14 oz can plum tomatoes
1 onion, chopped,
½ fennel bulb, sliced
3 large garlic cloves, crushed
100 g/4 oz uncooked orzo or other small soup pasta
225 g/8 oz cubed skinless white fish fillets, such as cod, monkfish, haddock or whiting
225 g/8 oz raw prawns, peeled, thawed if frozen
salt and freshly ground black pepper

Combine the stock, tomatoes, onion, fennel and garlic in the slow cooker. Cover and cook on High for 4–5 hours, adding the pasta during the last 20 minutes and the seafood during the last 10 minutes. Season to taste with salt and pepper.

Scallop and Pasta Soup

The rich flavour of scallops is lovely with tomatoes, peppers and mushrooms.

SERVES 6

450 ml/¾ pint chicken stock
400 g/14 oz can chopped plum tomatoes
120 ml/4 fl oz dry white wine or chicken stock
1 onion, chopped
½ green pepper, diced
½ red pepper, diced
1 small garlic clove, crushed
225 g/8 oz mushrooms, sliced
100 g/4 oz uncooked small soup pasta
450 g/1 lb scallops, halved if large
50 g/2 oz freshly grated Parmesan cheese
salt and freshly ground black pepper

Combine all the ingredients, except the pasta, scallops, cheese, salt and pepper, in the slow cooker. Cover and cook on Low for 6–8 hours, adding the pasta during the last 30 minutes and the scallops during the last 15 minutes. Stir in the cheese. Season to taste with salt and pepper.

Squash and Scallop Soup

Butternut squash makes an unusual partner to scallops in this creamy soup.

SERVES 6

250 ml/8 fl oz chicken stock
350 g/12 oz butternut squash, peeled and cubed
1 large celery stick, chopped
1 onion, chopped
¼ tsp fresh root ginger, finely grated
450 ml/¾ pint full-fat milk
450 g/1 lb scallops, halved if large
2 tbsp cornflour
1–2 tsp Worcestershire sauce
salt and white pepper, to taste

Combine the stock, vegetables and ginger in the slow cooker. Cover and cook on Low for 6–8 hours, adding 375 ml/13 fl oz milk and the scallops during the last 15 minutes. Stir in the combined remaining milk and the cornflour, stirring for 2–3 minutes. Season to taste with Worcestershire sauce, salt and white pepper.

Oyster and Mushroom Bisque

A creamy mushroom soup is enhanced with oysters and sherry.

SERVES 4

250 ml/8 fl oz chicken stock
24 fresh oysters, shucked,
liquor reserved
225 g/8 oz mushrooms, sliced
250 ml/8 fl oz full-fat milk
50 ml/2 fl oz dry sherry or water
2 tbsp cornflour
salt and white pepper, to taste
oyster crackers

Combine the stock, reserved oyster liquor and mushrooms in the slow cooker. Cover and cook on High for 2–3 hours, adding the milk during the last 30 minutes and oysters during the last 15 minutes. Stir in the combined sherry and cornflour, stirring for 2–3 minutes. Season to taste with salt and white pepper. Serve with oyster crackers.

Mardi Gras Oyster Soup

In this New Orleans recipe, oysters are combined with wine to make a celebration soup. A home-made, or good-quality bought, fish stock will give you the best results.

SERVES 6

1 litre/1¾ pints fish stock
36 fresh oysters, shucked, liquor reserved
1 onion, chopped
120 ml/4 fl oz dry white wine or fish stock
2 tbsp cornflour
salt and cayenne pepper, to taste
chopped chives, to garnish

Combine the fish stock, reserved oyster liquor and onion in the slow cooker. Cover and cook on High for 2–3 hours. Stir in the oysters and combined wine and cornflour. Cover and cook for 15 minutes. Season to taste with salt and cayenne pepper. Sprinkle each bowl of soup with chives.

Mussel Soup with Saffron

Saffron's unique flavour and brilliant colour makes this soup of mussels, spring onions and fresh tomatoes especially attractive.

SERVES 4

450 ml/¾ pint fish stock
175 ml/6 fl oz dry white wine or water
1 carrot, finely chopped
1 celery stick, finely chopped
100 g/4 oz tomatoes, finely chopped
4 spring onions, sliced
1 large garlic clove, crushed
1 bay leaf
10 saffron threads, crumbled
900 g/2 lb mussels, scrubbed and beards removed (discard any that remain open when tapped)
salt and cayenne pepper, to taste

Combine all the ingredients, except the mussels, salt and cayenne pepper, in the slow cooker. Cover and cook on High for 4 hours, adding the mussels during the last 15 minutes. Discard the bay leaf and any mussels that have not opened. Season to taste with salt and cayenne pepper.

Chinese Oyster Soup

Enjoy the flavour accents of shiitake mushrooms, garlic and ginger of the Oriental Stock to make the most of this oyster soup.

SERVES 4

600 ml/1 pint Oriental Stock (see page 29) or chicken stock
2 tbsp soy sauce
175 g/6 oz Chinese cabbage, sliced
225 g/8 oz mushrooms, sliced
25 g/1 oz beansprouts
4 spring onions, sliced
2.5 cm/1 in piece fresh root ginger, finely grated
24 fresh oysters, shucked, liquor reserved
salt and freshly ground black pepper

Combine all the ingredients, except the oysters, salt and pepper, in the slow cooker. Cover and cook on Low for 6–8 hours, adding the oysters and liquor during the last 10–15 minutes. Season to taste with salt and pepper.

Clam Soup

Fresh clams make an exceptional soup! This dish also works well using mussels or with 450 g/1 lb peeled prawns added during the last 10 minutes of cooking.

SERVES 4

250 ml/8 fl oz fish stock or chicken stock
250 ml/8 fl oz ready-made tomato sauce
250 ml/8 fl oz dry white wine or fish stock
3 large garlic cloves
¼ tsp crushed chilli flakes
1 tsp dried oregano
1 tsp dried thyme
48 clams, scrubbed (discard any that remain open when tapped)
15 g/½ oz fresh chopped parsley

salt and freshly ground black pepper, to taste
4 ciabatta slices, toasted

Combine all the ingredients, except the clams, parsley, salt, pepper and bread, in the slow cooker. Cover and cook on High for 4 hours, adding the clams and parsley during the last 15 minutes. Discard any clams that have not opened. Season the soup to taste with salt and pepper. Serve the stock and clams in shallow bowls with toasted ciabatta.

Potato and Mussel Saffron Soup

The texture of mussels and their rich flavour make a good contrast to the vegetables in this homely coastal soup.

SERVES 8

1 litre/1¾ pints water
400 g/14 oz can chopped tomatoes
3 potatoes, peeled and diced
3 carrots, thinly sliced
3 small leeks (white parts only), thinly sliced
3 garlic cloves, crushed
3 shallots, thinly sliced
2 bay leaves
1 tsp fennel seeds
¼ tsp saffron
25 g/1 oz fresh chopped parsley
32 mussels, scrubbed and beards removed (discard any that remain open when tapped)
salt and white pepper, to taste

Combine all the ingredients, except the parsley, mussels, salt and pepper in the slow cooker. Cover and cook on Low for 6–7 hours. Turn the heat to High and cook for 10 minutes. Add the parsley and mussels, cover and cook for 15 minutes. Discard the bay leaves and any mussels that have not opened. Season to taste with salt and pepper.

Vegetarian Soups

So many people are cutting down on their consumption of meat and enjoying more vegetable dishes – whether or not they are vegetarian – so even the most committed carnivore will find meals to enjoy here. Note that the recipes do contain dairy products so look out for brands that are suitable for vegetarians. The same applies to Worcestershire sauce.

Brussels Sprouts Soup Ⓥ

A perfect autumn soup to make when tiny fresh Brussels sprouts are available.

SERVES 4

450 g/1 lb Brussels sprouts, halved
1 onion, chopped
2 garlic cloves, crushed
½ tsp dried rosemary leaves
250 ml/8 fl oz vegetable stock
250 ml/8 fl oz semi-skimmed milk
salt and white pepper, to taste
freshly grated nutmeg, to garnish

Combine the Brussels sprouts, onion, garlic, rosemary and stock in the slow cooker. Cover and cook on High until the Brussels sprouts are very tender, 2–4 hours. Process the soup and milk in a food processor or blender until smooth. Season to taste with salt and pepper. Sprinkle each bowl of soup lightly with nutmeg.

Cream of Artichoke and Mushroom Soup Ⓥ

A delicate blend of mild artichoke hearts and succulent portabella mushrooms. Shiitake or brown cap mushrooms can be substituted for the portabella mushrooms, if you prefer a stronger flavour.

SERVES 4

450 ml/¾ pint vegetable stock
250 g/9 oz artichoke hearts from a jar or can, finely chopped
75 g/3 oz portabella mushrooms, chopped
½ onion, chopped
250 ml/8 fl oz single cream or full-fat milk
2 tbsp cornflour
salt and white pepper, to taste
paprika, to garnish

Combine all the ingredients, except the cream, cornflour, salt, pepper and paprika, in the slow cooker. Cover and cook on Low for 6–8 hours. Stir in the combined cream and cornflour, stirring occasionally for 5 minutes. Season to taste with salt and pepper. Sprinkle each bowl of soup with paprika.

Creamy Cabbage Soup Ⓥ

Flavoured with dill and rosemary, this soup is easy to make and satisfying to eat.

SERVES 6

1 litre/1¾ pints vegetable stock
1 small cabbage, thinly sliced
2 large onions, thinly sliced
2 carrots, sliced
1 large potato, peeled and sliced
1 bay leaf
½ tsp dried dill
½ tsp dried rosemary leaves
250 ml/8 fl oz soured cream
2 tbsp cornflour
salt and freshly ground black pepper,
  to taste

Combine all the ingredients, except the soured cream, cornflour, salt and pepper, in a 5.5 litre/9½ pint slow cooker. Cover and cook on Low for 6–8 hours. Discard the bay leaf. Stir in the combined soured cream and cornflour, stirring until thickened, 2–3 minutes. Season to taste with salt and pepper.

Cabbage and White Bean Soup Ⓥ

A tasty combination of vegetables and pulses.

SERVES 6

750 ml/1¼ pints vegetable stock
1 small cabbage, thinly sliced
400 g/14 oz can drained and rinsed
  cannellini beans
400 g/14 oz chopped tomatoes
2 large onions, thinly sliced
2 carrots, sliced
1 large potato, peeled and sliced
1 bay leaf
½ tsp dried dill
½ tsp dried rosemary leaves
salt and freshly ground black pepper,
  to taste

Combine all the ingredients, except the salt and pepper, in the slow cooker. Cover and cook on Low for 6–8 hours. Discard the bay leaf. Season to taste with salt and pepper.

Creamed Sweetcorn Soup Ⓥ

A filling dish that should prove popular with the family. Garnish bowls of soup generously with finely chopped fresh coriander or parsley, if you like.

SERVES 4

900 ml/1½ pints vegetable stock
1 onion, chopped
1 floury potato, peeled and cubed
2 garlic cloves, crushed
½ tsp ground coriander
400 g/14 oz can sweetcorn, drained
2 medium tomatoes, chopped
250 ml/8 fl oz milk
2 tbsp cornflour
salt and cayenne pepper, to taste
paprika, to garnish

Combine the stock, onion, potato, garlic and coriander in the slow cooker. Cover and cook on Low for 8 hours. Process the soup in a food processor or blender until almost smooth. Return to the slow cooker. Add the sweetcorn and tomatoes. Cover and cook on High for 30 minutes. Stir in the combined milk and cornflour, stirring for 2–3 minutes. Season to taste with salt and pepper. Sprinkle each bowl of soup with paprika.

Latin American Sweetcorn and Avocado Soup

An unusual combination but one that works beautifully.

SERVES 4

900 ml/1½ pints vegetable stock
½ tsp crushed saffron
1 onion, chopped
1 floury potato, peeled and cubed
2 garlic cloves, crushed
½ tsp ground coriander
2 eggs
100 g/4 oz soft cheese
2 tbsp chilli sauce
400 g/14 oz can sweetcorn, drained
250 ml/8 fl oz milk
2 tbsp cornflour
salt and cayenne pepper, to taste
avocado slices, to garnish

Combine the stock, saffron, onion, potato, garlic and coriander in the slow cooker. Cover and cook on Low for 8 hours. Process the soup in a food processor or blender until almost smooth. Beat together the eggs, cheese and chilli sauce, then whisk into the puréed soup. Return to the slow cooker. Add the sweetcorn and tomatoes. Cover and cook on High for 30 minutes. Stir in the combined milk and cornflour, stirring for 2–3 minutes. Season to taste with salt and cayenne pepper. Garnish each bowl of soup with avocado slices.

Black Bean Garlic Chowder

Garlic lovers take note – this is a colourful chowder with oodles of flavour.

SERVES 4

400 g/14 oz can black beans, drained and rinsed
400 ml/14 fl oz vegetable stock
1 garlic bulb, cloves peeled and thinly sliced or chopped
1–2 small Serrano or other very hot chillies, seeded and finely chopped
450 g/1 lb plum tomatoes, coarsely chopped
salt and freshly ground black pepper, to taste
Chilli Croûtons (see below)
15 g/½ oz fresh chopped parsley
50 ml/2 fl oz soured cream

Process 130 g/4½ oz of the beans and 175 ml/6 fl oz of the stock in a food processor or blender until smooth. Combine the puréed and whole black beans with the remaining stock, the garlic, chillies and tomatoes in the slow cooker. Cover and cook on Low for 6–8 hours. Season to taste with salt and pepper. Top each bowl of chowder with Chilli Croûtons, parsley and a dollop of soured cream.

Chilli Croûtons

SERVES 4 AS AN ACCOMPANIMENT

3 slices firm or day-old French bread, cubed (1 cm/½ in)
vegetable cooking spray
chilli powder

Spray the bread cubes with cooking spray. Sprinkle lightly with chilli powder and toss. Arrange in a single layer in a baking tray. Bake at 190°C/gas 5/ fan oven 170°C until browned, 8–10 minutes, stirring occasionally.

Easy Mexican Sweetcorn and Bean Soup Ⓥ

Red kidney beans and lots of chilli go with the sweetcorn to make a typical Mexican dish.

SERVES 4

600 ml/1 pint tomato juice
400 g/14 oz can chopped tomatoes, puréed
225 g/8 oz sweetcorn, thawed if frozen
275 g/10 oz drained canned red kidney beans
1 finely chopped onion
1 small green pepper, finely chopped
1 garlic clove, crushed
½–1 tbsp chilli powder
1 tsp ground cumin
1 tsp sugar
salt and freshly ground black pepper, to taste

Combine all the ingredients, except the salt and pepper, in the slow cooker. Cover and cook on Low for 6–8 hours. Season to taste with salt and pepper.

Garlic Vegetable Soup Ⓥ

Haricot and French beans with potato make a lovely soup with lashings of garlic. You can add even more garlic, if you like!

SERVES 8

2.25 litres/4 pints water
400 g/14 oz can haricot or cannellini beans, drained and rinsed
450 g/1 lb tomatoes, peeled, seeded and coarsely chopped
175 g/6 oz new potatoes, scrubbed and diced
1 large carrot, coarsely chopped
150 g/5 oz French beans, cut into short lengths
100 g/4 oz chopped leeks (white parts only)
½ celery stick, chopped
6 large garlic cloves, crushed
2 tbsp tomato purée
2 tbsp dried basil leaves
salt and freshly ground black pepper, to taste

Combine all the ingredients, except the salt and pepper, in the slow cooker. Cover and cook on Low for 6–8 hours. Season to taste with salt and pepper.

Savoury Mushroom and Barley Soup Ⓥ

Other grains, such as wild rice or oat groats, can be substituted for the barley. Cook according to the packet instructions and add to the soup during the last 30 minutes of cooking time.

SERVES 4

750 ml/1¼ pints water
400 g/14 oz can chopped tomatoes
2 small onions, chopped
1 celery stick, chopped
2 small carrots, chopped
1 tsp dried thyme leaves
¾ tsp crushed fennel seeds
175 g/6 oz brown cap or button
  mushrooms, sliced
90 g/3½ oz pearl barley
salt and freshly ground black pepper,
  to taste

Combine all the ingredients, except the salt and pepper, in the slow cooker. Cover and cook on High for 4–6 hours. Season to taste with salt and pepper.

Savoury Mushroom and Spinach Soup Ⓥ

You can make this with spinach or kale.

SERVES 4

750 ml/1¼ pints water
400 g/14 oz can chopped tomatoes
2 small onions, chopped
1 celery stick, chopped
2 small carrots, chopped
2–3 garlic cloves, sliced
1 tsp dried thyme leaves
¾ tsp crushed fennel seeds
175 g/6 oz brown cap or button
  mushrooms, sliced
90 g/3½ oz spinach, torn
salt and freshly ground black pepper,
  to taste

Combine all the ingredients, except the spinach, salt and pepper, in the slow cooker. Cover and cook on High for 4–6 hours, addng the spinach for the last 15 minutes. Season to taste with salt and pepper.

Maple, Bean and Mushroom Soup Ⓥ

Delicious – and with the distinctive hint of maple syrup.

SERVES 4

750 ml/1¼ pints water
400 g/14 oz can chopped tomatoes
400 g/14 oz can drained cannellini
    beans
2 small onions, chopped
2 small carrots, chopped
2 garlic cloves, crushed
1 celery stick, chopped
1 tsp dried thyme leaves
1–2 tbsp maple syrup
¾ tsp crushed fennel seeds
175 g/6 oz brown cap or button
    mushrooms, sliced
salt and freshly ground black pepper,
    to taste

Combine all the ingredients, except the salt and pepper, in the slow cooker. Cover and cook on High for 4–6 hours. Season to taste with salt and pepper.

Shiitake and Mushroom Chowder Ⓥ

Marsala is a dark, sweet wine, that goes well with the pronounced flavours of shiitake mushrooms and Swiss cheese in this chowder.

SERVES 4

750 ml/1¼ pints vegetable stock
4 shallots, thinly sliced
2 large potatoes, peeled and
    cubed (5 mm/¼ in)
175 g/6 oz shiitake mushroom
    caps, sliced
175 g/6 oz portabella mushrooms, cubed
2 tbsp Marsala wine (optional)
salt and white pepper, to taste
25 g/1 oz Gruyère or Emmental
    cheese, grated

Combine all the ingredients, except the Marsala, salt, pepper and cheese, in the slow cooker. Cover and cook on Low for 8–9 hours. Stir in the Marsala. Season to taste with salt and pepper. Sprinkle each bowl of soup with cheese.

Sweet Red Pepper Soup Ⓥ

Convenient roasted peppers from a jar are perked up with some hot chilli in this creamy soup.

SERVES 4

400 ml/14 fl oz vegetable stock
425 g/15 oz roasted red peppers from
    a jar, drained
250 ml/8 fl oz tomato juice
1 onion, chopped
½ small jalapeño or other medium-
    hot chilli, seeded and finely
    chopped
1 garlic clove, crushed
½ tsp dried marjoram
salt and freshly ground black pepper,
    to taste
50–120 ml/2–4 fl oz soured cream
sliced spring onions, to garnish

Combine all the ingredients, except the salt, pepper and soured cream, in the slow cooker. Cover and cook on Low for 4–6 hours. Process the soup in a food processor or blender. Season to taste with salt and pepper. Serve warm or refrigerate and serve chilled. Top each bowl of soup with a dollop of soured cream and sprinkle with spring onions.

Potato Pistou (V)

Fresh basil leaves add their unmistakeable flavour to this rich and flavourful soup with a beautifully soft texture.

SERVES 6

2.25 litres/4 pints water
4 onions, chopped
5 tomatoes, peeled, seeded and chopped
4 waxy potatoes, peeled and diced
100 g/4 oz French beans, halved
2 courgettes, sliced
½ tsp dried marjoram
40 g/1½ oz fresh basil leaves
5 garlic cloves, halved
25 g/1 oz freshly grated Parmesan cheese
salt and freshly ground black pepper, to taste

Combine the water, vegetables and marjoram in a 5.5 litre/9½ pint slow cooker. Cover and cook on Low for 6–8 hours. Process the soup in a food processor or blender until smooth. Add the basil, garlic and cheese, processing until smooth. Return the soup to the slow cooker. Cover and cook on High for 15 minutes. Season to taste with salt and pepper.

Vichyssoise (V)

This classic French potato soup is traditionally served chilled, but it's good warm, too! Top with soured cream and chives to make it extra flavoursome.

SERVES 4

1.5 litres/2½ pints vegetable stock
900 g/2 lb floury potatoes, peeled and cubed
75 g/3 oz leeks or 6 spring onions, sliced
1 large celery stick, sliced
½ tsp dried thyme
salt and white pepper, to taste

4 tbsp soured cream
snipped fresh chives, to garnish

Combine all the ingredients, except the salt, pepper and soured cream, in the slow cooker. Cover and cook on Low for 8–9 hours. Process the soup in a food processor or blender until smooth. Season to taste with salt and pepper. Serve warm, or refrigerate and serve chilled. Top each bowl of soup with 1 tbsp of soured cream, and sprinkle with chives.

Cucumber Vichyssoise with Roasted Red Pepper Swirl (V)

Yoghurt gives this soup a refreshing tang, and roasted peppers add a flavour perk.

SERVES 4

375 ml/13 fl oz vegetable stock
250 ml/8 fl oz water
2 onions, chopped
175 g/6 oz potato, peeled and cubed
150 g/5 oz cucumber, peeled and sliced
1 tsp ground cumin
375 ml/13 fl oz plain yoghurt
2 tbsp cornflour
salt and white pepper, to taste
Roasted Red Pepper Swirl (see page 121)

Combine all the ingredients, except the yoghurt, cornflour, salt, pepper and Roasted Red Pepper Swirl, in the slow cooker. Cover and cook on Low for 4–6 hours. Stir in the combined yoghurt and cornflour, stirring for 2–3 minutes. Process the mixture in a food processor or blender until smooth. Season to taste with salt and pepper. Serve warm or refrigerate and serve chilled. Spoon 2 tbsp of Roasted Red Pepper Swirl into each bowl of soup and swirl with a knife.

Roasted Red Pepper Swirl ⓥ

A delicious garnish to swirl into soups before serving.

SERVES 4 AS AN ACCOMPANIMENT

2 roasted red peppers from a jar
½ small pickled jalapeño chilli
1 garlic clove
2 tsp balsamic vinegar
2–4 tbsp water

Process all the ingredients, except the water, in a food processor or blender until smooth. Add the water, if needed, to make the consistency of double cream.

Avocado Vichyssoise ⓥ

A delicious soup to serve warm or cold.

SERVES 4

375 ml/13 fl oz vegetable stock
250 ml/8 fl oz water
2 onions, chopped
175 g/6 oz potato, peeled and cubed
1 tsp ground cumin
375 ml/13 fl oz plain yoghurt
2 tbsp cornflour
2 medium avocados, roughly chopped
¼ tsp hot chilli powder
2 tbsp dry sherry
salt and white pepper, to taste
4 tbsp crumbled Feta cheese
1 tbsp chopped fresh coriander

Combine the stock, water, vegetables and cumin in the slow cooker. Cover and cook on Low for 4–6 hours. Stir in the combined yoghurt and cornflour, stirring for 2–3 minutes. Add the avocados, chili powder and sherry and process the mixture in a food processor or blender until smooth. Season to taste with salt and pepper. Serve warm or refrigerate and serve chilled. Garnish each bowl with crumbled Feta and coriander.

Bean Gazpacho ⓥ

Enjoy this bean soup, served gazpacho-style, with avocado and cucumber pieces, soured cream and croûtons.

SERVES 8

2 x 400 g/14 oz cans pinto beans, drained and rinsed
1 litre/1¾ pints tomato juice
225 g/8 oz ready-made thick and chunky salsa
1 large celery stick, sliced
4 spring onions, sliced
½ green pepper, chopped
2 garlic cloves, roasted if possible, crushed
3–4 tbsp lime juice
salt and freshly ground black pepper, to taste
½ avocado, chopped
50 g/2 oz cucumber, peeled, seeded and chopped
120 ml/4 fl oz soured cream
Crispy Croûtons, to garnish (see page 30)

Combine all the ingredients, except the lime juice, salt, pepper, avocado, cucumber and soured cream, in the slow cooker. Cover and cook on Low for 6–8 hours. Season to taste with lime juice, salt and pepper. Process the soup in a food processor or blender until smooth. Serve hot or refrigerate and serve chilled. Mix the avocado and cucumber into the soup. Garnish each bowl of soup with a dollop of soured cream and some Crispy Croûtons.

121

Tomato and Vegetable Soup with Soured Cream Ⓥ

Serve this chunky soup with home-made croûtons.

SERVES 6

1.2 litres/2 pints vegetable stock
120 ml/4 fl oz dry white wine or
   water
8 large tomatoes, peeled and
   quartered
1 large onion, thinly sliced
225 g/8 oz potatoes, peeled and
   cubed
225 g/8 oz butternut squash, peeled
   and cubed
1 bay leaf
2 tsp dried basil leaves
50 g/2 oz frozen peas, thawed
375 ml/13 fl oz soured cream
2 tbsp cornflour
salt and freshly ground black pepper,
   to taste
Crispy Croûtons, to garnish
   (see page 30)

Combine all the ingredients, except
the peas, soured cream, cornflour, salt
and pepper, in a 5.5 litre/9½ pint slow
cooker. Cover and cook on High for 4–5
hours, adding the peas during the last 20
minutes. Stir in the combined 250 ml/8 fl
oz soured cream and cornflour, stirring for
2–3 minutes. Discard the bay leaf. Season
to taste with salt and pepper. Garnish
each bowl of soup with the remaining
soured cream and some Crispy Croûtons.

Orange-scented Squash Soup Ⓥ

Subtly seasoned with orange and spices, this unusual soup can be served warm or chilled.

SERVES 6

375 ml/13 fl oz water
120 ml/4 fl oz orange juice
2 small onions, chopped
1.5 kg/3 lb pumpkin or winter squash,
   peeled and cubed
1 large cooking apple, peeled and
   cubed
1 strip of orange zest
1 tsp ground cinnamon
¼ tsp freshly grated nutmeg
¼ tsp ground cloves
375–450 ml/13–15 fl oz semi-skimmed
   milk
2 tbsp cornflour
salt and white pepper, to taste
6 thin orange slices and snipped fresh
   chives, to garnish

Combine all the ingredients, except the
milk, cornflour, salt and pepper, in the
slow cooker. Cover and cook on Low
for 6–8 hours, adding 250 ml/8 fl oz of
the milk during the last 30 minutes. Stir
in the remaining milk and the cornflour
together, stirring for 2–3 minutes. Discard
the orange zest. Process the soup in a
food processor or blender until smooth.
Season to taste with salt and pepper.
Serve warm or refrigerate and serve
chilled. Garnish each bowl of soup with
an orange slice and chives.

Winter Squash Soup Ⓥ

Delicious warm or chilled. You could use pumpkin instead of winter squash.

SERVES 6

375 ml/13 fl oz water
2 small onions, chopped
1.5 kg/3 lb winter squash, peeled and cubed
1 large cooking apple, peeled and cubed
1 tsp ground cinnamon
¼ tsp ground ginger
¼ tsp cumin,
250 ml/8 fl oz cider
¼ tsp freshly grated nutmeg
250 ml/8 fl oz semi-skimmed milk
2 tbsp cornflour
salt and white pepper, to taste
snipped fresh chives, to garnish

Combine all the ingredients, except the milk, cornflour, salt and pepper, in the slow cooker. Cover and cook on Low for 6–8 hours, adding 250 ml/8 fl oz of the milk during the last 30 minutes. Stir in the remaining milk and the cornflour together, stirring for 2–3 minutes. Process the soup in a food processor or blender until smooth. Season to taste with salt and pepper. Serve warm or refrigerate and serve chilled. Garnish each bowl of soup with chives.

Sherried Butternut Squash Soup Ⓥ

Any type of winter squash can be used in this Italian-accented soup.

SERVES 4

1.2 litres/2 pints Roasted Vegetable Stock (see page 28) or vegetable stock
2 x 400 g/14 oz cans chopped tomatoes
1 large butternut squash, peeled, seeded and cubed
4 potatoes, peeled and cubed
1 onion, chopped
2 garlic cloves, crushed
1 tsp dried basil leaves
½ tsp dried thyme
25 g/1 oz chopped fresh parsley
2–4 tbsp dry sherry
salt and freshly ground black pepper, to taste

Combine all the ingredients, except the parsley, sherry, salt and pepper, in the slow cooker. Cover and cook on Low for 8–9 hours, adding the parsley during the last 20 minutes. Season to taste with sherry, salt and pepper.

Cider Soup Ⓥ

An unusual soup and a great choice for sipping when you come in from the winter cold.

SERVES 6

375 ml/13 fl oz vegetable stock
250 ml/8 fl oz cider
2 leeks, thinly sliced (white part only)
½ celery stick, chopped
¼ green pepper, chopped
½ tsp dried thyme
¼ tsp dry mustard powder
2–3 tsp vegetarian Worcestershire or mushroom sauce
75 ml/2½ fl oz semi-skimmed milk
2 tbsp cornflour
100 g/4 oz Cheddar cheese, grated
salt and white pepper, to taste
finely chopped thyme or parsley, to garnish

Combine all the ingredients, except the milk, cornflour, cheese, salt and pepper, in the slow cooker. Cover and cook on Low for 4–6 hours. Stir in the combined milk and cornflour, stirring for 2–3 minutes. Add the cheese, stirring until melted. Season to taste with salt and pepper. Sprinkle each bowl of soup with thyme or parsley.

Caramel Apple Soup Ⓥ

Delicious fried sweet apples are served as part of this soup.

SERVES 6

375 ml/13 fl oz vegetable stock
250 ml/8 fl oz cider
2 leeks, thinly sliced (white part only)
½ celery stick, chopped
¼ green pepper, chopped
½ tsp dried thyme
¼ tsp dry mustard powder
2–3 tsp vegetarian Worcestershire or mushroom sauce
275 g/10 oz apples, peeled and sliced
1–2 tbsp butter
65 g/2½ oz light brown sugar
75 ml/2½ fl oz semi-skimmed milk
2 tbsp cornflour
100 g/4 oz Cheddar cheese, grated
salt and white pepper, to taste
finely chopped thyme or parsley, to garnish

Combine all the ingredients, except the apples, butter, sugar, milk, cornflour, cheese, salt and pepper, in the slow cooker. Cover and cook on Low for 4–6 hours. When the soup is almost ready, fry the apples in the butter for 2 minutes. Sprinkle with the sugar and cook over medium heat, stirring occasionally, until the apples are tender, 3–4 minutes. Stir the combined milk and cornflour into the soup, stirring for 2–3 minutes. Add the cheese, stirring until melted. Season to taste with salt and pepper. Spoon the apples into six soup bowls, then ladle the warm soup over. Sprinkle each bowl of soup with thyme or parsley.

Green Vegetable Soup Ⓥ

Sun-dried tomato pesto is an excellent alternative to basil pesto in this colourful soup.

SERVES 6

1 litre/1¾ pints vegetable stock
50 g/2 oz green cabbage, thinly sliced
1 celery stick, chopped
1 onion, chopped
75 g/3 oz broccoli florets
65 g/2½ oz French beans, cut into short lengths
75 g/3 oz courgette, cubed
75 g/3 oz potato, peeled and cubed
50 g/2 oz uncooked ditalini
salt and freshly ground black pepper, to taste
50 ml/2 fl oz basil pesto

Combine all the ingredients, except the ditalini, salt, pepper and pesto, in the slow cooker. Cover and cook on Low for 8–9 hours, adding the ditalini during the last 30 minutes. Season to taste with salt and pepper. Stir in the basil pesto.

Random Soup (V)

The perfect soup to use up the odd pieces of fresh and frozen veg you have left – and it tastes great.

SERVES 8

1.75 litres/3 pints vegetable stock
400 g/14 oz can chopped tomatoes with roasted garlic
350 g/12 oz potatoes, peeled and cubed
225 g/8 oz cabbage, sliced
350 g/12 oz small broccoli florets
1 large carrot, sliced
175 g/6 oz sweet potato, peeled and cubed
2 celery sticks, sliced
½ tsp dried thyme
½ tsp dried rosemary
½ tsp dried oregano
100 g/4 oz frozen peas, thawed
100 g/4 oz sweetcorn, thawed if frozen
salt and freshly ground black pepper, to taste

Combine all the ingredients, except the peas, sweetcorn, salt and pepper, in a 5.5 litre/9½ pint slow cooker. Cover and cook on Low for 6–8 hours, adding the peas and sweetcorn during the last 30 minutes. Season to taste with salt and pepper.

Spicy Bean and Vegetable Soup (V)

Two kinds of bean, plus mushrooms and mixed vegetables, make a filling soup. Cooked, crumbled vegetarian burgers can be added to it for additional texture, if you like.

SERVES 6

2 x 400 g/14 oz cans red kidney beans, drained and rinsed
400 g/14 oz can chickpeas, drained and rinsed
250 ml/8 fl oz tomato purée
2 large tomatoes, peeled and seeded
1 onion, chopped
1 large carrot, chopped
100 g/4 oz mushrooms, chopped
½ green pepper, chopped
1 celery stick, chopped
2 garlic cloves, crushed
1 tsp ground cumin
1–2 tbsp chilli powder
salt and freshly ground black pepper, to taste

Combine all the ingredients, except the salt and pepper, in the slow cooker. Cover and cook on Low for 6–8 hours. Season to taste with salt and pepper.

Pistou (V)

Stir into Mediterranean-style soups for added flavour

SERVES 4 AS AN ACCOMPANIMENT

3 garlic cloves, crushed
2 tsp olive oil
25 g/1 oz fresh basil, finely chopped
25 g/1 oz blue cheese, crumbled

Combine all the ingredients in a bowl. Mash with a fork.

Vegetable Soup Ⓥ

Load your shopping trolley with healthy vegetables to make this tasty soup.

SERVES 6

1.5 litres/2½ pints vegetable stock
400 g/14 oz can chopped tomatoes
500 g/18 oz baking potatoes, peeled
   and diced
100 g/4 oz French beans, cut into
   short lengths
2 small onions, chopped
2 small carrots, chopped
1 large celery stick, chopped
130 g/4½ oz sweet potato, peeled
   and cubed
130 g/4½ oz butternut squash, peeled
   and cubed
250 g/9 oz courgettes, diced
1 tbsp tomato purée
1 tsp white wine vinegar
1 tsp sugar
1 bay leaf
¾ tsp dried thyme
¾ tsp dried marjoram leaves
50 g/2 oz sweetcorn, thawed if frozen
50 g/2 oz frozen peas, thawed
salt and freshly ground black pepper,
   to taste

Combine all the ingredients, except the sweetcorn, peas, salt and pepper, in a 5.5 litre/9½ pint slow cooker. Cover and cook on Low for 6–8 hours, adding the sweetcorn and peas during the last 20 minutes. Discard the bay leaf. Season to taste with salt and pepper.

Mediterranean Vegetable Soup Ⓥ

Orange zest and fennel seeds give this sunny soup of vegetables and tofu a fragrant accent.

SERVES 6

1 litre/1¾ pints Mediterranean Stock
   (see page 34) or vegetable stock
400 g/14 oz can chopped tomatoes
225 g/8 oz ready-made tomato sauce
450 g/1 lb tofu, cubed (2 cm/¾ in)
175 g/6 oz mushrooms, sliced
1 onion, chopped
½ green pepper, chopped
3 garlic cloves, crushed
2 strips of orange zest
2 bay leaves
1 tsp dried marjoram
¼–½ tsp crushed fennel seeds
salt and freshly ground black pepper,
   to taste

Combine all the ingredients, except the salt and pepper, in a 5.5 litre/9½ pint slow cooker. Cover and cook on Low for 6–8 hours. Discard the bay leaves. Season to taste with salt and pepper.

Potato and Sweetcorn Chowder Ⓥ

Mild green chillies, marjoram, mustard and a mature Cheddar give this simple vegetarian chowder plenty of flavour.

SERVES 4

750 ml/1¼ pints vegetable stock
600 g/1 lb 6 oz potatoes, peeled and cubed
1 onion, chopped
275 g/10 oz frozen sweetcorn, thawed
100 g/4 oz chopped mild green chillies from a jar, drained
1 bay leaf
½ tsp dry mustard powder
½ tsp dried marjoram
450 ml/¾ pint semi-skimmed milk
3 tbsp cornflour
75 g/3 oz mature cheese, grated
salt and white pepper, to taste
snipped chives, to garnish

Combine all the ingredients, except the milk, cornflour, cheese, salt and pepper, in the slow cooker. Cover and cook on Low for 6–8 hours. Stir in the combined milk and cornflour, stirring for 5 minutes. Discard the bay leaf. Add the cheese, stirring until melted. Season to taste with salt and pepper. Garnish each bowl of soup with chives.

French Vegetable Chowder with Pistou Ⓥ

Pistou, the French version of Italy's pesto, gives this chowder a lively boost. Bon appétit!

SERVES 4

400 ml/14 fl oz vegetable stock
400 g/14 oz can cannellini or haricot beans, drained and rinsed
150 g/5 oz French beans, cut into short lengths
350 g/12 oz small cauliflower florets

175 g/6 oz courgettes, cubed
175 g/6 oz potatoes, peeled and cubed
2 carrots, thinly sliced
3 plum tomatoes, coarsely chopped
4 spring onions, sliced
100 g/4 oz cooked elbow macaroni
Pistou (see page 125)
salt and freshly ground black pepper, to taste

Combine all the ingredients, except the macaroni, Pistou, salt and pepper, in the slow cooker. Cover and cook on Low for 6–8 hours, adding the macaroni and Pistou during the last 15 minutes. Season to taste with salt and pepper.

Monterey Spicy Soup with Pasta Ⓥ

A vegetarian brand of the mild American cheese called Monterey Jack goes well with this hearty chilli soup, but you can use a mild Cheddar if you prefer.

SERVES 4

400 g/14 oz can pinto beans, drained and rinsed
400 g/14 oz can chopped tomatoes
1 onion, chopped
½ green pepper, chopped
½–1 tbsp chilli powder
1 tsp dried oregano
1 tsp cocoa powder
50 g/2 oz small soup pasta, cooked
15 g/½ oz chopped fresh coriander
salt and freshly ground black pepper, to taste
75 g/3 oz Monterey Jack or mild Cheddar cheese, grated

Combine all the ingredients, except the pasta, coriander, salt, pepper and cheese, in the slow cooker. Cover and cook on Low for 6–8 hours, adding the pasta and fresh coriander during the last 30 minutes. Season to taste with salt and pepper. Sprinkle each bowl of chilli with cheese.

Gingered Asian Noodle Soup Ⓥ

Light and fragrant Asian flavours meld in this tempting soup.

SERVES 4

1 litre/1¾ pints vegetable stock
75 g/3 oz brown cap mushrooms, sliced
1 onion, chopped
1 small carrot, sliced
2 spring onions, thinly sliced
1 cm/½ in piece fresh root ginger, finely grated
1 garlic clove, crushed
1 tbsp soy sauce
a pinch of dried chilli flakes
1–2 tsp rice wine vinegar
75 g/3 oz baby spinach leaves
150 g/5 oz mangetouts
1 tsp toasted sesame oil
salt, to taste
100 g/4 oz cellophane noodles

Combine all the ingredients, except the spinach, mangetouts, sesame oil, salt and noodles, in the slow cooker. Cover and cook on Low for 4–6 hours, adding the spinach and mangetouts during the last 15 minutes. Stir in the sesame oil. Season to taste with salt.

Pour boiling water over the noodles to cover in a large bowl. Leave to stand for 5 minutes, then drain. Spoon the noodles into bowls and pour the hot soup over.

Alsatian Peasant Soup Ⓥ

Root vegetables, cabbage and beans combine for a robust soup that is almost a stew. Serve with a crusty rye bread and a good beer.

SERVES 6

750 ml/1¼ pints vegetable stock
2 x 400 g/14 oz cans cannellini beans, drained and rinsed
225 g/8 oz thinly sliced cabbage
175 g/6 oz potato, peeled and cubed
150 g/5 oz parsnip, sliced
1 large carrot, sliced
1 onion, chopped
1 celery stick, chopped
1 tsp dried thyme
½ tsp caraway seeds, crushed
1 bay leaf
salt and freshly ground black pepper, to taste
75 g/3 oz Emmental or Gruyère cheese, grated
Crispy Croûtons, to garnish (see page 30)

Combine all the ingredients, except the salt, pepper and cheese, in a 5.5 litre/9½ pint slow cooker. Cover and cook on Low for 6–8 hours. Discard the bay leaf. Season to taste with salt and pepper. Sprinkle each bowl of soup with 2 tbsp of grated cheese and some Crispy Croûtons.

Tortellini Soup with Kale Ⓥ

Fresh pasta, such as tortellini used here, can be cooked in the slow cooker if there is adequate stock and if it's added near to the end of cooking time.

SERVES 8

2.75 litres/4¾ pints Roasted Vegetable Stock (see page 28) or vegetable stock
75 g/3 oz mushrooms, sliced
100 g/4 oz leek (white part only) or 8 spring onions, sliced
3 garlic cloves, crushed
250 g/9 oz fresh mushroom or herb tortellini
100 g/4 oz kale, coarsely chopped
salt and freshly ground black pepper, to taste

Combine the stock, mushrooms, leek and garlic in a 5.5 litre/9½ pint slow cooker. Cover and cook on Low for 6–8 hours. Add the tortellini and kale. Cover and cook until the tortellini float to the top of the soup, about 40 minutes. Season to taste with salt and pepper.

Spinach and Tortellini Soup Ⓥ

A hint of nutmeg and a dash of lemon bring out the flavour of spinach in this unusual combination of vegetables with fresh tortellini. Fresh vegetarian ravioli would also work well.

SERVES 6

900 ml/1½ pints vegetable stock
375 ml/13 fl oz water
2 large carrots sliced
2 spring onions, sliced
2 garlic cloves, crushed
1 tsp dried basil
250 g/9 oz fresh tomato and cheese tortellini, cooked

225 g/8 oz spinach leaves, torn
2–3 tsp lemon juice
¼ tsp freshly grated nutmeg
salt and freshly ground black pepper, to taste

Combine the stock, water, vegetables, garlic and basil in a 5.5 litre/9½ pint slow cooker. Cover and cook on Low for 6–8 hours, adding the tortellini and spinach during the last 30 minutes. Season to taste with lemon juice, nutmeg, salt and pepper.

Ditalini Soup with Haricot Beans and Greens Ⓥ

Pasta and beans are familiar partners and taste wonderful in this satisfying vegetarian soup, with its hint of Tabasco and fresh greens. Kale or cabbage can be substituted for the spring greens.

SERVES 4

400 ml/14 fl oz vegetable stock
400 g/14 oz can haricot beans, drained and rinsed
400 g/14 oz can chopped tomatoes
1 tsp olive oil
2 onions, chopped
1 tsp dried oregano
200 g/7 oz spring greens, torn
75 g/3 oz ditalini
2 tbsp grated Provolone cheese
salt and Tabasco sauce, to taste

Combine all the ingredients, except the spring greens, ditalini, cheese, salt and Tabasco sauce, in the slow cooker. Cover and cook on Low for 6–8 hours, adding the spring greens and ditalini during the last 40 minutes. Stir in the Provolone cheese. Season to taste with salt and Tabasco sauce.

Pasta e Fagioli ⓥ

Perhaps the only soup that's better than this pasta e fagioli is the same soup the next day. If you make it a day ahead, wait to add the pasta until just before you serve it.

SERVES 12 AS A FIRST COURSE

2.5 litres/4¼ pints water
350 g/12 oz dried cannellini beans
450 g/1 lb tomatoes, peeled, seeded and chopped
2 onions, chopped
1 celery stick, diced
1 small carrot, diced
4 large garlic cloves, crushed
150 g/5 oz elbow macaroni, cooked
salt and freshly ground black pepper, to taste
freshly grated Parmesan cheese, to garnish

Combine all the ingredients, except the pasta, salt, pepper and Parmesan cheese, in a 5.5 litre/9½ pint slow cooker. Cover and cook on Low until the beans are tender, 7–8 hours, adding the pasta during the last 20 minutes. Season to taste with salt and pepper. Sprinkle each bowl of soup with Parmesan cheese.

Green Vegetable Minestrone ⓥ

This green soup is wonderful in spring, when fresh asparagus and peas are in season, but make it whenever you're in the mood for delicious soup!

SERVES 6

1.5 litres/2½ pints vegetable stock
2 x 400 g/14 oz cans cannellini beans, drained and rinsed
250 g/9 oz courgettes, sliced
250 g/9 oz small broccoli florets
200 g/7 oz asparagus, cut into 2.5 cm/1 in pieces
2 onions, thinly sliced
150 g/5 oz French beans, cut into short lengths
2 tbsp chopped fresh basil, or 2 tsp dried
2 tbsp chopped fresh basil rosemary, or 2 tsp dried
2 large garlic cloves
50 g/2 oz spinach fettuccine, broken into 2.5 cm/1 in pieces, cooked
100 g/4 oz fresh or thawed frozen peas
salt and freshly ground black pepper, to taste
freshly grated Parmesan cheese, to garnish

Combine all the ingredients, except the fettuccine, peas, salt and pepper, in a 5.5 litre/9½ pint slow cooker. Cover and cook on Low for 6–8 hours, adding the fettuccine and peas during the last 20 minutes. Season to taste with salt and pepper. Sprinkle each bowl of soup with Parmesan cheese.

Two-bean Minestrone ⓥ

Cannellini beans and chickpeas enrich this nutritious soup.

SERVES 8

1.5 litres/2½ pints water
400 g/14 oz can cannellini beans, drained and rinsed
400 g/14 oz can chickpeas, drained and rinsed
400 g/14 oz can plum tomatoes, roughly chopped, with juice
120 ml/4 fl oz dry red wine
175 g/6 oz courgettes, sliced
175 g/6 oz cabbage, thinly sliced
175 g/6 oz potato, peeled and diced
100 g/4 oz leek, sliced
1 small carrot, sliced
1 celery stick, sliced
1 onion, chopped
25 g/1 oz fresh parsley, chopped
2 garlic cloves, crushed
1 tbsp dried oregano
1 tbsp dried basil
50 g/2 oz small elbow macaroni, cooked
salt and freshly ground black pepper, to taste
8 tsp freshly grated Parmesan cheese, to garnish

Combine all the ingredients, except the macaroni, salt and pepper, in a 5.5 litre/9½ pint slow cooker. Cover and cook on High for 4–5 hours, adding the macaroni during the last 20 minutes. Season to taste with salt and pepper. Sprinkle each bowl of soup with 1 tsp of Parmesan cheese.

Italian Bean Soup ⓥ

For a creamy textured soup, purée half the cooked bean mixture before adding the macaroni and chickpeas.

SERVES 6

1.5 litres/2½ pints vegetable stock
1 litre/1¾ pints water
175 g/6 oz dried cannellini or haricot beans
2 onions, chopped
1 green pepper, chopped
1 large carrot, chopped
1 celery stick, chopped
2 garlic cloves, crushed
1 tsp dried basil
1 tsp dried oregano
¼ tsp dry mustard powder
225 g/8 oz ready-made tomato sauce
50 g/2 oz wholemeal elbow macaroni, cooked
400 g/14 oz can chickpeas, drained and rinsed
salt and freshly ground black pepper, to taste

Combine all the ingredients, except the tomato sauce, macaroni, chickpeas, salt and pepper, in a 5.5 litre/9½ pint slow cooker. Cover and cook on Low until the beans are tender, 7–8 hours, adding the tomato sauce, macaroni and chickpeas during the last 20 minutes. Season to taste with salt and pepper.

Summer Minestrone Ⓥ

Thick and savoury, this traditional Italian soup is always popular.

SERVES 8

1 litre/1¾ pints vegetable stock
450 ml/¾ pint water
400 g/14 oz can red kidney beans, drained and rinsed
400 g/14 oz can tomatoes
350 g/12 oz potatoes, peeled and cubed
2 large carrots, sliced
150 g/5 oz French beans, halved
130 g/4½ oz courgettes, sliced
100 g/4 oz cabbage, sliced
2 onions, chopped
1 celery stick, sliced
3–4 garlic cloves, crushed
2 tsp dried Italian herb seasoning
175 g/6 oz cooked macaroni
salt and freshly ground black pepper, to taste
2 tbsp freshly grated Parmesan or Romano cheese, to garnish

Combine all the ingredients, except the pasta, salt and pepper, in a 5.5 litre/9½ pint slow cooker. Cover and cook on Low for 6–8 hours, adding the pasta during the last 20 minutes. Season to taste with salt and pepper. Sprinkle each bowl of soup with Parmesan cheese.

Tuscan Bean Soup Ⓥ

This hearty well-seasoned bean soup with potato and barley makes a satisfying family meal.

SERVES 8

1.6 litres/2¾ pints vegetable stock
2 x 400 g/14 oz cans cannellini or haricot beans, drained and rinsed
175 g/6 oz potato, unpeeled and cubed
1 large carrot, sliced
2 onions, chopped
1 celery stick, chopped
½ green pepper, chopped
2 garlic cloves, roasted if possible, crushed
2 tbsp tomato purée
1½ tsp dried Italian herb seasoning
90 g/3½ oz pearl barley
75 g/3 oz baby spinach leaves
salt and freshly ground black pepper, to taste

Combine all the ingredients, except the barley, spinach, salt and pepper, in a 5.5 litre/9½ pint slow cooker. Cover and cook on Low for 6–8 hours, adding the barley and spinach during the last 30 minutes. Season to taste with salt and pepper.

Black Bean Soup Ⓥ

Dried beans can be cooked in a slow cooker without soaking, saving advance preparation time.

SERVES 4

250 g/9 oz dried black beans, rinsed
1.5 litres/2½ pints water
1 large onion, chopped
4 garlic cloves, crushed
1 tsp dried oregano
½ tsp dried thyme
1 large tomato, chopped
salt and freshly ground black pepper, to taste
6 tbsp soured cream
chopped oregano or parsley, to garnish

Combine the beans, water, onion, garlic and herbs in the slow cooker. Cover and cook on Low until the beans are tender, 7–8 hours, adding the tomato during the last 30 minutes. Process the soup in a food processor or blender until smooth. Season to taste with salt and pepper. Top each bowl of soup with a dollop of soured cream and sprinkle with oregano or parsley.

Chickpea and Pasta Soup ⓥ

Use any fresh vegetables instead of the courgettes and celery in this soup – carrots, cauliflower or broccoli florets, mushrooms, peas and French beans are possible choices.

SERVES 4

400 ml/14 fl oz vegetable stock,
400 g/14 oz can chickpeas, drained
   and rinsed
400 g/14 oz can tomatoes
2 small onions, chopped
250 g/9 oz courgettes, cubed
1 large celery stick, sliced
3–4 garlic cloves, crushed
1 tsp dried rosemary
1 tsp dried thyme
a pinch of crushed chilli flakes
100 g/4 oz farfalle
2–3 tsp lemon juice
salt, to taste

Combine all the ingredients, except the pasta, lemon juice and salt, in the slow cooker. Cover and cook on Low for 6–8 hours, adding the pasta during the last 20 minutes. Season to taste with lemon juice and salt.

Two-bean and Pasta Soup ⓥ

This substantial soup thickens upon standing. Thin with additional stock or water, if necessary.

SERVES 6

900 ml/1½ pints vegetable stock
250 ml/8 fl oz water
400 g/14 oz can tomatoes
400 g/14 oz can cannellini beans,
   drained and rinsed
400 g/14 oz can pinto beans, drained
   and rinsed
2 carrots, cubed
½ green pepper, chopped
4 spring onions, sliced
3 garlic cloves, crushed
2 tsp dried basil
2 tsp dried oregano
100 g/4 oz rigatoni, cooked
2–3 tsp lemon juice
salt and freshly ground black pepper,
   to taste

Combine all the ingredients, except the pasta, lemon juice and salt, in a 5.5 litre/9½ pint slow cooker. Cover and cook on Low for 6–8 hours, adding the pasta during the last 30 minutes. Season to taste with lemon juice, salt and pepper.

Haricot Bean and Sweet Potato Soup with Cranberry Coulis Ⓥ

This smooth and sweet soup flavoured with ginger tastes great with a swirl of tart Cranberry Coulis.

SERVES 6

750 ml/1¼ pints vegetable stock
2 x 400 g/14 oz cans haricot or cannellini beans, drained and rinsed
450 g/1 lb sweet potatoes, peeled and cubed
2 onions, chopped
1 tart eating apple, peeled and chopped
2 cm/¾ in fresh root ginger, finely grated
½ tsp dried marjoram
salt and white pepper, to taste
Cranberry Coulis (see below)

Combine all the ingredients, except the salt, white pepper and Cranberry Coulis, in a 5.5 litre/9½ pint slow cooker. Cover and cook on Low for 7–9 hours. Process the soup in a food processor or blender until smooth. Season to taste with salt and white pepper. Swirl 2 tbsp Cranberry Coulis into each bowl of soup.

Cranberry Coulis Ⓥ

Rememer to allow time for the cranberries to thaw, if using frozen.

SERVES 6 AS AN ACCOMPANIMENT

175 g/6 oz fresh or thawed frozen cranberries
250 ml/8 fl oz orange juice
2 tbsp sugar
2 tbsp honey

Heat the cranberries and orange juice to boiling in a small pan. Reduce the heat and simmer, covered, until the cranberries are tender, 5–8 minutes. Process with the sugar and honey in a food processor or blender until almost smooth.

Tangy Three-bean Soup Ⓥ

The spicy barbecue flavour of this dish is a nice departure from the usual bean soups.

SERVES 6

2.25 litres/4 pints water
75 g/3 oz dried black-eyed peas, rinsed
75 g/3 oz baby butter beans
75 g/3 oz cannellini beans
1 onion, chopped
1 small carrot, sliced
1 celery stick, sliced
1 garlic clove, crushed
a pinch of ground cloves
1 bay leaf
½ tsp dry mustard powder
½ tsp chilli powder
¼ tsp ground celery seeds
¼ tsp dried thyme
¼ tsp paprika
¼ tsp black pepper
400 g/14 oz ready-made tomato sauce
1–2 tbsp brown sugar
1 tbsp cider vinegar
1 tbsp light black treacle
salt and cayenne pepper, to taste

Combine all the ingredients, except the tomato sauce, brown sugar, vinegar, black treacle, salt and cayenne pepper, in the slow cooker. Cover and cook on Low until the beans are tender, 7–8 hours, adding the remaining ingredients, except the salt and cayenne pepper, during the last 30–45 minutes. Discard the bay leaf. Season to taste with salt and cayenne pepper.

Bean Soup with Many Garnishes Ⓥ

Colourful and delicious with a range of flavours and textures.

SERVES 4

250 g/9 oz dried black beans, rinsed
1.5 litres/2½ pints water
1 large onion, chopped
4 garlic cloves, crushed
1 tsp dried oregano
½ tsp dried thyme
1 large tomato, chopped
1 tbsp dry sherry
1 tbsp soy sauce
1 tbsp balsamic vinegar
salt and freshly ground black pepper, to taste
6 tbsp soured cream
cubed avocado, sliced spring onions, toasted pumpkin seeds and lime wedges, to garnish

Combine the beans, water, onion, garlic and herbs in the slow cooker. Cover and cook on Low until the beans are tender, 7–8 hours, adding the tomato, sherry, soy sauce and balsamic vinegar during the last 30 minutes. Season to taste with salt and pepper. Top each bowl of soup with a dollop of soured cream and sprinkle with the garnishes.

Black Bean Soup with Sun-dried Tomatoes and Coriander and Lemon Cream Ⓥ

Coriander and Lemon Cream adds a fresh accent to this spicy favourite.

SERVES 4

750 ml/1¼ pints vegetable stock
2 x 400 g/14 oz cans black beans, drained and rinsed
2 onions, chopped
2 garlic cloves, crushed
1 jalapeño or other medium-hot chilli, finely chopped
20 g/¾ oz sun-dried tomatoes (not in oil), at room temperature
¾ tsp ground cumin
¾ tsp dried oregano
¼–½ tsp Tabasco sauce
salt and freshly ground black pepper, to taste
15 g/½ oz fresh coriander, chopped
Coriander and Lemon Cream, to garnish (see page 136)

Combine all the ingredients, except the Tabasco sauce, salt, pepper and fresh coriander, in the slow cooker. Cover and cook on Low for 6–8 hours. Process the soup in a food processor or blender until smooth. Season to taste with Tabasco sauce, salt and pepper. Stir in the fresh coriander. Garnish each bowl of soup with dollops of Coriander and Lemon Cream.

Coriander and Lemon Cream Ⓥ

A slightly sharp garnish to stir into spicy casseroles.

SERVES 4 AS AN ACCOMPANIMENT

75 ml/2½ fl oz soured cream
2 tbsp fresh finely chopped coriander
1 tsp lemon or lime juice
¾ tsp ground coriander
2–3 dashes white pepper

Combine all the ingredients.

Country Bean Soup Ⓥ

Butter beans have a lovely floury texture that goes well in a vegetable soup.

SERVES 4

1 litre/1¾ pints vegetable stock
400 g/14 oz can chopped tomatoes
400 g/14 oz can butter beans, drained and rinsed
2 onions, chopped
1 leek, sliced
1 large carrot, chopped
2 garlic cloves, crushed
¾ tsp dried oregano
¼ tsp dried thyme
salt and freshly ground black pepper, to taste
100 g/4 oz grated Cheddar cheese
chopped fresh coriander, to garnish

Combine all the ingredients, except the salt, pepper and cheese, in the slow cooker. Cover and cook on High for 4–5 hours. Season to taste with salt and pepper. Sprinkle each bowl of soup with cheese and fresh coriander.

Ancho Black Bean and Pumpkin Soup Ⓥ

A great way to use your home-grown pumpkins.

SERVES 4

750 ml/1¼ pints vegetable stock
2 x 400 g/14 oz cans black beans, drained and rinsed
2 onions, chopped
2 garlic cloves, crushed
¾ tsp ground cumin
¾ tsp dried oregano
1 jalapeño or other medium-hot chilli, finely chopped
1 medium-hot chilli
400 g/14 oz cooked pumpkin or squash
¼–½ tsp Tabasco sauce
salt and freshly ground black pepper, to taste
15 g/½ oz fresh coriander, chopped

Combine the stock, black beans, onions, garlic, cumin and oregano in the slow cooker. Heat both the chillies in a dry frying pan over medium heat until softened. Remove the chillies and discard the veins and seeds. Purée with the cooked pumpkin or squash, then add to the slow cooker. Cover and cook on Low for 6–8 hours. Process the soup in a food processor or blender until smooth. Season to taste with Tabasco sauce, salt and pepper. Serve garnished with coriander.

Cuban Black Bean Soup ⓥ

The spicy, authentic Caribbean flavour is ample reward for making this soup.

SERVES 8

350 g/12 oz dried black beans, rinsed
2.25 litres/4 pints water
3 medium onions, chopped
3 garlic cloves, crushed
4–5 drops Tabasco sauce
1 large green pepper, finely chopped
2 tsp ground cumin
2 tsp dried oregano
salt and freshly ground black pepper, to taste
Cuban Rice, warm (see below)

Combine all the ingredients, except the salt, pepper and Cuban Rice, in a 5.5 litre/9½ pint slow cooker. Cover and cook on Low until the beans are tender, 7–8 hours. Season to taste with salt and pepper. Serve the soup over Cuban Rice in bowls.

Cuban Rice ⓥ

Delicious in soup or as a side dish, this rice is delicately flavoured with cider vinegar.

SERVES 8 AS AN ACCOMPANIMENT

225 g/8 oz long-grain white rice
¼ onion, finely chopped
450 ml/¾ pint water
2 tsp olive oil
1½ tbsp cider vinegar

Combine the rice, onion and water in a large pan. Heat to boiling. Reduce the heat and simmer, covered, for 20 minutes or until the rice is tender. Stir in the oil and vinegar.

Split Pea Soup with Three Accompaniments ⓥ

This thick and beautiful green soup is served with cubed sweet potatoes, fresh peas and croûtons.

SERVES 6

1.5 litres/2½ pints water
120 ml/4 fl oz dry white wine or water
450 g/1 lb dried split peas
1 onion, finely chopped
1 celery stick, chopped
2 vegetable stock cubes
¾ tsp dried thyme
1 bay leaf
salt and freshly ground black pepper, to taste

toppings: 100 g/4 oz cooked warm peas, 150 g/5 oz cooked cubed and peeled sweet potatoes, Crispy Croûtons (see page 30)

Combine all the ingredients, except the salt and pepper, in a 5.5 litre/9½ pint slow cooker. Cover and cook on Low for 6–8 hours. Process the soup in a food processor or blender until smooth. Discard the bay leaf. Season to taste with salt and pepper. Sprinkle each bowl of soup with peas, sweet potatoes and Crispy Croûtons.

Easy Black-eyed Pea and Lentil Soup Ⓥ

Black-eyed peas and lentils combine in this satisfying soup.

SERVES 6

2 litres/3½ pints vegetable stock
250 g/9 oz dried red lentils
130 g/4½ oz dried black-eyed peas, rinsed
3 medium tomatoes, chopped
1 small carrot, chopped
1 celery stick, chopped
1 onion, chopped
1 garlic clove, crushed
¾ tsp dried thyme
¾ tsp dried oregano
1 bay leaf
salt and freshly ground black pepper, to taste

Combine all the ingredients, except the salt and pepper, in a 5.5 litre/9½ pint slow cooker. Cover and cook on Low for 6–8 hours. Discard the bay leaf. Season to taste with salt and pepper.

Easy Indian Lentil Soup Ⓥ

This hearty soup tastes best made with tiny beige Indian lentils, which are available in Indian food stores. However, regular brown lentils can also be used.

SERVES 4

2.5 litres/4¼ pints water
350 g/12 oz dried Indian or brown lentils
1 large onion, finely chopped
1 celery stick, thinly sliced
1 small carrot, thinly sliced
1 garlic clove, crushed
2–3 tsp mild curry powder
1 tsp sugar
salt and freshly ground black pepper, to taste

Combine all the ingredients, except the salt and pepper, in a 5.5 litre/9½ pint slow cooker. Cover and cook on Low for 6–8 hours. Season to taste with salt and pepper.

Country Lentil Soup Ⓥ

Red lentils with vegetables and a selection of Mediterranean herbs make a bright soup that's wholesome and sustaining.

SERVES 6

750 ml/1¼ pints vegetable stock
450 ml/¾ pint water
175 g/6 oz dried red lentils
400 g/14 oz can chopped tomatoes
3 onions, chopped
1 large celery stick, sliced
1 large carrot, sliced
2 garlic cloves, crushed
½ tsp dried marjoram
½ tsp dried oregano
½ tsp dried thyme
salt and freshly ground black pepper, to taste
6 tbsp freshly grated Parmesan cheese

Combine all the ingredients, except the salt, pepper and Parmesan cheese, in a 5.5 litre/9½ pint slow cooker. Cover and cook on Low for 6–8 hours. Season to taste with salt and pepper. Sprinkle each bowl of soup with 1 tbsp of the cheese.

Curried Lentil and Spinach Soup Ⓥ

Lentils and spinach lend a delicious flavour and texture to this soup.

SERVES 6

2.25 litres/4 pints vegetable stock
400 g/14 oz can chopped tomatoes
175 g/6 oz dried brown lentils
4 chopped onions
½ celery stick, thinly sliced
½ carrot, thinly sliced
2 large garlic cloves, crushed
2–2½ tsp mild curry powder
1 tsp chilli powder
275 g/10 oz frozen chopped spinach,
    thawed and drained
salt and freshly ground black pepper,
    to taste

Combine all the ingredients, except the spinach, salt and pepper, in a 5.5 litre/ 9½ pint slow cooker. Cover and cook on Low for 6–8 hours, adding the spinach during the last 30 minutes. Season to taste with salt and pepper.

Bean and Barley Soup Ⓥ

Barley makes a soup substantial and also adds texture. This soup is a meal in itself.

SERVES 6

1.5 litres/2½ pints vegetable stock
2 x 400 g/14 oz cans haricot or
    cannellini beans, drained and rinsed
175 g/6 oz floury potato, unpeeled
    and cubed
1 large carrot, sliced
2 small onions, chopped
1 red pepper, chopped
2 garlic cloves, crushed
2 tbsp tomato purée
1½ tsp dried Italian herb seasoning
90 g/3½ oz pearl barley
75 g/3 oz baby spinach leaves
salt and freshly ground black pepper,
    to taste

Combine all the ingredients, except the barley, spinach, salt and pepper, in a 5.5 litre/9½ pint slow cooker. Cover and cook on High for 4–5 hours, adding the barley during the last 30 minutes and the spinach during the last 15 minutes. Season to taste with salt and pepper.

Potato Barley Soup Ⓥ

You can vary the flavour of this homely soup by using different stocks, as well as different vegetables.

SERVES 8

1.2 litres/2 pints vegetable stock
250 ml/8 fl oz tomato juice
2 onions, chopped
500 g/18 oz potatoes, peeled and
    chopped
1 small carrot, sliced
1 celery stick, sliced
1 small parsnip, sliced
1 garlic clove, crushed
2 bay leaves
¼ tsp dried thyme
¼ tsp dried marjoram
150 g/5 oz pearl barley
salt and freshly ground black pepper,
    to taste

Combine all the ingredients, except the barley, salt and pepper, in a 5.5 litre/9½ pint slow cooker. Cover and cook on Low for 6–8 hours, stirring in the barley during the last 30 minutes. Discard the bay leaves. Season to taste with salt and pepper.

Potato and Portabella Mushroom Soup Ⓥ

Portabella are best, but you can use any kind of mushrooms for this soup.

SERVES 8

1.2 litres/2 pints vegetable stock
2 onions, chopped
500 g/18 oz potatoes, peeled and
  chopped
150 g/5 oz portabella mushrooms,
  chopped
1 small carrot, sliced
1 celery stick, sliced
1 small parsnip, sliced
1 garlic clove, crushed
2 bay leaves
¼ tsp dried thyme
¼ tsp dried marjoram
salt and freshly ground black pepper,
  to taste

Combine all the ingredients, except the salt and pepper, in a 5.5 litre/9½ pint slow cooker. Cover and cook on Low for 6–8 hours. Discard the bay leaves. Season to taste with salt and pepper.

Polish-style Mushroom and Barley Soup Ⓥ

Dried mushrooms add an earthy, woody flavour to the soup. You can try it with other dried mushrooms if you like. Porcini and shiitake have strong flavours that permeate the whole soup.

SERVES 4–6

2.25 litres/4 pints vegetable stock
3 medium potatoes, peeled and diced
1 small onion, coarsely chopped
1 celery stick, sliced
100 g/4 oz halved baby carrots
90 g/3½ oz pearl barley
120 ml/4 fl oz dry white wine
  (optional)

10 g/¼ oz dried mushrooms, coarsely
  chopped
100 g/4 oz frozen peas, thawed
salt and white pepper, to taste
120 ml/4 fl oz soured cream
chopped fresh dill, to garnish

Combine all the ingredients, except the peas, salt, pepper and soured cream, in a 5.5 litre/9½ pint slow cooker. Cover and cook on Low for 6–8 hours, adding the peas during the last 20 minutes. Season to taste with salt and pepper. Garnish each bowl of soup with soured cream and dill.

Spicy Barley Soup Ⓥ

Herbs and mustard give this barley soup its savoury flavour.

SERVES 6

2.25 litres/4 pints vegetable stock
3 onions, chopped
130 g/4½ oz mushrooms, sliced
1 small carrot, sliced
1 celery stick, sliced
1 small turnip, sliced
1 large garlic clove, crushed
3 tbsp tomato purée
50 g/2 oz pearl barley
2 bay leaves
1 tsp dried marjoram
½ tsp dried thyme
½ tsp celery seeds
½ tsp dry mustard powder
salt and freshly ground black pepper,
  to taste

Combine all the ingredients, except the salt and pepper, in a 5.5 litre/9½ pint slow cooker. Cover and cook on Low for 6–8 hours. Discard the bay leaves. Season to taste with salt and pepper.

Chowders

Rich and filling, these traditionally American main-meal dishes can be served on their own, with crusty bread or your favourite side salad. They often combine a variety of meats and vegetables.

Florida Avocado and Tomato Chowder

Colourful ingredients create a kaleidoscope of fresh colours and flavours.

SERVES 4

400 ml/14 fl oz chicken stock
500 g/18 oz potatoes, peeled and cubed
100 g/4 oz sweetcorn, thawed if frozen
200 g/7 oz plum tomatoes, chopped
225 g/8 oz smoked turkey breast, cubed
1 tsp dried thyme
1 avocado, cubed
juice of 1 lime
3 bacon rashers, cooked and crumbled
salt and freshly ground black pepper, to taste

Combine all the ingredients, except the avocado, lime, bacon, salt and pepper, in the slow cooker. Cover and cook on High for 4–5 hours. Stir in the avocado, lime and bacon. Season to taste with salt and pepper.

Sweetcorn Chowder with Cheese

A satisfying chowder, rich with sausage, cheese and the flavour of sweetcorn.

SERVES 6

450 ml/¾ pint chicken stock
225 g/8 oz smoked sausage, sliced
400 g/14 oz can sweetcorn
400 g/14 oz can creamed sweetcorn
300 g/11 oz tomatoes, chopped
1 onion, chopped
1 red pepper, chopped
1 potato, peeled and chopped
1 garlic clove, crushed
450 ml/¾ pint full-fat milk
2 tbsp cornflour
50–75 g/2–3 oz Cheddar cheese, grated
salt and freshly ground black pepper, to taste
Garlic Croûtons, to garnish (see page 34)

Combine all the ingredients, except the milk, cornflour cheese, salt and pepper, in the slow cooker. Cover and cook on High for 4–5 hours, adding 250 ml/8 fl oz of the milk during the last 30 minutes. Stir in the remaining combined milk and the cornflour, stirring for 2–3 minutes. Add the cheese, stirring until melted. Season to taste with salt and pepper. Sprinkle each bowl of chowder with some Garlic Croûtons.

Hearty Sweetcorn and Potato Chowder Ⓥ

Make this thick, hearty chowder with storecupboard ingredients.

SERVES 4

450 ml/¾ pint vegetable stock
350 g/12 oz potatoes, peeled and cubed
225 g/8 oz sweetcorn, thawed if frozen
1 onion, chopped
1 celery stick, sliced
½ tsp dried thyme
325 ml/11 fl oz full-fat milk
2 tbsp cornflour
salt and freshly ground black pepper, to taste

Combine all the ingredients, except the milk, cornflour, salt and pepper, in the slow cooker. Cover and cook on High for 4–5 hours, adding the 300 ml/½ pint milk during the last 30 minutes. Stir in the combined remaining milk and the cornflour, stirring for 2–3 minutes. Season to taste with salt and pepper.

Sweet Onion and Bean Chowder

The onions can be caramelised to enhance the flavour, if you like. Sauté the onions in 2 tbsp butter in a large frying pan for 2 minutes. Reduce the heat to medium-low and cook until golden, about 10 minutes.

SERVES 8

450 ml/¾ pint vegetable or chicken stock
450 ml/¾ pint beef stock
400 g/14 oz can cannellini beans, drained and rinsed
700 g/1½ lb onions, thinly sliced
¾ tsp dried thyme
50 ml/2 fl oz dry sherry (optional)
salt and freshly ground black pepper, to taste
Garlic Croûtons, to garnish (see page 34)

Combine all the ingredients, except the sherry, salt and pepper, in the slow cooker. Cover and cook on High for 5–6 hours, adding the sherry during the last 15 minutes. Season to taste with salt and pepper. Sprinkle each bowl of chowder with some Garlic Croûtons.

Easy Vichyssoise

This is a quick and easy version of the traditional dish.

SERVES 6

750 ml/1¼ pints vegetable stock
600 g/1 lb 6 oz floury potatoes, peeled and cubed
2 leeks, chopped
250 ml/8 fl oz full-fat milk
2 tbsp cornflour
salt and freshly ground black pepper, to taste
snipped fresh chives, to garnish

Combine all the ingredients, except the milk, cornflour, salt and pepper, in the slow cooker. Cover and cook on Low for 6–8 hours. Stir in the combined milk and cornflour during the last 20 minutes. Process the chowder in a food processor or blender until smooth. Season to taste with salt and pepper. Serve warm, or refrigerate and serve chilled. Sprinkle each bowl of chowder with chives.

Potato Chowder

Substitute any vegetables you like for the potatoes in this versatile chowder, such as carrots, courgettes, French beans or sweetcorn, for a delectable vegetable chowder.

SERVES 6

750 ml/1¼ pints vegetable stock
600 g/1 lb 6 oz floury potatoes, peeled and cubed
2 onions, chopped
½ celery stick, thinly sliced
¼–½ tsp celery seeds
250 ml/8 fl oz full-fat milk
2 tbsp cornflour
salt and freshly ground black pepper, to taste

Combine all the ingredients, except the milk, cornflour, salt and pepper, in the slow cooker. Cover and cook on Low for 6–8 hours. Stir in the combined milk and cornflour during the last 20 minutes. Season to taste with salt and pepper.

Potato au Gratin Chowder (V)

Sprinkle with nutmeg for a lovely accent.

SERVES 6

750 ml/1¼ pints vegetable stock
600 g/1 lb 6 oz floury potatoes,
 peeled and cubed
2 onions, chopped
½ celery stick, thinly sliced
¼–½ tsp celery seeds
250 ml/8 fl oz full-fat milk
2 tbsp cornflour
75 g/3 oz Cheddar cheese, grated
salt and freshly ground black pepper,
 to taste
freshly grated nutmeg, to garnish

Combine all the ingredients, except the milk, cornflour, cheese, salt and pepper, in the slow cooker. Cover and cook on Low for 6–8 hours. Stir in the combined milk and cornflour during the last 20 minutes. Process half the chowder in a food processor or blender until almost smooth. Return to the slow cooker and cook on High for 10 minutes. Add the cheese, stirring until melted. Season to taste with salt and pepper. Sprinkle each bowl of chowder with freshly grated nutmeg.

Potato Curry Chowder (V)

The curry flavour in this chowder is subtle. Increase the amount if you prefer.

SERVES 4

1 litre/1¾ pints vegetable stock
8 spring onions, chopped
3 large potatoes, peeled and cubed
3 garlic cloves, crushed
¾ tsp curry powder
½ tsp ground cumin
250 ml/8 fl oz semi-skimmed milk
2 tbsp cornflour
salt and freshly ground black pepper,
 to taste

Combine all the ingredients, except the milk, cornflour, salt and pepper, in the slow cooker. Cover and cook on Low for 6–8 hours. Turn the heat to High and cook for 10 minutes. Stir in the combined milk and cornflour, stirring for 2–3 minutes. Season to taste with salt and pepper.

Onion Chowder with Cheese (V)

Fragrant rosemary gives this chowder an aromatic flavour.

SERVES 8

1 litre/1¾ pints vegetable stock
6 large floury potatoes, peeled and
 cubed (1 cm/½ in)
8 onions, chopped
1 large celery stick, chopped
6 garlic cloves, crushed
½ tsp dried rosemary
450 ml/¾ pint full-fat milk
2 tbsp cornflour
a pinch of freshly grated nutmeg
2 tsp Worcestershire sauce
100 g/4 oz Emmental or Gruyère
 cheese, grated
salt and white pepper, to taste

Combine the stock, potatoes, onions, celery, garlic and rosemary in a 5.5 litre/9½ pint slow cooker. Cover and cook on High for 4–5 hours, adding 250 ml/8 fl oz of the milk during the last 30 minutes. Stir in the combined remaining milk and the cornflour, nutmeg and Worcestershire sauce, stirring for 2–3 minutes. Add the cheese, stirring until melted. Season to taste with salt and white pepper.

Three-cheese and Potato Chowder ⓥ

You can vary the cheeses depending on what is available.

SERVES 8

1 litre/1¾ pints vegetable stock
6 large floury potatoes, peeled and
   cubed (1 cm/½ in)
8 onions, chopped
1 large celery stick, chopped
6 garlic cloves, crushed
½ tsp dried rosemary
450 ml/¾ pint full-fat milk
2 tbsp cornflour
a pinch of freshly grated nutmeg
2 tsp Worcestershire sauce
50 g/2 oz hard Mozzarella cheese,
   grated
50 g/2 oz Cheddar cheese
2–4 tbsp crumbled blue cheese
salt and white pepper, to taste

Combine the stock, potatoes, onions, celery, garlic and rosemary in a 5.5 litre/ 9½ pint slow cooker. Cover and cook on High for 4–5 hours, adding 250 ml/8 fl oz of the milk during the last 30 minutes. Stir in the combined remaining milk and the cornflour, nutmeg and Worcestershire sauce, stirring for 2–3 minutes. Add the cheeses, stirring until melted. Season to taste with salt and pepper.

Potato, Sweetcorn and Bacon Chowder

If you like, the bacon can be sautéed in 1 tsp butter or margarine. When crisp, sprinkle on the chowder as a garnish.

SERVES 6

750 ml/1¼ pints chicken stock
500 g/18 oz waxy potatoes, peeled
   and cubed
225 g/8 oz sweetcorn, thawed if frozen
1 large onion, chopped
1 garlic clove, crushed
175 g/6 oz back bacon, cut into strips
1 large bay leaf
¾ tsp dried thyme
¼ tsp dry mustard powder
450 ml/¾ pint full-fat milk
2 tbsp cornflour
salt and white pepper, to taste

Combine all the ingredients, except the milk, cornflour, salt and pepper, in the slow cooker. Cover and cook on High for 4–5 hours, adding 375 ml/13 fl oz of the milk during the last 30 minutes. Discard the bay leaf. Process half the chowder in a food processor or blender until smooth. Return to the slow cooker. Cover and cook on High for 10 minutes. Stir in the combined remaining milk and the cornflour, stirring for 2–3 minutes. Season to taste with salt and white pepper.

Colcannon Chowder

A lovely chowder with an Irish lilt!

SERVES 6

750 ml/1¼ pints chicken stock
500 g/18 oz waxy potatoes, peeled
and cubed
225 g/8 oz thinly sliced cabbage
1 large onion, chopped
1 garlic clove, crushed
175 g/6 oz back bacon, cut into strips
1 large bay leaf
¾ tsp dried thyme
¼ tsp dry mustard powder
375 ml/13 fl oz full-fat milk
120 ml/4 fl oz soured cream
2 tbsp cornflour
salt and white pepper, to taste

Combine all the ingredients, except the
milk, cornflour, salt and pepper, in the
slow cooker. Cover and cook on High
for 4–5 hours, adding the milk during
the last 30 minutes. Discard the bay leaf.
Stir in the combined soured cream and
the cornflour, stirring for 2–3 minutes.
Season to taste with salt and pepper.

Fresh Tomato and Courgette Chowder

*Savour summer's bounty in this lively
chowder of basil, tomatoes and
courgettes. The bacon adds a delightful
smoky accent.*

SERVES 4

400 ml/14 fl oz vegetable stock
450 g/1 lb plum tomatoes, chopped
2 onions, chopped
1 potato, peeled and cubed
1 courgette, cubed
25 g/1 oz sweetcorn, thawed if frozen
1 tbsp dried basil
salt and cayenne pepper, to taste
2 rashers smoked bacon, cooked until
crisp, and crumbled

Combine all the ingredients, except the
salt, cayenne pepper and bacon, in the
slow cooker. Cover and cook on High
for 4–5 hours. Season to taste with salt
and cayenne pepper. Sprinkle each bowl
of chowder with crumbled bacon.

Green Garden Chowder

*A fresh chowder full of healthy
vegetables.*

SERVES 4

400 ml/14 fl oz vegetable stock
450 g/1 lb plum tomatoes, chopped
2 onions, chopped
1 potato, peeled and cubed
1 courgette, cubed
1 tbsp dried basil
175 g/6 oz small broccoli florets
150 g/5 oz French beans, cut into
short lengths
75 g/3 oz spinach, sliced
salt and cayenne pepper, to taste
2 rashers smoked bacon, cooked until
crisp, and crumbled
4 tbsp grated Parmesan cheese

Combine the stock, tomatoes, onions,
potato, courgette and basil in the slow
cooker. Cover and cook on High for
4–5 hours, adding the broccoli, beans and
spinach for the last 30 minutes. Season
to taste with salt and cayenne pepper.
Sprinkle each bowl of chowder with
crumbled bacon and Parmesan cheese.

Black-eyed Pea and Sweetcorn Chowder

Roasted red peppers and bacon enliven this fuss-free chowder.

SERVES 4

375 ml/13 fl oz vegetable or chicken stock
3 onions, chopped
400 g/14 oz can black-eyed peas, drained and rinsed
400 g/14 oz can creamed sweetcorn
2 garlic cloves, crushed
1 tsp dried thyme
2 roasted red peppers from a jar, coarsely chopped
salt and freshly ground black pepper, to taste
4 bacon rashers, cooked until crisp and crumbled

Combine all the ingredients, except the roasted red peppers, salt, pepper and bacon, in the slow cooker. Cover and cook on High for 2–3 hours, adding the roasted peppers during the last 15 minutes. Season to taste with salt and pepper. Sprinkle each bowl of chowder with bacon.

Red Kidney Beans and Greens Chowder

An easy and delicious dish.

SERVES 4

375 ml/13 fl oz vegetable or chicken stock
3 onions, chopped
400 g/14 oz can red kidney beans, drained and rinsed
400 g/14 oz okra, sliced
2 garlic cloves, crushed
1 tsp dried thyme
176 g/6 oz spring greens, sliced

salt and freshly ground black pepper, to taste
4 bacon rashers, cooked until crisp and crumbled

Combine all the ingredients, except the spring greens, salt, pepper and bacon, in the slow cooker. Cover and cook on High for 2–3 hours, adding the spring greens during the last 15 minutes. Season to taste with salt and pepper. Sprinkle each bowl of chowder with bacon.

Haricot Bean and Bacon Chowder

Milk adds a creamy smoothness to this bean chowder.

SERVES 8

1.5 litres/2½ pints chicken stock
250 g/9 oz dried haricot beans, rinsed
1 carrot, chopped
1 onion, chopped
2 large garlic cloves, crushed
½ tsp dried oregano
½ tsp dried basil
½ tsp dried rosemary
250 ml/8 fl oz full-fat milk
2 tbsp cornflour
salt and freshly ground black pepper, to taste
8 bacon rashers, cooked until crisp and crumbled

Combine the stock, beans, vegetables and herbs in a 5.5 litre/9½ pint slow cooker. Cover and cook on Low until the beans are tender, 6–8 hours. Turn the heat to High and cook for 10 minutes. Stir in the combined milk and cornflour, stirring for 2–3 minutes. If you like, process half the chowder in a food processor or blender until smooth. Stir back into the slow cooker. Season to taste with salt and pepper. Sprinkle each bowl of chowder with bacon.

Mixed Bean Chowder

Vary the beans according to what you have in your storecupboard.

SERVES 8

1.5 litres/2½ pints chicken stock
75 g/3 oz dried cannellini beans
75 g/3 oz dried pinto beans
75 g/3 oz dried red kidney beans, soaked overnight then boiled for 10 minutes
1 carrot, chopped
1 onion, chopped
2 large garlic cloves, crushed
½ tsp dried oregano
½ tsp dried basil
½ tsp dried rosemary
250 ml/8 fl oz full-fat milk
2 tbsp cornflour
salt and freshly ground black pepper, to taste
8 bacon rashers, cooked until crisp and crumbled

Combine the stock, beans, vegetables and herbs in a 5.5 litre/9½ pint slow cooker. Cover and cook on Low until the beans are tender, 6–8 hours. Turn the heat to High and cook for 10 minutes. Stir in the combined milk and cornflour, stirring for 2–3 minutes. If you like, process half the chowder in a food processor or blender until smooth. Stir back into the slow cooker. Season to taste with salt and pepper. Sprinkle each bowl of chowder with bacon.

Tex-Mex Chicken and Cheese Chowder

If you are able to buy pepper-Jack cheese, use this instead of the Monterey Jack or Cheddar and omit the chilli, for a more authentic version.

SERVES 4

375 ml/13 fl oz chicken stock
2 x 400 g/14 oz cans creamed sweetcorn
450 g/1 lb skinless chicken breast fillet, cubed (1 cm/½ in)
1 onion, finely chopped
1 medium-hot chilli, finely chopped
1 courgette, cubed
375 ml/13 fl oz semi-skimmed milk
2 tbsp cornflour
175 g/6 oz Monterey Jack or Cheddar cheese, grated
salt and freshly ground black pepper, to taste

Combine the stock, sweetcorn, chicken, onion and chilli in the slow cooker. Cover and cook on High for 4–5 hours, adding the courgette during the last 30 minutes. Stir in the combined milk and cornflour, stirring for 2–3 minutes. Add the cheese, stirring until melted. Season to taste with salt and pepper.

Chicken Chowder Hispaniola

This enticing chowder boasts sofrito, a popular Cuban seasoning found in the ethnic section of many supermarkets.

SERVES 4

400 g/14 oz can chopped tomatoes
400 ml/14 fl oz chicken stock
400 g/14 oz can chickpeas, drained and rinsed
350 g/12 oz skinless chicken breast fillet, cubed (2 cm/¾ in)
1 onion, chopped
150 g/5 oz spinach, sliced
2 tbsp sofrito sauce (optional)
salt and freshly ground black pepper, to taste
25 g/1 oz flaked almonds, toasted

Combine all the ingredients, except the spinach, sofrito sauce, salt, pepper and almonds, in the slow cooker. Cover and cook on High for 4–5 hours, stirring in the spinach and sofrito sauce during the last 15 minutes. Season to taste with salt and pepper. Sprinkle each bowl with almonds.

Creamy Chicken and Sweetcorn Chowder

A delightfully creamy and filling chowder that makes for real comfort food!

SERVES 4

375 ml/13 fl oz chicken stock
2 x 400 g/14 oz cans creamed sweetcorn
450 g/1 lb skinless chicken breast fillet, cubed (1 cm/½ in)
1 onion, finely chopped
1 celery stick, thinly sliced
1 carrot, thinly sliced
375 ml/13 fl oz semi-skimmed milk
2 tbsp cornflour
175 g/6 oz Monterey Jack or Cheddar cheese, grated
salt and freshly ground black pepper, to taste

Combine the stock, sweetcorn, chicken, onion, celery and carrot in the slow cooker. Cover and cook on High for 4–5 hours. Stir in the combined milk and cornflour, stirring for 2–3 minutes. Add the cheese, stirring until melted. Season to taste with salt and pepper.

Chicken and Sweetcorn Chowder

A piquant hint of hot chilli gives a little fire to this flavoursome chowder.

SERVES 8

1 litre/1¾ pints chicken stock
450 g/1 lb skinless chicken breast fillet, cubed (1 cm/½ in)
350 g/12 oz sweetcorn, thawed if frozen
2 medium tomatoes, chopped
1 onion, chopped
½ green pepper, chopped
1 carrot, chopped
1–2 tsp finely chopped jalapeño or other medium-hot chilli, finely chopped
2 garlic cloves, crushed
1 tsp dried thyme
250 ml/8 fl oz semi-skimmed milk
2 tbsp cornflour
salt and freshly ground black pepper, to taste

Combine all the ingredients, except the milk, cornflour, salt and pepper, in a 5.5 litre/9½ pint slow cooker. Cover and cook on Low for 6–8 hours. Turn the heat to High and cook for 10 minutes. Stir in the combined milk and cornflour, stirring for 2–3 minutes. Season to taste with salt and pepper.

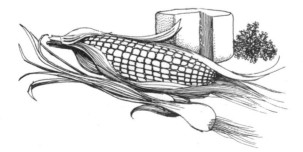

Hearty Chicken and Sweetcorn Chowder

Salsa and black olives are surprising flavour accents in this satisfying chowder.

SERVES 6

450 ml/¾ pint chicken stock
2 x 400 g/14 oz cans cream-style
sweetcorn
450 g/1 lb skinless chicken breast
fillet, cubed
350 g/12 oz potatoes, peeled and cubed
1 onion, chopped
½ red pepper, chopped
2 garlic cloves, crushed
75 ml/2½ fl oz ready-made mild or
hot salsa
salt and freshly ground black pepper,
to taste
chopped black olives, to garnish

Combine all the ingredients, except the salt and pepper, in a 5.5 litre/9½ pint slow cooker. Cover and cook on High for 3–4 hours. Season to taste with salt and pepper. Sprinkle each serving with olives.

Mediterranean-style Chicken and Prawn Chowder

The enticing flavours of the Mediterranean, brought to you courtesy of the chickpeas, red pepper, garlic and oregano.

SERVES 6

450 ml/¾ pint chicken stock
2 x 400 g/14 oz cans chickpeas,
drained
400 g/14 oz can creamed sweetcorn
225 g/8 oz skinless chicken breast
fillet, cubed
225 g/8 oz large, peeled and deveined
raw prawns
350 g/12 oz potatoes, peeled and
cubed
1 onion, chopped
1 roasted red pepper, chopped
2 garlic cloves, crushed
¾ tsp dried oregano
salt and freshly ground black pepper,
to taste
chopped black olives, to garnish

Combine all the ingredients, except the salt and pepper, in a 5.5 litre/9½ pint slow cooker. Cover and cook on High for 3–4 hours. Season to taste with salt and pepper. Sprinkle each serving with olives.

Chicken and Vegetable Chowder

If you have chicken fillets in the freezer, this would make a good convenience meal.

SERVES 6

450 ml/¾ pint chicken stock
400 g/14 oz can cream of chicken or potato and leek soup
450 g/1 lb skinless chicken breast fillet, cubed (2 cm/¾ in)
1 large carrot, sliced
50 g/2 oz Mexican-style sweetcorn
1 onion, chopped
2 garlic cloves, crushed
1 tsp dried thyme
350 g/12 oz small broccoli florets
120 ml/4 fl oz semi-skimmed milk
salt and freshly ground black pepper, to taste

Combine all the ingredients, except the broccoli, milk, salt and pepper, in the slow cooker. Cover and cook on High for 3–4 hours, adding the broccoli and milk during the last 20 minutes. Season to taste with salt and pepper.

Chicken and Fresh Vegetable Chowder

A good family meal of chicken and vegetables cooked to tenderness.

SERVES 8

1 litre/1¾ pints chicken stock
700 g/1½ lb skinless chicken breast fillet, cubed (2.5 cm/1 in)
1 onion, chopped
1 pepper, chopped
1 celery stick, chopped
1 carrot, chopped
75 g/3 oz courgettes, chopped
2 garlic cloves, crushed
¾ tsp dried thyme
¾ tsp dried marjoram
1 bay leaf
175 ml/6 fl oz semi-skimmed milk
2 tbsp cornflour
salt and freshly ground black pepper, to taste

Combine all the ingredients, except the milk, cornflour, salt and pepper, in the slow cooker. Cover and cook on High for 3–4 hours. Stir in the combined milk and cornflour, stirring for 2–3 minutes. Discard the bay leaf. Season to taste with salt and pepper.

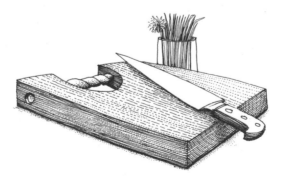

Chicken and Prawn Chowder with Lime

Lime provides the flavour accent in this chowder, while tomatoes and avocado contribute colour and texture contrasts.

SERVES 4

1.2 litres/2 pints chicken stock
225 g/8 oz skinless chicken breast
   fillet, cubed (2 cm/¾ in)
4 spring onions, sliced
4 plum tomatoes, chopped
¼ tsp crushed chilli flakes
a pinch of celery seeds
100 g/4 oz easy-cook long-grain rice
225 g/8 oz large prawns, peeled,
   deveined and halved crossways
1 avocado, cubed
juice of 1 lime
1 tsp grated lime zest
salt and freshly ground black pepper,
   to taste

Combine the stock, chicken, spring onions, tomatoes, chilli flakes and celery seeds in the slow cooker. Cover and cook on High for 4–5 hours, adding the rice during the last 2 hours and the prawns during the last 20 minutes. Stir in the avocado, lime juice and zest. Season to taste with salt and pepper.

Prawn and Vegetable Chowder

The rich flavour of this chowder comes from a combination of herbs, spices and tomato sauce.

SERVES 6

750 ml/1¼ pints chicken stock
350 g/12 oz sweetcorn, thawed if frozen
225 g/8 oz ready-made tomato sauce
350 g/12 oz waxy potatoes, peeled
   and diced
2 onions, chopped

1 green or red pepper, chopped
2 garlic cloves, crushed
50 ml/2 fl oz dry sherry (optional)
1–2 tsp dried Italian seasoning
¼ tsp chilli powder
¼ tsp dry mustard powder
3–4 drops Tabasco sauce
175 g/6 oz cooked peeled prawns,
   thawed if frozen, halved
120 ml/4 fl oz full-fat milk
salt and freshly ground black pepper,
   to taste

Combine all the ingredients, except the prawns, milk, salt and pepper, in a 5.5 litre/9½ pint slow cooker. Cover and cook on High for 4–5 hours, adding the prawns and milk during the last 10 minutes. Season to taste with salt and pepper.

Bean and Prawn Chowder

It's worth keeping some frozen prawns in the freezer for dishes such as this, but remember to let them thaw before you use them.

SERVES 8

2 x 400 g/14 oz cans cannellini beans,
   drained and rinsed
375 ml/13 fl oz chicken stock
400 g/14 oz can creamed sweetcorn
½ onion, chopped
½–¾ tsp dried thyme
¼ tsp dry mustard powder
700 g/1½ lb medium prawns, peeled
375 ml/13 fl oz semi-skimmed milk
2 tbsp cornflour
salt and cayenne pepper, to taste

Combine the beans, stock, sweetcorn, onion, thyme and mustard in the slow cooker. Cover and cook on Low for 6–8 hours, stirring in the prawns and combined milk and cornflour during the last 15–20 minutes. Season to taste with salt and cayenne pepper.

Lobster and Prawn Chowder

Here is a special treat for when lobster is available. It's worth making a really good home-made stock for this one, if you can.

SERVES 4

375 ml/13 fl oz fish stock
400 g/14 oz can chopped tomatoes
2 large potatoes, peeled and cubed
1 onion, chopped
1 tsp dried tarragon
225 g/8 oz cooked lobster meat, cut into small chunks
100 g/4 oz small cooked peeled prawns
250 ml/8 fl oz semi-skimmed milk
15 g/½ oz chopped parsley
salt and freshly ground black pepper, to taste

Combine the stock, tomatoes, potatoes, onion and tarragon in the slow cooker. Cover and cook on Low for 6–8 hours, adding the remaining ingredients, except the salt and pepper, during the last 10–15 minutes. Season to taste with salt and pepper.

Crabmeat Chowder

You can use fresh crabmeat in this recipe, but canned is also good and very convenient.

SERVES 4

375 ml/13 fl oz fish stock
400 g/14 oz can chopped tomatoes
2 large potatoes, peeled and cubed
1 onion, chopped
½ tsp dried thyme
300 g/11 oz white crabmeat
250 ml/8 fl oz semi-skimmed milk
15 g/½ oz chopped parsley
salt and freshly ground black pepper, to taste

Combine the stock, tomatoes, potatoes, onion and thyme in the slow cooker. Cover and cook on Low for 6–8 hours, adding the remaining ingredients, except the salt and pepper, during the last 10–15 minutes. Season to taste with salt and pepper.

Curried Scallop and Potato Chowder

This chowder has a lively curry flavour and a bright yellow colour!

SERVES 4

375 ml/13 fl oz fish stock
120 ml/4 fl oz dry white wine or water
450 g/1 lb potatoes, peeled and cubed
1 tsp curry powder
1 small garlic clove, crushed
450 g/1 lb scallops, halved if large
100 g/4 oz frozen peas, thawed
50–120 ml/2–4 fl oz semi-skimmed milk
salt and freshly ground black pepper, to taste

Combine the stock, wine, potatoes, curry powder and garlic in the slow cooker. Cover and cook on Low for 6–8 hours. Process the mixture in a food processor or blender until smooth. Return to the slow cooker. Stir in the scallops, peas and milk. Cover and cook on High until the scallops are cooked, about 10 minutes. Season to taste with salt and pepper.

Sherried Crab and Mushroom Chowder

Succulent, sweet crabmeat and fresh mushrooms complement one another in this elegant dish.

SERVES 4

600 ml/1 pint chicken stock
450 g/1 lb mushrooms, sliced
130 g/4¼ oz waxy potato, peeled and diced
2 small onions, chopped
½ celery stick, finely chopped
½ carrot, finely chopped
a pinch of dried thyme
1 tbsp tomato purée
1½ tsp soy sauce
350 ml/12 fl oz full-fat milk
175 g/6 oz fresh white crabmeat, coarsely chopped
2 tbsp dry sherry or water
1 tbsp cornflour
salt and white pepper, to taste

Combine the stock, vegetables, thyme, tomato purée and soy sauce in the slow cooker. Cover and cook on High for 4–5 hours, adding 250 ml/8 fl oz of the milk and the crabmeat during the last 30 minutes. Stir in the combined remaining milk, sherry and cornflour, stirring for 2–3 minutes. Season to taste with salt and pepper.

Spicy Crab and Scallop Chowder

The flavour kick in this seafood chowder comes from pickling spice.

SERVES 4

375 ml/13 fl oz fish stock
400 g/14 oz can tomatoes
1 onion, chopped
1 celery stick, chopped
2 tsp pickling spice

100 g/4 oz white crabmeat
225 g/8 oz scallops, halved if large
120 ml/4 fl oz semi-skimmed milk
salt and freshly ground black pepper, to taste

Combine the stock, tomatoes, onion, celery and pickling spice tied in a muslin bag in the slow cooker. Cover and cook on Low for 6–8 hours, adding the crabmeat, scallops and milk during the last 15 minutes. Discard the spice bag. Season to taste with salt and pepper.

Seafood Sampler Chowder

This delicately seasoned chowder is great with Crispy Croûtons (see page 30).

SERVES 4

400 g/14 oz can chopped tomatoes
250 ml/8 fl oz fish or chicken stock
2 medium potatoes, peeled and cubed
½ yellow pepper, chopped
1 onion, chopped
120 ml/4 fl oz dry white wine or water
½ tsp celery seeds
1 tsp herbes de Provence
225 g/8 oz haddock or halibut, cubed (2.5 cm/1 in)
100 g/4 oz scallops, quartered
100 g/4 oz peeled prawns
½ tsp Tabasco sauce
salt, to taste

Combine the tomatoes with the stock, potatoes, pepper, onion, wine or water, celery seeds and herbs in the slow cooker. Cover and cook on Low for 6–8 hours, adding the seafood during the last 20 minutes. Stir in the Tabasco sauce. Season to taste with salt.

Seafood Chowder

Worcestershire sauce adds piquancy to this chowder, which is topped with crispy bacon.

SERVES 8

450 ml/¾ pint fish stock
2 x 400 g/14 oz cans chopped
  tomatoes
120–250 ml/4–8 fl oz ready-made
  tomato sauce
700 g/1½ lb potatoes, peeled and
  chopped
2 onions, sliced
1 large celery stick, sliced
1 tbsp Worcestershire sauce
1 tsp dried rosemary
700 g/1½ lb cod or halibut steaks,
  cubed (2.5 cm/1 in)
250 ml/8 fl oz full-fat milk
3 tbsp cornflour
salt and freshly ground black pepper,
  to taste
4 bacon rashers, cooked until crisp
  and crumbled

Combine the stock, tomatoes, tomato sauce, potatoes, onions, celery, Worcestershire sauce and rosemary in a 5.5 litre/9½ pint slow cooker. Cover and cook on High for 4–5 hours, adding the fish during the last 15 minutes. Stir in the combined milk and cornflour, stirring for 2–3 minutes. Season to taste with salt and pepper. Sprinkle each bowl of chowder with bacon.

Rich Prawn Chowder

Remember to allow the prawns to thaw, if using frozen, before adding them to the slow cooker.

SERVES 8

450 ml/¾ pint fish stock
2 x 400 g/14 oz cans chopped
  tomatoes
120–250 ml/4–8 fl oz ready-made
  tomato sauce
350 g/12 oz potatoes, peeled and
  chopped
100 g/4 oz thawed frozen peas
2 onions, sliced
1 large celery stick, sliced
1 tbsp Worcestershire sauce
1 tsp dried rosemary
700 g/1½ lb large, peeled, deveined
  prawns
250 ml/8 fl oz full-fat milk
3 tbsp cornflour
salt and freshly ground black pepper,
  to taste
4 bacon rashers, cooked until crisp
  and crumbled

Combine the stock, tomatoes, tomato sauce, potatoes, peas, onions, celery, Worcestershire sauce and rosemary in a 5.5 litre/9½ pint slow cooker. Cover and cook on High for 4–5 hours, adding the prawns during the last 15 minutes. Stir in the combined milk and cornflour, stirring for 2–3 minutes. Season to taste with salt and pepper. Sprinkle each bowl of chowder with bacon.

Salmon and Roasted Pepper Chowder

Salmon is paired with sweetcorn and seasoned with chilli, cumin and oregano for a fabulous feast.

SERVES 4

225 g/8 oz sweetcorn, thawed if frozen
450 ml/¾ pint vegetable stock
2 medium potatoes, peeled and cubed
2 roasted red peppers, chopped
½–1 jalapeño or other medium-hot chilli, finely chopped
2 garlic cloves, crushed
1 tsp cumin seeds
1 tsp dried oregano
350 g/12 oz thick salmon fillet, skinned and cubed (2.5 cm/1 in)
salt and freshly ground black pepper, to taste

Combine all the ingredients, except the salmon, salt and pepper, in the slow cooker. Cover and cook on High for 4–5 hours, adding the salmon during the last 15 minutes. Season to taste with salt and pepper.

Bermuda Fish Chowder

With bay and thyme, and a good splash of Worcestershire sauce, this chowder is certainly robust in flavour.

SERVES 6

1 litre/1¾ pints fish stock
400 g/14 oz can plum tomatoes, roughly chopped, with juice
75 ml/2½ fl oz tomato ketchup
2 small smoked pork hocks
550 g/1¼ lb potatoes, peeled and cubed
2 onions, chopped
1 large celery stick, chopped
1 large carrot, chopped
½ green pepper, chopped
2½ tsp Worcestershire sauce
2 large bay leaves
½–¾ tsp dried thyme
1 tsp curry powder
450 g/1 lb lean fish fillets such as haddock, cod, hake, whiting, cubed (2.5 cm/1 in)
salt and freshly ground black pepper, to taste

Combine all the ingredients, except the fish, salt and pepper, in a 5.5 litre/ 9½ pint slow cooker. Cover and cook on Low for 6–8 hours, adding the fish during the last 15 minutes. Discard the pork hocks and bay leaves. Season to taste with salt and pepper.

Fresh Salmon Chowder with Potatoes

Salmon has a good flavour that's perfect for fine chowders like this one.

SERVES 4

750 ml/1¼ pints fish stock
550 g/1¼ lb potatoes, peeled and cubed
2 onions, chopped
½ tsp dry mustard powder
½ tsp dried marjoram
450 g/1 lb thick salmon fillet, skinned and cubed (2.5 cm/1 in)
250 ml/8 fl oz full-fat milk
2 tbsp cornflour
salt and white pepper, to taste

Combine the stock, potatoes, onions, mustard and marjoram in the slow cooker. Cover and cook on High for 5–6 hours. Process the chowder in a food processor or blender until smooth. Return to the slow cooker. Stir in the salmon. Cover and cook on High until the fish is cooked, 10–15 minutes. Stir in the combined milk and cornflour, stirring for 2–3 minutes. Season to taste with salt and white pepper.

Monkfish and Cheddar Chowder

Use any favourite firm-textured fish in this creamy chowder enriched with cheese.

SERVES 4

400 ml/14 fl oz chicken stock
450 g/1 lb potatoes, peeled and cubed
1 onion, chopped
1 carrot, sliced
450 g/1 lb monkfish, membrane removed, cubed (2 cm/¾ in)
120 ml/4 fl oz semi-skimmed milk
50 g/2 oz Cheddar cheese, grated
½–1 tsp Tabasco sauce
salt, to taste

Combine the stock and vegetables in the slow cooker. Cover and cook on Low for 6–8 hours. Process the chowder in a food processor or blender until smooth. Return to the slow cooker. Cover and cook on High for 25 minutes, adding the fish and milk during the last 15 minutes. Add the cheese and Tabasco sauce, stirring until the cheese has melted. Season to taste with salt.

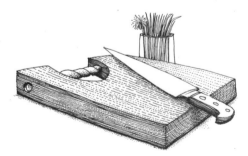

Flounder Chowder

Although this dish calls for flounder, you could also use plaice, lemon sole, cod, haddock, whiting or halibut.

SERVES 6

450 ml/¾ pint fish or vegetable stock
350 g/12 oz potatoes, peeled and
    cubed (2 cm/¾ in)
2 onions, chopped
1 large carrot, chopped
1 large celery stick, chopped
175 g/6 oz dried butter beans, rinsed
50 g/2 oz sweetcorn, thawed if frozen
1 garlic clove, crushed
1½ tsp dried basil
½ tsp dried marjoram
¼ tsp dry mustard powder
¼ tsp crushed celery seeds
450 ml/¾ pint semi-skimmed milk
450 g/1 lb skinless flounder fillets,
    diced (2.5 cm/1 in)
1 tbsp cornflour
salt and freshly ground black pepper,
    to taste

Combine all the ingredients, except the milk, fish, cornflour, salt and pepper, in a 5.5 litre/9½ pint slow cooker. Cover and cook on Low for 6–8 hours, adding 375 ml/13 fl oz of the milk during the last 30 minutes. Add the fish. Cover and cook on High for 10–15 minutes. Stir in the combined remaining milk and the cornflour, stirring for 2–3 minutes. Season to taste with salt and pepper.

Canadian Fish Chowder

Mace is the secret flavour in this easy chowder. Try some of the cheaper and less well-known fish for an economical family meal.

SERVES 6

2 x 400 g/14 oz cans chopped tomatoes
450 ml/¾ pint water
2 onions, finely chopped
1 large carrot, finely chopped
1 large celery stick, finely chopped
2 leeks (white parts only), thinly sliced
450 g/1 lb cod, haddock, whiting or
    pollack, cubed (2.5 cm/1 in)
250 ml/8 fl oz semi-skimmed milk
¼–½ tsp ground mace
salt and white pepper, to taste
2 spring onions, thinly sliced

Combine the tomatoes, water and vegetables in the slow cooker. Cover and cook on High for 4–5 hours, adding the fish, milk and mace during the last 15 minutes. Season to taste with salt and white pepper. Sprinkle each bowl of chowder with spring onions.

Potato Seafood Chowder

Saffron adds a subtle flavour and a beautiful colour to this chowder of haddock, cod and prawns.

SERVES 4

450 ml/¾ pint fish stock
3 medium floury potatoes, unpeeled
    and cubed
1 onion, sliced
1 celery stick, sliced
1 tsp saffron threads
450 ml/¾ pint semi-skimmed milk
225 g/8 oz haddock fillets
225 g/8 oz cod fillets
50 g/2 oz raw or cooked peeled
    prawns, thawed if frozen
1 tbsp cornflour
salt and white pepper, to taste

Combine the stock, vegetables and saffron in the slow cooker. Cover and cook on High for 4–5 hours, adding 375 ml/13 fl oz of the milk during the last 30 minutes and the seafood during the last 15 minutes. Stir in the combined remaining milk and the cornflour, stirring for 2–3 minutes. Season to taste with salt and pepper.

Cod and Vegetable Chowder

You could use another firm white fish instead of cod, for a change.

SERVES 4

400 ml/14 fl oz chicken stock
350 g/12 oz potatoes, peeled and cubed
1 onion, chopped
1 carrot, sliced
175 g/6 oz small broccoli florets
50 g/2 oz thawed frozen peas
65 g/2½ oz French beans, cut into short lengths
450 g/1 lb cod, cubed (2 cm/¾ in)
120 ml/4 fl oz semi-skimmed milk
50 g/2 oz Cheddar cheese, grated
½–1 tsp Tabasco sauce
salt, to taste

Combine the stock and vegetables in the slow cooker. Cover and cook on Low for 6–8 hours. Process the chowder in a food processor or blender until smooth. Return to the slow cooker. Cover and cook on High for 25 minutes, adding the fish and milk during the last 15 minutes. Add the cheese and Tabasco sauce, stirring until the cheese has melted. Season to taste with salt.

Nova Scotia Seafood Chowder

Hearty chowders are a hallmark of the cuisine in Canada's Atlantic provinces and the seafood they contain depends on the day's catch. This combination is typical.

SERVES 4

450 ml/¾ pint fish stock
350 g/12 oz potatoes, peeled and cubed
½ cauliflower, in florets
1 large onion, chopped
1 carrot, chopped
1 celery stick, chopped
1 garlic clove, crushed
1½ tsp dried basil
½ tsp dried marjoram
¼ tsp dry mustard powder
450 ml/¾ pint full-fat milk
225 g/8 oz skinless white fish fillets such as cod, haddock, whiting, plaice or flounder, cubed
100 g/4 oz raw prawns, peeled
100 g/4 oz white crabmeat
1 tbsp cornflour
salt and white pepper, to taste

Combine the stock, vegetables, garlic, herbs and mustard in the slow cooker. Cover and cook on Low for 6–8 hours, adding 375 ml/13 fl oz of the milk during the last 30 minutes. Turn the heat to High and add the seafood. Cover and cook for 10 minutes. Stir in the combined remaining milk and the cornflour, stirring for 2–3 minutes. Season to taste with salt and pepper.

Cod and Potato Chowder

This chunky chowder has a thick, flavourful base of puréed vegetables.

SERVES 4

375 ml/13 fl oz fish stock
700 g/1½ lb potatoes, peeled and cubed
1 large onion, chopped
1 celery stick, chopped
1 carrot, chopped
1 tsp dried thyme
250 ml/8 fl oz semi-skimmed milk
450 g/1 lb cod, cubed (2 cm/¾ in)
½–1 tsp Tabasco sauce
salt, to taste
2 bacon rashers, cooked until crisp and crumbled

Combine the stock, vegetables and thyme in the slow cooker. Cover and cook on High for 4–5 hours. Process the chowder and milk in a food processor or blender until smooth. Return to the slow cooker. Add the cod and the Tabasco sauce. Cover and cook on High for 10–15 minutes. Season to taste with salt. Sprinkle each bowl of chowder with bacon.

Salmon, Prawn and Sweet Potato Chowder

Cod, whiting and red snapper are other possible fish choices for this herb-scented chowder.

SERVES 8

2 x 400 g/14 oz cans chopped tomatoes
450 ml/¾ pint chicken stock
120 ml/4 fl oz dry white wine or chicken stock
700 g/1½ lb sweet potatoes, peeled and cubed
1 onion, chopped
½ green pepper, chopped
50 g/2 oz sweetcorn, thawed if frozen
2 garlic cloves, crushed
1 tsp dried basil
1 tsp dried oregano
¼ tsp dried thyme
350 g/12 oz thick salmon fillet, skinned and cubed (2.5 cm/1 in)
350 g/12 oz large raw prawns, peeled and deveined
salt and freshly ground black pepper, to taste

Combine all the ingredients, except the salmon, prawns, salt and pepper, in a 5.5 litre/9½ pint slow cooker. Cover and cook on Low for 6–8 hours, adding the salmon and prawns during the last 15–20 minutes. Season to taste with salt and pepper.

Scandinavian Fish Chowder

This fish chowder features cod, with accents of dill, cucumber and hard-boiled eggs.

SERVES 8

450 ml/¾ pint water
350 g/12 oz potatoes, peeled and diced
1 large celery stick, chopped
1 onion, chopped
1 tsp dried dill
½ tsp paprika
¼ tsp ground allspice
450 ml/¾ pint semi-skimmed milk
450 g/1 lb skinless cod fillets, sliced
150 g/5 oz cucumber, seeded and chopped
2 tbsp cornflour
2 tbsp lemon juice
salt and freshly ground black pepper, to taste
hard-boiled egg slices, to garnish

Combine the water, potatoes, celery, onion, dill, paprika and allspice in a 5.5 litre/9½ pint slow cooker. Cover and cook on Low for 6–8 hours, stirring in 375 ml/13 fl oz of the milk during the last 30 minutes. Stir in the cod and cucumber. Cover and cook on High for 10 minutes. Stir in the combined remaining milk and the cornflour, stirring for 2–3 minutes. Stir in the lemon juice. Season to taste with salt and pepper. Garnish the bowls of chowder with egg slices.

Red Clam Chowder

Adding tomato juice gives a fuller flavour. Use sweet potatoes instead of the white for a change.

SERVES 8

450 ml/¾ pint fish stock
450 ml/¾ pint tomato juice
350 g/12 oz potatoes, peeled and diced
400 g/14 oz can chopped tomatoes
2 onions, chopped
1 large carrot, sliced
½ green pepper, chopped
1 celery stick, chopped
1 garlic clove
1 bay leaf
1 tsp dried basil
½ tsp dried oregano
½ tsp sugar
375 g/13 oz clams from a jar, drained and chopped, with juice
salt and cayenne pepper, to taste

Combine all the ingredients, except the clams, salt and cayenne pepper, in a 5.5 litre/9½ pint slow cooker. Cover and cook on High for 4–5 hours, adding the clams during the last 30 minutes. Discard the bay leaf. Season to taste with salt and cayenne pepper.

Manhattan-style Clam Chowder with Sweetcorn

The mild smokiness of bacon adds a subtle flavour to this chowder.

SERVES 4

2 x 400 g/14 oz cans chopped tomatoes
250 ml/8 fl oz chicken stock
175 g/6 oz potatoes, peeled and cubed
1 onion, finely chopped
100 g/4 oz sweetcorn, thawed if frozen
1 celery stick, chopped
½ green pepper, chopped
50 g/2 oz smoked back bacon, cut into thin strips
1 garlic clove, crushed
1 bay leaf
½ tsp dried thyme
½ tsp dried basil
½ tsp sugar
375 g/13 oz clams from a jar, drained and chopped, with juice
salt and cayenne pepper, to taste

Combine all the ingredients, except the clams, salt and cayenne pepper, in the slow cooker. Cover and cook on High for 4–6 hours, adding the clams during the last 45 minutes. Discard the bay leaf. Season to taste with salt and cayenne pepper.

Manhattan-style Fish and Vegetable Chowder

A delicious chowder with a flavour of the sea.

SERVES 6

1 litre/1¾ pints tomato juice
450 ml/¾ pint chicken stock
150 g/5 oz frozen French beans, thawed
100 g/4 oz sweetcorn, thawed if frozen
175 g/6 oz potato, peeled and cubed
2 onions, chopped
1 celery stick, chopped
1 carrot, chopped
1 bay leaf
½ tsp dried thyme
½ tsp dried marjoram
¼ tsp dry mustard powder
¼ tsp black pepper
350 g/12 oz skinless haddock or halibut fillets, cubed (2 cm/¾ in)
salt and cayenne pepper, to taste

Combine all the ingredients, except the fish, salt and cayenne pepper, in a 5.5 litre/9½ pint slow cooker. Cover and cook on Low for 6–8 hours, adding the fish during the last 15–20 minutes. Discard the bay leaf. Season to taste with salt and pepper.

White Clam and Sweetcorn Chowder

If you keep a jar or two of clams, or even cockles, in your storecupboard you can make this hearty chowder at any time.

SERVES 4

250 ml/8 fl oz fish or chicken stock
350 g/12 oz waxy potatoes, peeled and cubed (1 cm/½ in)
100 g/4 oz sweetcorn, thawed if frozen
1 medium onion, chopped
1 large celery stick, chopped
1 large bay leaf
½ tsp dried marjoram
250 ml/8 fl oz semi-skimmed milk
275 g/10 oz clams from a jar, drained and finely chopped, with juice
2 tsp cornflour
salt and freshly ground black pepper, to taste

Combine all the ingredients, except the milk, clams, cornflour, salt and pepper, in the slow cooker. Cover and cook on High for 4–5 hours. Discard the bay leaf. Process the chowder in a food processor or blender until smooth. Return to the slow cooker. Stir in 175 ml/6 fl oz of the milk and the clams. Cover and cook on High for 15 minutes. Stir in the combined remaining milk and the cornflour, stirring for 2–3 minutes. Season to taste with salt and pepper.

International Flavours

These dishes focus on flavours from around the world – from American favourites to spicy offerings from the East. Remember to keep your spices in a dark cupboard or pantry so they retain their flavour; and don't keep them too long as they do lose their pungency over time.

Yankee Bean Stew

Lamb and haricot beans with the smokiness of ham make a substantial dish.

SERVES 6

1 litre/1¾ pints chicken stock
2 x 400 g/14 oz cans haricot beans, drained and rinsed
450 g/1 lb lean stewing lamb, cubed (1 cm/½ in)
225–350 g/8–12 oz smoked ham, cubed (1 cm/½ in)
1 large onion, chopped
1 celery stick, chopped
2 carrots, chopped
2 garlic cloves, crushed
1 tsp herbes de Provence or dried Italian herb seasoning
400 g/14 oz can chopped tomatoes
salt and freshly ground black pepper, to taste

Combine all the ingredients, except the salt and pepper, in a 5.5 litre/9½ pint slow cooker. Cover and cook on Low for 6–8 hours. Season to taste with salt and pepper.

Tennessee Gumbo

To please all palates, serve this soup with an assortment of hot sauces.

SERVES 12

1.5 litres/2½ pints Rich Chicken Stock (see page 25) or chicken stock
2 x 400 g/14 oz cans chopped tomatoes
350 g/12 oz skinless chicken breast fillets, cubed
350 g/12 oz lean ham, cubed
4 onions, chopped
1 large celery stick, chopped
1 green pepper, chopped
3 large garlic cloves, crushed
2 tsp Worcestershire sauce
a pinch of ground cloves
1 tsp dried thyme
2 bay leaves
225 g/8 oz easy-cook long-grain rice
350 g/12 oz raw prawns, peeled
salt and Tabasco sauce, to taste

Combine all the ingredients, except the rice, prawns, salt and Tabasco sauce, in a 5.5 litre/9½ pint slow cooker. Cover and cook on Low for 6–8 hours, adding the rice during the last 2 hours and the prawns during the last 20 minutes. Discard the bay leaves. Season to taste with salt and Tabasco sauce.

Bourbon Street Soup

Okra, rice, tomatoes and chilli bring a hint of New Orleans to this vegetable beef soup.

SERVES 6

1 litre/1¾ pints water
450 g/1 lb lean stewing or braising
  steak, cubed (2.5 cm/1 in)
2 x 400 g/14 oz cans chopped tomatoes
3 onions, chopped
1 small green pepper, chopped
3 garlic cloves, crushed
1 tsp dried thyme
¼–½ tsp crushed chilli flakes
1 bay leaf
65 g/2½ oz easy-cook long-grain rice
175 g/6 oz sweetcorn, thawed if frozen
175 g/6 oz sliced fresh or thawed
  frozen okra
salt and freshly ground black pepper,
  to taste
Tabasco sauce, to taste

Combine all the ingredients, except the rice, sweetcorn, okra, salt, pepper and Tabasco sauce, in a 5.5 litre/9½ pint slow cooker. Cover and cook on Low for 6–8 hours, adding the rice during the last 2 hours and the sweetcorn and okra during the last 30 minutes. Discard the bay leaf. Season to taste with salt, pepper and Tabasco sauce.

Southern Sweetcorn and Bean Soup with Bean Cookies

Smoky chipotle chillies, available from specialist suppliers, give this soup a unique flavour, although the dish can also be made with fresh chillies. Serve with some moist, savoury cookies made with puréed beans.

SERVES 6

1.5 litres/2½ pints Rich Chicken Stock
  (see page 25) or chicken stock

2 x 400 g/14 oz cans cannellini beans,
  drained, rinsed and coarsely mashed
225 g/8 oz sweetcorn, thawed if frozen
2 onions, chopped
1 red pepper chopped
1 garlic clove, crushed
¼–½ small chipotle chilli in adobo, or
  ½ hot chilli, chopped
1 tsp dried thyme
salt and freshly ground black pepper,
  to taste
120 ml/4 fl oz soured cream
Bean Cookies (see below)

Combine all the ingredients, except the salt, pepper, soured cream and Bean Cookies, in a 5.5 litre/9½ pint slow cooker. Cover and cook on High for 4–5 hours. Season to taste with salt and pepper. Garnish each bowl of soup with dollops of soured cream and serve with Bean Cookies.

Bean Cookies Ⓥ

Delicious cookies from the southern states of the US

SERVES 6 AS AN ACCOMPANIMENT

75 g/3 oz plain flour
2 tsp baking powder
1½ tsp sugar
¼ tsp salt
40 g/1½ oz white vegetable fat
½ x 400 g/14 oz can cannellini beans,
  drained and rinsed
3 tbsp skimmed milk

Combine the flour, baking powder, sugar and salt in a medium bowl. Cut in the white vegetable fat until the mixture resembles coarse crumbs. Process the beans and milk in a food processor or blender until almost smooth. Add to the flour mixture and mix just until the dough comes together. Drop spoonfuls of the dough on to an ungreased baking sheet. Bake at 190°C/gas 5/fan oven 170°C until light brown, about 12 minutes.

163

Red Bean, Rice and Sausage Soup

It's the smoked sausage that gives this easy but satisfying soup an edge.

SERVES 6

1.2 litres/2 pints chicken stock
2 x 400 g/14 oz cans red kidney
    beans, drained and rinsed
400 ml/14 fl oz ready-made tomato
    sauce
175 g/6 oz smoked sausage, sliced
1 small carrot, diced
1 small celery stick, diced
½ small red pepper, diced
1 large onion, finely chopped
1 garlic clove, crushed
¼ tsp dried thyme
1 bay leaf
65 g/2½ oz easy-cook long-grain rice
salt and freshly ground black pepper,
    to taste

Combine all the ingredients, except the rice, salt and pepper, in a 5.5 litre/9½ pint slow cooker. Cover and cook on High for 4–5 hours, adding the rice during the last 2 hours. Discard the bay leaf and season to taste with salt and pepper.

Creole-style Lamb Soup

The lamb cooks to a luscious tenderness accentuated by herbs and mustard.

SERVES 6

1 litre/1¾ pints beef stock
700 g/1½ lb ready-made tomato sauce
    or passata
450 g/1 lb lean stewing lamb, cubed
    (1 cm/½ in)
2 onions, chopped
1 courgette, chopped
½ green pepper, chopped
1 celery stick, chopped
2 large garlic cloves, crushed
1 bay leaf

1 tsp dried marjoram
½ tsp dried thyme
½ tsp dried basil
¼ tsp dry mustard powder
65 g/2½ oz easy-cook long-grain rice
salt and freshly ground black pepper,
    to taste
Tabasco sauce, to taste

Combine all the ingredients, except the rice, salt, pepper and Tabasco sauce, in a 5.5 litre/9½ pint slow cooker. Cover and cook on Low for 6–8 hours, adding the rice during the last 2 hours. Discard the bay leaf. Season to taste with salt and pepper. Serve with Tabasco sauce.

Vegetable Soup with Chilli Crisps ⓥ

This vegetable soup is enhanced with a garnish of fresh coriander.

SERVES 8

2.25 litres/4 pints vegetable stock
4 onions, sliced
2 large carrots, sliced
175 g/6 oz mushrooms, sliced
350 g/12 oz waxy potatoes, unpeeled
    and cubed
400 g/14 oz tomatoes, chopped
3 large garlic cloves, crushed
2 tsp dried oregano
1 tsp ground cumin
¼ tsp crushed chilli flakes
salt and freshly ground black pepper,
    to taste
Chilli Crisps (see page 165)
15 g/½ oz chopped fresh coriander

Combine all the ingredients, except the Chilli Crisps and coriander, in a 5.5 litre/9½ pint slow cooker. Cover and cook on High for 4–5 hours. Season to taste with salt and pepper. Sprinkle each bowl of soup with Chilli Crisps and fresh coriander.

Chilli Crisps (V)

Crunchy tortilla chips to accompany dips or soups.

SERVES 8 AS AN ACCOMPANIMENT

3 corn tortillas (15 cm/6 in)
olive oil cooking spray
½ tsp garlic powder
½ tsp chilli powder

Spray both sides of the tortillas with cooking spray. Sprinkle the tops with garlic and chilli powder. Cut the tortillas in half, and then into thin strips. Arrange on a baking sheet and bake at 220°C/gas 7/fan oven 200°C until crisp, about 10 minutes.

Mexican-style Chicken and Lime Soup

Lightly seasoned with lime and fresh coriander, this soup is packed with chicken and vegetables.

SERVES 8

2.25 litres/4 pints chicken stock
700 g/1½ lb skinless chicken breast fillets, cubed
2 large tomatoes, peeled, seeded and chopped
100 g/4 oz sweetcorn, thawed if frozen
1 courgette, diced
1 onion, chopped
½ green pepper, chopped
2 tbsp chopped fresh coriander
2 tbsp lime juice
salt and freshly ground black pepper, to taste
4 corn tortillas (15 cm/6 in), each cut into 10 wedges
vegetable cooking spray
thin lime slices, to garnish

Combine the stock, chicken and vegetables in a 5.5 litre/9½ pint slow cooker. Cover and cook on Low for 6–8 hours, stirring in the fresh coriander and lime juice during the last 30 minutes. Season to taste with salt and pepper. Spray the tortillas lightly with cooking spray and toss. Cook in a lightly greased large frying pan over medium heat until browned and crisp, about 5 minutes. Add the tortilla wedges to eight soup bowls, and ladle the soup over. Float the lime slices on top.

Prawn and Black Bean Soup

Oregano, thyme, cumin and lots of garlic give this soup plenty of impact. Try using red kidney beans instead of black beans, for a change.

SERVES 6

1.2 litres/2 pints chicken stock
2 x 400 g/14 oz cans black beans, drained and rinsed
2 onions, chopped
2 tomatoes, cut into wedges
4 garlic cloves, crushed
1 tsp dried oregano
1 tsp dried thyme
1 tsp ground cumin
1 bay leaf
225 g/8 oz raw prawns, peeled
salt and freshly ground black pepper, to taste
chopped fresh coriander, to garnish

Combine all the ingredients, except the prawns, salt and pepper, in the slow cooker. Cover and cook on High for 4–5 hours, adding the prawns during the last 15 minutes. Discard the bay leaf. Season to taste with salt and pepper. Sprinkle each bowl of soup with fresh coriander.

165

Sopa de Casa

Creamed sweetcorn and cheese give this soup a pleasingly smooth texture.

SERVES 6

400 ml/14 fl oz chicken stock
350 g/12 oz sweetcorn, thawed if frozen
100 g/4 oz green chillies from a jar, chopped
450 g/1 lb skinless chicken breast fillets, cubed (2 cm/¾ in)
2 chopped onions
1 large tomato, chopped
½ jalapeño, or other medium-hot, chilli, finely chopped
2 large garlic cloves, crushed
¾ tsp dried oregano
½ tsp ground cumin
250 ml/8 fl oz full-fat milk
100 g/4 oz Monterey Jack or mild Cheddar cheese, grated
salt and freshly ground black pepper, to taste

Process the chicken stock and 175 g/ 6 oz of the sweetcorn in a food processor or blender until smooth. Combine the puréed sweetcorn and the remaining ingredients, except the milk, cheese, salt and pepper, in the slow cooker. Cover and cook on Low for 6–8 hours, adding the milk during the last 30 minutes. Stir in the cheese, stirring until melted. Season to taste with salt and pepper.

Spicy Pork and Chicken Soup

Garnish with thinly sliced vegetables for a colourful supper dish.

SERVES 4

2 ancho or other medium-hot chillies, seeds and veins discarded
250 ml/8 fl oz boiling water
750 ml/1¼ pints chicken stock
225 g/8 oz pork loin, cubed
225 g/8 oz skinless chicken breast fillets, cubed
400 g/14 oz can chopped tomatoes
400 g/14 oz can pinto beans, drained and rinsed
2 onions, chopped
1 garlic clove, crushed
½ tsp dried oregano
½ tsp dried thyme
salt and freshly ground black pepper, to taste
6 lime wedges

garnishes: thinly sliced lettuce, cabbage, spring onion, radish, grated carrot

Cover the chillies with boiling water in a small bowl. Leave to stand until softened, about 10 minutes. Process the chillies and water in a food processor or blender until smooth. Combine the chilli mixture and remaining ingredients, except the salt, pepper and lime wedges in the slow cooker. Cover and cook on Low for 6–8 hours. Season to taste with salt and pepper. Serve with lime wedges and the garnishes.

Mexican Meatballs

These are great with any spicy soups.

MAKES 24 MEATBALLS

450 g/1 lb lean minced beef
15 g/½ oz rice, cooked
1 small onion, finely chopped
1 garlic clove, crushed
½ tsp dried mint
½ tsp dried oregano
⅛ tsp ground cumin
½ tsp salt
¼ tsp pepper

Combine all the ingredients in a bowl. Shape the mixture into 24 small meatballs.

Mexican Meatball Soup

A great favourite in Mexico, this soup is traditionally delicately seasoned with mint.

SERVES 4

750 ml/1¼ pints chicken stock
450 ml/¾ pint tomato juice
450 ml/¾ pint water
Mexican Meatballs (see below)
2 courgettes, sliced
1 onion, chopped
1 carrot, chopped
2 garlic cloves, crushed
1 small jalapeño or other medium-hot chilli, seeds and veins discarded, finely chopped
1½ tsp dried mint
salt and freshly ground black pepper, to taste

Combine all the ingredients, except the salt and pepper, in the slow cooker. Cover and cook on High for 4–5 hours. Season to taste with salt and pepper.

French Onion Soup

Browning the onions in butter gives this soup its richness and full, traditional flavour.

SERVES 4

450 g/1 lb onions, thinly sliced
1–2 tbsp butter or margarine
½ tsp dry mustard powder
2 tsp flour
1 litre/1¾ pints Fragrant Beef Stock (see page 26) or beef stock
120 ml/4 fl oz dry white wine (optional)
salt and freshly ground black pepper, to taste
4 slices French bread, toasted
50 g/2 oz freshly grated Parmesan cheese

Cook the onions in the butter in a large pan over medium to medium-low heat until golden, 15–20 minutes. Stir in the mustard and flour and cook for 1–2 minutes.

Combine the onion mixture and remaining ingredients, except the salt, pepper, bread and cheese, in the slow cooker. Cover and cook on Low for 6–8 hours. Season to taste with salt and pepper. Sprinkle the bread with cheese. Grill until melted, 1–2 minutes. Top each bowl of soup with bread slices.

Mexican Chicken and Sweetcorn Soup

Monterey Jack cheese gives this chicken-based soup richness.

SERVES 8

1 litre/1¾ pints Rich Chicken Stock (see page 31) or chicken stock
450 g/1 lb skinless chicken breast fillets, cubed
225 g/8 oz sweetcorn, thawed if frozen
3 onions, chopped
1 red or green pepper, chopped
1 small jalapeño or other medium-hot chilli, finely chopped
1 garlic clove
1 tsp ground cumin
salt and freshly ground black pepper, to taste
100–175 g/4–6 oz Monterey Jack or mild Cheddar cheese, grated

Combine all the ingredients, except the salt, pepper and cheese, in the slow cooker. Cover and cook on Low for 6–8 hours. Season to taste with salt and pepper. Add the cheese, stirring until melted.

El Paso Pork and Sweetcorn Soup

If you cannot get a poblano chilli, any mildish variety will be an acceptable substitute.

SERVES 8

1 litre/1¾ pints Rich Chicken Stock (see page 25) or chicken stock
450 g/1 lb lean pork, cubed
225 g/8 oz sweetcorn, thawed if frozen
3 onions, chopped
1 small poblano chilli
1 small jalapeño or other medium-hot chilli, finely chopped
1 garlic clove
1 tsp ground cumin
salt and freshly ground black pepper, to taste
100 g/4 oz Feta cheese, crumbled

Combine all the ingredients, except the salt, pepper and cheese, in the slow cooker. Cover and cook on Low for 6–8 hours. Season to taste with salt and pepper. Spinkle each serving with the Feta.

French Vegetable Soup

Made with veal stock, cubes of veal and lots of fresh vegetables, this soup is a special treat.

SERVES 8

2.25 litres/4 pints Veal Stock (see page 26) or chicken stock
400 g/14 oz can chopped tomatoes
450 g/1 lb lean stewing veal, cubed
250 g/9 oz potatoes, peeled and cubed
150 g/5 oz French beans, cut into short lengths
100 g/4 oz cauliflower florets
1 onion, chopped
1 celery stick, sliced
1 carrot, sliced
1 tsp dried thyme
½ tsp dried rosemary
175 g/6 oz small broccoli florets
100 g/4 oz frozen peas, thawed
salt and freshly ground black pepper, to taste

Combine all the ingredients, except the broccoli, peas, salt and pepper, in a 5.5 litre/9½ pint slow cooker. Cover and cook on Low for 6–8 hours, adding the broccoli and peas during the last 20–30 minutes. Season to taste with salt and pepper.

Onion and White Bean Soup

Manchego cheese hails from Spain and is a lovely finishing touch in this recipe, but you could use another firm medium-strong white cheese in its place.

SERVES 4

450 g/1 lb onions, thinly sliced
1–2 tbsp butter or margarine
½ tsp dry mustard powder
2 tsp flour
400 g/14 oz can haricot or cannellini beans, drained and rinsed
1 litre/1¾ pints Fragrant Beef Stock (see page 26) or beef stock
120 ml/4 fl oz dry white wine (optional)
½ tsp dried rosemary
¼ tsp dried thyme
salt and freshly ground black pepper, to taste
4 tbsp grated Manchego cheese

Cook the onions in the butter in a large pan over medium to medium-low heat until golden, 15–20 minutes. Stir in the mustard and flour and cook for 1–2 minutes. Combine the onion mixture and remaining ingredients, except the salt, pepper and cheese, in the slow cooker. Cover and cook on Low for 6–8 hours. Season to taste with salt and pepper. Sprinkle each serving with 1 tbsp of the cheese.

White Bean Soup Provençal ⓥ

Serve warm focaccia as the perfect accompaniment to this herb-infused soup.

SERVES 8

1.5 litres/2½ pints vegetable stock
450 ml/¾ pint water
450 g/1 lb dried cannellini or haricot beans
2 onions, chopped
1 large celery stick, chopped
3 garlic cloves, crushed
2 tsp dried sage
3 large plum tomatoes, chopped
2 tsp lemon juice
salt and freshly ground black pepper, to taste
Mixed Herb Pesto (see below)

Combine all the ingredients, except the tomatoes, lemon juice, salt, pepper and Mixed Herb Pesto, in a 5.5 litre/9½ pint slow cooker. Cover and cook on Low until the beans are tender, 7–8 hours, adding the tomatoes and lemon juice during the last 30 minutes. Season to taste with salt and pepper. Stir 1 tbsp of Mixed Herb Pesto into each bowl of soup.

Mixed Herb Pesto ⓥ

Swirl this into soups and stews for extra flavour.

SERVES 8 AS AN ACCOMPANIMENT

15 g/½ oz fresh basil leaves
15 g/½ oz fresh parsley sprigs
10 g/¼ oz fresh oregano leaves
3 garlic cloves
2–3 tbsp freshly grated Parmesan cheese
2–3 tbsp walnut pieces
2–3 tbsp olive oil
2 tsp lemon juice
salt and freshly ground black pepper, to taste

Process the herbs, garlic, Parmesan cheese and walnuts in a food processor, adding the oil and lemon juice gradually, until the mixture is very finely chopped. Season to taste with salt and pepper.

Minestrone

Make this chunky soup, containing cubes of beef, the centrepiece of an Italian-style family supper. Serve with a tossed salad and crusty bread.

SERVES 8

2.25 litres/4 pints beef stock
2 x 400 g/14 oz cans cannellini beans, drained and rinsed
175 g/6 oz tomato purée
450 g/1 lb lean braising steak, cubed (2 cm/¾ in)
350 g/12 oz courgettes, coarsely diced
225 g/8 oz cabbage, chopped
1 large onion, chopped
2 carrots, sliced
2 garlic cloves, crushed
2 bay leaves
1 tbsp dried Italian herb seasoning
350 g/12 oz cooked elbow macaroni
salt and freshly ground black pepper, to taste

Combine all the ingredients, except the macaroni, salt and pepper, in a 5.5 litre/9½ pint slow cooker. Cover and cook on Low for 6–8 hours, adding the macaroni during the last 15 minutes. Discard the bay leaves. Season to taste with salt and pepper.

Minestrone Primavera Ⓥ

This version of the famous Italian soup is a medley of vegetables and has chickpeas to make it substantial.

SERVES 8

1.2 litres/2 pints vegetable stock
400 g/14 oz can chickpeas, drained and rinsed
225 g/8 oz cabbage, coarsely grated or finely chopped
400 g/14 oz can chopped tomatoes
150 g/5 oz French beans, cut into short lengths
6 small new potatoes, scrubbed and quartered
2 small onions, chopped
75 g/3 oz leeks (white part only), thinly sliced
2 small carrots, sliced
1 tsp dried Italian herb seasoning
130 g/4½ oz small broccoli florets
75 g/3 oz frozen peas, thawed
100 g/4 oz macaroni, cooked
25 g/1 oz finely chopped parsley (optional)
salt and freshly ground black pepper, to taste
freshly grated Parmesan cheese, to garnish

Combine all the ingredients, except the broccoli, peas, macaroni, parsley, salt and pepper, in a 5.5 litre/9½ pint slow cooker. Cover and cook on Low for 6–8 hours, adding the broccoli, peas and macaroni during the last 30 minutes. Stir in the parsley. Season to taste with salt and pepper. Sprinkle each bowl of soup with Parmesan cheese.

Chickpea and Pasta Minestrone

Flavoured with smoked ham, this vegetable and chickpea soup is filling and tastes great.

SERVES 6

1.5 litres/2½ pints chicken stock
400 g/14 oz can chickpeas, drained and rinsed
400 g/14 oz can tomatoes with herbs, coarsely chopped, with juice
100–150 g/4–5 oz smoked ham, diced
225 g/8 oz cabbage, chopped
1 large onion, chopped
2 large carrots, thinly sliced
2 celery sticks, thinly sliced
2 garlic cloves, crushed
1 tbsp dried Italian herb seasoning
25 g/1 oz orzo
salt and freshly ground black pepper, to taste

Combine all the ingredients, except the orzo, salt and pepper, in a 5.5 litre/9½ pint slow cooker. Cover and cook on Low for 6–8 hours, adding the orzo during the last 20 minutes. Season to taste with salt and pepper.

Meaty Minestrone

The combination of cubes of beef and chunks of pork sausage makes this easy soup extra hearty.

SERVES 8

1.5 litres/2½ pints beef stock
400 g/14 oz can cannellini beans, drained and rinsed
400 g/14 oz can chopped tomatoes
700 g/1½ lb lean stewing or braising steak, cubed
100 g/4 oz herby pork sausage, cut into chunks
1 large onion, chopped
1 celery stick, sliced
2 carrots, sliced
2 garlic cloves, crushed
2 tsp dried basil
1 tsp dried oregano
1 bay leaf
275 g/10 oz French beans, cut into short lengths
50 g/2 oz rotini or shell pasta, cooked
salt and freshly ground black pepper, to taste
freshly grated Parmesan cheese, to garnish

Combine all the ingredients, except the pasta, salt and pepper in a 5.5 litre/9½ pint slow cooker. Cover and cook on Low for 6–8 hours, adding the pasta during the last 15 minutes. Discard the bay leaf. Season to taste with salt and pepper. Sprinkle each bowl of soup with Parmesan cheese.

Vegetarian Minestrone Gratin

Minestrone soups are far too good for vegetarians to miss out on. This is just as satisfying as one created with meat-eaters in mind.

SERVES 8

1.5 litres/2½ pints vegetable stock
400 g/14 oz can cannellini beans, drained and rinsed
400 g/14 oz can red kidney beans, drained and rinsed
400 g/14 oz can chopped tomatoes
1 large onion, chopped
1 celery stick, sliced
2 carrots, sliced
1 large courgette, diced
2 garlic cloves, crushed
2 tsp dried basil
1 tsp dried oregano
1 bay leaf
275 g/10 oz French beans, cut into short lengths
50 g/2 oz rotini or shell pasta, cooked
8 slices French bread
225 g/8 oz Mozzarella cheese, grated
salt and freshly ground black pepper, to taste
chopped fresh parsley, to garnish

Combine all the ingredients, except the pasta, salt, pepper, French bread and cheese, in a 5.5 litre/9½ pint slow cooker. Cover and cook on Low for 6–8 hours, adding the pasta during the last 15 minutes. Toast the French bread under the grill. Sprinkle each slice with 2 tbsp of the Mozzarella and grill until melted, 1–2 minutes. Discard the bay leaf and season the soup to taste with salt and pepper. Spoon into bowls and top each with a bread slice and a sprinkling of chopped parsley.

Hearty Minestrone with Pepperoni

Pepperoni adds depth to this full-bodied soup. Serve with crusty bread and a salad for an easy, satisfying supper.

SERVES 4

1.5 litres/2½ pints chicken stock
2 x 400 g/14 oz cans plum tomatoes
400 g/14 oz can cannellini or borlotti beans, drained and rinsed
1 large onion, chopped
1 celery stick, coarsely diced
1 red pepper, coarsely diced
2 carrots, coarsely chopped
2 courgettes, coarsely chopped
2 garlic cloves, crushed
50 g/2 oz pepperoni or hard salami, finely diced
1 tbsp dried Italian herb seasoning
90 g/3½ oz cooked elbow macaroni
salt and freshly ground black pepper, to taste

Combine all the ingredients, except the macaroni, salt and pepper, in a 5.5 litre/9½ pint slow cooker. Cover and cook on Low for 6–8 hours, adding the macaroni during the last 15 minutes. Season to taste with salt and pepper.

Italian-style Vegetable Soup Ⓥ

Convenience foods, plus some vegetables you may already have, make this soup so easy to assemble.

SERVES 8

1.5 litres/2½ pints vegetable stock
2 x 400 g/14 oz cans cannellini beans, drained and rinsed
400 g/14 oz ready-made tomato sauce
175 g/6 oz cabbage, chopped
2 onions, chopped
1 large carrot, sliced
1 garlic clove, crushed
1 tsp dried Italian herb seasoning
450 g/1 lb frozen mixed broccoli, sweetcorn and red peppers, thawed
salt and freshly ground black pepper, to taste
Crispy Croûtons (see page 30) or Garlic Croûtons (see page 34), to garnish

Combine all the ingredients, except the thawed vegetables, salt and pepper, in a 5.5 litre/9½ pint slow cooker. Cover and cook on High for 4–5 hours, adding the thawed vegetables during the last 20 minutes. Season to taste with salt and pepper. Divide the croûtons between the soup bowls, then ladle the soup over.

Chickpea and Couscous Soup Ⓥ

Couscous is a traditional partner to chickpeas in this filling soup.

SERVES 6

1.2 litres/2 pints vegetable stock
400 g/14 oz can chopped tomatoes
400 g/14 oz can chickpeas, drained and rinsed
1 courgette, diced
100 g/4 oz small cauliflower florets
½ medium green pepper, diced
1 onion, chopped
1 celery stick, chopped
1 large carrot, chopped
1 bay leaf
1 garlic clove, crushed
¾ tsp ground cumin
¾ tsp dried thyme
a generous pinch of ground cloves
50 g/2 oz couscous
salt and freshly ground black pepper, to taste

Combine all the ingredients, except the couscous, salt and pepper, in a 5.5 litre/9½ pint slow cooker. Cover and cook on High for 4–5 hours. Turn the heat to off and stir in the couscous. Cover and leave to stand for 5–10 minutes. Discard the bay leaf. Season to taste with salt and pepper.

Portuguese Soup

This tasty kale soup is a simplified version of the Portuguese favourite caldo verde. Use linguiça, a Portuguese sausage, for the most authentic flavour, if possible. Brown it in a frying pan, if you like, and drain well. Try spinach instead of kale, for a change.

SERVES 4

1 litre/1¾ pints beef stock
400 g/14 oz can red kidney beans, drained and rinsed
50 g/2 oz ready-made tomato sauce
225 g/8 oz smoked sausage, sliced
3 potatoes, peeled and cubed
2 onions, chopped
½ red pepper, chopped
6 large garlic cloves, crushed
225 g/8 oz kale, sliced
salt and freshly ground black pepper, to taste
Tabasco sauce, to taste

Combine all the ingredients, except the kale, salt, pepper and Tabasco sauce, in the slow cooker. Cover and cook on High for 4–5 hours, adding the kale during the last 15 minutes. Season to taste with salt, pepper and Tabasco sauce.

Pasta Fagioli Ⓥ

A traditional pasta fagioli, with some Mexican-style taste twists!

SERVES 6

750 ml/1¼ pints vegetable stock
2 x 400 g/14 oz cans pinto beans, drained and rinsed
500 g/18 oz tomatoes, chopped
2 onions, chopped
1 green pepper, chopped
1 large carrot, sliced
1 celery stick, chopped
1 garlic clove, crushed
1 jalapeño or other medium-hot chilli, finely chopped
2 tsp dried oregano
175 g/6 oz cooked elbow macaroni
15 g/½ oz chopped fresh coriander
salt and cayenne pepper, to taste

Combine all the ingredients, except the macaroni, coriander, salt and cayenne pepper, in the slow cooker. Cover and cook on High for 4–5 hours, adding the macaroni and coriander during the last 15 minutes. Season to taste with salt and cayenne pepper.

Italian Cannellini and Cabbage Soup Ⓥ

Any white bean, such as butter or haricot, may be substituted for the cannelloni in this caraway-accented soup.

SERVES 8

750 ml/1¼ pints vegetable stock
250 ml/8 fl oz water
400 g/14 oz can cannellini beans, drained and rinsed
350 g/12 oz cabbage, thinly sliced or chopped
1 small onion, coarsely chopped
3 garlic cloves, crushed
1 tsp caraway seeds, crushed

90 g/3½ oz cooked penne
salt and freshly ground black pepper, to taste

Combine all the ingredients, except the pasta, salt and pepper, in the slow cooker. Cover and cook on High for 4–5 hours, adding the pasta during the last 20 minutes. Season to taste with salt and pepper.

Sicilian Summer Tomato Soup

Sun-ripened tomatoes, lots of garlic and a hint of citrus make this Mediterranean soup perfect for a summer's day when tomatoes are at their best.

SERVES 10

1 litre/1¾ pints chicken stock
120 ml/4 fl oz dry white wine or extra chicken stock
50 ml/2 fl oz orange juice
2 tbsp tomato purée
18 plum or vine-ripened tomatoes, peeled, seeded and chopped
2 red onions, finely chopped
2 yellow onions, finely chopped
75 g/3 oz mushrooms, sliced
4 spring onions, chopped
1 carrot, chopped
1 celery stick, chopped
15 g/½ oz chopped fresh parsley
9 large garlic cloves, chopped
1–2 tbsp dried basil
1 tsp sugar
grated zest of 1 orange
700 g/1½ lb spinach, coarsely chopped
salt and freshly ground black pepper, to taste

Combine all the ingredients, except the spinach, salt and pepper, in a 5.5 litre/9½ pint slow cooker. Cover and cook on High for 4–5 hours, adding the spinach during the last 30 minutes. Season to taste with salt and pepper.

Red and White Bean Soup with Bacon and Pasta

The tiny rice-shaped pasta, orzo, goes with many Mediterranean dishes but any small soup pasta works just as well.

SERVES 6

1.5 litres/2½ pints chicken stock
2 x 400 g/14 oz cans cannellini beans, drained and rinsed
400 g/14 oz cans red kidney beans, rinsed and drained
400 g/14 oz ready-made tomato sauce
175 g/6 oz back bacon, thinly sliced
2 onions, chopped
1 large celery stick, chopped
2 tsp dried Italian herb seasoning
50 g/2 oz orzo or soup pasta
salt and freshly ground black pepper, to taste

Combine all the ingredients, except the orzo, salt and pepper, in a 5.5 litre/9½ pint slow cooker. Cover and cook on Low for 6–8 hours, adding the orzo during the last 20 minutes. Season to taste with salt and pepper.

Cannellini Bean and Pasta Soup

If you always keep a couple of cans of cannellini beans in the storecupboard, you will always have what you need for a simple evening meal.

SERVES 4

1 litre/1¾ pints chicken stock
2 x 400 g/14 oz cans cannellini beans, drained and rinsed
130 g/4½ oz back bacon, diced
½ small red pepper, diced

2 garlic cloves, crushed
½ tsp dried marjoram
½ tsp dried sage
100 g/4 oz ditalini
salt and freshly ground black pepper, to taste
Parmesan Croûtons, to garnish (see page 71)

Combine all the ingredients, except the ditalini, salt and pepper, in the slow cooker. Cover and cook on Low for 6–8 hours, adding the pasta during the last 30 minutes. Season to taste with salt and pepper. Sprinkle each bowl of soup with Parmesan Croûtons.

Italian Meatball Soup

Substitute other pastas for the spaghetti, if you like, such as orecchiette (little ears) or conchiglie (shells).

SERVES 8

Italian Turkey Meatballs (see page 176)
2.25 litres/4 pints chicken stock
275 g/10 oz French beans, cut into short lengths
1 large carrot, sliced
4 onions, chopped
5 plum tomatoes, coarsely chopped
2 garlic cloves, crushed
1–2 tsp dried Italian herb seasoning
225 g/8 oz thin spaghetti, broken into 7.5 cm/3 in pieces, cooked
salt and freshly ground black pepper, to taste

Combine all the ingredients, except the pasta, salt and pepper, in a 5.5 litre/ 9½ pint slow cooker. Cover and cook on Low for 6–8 hours, adding the pasta during the last 15–20 minutes. Season to taste with salt and pepper.

Italian Turkey Meatballs

So easy to make, and so delicious in Italian-inspired soups.

MAKES 24–32 MEATBALLS

700 g/1½ lb minced turkey
1 egg
15 g/½ oz seasoned dry breadcrumbs
2 garlic cloves, crushed
1 tbsp dried Italian herb seasoning
¾ tsp salt
½ tsp pepper

Combine all the ingredients in a bowl. Shape the mixture into 24–32 meatballs.

Italian Mushroom and Barley Soup ⓥ

For variation, substitute a 400 g/14 oz can drained, rinsed borlotti beans for the barley in this comforting Italian soup.

SERVES 6

1.5 litres/2½ pints vegetable stock
450 ml/¾ pint tomato juice
400 g/14 oz can chopped tomatoes
90 g/3½ oz pearl barley
250 g/9 oz mushrooms, sliced
2 small carrots, chopped
2 small onions, chopped
2 garlic cloves, crushed
1 tsp dried basil
1 tsp dried oregano
salt and freshly ground black pepper, to taste
soured cream, to garnish

Combine all the ingredients, except the salt and pepper, in a 5.5 litre/9½ pint slow cooker. Cover and cook on Low for 6–8 hours. Season to taste with salt and pepper. Top each bowl of soup with a dollop of soured cream.

Kale and Ravioli Soup ⓥ

Fresh ravioli or tortellini can be cooked in the slow cooker or cooked in advance and added to the slow cooker at the end of cooking time. You could use spinach instead of kale.

SERVES 6

1 litre/1¾ pints vegetable stock
450 ml/¾ pint water
1 carrot, sliced
200 g/7 oz plum or vine-ripened tomatoes, chopped
2 onions, chopped
1 large celery stick, chopped
2 garlic cloves, crushed
¾ tsp dried basil
¾ tsp dried rosemary
250 g/9 oz fresh herb ravioli
225 g/8 oz kale, coarsely chopped
2–3 tsp lemon juice
salt and freshly ground black pepper, to taste

Combine all the ingredients, except the ravioli, kale, lemon juice, salt and pepper, in a 5.5 litre/9½ pint slow cooker. Cover and cook on Low for 6–8 hours. Add the ravioli and kale, and continue cooking until the ravioli float to the top, about 10–15 minutes. Season to taste with lemon juice, salt and pepper.

Curry Meatballs

You can use a little more or less curry powder according to your preference.

MAKES 12–16 MEATBALLS

225 g/8 oz lean minced beef
1 small onion, minced or very finely chopped
1½ tsp curry powder
½ tsp salt
¼ tsp pepper

Combine all the ingredients in a bowl. Shape the mixture into 12–16 meatballs.

Curry Soup with Meatballs

This lightly thickened soup is delicately flavoured with curry and mint and tastes good with Curry Meatballs.

SERVES 4

Curry Meatballs (see page 176)
1.2 litres/2 pints beef stock
1 onion, chopped
2 tsp crushed garlic
2 tsp curry powder
50 g/2 oz vermicelli, broken into 5 cm/2 in pieces, cooked
salt and freshly ground black pepper, to taste
15 g/½ oz fresh mint, chopped

Combine all the ingredients, except the pasta, salt, pepper and mint, in the slow cooker. Cover and cook on High for 4–5 hours, adding the pasta during the last 15 minutes. Season to taste with salt and pepper. Stir in the mint.

Mulligatawny

A colourful soup, lightly spiced with curry powder.

SERVES 8

1.2 litres/2 pints chicken stock
450 g/1 lb skinless chicken breast fillets, halved
400 g/14 oz can chopped tomatoes
3 onions, coarsely chopped
175 g/6 oz cooking apples, coarsely chopped
1 celery stick, sliced
1 carrot, sliced
½ red pepper, sliced
75 g/3 oz waxy potatoes, peeled and diced
1 large garlic clove, crushed
2½ tsp curry powder
1 tsp chilli powder
½ tsp ground allspice

½ tsp dried thyme
15 g/½ oz fresh parsley, coarsely chopped
salt and freshly ground black pepper, to taste

Combine all the ingredients, except the parsley, salt and pepper, in a 5.5 litre/9½ pint slow cooker. Cover and cook on Low for 6–8 hours. Stir in the parsley. Season to taste with salt and pepper.

Indian-style Potato and Spinach Soup with Chicken

The combination of herbs and spices gives this soup an exotic flavour and aroma.

SERVES 6

750 ml/1¼ pints chicken stock
350 g/12 oz skinless chicken breast fillets, diced
400 g/14 oz can chopped tomatoes
350 g/12 oz baking potatoes, peeled and cubed
2 onions, chopped
2 large garlic cloves, crushed
½ tsp caraway seeds
½ tsp ground cardamom
1½ tbsp mild or hot curry powder
2 tsp ground coriander
275 g/10 oz frozen chopped spinach, thawed and drained
salt and freshly ground black pepper, to taste

Combine all the ingredients, except the spinach, salt and pepper, in the slow cooker. Cover and cook on Low for 6–8 hours, adding the spinach during the last 20 minutes. Season to taste with salt and pepper.

Indian Lentil Soup Ⓥ

This soup from India, dal shorba, is flavoured with curry spices. Red or green lentils can also be used.

SERVES 8

1 litre/1¾ pints vegetable stock
1 litre/1¾ pints water
350 g/12 oz dried brown lentils
1 onion, chopped
1 garlic clove, crushed
2 tsp curry powder
1 tsp coriander seeds, crushed
1 tsp cumin seeds, crushed
½ tsp ground turmeric
¼ tsp crushed chilli flakes
salt and freshly ground black pepper, to taste
6 tbsp plain yoghurt

Combine all the ingredients, except the salt, pepper and yoghurt, in a 5.5 litre/9½ pint slow cooker. Cover and cook on Low for 6–8 hours. Season to taste with salt and pepper. Top each bowl of soup with a tablespoonful of yoghurt.

Spiced Chicken Soup

This piquant chicken soup is delicious served with warm pitta bread for a light meal.

SERVES 8

2.25 litres/4 pints chicken stock
700 g/1½ lb skinless chicken breast fillets, cubed (2 cm/¾ in)
1 onion, thinly sliced
6 peppercorns
2 tsp ground coriander
1 tsp ground turmeric
1 tsp ground ginger
¼ tsp crushed chilli flakes
1½ tsp cider vinegar
salt and freshly ground black pepper, to taste
chopped fresh coriander, to garnish

Combine all the ingredients, except the chilli, vinegar, salt and pepper, in a 5.5 litre/9½ pint slow cooker. Cover and cook on Low for 6–8 hours, adding the chilli flakes and vinegar during the last 30 minutes. Season to taste with salt and pepper. Garnish each bowl of soup with chopped fresh coriander.

Russian Cabbage Soup

Red cabbage and beetroot gives this soup a bright colour and good flavour. You can use green cabbage instead of red if you like.

SERVES 8

1.5 litres/2½ pints beef stock
400 g/14 oz can chopped tomatoes
700 g/1½ lb red cabbage, thinly sliced
4 large beetroots, peeled and cubed (1 cm/½ in)
1 large carrot, sliced
2 onions, sliced
150 g/5 oz turnip, cubed
175 g/6 oz potato, peeled and cubed
1 tbsp cider vinegar
salt and freshly ground black pepper, to taste
8 tbsp soured cream

Combine all the ingredients, except the salt, pepper and soured cream, in a 5.5 litre/9½ pint slow cooker. Cover and cook on Low for 6–8 hours. Season to taste with salt and pepper. Top each bowl of soup with a tablespoonful of soured cream.

Hearty Beef and Vegetable Soup

A delicious and convenient use for leftover cooked beef. If using raw beef, add it at the beginning.

SERVES 8

1 litre/1¾ pints Fragrant Beef Stock (see page 26) or beef stock
450 ml/¾ pint tomato juice
350 g/12 oz green or red cabbage, shredded
2 onions, thinly sliced
1 large carrot, thinly sliced
75 g/3 oz mushrooms, thinly sliced
175 g/6 oz potatoes, unpeeled and cubed
1 tsp caraway seeds
1 tsp paprika
600 g/1 lb 6 oz cooked lean beef, cubed
2 tbsp raisins
1 tbsp sugar
2–3 tsp vinegar
salt and freshly ground black pepper, to taste
Dill Soured Cream (see below)

Combine the stock, tomato juice, vegetables, caraway seeds and paprika in a 5.5 litre/9½ pint slow cooker. Cover and cook on Low for 6–8 hours, adding the beef, raisins, sugar and vinegar during the last 30 minutes. Season to taste with salt and pepper. Garnish the bowls of soup with dollops of Dill Soured Cream.

Dill Soured Cream Ⓥ

A delicious mix to swirl into borscht or use as a dip.

SERVES 6 AS AN ACCOMPANIMENT

175 ml/6 fl oz soured cream
2 tbsp fresh or 1 tbsp dried dill
1–2 tsp lemon juice

Mix all the ingredients.

Cabbage and Vegetable Soup Ⓥ

Garlic Croûtons are the ideal finishing touch for this soup, but it would also be good with chunks of fresh crusty white or wholemeal bread.

SERVES 8

1 litre/1¾ pints vegetable stock
450 ml/¾ pint tomato juice
400 g/14 oz can haricot beans, rinsed and drained
400 g/14 oz can red kidney beans, rinsed and drained
350 g/12 oz green or red cabbage, shredded
2 onions, thinly sliced
1 large carrot, thinly sliced
75 g/3 oz mushrooms, thinly sliced
175 g/6 oz potatoes, unpeeled and cubed
1 tsp caraway seeds
1 tsp paprika
2 tbsp raisins
1 tbsp sugar
2–3 tsp vinegar
salt and freshly ground black pepper, to taste
Garlic Croûtons, to garnish (see page 34)

Combine the stock, tomato juice, beans, vegetables, caraway seeds and paprika in a 5.5 litre/9½ pint slow cooker. Cover and cook on Low for 6–8 hours, adding the raisins, sugar and vinegar during the last 30 minutes. Season to taste with salt and pepper. Garnish the bowls of soup with Garlic Croûtons.

Beef Borscht

The traditional beetroot soup tastes good with the cubes of lean beef, which makes it a sustaining meal.

SERVES 8

2.25 litres/4 pints beef stock
350 g/12 oz lean braising beef, cubed
450 g/1 lb beetroots, peeled and cubed
350 g/12 oz red or green cabbage,
    shredded
3 small carrots, sliced
2 onions, chopped
1 tbsp dried dill
50–75 ml/2–2½ fl oz cider vinegar
salt and freshly ground black pepper,
    to taste
soured cream, to garnish

Combine all the ingredients, except the vinegar, salt and pepper, in a 5.5 litre/9½ pint slow cooker. Cover and cook on Low for 6–8 hours, adding the vinegar during the last hour. Season to taste with salt and pepper. Garnish each bowl of soup with a dollop of soured cream.

Borscht with Sausage

This traditional soup contains garlicky Polish sausage. Choose one that has a high meat content for the best flavour.

SERVES 8

1.5 litres/2½ pints beef stock
225 g/8 oz smoked Polish sausage
1 small red cabbage, thinly sliced
4 medium beetroots, peeled and
    cubed
2 carrots, sliced
1 garlic clove, crushed
1 bay leaf
2–3 tsp sugar
2 tbsp cider vinegar
salt and freshly ground black pepper,
    to taste
chopped fresh dill, to garnish

Combine all the ingredients, except the sugar, vinegar, salt and pepper, in a 5.5 litre/9½ pint slow cooker. Cover and cook on High for 4–5 hours, adding the sugar and vinegar during the last hour. Remove the sausage, then slice it and return it to the soup. Discard the bay leaf. Season to taste with salt and pepper. Sprinkle each bowl of soup with dill.

Russian Borscht

This Russian soup makes a hearty cold weather meal.

SERVES 6

1.2 litres/2 pints beef stock
400 g/14 oz can chopped tomatoes
450 g/1 lb cabbage, thinly sliced
275 g/10 oz beetroots, grated
2 large carrots, grated
2 onions, chopped
150 g/5 oz turnip, grated
1 tbsp sugar
2 bay leaves
1 tsp dried thyme
3–4 tbsp red wine vinegar
salt and freshly ground black pepper,
    to taste
Dill Soured Cream (see page 179)

Combine all the ingredients, except the vinegar, salt, pepper and Dill Soured Cream, in a 5.5 litre/9½ pint slow cooker. Cover and cook on Low for 6–8 hours. Season to taste with vinegar, salt and pepper. Discard the bay leaves. Dollop each bowl of soup with Dill Soured Cream.

Eastern European Borscht

Slow cooking enhances the flavours in this favourite borscht that includes beef and smoked sausage.

SERVES 12

2.25 litres/4 pints water
450 g/1 lb lean stewing or braising steak, cubed
700 g/1½ lb smoked sausage, sliced
450 g/1 lb cabbage, shredded
500 g/18 oz beetroots, cooked, peeled and coarsely grated
450 g/1 lb potatoes, peeled and grated
1 large carrot, grated
2 onions, sliced
2 tbsp red wine vinegar
1 tsp sugar
2 tsp dried marjoram
2 tsp dried dill
salt and freshly ground black pepper, to taste
250 ml/8 fl oz soured cream
15 g/½ oz chopped fresh dill

Combine all the ingredients, except the salt, pepper, soured cream and dill, in a 5.5 litre/9½ pint slow cooker. Cover and cook on Low for 6–8 hours. Season to taste with salt and pepper. Garnish each bowl of soup with a generous dollop of soured cream and sprinkle with dill.

Goulash Soup

If you like, stir combined 175 ml/6 fl oz of soured cream and 1 tbsp of cornflour into the soup at the end of the cooking time. Stir for 2–3 minutes.

SERVES 6

1.5 litres/2½ pints beef stock
450 g/1 lb lean braising steak, cubed
350 g/12 oz potatoes, peeled and diced
2 onions, chopped
150 g/5 oz French beans, cut into 2 cm/¾ in lengths
1 carrot, thinly sliced
1 celery stick, diced
2 large garlic cloves, crushed
50 g/2 oz pearl barley
1 bay leaf
1½ tsp paprika
½ tsp dried thyme
½ tsp dry mustard powder
400 g/14 oz ready-made tomato sauce
salt and freshly ground black pepper, to taste

Combine all the ingredients, except the tomato sauce, salt and pepper, in a 5.5 litre/9½ pint slow cooker. Cover and cook on Low for 6–8 hours, adding the tomato sauce during the last hour. Discard the bay leaf. Season to taste with salt and pepper.

Goulash Bean Soup

Caraway seeds and paprika give a Hungarian accent to this vegetable, beef and bean soup.

SERVES 8

1 litre/1¾ pints beef stock
2 x 400 g/14 oz cans red kidney
    beans, drained and rinsed
400 g/14 oz can chopped tomatoes
700 g/1½ lb lean rump steak, cubed
350 g/12 oz cabbage, sliced
4 onions, chopped
1 large carrot, chopped
1 red pepper, chopped
3 large garlic cloves, crushed
1 tbsp paprika
2 tsp caraway seeds, crushed
1 tsp dried thyme
salt and freshly ground black pepper,
    to taste
120 ml/4 fl oz soured cream

Combine all the ingredients, except the salt, pepper and soured cream, in a 5.5 litre/9½ pint slow cooker. Cover and cook on Low for 6–8 hours. Season to taste with salt and pepper. Top each bowl of soup with dollops of soured cream.

Spicy North African-style Chicken Soup

Here are the tangy flavours and hearty textures of North African cuisine.

SERVES 6

1.5 litres/2½ pints chicken stock
400 g/14 oz can tomatoes
450 g/1 lb skinless chicken breast
    fillets, cubed
6 onions, coarsely chopped
1 celery stick, sliced
50 g/2 oz bulghar wheat
2 large garlic cloves, crushed
1 cinnamon stick
2 large bay leaves
¾ tsp dried marjoram
¾ tsp dried thyme
a pinch of ground cloves
salt and freshly ground black pepper,
    to taste

Combine all the ingredients, except the salt and pepper, in a 5.5 litre/ 9½ pint slow cooker. Cover and cook on Low for 6–8 hours. Discard the cinnamon stick and bay leaves. Season to taste with salt and pepper.

Basque Vegetable Soup

Lots of garlic and thyme gives this tasty chickpea soup a Spanish theme.

SERVES 8

2.5 litres/4¼ pints chicken stock
120 ml/4 fl oz dry red wine or chicken
  stock
700 g/1½ lb skinless chicken breast
  fillets, cubed
2 x 400 g/14 oz cans chickpeas,
  drained and rinsed
450 g/1 lb cabbage, coarsely shredded
2 onions, chopped
100 g/4 oz leeks (white parts only),
  chopped
175 g/6 oz potatoes, unpeeled and
  cubed
65 g/2½ oz turnip, cubed
1 carrot, chopped
½ red pepper, chopped
½ green pepper, chopped
5 large garlic cloves, chopped
2 tsp dried thyme
salt and freshly ground black pepper,
  to taste
Garlic Croûtons, to garnish (see page 34)

Combine all the ingredients, except
the salt and pepper, in a 5.5 litre/
9½ pint slow cooker. Cover and cook on
Low for 6–8 hours. Season to taste with
salt and pepper. Sprinkle each bowl of
soup with Garlic Croûtons.

Oriental Soup with Noodles and Chicken

Just a few dried oriental mushrooms will give a dish a good, strong flavour.

SERVES 4

25 g/1 oz dried cloud ear or shiitake
  mushrooms
750 ml/1¼ pints chicken stock
2 tbsp dry sherry (optional)
225 g/8 oz skinless chicken breast
  fillets, cubed
50 g/2 oz button mushrooms, sliced
1 carrot, sliced
1½ tsp light soy sauce
½ tsp Chinese five-spice powder
50 g/2 oz mangetouts, trimmed
150 g/5 oz dried medium egg noodles
salt and freshly ground black pepper,
  to taste

Put the dried mushrooms in a bowl
and pour hot water over to cover.
Leave to stand until the mushrooms
are soft, about 15 minutes. Drain.
Slice the mushrooms, discarding any
tough parts and the stalks of shiitake.

Combine the mushrooms and remaining
ingredients, except the mangetouts,
noodles, salt and pepper, in the slow
cooker. Cover and cook on High for
4–5 hours, adding the mangetouts and
noodles during the last 20 minutes.
Season to taste with salt and pepper.

East Meets West Soup

This creamy, hotly spiced soup is garnished with crisp Chilli-seasoned Wontons.

SERVES 6

1 litre/1¾ pints chicken stock
225 g/8 oz green chillies from a jar,
    drained and chopped
2 onions, thinly sliced
1 large celery stick, thinly sliced
1 small jalapeño or other medium-hot
    chilli, finely chopped
2.5 cm/1 in piece fresh root ginger,
    finely grated
3 large garlic cloves, crushed
1 tsp ground cumin
250 ml/8 fl oz semi-skimmed milk
2 tbsp cornflour
salt and freshly ground black pepper,
    to taste
15 g/½ oz fresh coriander, chopped
Chilli-seasoned Wontons (see below)

Combine all the ingredients, except the milk, cornflour, salt, pepper, coriander and Chilli-seasoned Wontons, in the slow cooker. Cover and cook on Low for 6–8 hours. Stir in the combined milk and cornflour, stirring for 2–3 minutes. Season to taste with salt and pepper. Stir in the coriander. Serve with Chilli-seasoned Wontons.

Chilli-seasoned Wontons

These are great in soups, as above, but also make tasty finger-food.

MAKES 36

1 tsp hot chilli powder
½ tsp garlic powder
¼ tsp cayenne pepper
2 tsp canola oil
2 tsp water
18 wonton wrappers, cut diagonally
    into halves.

To make the wontons, combine all the wonton ingredients, except the wrappers. Brush both sides of the wrappers with the mixture and put on a baking sheet. Bake at 190°C/gas 5/fan oven 170°C until crisp, about 5 minutes. Cool on wire racks.

Chicken Wonton Soup

The wontons can be prepared ahead and refrigerated, covered, for several hours before cooking.

SERVES 6

1 litre/1¾ pints chicken stock
225 g/8 oz baby sweetcorn, fresh or
    canned drained and rinsed
½ red pepper, chopped
1 carrot, chopped
2 cm/¾ in piece fresh root ginger,
    finely grated
2 tsp soy sauce
1 tsp toasted sesame oil
65 g/2½ oz spinach leaves, sliced
Chicken Wontons (see page 185)
salt and cayenne pepper, to taste

Combine all the ingredients, except the sesame oil, spinach, Chicken Wontons, salt and cayenne pepper, in the slow cooker. Cover and cook on Low for 4–5 hours, adding the spinach during the last 10 minutes. Stir in the Chicken Wontons. Season to taste with salt and cayenne pepper.

Chicken Wontons

Chicken wontons are first-class in the previous soup recipe and they also make tasty finger-food at parties.

MAKES 24

225 g/8 oz skinless chicken breast fillets
3 spring onions, sliced
1 cm/½ in piece fresh root ginger, finely grated
24 wonton wrappers

Process all the ingredients, except the wrappers, in a food processor until finely chopped. Place 1 mounded teaspoonful of the chicken mixture on to each wrapper. Moisten the edges with water and fold in half diagonally to create triangles, sealing the edges. Cook the wontons in a large pan of boiling water until they float to the top, 5–7 minutes. Drain and serve.

Sour Sauce Ⓥ

A very delicate balance of sweet and sour. You can substitute distilled white vinegar for the rice vinegar and soy sauce for the tamari sauce if you wish.

SERVES 6 AS AN ACCOMPANIMENT

3 tbsp rice vinegar
1 tbsp tamari sauce
2 tbsp light brown sugar

Mix all the ingredients together until the sugar has dissolved.

Hot-and-sour Soup Ⓥ

The hot-and-sour contrasts makes this Mandarin soup a unique dish. The hot chilli sesame oil and Sour Sauce that accompany it are intensely flavoured, so use them sparingly.

SERVES 6

25 g/1 oz dried Chinese black mushrooms
175 ml/6 fl oz boiling water
1 litre/1¾ pints vegetable stock
350 g/12 oz tempeh or tofu, cubed
100 g/4 oz bamboo shoots
50 ml/2 fl oz rice vinegar or white distilled vinegar
2 tbsp tamari or soy sauce
2.5 cm/1 in piece fresh root ginger, finely grated
1 tbsp brown sugar
1 tbsp cornflour
3 tbsp water
salt and freshly ground black pepper, to taste
1 egg, lightly beaten
1 tsp toasted sesame oil
12–18 drops hot chilli sesame oil or Szechuan chilli sauce
Sour Sauce (see opposite)

Put the mushrooms in a small bowl and pour the boiling water over. Leave to stand until the mushrooms have softened, 15–20 minutes. Drain, reserving the liquid. Slice the mushrooms, discarding the tough stems. Combine the mushrooms and reserved liquid, stock, tempeh or tofu, bamboo shoots, vinegar, tamari or soy sauce, ginger and brown sugar in the slow cooker. Cover and cook on High for 2–3 hours. Stir in the combined cornflour and water, stirring for 2–3 minutes. Season to taste with salt and pepper. Slowly stir the egg into the soup. Stir in the sesame oil. Serve with hot chilli oil and Sour Sauce.

Asian Mushroom Soup with Soba Noodles Ⓥ

The pungent taste of just a few shiitake mushrooms lifts the overall mushroom flavour of this light Asian soup. Thin egg noodles or spaghetti can be substituted for the soba noodles.

SERVES 6

750 ml/1¼ pints boiling water
25 g/1 oz dried shiitake mushrooms
1 litre/1¾ pints vegetable stock
700 g/1½ lb brown cap mushrooms, finely chopped
½ small onion, finely chopped
1 garlic clove, crushed
½ tsp dried thyme
120 ml/4 fl oz dry white wine (optional)
100 g/4 oz soba noodles, cooked
225 g/8 oz mangetouts, trimmed
10 radishes, sliced
1 tbsp red wine vinegar
salt and freshly ground black pepper, to taste

Pour the boiling water over the shiitake mushrooms in a bowl and leave to stand until softened, about 15 minutes. Drain the liquid into a bowl. Strain the liquid through a fine sieve and reserve. Finely chop the mushrooms, discarding the tough stalks.

Combine the shiitake mushrooms, reserved liquid and remaining ingredients, except the noodles, mangetouts, radishes, vinegar, salt and pepper, in a 5.5 litre/9½ pint slow cooker. Cover and cook on High for 4–5 hours, adding the noodles, mangetouts, radishes and vinegar during the last 20 minutes. Season to taste with salt and pepper.

Asian Shiitake and Noodle Soup

Shiitake mushrooms and Japanese udon noodles give this soup its distinctively full flavour.

SERVES 6

1 litre/1¾ pints beef stock
75 g/3 oz thinly sliced shiitake or other wild mushrooms, tough stems discarded
1 red pepper, chopped
1 large carrot, chopped
2 spring onions, sliced
1 cm/½ in piece fresh root ginger, finely grated
1 garlic clove, crushed
1 tsp toasted sesame oil
1 tsp tamari or soy sauce
65 g/2½ oz spinach, sliced
salt and freshly ground black pepper, to taste
225 g/8 oz Japanese udon noodles, cooked, warm

Combine all the ingredients, except the sesame oil, tamari or soy sauce, spinach, salt, pepper and noodles, in the slow cooker. Cover and cook on High for 4–6 hours, adding the sesame oil, tamari or soy sauce and spinach during the last 10 minutes. Season to taste with salt and pepper. Put the noodles in bowls and ladle the soup over.

Chillies

For those who like their dishes spicy, here's a selection of hot chillies – although you can vary the heat according to your own taste.

Chicken Chilli with Orange Coriander Rice

A piquant, aromatic chilli.

SERVES 6

450 g/1 lb skinless chicken breast fillets, cubed
2 x 400 g/14 oz cans chopped tomatoes
400 g/14 oz can cannellini beans, drained and rinsed
1 onion, chopped
1 garlic clove, crushed
2 tsp chilli powder
½ tsp ground cumin
¼ tsp ground allspice
1 strip orange zest
salt and freshly ground black pepper
chopped fresh coriander, to garnish
Orange Coriander Rice (see below)

Combine all the ingredients, except the salt, pepper, coriander and Orange Coriander Rice, in the slow cooker. Cover and cook on Low for 6–8 hours. Season to taste with salt and pepper. Garnish the chilli with fresh coriander and serve with Orange Coriander Rice.

Orange Coriander Rice Ⓥ

A beautifully fragrant rice dish.

SERVES 6

4 spring onions, sliced
oil, for greasing
225 g/8 oz long-grain rice
grated zest of 1 small orange
500 ml/17 fl oz water
2 tbsp finely chopped fresh coriander
salt and freshly ground black pepper

Sauté the onions in a lightly greased medium pan until tender, 3–5 minutes. Add the rice and orange zest. Stir over medium heat until the rice is lightly browned, 2–3 minutes. Add the water and heat to boiling. Reduce the heat and simmer, covered, until the rice is tender, 20–25 minutes. Stir in the coriander. Season to taste with salt and pepper.

White Chilli

Tomatillos can occasionally be bought, when in season, at ethnic markets, so if you are lucky enough to find them try the Tomatillo Salsa to serve with this chicken chilli, although a bought salsa also works very well.

SERVES 8

450 g/1 lb skinless chicken breast fillets, cubed (2 cm/¾ in)
450 ml/¾ pint chicken stock
2 x 400 g/14 oz cans cannellini beans, drained and rinsed
1 red or green pepper, chopped
2 onions, chopped
2 garlic cloves, crushed
2 tsp finely chopped jalapeño or other medium-hot chilli
2 cm/¾ in piece fresh root ginger, finely grated
1 tsp dried thyme
1 tsp dried oregano
1 tbsp cornflour
salt and freshly ground black pepper
Tomatillo Salsa (see page 188)
soured cream, to garnish

Combine all the ingredients, except 120 ml/4 fl oz of the stock, the cornflour, salt, pepper and Tomatillo Salsa, in the slow cooker. Cover and cook on Low for 6–8 hours. Cook on High for 10 minutes. Stir in the combined remaining stock and the cornflour, stirring for 2–3 minutes. Season to taste with salt and pepper. Serve with Tomatillo Salsa and soured cream.

Tomatillo Salsa Ⓥ

You can buy tomatillos in major supermarkets or ethnic stores.

SERVES 8 AS AN ACCOMPANIMENT

350 g/12 oz tomatillos, husked
½ small onion, chopped
1 tbsp finely chopped fresh coriander
1 tsp crushed jalapeño or other
   medium-hot chilli
1 garlic clove, crushed
¼ tsp ground cumin
a pinch of sugar
salt, to taste

Simmer the tomatillos in water to cover in a large pan until tender, 5–8 minutes. Cool and drain, reserving the liquid. Process the tomatillos and the remaining ingredients, except the salt, in a food processor or blender until almost smooth, adding enough reserved liquid to make a medium dipping consistency. Season to taste with salt.

Sweet and Spicy Chilli

Chicken with sweet potatoes and warm spices, combined with chilli and fresh root ginger, make a dish that really packs a punch.

SERVES 6

450 g/1 lb skinless chicken breast
   fillets, cubed (2 cm/¾ in)
750 ml/1¼ pints chicken stock
2 x 400 g/14 oz cans cannellini beans,
   drained and rinsed
3 onions, chopped
225 g/8 oz mushrooms, quartered
2 sweet potatoes, peeled and cubed
   (2 cm/¾ in)
2 garlic cloves, crushed
2 cm/¾ in piece fresh root ginger,

finely grated
2 tsp finely grated jalapeño or other
   medium-hot chilli
1 tsp dried oregano
1 tsp dried ground cumin
½ tsp ground coriander
½ tsp ground cinnamon
salt and white pepper, to taste
soured cream, to garnish

Combine all the ingredients, except the salt and pepper in a 5.5 litre/9½ pint slow cooker. Cover and cook on Low for 6–8 hours. Season to taste with salt and pepper. Serve with soured cream.

Roasted Pepper Chilli

Here's a turkey chilli with a lean and healthful profile. For crunch, serve it topped with crumbled tortilla chips.

SERVES 4

450 g/1 lb minced turkey
2 x 400 g/14 oz cans tomatoes
400 g/14 oz can black beans or red
   kidney beans, drained and rinsed
2 red onions, chopped
½ roasted red pepper from a jar,
   coarsely chopped
1 small jalapeño or other medium-hot
   chilli, finely chopped
1 tbsp chilli powder (optional)
½ tsp ground cumin
¼ tsp ground allspice
salt and freshly ground black pepper,
   to taste

Cook the turkey in a lightly greased frying pan over medium heat until browned, about 5 minutes, crumbling it with a fork. Combine the turkey and the remaining ingredients, except the salt and pepper, in the slow cooker. Cover and cook on Low for 6–8 hours. Season to taste with salt and pepper.

California Chilli

This hot and zesty chicken chilli has the crunch of sunflower seeds and the smoothness of avocado to top it off.

SERVES 6

450 g/1 lb skinless chicken breast fillets, cubed (2.5 cm/1 in)
750 g/1¾ lb plum or vine-ripened tomatoes, sliced
50 g/2 oz softened sun-dried tomatoes (not in oil), diced
250 ml/8 fl oz dry red wine or chicken stock
1–2 tbsp chilli powder
1 tsp crushed mixed peppercorns
¼–½ tsp crushed chilli flakes
1 avocado, chopped
2 tbsp sunflower seeds, toasted
salt, to taste
6 tbsp chopped fresh basil, to garnish

Combine all the ingredients, except the avocado, sunflower seeds and salt, in the slow cooker. Cover and cook on Low for 6–8 hours. Stir in the avocado and sunflower seeds. Season to taste with salt. Sprinkle each bowl of chilli with basil.

Big Red Chilli

A spicy beef chilli with lots of kick that includes red onion, red kidney beans, red pepper and chopped tomatoes.

SERVES 4

225 g/8 oz lean minced beef
2 x 400 g/14 oz cans chopped tomatoes
400 g/14 oz can red kidney beans, drained and rinsed
1 large red onion, chopped
1 red pepper, chopped
2 tbsp red wine vinegar
2 tbsp chilli powder

¼ tsp ground allspice
150 g/5 oz ready-made tomato and chilli pasta sauce
salt and freshly ground black pepper, to taste

Cook the beef in a lightly greased large frying pan over medium heat until browned, about 5 minutes, crumbling it with a fork. Combine the beef and the remaining ingredients, except the salt and pepper, in the slow cooker. Cover and cook on Low for 6–8 hours. Season to taste with salt and pepper.

Farmhouse Chilli

A lovely pork chilli with sage and sweetened with maple syrup.

SERVES 4

225 g/8 oz crumbled pork sausage
2 x 400 g/14 oz cans chopped tomatoes
400 g/14 oz can red kidney beans, drained and rinsed
1 large red onion, chopped
1 red pepper, chopped
2 tbsp red wine vinegar
1–2 tbsp maple syrup
1 tbsp chilli powder
¾ tsp ground cumin
¾ tsp dried sage
150 ml/¼ pint tomato juice
salt and freshly ground black pepper, to taste

Cook the pork in a lightly greased large frying pan over medium heat until browned, about 5 minutes, crumbling it with a fork. Combine the pork and the remaining ingredients, except the salt and pepper, in the slow cooker. Cover and cook on Low for 6–8 hours. Season to taste with salt and pepper.

Corn and Bean con Carne

As with all recipes with minced beef, try to buy the best quality with very little fat. Serve this dish with Cornmeal Crisps.

SERVES 8

350 g/12 oz lean minced beef
oil, for greasing
2 x 400 g/14 oz cans chopped tomatoes
2 x 400 g/14 oz cans kidney beans, drained and rinsed
1 litre/1¾ pints beef stock
225 g/8 oz sweetcorn, thawed if frozen
1 large onion, finely chopped
1–2 tbsp chilli powder, or to taste
1 tsp ground cumin
1 tsp sugar
salt and freshly ground black pepper, to taste
Cornmeal Crisps (see below)

Cook the beef in a lightly greased large frying pan over medium heat until browned, about 8 minutes, crumbling it with a fork. Combine the beef and the remaining ingredients, except the salt, pepper and Cornmeal Crisps, in a 5.5 litre/9½ pint slow cooker. Cover and cook on Low for 6–8 hours. Season to taste with salt and pepper. Serve with Cornmeal Crisps.

Cornmeal Crisps Ⓥ

Perfect with chilli.

SERVES 8 AS AN ACCOMPANIMENT

100 g/4 oz self-raising flour
40 g/1½ oz polenta
1 tbsp sugar
50 g/2 oz chilled butter or margarine, cut into pieces
1 tbsp distilled white vinegar
50 ml/2 fl oz iced water
oil, for greasing
1 egg white, beaten
2–3 tbsp freshly grated Parmesan cheese

Combine the flour, polenta and sugar in a small bowl. Cut in the butter with a pastry cutter, or rub in with your fingers, until the mixture resembles coarse crumbs. Mix in the vinegar and enough iced water for the mixture to form a dough. Roll out the dough on a floured surface to about 5 mm/¼ in thickness. Cut into rounds with a biscuit cutter and put on a greased baking sheet. Brush with egg white and sprinkle with Parmesan cheese. Bake at 190°C/gas 5/fan oven 170°C until golden, 7–10 minutes. Cool on a wire rack.

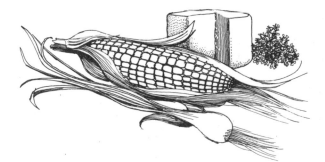

Chilli with Squash and Beans

A squeeze of lime adds a cooling touch to this spicy beef chilli.

SERVES 6

450 g/1 lb lean minced beef
oil, for greasing
750 ml/1¼ pints tomato juice
400 g/14 oz ready-made chunky
    tomato sauce
400 g/14 oz can red kidney beans,
    drained and rinsed
4 onions, sliced
2 large celery sticks, chopped
350 g/12 oz butternut squash, cubed
    (2.5 cm/1 in)
1 red pepper, sliced
130 g/4½ oz courgettes, sliced
75 g/3 oz mushrooms, sliced
½ jalapeño or other medium-hot
    chilli, finely chopped
2 garlic cloves, crushed
1½ tsp chilli powder, or to taste
1½ tsp ground cumin
salt and freshly ground black pepper,
    to taste
6 lime wedges

Cook the minced beef in a lightly greased large frying pan over medium heat until browned, about 8 minutes, crumbling it with a fork. Combine the beef and the remaining ingredients, except the salt, pepper and lime wedges, in a 5.5 litre/ 9½ pint slow cooker. Cover and cook on Low for 6–8 hours. Season to taste with salt and pepper. Serve with lime wedges.

Blizzard Chilli

A great chilli for winter evenings. If you keep some minced beef in the freezer, you'll always be able to cook up a chilli.

SERVES 6

450 g/1 lb lean minced beef
oil, for greasing
750 g/1¾ lb ready-made tomato sauce
275 g/10 oz canned kidney beans,
    drained and rinsed
275 g/10 oz canned black beans or
    black-eyed peas, drained and rinsed
275 g/10 oz canned cannellini beans,
    drained and rinsed
4 onions, finely chopped
1 garlic clove, crushed
1 bay leaf
1 tbsp chilli powder
2 tsp sugar
1 tsp ground cumin
salt and freshly ground black pepper,
    to taste

Cook the minced beef in a lightly greased large frying pan over medium heat until browned, 8–10 minutes, crumbling it with a fork. Combine the beef and the remaining ingredients, except the salt and pepper, in a 5.5 litre/9½ pint slow cooker. Cover and cook on Low for 6–8 hours. Discard the bay leaf. Season to taste with salt and pepper.

Family-favourite Chilli

This very easy chilli will appeal to all ages.

SERVES 8

700 g/1½ lb lean minced beef or turkey
oil, for greasing
2 x 400 g/14 oz cans pinto beans,
   drained and rinsed
2 x 400 g/14 oz cans tomatoes
225 g/8 oz sweetcorn, thawed if frozen
2 onions, chopped
½ green pepper, chopped
2 tbsp taco seasoning mix
1 garlic clove, crushed
½ tsp dried thyme
salt and freshly ground black pepper,
   to taste
soured cream
tortilla chips

Cook the minced beef in a lightly greased
large frying pan over medium heat until
browned, about 10 minutes, crumbling
it with a fork. Combine the beef and the
remaining ingredients, except the salt,
pepper, soured cream and tortilla chips,
in a 5.5 litre/9½ pint slow cooker. Cover
and cook on Low for 6–8 hours. Season
to taste with salt and pepper. Serve
with soured cream and tortilla chips.

Cincinnati Chilli

*The Five-Way Cincinnati Chilli gained
fame in the chilli parlours of that city. The
sauce is seasoned with sweet spices and
a hint of dark chocolate and is served
alone (1 way), over spaghetti (2 ways),
with added beans (3 ways), with chopped
onions (4 ways) and with grated cheese
(5 ways).*

SERVES 8

350 g/12 oz lean ground turkey or beef
oil, for greasing
2 x 400 g/14 oz cans chopped tomatoes
225 g/8 oz tomato sauce
120 ml/4 fl oz water
1 onion, chopped
4 garlic cloves, crushed
2–3 tbsp chilli powder, or to taste
1 tbsp cocoa powder
2 tsp dried oregano
1 tsp ground cinnamon
1 tsp ground allspice
salt and freshly ground black pepper,
   to taste
450 g/1 lb spaghetti, cooked, warm
toppings: canned pinto beans,
   chopped onions, grated Cheddar
   cheese

Cook the turkey in a lightly greased
large frying pan over medium heat until
browned, about 5 minutes, crumbling it
with a fork. Combine the turkey and the
remaining ingredients, except the salt,
pepper and spaghetti, in the slow cooker.
Cover and cook on Low for 6–8 hours.
Season to taste with salt and pepper.
Serve with spaghetti and the toppings.

Chunky Chilli for a Crowd

Make this big batch of chilli for a party and serve it with a do-it-yourself array of garnishes. Or make it for dinner and freeze some for later use.

SERVES 16

1.75 kg/4 lb lean stewing or braising steak, cubed (2.5 cm/1 in)
3 onions, sliced
1½ green peppers, sliced
10 garlic cloves, crushed,
2 jalapeño or other medium-hot chillies, chopped
4 x 400 g/14 oz cans chopped tomatoes
2 x 400 g/14 oz cans pinto beans, drained and rinsed
175 g/6 oz tomato purée
3–4 tbsp chilli powder
1 tsp beef bouillon granules
120 ml/4 fl oz water
25 g/1 oz cornflour
salt and freshly ground black pepper, to taste
Tabasco sauce, to taste

garnishes: baked tortilla chips, grated Cheddar cheese, soured cream, chopped tomatoes, diced avocado, sliced black olives

Combine all the ingredients, except the water, cornflour, salt, pepper and Tabasco sauce, in a 5.5 litre/9½ pint slow cooker. Cover and cook on Low for 6–8 hours. Turn the heat to High. Cook for 10 minutes. Stir in the combined water and cornflour, stirring for 2–3 minutes. Season to taste with salt, pepper and Tabasco sauce. Serve with the garnishes.

Macho Chilli

A real man's chilli – but women will love it too!

SERVES 8

225 g/8 oz pork sausages, casings removed
225 g/8 oz lean minced beef
3 x 400 g/14 oz cans chopped tomatoes
400 g/14 oz can pinto beans, drained and rinsed
400 g/14 oz black beans, drained and rinsed
400 g/14 oz can chickpeas, drained and rinsed
250 ml/8 fl oz dry red wine or tomato juice
3 onions, coarsely chopped
1 green pepper, coarsely chopped
2 garlic cloves, crushed
1 small jalapeño or other medium-hot chilli, finely chopped
50–120 ml/2–4 fl oz Worcestershire sauce
1 tsp dry mustard powder
1 tsp celery seeds
1–2 tbsp chilli powder, or to taste
½ tsp ground cumin
8 bacon rashers, cooked until crisp and crumbled
salt and freshly ground black pepper, to taste

Cook the sausagemeat and minced beef in a lightly greased large frying pan over medium heat until browned, about 10 minutes, crumbling with a fork. Combine the meat and the remaining ingredients, except the bacon, salt and pepper, in a 5.5 litre/9½ pint slow cooker. Cover and cook on Low for 6–8 hours. Stir in the bacon. Season to taste with salt and pepper.

Chilli con Carne

Beer, as well as cumin and oregano, gives this chilli depth of flavour.

SERVES 8

450 g/1 lb lean minced beef
oil, for greasing
2 onions, chopped
1 green pepper, chopped
2 garlic cloves, crushed
1–2 tbsp chilli powder, or to taste
2 tsp ground cumin
2 tsp dried oregano
2 x 400 g/14 oz cans chopped tomatoes
400 g/14 oz can red kidney beans, drained and rinsed
175 g/6 oz tomato purée
175 ml/6 fl oz beer or water
1 tbsp light brown sugar
1 tbsp cocoa powder
salt and freshly ground black pepper, to taste
50 g/2 oz Cheddar cheese, grated
2 spring onions, sliced
120 ml/4 fl oz soured cream

Cook the minced beef in a lightly greased large frying pan over medium heat until the meat is browned, about 10 minutes, crumbling it with a fork. Combine the beef and the remaining ingredients, except the salt, pepper, cheese, spring onions and soured cream, in the slow cooker. Cover and cook on Low for 6–8 hours. Season to taste with salt and pepper. Sprinkle each bowl of chilli with cheese, spring onions and soured cream.

Chilli Mac

This chilli needs no other accompaniment, making it a wonderfully easy meal in itself.

SERVES 8

450 g/1 lb lean minced beef
oil, for greasing
2 onions, chopped
1 green pepper, chopped
2 garlic cloves, crushed
1–2 tbsp chilli powder, or to taste
2 tsp ground cumin
2 tsp dried oregano
2 x 400 g/14 oz cans chopped tomatoes
400 g/14 oz can red kidney beans, drained and rinsed
175 g/6 oz tomato purée
175 ml/6 fl oz beer or water
1 tbsp light brown sugar
1 tbsp cocoa powder
salt and freshly ground black pepper, to taste
200 g/7 oz cooked elbow macaroni
50 g/2 oz Cheddar cheese, grated
2 spring onions, sliced
120 ml/4 fl oz soured cream

Cook the minced beef in a lightly greased large frying pan over medium heat until the meat is browned, about 10 minutes, crumbling it with a fork. Combine the beef and the remaining ingredients, except the salt, pepper, macaroni, cheese, spring onions and soured cream, in the slow cooker. Cover and cook on Low for 6–8 hours. Turn the slow cooker to High, add the macaroni and 120ml/4 fl oz of water and cook for 15 minutes. Season to taste with salt and pepper. Sprinkle each bowl of chilli with cheese, spring onions and soured cream.

Pork Chilli with Greens

Leafy greens add nutrients and colour to this tasty chilli.

SERVES 8

700 g/1½ lb lean minced pork
2 x 400 g/14 oz cans kidney beans, drained and rinsed
2 x 400 g/14 oz cans chopped tomatoes
1 onion, chopped
½ tsp ground cinnamon
½ tsp ground cumin
½–1 tsp crushed chilli flakes
225 g/8 oz curly kale or spinach, coarsely chopped
salt and freshly ground black pepper, to taste

Cook the pork in a lightly greased large frying pan until browned, about 10 minutes, crumbling it with a fork. Combine the pork and the remaining ingredients, except the kale, salt and pepper, in the slow cooker. Cover and cook on Low for 6–8 hours, stirring in the kale during the last 20 minutes. Season to taste with salt and pepper.

South-western Chilli

If you don't have a jalapeño chilli, another hot variety of chilli will be fine.

SERVES 8

450 g/1 lb lean minced beef
oil, for greasing
2 onions, chopped
1 green pepper, chopped
2 garlic cloves, crushed
1 jalapeño chilli, finely chopped
1–2 tbsp chilli powder, or to taste
2 tsp ground cumin
2 tsp dried oregano
2 x 400 g/14 oz cans chopped tomatoes
400 g/14 oz can black or pinto beans, drained and rinsed
175 g/6 oz tomato purée
175 ml/6 fl oz beer or water
1 tbsp light brown sugar
1 tbsp cocoa powder
salt and freshly ground black pepper, to taste
50 g/2 oz Cheddar cheese, grated
2 spring onions, sliced
120 ml/4 fl oz soured cream
chopped fresh coriander, to garnish

Cook the minced beef in a lightly greased large frying pan over medium heat until the meat is browned, about 10 minutes, crumbling it with a fork. Combine the beef and the remaining ingredients, except the salt, pepper, cheese, spring onions and soured cream, in the slow cooker. Cover and cook on Low for 6–8 hours. Season to taste with salt and pepper. Sprinkle each bowl of chilli with cheese, spring onions, soured cream and a little coriander.

Tenderloin Chilli

This super easy chilli contains tender, lean pork and fresh tomatoes. If you prefer a less hot chilli, omit the chilli powder and just use the fresh chillies.

SERVES 4

450 g/1 lb pork tenderloin, cubed (1 cm/½ in)
400 ml/14 fl oz beef stock
400 g/14 oz can pinto beans, drained and rinsed
450 g/1 lb plum or vine-ripened tomatoes, sliced
2 jalapeño or other medium-hot chillies, finely chopped
1 tbsp chilli powder (optional)
1 tsp toasted cumin seeds
1 tsp Worcestershire sauce
salt and freshly ground black pepper, to taste

Combine all the ingredients, except the salt and pepper, in the slow cooker. Cover and cook on High for 4–6 hours. Season to taste with salt and pepper.

Chilli with Rajas

Some claim that raja mirchi chillies are the hottest in the world!·

SERVES 8

2 onions
700 g/1½ lb lean minced beef
2 x 400 g/14 oz cans kidney beans, drained and rinsed
2 x 400 g/14 oz cans chopped tomatoes
½ tsp ground cumin
1–2 tbsp chilli powder
½–1 tsp crushed chilli flakes
2 poblano chillies, thinly sliced
1–2 tbsp olive oil
salt and freshly ground black pepper, to taste

Finely chop one onion. Cook the beef in a lightly greased large frying pan until browned, about 10 minutes, crumbling it with a fork. Combine with the remaining ingredients, except the oil, salt, pepper, chillies and remaining onion, in the slow cooker. Cover and cook on Low for 6–8 hours. Thinly slice the remaining onion. Cook with the chillies in the olive oil in a pan over a medium heat until tender and the onions are caramelised, 15–20 minutes. Season the beef mixture to taste with salt and pepper and the chilli mixture with salt. Top the beef mixture with the chilli mixture.

Habanero Chilli

Substitute jalapeño chilli if you prefer a milder flavour.

SERVES 4

100 g/4 oz pork sausages, casings removed
oil, for greasing
400 g/14 oz can chopped tomatoes
400 g/14 oz can refried beans
1 large onion, chopped
1 medium green pepper, chopped
¼–½ habanero or other hot chilli, chopped

1 tbsp chilli powder
1 tsp ground cumin
salt, to taste
250 ml/8 fl oz soured cream

Cook the sausagemeat in a lightly greased small frying pan until browned, about 5 minutes, crumbling it with a fork. Combine the sausagemeat and the remaining ingredients, except the salt and soured cream, in the slow cooker. Cover and cook on Low for 4–5 hours. Season to taste with salt. Serve with soured cream.

Chilli Rio Grande

Lots of onions and a combination of minced and cubed meats gives this chilli loads of flavour and texture.

SERVES 12

450 g/1 lb lean minced beef
900 g/2 lb lean pork, cubed (2 cm/¾ in)
400 ml/14 fl oz beef stock
2 x 400 g/14 oz cans red kidney beans, drained and rinsed
2 x 400 g/14 oz cans chopped tomatoes
350 ml/12 fl oz beer or tomato juice
100 g/4 oz green chillies from a jar, chopped
8 onions, chopped
6 garlic cloves, crushed
25 g/1 oz chilli powder (optional)
1 tbsp ground cumin
2 tsp dried oregano
salt and freshly ground black pepper, to taste
1½ quantity Coriander-chilli Soured Cream (see page 200)

Cook the minced beef in a lightly greased large frying pan over medium heat until browned, crumbling it with a fork. Combine the beef and the remaining ingredients, except the salt, pepper and Coriander and Chilli Soured Cream, in a 5.5 litre/9½ pint slow cooker. Cover and cook on Low for 6–8 hours. Season to taste with salt and pepper. Serve with dollops of Coriander-chilli Soured Cream.

Texas Hot Chilli

Hot sausage, hot chillies and lots of spices make this chilli extra good.

SERVES 8

350 g/12 oz spicy pork sausages, casings removed
700 g/1½ lb coarsely minced lean beef
400 g/14 oz can chopped tomatoes
400 ml/14 fl oz beef stock
400 g/14 oz tomato sauce from a jar
400 g/14 oz can red kidney beans, drained and rinsed
400 g/14 oz chickpeas, drained and rinsed
100 g/4 oz chopped green chillies from a jar, with liquid
1 large onion, chopped
1 jalapeño or medium chilli, chopped
2 tbsp hot chilli powder
½ tsp ground cumin
½ tsp coriander
1 tbsp low-sodium Worcestershire sauce
salt and cayenne pepper, to taste
Tabasco sauce, to taste

Cook the sausagemeat and minced beef in a lightly greased large frying pan over medium heat until browned, about 10 minutes, crumbling it with a fork. Combine the meat and the remaining ingredients, except the salt, cayenne pepper and Tabasco sauce, in a 5.5 litre/9½ pint slow cooker. Cover and cook on Low for 6–8 hours. Season to taste with salt, cayenne pepper and Tabasco sauce.

Italian-style Chilli

The spicy pepperoni is a wonderful addition to the pork and beef.

SERVES 8

350 g/12 oz spicy pork sausages, casings removed
600 g/1 lb 6 oz minced lean beef
100 g/4 oz sliced pepperoni
400 g/14 oz can chopped tomatoes
400 ml/14 fl oz beef stock
400 g/14 oz tomato sauce from a jar
400 g/14 oz can red kidney beans, drained and rinsed
400 g/14 oz chickpeas, drained and rinsed
1 large onion, chopped
2 tbsp hot chilli powder
1–1½ tsp dried Italian herb seasoning
1 tbsp Worcestershire sauce
salt, to taste
cayenne pepper, to taste
Tabasco sauce, to taste

Cook the sausagemeat and minced beef in a lightly greased large frying pan over medium heat until browned, about 10 minutes, crumbling it with a fork. Combine the meat and the remaining ingredients, except the salt, cayenne pepper and Tabasco sauce, in a 5.5 litre/9½ pint slow cooker. Cover and cook on Low for 6–8 hours. Season to taste with salt, cayenne pepper and Tabasco sauce.

Mesquite Chicken Chilli

This differently delicious Tex-Mex dish will appeal to the adventurous!

SERVES 4

350 g/12 oz skinless chicken breast fillets, cubed
2 x 400 g/14 oz cans chopped tomatoes
400 g/14 oz can red kidney beans, drained and rinsed
225 g/8 oz tomatoes, coarsely chopped
2 small onions, chopped
1 poblano chilli, chopped
2 tbsp chilli powder
2 tsp minced garlic
1 tsp mesquite smoke flavouring
salt and freshly ground black pepper, to taste

Combine all the ingredients, except the salt and pepper, in the slow cooker. Cover and cook on Low for 6–8 hours. Season to taste with salt and pepper.

Veal Chilli Poblano

Minced veal, mild chilli and seasoning mix make this a fast-track favourite.

SERVES 4

450 g/1 lb lean minced veal
400 g/14 oz can chopped tomatoes
**400 g/14 oz can cannellini beans,
    drained and rinsed**
1 large onion, chopped
**1 small poblano or other mild chilli,
    chopped**
1 celery stick, chopped
39g packet chilli seasoning mix
Tortilla Wedges (see right)

Combine all the ingredients, except the Tortilla Wedges, in the slow cooker. Cover and cook on Low for 6–8 hours. Serve with Tortilla Wedges.

Easy Tortilla Chilli

Tortilla chips add crunch and texture here.

SERVES 8

225 g/8 oz lean minced beef
oil, for greasing
900 ml/1½ pints beef stock
**450 g/1 lb ready-made mild or medium
    salsa**
**400 g/14 oz can kidney beans, drained
    and rinsed**
4 onions, chopped
175 g/6 oz sweetcorn, thawed if frozen
1 tsp chilli powder
100 g/4 oz tortilla chips, crushed
salt and freshly ground black pepper
50 g/2 oz Cheddar cheese, grated

Cook the beef in a lightly greased large frying pan over medium heat until browned, about 5 minutes, crumbling it with a fork. Combine the beef, stock, salsa, beans, onions, sweetcorn and chilli powder in a 5.5 litre/9½ pint slow cooker. Cover and cook on Low for 6–8 hours. Stir in the tortilla chips. Season to taste with salt and pepper. Sprinkle with cheese.

Tortilla Wedges Ⓥ

Delicious to accompany Mexican dishes.

SERVES 4 AS AN ACCOMPANIMENT

2 x 15 cm/6 in flour tortillas
25 g/1 oz cheese with chilli, grated
25 g/1 oz Cheddar cheese, grated
3 sliced spring onions
25 g/1 oz mild or hot salsa
soured cream, to garnish

Put the tortillas on a baking sheet. Sprinkle with the combined cheeses and the spring onions. Bake at 230°C/gas 8/ fan oven 210°C until the edges of the tortillas are browned and the cheese has melted, 5–7 minutes. Cut each tortilla into six wedges. Top each with 1 tsp salsa and a small dollop of soured cream.

Texas Two-step Chilli

Pork and turkey get together in this straightforward and tasty dish. Fresh coriander adds a captivating pungency.

SERVES 4

225 g/8 oz lean minced pork
225 g/8 oz minced turkey breast
8 spring onions, sliced
oil, for greasing
400 g/14 oz can chilli beans, undrained
450 g/1 lb tomatoes, chopped
**1 small jalapeño or other medium-hot
    chilli, seeded and chopped**
salt, to taste
**finely chopped fresh coriander,
    to garnish**

Cook the pork, turkey and spring onions in a lightly greased large frying pan over medium heat until the meat is browned, about 8 minutes, crumbling it with a fork. Combine the meat mixture and the remaining ingredients, except the salt, in the slow cooker. Cover and cook on Low for 5–6 hours. Season to taste. Sprinkle each bowl of soup with fresh coriander.

Taco Chilli

Hominy can be found in ethnic markets or from specialist suppliers, or add a can of cannellini beans instead.

SERVES 8

900 g/2 lb lean minced beef
oil, for greasing
400 g/14 oz can pinto beans, drained and rinsed
100 g/4 oz hominy, drained and rinsed
400 g/14 oz can chopped tomatoes, undrained
275 g/10 oz canned chopped tomatoes with chilli, with juice
225 g/8 oz canned sweetcorn, drained
1 large onion, chopped
2 celery sticks, chopped
35g packet taco seasoning mix
1 garlic clove, crushed
½ tsp dried thyme

garnishes: soured cream, grated Cheddar cheese, taco chips

Cook the minced beef in a lightly greased large frying pan until browned, about 10 minutes, crumbling it with a fork. Combine the beef and the remaining ingredients in the slow cooker. Cover and cook on Low for 6–8 hours. Serve with the garnishes.

Baked Tortilla Chips Ⓥ

Make your own tortilla chips – it's so easy.

SERVES 6 AS AN ACCOMPANIMENT

6 x 15 cm/6 in corn tortillas
vegetable cooking spray
a pinch of ground cumin
a pinch of chilli powder
a pinch of dried oregano
a pinch of paprika
salt and cayenne pepper, to taste

Cut each tortilla into eight wedges. Arrange in a single layer on a baking tray. Spray the tortillas with cooking spray.

Sprinkle lightly with the combined herbs, paprika, salt and cayenne pepper. Bake at 180°C/gas 4/fan oven 160°C until lightly browned, 5–7 minutes.

Cream of Chilli

A chilli that's a little different – made with canned soup!

SERVES 6

450 g/1 lb skinless chicken breast fillets, cubed (2 cm/¾ in)
275 g/10 oz ready-made cream of chicken soup
120 ml/4 fl oz ready-made tomato sauce
1 onion, chopped
3 spring onions, chopped
½ red pepper, chopped
1 small jalapeño or other medium-hot chilli, seeded and finely chopped
2 garlic cloves, crushed
100 g/4 oz chopped green chillies from a jar, drained
1 tbsp chilli powder
½ tsp ground cumin
250 ml/8 fl oz semi-skimmed milk
salt and freshly ground black pepper, to taste
50 g/2 oz Monterey Jack or Cheddar cheese, grated
Baked Tortilla Chips (see left)

Combine all the ingredients, except the milk, salt, pepper, cheese and Baked Tortilla Chips, in the slow cooker. Cover and cook on Low for 6–8 hours, adding the milk during the last 20 minutes. Season to taste with salt and pepper. Sprinkle each bowl of chilli with cheese. Serve with Baked Tortilla Chips.

Chilli Mole

This chilli boasts the intriguing flavours of a traditional Mexican mole. Use chicken, pork or beef, or a combination of all three meats.

SERVES 6

450 g/1 lb lean pork, fat trimmed, cubed
250 ml/8 fl oz chicken stock
400 g/14 oz can chopped tomatoes
400 g/14 oz can black beans, drained and rinsed
Mole Sauce (see page 268)
salt and freshly ground black pepper, to taste
Guacamole (see below)
finely chopped fresh coriander, to garnish

Combine all the ingredients, except the salt, pepper and Guacamole, in the slow cooker. Cover and cook on Low for 6–8 hours. Season to taste with salt and pepper. Top each bowl of chilli with Guacamole. Sprinkle generously with fresh coriander.

Guacamole Ⓥ

Traditional with chilli dishes.

SERVES 6 AS AN ACCOMPANIMENT

1 ripe avocado, coarsely mashed
½ small onion, finely chopped
½ jalapeño or other medium-hot chilli, seeded and finely chopped
1 tbsp finely chopped fresh coriander
Tabasco sauce, to taste
salt, to taste

Mix the avocado, onion, chilli and coriander. Season to taste with Tabasco sauce and salt.

Chilli Verde

This 'green chilli' is made with tomatillos, which are also called Mexican green tomatoes. They are available canned from ethnic markets and specialist suppliers.

SERVES 8

450 g/1 lb boneless lean pork, cubed (1 cm/½ in)
900 ml/1½ pints chicken stock
2 x 400 g/14 oz cans cannellini beans, drained and rinsed
100–225 g/4–8 oz green chillies from a jar, diced
250 ml/8 fl oz water
900 g/2 lb canned tomatillos, quartered
2 large onions, thinly sliced
6–8 garlic cloves, chopped
2 tsp ground cumin
25 g/1 oz fresh coriander, chopped
Coriander-chilli Soured Cream (see below)

Combine all the ingredients, except the coriander and the Coriander-chilli Soured Cream, in a 5.5 litre/9½ pint slow cooker. Cover and cook on Low for 6–8 hours. Stir in the coriander. Serve with Coriander-chilli Soured Cream.

Coriander-chilli Soured Cream Ⓥ

Great with spicy dishes.

SERVES 8 AS AN ACCOMPANIMENT

120 ml/4 fl oz soured cream
1 tbsp chopped fresh coriander
1 tsp chopped pickled jalapeño or other medium-hot chilli

Combine all the ingredients.

Mexican Chorizo

This is not a slow-cooker recipe but one that forms the basis of many delicious dishes, such as the one that follows.

SERVES 6

½ tsp coriander seeds, crushed
½ tsp cumin seeds, crushed
oil, for greasing
2 dried ancho or other medium-hot chillies
700 g/1½ lb pork tenderloin, finely chopped or minced
4 garlic cloves, crushed
2 tbsp paprika
2 tbsp cider vinegar
2 tbsp water
1 tsp dried oregano
½ tsp salt

Cook the coriander and cumin seeds in a lightly greased small frying pan over medium heat, stirring frequently until toasted, 2–3 minutes. Remove from the frying pan and reserve. Add the ancho chillies to the frying pan. Cook over medium heat until softened, about 1 minute on each side, turning the chillies often so that they do not burn. Remove and discard the stems, veins and seeds. Chop finely. Combine all the ingredients, mixing well.

Mexican Chorizo Chilli

The Chorizo can be used in many Mexican recipes, or formed into patties and cooked for a dinner main course.

SERVES 6

Mexican Chorizo (see above)
1 onion, chopped
oil, for greasing
2 x 400 g/14 oz cans chopped tomatoes
2 x 400 g/14 oz cans pinto or black beans, drained and rinsed
salt and pepper to taste

Cook the Mexican Chorizo and onion in a lightly greased large frying pan over medium heat until browned, 8–10 minutes, crumbling it with a fork. Combine the chorizo and the remaining ingredients, except the salt and pepper, in the slow cooker. Cover and cook on Low for 4–6 hours. Season to taste with salt and pepper.

Cheese and Chilli Blanco with Red Tomato Salsa

This white chilli is made extra-creamy with the addition of soured cream and Monterey Jack or Cheddar cheese.

SERVES 8

700 g/1½ lb skinless chicken breast fillets, cubed
2 x 400 g/14 oz cans cannellini beans, drained and rinsed
400 ml/14 fl oz chicken stock
100 g/4 oz diced green chillies from a jar, drained
4 onions, chopped
1 tbsp chopped garlic
1 tbsp dried oregano
1 tsp ground cumin
250 ml/8 fl oz soured cream
225 g/8 oz Monterey Jack or Cheddar cheese, grated
salt and cayenne pepper, to taste
Red Tomato Salsa (see page 202)

Combine all the ingredients, except the soured cream, cheese, salt, cayenne pepper and Red Tomato Salsa, in the slow cooker. Cover and cook on Low for 6–8 hours. Stir in the soured cream and cheese, stirring until the cheese has melted. Season to taste with salt and cayenne pepper. Serve with Red Tomato Salsa.

Red Tomato Salsa Ⓥ

A great salsa with a touch of bite.

SERVES 8 AS AN ACCOMPANIMENT

2 large tomatoes, chopped
1 small onion, finely chopped
1 green pepper, finely chopped
2 tbsp finely chopped poblano or
**   other mild chilli**
1 garlic clove, crushed
2 tbsp finely chopped fresh coriander
salt, to taste

Mix all the ingredients, seasoning to taste with salt.

Ranchero Chilli

A hearty chilli with flavours of the Wild West. Definitely one for the boys!

SERVES 6

450 g/1 lb lean minced beef
100 g/4 oz smoked sausage, sliced
oil, for greasing
600 ml/1 pint beef stock
250 ml/8 fl oz beer or extra beef stock
450 g/1 lb chopped tomatoes, undrained
400 g/14 oz can chilli beans in chilli sauce
400 g/14 oz can pinto beans, drained
**   and rinsed**
1 onion, chopped
1 green pepper, chopped
1 jalapeño chilli, finely chopped
3 large garlic cloves, crushed
1 tbsp ground cumin
3 tbsp chilli powder, or to taste
1 tsp dried oregano
salt and freshly ground black pepper
soured cream, to garnish

Cook the beef and sausage in a greased frying pan over medium heat until browned, about 8 minutes, crumbling it with a fork. Combine with the remaining ingredients, except the salt and pepper, in the slow cooker. Cover and cook on Low for 6–8 hours. Season to taste with salt and pepper. Top each serving with a dollop of soured cream.

Yellow Squash and Cannellini Bean Chilli

Packed with vegetables and pork, this vibrant chilli makes a good family meal. You could use yellow courgettes instead of the squash.

SERVES 6

450 g/1 lb lean minced pork
oil, for greasing
1 litre/1¾ pints chicken stock
250 ml/8 fl oz dry white wine or
**   chicken stock**
100 g/4 oz dried cannellini beans
100 g/4 oz dried chickpeas
2 onions, chopped
1 yellow pepper, chopped
100 g/4 oz leeks, thinly sliced
175 g/6 oz yellow summer squash,
**   such as patty pan, cubed**
175 g/6 oz waxy potatoes, peeled and
**   cubed**
2 garlic cloves, crushed
2 tsp finely chopped jalapeño or other
**   medium-hot chilli**
2 tsp cumin seeds
1 tsp dried oregano
1 tsp chilli powder
½ tsp ground coriander
½ tsp ground cinnamon
1 bay leaf
salt and freshly ground black pepper,
**   to taste**
1 small tomato, finely chopped
2 spring onions, thinly sliced
3 tbsp finely chopped fresh coriander

Cook the pork in a lightly greased large frying pan until browned, about 8 minutes, crumbling it with a fork. Combine the pork and the remaining ingredients, except the salt, pepper, chopped tomato, spring onions and fresh coriander, in a 5.5 litre/9½ pint slow cooker. Cover and cook on Low until the beans are tender, 7–8 hours. Season to taste with salt and pepper. Discard the bay leaf. Sprinkle each bowl of chilli with tomato, spring onions and fresh coriander.

Mediterranean Chilli

This variation on a standard chilli recipe is just bursting with healthy vegetables and pulses.

SERVES 6

**450 g/1 lb lean minced lamb or beef
oil, for greasing
1 litre/1¾ pints chicken stock
250 ml/8 fl oz dry white wine or
chicken stock
100 g/4 oz dried cannellini beans
100 g/4 oz dried chickpeas
2 onions, chopped
1 yellow pepper, chopped
200 g/7 oz Kalamata or other black
olives, sliced
100 g/4 oz leeks, thinly sliced
175 g/6 oz yellow summer squash,
such as patty pan, or yellow
courgette, cubed
175 g/6 oz waxy potatoes, peeled and
cubed
2 garlic cloves, crushed
2 tsp finely chopped jalapeño or other
medium-hot chilli
2 tsp cumin seeds
1 tsp dried oregano
1 tsp chilli powder
½ tsp ground coriander
½ tsp ground cinnamon
1 bay leaf
salt and freshly ground black pepper,
to taste
175 g/6 oz couscous
1 small tomato, finely chopped
2 spring onions, thinly sliced
3 tbsp finely chopped fresh coriander
6 tbsp crumbed Feta cheese**

Cook the lamb or beef in a lightly greased large frying pan until browned, about 8 minutes, crumbling it with a fork. Combine the meat and the remaining ingredients, except the salt, pepper, chopped tomato, spring onions, fresh coriander, couscous and Feta, in a 5.5 litre/9½ pint slow cooker. Cover and cook on Low until the beans are tender, 7–8 hours. Season to taste with salt and pepper. Make up the couscous according to the packet directons. Discard the bay leaf from the chilli mixture. Serve the chilli over the couscous and sprinkle each serving with tomato, spring onions, fresh coriander and Feta.

Chilli with Beans

This simple beef and turkey chilli is great to come home to at the end of a busy day.

SERVES 8

**450 g/1 lb lean minced beef
450 g/1 lb minced turkey
oil, for greasing
2 large onions, chopped
3 garlic cloves, crushed
175 g/6 oz tomato purée
550 g/1¼ lb tomato sauce with herbs
from a jar
2 x 400 g/14 oz cans kidney beans,
drained and rinsed
2 tbsp chilli powder, or to taste
1 tsp dried oregano
salt and freshly ground black pepper,
to taste**

Cook the minced beef and turkey in a lightly greased large frying pan over medium heat until the meat is browned, about 10 minutes, crumbling the meat with a fork. Combine the meat and the remaining ingredients, except the salt and pepper, in the slow cooker. Cover and cook on Low for 6–8 hours. Season to taste with salt and pepper.

Black and White Bean Chilli

Made with black and cannellini beans, this chilli is accented in flavour and colour with sun-dried tomatoes.

SERVES 4

350 g/12 oz lean minced beef
oil, for greasing
2 x 400 g/14 oz cans chopped tomatoes
400 g/14 oz can cannellini beans, drained and rinsed
400 g/14 oz can black beans or red kidney beans, drained and rinsed
2 onions, chopped
½ green pepper, chopped
15 g/½ oz sun-dried tomatoes (not in oil), chopped
1 jalapeño or other medium-hot chilli, finely chopped
2 garlic cloves, crushed
2–3 tbsp chilli powder, or to taste
1–1½ tsp ground cumin
1–1½ tsp dried oregano
1 bay leaf
salt and freshly ground black pepper, to taste
15 g/½ oz fresh coriander, finely chopped

Cook the beef in a lightly greased large frying pan over medium heat until browned, 8–10 minutes, crumbling it with a fork. Combine the beef and the remaining ingredients, except the salt, pepper and fresh coriander, in the slow cooker. Cover and cook on Low for 6–8 hours. Discard the bay leaf. Season to taste with salt and pepper. Stir in the fresh coriander.

Chilli with Beans and Beer

This chilli is very easy to make. Beer adds richness to the sauce, which improves when cooked for a long time.

SERVES 6

450 g/1 lb lean minced beef
oil, for greasing
600 ml/1 pint beef stock
250 ml/8 fl oz beer
450 g/1 lb chopped tomatoes, undrained
400 g/14 oz can chilli beans in chilli sauce
400 g/14 oz can pinto beans, drained and rinsed
3 large garlic cloves, crushed
1 tbsp ground cumin
3 tbsp chilli powder, or to taste
1 tsp dried oregano
salt and freshly ground black pepper, to taste

Cook the minced beef in a lightly greased large frying pan over medium heat until browned, about 8 minutes, crumbling it with a fork. Combine the minced beef and the remaining ingredients, except the salt and pepper, in the slow cooker. Cover and cook on Low for 6–8 hours. Season to taste with salt and pepper.

Spiced Bean Chilli with Fusilli

Use your favourite beans and pasta shapes in this versatile chilli.

SERVES 8

450 g/1 lb lean minced beef
oil, for greasing
2 x 400 g/14 oz cans chopped
 tomatoes with garlic
400 g/14 oz can chickpeas, drained
 and rinsed
400 g/14 oz can red kidney beans,
 drained and rinsed
4 onions, chopped
100 g/4 oz button mushrooms, sliced
1 celery stick, sliced
120 ml/4 fl oz white wine or water
2 tbsp chilli powder, or to taste
¾ tsp dried oregano
¾ tsp dried thyme
¾ tsp ground cumin
225 g/8 oz fusilli, cooked
salt and freshly ground black pepper,
 to taste
3–4 tbsp sliced green or black olives

Cook the beef in a lightly greased large frying pan over medium heat until browned, 8–10 minutes, crumbling it with a fork. Combine the beef and the remaining ingredients, except the fusilli, salt, pepper and olives, in a 5.5 litre/9½ pint slow cooker. Cover and cook on Low for 6–8 hours, adding the pasta during the last 20 minutes. Season to taste with salt and pepper. Sprinkle each bowl of soup with olives.

Lentil Chilli with Bacon and Beer

Lime, beer and bacon make this chilli different and delicious.

SERVES 4

750 ml/1¼ pints beef stock
250 ml/8 fl oz beer or beef stock
75 g/3 oz dried lentils, rinsed
75 g/3 oz dried black beans, rinsed
1 medium onion, chopped
3 large garlic cloves, crushed
1 tbsp finely chopped jalapeno or
 other medium-hot chilli
1 tbsp chilli powder
1 tsp ground cumin
1 tsp dried rosemary, crushed
225 g/8 oz canned chopped tomatoes
juice of 1 lime
salt and freshly ground black pepper,
 to taste
4 bacon rashers, cooked until crisp
 and crumbled

Combine all the ingredients, except the tomatoes, lime juice, salt, pepper and bacon, in the slow cooker. Cover and cook on High until the beans are tender, 5–6 hours, adding the tomatoes during the last 30 minutes. Stir in the lime juice. Season to taste with salt and pepper. Sprinkle each bowl of chilli with bacon.

Vegetable and Lentil Chilli Ⓥ

Lentils add great texture to this nutritious and satisfying meatless chilli.

SERVES 4

1 litre/1¾ pints vegetable stock
250 ml/8 fl oz water
400 g/14 oz can chopped tomatoes
130 g/4½ oz dried brown lentils
100 g/4 oz sweetcorn, thawed if frozen
2 onions, chopped
1 red or green pepper, chopped
1 small carrot, sliced
½ celery stick, sliced
1 garlic clove, crushed
½–1 tbsp chilli powder
¾ tsp ground cumin
1 bay leaf
salt and freshly ground black pepper, to taste

Combine all the ingredients, except the salt and pepper, in the slow cooker. Cover and cook on Low for 6–8 hours. Discard the bay leaf. Season to taste with salt and pepper.

Vegetarian Black and White Bean Chilli Ⓥ

Black and white beans give this vegetarian chilli texture and an attractive appearance. Its warm flavour comes from toasted cumin seeds.

SERVES 4

450 ml/¾ pint tomato juice
250 ml/8 fl oz vegetable stock
2 tbsp tomato purée
400 g/14 oz can black beans, drained and rinsed
400 g/14 oz can cannellini or haricot beans, drained and rinsed
1 onion, chopped
1 mild chilli, seeded and finely chopped
1 tsp paprika
1 tsp toasted cumin seeds
50 g/2 oz wild rice, cooked
salt and freshly ground black pepper, to taste

Combine all the ingredients, except the wild rice, salt and pepper, in the slow cooker. Cover and cook on Low for 6–8 hours, adding the wild rice during the last 30 minutes. Season to taste with salt and pepper.

Chilli-bean and Sweetcorn Chilli Ⓥ

This easy chilli is seriously spicy! For a less spicy version, substitute a can of drained and rinsed pinto or kidney beans for the chilli beans.

SERVES 4

400 g/14 oz can chilli beans
250 ml/8 fl oz vegetable stock
400 g/14 oz can chopped tomatoes
1 green pepper, chopped
100 g/4 oz sweetcorn, thawed if frozen
1 onion, chopped
2 garlic cloves, crushed
1–3 tsp chilli powder
salt and freshly ground black pepper, to taste

Combine all the ingredients, except the salt and pepper, in the slow cooker. Cover and cook on Low for 6–8 hours. Season to taste with salt and pepper.

Chilli sin Carne Ⓥ

The variety of toppings makes this chilli fun to serve – add other toppings, too, such as chopped peppers and tomatoes and chopped fresh oregano or fresh coriander.

SERVES 6–8

6 x 400 g/14 oz cans chopped tomatoes
400 g/14 oz can red kidney beans, drained and rinsed
175 g/6 oz tomato purée
175 ml/6 fl oz beer or water
350 g/12 oz Quorn or beef-flavoured soya mince
2 onions, chopped
1 green pepper, chopped
2 garlic cloves, crushed
1 tbsp light brown sugar
1 tbsp cocoa powder
1–2 tbsp chilli powder
1–2 tsp ground cumin
1–2 tsp dried oregano
¼ tsp ground cloves
salt and freshly ground black pepper, to taste
toppings: grated cheese, soured cream, thinly sliced spring onions

Combine all the ingredients, except the salt and pepper, in a 5.5 litre/9½ pint slow cooker. Cover and cook on Low for 6–8 hours. Season to taste with salt and pepper. Serve with the toppings.

Tortilla Chilli Ⓥ

A tasty tomato dish sprinkled with tortilla chips.

SERVES 6–8

6 x 400 g/14 oz cans chopped tomatoes
400 g/14 oz can black or pinto beans, drained and rinsed
175 g/6 oz tomato purée
175 ml/6 fl oz beer or water
350 g/12 oz Quorn or beef-flavoured soya mince
2 onions, chopped
1 jalapeño or other medium-hot chilli, finely chopped
1 green pepper, chopped
2 garlic cloves, crushed
1 tbsp light brown sugar
1 tbsp cocoa powder
1–2 tbsp chilli powder
1–2 tsp ground cumin
1–2 tsp dried oregano
¼ tsp ground cloves
salt and freshly ground black pepper, to taste
crushed tortilla chips and chopped fresh coriander leaves, to garnish

Combine all the ingredients, except the salt, pepper and garnishes, in a 5.5 litre/9½ pint slow cooker. Cover and cook on Low for 6–8 hours. Season to taste with salt and pepper. Serve sprinkled with tortilla chips and coriander.

207

Sweet Potato Chipotle Chilli Ⓥ

If you're a fan of Mexican food, you might like to add chipotle chillies – dried, smoked jalapeño chillies – in adobo sauce to your storecupboard. They are available from specialist suppliers. Taste before adding more, as they can be fiercely hot!

SERVES 4

2 x 400 g/14 oz cans black beans, drained and rinsed
400 g/14 oz can chopped tomatoes
250 ml/8 fl oz water or vegetable stock
500 g/18 oz sweet potatoes, peeled and cubed
2 onions, chopped
1 green pepper, chopped
1 cm/½ in piece fresh root ginger, finely grated
1 garlic clove, crushed
1 tsp cumin seeds, crushed
½–1 small chipotle chilli in adobo sauce, chopped
salt, to taste

Combine all the ingredients, except the chipotle chilli and salt, in the slow cooker. Cover and cook on Low for 6–8 hours, adding the chipotle chilli during the last 30 minutes. Season to taste with salt.

Sagebrush Chilli with Fresh Tomatoes Ⓥ

Fresh tomatoes and dried sage give this chilli a different edge. Chose ripe tomatoes in season for the best flavour.

SERVES 4

2 x 400 g/14 oz cans black-eyed peas, drained and rinsed
750 g/1¾ lb tomatoes, cut into wedges
4 spring onions, sliced

8 garlic cloves, thinly sliced
1 large hot, red chilli, roasted, seeded and finely chopped
½–2 tbsp chilli powder
1 tsp ground cumin
1 tsp ground coriander
¾ tsp dried sage
salt and freshly ground black pepper, to taste

Combine all the ingredients, except the salt and pepper, in the slow cooker. Cover and cook on Low for 8–9 hours. Season to taste with salt and pepper.

Black Bean, Rice and Sweetcorn Chilli Ⓥ

For a taste of Mexican cuisine, use black beans in this quick and simple vegetarian chilli, but red kidney beans will work as well.

SERVES 4

2 x 400 g/14 oz cans chopped tomatoes
400 g/14 oz can black beans, drained and rinsed
50 g/2 oz sweetcorn, thawed if frozen
3 onions, chopped
1 large red pepper, chopped
1 jalapeño or other medium-hot chilli, finely chopped
3 garlic cloves, crushed
½–1 tbsp chilli powder
1 tsp ground allspice
25 g/1 oz rice, cooked
salt and freshly ground black pepper, to taste

Combine all the ingredients, except the rice, salt and pepper, in the slow cooker. Cover and cook on Low for 8–9 hours, adding the rice during the last 15 minutes. Season to taste with salt and pepper.

Salsa Chilli Ⓥ

Ready-made salsa is handy to keep in the storecupboard to add flavour and texture to dishes such as this.

SERVES 4

400 g/14 oz can chopped tomatoes
400 g/14 oz can red kidney beans, drained and rinsed
250 ml/8 fl oz water
120 ml/4 fl oz ready-made medium or hot salsa
50 g/2 oz sweetcorn, thawed if frozen
½–1 tbsp chilli powder
½–1 tsp jalapeño or other medium-hot chilli, finely chopped
90 g/3½ oz pearl barley
salt and freshly ground black pepper, to taste
50 g/2 oz mature Cheddar cheese, grated

Combine all the ingredients, except the barley, salt, pepper and cheese, in the slow cooker. Cover and cook on Low for 6–8 hours, adding the barley during the last 40 minutes. Season to taste with salt and pepper. Sprinkle each bowl with grated cheese.

Mango Salsa Ⓥ

A lovely sweet-hot salsa to serve with spicy dishes.

SERVES 6 AS AN ACCOMPANIMENT

1 mango, cubed
1 banana, cubed
15 g/½ oz fresh coriander, chopped
½ small jalapeño or other medium-hot chilli, finely chopped
1 tbsp pineapple or orange juice concentrate
1 tsp lime juice

Combine all the ingredients.

Caribbean Chilli Ⓥ

This hearty meatless three-bean chilli is accented with Mango Salsa. Serve with brown rice, if you like.

SERVES 6

2 x 400 g/14 oz cans chopped tomatoes
400 g/14 oz can pinto beans, drained and rinsed
400 g/14 oz can cannellini beans, drained and rinsed
400 g/14 oz can black beans, drained and rinsed
2 red or green peppers, chopped
2 onions, chopped
1 jalapeño or other medium-hot chilli, finely chopped
2 cm/¾ in piece fresh root ginger, finely grated
2 tsp sugar
3 large garlic cloves, crushed
1 tbsp ground cumin
2 tbsp paprika
½–2 tbsp chilli powder
¼ tsp ground cloves
1 tbsp lime juice
salt and freshly ground black pepper, to taste
Mango Salsa (see below)

Combine all the ingredients, except the salt, pepper and Mango Salsa, in a 5.5 litre/9½ pint slow cooker. Cover and cook on Low for 6–8 hours. Season to taste with salt and pepper. Serve with Mango Salsa.

Beef and Veal Dishes

Beef cooks beautifully in the slow cooker, with the great advantage that you don't have to use the most expensive cuts of meat. Braising and stewing cuts give superb flavour and are meltingly tender when cooked in the slow cooker.

Roast Beef with Fettuccine

Slice this perfectly cooked roast and serve with fettuccine.

SERVES 8

1 boneless beef joint, such as topside (about 1.5 kg/3 lb)
salt and freshly ground black pepper, to taste
2 onions, sliced
120 ml/4 fl oz beef stock
50 g/2 oz frozen petits pois, thawed
1 tbsp cornflour
2 tbsp water
50 g/2 oz freshly grated Parmesan or Romano cheese
450 g/1 lb fettuccine, cooked, hot

Sprinkle the beef lightly with salt and pepper. Put in the slow cooker with the onions and stock. Insert a meat thermometer so that the tip is in the centre of the roast. Cover and cook on Low until the meat thermometer registers 68°C for medium rare, about 4 hours. Remove to a serving platter and cover loosely with foil.

Add the peas to the slow cooker. Cover and cook on High for 10 minutes. Stir in the combined cornflour and water, stirring for 2–3 minutes. Stir in the cheese. Season to taste with salt and pepper. Toss with the fettuccine and serve with the beef.

Roast Beef Horseradish Sauce

You can use Romano cheese instead of Parmesan, if you prefer. Use more or less horseradish according to your taste.

SERVES 8

1 boneless beef joint, such as topside (about 1.5 kg/3 lb)
salt and freshly ground black pepper, to taste
2 onions, sliced
120 ml/4 fl oz beef stock
50 g/2 oz frozen petits pois, thawed
1 tbsp cornflour
2 tbsp water
50 g/2 oz freshly grated Parmesan cheese
2 tbsp prepared horseradish
a generous pinch of cayenne pepper
250 ml/8 fl oz whipped cream

Sprinkle the beef lightly with salt and pepper. Put in the slow cooker with the onions and stock. Insert a meat thermometer so that the tip is in the centre of the roast. Cover and cook on Low until the meat thermometer registers 68°C for medium rare, about 4 hours. Remove to a serving platter and cover loosely with foil. Add the peas to the slow cooker. Cover and cook on High for 10 minutes. Stir in the combined cornflour and water, stirring for 2–3 minutes. Stir in the Parmesan cheese. Season to taste with salt and pepper. Mix together the horseradish, cayenne pepper and whipped cream and serve with the beef.

Sauerbraten

The longer you can marinate the beef, the more flavourful it will be. Many sauerbraten recipes do not include soured cream – omit it if you prefer.

SERVES 8–10

450 ml/¾ pint water
250 ml/8 fl oz dry red wine
1 large onion, thinly sliced
2 tbsp pickling spice
12 whole cloves
12 peppercorns
2 bay leaves
1½ tsp salt
1 boneless beef joint, such as topside or silverside (about 1.5 kg/3 lb)
75 g/3 oz ginger nut biscuits, finely crushed
150 ml/¼ pint soured cream
2 tbsp cornflour

Heat the water, wine, onion, seasonings and salt to boiling in a large pan. Cool. Pour the mixture over the beef in the slow cooker. Refrigerate the crock, covered, for at least 1 day.

Put the crock in the slow cooker. Cover and cook on Low for 6–8 hours. Remove the meat to a serving platter and keep warm. Stir the ginger nut biscuits into the stock. Stir in the combined soured cream and cornflour, stirring for 2–3 minutes. Serve the sauce over the sliced meat.

One-pot Roast

Pot roast with vegetables can't be beaten for a cold weather meal – add red wine for extra flavour.

SERVES 8

1.5 kg/3 lb braising steak
2 large onions, halved and sliced
1 packet onion soup mix
450 g/1 lb carrots, thickly sliced
1 kg/2¼ lb waxy potatoes, unpeeled

½ small cabbage, cut into 6–8 wedges
salt and freshly ground black pepper, to taste
120 ml/4 fl oz dry red wine or beef stock

Put the beef on top of the onions in a 5.5 litre/9½ pint slow cooker and sprinkle with the soup mix. Arrange the vegetables around the beef and sprinkle lightly with salt and pepper. Add the wine or stock, cover and cook on Low for 6–8 hours. Serve the beef and vegetables with the stock, or use to make gravy. Note: to make gravy, measure the stock and pour into a small pan. Heat to boiling. For every 250 ml/8 fl oz of stock, whisk in 2 tbsp of flour mixed with 50 ml/2 fl oz of cold water, whisking until thickened, about 1 minute.

Coffee Pot Roast

A favourite recipe of a good friend, Judy Pompei, the beef is given incredible richness by adding coffee and soy sauce.

SERVES 10

2 large onions, sliced
1 boneless beef joint, such as rump (about 1.5 kg/3 lb)
250 ml/8 fl oz strong coffee
50 ml/2 fl oz soy sauce
1 garlic clove, crushed
1 tsp dried oregano
2 bay leaves

Put half the onions into the slow cooker. Top with the beef and remaining onions. Add the remaining ingredients. Cover and cook on Low for 6–8 hours. Serve the beef with the stock.

Boeuf Bourguignon

This is Catherine Atkinson's version of this robust and much-loved classic from the Burgundy region of France.

SERVES 4

175 g/6 oz button onions, unpeeled
2 tbsp olive oil
100 g/4 oz rindless smoked streaky bacon, cut into small pieces
100 g/4 oz baby button mushrooms
2 garlic cloves, crushed, or 10 ml/2 tsp garlic purée
250 ml/8 fl oz beef stock
700 g/1½ lb lean braising or chuck steak, trimmed and cut into 5 cm/ 2 in cubes
2 tsp plain flour
250 ml/8 fl oz red wine
1 sprig of fresh thyme or 2.5 ml/½ tsp dried thyme
1 bay leaf
salt and freshly ground black pepper
2 tbsp chopped fresh parsley
creamy mashed potatoes and a green vegetable, to serve

Put the onions in a heatproof bowl and pour over enough boiling water to cover. Leave for 5 minutes. Meanwhile, heat 1 tbsp of the oil in a frying pan, add the bacon and fry until lightly browned. Transfer to the slow cooker using a slotted spoon, leaving all the fat and juices behind. Drain the onions and peel off the skins when cool enough to handle. Add to the frying pan and cook gently until they begin to brown. Add the mushrooms and garlic and cook for 2 minutes, stirring. Transfer the vegetables to the cooking pot. Pour the stock over, cover with the lid and switch on the slow cooker to High or Low.

Heat the remaining oil in the frying pan and fry the beef cubes until a rich, dark-brown colour on all sides. Sprinkle the flour over the meat and stir well. Gradually pour in the wine, stirring all the time, until the sauce is bubbling and thickened. Add to the slow cooker with the thyme, bay leaf, salt and pepper. Cook the casserole for 3–4 hours on High or 6–8 hours on Low, or until the meat and vegetables are very tender. Remove the thyme sprig and bay leaf. Sprinkle with parsley and serve with creamy mashed potatoes and a green vegetable.

Barbecued Brisket

This delicious brisket is prepared with an easy spice rub and slow cooked to perfection in barbecue sauce.

SERVES 10

1 beef brisket, fat trimmed (about 1.5 kg/3 lb)
Spice Rub (see page 213)
450 ml/¾ pint ready-made barbecue sauce
50 ml/2 fl oz red wine vinegar
50 g/2 oz light brown sugar
2 medium onions, sliced
120 ml/4 fl oz water
450 g/1 lb fettuccine, cooked, hot

Rub the brisket with the Spice Rub and put in the slow cooker. Pour in the combined remaining ingredients, except the fettuccine. Cover and cook on Low for 6–8 hours, turning the heat to High during the last 20–30 minutes. Remove the brisket to a serving platter and leave to stand, covered with foil, for about 10 minutes. Slice and serve with the barbecue sauce and onions over fettuccine.

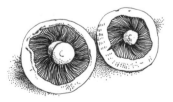

Barbecued Beef Sandwiches

The humble sandwich is transformed into a true feast in this recipe.

SERVES 10

1 beef brisket, fat trimmed (about 1.5 kg/3 lb)
Spice Rub (see below)
450 ml/¾ pint ready-made barbecue sauce
50 ml/2 fl oz red wine vinegar
50 g/2 oz light brown sugar
2 medium onions, sliced
120 ml/4 fl oz water
baguettes or rolls
coleslaw

Rub the brisket with the Spice Rub and put in the slow cooker. Pour in the combined remaining ingredients, except the baguettes or rolls and coleslaw. Cover and cook on Low for 6–8 hours, turning the heat to High during the last 20–30 minutes. Remove the brisket to a serving platter and leave to stand, covered with foil, for about 10 minutes. Shred the brisket using a fork and mix with the barbecue mixture. Spoon the beef inside chunks of split baguette or roll and top with coleslaw.

Spice Rub Ⓥ

Great for beef dishes.

MAKES 3 TBSP

2 tbsp finely chopped fresh parsley
1 garlic clove, crushed
½ tsp seasoned salt
½ tsp ground ginger
½ tsp freshly grated nutmeg
½ tsp pepper

Mix all the ingredients together until thoroughly combined.

Mushroom-stuffed Flank Steak

A bacon, mushroom and thyme stuffing tastes very good indeed inside tenderly cooked beef.

SERVES 6

3 bacon rashers
225 g/8 oz brown cap mushrooms, sliced
½ onion, chopped
¾ tsp dried thyme
salt and freshly ground black pepper, to taste
700 g/1½ lb boneless beef thick flank
175 ml/6 fl oz dry red wine or beef stock
100 g/4 oz rice, cooked, hot

Cook the bacon in a large frying pan until crisp. Drain and crumble. Discard all but 1 tbsp of the bacon fat. Add the mushrooms, onion and thyme to the frying pan and sauté until tender, 5–8 minutes. Mix in the bacon. Season to taste with salt and pepper.

Pound the meat with a meat mallet, if necessary, to make it even in thickness. Spoon the stuffing over the meat and roll up, beginning from the long side. Secure with short skewers and put in the slow cooker. Add the wine or stock. Cover and cook on Low for 6–8 hours. Slice and serve over rice, spooning the juices over the top.

Pot-roasted Brisket in Beer

Marinating is the key to success for this tender, juicy beef.

SERVES 4–6

1.25 kg/2½ lb rolled brisket
300 ml/½ pint pale ale
salt and freshly ground black pepper
25 g/1 oz beef dripping, white
   vegetable fat or sunflower oil
2 onions, each cut into 8 wedges
2 carrots, quartered
2 celery sticks, thickly sliced
2 sprigs of fresh thyme
2 bay leaves
2 whole cloves
150 ml/¼ pint boiling beef stock
1 tbsp cornflour (cornstarch)

Place the meat in a bowl just large enough to hold it and pour the ale over. Cover and leave to marinate in the refrigerator for at least 8 hours, or overnight if preferred, turning several times if possible. Drain the meat, reserving the ale and wipe it dry. Season the meat well with salt and pepper. Heat the dripping, vegetable fat or oil in a large, heavy pan until hot. Add the meat and turn frequently until well browned all over. Lift the meat on to a plate.

Pour away some of the fat in the pan, then add the onions, carrots and celery. Cook for a few minutes until lightly browned and beginning to soften. Arrange a single layer of vegetables in the base of the ceramic cooking pot. Put the beef on top, then add the remaining vegetables around the sides of the meat. Tuck in the thyme, bay leaves and cloves. Pour the beer marinade over the beef, followed by the beef stock. Cover with the lid and cook for 5–8 hours on Low, or until the meat and vegetables are cooked through and tender. Turn the meat and baste with the gravy once or twice during cooking.

Lift out the meat and place on a warmed serving plate or board. Cover with foil and leave to rest for 10 minutes before carving into thick slices. Meanwhile, skim any fat from the juices and gravy in the ceramic cooking pot. Blend the cornflour with a little cold water in a saucepan, then strain in the stock (keeping the vegetables, discarding the bay leaves and thyme). Bring to the boil, whisking until bubbling and thickened. Taste and adjust the seasoning if necessary. Serve the rich gravy with the beef and vegetables.

Vegetable-stuffed Beef Flank

The meat will be extremely tender after the long slow cooking and wonderful stuffed with this exciting selection of vegetables.

SERVES 6

40 g/1½ oz mushrooms, sliced
½ onion, chopped
½ carrot, chopped
50 g/2 oz courgette, chopped
25 g/1 oz sweetcorn, thawed if frozen
¾ tsp dried rosemary
1 tbsp olive oil
salt and freshly ground black pepper,
   to taste
700 g/1½ lb boneless beef thick flank
400 g/14 oz can chopped tomatoes
100 g/4 oz rice, cooked, hot

Sauté the mushrooms, onion, carrot, courgette, sweetcorn and rosemary in the olive oil in a frying pan until tender, 5–8 minutes. Season to taste with salt and pepper.

Pound the meat with a meat mallet, if necessary, to make it even in thickness. Spoon the stuffing over the meat and roll up, beginning from the long side. Secure with short skewers and put in the slow cooker. Add the tomatoes. Cover and cook on Low for 6–8 hours. Slice and serve over rice, spooning the juices over the top.

Beef Carbonnade

You need only a small amount of beer to enrich this well known Belgian dish, so it's a good idea to choose one that you enjoy drinking as well.

SERVES 4

700 g/1½ lb lean braising or chuck steak, trimmed
2 tbsp sunflower oil
1 large onion, thinly sliced
2 garlic cloves, crushed, or 2 tsp garlic purée
2 tsp soft brown sugar
1 tbsp plain flour
250 ml/8 fl oz light ale
250 ml/8 fl oz beef stock
1 tsp wine vinegar
1 bay leaf
salt and freshly ground black pepper
chopped fresh parsley, to garnish
crusty French bread, to serve

Cut the meat into pieces about 5 cm/2 in square and 1 cm/½ in thick. Heat 1 tbsp of the oil in a frying pan and brown the meat on all sides. Transfer to the ceramic cooking pot with a slotted spoon, leaving the juices behind in the pan. Add the remaining oil to the pan. Add the onion and cook gently for 5 minutes. Stir in the garlic and sugar, then sprinkle the flour over, stirring to mix. Gradually add the ale and bring to the boil. Let it bubble for a minute, then turn off the heat. Pour the mixture over the beef, then stir in the stock and vinegar. Add the bay leaf and season with salt and pepper. Cover with the lid. Cook for 1 hour on High, then reduce the heat to Low and cook for a further 5–7 hours or until the beef is very tender. Remove the bay leaf and adjust the seasoning, if necessary. Serve the casserole straight away, garnished with a little chopped fresh parsley and accompanied with crusty French bread.

Rouladen

Thin sandwich steaks make easy work of these beef and ham rolls

SERVES 4

4 small or 2 large thin beef sandwich steaks (about 450 g/1 lb total weight)
salt and freshly ground black pepper, to taste
4 slices smoked ham (about 25 g/1 oz each)
100 g/4 oz mushrooms, finely chopped
3 tbsp finely chopped cornichons
½ onion, chopped
1–2 tbsp Dijon mustard
1 tsp dried dill
120 ml/4 fl oz beef stock

Sprinkle the sandwich steaks lightly with salt and pepper. Top each steak with a ham slice. Mix the remaining ingredients, except the stock, and spread over the ham slices. Roll up the steaks, securing them with cocktail sticks. Place, seam sides down, in the slow cooker. Add the stock. Cover and cook on Low for 5–6 hours.

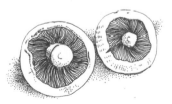

215

Italian-style Rouladen

Provolone is an Italian cheese that is similar to Mozzarella but with a much fuller flavour.

SERVES 4

4 small or 2 large thin beef sandwich steaks (about 450 g/1 lb total weight)
salt and freshly ground black pepper, to taste
4 slices smoked ham (about 25 g/1 oz each)
4 slices Provolone cheese
4 tbsp chopped sun-dried tomatoes
2 tsp dried dill
120 ml/4 fl oz beef stock

Sprinkle the sandwich steaks lightly with salt and pepper. Top each steak with a ham slice. Mix together the cheese and tomatoes and spread over the ham slices. Sprinkle with the dill. Roll up the steaks, securing them with cocktail sticks. Place, seam sides down, in the slow cooker. Add the stock. Cover and cook on Low for 5–6 hours.

Greek-style Rouladen

A taste of Greece, brought to you courtesy of Feta cheese and olives.

SERVES 4

4 small or 2 large thin beef sandwich steaks (about 450 g/1 lb total weight)
salt and freshly ground black pepper, to taste
50 g/2 oz Feta cheese
2 spring onions, finely chopped
4 sun-dried tomatoes, chopped
25 g/1 oz Greek olives, sliced
120 ml/4 fl oz beef stock

Sprinkle the sandwich steaks lightly with salt and pepper. Mash the cheese with the onions, sun-dried tomatoes and olives and spread over the steaks. Roll up the steaks, securing them with cocktail sticks. Place, seam sides down, in the slow cooker. Add the stock. Cover and cook on Low for 5–6 hours.

Braised Short Ribs

You'll find these short ribs especially tasty and juicy. Nibbling on the bones is allowed!

SERVES 4

250 ml/8 fl oz dry red wine or beef stock
4 large carrots, thickly sliced
1 large onion, cut into wedges
2 bay leaves
1 tsp dried marjoram
900 g/2 lb beef short ribs

Combine all the ingredients in the slow cooker, putting the short ribs on the top. Cover and cook on Low for 7–8 hours.

Spiced Beef with Horseradish

The warm spiciness of this casserole from Catherine Atkinson is achieved with a mixture of creamed horseradish, ginger and curry powder.

SERVES 4

1 onion, chopped
2 tbsp creamed horseradish sauce
1 tbsp Worcestershire sauce
450 ml/¾ pint hot (not boiling) beef stock
1 tbsp plain flour
1 tsp medium curry powder
½ tsp ground ginger
1 tsp dark brown sugar
700 g/1½ lb lean braising or chuck steak, cubed
salt and freshly ground black pepper
2 tbsp chopped fresh or frozen parsley
new potatoes and a green vegetable, to serve

Put the onion into the ceramic cooking pot. Stir the horseradish and Worcestershire sauce into the stock and pour over the onion. Switch on the slow cooker to Low and leave for 3–4 minutes while preparing and measuring the remaining ingredients.

Mix the flour, curry powder, ginger and sugar together in a bowl. Add the beef and toss to coat the cubes evenly in the spice mixture. Add to the slow cooker and season with salt and pepper. Cover and cook for 6–7 hours on Low or until the beef is really tender.

Stir in the parsley and adjust the seasoning, if necessary. Serve with new potatoes and a green vegetable such as steamed shredded cabbage.

Simple Meatloaf

Moist, the way meatloaf should be, with plenty of leftovers for sandwiches, too! Serve with Real Mashed Potatoes (see page 264).

SERVES 6

700 g/1½ lb lean minced beef
100 g/4 oz porridge oats
120 ml/4 fl oz semi-skimmed milk
1 egg
50 ml/2 fl oz tomato ketchup or chilli sauce
1 onion, chopped
½ green pepper, chopped
1 garlic clove, crushed
1 tsp dried Italian herb seasoning
1 tsp salt
½ tsp pepper

Make foil handles (see page 10) and fit them into the slow cooker. Mix all the ingredients until blended. Pat the mixture into a loaf shape and put into the slow cooker, making sure the sides of the loaf do not touch the crock. Insert a meat thermometer so that the tip is in the centre of the loaf. Cover and cook on Low until the meat thermometer registers 76°C, about 6–7 hours. Remove, using the foil handles and leave to stand, loosely covered with foil, for 10 minutes.

Italian Meatloaf

Classic meatloaf but with an Italian twist. You could use chilli sauce instead of ketchup.

SERVES 6

700 g/1½ lb lean minced beef
100 g/4 oz porridge oats
120 ml/4 fl oz semi-skimmed milk
1 egg
50 ml/2 fl oz tomato ketchup
1 onion, chopped
½ green pepper, chopped
1 garlic clove, crushed
1 tbsp freshly grated Parmesan cheese
50 g/2 oz grated Mozzarella cheese
2 tbsp pitted black olives, chopped
1 tsp dried Italian herb seasoning
1 tsp salt
½ tsp pepper
2 tbsp ready-made tomato sauce or ketchup
grated Parmesan cheese and grated hard Mozzarella cheese, to garnish

Make foil handles (see page 10) and fit them into the slow cooker. Mix all the ingredients until blended. Pat the mixture into a loaf shape and put into the slow cooker, making sure the sides of the loaf do not touch the crock. Insert a meat thermometer so that the tip is in the centre of the loaf. Cover and cook on Low until the meat thermometer registers 76°C, about 6–7 hours. Top with the tomato sauce or ketchup and sprinkle with the cheeses. Cover and cook on Low until the cheese has melted, 5–10 minutes. Remove, using the foil handles.

Savoury Cheese Meatloaf

This meatloaf has a very full cheesy flavour, making it rich and extremely satisfying. You could use chilli sauce instead of ketchup.

SERVES 6

450 g/1 lb lean minced beef
225 g/8 oz lean minced pork
100 g/4 oz soft cheese
75 g/3 oz Cheddar cheese, grated
100 g/4 oz porridge oats
120 ml/4 fl oz semi-skimmed milk
1 egg
50 ml/2 fl oz tomato ketchup
2 tbsp Worcestershire sauce
1 onion, chopped
½ green pepper, chopped
1 garlic clove, crushed,
1 tsp dried Italian herb seasoning
1 tsp salt
½ tsp pepper

Make foil handles (see page 10) and fit them into the slow cooker. Mix all the ingredients, except 25 g/1 oz of the Cheddar cheese, until blended. Pat the mixture into a loaf shape and put into the slow cooker, making sure the sides of the loaf do not touch the crock. Insert a meat thermometer so that the tip is in the centre of the loaf. Cover and cook on Low until the meat thermometer registers 76°C, about 6–7 hours. Sprinkle with the reserved Cheddar cheese, cover and cook on Low until the cheese has melted, 5–10 minutes. Remove, using the foil handles.

Chutney and Peanut Meatloaf

If you don't have Branston Pickle, you can use the same measure of chopped chutney.

SERVES 6

700 g/1½ lb lean minced beef
100 g/4 oz porridge oats
120 ml/4 fl oz semi-skimmed milk
1 egg
100 g/4 oz Branston Pickle
1 onion, chopped
½ green pepper, chopped
1 garlic clove, crushed,
50 g/2 oz chopped peanuts
1 tsp curry powder
½ tsp ground ginger
1 tsp dried Italian herb seasoning
1 tsp salt
½ tsp pepper

Make foil handles (see page 10) and fit them into the slow cooker. Mix all the ingredients until blended. Pat the mixture into a loaf shape and put into the slow cooker, making sure the sides of the loaf do not touch the crock. Insert a meat thermometer so that the tip is in the centre of the loaf. Cover and cook on Low until the meat thermometer registers 76°C, about 6–7 hours. Remove, using the foil handles and leave to stand, loosely covered with foil, for 10 minutes.

Egg Lemon Sauce

This delicate, lemony sauce can be made with vegetable stock.

SERVES 6 AS AN ACCOMPANIMENT

1 tbsp butter or margarine
2 tbsp flour
120 ml/4 fl oz chicken stock
120 ml/4 fl oz semi-skimmed milk
1 egg, lightly beaten
3–4 tbsp lemon juice
1 tsp grated lemon zest
salt and white pepper, to taste

Melt the butter in a medium pan. Whisk in the flour and cook for 1 minute. Whisk in the stock and milk. Heat to boiling, whisking until thickened, about 1 minute. Whisk about half the stock mixture into the egg. Whisk the mixture back into the pan. Whisk over medium heat for 1 minute. Add the lemon juice and zest. Season to taste with salt and pepper.

Lemon Meatloaf with Egg Lemon Sauce

Meatloaf takes on a new dimension with a lemon accent and a smooth egg and lemon sauce to accompany.

SERVES 6

700 g/1½ lb lean minced beef
50 g/2 oz fresh breadcrumbs
1 egg
1 small onion, chopped
½ small green pepper, chopped
1 garlic clove, crushed
1 tbsp lemon juice
1 tbsp grated lemon zest
1 tsp Dijon mustard
½ tsp dried thyme
½ tsp pepper
¾ tsp salt
Egg Lemon Sauce (see left)

Make foil handles (see page 10) and fit into the slow cooker. Mix all the ingredients, except the Egg Lemon Sauce, until blended. Pat the mixture into a loaf shape and put into the slow cooker, making sure the sides of the loaf do not touch the crock. Insert a meat thermometer so that the tip is in the centre of the loaf. Cover and cook on Low until the meat thermometer registers 76°C, 6–7 hours. Remove, using the foil handles, and leave to stand, loosely covered with foil, for 10 minutes. Serve with Egg Lemon Sauce.

Sweet-sour Ham Loaf

Meatloaf can also be cooked in a 23 x 13 cm/9 x 5 in loaf tin or two smaller loaf tins, if they fit into your slow cooker. Put pans on a rack or on empty tuna cans with both ends removed.

SERVES 6

450 g/1 lb lean minced beef
225 g/8 oz minced or finely chopped smoked ham
50 g/2 oz fresh breadcrumbs
1 egg
1 small onion, chopped
½ small green pepper, chopped
1 garlic clove, crushed
1 tsp Dijon mustard
2 chopped cornichons
50 g/2 oz almonds, coarsely chopped
50 g/2 oz dried mixed fruit
90 g/3½ oz apricot preserve
1 tbsp cider vinegar
2 tsp soy sauce
½ tsp pepper
¾ tsp salt

Make foil handles (see page 10) and fit into the slow cooker. Mix all the ingredients until blended. Pat the mixture into a loaf shape and put into the slow cooker, making sure the sides of the loaf do not touch the crock. Insert a meat thermometer so that the tip is in the centre of the loaf. Cover and cook on Low until the meat thermometer registers 76°C, 6–7 hours. Remove, using the foil handles, and leave to stand, loosely covered with foil, for 10 minutes.

Easy Beef with Wine and Vegetables

A simple yet satisfying beef casserole. Serve over noodles, if you like.

SERVES 4

450 g/1 lb rump steak, cut into 1 cm/½ in strips

250 ml/8 fl oz beef stock
120 ml/4 fl oz dry red wine
275 g/10 oz French beans, cut into short lengths
2 potatoes, cubed
2 small onions, cut into wedges
3 carrots, thickly sliced
¾ tsp dried thyme
salt and freshly ground black pepper, to taste

Combine all the ingredients, except the salt and pepper, in the slow cooker. Cover and cook on Low for 6–8 hours. Season to taste with salt and pepper.

Stuffed Cabbage Leaves

Choose good-quality lean minced beef to mix with pepper, onion and rice for a tasty stuffing for cabbage leaves cooked in a tomato sauce.

SERVES 4

8 large cabbage leaves
450 g/1 lb lean minced beef
½ onion, finely chopped
¼ green pepper, finely chopped
15 g/½ oz rice, cooked
50 ml/2 fl oz water
1 tsp salt
¼ tsp freshly ground black pepper
400 g/14 oz ready-made tomato sauce
450 g/1 lb can chopped tomatoes

Put the cabbage leaves in boiling water until softened, 1–2 minutes. Drain well. Trim the thick veins from the leaves so that they lay flat. Mix the minced beef and the remaining ingredients, except the tomato sauce and chopped tomatoes. Divide the meat mixture into eight equal parts, moulding each into a loaf shape. Wrap each in a cabbage leaf, folding the ends and sides over. Pour half the combined tomato sauce and chopped tomatoes into the slow cooker. Add the cabbage rolls, seam sides down. Pour the remaining tomato mixture over. Cover and cook on Low for 6–8 hours.

Meatballs Florentine

Ricotta cheese, spinach and Mediterranean flavourings make these meatballs exceptionally tasty.

SERVES 4

**65 g/2½ oz spinach leaves
100 g/4 oz Ricotta cheese
1 egg
2 spring onions, chopped
2 garlic cloves
2 tsp dried oregano
½ tsp dried dill
½ tsp freshly grated nutmeg
½ tsp salt
½ tsp pepper
450 g/1 lb lean minced beef
25 g/1 oz fresh breadcrumbs
1 litre/1¾ pints ready-made pasta
  sauce with herbs
225 g/8 oz fettuccine, cooked, hot**

Process the spinach, Ricotta, egg, spring onions, garlic, seasonings, salt and pepper in a food processor or blender until smooth. Mix with the minced beef and breadcrumbs. Shape the mixture into 8–12 meatballs. Combine the meatballs and pasta sauce in the slow cooker, covering the meatballs with sauce. Cover and cook on Low for 5–6 hours. Serve on fettuccine.

Rigatoni with Aubergine Meatballs

Aubergine is a surprise ingredient in these fabulous meatballs.

SERVES 6

**Aubergine Meatballs (see below)
700 g/1½ lb pasta sauce from a jar
350 g/12 oz rigatoni or other pasta
  shapes, cooked, hot
2–3 tbsp olive oil
2 tbsp drained capers
15 g/½ oz chopped fresh flatleaf
  parsley**

Combine the Aubergine Meatballs and pasta sauce in the slow cooker, covering the meatballs with sauce. Cover and cook on Low for 6–8 hours. Toss the rigatoni with oil, capers and parsley. Serve with the meatballs and sauce.

Aubergine Meatballs

The cubed aubergine add a superb richness to these beef-based meatballs.

MAKES 18 MEATBALLS

**1 small aubergine (about 350 g/12
  oz), cubed
700 g/1½ lb lean minced beef
50 g/2 oz freshly grated Parmesan or
  Romano cheese
25 g/1 oz dry breadcrumbs
2 eggs
1½ tsp dried Italian herb seasoning
1 tsp salt
½ tsp pepper**

Cook the aubergine in 5 cm/2 in of simmering water in a medium pan until tender, about 10 minutes. Drain, cool and mash. Combine the aubergine with the remaining meatball ingredients. Shape into 18 meatballs.

221

South African Bobotie

A traditional recipe from southern Africa.

SERVES 4

2 slices of stale bread, crusts removed
2 tbsp oil
1 onion, sliced
2 garlic cloves, crushed
10 ml/2 tsp curry powder
2.5 ml/½ tsp ground cloves
5 ml/1 tsp ground turmeric
2 eggs
450 g/1 lb minced beef
2 tbsp hot water
2 tbsp lemon juice
2 tbsp sugar
salt and freshly ground black pepper

for the topping:
1 egg
150 ml/¼ pt milk
a handful of flaked almonds
rice and a green vegetable, to serve

Soak the bread in warm water for
10 minutes, then squeeze out the excess
water and crumble. Heat the oil in a
frying pan and fry the onion until soft.
Add the garlic, curry powder, cloves and
turmeric and fry for a further 5 minutes,
stirring frequently. Beat the eggs in a
bowl, then stir in the mince. Add the
onion and spice mixture, the bread, hot
water, lemon juice and sugar. Season
with salt and pepper and mix well. Turn
the mixture into a greased 450 g/1 lb
loaf tin (pan) and cover with foil. Place
in the slow cooker and add enough
boiling water to come half-way up the
sides of the pan. Cover and cook on Low
for 8–10 hours until cooked through.
Mix the egg, milk and almonds and pour
over the top. Cover and cook on High for
a further 30 minutes until set. Serve sliced
with rice and a green vegetable.

Country Beef

Root vegetables, plus herbs, garlic and
peas give this casserole lots of flavour and
texture. It's delicious served over noodles
or rice.

SERVES 4

900 g/2 lb lean braising steak, cubed
250 ml/8 fl oz beef stock
150 g/5 oz parsnip, cubed
2 onions, chopped
1 large celery stick, chopped
120 ml/4 fl oz dry red wine or
  beef stock
350 g/12 oz potatoes, unpeeled and
  cubed
2 large carrots, thickly sliced
3 garlic cloves, crushed
2 tbsp tomato purée
½ tsp dried thyme
½ tsp dried rosemary
1 large bay leaf
50 g/2 oz frozen peas, thawed
2 tbsp cornflour
50 ml/2 fl oz cold water
salt and freshly ground black pepper,
  to taste

Combine all the ingredients, except the
peas, cornflour, water, salt and pepper,
in a 5.5 litre/9½ pint slow cooker. Cover
and cook on High for 4–5 hours. Add
the peas, turn the heat to High and cook
for 10 minutes. Stir in the combined
cornflour and water, stirring for 2–3
minutes. Discard the bay leaf. Season to
taste with salt and pepper.

Hearty Beef

Red kidney beans make this one of the tastiest casseroles you could rustle up.

SERVES 6

450 g/1 lb lean rump steak, cubed (2 cm/¾ in)
175 ml/6 fl oz beef stock
400 g/14 oz can chopped tomatoes
400 g/14 oz can red kidney beans, drained and rinsed
1 onion, chopped
3 small waxy potatoes, unpeeled and cubed
3 carrots, sliced
1 tbsp cornflour
2 tbsp cold water
2–3 tsp Worcestershire sauce
salt and freshly ground black pepper, to taste

Combine all the ingredients, except the cornflour, water, Worcestershire sauce, salt and pepper, in the slow cooker. Cover and cook on Low for 6–8 hours. Turn the heat to High and cook for 10 minutes. Stir in the combined cornflour and water, stirring for 2–3 minutes. Season to taste with Worcestershire sauce, salt and pepper.

Simple Beef Casserole

Serve this Italian-seasoned beef casserole over noodles, rice or Microwave Polenta (see page 296).

SERVES 6

900 g/2 lb lean braising steak, cubed (2.5 cm/1 in)
400 g/14 oz can chopped tomatoes
120 ml/4 fl oz beef stock
120 ml/4 fl oz dry red wine or beef stock
2 onions, chopped
2 garlic cloves, crushed
2 tsp dried Italian herb seasoning
salt and freshly ground black pepper, to taste

Combine all the ingredients, except the salt and pepper, in the slow cooker. Cover and cook on Low for 6–8 hours. Season to taste with salt and pepper.

Family Favourite Beef with Herbs

Lots of vegetables, cooked until tender, taste great in this wholesome casserole.

SERVES 8

900 g/2 lb lean braising steak, cubed (2.5 cm/1 in)
400 g/14 oz can chopped tomatoes
250 ml/8 fl oz beef stock
350 g/12 oz potatoes, unpeeled and cubed
275 g/10 oz swede or turnips, cubed
3 onions, chopped
1 large carrot, thickly sliced
2 large celery sticks, sliced
4 garlic cloves, crushed
½–¾ tsp dried marjoram
½–¾ tsp dried thyme
1 bay leaf
2 tbsp cornflour
50 ml/2 fl oz cold water
2–3 tsp Worcestershire sauce
salt and freshly ground black pepper, to taste

Combine all the ingredients, except the cornflour, water, Worcestershire sauce, salt and pepper, in a 5.5 litre/9½ pint slow cooker. Cover and cook on Low for 6–8 hours. Turn the heat to High and cook for 10 minutes. Stir in the combined cornflour and water, stirring for 2–3 minutes. Discard the bay leaf. Season to taste with Worcestershire sauce, salt and pepper.

Beef and Vegetable Casserole

Courgettes, button mushrooms and root vegetables make a good combination in this well-rounded meal.

SERVES 6

700 g/1½ lb lean rump steak, cubed
   (2.5 cm/1 in)
250 ml/8 fl oz beef stock
120 ml/4 fl oz red wine or beef stock
6 carrots, quartered
4 small potatoes, quartered
4 onions, quartered
2 small courgettes, sliced
100 g/4 oz button mushrooms
1 garlic clove, crushed
1 tsp Worcestershire sauce
2 bay leaves
1 tbsp cornflour
50 ml/2 fl oz cold water
salt and freshly ground black pepper,
   to taste

Combine all the ingredients, except the cornflour, water, salt and pepper, in a 5.5 litre/9½ pint slow cooker. Cover and cook on Low for 6–8 hours. Turn the heat to High and cook for 10 minutes. Stir in the combined cornflour and water, stirring for 2–3 minutes. Discard the bay leaves. Season to taste with salt and pepper.

Beef and Mushrooms

Wine adds richness to a sauce, and here white wine is used to give a light touch to this beef dish to serve with tagliatelle.

SERVES 6

450 g/1 lb lean rump steak, cubed
450 ml/¾ pint beef stock
120 ml/4 fl oz dry white wine
225 g/8 oz mushrooms, thinly sliced
½ onion, chopped
1 garlic clove, crushed
1 tbsp dried Italian herb seasoning
2 tbsp cornflour

120 ml/4 fl oz cold water
salt and freshly ground black pepper,
   to taste
225 g/8 oz tagliatelle, cooked, hot

Combine all the ingredients, except the cornflour, water, salt, pepper and pasta, in the slow cooker. Cover and cook on Low for 6–8 hours. Turn the heat to High and cook for 10 minutes. Stir in the combined cornflour and water, stirring for 2–3 minutes. Season to taste with salt and pepper. Serve over the pasta.

Beef with Potatoes and Rice

A robust beef casserole that includes both potatoes and rice. The potatoes add a chunky texture and the rice helps to thicken the flavourful sauce.

SERVES 4

450 g/1 lb lean rump steak, cubed
120 ml/4 fl oz beef stock
50 g/2 oz cabbage, coarsely shredded
2 small potatoes, unpeeled and sliced
1 large onion, finely chopped
1 carrot, sliced
2 garlic cloves, crushed
120 ml/4 fl oz dry red wine or beef stock
50 ml/2 fl oz tomato ketchup
2 tsp brown sugar
1½ tsp cider vinegar
1½ tsp dried thyme
½ tsp dry mustard powder
50 g/2 oz easy-cook long-grain rice
2 tbsp cornflour
50 ml/2 fl oz cold water
salt and freshly ground black pepper,
   to taste

Combine all the ingredients, except the rice, cornflour, water, salt and pepper, in the slow cooker. Cover and cook on Low for 6–8 hours, adding the rice during the last 2 hours. Turn the heat to High and cook for 10 minutes. Stir in the combined cornflour and water, stirring for 2–3 minutes. Season to taste with salt and pepper.

Beef and Squash with Polenta

If you don't have a second slow cooker, the polenta can be made in the microwave (see page 296), or you can cook polenta conventionally, following the packet instructions.

SERVES 8

900 g/2 lb lean braising steak, cubed (2.5 cm/1 in)
250 ml/8 fl oz beef stock
500 g/18 oz butternut squash, peeled and cubed
4 medium tomatoes, chopped
1 onion, chopped
¾ tsp dried marjoram
¾ tsp dried thyme
3 courgettes, cubed
salt and freshly ground black pepper, to taste
700 g/1½ lb polenta (see page 356)

Combine all the ingredients, except the courgettes, salt, pepper and polenta, in a 5.5 litre/9½ pint slow cooker. Cover and cook on Low for 6–8 hours, adding the courgettes during the last 45 minutes. Season to taste with salt and pepper. Serve over polenta.

Wine-braised Beef Casserole

Bay leaves, garlic, mushrooms and red wine together bring a good strong flavour to this dish.

SERVES 6

700 g/1½ lb rump steak, cubed
250 ml/8 fl oz beef stock
250 g/9 oz ready-made tomato sauce
120 ml/4 fl oz dry red wine
175 g/6 oz mushrooms, sliced
2 onions, chopped
1 celery stick, thinly sliced
12 baby carrots
6 small potatoes, halved

1 garlic clove, crushed
1 tsp dried thyme
2 large bay leaves
1–2 tbsp cornflour
50 ml/2 fl oz cold water
salt and freshly ground black pepper, to taste

Combine all the ingredients, except the cornflour, water, salt and pepper, in a 5.5 litre/9½ pint slow cooker. Cover and cook on Low for 6–8 hours. Turn the heat to High and cook for 10 minutes. Stir in the combined cornflour and water, stirring for 2–3 minutes. Discard the bay leaves. Season to taste with salt and pepper.

Rosemary Beef Casserole

Fragrant rosemary is the highlight of this delicious casserole.

SERVES 6

700 g/1½ lb lean braising steak, cubed
375 ml/13 fl oz beef stock
225 g/8 oz ready-made tomato sauce
2 tbsp dry sherry (optional)
425 g/15 oz French beans, cut into short lengths
2 onions, finely chopped
1 carrot, sliced
1 celery stick, sliced
1 large garlic clove, crushed
1 tsp dried rosemary
1 bay leaf
1–2 tbsp cornflour
50 ml/2 fl oz cold water
salt and freshly ground black pepper, to taste
175 g/6 oz rice, cooked, hot

Combine all the ingredients, except the cornflour, water, salt, pepper and rice, in a 5.5 litre/9½ pint slow cooker. Cover and cook on Low for 6–8 hours. Turn the heat to High and cook for 10 minutes. Stir in the combined cornflour and water, stirring for 2–3 minutes. Discard the bay leaf. Season to taste with salt and pepper. Serve over the rice.

225

Autumn Steak and Sweet Potato Casserole

Apples give this autumn casserole a touch of sweetness.

SERVES 4

450 g/1 lb lean rump steak, cubed (2 cm/¾ in)
375 ml/13 fl oz beef stock
450 g/1 lb sweet potatoes, peeled and cubed
2 onions, cut into thin wedges
1 tsp dried rosemary
2 eating apples, peeled and thickly sliced
50 g/2 oz frozen peas, thawed
2 tbsp cornflour
50 ml/2 fl oz cold water
salt and freshly ground black pepper, to taste

Combine all the ingredients, except the apples, peas, cornflour, water, salt and pepper, in the slow cooker. Cover and cook on Low for 6–8 hours, adding the apples during the last 15 minutes. Add the peas, turn the heat to High and cook for 10 minutes. Stir in the combined cornflour and water, stirring for 2–3 minutes. Season to taste with salt and pepper.

Barbecued Beef and Bean Dinner

Use a ready-made sauce and salsa, plus a can of kidney beans to make this tasty dish using storecupboard and freezer ingredients.

SERVES 6

450 g/1 lb lean rump steak, cut into 1 cm/½ in strips)
3 x 400 g/14 oz cans red kidney beans, drained and rinsed
225 g/8 oz ready-made tomato sauce
100 g/4 oz ready-made mild or medium salsa
3 onions, finely chopped
2 garlic cloves, crushed
2 tbsp cider vinegar
2–3 tbsp brown sugar
1–3 tsp chilli powder
2 tsp Worcestershire sauce
100 g/4 oz sweetcorn, thawed if frozen
salt and freshly ground black pepper, to taste

Combine all the ingredients, except the sweetcorn, salt and pepper, in the slow cooker. Cover and cook on Low for 6–8 hours, stirring in the sweetcorn during the last 30 minutes. Season to taste with salt and pepper.

Paprika Sirloin Casserole with Soured Cream

Enjoy tender beef and vegetables in a paprika-spiked soured cream sauce.

SERVES 4

450 g/1 lb boneless beef sirloin steak, fat trimmed, cut into 1 cm/½ in strips
250 ml/8 fl oz beef stock
400 g/14 oz can chopped tomatoes
500 g/18 oz waxy potatoes, cubed
225 g/8 oz French beans, halved
100 g/4 oz baby onions or shallots
2 bay leaves
1 tbsp paprika
120 ml/4 fl oz soured cream
1 tbsp cornflour
salt and freshly ground black pepper, to taste

Combine all the ingredients, except the soured cream, cornflour, salt and pepper, in the slow cooker. Cover and cook on Low for 6–8 hours. Stir in the combined soured cream and cornflour, stirring for 2–3 minutes. Discard the bay leaves. Season to taste with salt and pepper.

Minced Beef and Vegetable Stroganoff

Soured cream and a medley of mushrooms provide a rich flavour and creamy texture to this favourite dish.

SERVES 8

700 g/1½ lb lean minced beef
oil, for greasing
120 ml/4 fl oz water
50 ml/2 fl oz dry red wine or water
2 onions, thinly sliced
2 garlic cloves, crushed
225 g/8 oz mixed wild mushrooms, such as shiitake, oyster, enoki, or brown cap, sliced
1½ tsp Dijon mustard
½ tsp dried dill
225 g/8 oz broccoli florets
250 ml/8 fl oz soured cream
2 tbsp cornflour
salt and freshly ground black pepper, to taste
450 g/1 lb noodles, cooked, hot

Cook the minced beef in a lightly greased large frying pan over medium heat until browned, about 10 minutes, crumbling it with a fork. Combine the beef and the remaining ingredients, except the broccoli, soured cream, cornflour, salt, pepper and noodles, in the slow cooker. Cook on Low for 6–8 hours, adding the broccoli during the last 30 minutes. Stir in the combined soured cream and cornflour, stirring for 2–3 minutes. Season to taste with salt and pepper. Serve over noodles.

Cumin and Chilli Beef

Complement this delicious casserole with soured cream and serve with warm tortillas.

SERVES 8

600 ml/1 pint boiling water
2–6 ancho or other medium-hot chillies, stems, seeds and veins discarded
4 tomatoes, cut into wedges
900 g/2 lb lean beef silverside, cubed (2 cm/¾ in)
1 large onion, chopped
2 garlic cloves, crushed
1 tsp finely chopped jalapeño or other medium-hot chilli
1 tsp dried oregano
1 tsp crushed cumin seeds
1 tbsp cornflour
3 tbsp cold water
salt and freshly ground black pepper, to taste
Red Pepper Rice (see page 309)

Pour boiling water over the ancho chillies in a bowl. Leave to stand until softened, about 10 minutes. Process the chillies, water and tomatoes in a food processor or blender until smooth. Combine the chilli mixture and the remaining ingredients, except the cornflour, water, salt, pepper and Red Pepper Rice, in the slow cooker. Cover and cook on Low for 6–8 hours. Turn the heat to High and cook for 10 minutes. Stir in the combined cornflour and water, stirring for 2–3 minutes. Season to taste with salt and pepper. Serve over Red Pepper Rice.

Burgundy Beef

This French-inspired casserole is perfect for a stress-free special occasion.

SERVES 8

900 g/2 lb lean braising steak
250 ml/8 fl oz Burgundy or
    other red wine
250 ml/8 fl oz beef stock
1 tbsp tomato purée
2 onions, chopped
1 tsp dried thyme
1 tsp dried rosemary
1 tsp dried tarragon
175 g/6 oz baby onions or shallots
130 g/4½ oz mushrooms, sliced
2 tbsp cornflour
50 ml/2 fl oz cold water
25 g/1 oz fresh parsley, chopped
salt and freshly ground black pepper,
    to taste

Combine the beef, wine, stock, tomato purée, chopped onions, and herbs in a 5.5 litre/9½ pint slow cooker. Cover and cook on Low for 6–8 hours, adding the baby onions and mushrooms during the last 2 hours. Turn the heat to High and cook for 10 minutes. Stir in the combined cornflour and water, stirring for 2–3 minutes. Stir in the parsley and season to taste with salt and pepper.

Beef Stroganoff

Always a popular dish, using the slow cooker makes the beef meltingly tender and an ideal main course for entertaining.

SERVES 4

450 g/1 lb beef silverside or sirloin
    steak, cut into 1 cm/½ in strips
250 ml/8 fl oz beef stock
250 g/9 oz mushrooms, sliced
1 onion, sliced
2 garlic cloves, crushed
1 tsp Dijon mustard

½ tsp dried thyme
120 ml/4 fl oz soured cream
1 tbsp cornflour
salt and freshly ground black pepper,
    to taste
425 g/15 oz noodles, cooked, hot

Combine all the ingredients, except the soured cream, cornflour, salt, pepper and noodles, in the slow cooker. Cover and cook on Low for 6–8 hours. Stir in the combined soured cream and cornflour, stirring for 2–3 minutes. Season to taste with salt and pepper. Serve over noodles.

Creamy Beef Stroganoff with Rice

Horseradish adds a pleasant sharpness of flavour. Increase the amount if you like.

SERVES 4

450 g/1 lb lean beef silverside, cubed
    (2.5 cm/1 in)
250 ml/8 fl oz beef stock
50 ml/2 fl oz red Burgundy wine
    (optional)
3 tbsp tomato purée
225 g/8 oz mushrooms, sliced
2 onions, chopped
2 large garlic cloves, crushed
1 tsp creamed horseradish
½ tsp dried thyme
1 bay leaf
175 ml/6 fl oz soured cream
2 tbsp cornflour
salt and freshly ground black pepper,
    to taste
100 g/4 oz rice, cooked, hot

Combine all the ingredients, except the soured cream, cornflour, salt, pepper and rice, in the slow cooker. Cover and cook on Low for 6–8 hours. Stir in the combined soured cream and cornflour, stirring for 2–3 minutes. Discard the bay leaf. Season to taste with salt and pepper. Serve over rice.

Beef and Mushroom Stroganoff

Serve in shallow bowls with warm crusty bread to soak up the juices.

SERVES 4

450 g/1 lb lean rump steak, cut into 1 cm/½ in strips
375 ml/13 fl oz beef stock
225 g/8 oz mushrooms, sliced
1 onion, chopped
3 shallots or spring onions, chopped
1 garlic clove, crushed
120–250 ml/4–8 fl oz soured cream
2 tbsp cornflour
salt and freshly ground black pepper, to taste

Combine all the ingredients, except the soured cream, cornflour, salt and pepper, in the slow cooker. Cover and cook on Low for 6–8 hours. Stir in the combined soured cream and cornflour, stirring for 2–3 minutes. Season to taste with salt and pepper.

Beef Ragout

Serve this casserole over rice, noodles or a cooked grain, such as barley, wheat berries or oat groats.

SERVES 8

900 g/2 lb lean braising steak, cubed (2.5 cm/1 in)
375 ml/13 fl oz beef stock
2 large carrots, sliced
2 celery sticks, sliced
225 g/8 oz baby onions or shallots
1 garlic clove, chopped
1 tsp dried oregano
1 tsp dried thyme
2 tbsp cornflour
50 ml/2 fl oz cold water
salt and freshly ground black pepper, to taste

Combine all the ingredients, except the cornflour, water, salt and pepper, in a 5.5 litre/9½ pint slow cooker. Cover and cook on Low for 6–8 hours. Turn the heat to High and cook for 10 minutes. Stir in the combined cornflour and water, stirring for 2–3 minutes. Season to taste with salt and pepper.

Beef Goulash

In Hungary, this paprika-seasoned casserole is called gulyas, and it's often served with dollops of soured cream.

SERVES 4

12–450 g/1 lb lean rump steak, cubed (2 cm/¾ in)
400 g/14 oz chopped tomatoes
225 g/8 oz cabbage, coarsely sliced
3 onions, cut into thin wedges
100 g/4 oz portabella mushrooms, chopped
1 tbsp paprika
2 tsp caraway seeds
1–2 tbsp cornflour
50 ml/2 fl oz cold water
salt and freshly ground black pepper, to taste
225 g/8 oz medium egg noodles, cooked, hot

Combine all the ingredients, except the cornflour, water, salt, pepper and noodles, in the slow cooker. Cover and cook on Low for 6–8 hours. Turn the heat to High and cook for 10 minutes. Stir in the cornflour and water, stirring for 2–3 minutes. Season to taste with salt and pepper. Serve over the noodles.

Hungarian Goulash

This traditional dish of tenderly cooked beef is flavoured with paprika and enriched with soured cream.

SERVES 6

900 g/2 lb lean rump steak, cubed (2.5 cm/1 in)
400 g/14 oz can chopped tomatoes
1 onion, finely chopped
1 garlic clove, crushed
1½ tsp paprika
1 bay leaf
250 ml/8 fl oz soured cream
2 tbsp cornflour
salt and freshly ground black pepper, to taste
350 g/12 oz egg noodles, cooked, hot

Combine all the ingredients, except the soured cream, cornflour, salt, pepper and noodles, in the slow cooker. Cover and cook on Low for 6–8 hours. Stir in the combined soured cream and cornflour, stirring for 2–3 minutes. Discard the bay leaf. Season to taste with salt and pepper. Serve over noodles.

Beef Casserole with Port

Catherine Atkinson's rich and delicious dish has just a hint of sweetness from the treacle, giving it almost a Caribbean flavour.

SERVES 4

175 g/6 oz button onions, unpeeled
2 tbsp sunflower oil
700 g/1½ lb lean braising or chuck steak, trimmed and cubed (5 cm/2 in)
150 g/5 oz baby button mushrooms
1 garlic clove, crushed, or 1 tsp garlic purée
1 tbsp plain flour
300 ml/½ pint beef stock
2 oranges
1 tbsp tomato purée
1 tbsp black treacle
2 tbsp port
salt and freshly ground black pepper
rice and a green vegetable, to serve

Put the onions in a heatproof bowl and pour over enough boiling water to cover. Leave for 5–10 minutes while browning the beef. Heat the oil in a frying pan. Add the beef and cook for 5 minutes, turning the pieces frequently until browned all over. Transfer to the ceramic cooking pot with a slotted spoon, leaving any fat and juices behind.

Drain the onions and peel off the skins when cool enough to handle. Add to the frying pan with the mushrooms and cook gently until they begin to brown. Stir in the garlic, then push the mixture to one side. Sprinkle the flour over the fat and juices in the pan. Stir well, then gradually add the stock and bring to the boil. Remove from the heat.

Remove the zest from the oranges using a zester. Cut the oranges in half and squeeze out the juice. Add the zest and juice to the pan. Stir in the tomato purée, treacle and port. Season with salt and pepper. Pour the mixture over the beef in the ceramic cooking pot. Cover with the lid and cook on Low for 6–8 hours or until the beef and onions are very tender. Serve with rice and a green vegetable such as runner beans.

Hungarian-style Beef

Serve this rich-tasting beef and vegetable casserole with warm crusty bread to soak up the wonderful sauce.

SERVES 6

450 g/1 lb lean rump steak, cut into thin strips
120 ml/4 fl oz beef stock
120 ml/4 fl oz dry red wine or extra beef stock
225 g/8 oz ready-made tomato sauce
450 g/1 lb potatoes, peeled and cubed
2 large carrots, sliced
2 celery sticks, sliced
2 onions, finely chopped
1 large garlic clove, crushed
1 tsp dried thyme
1 tsp paprika
1 bay leaf
¼ tsp dry mustard powder
120 ml/4 fl oz soured cream
1 tbsp cornflour
salt and freshly ground black pepper

Combine all the ingredients, except the soured cream, cornflour, salt and pepper, in the slow cooker. Cover and cook on Low for 6–8 hours. Stir in the combined soured cream and cornflour, stirring for 2–3 minutes. Discard the bay leaf. Season to taste with salt and pepper.

Italian-style Beef Casserole

Green pepper, mushrooms, tomatoes and basil flavour this beef dish. Serve over linguine.

SERVES 4

550 g/1¼ lb lean rump steak, cubed (2.5 cm/1 in)
400 g/14 oz can chopped tomatoes
2 onions, chopped
1 green pepper, chopped
75 g/3 oz mushrooms, sliced
3 shallots or spring onions, chopped
1 tsp beef bouillon granules, or a beef stock cube
1 tsp dried basil
1 tsp garlic powder
2 tbsp cornflour
50 ml/2 fl oz cold water
salt and freshly ground black pepper, to taste
175 g/6 oz linguine, cooked, hot
3 tbsp chopped fresh parsley
3 tbsp freshly grated Parmesan cheese

Combine all the ingredients, except the cornflour, water, salt, pepper, linguine, parsley and cheese, in the slow cooker. Cover and cook on Low for 6–8 hours. Turn the heat to High and cook for 10 minutes. Stir in the combined cornflour and water, stirring for 2–3 minutes. Season to taste with salt and pepper. Serve over linguine, sprinkled with parsley and Parmesan cheese.

Five-spice Beef Casserole

A simple-to-make dish with lots of Asian flavour, thanks to Chinese five-spice powder and Chinese chilli sauce.

SERVES 4

450 g/1 lb lean rump steak, cubed (2.5 cm/1 in)
175 ml/6 fl oz orange juice
175 ml/6 fl oz beef stock
225 g/8 oz coarsely sliced Chinese leaves
1 onion, cut into thin wedges
1 red pepper, thinly sliced
1 tbsp teriyaki sauce
1 tsp Chinese chilli sauce with garlic
1¼ tsp Chinese five-spice powder
100 g/4 oz bean thread noodles
salt and freshly ground black pepper, to taste

Combine all the ingredients, except the noodles, salt and pepper, in the slow cooker. Cover and cook for 6–8 hours. During the last hour of cooking time, soak the bean thread noodles in hot water to cover in a large bowl for 15 minutes. Drain and stir into the stew during the last 30 minutes of cooking time. Season to taste with salt and pepper.

Asian Beef with Sesame Noodles

Sesame Noodles are the perfect accompaniment for this fragrant dish.

SERVES 8

900 g/2 lb lean braising steak, cubed (2.5 cm/1 in)
250 ml/8 fl oz water
2 thin slices fresh root ginger
2 garlic cloves, halved
2 spring onions, sliced
3–4 tbsp soy sauce
2–3 tsp sugar
3 tbsp dry sherry (optional)
50 g/2 oz frozen peas, thawed
2 tbsp cornflour
50 ml/2 fl oz cold water
salt and freshly ground black pepper, to taste
Sesame Noodles (see right)
1 tbsp sesame seeds, toasted
finely chopped fresh coriander, to garnish

Combine all the ingredients, except the peas, cornflour, cold water, salt, pepper, Sesame Noodles and sesame seeds, in the slow cooker. Cover and cook on Low for 6–8 hours. Add the peas, turn the heat to High and cook for 10 minutes. Stir in the combined cornflour and water, stirring for 2–3 minutes. Season to taste with salt and pepper. Serve the beef over hot Sesame Noodles and sprinkle with sesame seeds and fresh coriander.

Sesame Noodles Ⓥ

Use light or dark sesame oil according to your preference. Dark is generally lower in salt.

SERVES 8 AS AN ACCOMPANIMENT

350 g/12 oz thin noodles, cooked, hot
2–4 tsp soy sauce
2 tsp toasted sesame oil
2 spring onions, thinly sliced

Cook the noodles according to the packet instructions. Toss the hot noodles with the remaining ingredients. Serve hot.

Teriyaki Beef and Broccoli

Japanese teriyaki sauce and ginger give this dish plenty of flavour. It can also be served over rice, pasta or any grain.

SERVES 4

12–450 g/1 lb lean rump steak, cut into 1 cm/½ in strips
250 ml/8 fl oz beef stock
1 onion, cut into thin wedges
2 carrots, sliced
2.5 cm/1 in piece fresh root ginger, finely grated
2 tbsp teriyaki sauce
350 g/12 oz small broccoli florets
2 tbsp cornflour
50 ml/2 fl oz cold water
salt and freshly ground black pepper, to taste
225 g/8 oz noodles, cooked, hot

Combine all the ingredients, except the broccoli, cornflour, water, salt, pepper and noodles, in the slow cooker. Cover and cook on Low for 6–8 hours, adding the broccoli during the last 30 minutes. Turn the heat to High and cook for 10 minutes. Stir in the combined cornflour and water, stirring for 2–3 minutes. Season to taste with salt and pepper. Serve over noodles.

Middle Eastern Beef and Bean Hot Pot

Sweet spices give Middle Eastern flavour accents to succulent steak.

SERVES 8

450 g/1 lb lean braising steak, cubed
175 g/6 oz dried cannellini beans
1 litre/1¾ pints beef stock
4 onions, chopped
2 garlic cloves, crushed
2 bay leaves
1 tsp dried thyme
½ tsp ground cinnamon
a pinch of ground cloves
275 g/10 oz tomatoes, chopped
75 g/3 oz rice, cooked
**salt and freshly ground black pepper,
    to taste**

Combine all the ingredients, except the tomatoes, rice, salt and pepper, in a 5.5 litre/9½ pint slow cooker. Cover and cook on Low until the beans are tender, 7–8 hours, adding the tomatoes and rice during the last 30 minutes. Discard the bay leaves. Season to taste with salt and pepper.

Curried Beef Casserole with Chive Scones

Part of the beef in this aromatic casserole is coarsely chopped, giving the casserole an extra-rich texture.

SERVES 8

900 g/2 lb lean braising steak
375 ml/13 fl oz beef stock
3 onions, chopped
1 large tomato, coarsely chopped
1½ tsp curry powder
2 bay leaves
**salt and freshly ground black pepper,
    to taste**
275 g/10 oz frozen peas, thawed

4 plain scones, halved
melted butter or cooking spray
**chopped fresh or dried chives,
    to garnish**

Cut half the beef into 2.5 cm/1 in cubes. Coarsely chop the remaining beef. Combine the beef and the remaining ingredients, except the salt, pepper, peas, scones and butter or cooking spray, in the slow cooker. Cover and cook on Low for 6–8 hours. Discard the bay leaves. Season to taste with salt and pepper. Add the peas and put the scone halves, cut sides down, on the stew. Brush the scones lightly with butter or spray with oil and sprinkle with chives. Cover and cook for 15 minutes.

Greek Beef with Lentils

Lentils and fresh vegetables make delicious partners in this easy casserole.

SERVES 6

**450 g/1 lb beef silverside, cubed
    (2 cm/¾ in)**
750 ml/1¼ pints beef stock
400 g/14 oz can chopped tomatoes
350 g/12 oz floury potatoes, cubed
**275 g/10 oz French beans, cut into
    short lengths**
175 g/6 oz dried green or brown lentils
2 onions, chopped
1 green pepper, chopped
2 garlic cloves, crushed
1 tsp dried oregano
1 tsp dried mint
½ tsp ground turmeric
½ tsp ground coriander
1 courgette, cubed
**salt and freshly ground black pepper,
    to taste**

Combine all the ingredients, except the courgette, salt and pepper, in a 5.5 litre/9½ pint slow cooker. Cover and cook on Low for 6–8 hours, adding the courgette during the last 30 minutes. Season to taste with salt and pepper.

Romano Meatballs with Pasta

Meatballs combined with vegetables and tricolour pasta in a delectable casserole. The meatballs will be less fragile to handle if you first brown them in a lightly greased frying pan.

SERVES 4

Romano Meatballs (see below)
900 ml/1½ pints beef stock
400 g/14 oz can chopped plum tomatoes
½ onion, chopped
1 tsp dried Italian herb seasoning
100 g/4 oz tricolour fusilli, cooked
350 g/12 oz small broccoli florets
3 tbsp cornflour
75 ml/2½ fl oz cold water
salt and freshly ground black pepper,
** to taste**

Combine all the ingredients, except the pasta, broccoli, cornflour, water, salt and pepper, in the slow cooker, making sure the meatballs are submerged. Cover and cook on Low for 6–8 hours, adding the pasta and broccoli during the last 15 minutes. Turn the heat to High and cook for 10 minutes. Stir in the combined cornflour and water, stirring for 2–3 minutes. Season to taste with salt and pepper.

Romano Meatballs

These tasty beef meatballs have added texture from the oats.

MAKES 16 MEATBALLS

225 g/8 oz lean minced beef
1 egg white
50 g/2 oz porridge oats
1 tbsp dried minced onion
½ tsp dried Italian herb seasoning
50 g/2 oz freshly grated Parmesan or
** Romano cheese**

Combine all the ingredients in a bowl. Shape the mixture into 16 meatballs.

Pasta Bolognese

Bolognese sauce must surely be the best known and most popular of pasta sauces.

SERVES 6

450 g/1 lb lean minced beef
oil, for greasing
½ onion, chopped
½ carrot, chopped
½ celery stick, chopped
3 garlic cloves, crushed
1½ tsp dried Italian herb seasoning
a pinch of freshly grated nutmeg
225 g/8 oz ready-made tomato sauce
225 g/8 oz chopped tomatoes
50 ml/2 fl oz dry red wine or tomato
** juice**
½ tsp salt
freshly ground black pepper, to taste
350 g/12 oz spaghetti, cooked, hot

Cook the minced beef in a lightly greased medium pan over medium heat until browned, 5–8 minutes, crumbling it with a fork. Combine the beef and the remaining ingredients, except the spaghetti, in the slow cooker. Cover and cook on Low for 6–7 hours. If a thicker consistency is desired, cook uncovered, turning the heat to High, during the last 30 minutes. Serve the sauce over the spaghetti.

Steak in Tomato Sauce

Strips of steak are cooked with potatoes, peas and carrots in a tomato sauce.

SERVES 6

700 g/1½ lb lean braising steak, cut into 1 cm/½ in strips
400 g/14 oz can chopped tomatoes with herbs
225 g/8 oz ready-made tomato sauce
4 waxy potatoes, cubed
1 large onion, thinly sliced
½ tsp garlic powder
275 g/10 oz frozen peas and carrots, thawed
2 tbsp cornflour
50 ml/2 fl oz water
salt and freshly ground black pepper, to taste

Combine all the ingredients, except the frozen vegetables, cornflour, water, salt and pepper, in a 5.5 litre/9½ pint slow cooker. Cover and cook on Low for 6–8 hours, adding the thawed frozen vegetables during the last 10 minutes. Turn the heat to High and cook for 10 minutes. Stir in the combined cornflour and water, stirring for 2–3 minutes. Season to taste with salt and pepper.

Garden Vegetables with Hearty Meatballs

If you have time, brown the meatballs in a lightly greased large frying pan, or bake them at 180°C/gas 4/fan oven 160°C until browned – they will be less fragile and more attractive. Add the meatballs to the slow cooker carefully, so that they don't break apart.

SERVES 6

Hearty Meatballs (see page 86)
250 ml/8 fl oz beef stock
2 x 400 g/14 oz cans chopped tomatoes
3 carrots, thickly sliced
1 tsp dried basil
2 small courgettes, sliced
50 g/2 oz frozen peas, thawed
2 tbsp cornflour
50 ml/2 fl oz cold water
salt and freshly ground black pepper, to taste
350 g/12 oz noodles or fettuccine, cooked, hot

Combine all the ingredients, except the courgettes, peas, cornflour, water, salt, pepper and noodles, in a 5.5 litre/9½ pint slow cooker, making sure the meatballs are submerged. Cover and cook on Low for 6–8 hours, adding the courgettes and peas during the last 20 minutes. Turn the heat to High and cook for 10 minutes. Stir in the combined cornflour and water, stirring for 2–3 minutes. Season to taste with salt and pepper. Serve over the noodles.

Salt Beef and Red Cabbage

Root vegetables and cabbage make a good base for salt beef.

SERVES 4

450 g/1 lb salt beef or brisket, cubed
450 g/1 lb red cabbage, coarsely sliced
120 ml/4 fl oz chicken stock
4 waxy potatoes, cubed
1 large carrot, sliced
150 g/5 oz turnip, cubed
1 tbsp cider vinegar
1 tsp pickling spice
salt and freshly ground black pepper, to taste

Combine all the ingredients, except the salt and pepper, in the slow cooker. Cover and cook on Low for 6–8 hours. Season to taste with salt and pepper.

Veal with Sage

Sage and dry white wine give this dish a delicate touch.

SERVES 6

550 g/1¼ lb boneless veal leg, cubed
250 ml/8 fl oz chicken stock
120 ml/4 fl oz dry white wine
1 onion, chopped
2 celery sticks, sliced
2 carrots, sliced
2 garlic cloves, chopped
½ tsp dried sage
½ tsp dried thyme
salt and freshly ground black pepper, to taste
350 g/12 oz egg noodles, cooked, hot

Combine all the ingredients, except the salt, pepper and noodles, in the slow cooker. Cover and cook on Low for 6–8 hours. Season to taste with salt and pepper. Serve over the noodles.

Creamed Veal with Peas and Mushrooms

This would also be lovely served with Real Mashed Potatoes (see page 258).

SERVES 6

550 g/1¼ lb boneless veal leg, cubed
250 ml/8 fl oz chicken stock
1 onion, chopped
2 celery sticks, sliced
175 g/6 oz mushrooms, sliced
2 garlic cloves, chopped
½ tsp dried sage
½ tsp dried thyme
75 g/3 oz frozen petits pois, thawed
175 ml/6 fl oz milk
2 tbsp cornflour
50 ml/2 fl oz cold water
salt and freshly ground black pepper, to taste
350 g/12 oz egg noodles, cooked, hot

Combine all the ingredients, except the petits pois, milk, cornflour, water, salt, pepper and noodles, in the slow cooker. Cover and cook on Low for 5–7 hours. Add the petits pois and milk and cook on Low for a further 1 hour. Turn the slow cooker to High and cook for 10 minutes. Stir in the combined cornflour and cold water and stir for 2–3 minutes. Season to taste with salt and pepper. Serve over noodles.

Veal Marsala

Chicken breast can be substituted for the veal in this casserole, and chicken stock for the Marsala. Serve over rice, if you like.

SERVES 4

450 g/1 lb lean veal leg, cubed
250 ml/8 fl oz chicken stock
50–120 ml/2–4 fl oz Marsala
175 g/6 oz mushrooms, sliced
2 garlic cloves, crushed
¼–½ tsp dried rosemary, crushed
2 tbsp cornflour
50 ml/2 fl oz cold water
salt and freshly ground black pepper, to taste

Combine all the ingredients, except the cornflour, water, salt and pepper, in the slow cooker. Cover and cook on Low for 6–8 hours. Turn the heat to High and cook for 10 minutes. Stir in the combined cornflour and water, stirring for 2–3 minutes. Season to taste with salt and pepper.

Veal and Vegetable Paprikash

Use either hot or sweet paprika in this recipe according to your preference.

SERVES 6

700 g/1½ lb boneless veal leg, cubed (1 cm/½ in)
250 ml/8 fl oz chicken stock
225 g/8 oz cabbage, thinly sliced
2 onions, sliced
1 large carrot, sliced
1 green peppers, sliced
75 g/3 oz mushrooms, sliced
200 g/7 oz tomatoes, chopped
1 tbsp paprika
1 courgette, sliced
120 ml/4 fl oz soured cream
2 tbsp cornflour
salt and freshly ground black pepper, to taste
350 g/12 oz noodles, cooked, hot

Combine all the ingredients, except the courgette, soured cream, cornflour, salt, pepper and noodles, in a 5.5 litre/9½ pint slow cooker. Cover and cook on Low for 6–8 hours, adding the courgette during the last 30 minutes. Stir in the combined soured cream and cornflour, stirring for 2–3 minutes. Season to taste with salt and pepper. Serve over noodles.

Veal with Wine

Chicken breast can be substituted for the veal in this recipe. Serve over rice or pasta, with a green salad and warm crusty bread.

SERVES 6

700 g/1½ lb boneless veal leg, cubed (2 cm/¾ in)
120 ml/4 fl oz chicken stock
120 ml/4 fl oz ready-made tomato sauce
120 ml/4 fl oz dry white wine
175 g/6 oz sweet potatoes, peeled and cubed
1 large onion, chopped
1 garlic clove, crushed
¼ red pepper, chopped
¼ green pepper, chopped
100 g/4 oz frozen peas, thawed
2 tbsp cornflour
50 ml/2 fl oz cold water
salt and freshly ground black pepper, to taste

Combine all the ingredients, except the peas, cornflour, water, salt and pepper, in the slow cooker. Cover and cook on Low for 6–8 hours. Add the peas, turn the heat to High and cook for 10 minutes. Stir in the combined cornflour and water, stirring for 2–3 minutes. Season to taste with salt and pepper.

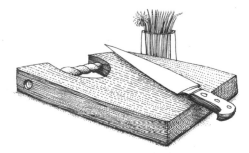

237

Savoury Veal with Caraway

Caraway and anise seeds bring a warm and spicy flavour to this casserole.

SERVES 8

900 g/2 lb lean veal leg, cubed (2 cm/¾ in)
120 ml/4 fl oz chicken stock
120 ml/4 fl oz dry white wine or extra chicken stock
1 small cabbage, cut into 8 wedges
3 leeks (white parts only), thickly sliced
175 g/6 oz mushrooms, sliced
3 garlic cloves, crushed
1 tsp caraway seeds, crushed
¾ tsp anise seeds, crushed
2 bay leaves
1 tbsp cornflour
120 ml/4 fl oz soured cream
salt and freshly ground black pepper, to taste

Combine all the ingredients, except the cornflour, soured cream, salt and pepper, in a 5.5 litre/9½ pint slow cooker. Cover and cook on Low for 6–8 hours. Stir in the combined cornflour and soured cream, stirring for 2–3 minutes. Discard the bay leaves. Season to taste with salt and pepper.

Veal Sauvignon

This fragrant casserole is also delicious served over an aromatic rice, such as basmati or jasmine.

SERVES 4

450 g/1 lb boneless veal cutlets, cut into thin strips
120 ml/4 fl oz chicken stock
120 ml/4 fl oz dry white wine
1 onion, halved and thinly sliced
1 garlic clove, crushed
1 tsp dried marjoram
1 tbsp tomato purée

½ cauliflower, broken into small florets
150 g/5 oz Swiss chard or spinach, torn
salt and freshly ground black pepper, to taste
225 g/8 oz fettuccine, cooked, hot

Combine all the ingredients, except the cauliflower, Swiss chard, salt, pepper and pasta, in the slow cooker. Cover and cook on Low for 6–8 hours, adding the cauliflower and Swiss chard during the last 30 minutes. Season to taste with salt and pepper. Serve over fettuccine.

Mediterranean Veal

Beef or pork can be substituted for the veal in this recipe. If you prefer a thicker consistency of sauce, thicken at the end of cooking time with 1–2 tbsp cornflour combined with 50 ml/2 fl oz cold water.

SERVES 6

700 g/1½ lb lean veal leg, cubed
250 ml/8 fl oz chicken stock
400 g/14 oz can chopped tomatoes
2 tbsp tomato purée
1 onion, coarsely chopped
1 carrot, coarsely chopped
2 garlic cloves, crushed
¾ tsp dried thyme
¾ tsp dried basil
1 bay leaf
50 g/2 oz pitted olives
2 tbsp drained capers
salt and freshly ground black pepper, to taste
350 g/12 oz linguine, cooked, hot

Combine all the ingredients, except the olives, capers, salt, pepper and pasta, in the slow cooker. Cover and cook on Low for 6–8 hours, adding the olives and capers during the last 30 minutes. Discard the bay leaf. Season to taste with salt and pepper. Serve over pasta.

Veal Meatballs with Soured Cream Mushroom Sauce

Delicate veal is enhanced by a cream sauce to serve with fettuccine.

SERVES 4

**225 g/8 oz mushrooms, sliced
Veal Meatballs (see below)
120 ml/4 fl oz chicken stock
250 ml/8 fl oz soured cream
3 tbsp cornflour
salt and freshly ground black pepper,
    to taste
225 g/8 oz fettuccine, cooked, hot**

Put three-quarters of the mushrooms in the slow cooker. Top with the meatballs and remaining mushrooms. Pour the stock over. Cover and cook on Low for 5–6 hours. Remove the meatballs and keep warm. Stir the combined soured cream and cornflour into the stock, stirring for 2–3 minutes. Season to taste with salt and pepper. Serve the meatballs and sauce over fettuccine.

Veal Meatballs

Minced chicken, pork or beef can be substituted for the veal.

MAKES 12–16 MEATBALLS

**700 g/1½ lb minced veal
2 spring onions, finely chopped
1 garlic clove, crushed
2 eggs
50 ml/2 fl oz chicken stock or milk
40 g/1½ oz dry breadcrumbs
1 tsp salt
¼ tsp pepper**

Combine all the ingredients in a bowl. Shape the mixture into 12–16 meatballs.

Osso Bucco

Gremolata, a pungent mixture of finely chopped parsley, lemon zest and garlic, is traditionally added to this classic northern Italian dish.

SERVES 6

**1.75 kg/4 lb shin of veal cut into
    6 pieces, fat trimmed
2 x 400 g/14 oz cans chopped
    tomatoes
120 ml/4 fl oz dry white wine or water
3 carrots, chopped
3 garlic cloves, crushed
2 celery sticks, thinly sliced
1 onion, chopped
¾ tsp dried basil
¾ tsp dried thyme
2 bay leaves
Gremolata (see page 245)
salt and freshly ground black pepper,
    to taste
225 g/8 oz rice, cooked, hot**

Combine all the ingredients, except the Gremolata, salt, pepper and rice, in a 5.5 litre/9½ pint slow cooker. Cover and cook on Low for 6–8 hours. Discard the bay leaves. Stir in half the Gremolata and season to taste with salt and pepper. Serve over rice and hand round the remaining Gremolata.

Pork and Lamb Dishes

Bring variety and imagination to your slow cooking by trying all the various cuts of meat for your slow cooking recipes.

Fruit-stuffed Pork Loin

Pork always tastes perfect contrasting with fruit, and prunes make an especially rich accompaniment. Any dried fruit can be used in this fragrant filling if you prefer.

SERVES 6–8

**130 g/4½ oz pitted prunes
900 g/2 lb boneless pork loin
½ apple, peeled and chopped
½ tsp dried marjoram
½ tsp dried sage
salt and freshly ground black pepper, to taste
120 ml/4 fl oz dry white wine or apple juice
2 tbsp cornflour
2 tbsp honey
175 ml/6 fl oz full-fat milk or single cream**

Soak the prunes in hot water to cover until softened, 10–15 minutes. Drain well. Chop coarsely. Push the handle of a long wooden spoon through the centre of the loin to make an opening for the stuffing.

Combine the prunes, apple and herbs. Push the mixture through the meat, using the handle of a wooden spoon. Sprinkle the outside of the roast lightly with salt and pepper. Put a meat thermometer in the meat, making sure the tip does not rest in the stuffing.

Put the pork and wine or apple juice in the slow cooker. Cover and cook on Low until the temperature registers 71°C, about 3 hours. Remove the meat to a platter and keep warm. Turn the heat to High and cook for 10 minutes. Stir in the combined cornflour, honey and milk or cream, stirring for 2–3 minutes.

Pork Loin Braised in Milk

Pork is exceedingly tender and moist when roasted in milk. The milk and cooking juices are then strained and the milk curds discarded, to make a tasty gravy.

SERVES 8

**1.5 kg/3 lb boneless pork loin
salt and freshly ground black pepper, to taste
120 ml/4 fl oz full-fat milk
50 ml/2 fl oz dry white wine or milk
2 large fresh rosemary sprigs
2 fresh sage sprigs
2 garlic cloves, crushed**

Sprinkle the pork lightly with salt and pepper. Insert a meat thermometer in the centre of the roast so that the tip is in the centre of the meat. Put the meat and the remaining ingredients into the slow cooker. Cover and cook on Low until the meat thermometer registers 71°C, about 4 hours. Remove to a serving platter. Strain the stock, discarding the milk curds and herbs. Make gravy with the stock or reserve for another use.

Note: to make gravy, measure the strained stock and pour into a small pan. Heat to boiling. For every 250 ml/8 fl oz of stock, whisk in 2 tbsp of flour mixed with 50 ml/2 fl oz of cold water, whisking until thickened, about 1 minute.

Pork Sandwiches

I suggest using burger buns here, but you could also try crusty white or wholemeal French bread.

SERVES 10

1 bonless pork loin, fat trimmed (about 1.5 kg/3 lb)
Spice Rub (see page 208)
450 ml/¾ pint ready-made barbecue sauce
50 ml/2 fl oz red wine vinegar
50 g/2 oz light brown sugar
2 medium onions, sliced
120 ml/4 fl oz water
toasted burger buns
dill pickles

Rub the pork loin with the Spice Rub and put in the slow cooker. Pour in the combined remaining ingredients, except the burger buns and dill pickles. Cover and cook on Low for 6–8 hours, turning the heat to High during the last 20–30 minutes. Remove the pork to a serving platter and leave to stand, covered with foil, for about 10 minutes. Shred the pork using a fork and mix with the barbecue mixture. Spoon the pork inside toasted burger buns and top with dill pickles.

Roast Pork with Mango Chutney

A home-made Mango Chutney tastes wonderful with roast pork. Make the chutney in advance. It will keep in the fridge for several weeks. It's also excellent served with chicken.

SERVES 8

1 onion, finely chopped
120 ml/4 fl oz chicken stock
1.5 kg/3 lb boneless pork loin
paprika
salt and freshly ground black pepper
Mango Chutney (see below)

Put the onion and stock in the slow cooker. Sprinkle the pork lightly with paprika, salt and pepper. Insert a meat thermometer into centre of the pork so that the tip is in the centre of the meat. Put the pork into the slow cooker. Cover and cook on Low until the meat thermometer registers 71°C, about 4 hours. Remove the pork to a serving platter and leave to rest, loosely covered with foil, for about 10 minutes. Make gravy with the stock mixture or reserve for soup or another use. Serve the pork with Mango Chutney.
Note: To make gravy, measure the stock mixture and pour into a small pan. Heat to boiling. For every 250 ml/8 fl oz of stock mixture, whisk in 2 tbsp of flour mixed with 50 ml/2 fl oz of cold water, whisking until thickened, about 1 minute.

Mango Chutney ⓥ

Serve with curries or pork.

SERVES 8 AS AN ACCOMPANIMENT

3 mangoes, chopped
225 g/8 oz light brown sugar
120 ml/4 fl oz cider vinegar
40 g/1½ oz sultanas
2 tsp finely chopped jalapeño or other medium-hot chilli
4 cm/1½ in fresh root ginger, finely grated
1 large garlic clove, crushed
4 cardamom pods, crushed
1 small cinnamon stick
2 cloves
salt, to taste

Combine all the ingredients in the slow cooker. Cover and cook on High for 3½ hours. Uncover and cook until thickened, about 2 hours. Cool. Refrigerate. Season to taste with salt.

Pork Loin with Mustard Sauce

This pork loin cooks to perfect tenderness in about 4 hours and is just right served with Mustard Sauce.

SERVES 8

2 onions, chopped
120 ml/4 fl oz chicken stock
1.5 kg/3 lb boneless pork loin
paprika
salt and freshly ground black pepper
Mustard Sauce (see below)

Put the onions and stock in the slow cooker. Sprinkle the pork lightly with paprika, salt and pepper. Insert a meat thermometer in the centre of the roast so that the tip is in the centre of the meat. Put the pork in the slow cooker. Cover and cook on Low until the meat thermometer registers 71°C, about 4 hours. Remove the pork to a serving platter and leave to stand, loosely covered with foil, for about 10 minutes. Strain the stock and onions. Spoon the onions around the pork. Reserve the stock for soup or another use. Serve the pork with Mustard Sauce.

Mustard Sauce Ⓥ

The ideal sauce to serve with pork in any shape or form.

MAKES ABOUT 300 ML/½ PINT

200 g/7 oz caster sugar
25 g/1 oz dry mustard powder
1 tbsp flour
120 ml/4 fl oz cider vinegar
2 eggs
1 tbsp butter or margarine

Mix the sugar, mustard powder and flour in a small pan. Whisk in the vinegar and eggs. Cook over low heat until thickened, about 10 minutes. Stir in the butter or margarine.

Roast Pork with Marmalade Sauce

Reserve the stock left in the slow cooker for another use. If you don't have orange liqueur for the Marmalade Sauce, use the same measure of water.

SERVES 8

2 onions, chopped
120 ml/4 fl oz chicken stock
1.5 kg/3 lb boneless pork loin
paprika
salt and freshly ground black pepper
Marmalade Sauce (see below)

Put the onions and stock in the slow cooker. Sprinkle the pork lightly with paprika, salt and pepper. Insert a meat thermometer in the centre of the roast so that the tip is in the centre of the meat. Put the pork in the slow cooker. Cover and cook on Low until the meat thermometer registers 71°C, about 4 hours. Remove the pork to a serving platter and leave to stand, loosely covered with foil, for about 10 minutes. Strain the stock and onions. Spoon the onions around the pork. Serve the pork with Marmalade Sauce.

Marmalade Sauce Ⓥ

Lovely with roast pork, but also as a topping for countless cakes and puddings.

MAKES 450 G/1 LB

450 g/1 lb orange marmalade
2 tbsp butter or margarine
2 tbsp orange liqueur

Heat the marmalade, butter or margarine and liqueur in a small pan until hot.

Gingered Tomato Relish Ⓥ

If making this to accompany the pork loin recipe on this page, for simplicity you would use the onions strained from the stock at the end of cooking, instead of preparing them from scratch.

SERVES 8 AS AN ACCOMPANIMENT

2 onions, chopped
a little olive oil, for frying
275 g/10 oz tomatoes, chopped
75 g/3 oz courgette, finely chopped
1 carrot, finely chopped
2.5 cm/1 in piece fresh root ginger,
    finely grated
salt and freshly ground black pepper

Sauté the onions in a little olive oil until lightly browned in a medium frying pan. Add the tomatoes, courgette, carrot and ginger and heat, covered, until the tomatoes are soft and the mixture is bubbly, 3–4 minutes. Simmer rapidly, uncovered, until the excess liquid is gone, about 5 minutes. Season to taste with salt and pepper.

Pork Loin with Onion Gravy

Onion gravy goes supremely well with pork joints and also with beef roasts and sausages.

SERVES 8

2 onions, chopped
120 ml/4 fl oz chicken stock
1.5 kg/3 lb boneless pork loin
paprika
salt and freshly ground black pepper
plain flour
cold water or milk

Put the onions and stock in the slow cooker. Sprinkle the pork lightly with paprika, salt and pepper. Insert a meat thermometer in the centre of the roast

so that the tip is in the centre of the meat. Put the pork in the slow cooker. Cover and cook on Low until the meat thermometer registers 71°C, about 4 hours. Remove the pork to a serving platter and leave to stand, loosely covered with foil, for about 10 minutes. To make the onion gravy, strain the stock into a measuring jug, reserving the onions. Heat the stock to boiling point in a medium pan. For each 250 ml/8 fl oz of stock, stir in 2 tbsp of flour combined with 50 ml/2 fl oz of cold water or milk, stirring until thickened, about 1 minute. Season to taste with salt and pepper. Spoon the onions around the pork and serve with the onion gravy.

Pork Loin with Gingered Tomato Relish

Reserve the strained stock mixture for soup or another use.

SERVES 8

2 onions, chopped
120 ml/4 fl oz chicken stock
1.5 kg/3 lb boneless pork loin
paprika
salt and freshly ground black pepper
Gingered Tomato Relish (see below)

Put the onions and stock in the slow cooker. Sprinkle the pork lightly with paprika, salt and pepper. Insert a meat thermometer in the centre of the roast so that the tip is in the centre of the meat. Put the pork in the slow cooker. Cover and cook on Low until the meat thermometer registers 71°C, about 4 hours. Remove the pork to a serving platter and leave to stand, loosely covered with foil, for about 10 minutes. Strain the stock and reserve the onions for making Gingered Tomato Relish. Serve the pork with Gingered Tomato Relish.

Pork Loin with Cranberry Coulis

You might not have thought of a cranberry-based accompaniment for pork but the two do go extremely well together.

SERVES 8

120 ml/4 fl oz chicken stock
1.5 kg/3 lb boneless pork loin
paprika
salt and freshly ground black pepper
Cranberry Coulis (see below)

Put the stock in the slow cooker. Sprinkle the pork lightly with paprika, salt and pepper. Insert a meat thermometer in the centre of the roast so that the tip is in the centre of the meat. Put the pork in the slow cooker. Cover and cook on Low until the meat thermometer registers 71°C, about 4 hours. Remove the pork to a serving platter and leave to stand, loosely covered with foil, for about 10 minutes. Serve the pork with Cranberry Coulis.

Cranberry Coulis Ⓥ

Don't forget to allow time for the cranberries to thaw, if using frozen.

SERVES 8 AS AN ACCOMPANIMENT

175 g/6 oz fresh or thawed frozen
   cranberries
250 ml/8 fl oz orange juice
50 g/2 oz caster sugar
2–3 tbsp honey

Heat the cranberries with the orange juice, sugar and honey to boiling in a medium pan. Reduce the heat and simmer, covered, until the cranberries are tender, 5–8 minutes. Process in a food processor or blender until almost smooth.

Pork Loin with Brandied Cherry Sauce

Cherry sauces are more widely known as an accompaniment for duck but this one is great with pork loin.

SERVES 8

120 ml/4 fl oz chicken stock
1.5 kg/3 lb boneless pork loin
paprika
salt and freshly ground black pepper

Put the stock in the slow cooker. Sprinkle the pork lightly with paprika, salt and pepper. Insert a meat thermometer in the centre of the roast so that the tip is in the centre of the meat. Put the pork in the slow cooker. Cover and cook on Low until the meat thermometer registers 71°C, about 4 hours. Remove the pork to a serving platter and leave to stand, loosely covered with foil, for about 10 minutes. Serve the pork with Brandied Cherry Sauce.

Brandied Cherry Sauce Ⓥ

This sauce is lovely made with fresh cherries when they are in season, but thawed frozen will also be fine.

SERVES 8 AS AN ACCOMPANIMENT

2 tbsp sugar
2 tsp cornflour
¼ tsp ground allspice
120 ml/4 fl oz cold water
175 g/6 oz pitted dark sweet cherries
1 tbsp brandy
lemon juice, to taste

Mix the sugar, cornflour, allspice and cold water in a medium pan. Stir in the cherries and heat to boiling, stirring until thickened, about 1 minute. Stir in the brandy and add lemon juice to taste.

Roast Pork Shoulder with Noodles

This pork roast cooks to falling-apart tenderness, perfect for the following variations: Savoury Herb-rubbed Pork, Teriyaki Pork and Pork Tacos.

SERVES 8

2 onions, chopped
250 ml/8 fl oz chicken stock
1.5 kg/3 lb boneless pork shoulder
salt and freshly ground black pepper
3 tbsp cornflour
75 ml/2½ fl oz water
450 g/1 lb noodles, cooked, hot

Put the onion and stock in the slow cooker. Sprinkle the pork lightly with salt and pepper and put in the slow cooker. Cover and cook on Low for 7–8 hours. Remove the pork and shred the meat. Turn the slow cooker to High. Cook for 10 minutes. Stir in the combined cornflour and water, stirring for 2–3 minutes. Return the pork to the slow cooker and toss. Serve over the noodles.

Savoury Herb-rubbed Pork

Serve this fragrant herby pork over noodles or rice, or use it as a delicious sandwich filling.

SERVES 8

2 onions, chopped
1 green pepper, sliced
250 ml/8 fl oz chicken stock
3 garlic cloves, crushed
2 tsp olive oil
1 tsp dried sage
1 tsp dried thyme
salt and freshly ground black pepper
1.5 kg/3 lb boneless pork shoulder
3 tbsp cornflour
75 ml/2½ fl oz water

Put the onions, sliced pepper and stock in the slow cooker. Mix the garlic, olive oil, sage, thyme, ½ tsp salt and a good grinding of pepper and rub all over the pork. Put the pork in the slow cooker. Cover and cook on Low for 7–8 hours. Remove the pork and shred the meat. Turn the slow cooker to High. Cook for 10 minutes. Stir in the combined cornflour and water, stirring for 2–3 minutes. Return the pork to the slow cooker and toss.

Teriyaki Pork

This tender pork is lovely served with noodles or rice, or even rolled up in warm flour tortillas.

SERVES 8

2 onions, chopped
250 ml/8 fl oz chicken stock
1.5 kg/3 lb boneless pork shoulder
salt and freshly ground black pepper
50 ml/2 fl oz teriyaki marinade

Put the onion and stock in the slow cooker. Sprinkle the pork lightly with salt and pepper and put in the slow cooker. Cover and cook on Low for 7–8 hours. Remove the pork and shred the meat. Mix the meat with the teriyaki marinade, adding enough of the stock and onion mixture to moisten.

Pork Tacos

You could make your own taco seasoning, but I find the ready-made packets of mix are really very good.

SERVES 8

250 ml/8 fl oz chicken stock
1.5 kg/3 lb boneless pork shoulder
salt and freshly ground black pepper
½–1 packet taco seasoning mix
8 taco shells or flour tortillas
shredded lettuce, chopped tomato,
    diced or mashed avocado and
    soured cream

Put the stock in the slow cooker. Sprinkle the pork lightly with salt and pepper and put in the slow cooker. Cover and cook on Low for 7–8 hours. Remove the pork and shred the meat. Mix the shredded pork with the taco seasoning, adding enough of the stock to moisten. Serve in warm taco shells or flour tortillas with shredded lettuce, chopped tomato and avocado, and soured cream.

Pork Chops with Celery

Enjoy the convenience of canned soup to make a delectable sauce for pork chops.

SERVES 4

4 boneless loin pork chops, about
    100 g/4 oz each
1 tsp dried thyme
salt and freshly ground black pepper,
    to taste
1 small onion, halved and sliced
4 spring onions, thinly sliced
1 small celery stick, sliced
300 g/11 oz can cream of celery soup
120 ml/4 fl oz semi-skimmed milk

Sprinkle the pork chops with the thyme, salt and pepper. Put in the slow cooker, adding the onion and celery. Pour the combined soup and milk over. Cover and cook on Low for 4–5 hours.

Portabella Pork Chops

Portabella mushrooms are largish and have a silky, light brown skin. Use other closed-cup mushrooms if you prefer.

SERVES 4

4 boneless loin pork chops, about
    100 g/4 oz each
1 tsp dried thyme
salt and freshly ground black pepper,
    to taste
100 g/4 oz portabella mushrooms,
    chopped
300 g/11 oz can cream of mushroom soup
120 ml/4 fl oz semi-skimmed milk

Sprinkle the pork chops with the thyme, salt and pepper. Put in the slow cooker, adding the mushrooms. Pour the combined soup and milk over. Cover and cook on Low for 4–5 hours.

Pork Chops with Apricot and Hoisin Sauce

The easiest of dinners, slow cooker-style! Serve over rice, if you like.

SERVES 6

6 boneless loin pork chops, about
    100 g/4 oz each
salt and freshly ground black pepper,
    to taste
50 ml/2 fl oz chicken stock
150 g/5 oz apricot preserve
3 tbsp hoisin sauce
2–3 tsp cornflour
2 tbsp finely chopped fresh coriander
    or parsley

Sprinkle the pork chops very lightly with salt and pepper and put in the slow cooker. Add the stock. Cover and cook on Low until the chops are tender, about 3 hours. Remove the chops and keep warm. Turn the heat to High and cook for 10 minutes. Stir the combined remaining ingredients into the stock, stirring for 2–3 minutes. Serve the sauce over the pork chops.

Pork Chops with Sage

Sage is a perfect complement to pork, and mustard adds a piquant finishing touch.

SERVES 4

4 boneless loin pork chops (about 100 g/4 oz each)
½ onion, chopped
10 ml/2 tsp dried sage
120 ml/4 fl oz chicken stock
120 ml/4 fl oz dry white wine or extra chicken stock
1 tbsp cornflour
2 tbsp honey
2 tbsp water
1–2 tbsp Dijon mustard
1–2 tbsp lemon juice
salt and freshly ground black pepper, to taste

Combine the pork chops, onion, sage, stock and wine in the slow cooker. Cover and cook on Low until the chops are tender, 3–4 hours. Remove the chops and keep warm. Turn the heat to High. Stir the combined cornflour, honey and water into the stock. Cook, uncovered, until the juices are the consistency of a thin sauce, about 5 minutes. Season to taste with mustard, lemon juice, salt and pepper.

Pork with Prunes

Prunes may seem like a surprising addition, but they give a superbly rich dimension to the sauce.

SERVES 6–8

900 g/2 lb boneless pork loin, cubed (4 cm/1½ in)
225 g/8 oz pitted prunes
375 ml/13 fl oz chicken stock
120 ml/4 fl oz dry white wine or extra chicken stock
grated zest of 1 lemon
2 tbsp cornflour
50 ml/2 fl oz cold water
1–2 tsp lemon juice
salt and freshly ground black pepper, to taste
225 g/8 oz rice or couscous, cooked, hot

Combine all the ingredients, except the cornflour, water, lemon juice, salt, pepper and rice or couscous, in the slow cooker. Cover and cook on Low for 6–8 hours. Turn the heat to High and cook for 10 minutes. Stir in the combined cornflour and water, stirring for 2–3 minutes. Season to taste with lemon juice, salt and pepper. Serve over rice or couscous.

Pork with Pears and Apricots

As with the previous recipe, this is lovely spooned over rice, but it also works very well with couscous. You could also spike the finished dish with a little lemon juice, if liked.

SERVES 6–8

900 g/2 lb boneless pork loin, cubed (4 cm/1½ in)
100 g/4 oz dried pears
100 g/4 oz dried apricots
375 ml/13 fl oz chicken stock
120 ml/4 fl oz dry white wine or extra chicken stock
2 tbsp grated orange zest
2 tbsp cornflour
50 ml/2 fl oz orange juice
salt and freshly ground black pepper, to taste

Combine all the ingredients, except the cornflour, orange juice, salt and pepper, in the slow cooker. Cover and cook on Low for 6–8 hours. Turn the heat to High and cook for 10 minutes. Stir in the combined cornflour and orange juice, stirring for 2–3 minutes. Season to taste with salt and pepper.

Country-style Pork with Plum Sauce

Plum sauce and honey make these steaks sweet eating! If you want, they can be browned under the grill before serving.

SERVES 4

**4 pork shoulder steaks, about
   600 g/1 lb 6 oz total weight
200 g/7 oz plum sauce
100 g/4 oz honey
1 tbsp soy sauce
2 tbsp cornflour
50 ml/2 fl oz orange juice
salt and freshly ground black pepper,
   to taste**

Arrange the steaks in the slow cooker. Pour the combined plum sauce, honey and soy sauce over the steaks. Cover and cook on Low for 6–8 hours. Remove the steaks to a platter. Keep warm. Turn the heat to High and cook for 10 minutes. Stir in the combined cornflour and orange juice, stirring for 2–3 minutes. Season and serve the sauce over the steaks.

Orange and Honey Ham

This easy-to-make ham is subtly flavoured with orange and honey.

SERVES 8–10

**1.5 kg/3 lb boneless smoked ham
75 ml/2½ fl oz orange juice
75 ml/2½ fl oz honey
½ tsp ground cloves
1½ tbsp cornflour
50 ml/2 fl oz cold water
2 tbsp dry sherry (optional)**

Put a meat thermometer in the ham so that the tip is near the centre. Put in the slow cooker. Add the orange juice, honey and cloves. Cover and cook on Low until the temperature registers 68°C, about 3 hours. Remove the ham to a platter and keep warm.

Measure 375 ml/13 fl oz of the stock into a pan and heat to boiling. Whisk in the combined cornflour, water and sherry, whisking until thickened, about 1 minute. Serve the sauce over the ham.

Pork and Squash Ragout

Healthy Garlic Bread is delicious with this hearty casserole.

SERVES 4

**450 g/1 lb boneless pork loin, cubed
   (2 cm/¾ in)
2 x 400 g/14 oz cans chopped tomatoes
400 g/14 oz can red kidney beans,
   drained and rinsed
175 g/6 oz butternut or other winter
   squash, peeled and cubed
3 onions, chopped
1½ green peppers, chopped
2 garlic cloves, preferably roasted, crushed
2 tsp dried Italian herb seasoning
salt and freshly ground black pepper,
   to taste
Healthy Garlic Bread (see below)**

Combine all the ingredients, except the salt, pepper and Healthy Garlic Bread, in the slow cooker. Cover and cook on Low for 6–8 hours. Season to taste with salt and pepper. Serve with Healthy Garlic Bread.

Healthy Garlic Bread Ⓥ

Try this lower-fat garlic bread.

SERVES 4

**4 thick slices baguette or ciabatta
olive oil cooking spray
2 garlic cloves, halved**

Spray both sides of the bread generously with cooking spray. Grill until browned, about 1 minute on each side. Rub both sides of the hot toast with the cut sides of the garlic.

Pork with Peppers and Courgette

This sunny combination of pork and vegetables can be served over pasta.

SERVES 4

450 g/1 lb pork tenderloin or boneless pork loin, cubed (2.5 cm/1 in)
225 g/8 oz ready-made tomato sauce
120 ml/4 fl oz chicken stock
3 tbsp dry sherry (optional)
1 red pepper, sliced
1 green pepper, sliced
1 large onion, chopped
1 garlic clove, crushed
¾ tsp dried basil
¾ tsp dried thyme
1 bay leaf
1 courgette, sliced
1 tbsp cornflour
2 tbsp cold water
salt and freshly ground black pepper, to taste
225 g/8 oz fusilli, cooked, hot

Combine all the ingredients, except the courgette, cornflour, water, salt, pepper and fusilli, in the slow cooker. Cover and cook on Low for 6–8 hours, adding the courgette during the last 30 minutes. Stir in the combined cornflour and water, stirring for, 2–3 minutes. Discard the bay leaf. Season to taste with salt and pepper. Serve over fusilli.

Pork with Artichokes and White Beans

A hint of orange with aromatic rosemary add to these Tuscan flavours.

SERVES 6

700 g/1½ lb boneless pork loin, cubed (2 cm/¾ in)
400 g/14 oz can chopped tomatoes
400 g/14 oz can cannellini or haricot beans, drained and rinsed
150 ml/¼ pint chicken stock
2 garlic cloves, crushed
1 tsp dried rosemary
1 tsp grated orange zest
400 g/14 oz can artichoke hearts, drained, rinsed and quartered
1 tbsp cornflour
2 tbsp cold water
salt and freshly ground black pepper

Combine all the ingredients, except the artichokes, cornflour, water, salt and pepper, in the slow cooker. Cover and cook on Low for 6–8 hours, adding the artichoke hearts during the last 30 minutes. Turn the heat to High and cook for 10 minutes. Stir in the combined cornflour and water, stirring for 2–3 minutes. Season to taste with salt and pepper.

Peppered Pork in White Wine

Cubed boneless pork loin can be substituted for the tenderloin.

SERVES 4

450 g/1 lb pork tenderloin, sliced (1 cm/½ in)
250 ml/8 fl oz beef stock
120 ml/4 fl oz dry white wine
1 onion, finely chopped
½ red pepper, chopped
1 garlic clove, crushed
2 tsp finely crushed peppercorns
1 tbsp red wine vinegar
1 tbsp cornflour
2 tbsp cold water
salt and freshly ground black pepper
15 g/½ oz fresh chives or parsley, finely chopped

Combine all the ingredients, except the vinegar, cornflour, water, salt, pepper and chives, in the slow cooker. Cover and cook on Low for 6–8 hours. Stir in the combined vinegar, cornflour and water, stirring for 2–3 minutes. Season with salt and pepper. Sprinkle with the chives.

Austrian Pork with Apples and Cranberry Sauce

Enjoy this thyme-seasoned medley of lean pork and fruit.

SERVES 4

450 g/1 lb boneless pork loin, cubed (2 cm/¾ in)
200 g/7 oz cranberry sauce from a jar
200 ml/7 fl oz chicken stock
2 onions, chopped
2 large cooking apples, peeled, cored and thinly sliced
1 tbsp Worcestershire sauce
1 tbsp cider vinegar
1 tbsp brown sugar
½ tsp dried thyme
salt and freshly ground black pepper, to taste
225 g/8 oz egg noodles, cooked, hot

Combine all the ingredients, except the salt, pepper and noodles, in the slow cooker. Cover and cook on Low for 6–8 hours. Season to taste with salt and pepper. Serve over the noodles.

Orange Pork Ragout

The warm flavour of cloves complements the orange perfectly in this casserole of pork and peppers.

SERVES 4

450 g/1 lb boneless pork loin, cubed (2.5 cm/1 in)
250 ml/8 fl oz chicken stock
250 ml/8 fl oz orange juice
2 onions, sliced
1 red pepper, sliced
1 green pepper, sliced
2 tsp sugar
1 tsp dried thyme
¼ tsp ground cloves
2 tbsp cornflour
50 ml/2 fl oz cold water
salt and freshly ground black pepper, to taste
175 g/6 oz white or brown rice, cooked, hot

Combine all the ingredients, except the cornflour, water, salt, pepper and rice, in the slow cooker. Cover and cook on Low for 6–8 hours. Turn the heat to High and cook for 10 minutes. Stir in the combined cornflour and water, stirring for 2–3 minutes. Season to taste with salt and pepper. Serve over the rice.

Barbecued Pork

A quick cook-in barbecue sauce with cider makes a tasty base for apple, cabbage and pork flavoured with caraway.

SERVES 4

450 g/1 lb boneless pork loin, cubed (2 cm/¾ in)
375 ml/13 fl oz cider or apple juice
225 g/8 oz cook-in barbecue sauce
450 g/1 lb thinly sliced cabbage
1 medium onion, coarsely chopped
1 large tart apple, peeled and coarsely chopped
1 tsp crushed caraway seeds
1 tbsp cornflour
3 tbsp cold water
salt and freshly ground black pepper, to taste
225 g/8 oz noodles, cooked, hot

Combine all the ingredients, except the cornflour, water, salt, pepper and noodles, in the slow cooker. Cover and cook on Low for 6–8 hours. Turn the heat to High and cook for 10 minutes. Stir in the combined cornflour and water, stirring for 2–3 minutes. Season to taste with salt and pepper. Serve over the noodles.

Pork Loin with Gremolata

Gremolata is added at the table to give a fresh zing to pork cooked with tomatoes.

SERVES 4

450 g/1 lb boneless pork loin, cubed (2.5 cm/1 in)
250 ml/8 fl oz beef stock
400 g/14 oz can chopped tomatoes, undrained
2 potatoes, cubed
4 shallots, thinly sliced
2 garlic cloves, crushed
1 tsp dried thyme
1½ tbsp cornflour
50 ml/2 fl oz cold water
salt and freshly ground black pepper, to taste
Gremolata (see below)

Combine all the ingredients, except the cornflour, water, salt, pepper and Gremolata, in the slow cooker. Cover and cook on Low for 6–8 hours. Turn the heat to High and cook the meat for 10 minutes. Stir in the combined cornflour and water, stirring for 2–3 minutes. Season to taste with salt and pepper. Pass the Gremolata to stir into each serving.

Gremolata

Gremolata is a refreshing blend of garlic, lemon zest and parsley that goes so well with rich meats.

SERVES 4, AS AN ACCOMPANIMENT

25 g/1 oz fresh parsley sprigs
1–2 tbsp grated lemon zest
4 large garlic cloves, crushed

Process all the ingredients in a food processor or blender until finely minced.

Cantonese Pork

Lean beef or skinless chicken breast fillets can be substituted for the pork in this sweet-and-sour casserole.

SERVES 6

700 g/1½ lb lean pork steak, cut into thin strips
225 g/8 oz ready-made tomato sauce
1 onion, sliced
1 small red pepper, sliced
65 g/2½ oz mushrooms, sliced
3 tbsp brown sugar
1½ tbsp cider vinegar
2 tsp Worcestershire sauce
1 tbsp dry sherry (optional)
90 g/3½ oz pineapple chunks
65 g/2½ oz mangetouts, halved
2 tbsp cornflour
50 ml/2 fl oz cold water
salt and freshly ground black pepper, to taste
175 g/6 oz rice, cooked, hot

Combine all the ingredients, except the pineapple chunks, mangetouts, cornflour, water, salt, pepper and rice, in the slow cooker. Cover and cook on Low for 6–8 hours, adding the pineapple and mangetouts during the last 15 minutes. Turn the heat to High and cook for 10 minutes. Stir in the combined cornflour and water, stirring until thickened, 2–3 minutes. Season to taste with salt and pepper. Serve over the rice.

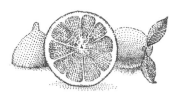

Golden Curried Pork

Brightly coloured Cuban Rice perfectly complements this dish of aubergines, squash, chickpeas and pork.

SERVES 6

450 g/1 lb pork tenderloin, cubed (2 cm/¾ in)
400 g/14 oz can chickpeas, drained and rinsed
2 x 400 g/14 oz cans chopped tomatoes
1 small aubergine, cubed (2.5 cm/1 in)
1 onion, sliced
½ green pepper, chopped
1 celery stick, chopped
2 garlic cloves, crushed
½ tsp ground cinnamon
½ tsp freshly grated nutmeg
½ tsp curry powder
½ tsp ground cumin
a pinch of cayenne pepper
1 courgette, cubed
175 g/6 oz butternut squash, cubed
1–2 tbsp cornflour
50 ml/2 fl oz cold water
salt and freshly ground black pepper, to taste
Cuban Rice (see page 137)
3 tbsp raisins
3 tbsp toasted flaked almonds

Combine all the ingredients, except the courgette, butternut squash, cornflour, water, salt, pepper, Cuban Rice, raisins and almonds in a 5.5 litre/9½ pint slow cooker. Cover and cook on High for 4–5 hours, adding the courgette and butternut squash during the last 20 minutes. Stir in the combined cornflour and water, stirring for 2–3 minutes. Season to taste with salt and pepper. Serve over Cuban Rice and sprinkle with raisins and almonds.

Caribbean Pork with Ginger and Beans

Fresh root ginger accents the flavour contrasts in this colourful dish.

SERVES 6

12–450 g/1 lb lean pork loin, cubed
120 ml/4 fl oz chicken stock
120 ml/4 fl oz orange juice
400 g/14 oz can black beans, drained and rinsed
400 g/14 oz can black-eyed peas, drained and rinsed
2 onions, chopped
1 red pepper, chopped
2 garlic cloves, crushed
2 tsp finely chopped jalapeño or other medium-hot chilli
2.5 cm/1 in piece fresh root ginger, finely grated
½ tsp dried thyme
75 g/3 oz okra, trimmed and cut into pieces
75 g/3 oz orange marmalade
300 g/11 oz mandarin orange segments, drained
salt and freshly ground black pepper, to taste
175 g/6 oz brown or white rice, cooked, hot

Combine all the ingredients, except the okra, marmalade, orange segments, salt, pepper and rice, in the slow cooker. Cover and cook on Low for 6–8 hours, adding the okra and marmalade during the last 30 minutes. Stir in the orange segments and season to taste with salt and pepper. Serve over the rice.

Savoury Pork and Mexican Chorizo

This chilli pork dish makes delicious tacos too.

SERVES 6–8

Mexican Chorizo (see page 205)
225 g/8 oz boneless pork loin, cubed
   (2.5 cm/1 in)
2 large tomatoes, chopped
1 small red onion, sliced
1 garlic clove, crushed
¼ tsp dried oregano
¼ tsp dried thyme
1 bay leaf
1–3 pickled jalapeño or other
   medium-hot chillies, finely chopped
1 tbsp pickled chilli juice
salt and freshly ground black pepper,
   to taste
225–350 g/8–12 oz rice, cooked, hot

Cook the Mexican Chorizo in a lightly greased medium frying pan over medium heat until browned, crumbling with a fork. Combine the Mexican Chorizo and the remaining ingredients, except the salt, pepper and rice, in the slow cooker. Cover and cook on High for 4–5 hours. Discard the bay leaf. Season to taste with salt and pepper. Serve over the rice.

Pork and Chorizo Tacos

You could wrap the mixture in warmed soft flour tortillas instead of taco shells.

SERVES 6–8

Mexican Chorizo (see page 205)
225 g/8 oz boneless pork loin, cubed
   (2.5 cm/1 in)
2 large tomatoes, chopped
1 small red onion, sliced
1 garlic clove, crushed
¼ tsp dried oregano
¼ tsp dried thyme
1 bay leaf
1–3 pickled jalapeño or other
   medium-hot chillies, finely chopped
1 tbsp pickled chilli juice
salt and freshly ground black pepper,
   to taste
1 tbsp cornflour
2 tbsp water
15 g/½ oz chopped fresh coriander
6–8 taco shells
soured cream
shredded iceberg lettuce

Cook the Mexican Chorizo in a lightly greased medium frying pan over medium heat until browned, crumbling with a fork. Combine the Mexican Chorizo and the remaining ingredients, except the salt, pepper, cornflour, water, coriander, taco shells, soured cream and lettuce, in the slow cooker. Cover and cook on High for 4–5 hours. At the end of cooking time, discard the bay leaf and season to taste with salt and pepper. Turn the heat to High and cook for 10 minutes. Stir in the combined cornflour and water, stirring for 2–3 minutes. Stir in the coriander. Serve in warm, crisp taco shells, topping with soured cream and shredded lettuce.

Pork with Potato and Cabbage

Serve this robust pork dish over noodles or rice.

SERVES 4

450 g/1 lb boneless lean pork loin
400 g/14 oz can tomatoes
225 g/8 oz ready-made tomato sauce
225 g/8 oz cabbage, thinly sliced
350 g/12 oz potatoes, peeled and
**   cubed**
1 large onion, finely chopped
2 garlic cloves, crushed
1 tbsp brown sugar
2 tsp balsamic vinegar
2 tsp dried thyme
1 bay leaf
salt and freshly ground black pepper,
**   to taste**

Combine all the ingredients, except the salt and pepper, in the slow cooker. Cover and cook on Low for 6–8 hours. Discard the bay leaf. Season to taste with salt and pepper.

Pork and Sauerkraut

This German-inspired casserole is best served in shallow bowls with crusty rye rolls to accompany.

SERVES 4

450 g/1 lb boneless lean pork loin,
**   cubed (2 cm/¾ in)**
400 g/14 oz can chopped tomatoes
450 g/1 lb sauerkraut, drained
350 g/12 oz waxy potatoes, thinly
**   sliced**
1 large onion, finely chopped
1 tsp caraway seeds
120 ml/4 fl oz soured cream
1 tbsp cornflour
salt and freshly ground black pepper,
**   to taste**

Combine all the ingredients, except the soured cream, cornflour, salt and pepper, in the slow cooker. Cover and cook on Low for 6–8 hours. Stir in the combined soured cream and cornflour, stirring for 2–3 minutes. Season to taste with salt and pepper.

Finnish Pork with Beetroot and Noodles

This Scandinavian dish is colourful and delicious.

SERVES 4

450 g/1 lb boneless lean pork loin,
**   cubed (5 cm/2 in)**
250 ml/8 fl oz beef stock
3 tbsp cider vinegar
2 onions, chopped
1½ tsp creamed horseradish
½ tsp dried thyme
450 g/1 lb cooked beetroot, cubed
2 tsp cornflour
50 ml/2 fl oz cold water
salt and freshly ground black pepper,
**   to taste**
225 g/8 oz egg noodles, cooked, hot

Combine all the ingredients, except the beetroot, cornflour, water, salt, pepper and noodles, in the slow cooker. Cover and cook on Low for 6–8 hours. Add the beetroot cubes, turn the heat to High and cook for 10 minutes. Stir in the combined cornflour and water, stirring for 2–3 minutes. Season to taste with salt and pepper. Serve over the noodles.

German-style Pork

Serve this dish over noodles or with thick slices of warm rye bread.

SERVES 4

450 g/1 lb boneless pork loin, cubed (2.5 cm/1 in)
250 ml/8 fl oz cider
2 onions, chopped
150 g/5 oz swede, cubed
275 g/10 oz sauerkraut, drained
350 g/12 oz potatoes, peeled and thinly sliced
2 bay leaves
1½ tbsp brown sugar
2 medium apples, peeled and sliced
50 g/2 oz frozen peas, thawed
salt and freshly ground black pepper, to taste

Combine all the ingredients, except the apples, peas, salt and pepper, in the slow cooker. Cover and cook on Low for 6–8 hours, adding the apples and peas during the last 30 minutes. Discard the bay leaves. Season to taste with salt and pepper.

Ham with Black-eyed Peas and Chickpeas

Serve this dish of ham, pulses and okra with Roasted Chilli Cornbread (see page 364).

SERVES 6

12–450 g/1 lb baked ham, cubed
400 g/14 oz can tomatoes
400 g/14 oz can chickpeas, drained and rinsed
400 g/14 oz can black-eyed peas, drained and rinsed
1 onion, chopped
2 garlic cloves, crushed
1 tsp dried marjoram
1 tsp dried thyme

¼ tsp Tabasco sauce
275 g/10 oz frozen spinach, thawed and drained
225 g/8 oz okra, trimmed and cut into pieces
salt and freshly ground black pepper, to taste

Combine all the ingredients, except the spinach, okra, salt and pepper, in the slow cooker. Cover and cook on High for 4–5 hours, adding the spinach and okra during the last 30 minutes. Season to taste with salt and pepper.

Ham and Peppers with Polenta

The microwave method for cooking polenta eliminates the constant stirring necessary when polenta is made on the hob. You can also make it in a slow cooker (see page 296).

SERVES 4

225 g/8 oz gammon steak, cubed
400 g/14 oz can chopped tomatoes
½ green pepper, chopped
½ red pepper, chopped
½ yellow pepper, chopped
1 onion, chopped
1 garlic clove, crushed
1 bay leaf
1–1½ tsp dried Italian herb seasoning
salt and freshly ground black pepper, to taste
Microwave Polenta (see page 296)
2 tbsp freshly grated Parmesan cheese

Combine all the ingredients, except the salt, pepper, Microwave Polenta and Parmesan cheese, in the slow cooker. Cover and cook on High for 4–5 hours. Discard the bay leaf. Season to taste with salt and pepper. Serve over Microwave Polenta and sprinkle with Parmesan cheese.

Smoked Sausage with Beans

Serve this hearty winter casserole over noodles or rice, with warm Buttermilk Bread (see page 359).

SERVES 8

450 g/1 lb smoked sausage, sliced (2 cm/¾ in)
2 x 400 g/14 oz cans red kidney beans, drained and rinsed
400 g/14 oz can cannellini beans, drained and rinsed
2 x 400 g/14 oz cans chopped tomatoes
120 ml/4 fl oz water
3 onions, chopped
½ green pepper, chopped
2 garlic cloves, crushed
½ tsp dried thyme
½ tsp sage
1 bay leaf
salt and freshly ground black pepper, to taste

Combine all the ingredients, except the salt and pepper, in a 5.5 litre/9½ pint slow cooker. Cover and cook on High for 4–5 hours. Discard the bay leaf. Season to taste with salt and pepper.

Squash with Smoked Sausage

Smoked sausage adds a great flavour to this chunky, vegetable-rich casserole.

SERVES 4

225 g/8 oz smoked sausage, sliced (2 cm/¾ in)
400 g/14 oz can tomatoes
120 ml/4 fl oz beef stock
700 g/1½ lb butternut or other winter squash, peeled, seeded and cubed (2 cm/¾ in)
1 onion, cut into thin wedges
100 g/4 oz frozen peas, thawed
salt and freshly ground black pepper, to taste
175 g/6 oz brown rice, cooked, hot (optional)

Combine all the ingredients, except the peas, salt, pepper and rice, in the slow cooker. Cover and cook on High for 4–6 hours, adding the peas during the last 20 minutes. Season to taste with salt and pepper. Serve over brown rice, if you like.

Italian Sausage and Vegetable Risotto

You could use meatless sausage to make this a risotto suitable for vegetarians.

SERVES 4

750 ml/1¼ pints vegetable stock
1 small onion, chopped
3 garlic cloves, crushed
75 g/3 oz brown cap or button mushrooms, sliced
1 tsp dried rosemary
1 tsp dried thyme
350 g/12 oz arborio rice
175 g/6 oz butternut squash, cubed
100 g/4 oz cooked Italian sausage
25 g/1 oz freshly grated Parmesan cheese
salt and freshly ground black pepper, to taste

Heat the stock to boiling in a small pan. Pour into the slow cooker. Add the remaining ingredients, except the Parmesan cheese, salt and pepper. Cover and cook on High until the rice is al dente and the liquid is almost absorbed, about 1¼ hours (watch carefully so that the rice does not overcook). Stir in the cheese. Season to taste with salt and pepper.

Sausage Lasagne

When you take the lasagne out of the slow cooker, you may find it has sunk a little in the centre. It will become more even as it cools.

SERVES 6

700 g/1½ lb ready-made tomato and basil pasta sauce
8 no-precook lasagne sheets
550 g/1¼ lb Ricotta cheese
275 g/10 oz Mozzarella cheese, grated
25 g/1 oz sautéed sliced mushrooms
25 g/1 oz cooked, crumbled Italian sausage
1 egg
1 tsp dried basil
25 g/1 oz freshly grated Parmesan cheese

Spread 75 g/3 oz of the sauce over the base of a 23 x 13 cm/9 x 5 in loaf tin. Top with 1 lasagne sheet and 75 g/3 oz of the Ricotta cheese and 40 g/1½ oz of the Mozzarella cheese. Then add half the mushrooms and half the sausage. Repeat the layers, ending with 75 g/3 oz of sauce on top. Sprinkle with the Parmesan cheese. Put the tin on the rack in a 5.5 litre/9½ pint slow cooker. Cover and cook on Low for 4 hours. Remove the tin and cool on a wire rack for 10 minutes.

Irish Lamb Stew

This simply seasoned stew is a welcome meal on cold winter evenings.

SERVES 6

700 g/1½ lb lean stewing lamb, cubed
450 ml/¾ pint chicken stock
2 onions, sliced
6 potatoes, quartered
6 carrots, thickly sliced
½ tsp dried thyme
1 bay leaf
50 g/2 oz frozen peas, thawed

2 tbsp cornflour
50 ml/2 fl oz cold water
1–1½ tsp Worcestershire sauce
salt and freshly ground black pepper, to taste

Combine all the ingredients, except the peas, cornflour, water, Worcestershire sauce, salt and pepper, in the slow cooker. Cover and cook on Low for 6–8 hours. Add the peas, turn the heat to High and cook for 10 minutes. Stir in the combined cornflour and water, stirring for 2–3 minutes. Discard the bay leaf. Season to taste with Worcestershire sauce, salt and pepper.

Rosemary Lamb with Sweet Potatoes

The pairing of rosemary and lamb is classic, distinctive and delightful.

SERVES 4

450 g/1 lb boneless lamb shoulder, fat trimmed, cubed (2 cm/¾ in)
375 ml/13 fl oz beef stock
450 g/1 lb sweet potatoes, peeled and cubed (2 cm/¾ in)
200 g/7 oz French beans, cut into short lengths
1 large onion, cut into thin wedges
1 tsp dried rosemary
2 bay leaves
1–2 tbsp cornflour
50 ml/2 fl oz cold water
salt and freshly ground black pepper, to taste

Combine all the ingredients, except the cornflour, water, salt and pepper, in the slow cooker. Cover and cook on Low for 6–8 hours. Turn the heat to High and cook for 10 minutes. Stir in the combined cornflour and water, stirring for 2–3 minutes. Discard the bay leaves. Season to taste with salt and pepper.

Lamb with White Beans and Sausage

Dried beans cook perfectly in the slow cooker – no need to soak or precook!

SERVES 6

450 g/1 lb boneless lamb shoulder, cubed (2.5 cm/1 in)
225 g/8 oz dried haricot, cannelloni or butter beans
450 ml/¾ pint chicken stock
120 ml/4 fl oz dry white wine or extra chicken stock
225 g/8 oz smoked sausage, sliced (2.5 cm/1 in)
2 onions, chopped
3 carrots, thickly sliced
1 garlic clove, crushed
¾ tsp dried rosemary
¾ tsp dried oregano
1 bay leaf
400 g/14 oz can chopped tomatoes
salt and freshly ground black pepper

Combine all the ingredients, except the tomatoes, salt and pepper, in a 5.5 litre/9½ pint slow cooker. Cover and cook on Low until the beans are tender, 7–8 hours, adding the tomatoes during the last 30 minutes. Discard the bay leaf. Season to taste with salt and pepper.

Lamb Shanks with Lentils

Enjoy this rich and flavourful combination.

SERVES 6

900 g/2 lb lamb shanks, fat trimmed
375 ml/13 fl oz chicken stock
400 g/14 oz can chopped tomatoes
75 g/3 oz brown dried lentils
1 carrot, sliced
½ green pepper, chopped
4 onions, chopped
2 garlic cloves, crushed
2 bay leaves
2 tsp dried thyme
¼ tsp ground cinnamon

¼ tsp ground cloves
salt and freshly ground black pepper
65 g/2½ oz brown rice, cooked, hot

Combine all the ingredients, except the salt, pepper and rice, in a 5.5 litre/9½ pint slow cooker. Cover and cook on Low for 6–8 hours. Discard the bay leaves. Remove the lamb shanks. Remove the lean meat and cut into bite-sized pieces. Return the meat to the slow cooker and season to taste with salt and pepper. Serve over the rice.

Lamb with Chillies

This dish could also be made using 1 or 2 fresh mild green chillies, if you prefer. It's also good made with braising steak and beef stock.

SERVES 4

450 g/1 lb boneless lamb shoulder, fat trimmed, cubed (2 cm/¾in)
2 x 400 g/14 oz cans chopped tomatoes
120 ml/4 fl oz chicken stock
100 g/4 oz mild green chillies from a jar, or to taste, chopped
175 g/6 oz potatoes, cubed
175 g/6 oz yellow or green courgettes, or patty pan squash, cubed
2 onions, sliced
50 g/2 oz sweetcorn, thawed if frozen
1 small jalapeño or other medium-hot chilli, chopped
4 garlic cloves, crushed
1½ tsp dried Italian herb seasoning
2 tbsp cornflour
50 ml/2 fl oz cold water
salt and freshly ground black pepper

Combine all the ingredients, except the cornflour, water, salt and pepper, in the slow cooker. Cover and cook on Low for 6–8 hours. Turn the heat to High and cook for 10 minutes. Stir in the combined cornflour and water, stirring for 2–3 minutes. Season to taste with salt and pepper.

Moroccan Lamb

Raisins, almonds and hard-boiled eggs provide a colourful garnish to this dish.

SERVES 8

**900 g/2 lb boneless lean leg of lamb,
  cubed (2 cm/¾ in)**
250 ml/8 fl oz chicken stock
3 onions, chopped
275 g/10 oz tomatoes, chopped
2 large garlic cloves, crushed
**2 cm/¾ in piece fresh root ginger,
  finely grated**
½ tsp ground cinnamon
¼ tsp ground turmeric
1 bay leaf
50 g/2 oz raisins
salt and freshly ground black pepper
**25 g/1 oz whole blanched almonds,
  toasted**
2 hard-boiled eggs, chopped
chopped fresh coriander, to garnish
275 g/10 oz couscous or rice, cooked, hot

Combine all the ingredients, except the raisins, salt, pepper, almonds, eggs, fresh coriander and couscous, in a 5.5 litre/9½ pint slow cooker. Cover and cook on Low for 6–8 hours, adding the raisins during the last 30 minutes. Discard the bay leaf, season to taste with salt and pepper. Spoon the casserole into a serving dish and sprinkle with the almonds, hard-boiled eggs and fresh coriander. Serve over the couscous or rice.

Lamb and Turnips with Coriander

Flavoured with red wine, fresh sage and coriander, serve over white or brown rice.

SERVES 4

**450 g/1 lb boneless lamb shoulder, fat
  trimmed, cubed (2.5 cm/1 in)**
250 ml/8 fl oz tomato juice
120 ml/4 fl oz dry red wine
350 g/12 oz potatoes, cubed
275 g/10 oz turnips, cubed
1 onion, chopped
3 large garlic cloves, crushed
1 tbsp fresh sage, or 1 tsp dried sage
salt and freshly ground black pepper
25 g/1 oz fresh coriander, chopped

Combine all the ingredients, except the salt, pepper and fresh coriander, in the slow cooker. Cover and cook on Low for 6–8 hours. Season to taste with salt and pepper. Stir in the fresh coriander.

Lamb and Vegetable Tajine

Enjoy the fragrant flavours of Moroccan cuisine. Serve with warm pitta bread.

SERVES 6

450 g/1 lb lean lamb or beef, cubed
2 x 400 g/14 oz cans chopped tomatoes
**400 g/14 oz can chickpeas, drained
  and rinsed**
200 g/7 oz French beans, halved
175 g/6 oz butternut squash, chopped
150 g/5 oz turnip, chopped
1 onion, chopped
1 celery stick, sliced
1 carrot, sliced
**1 cm/½ in piece fresh root ginger,
  finely grated**
1 garlic clove, crushed
1 cinnamon stick
2 tsp paprika
2 tsp ground cumin
2 tsp ground coriander
175 g/6 oz prunes, pitted
40 g/1½ oz small black pitted olives
salt and freshly ground black pepper
250 g/9 oz couscous, cooked, hot

Combine all the ingredients, except the prunes, olives, salt, pepper and couscous, in a 5.5 litre/9½ pint slow cooker. Cover and cook on Low for 6–8 hours, adding the prunes and olives during the last 30 minutes. Season to taste with salt and pepper. Serve over couscous.

Marrakech Lamb

Three 400 g/14 oz cans of haricot or cannellini beans can be substituted for the dried beans, if you like.

SERVES 8

900 g/2 lb boneless lean leg of lamb, cubed (2.5 cm/1 in)
750 ml/1¼ pints chicken stock
100 g/4 oz dried haricot or cannellini beans
100 g/4 oz portabella or brown cap mushrooms, coarsely chopped
1 carrot, sliced
1 onion, sliced
3 large garlic cloves, crushed
1 tsp ground cumin
1 tsp dried thyme
2 bay leaves
1 large roasted red pepper from a jar, sliced
225 g/8 oz baby spinach leaves
120 ml/4 fl oz dry white wine
2 tbsp cornflour
salt and freshly ground black pepper, to taste
275 g/10 oz couscous or rice, cooked, hot

Combine all the ingredients, except the roasted peppers, spinach, wine, cornflour, salt, pepper and couscous, in a 5.5 litre/9½ pint slow cooker. Cover and cook on Low until the beans are tender, 7–8 hours. Add the roasted peppers and spinach, turn the heat to High and cook for 10 minutes. Stir in the combined wine and cornflour, stirring until thickened, 2–3 minutes. Discard the bay leaves. Season to taste with salt and pepper. Serve over the couscous or rice.

Lamb Biriani

This traditional Indian meat and rice dish can also be made with chicken or beef.

SERVES 4

450 g/1 lb boneless lean lamb leg, cubed (2 cm/¾ in)
250 ml/8 fl oz chicken stock
4 onions, chopped
1 garlic clove, crushed
1 tsp ground coriander
1 tsp ground ginger
½ tsp chilli powder
¼ tsp ground cinnamon
¼ tsp ground cloves
175 ml/6 fl oz plain yoghurt
1 tbsp cornflour
salt and freshly ground black pepper, to taste
175 g/6 oz basmati or jasmine rice, cooked, hot

Combine all the ingredients, except the yoghurt, cornflour, salt, pepper and rice, in the slow cooker. Cover and cook on Low for 6–8 hours. Stir in the combined yoghurt and cornflour, stirring for 2–3 minutes. Season to taste with salt and pepper. Serve over rice.

Two-meat Goulash

The combination of caraway and fennel seeds enhances the traditional taste of paprika in this distinctive goulash.

SERVES 8

450 g/1 lb lean silverside or braising steak, cubed (2 cm/¾ in)
450 g/1 lb lean pork loin, cubed (2 cm/¾ in)
120 ml/4 fl oz beef stock
400 g/14 oz can chopped tomatoes
2 tbsp tomato purée
100 g/4 oz small mushrooms, halved
3 onions, chopped
2 garlic cloves, crushed
2 tbsp paprika
½ tsp crushed caraway seeds
½ tsp crushed fennel seeds
2 bay leaves
120 ml/4 fl oz soured cream
2 tbsp cornflour
salt and freshly ground black pepper, to taste
450 g/1 lb noodles, cooked, hot

Combine all the ingredients, except the soured cream, cornflour, salt, pepper and noodles, in the slow cooker. Cover and cook on Low for 6–8 hours. Stir in the combined soured cream and cornflour, stirring for 2–3 minutes. Discard the bay leaves. Season to taste with salt and pepper. Serve over the noodles.

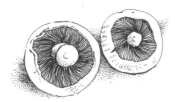

Pork and Chicken with Double Mushrooms

Just a few shiitake mushrooms add a distinctive, savoury flavour that enhances this casserole of pork, chicken and brown cap mushrooms.

SERVES 6

120 ml/4 fl oz boiling water
3 dried shiitake mushrooms
350 g/12 oz boneless pork loin, cubed (2 cm/¾ in)
350 g/12 oz chicken breast fillet, cubed (2 cm/¾ in)
120 ml/4 fl oz dry white wine
120 ml/4 fl oz chicken stock
100 g/4 oz small brown cap or white button mushrooms, halved
2 onions, chopped
½ tsp fennel seeds, lightly crushed
salt and freshly ground black pepper, to taste
225 g/8 oz brown or white rice, cooked, hot

Pour the boiling water over the dried mushrooms in a small bowl. Leave to stand until the mushrooms are softened, 5–10 minutes. Drain, reserving the liquid. Strain the liquid. Slice the mushrooms into thin strips, discarding the hard centres. Combine the dried mushrooms and reserved liquid and the remaining ingredients, except the salt, pepper and rice, in the slow cooker. Cover and cook on Low for 6–8 hours. Season to taste with salt and pepper. Serve over the rice.

Karelian Ragout

Allspice gently seasons beef, pork and lamb in this Finnish dish. Serve over cooked rice or noodles, if you wish.

SERVES 12

450 g/1 lb silverside or braising steak, cubed (2.5 cm/1 in)
450 g/1 lb lean lamb, cubed (2.5 cm/1 in)
450 g/1 lb pork loin, cubed (2.5 cm/1 in)
450 ml/¾ pint beef stock
4 onions, thinly sliced
½ tsp ground allspice
2 bay leaves
salt and freshly ground black pepper, to taste
15 g/½ oz parsley, finely chopped

Combine all the ingredients, except the salt, pepper and parsley, in a 5.5 litre/9½ pint slow cooker. Cover and cook on Low for 6–8 hours. Discard the bay leaves. Season to taste with salt and pepper and stir in the parsley.

Lamb and Beef with Cognac

The flavours of two meats, wine and cognac blend uniquely in this elegant dish.

SERVES 6

450 g/1 lb beef silverside or braising steak, cubed (2 cm/¾ in)
450 g/1 lb leg of lamb, cubed (2 cm/¾ in)
120 ml/4 fl oz beef stock
120 ml/4 fl oz dry white wine or beef stock
3 tbsp Cognac
450 g/1 lb baby carrots
½ tsp ground cinnamon
¼ tsp ground mace
225 g/8 oz baby onions or shallots
350 g/12 oz small broccoli florets
salt and freshly ground black pepper, to taste

Combine all the ingredients, except the baby onions or shallots, broccoli, salt and pepper, in the slow cooker. Cover and cook for 6–8 hours, adding the baby onions during the last 2 hours and the broccoli during the last 30 minutes. Season to taste with salt and pepper.

Beef, Pork and Chicken Goulash

The mingled juices of three kinds of meat, flavoured with caraway and dill, and smothered in a creamy tomato sauce, produce an amazing flavour.

SERVES 8

350 g/12 oz silverside or braising steak, cubed (2 cm/¾ in)
350 g/12 oz pork loin, cubed (2 cm/¾ in)
350 g/12 oz chicken breast fillet, cubed (2 cm/¾ in)
250 ml/8 fl oz beef stock
50 ml/2 fl oz tomato purée
3 large tomatoes, coarsely chopped
225 g/8 oz mushrooms, sliced
4 spring onions, thinly sliced
1 onion, chopped
1 tbsp paprika
¾ tsp caraway seeds, crushed
½ tsp dried dill
175 ml/6 fl oz soured cream
3 tbsp cornflour
salt and freshly ground black pepper, to taste
450 g/1 lb noodles, cooked, hot

Combine all the ingredients, except the soured cream, cornflour, salt, pepper and noodles, in a 5.5 litre/9½ pint slow cooker. Cover and cook on Low for 6–8 hours. Stir in the combined soured cream and cornflour, stirring until thickened, 2–3 minutes. Season to taste with salt and pepper. Serve over the noodles.

Chicken and Poultry Dishes

So versatile, light and readily available, we all enjoy lots of chicken in our diet so this chapter offers you a whole range of interesting dishes to delight your family and friends.

Chicken Risotto

You will need to use matured Asiago cheese for grating. It's very similar to Parmesan and Romano cheeses, either of which you could use if that's more convenient.

SERVES 4

750 ml/1¼ pints vegetable stock
1 small onion, chopped
3 garlic cloves, crushed
1 tomato, chopped
350 g/12 oz arborio rice
1 tsp dried marjoram
200 g/7 oz cooked, cubed chicken breast
225 g/8 oz frozen petits pois, thawed
50 g/2 oz freshly grated Asiago cheese
salt and freshly ground black pepper, to taste

Heat the stock to boiling in a small pan. Pour into the slow cooker. Add the remaining ingredients, except the chicken, peas, Asiago cheese, salt and pepper. Cover and cook on High until the rice is al dente and the liquid is almost absorbed, about 1¼ hours, adding the chicken and peas during the last 15 minutes (watch carefully so that the rice does not overcook). Stir in the cheese. Season to taste with salt and pepper.

Roast Chicken with Cranberry and Orange Relish

Using a meat thermometer ensures that the chicken will be cooked through and tender for perfect slicing. The Cranberry and Orange Relish recipe makes an ample amount.

SERVES 6

1 whole chicken, about 1.5 kg/3 lb
paprika
salt and freshly ground black pepper, to taste
120 ml/4 fl oz chicken stock
¼ quantity Cranberry and Orange Relish (see page 258)

Make foil handles (see page 10) and fit them into the slow cooker. Sprinkle the chicken lightly with paprika, salt and pepper. Insert a meat thermometer so that the tip is in the thickest part of the inside thigh, not touching the bone. Put the chicken in the slow cooker. Add the stock. Cover and cook on Low until the thermometer registers 80°C, 4–5 hours. Remove the chicken, using the foil handles. Put on a serving platter and cover loosely with foil. Reserve the stock for soup or another use. Serve the chicken with the Cranberry and Orange Relish.

Cranberry and Orange Relish Ⓥ

This keeps well in the refrigerator for several weeks.

SERVES 18

5 large navel oranges
250 ml/8 fl oz water
700 g/1½ lb granulated sugar
350 g/12 oz cranberries
50 g/2 oz coarsely chopped walnuts

Grate the zest from 3 oranges. Reserve. Peel the oranges and cut into sections. Combine all the ingredients in the slow cooker. Cover and cook on Low for 6–7 hours. If a thicker consistency is desired, cook uncovered until thickened.

Real Mashed Potatoes Ⓥ

Rich and fluffy – mashed potato as you've probably never tasted it before!

SERVES 6

900 g/2 lb floury potatoes, peeled and cooked, hot
75 ml/2½ fl oz semi-skimmed milk
75 ml/2½ fl oz soured cream
2 tbsp butter or margarine
salt and freshly ground black pepper, to taste

Mash the potatoes or beat until smooth, adding the milk, soured cream and butter or margarine. Season to taste with salt and pepper.

Roast Chicken with Mashed Potatoes and Gravy

Accompany this moist and perfectly cooked chicken with steamed broccoli and carrots, and the creamy potatoes.

SERVES 6

1 whole chicken, about 1.5 kg/3 lb
paprika
salt and freshly ground black pepper, to taste
120 ml/4 fl oz chicken stock or water
25 g/1 oz plain flour
120 ml/4 fl oz water
Real Mashed Potatoes (see left)

Make foil handles (see page 10) and fit into the slow cooker. Sprinkle the chicken lightly with paprika, salt and pepper. Insert a meat thermometer so that the tip is in the thickest part of the inside thigh, not touching the bone. Put the chicken in the slow cooker. Add the stock. Cover and cook on Low until the thermometer registers 80°C, 4–5 hours. Remove the chicken, using the foil handles. Put on a serving platter and cover loosely with foil.

Pour the stock into a measuring jug. Spoon off the fat. Measure 450 ml/¾ pint of the stock into a small pan and heat to boiling. Whisk in the combined flour and water, whisking until thickened, about 1 minute. Season to taste with salt and pepper. Serve the chicken with Real Mashed Potatoes and gravy.

Thai Green Chicken and Bean Curry

Thai curry pastes in jars are very useful additions to your storecupboard and make this a tasty recipe from Carolyn Humphries.

SERVES 4

a good handful of frozen diced onion, or 1 fresh onion or 4 spring onions, chopped
10 ml/2 tsp softened butter
450 g/1 lb diced chicken meat
200 g/7 oz frozen green beans, cut into short lengths
400 g/14 oz can of coconut milk
45 ml/3 tbsp Thai green curry paste
5 ml/1 tsp lemon grass from a jar
1 tbsp Thai fish sauce
salt and freshly ground black pepper
rice or egg noodles, to serve
a few dried chives, to garnish

Mix the onion with the butter in the slow cooker. Add the chicken and beans and spread out. Mix the coconut milk with the curry paste, lemon grass and fish sauce. Pour over the chicken and beans. Cover and cook on High for 3 hours or Low for 6 hours until really tender. Taste and re-season, if necessary. Spoon over rice or egg noodles and serve sprinkled with a few dried chives.

Chicken Breasts with Zesty Vegetables

Orange, rosemary and fennel accent these tender chicken breasts.

SERVES 4

4 skinless chicken breast fillets, about 175 g/6 oz each
12 baby carrots
8 small waxy potatoes, quartered
225 g/8 oz white or brown cap mushrooms, quartered
3 garlic cloves, thinly sliced
1–2 tsp grated orange zest
1 tsp crushed fennel seeds
1 tsp dried rosemary
1 bay leaf
120 ml/4 fl oz chicken stock or orange juice
120 ml/4 fl oz dry white wine or extra chicken stock
2 tbsp orange liqueur (optional)
1 tbsp cornflour
2 tbsp water
salt and freshly ground black pepper, to taste

Put all the ingredients, except the cornflour, water, salt and pepper in the slow cooker. Cover and cook on Low for 6–8 hours.

Remove the chicken and vegetables to a serving platter and keep hot. Measure 150 ml/¾ pint of the stock into a small pan. Whisk in the combined cornflour and water, whisking until thickened, about 1 minute. Season to taste with salt and pepper. Serve the gravy over the vegetables and chicken breasts.

Sherried Chicken

A lovely dish for entertaining or for special family meals. Serve over aromatic rice to absorb the flavourful juices.

SERVES 4

50 ml/2 fl oz dry sherry
175 g/6 oz sultanas
4 skinless chicken breast fillets, about 175 g/6 oz each
50 g/2 oz walnuts, coarsely chopped
1 tart cooking apple, peeled and chopped
1 small red onion, sliced
2 garlic cloves, crushed
250 ml/8 fl oz chicken stock
salt and freshly ground black pepper, to taste

Pour the sherry over the sultanas in a bowl. Leave to stand for 15–30 minutes. Put in the slow cooker with all the remaining ingredients, except the salt and pepper. Cover and cook on High or until the chicken is tender, 3–4 hours. Season to taste with salt and pepper.

Savoury Chicken and Rice

This is Catherine Atkinson's great way to use bought ready-cooked or leftover chicken – and also pork or beef.

SERVES 4

4 spring onions, sliced
200 g/7 oz can of chopped tomatoes
175 ml/6 fl oz boiling chicken or vegetable stock
½ red pepper, seeded and chopped, or 50 g/2 oz thawed frozen sliced mixed peppers
a pinch of dried mixed herbs
75 g/3 oz easy-cook long-grain rice
salt and freshly ground black pepper
75 g/3 oz roughly chopped cooked chicken

Put the spring onions in the ceramic cooking pot. Pour the tomatoes over, then the stock. Cover with the lid and switch on the slow cooker to High. Leave for a few minutes while measuring and preparing the rest of the ingredients. Stir in the chopped pepper and the herbs, then sprinkle the rice over. Season with salt and pepper and stir again. Re-cover with the lid and cook for 50–60 minutes or until the rice is just tender and has absorbed most of the liquid. Stir in the chicken and cook for a further 10 minutes to heat the chicken through before serving.

Mediterranean Chicken

Chicken breasts are topped with fennel, courgette and olives in a tomato-based sauce.

SERVES 4

4 skinless chicken breast fillets, about
   175 g/6 oz each
400 g/14 oz can chopped tomatoes
120 ml/4 fl oz chicken stock
120 ml/4 fl oz dry white wine or extra
   chicken stock
1 courgette, sliced
2 small onions, chopped
1 fennel bulb, sliced
1 tsp dried oregano
1 bay leaf
40 g/1½ oz pitted Kalamata olives,
   sliced
1–2 tsp lemon juice
salt and freshly ground black pepper,
   to taste
75 g/3 oz rice, cooked, hot

Put all the ingredients, except the olives, lemon juice, salt, pepper and rice, in the slow cooker. Cover and cook on Low for 6–8 hours, adding the olives during the last 30 minutes. Season to taste with lemon juice, salt and pepper. Discard the bay leaf. Serve the chicken and tomato mixture over the rice.

Indonesian Chicken with Courgette

Coconut milk, fresh root ginger, garlic, fresh coriander and cumin make a fragrant sauce for chicken.

SERVES 6

3 large skinless chicken breasts,
   175–225 g/6–8 oz each, halved
400 g/14 oz can coconut milk
50 ml/2 fl oz water
50 ml/2 fl oz lemon juice
1 onion, finely chopped
1 garlic clove, crushed
7.5 cm/3 in fresh root ginger, finely
   grated, or 2 tsp ground ginger
2 tsp ground coriander
1 tsp ground cumin
450 g/1 lb courgettes, halved
   lengthways, seeded and sliced
1 tbsp cornflour
2 tbsp water
15 g/½ oz fresh coriander, chopped
salt and freshly ground black pepper,
   to taste
100 g/4 oz rice, cooked, hot

Put all the ingredients, except the courgettes, cornflour, 2 tbsp water, fresh coriander, salt, pepper and rice, in the slow cooker. Cover and cook on Low for 3½–4 hours, adding the courgettes during the last 30 minutes. Remove the chicken breasts and keep warm. Turn the heat to High and cook for 10 minutes. Stir in the combined cornflour and 2 tbsp water, stirring for 2–3 minutes. Stir in the fresh coriander. Season to taste with salt and pepper. Serve the chicken and stock over the rice in shallow bowls.

Chicken Breasts with Figs

Figs and orange juice, heightened with soy sauce and sherry, complement tender chicken breasts.

SERVES 4

4 skinless chicken breast fillets (about 175 g/6 oz each)
8 dried figs, quartered
2 tbsp soy sauce
2 tbsp dry sherry
175 ml/6 fl oz orange juice
grated zest of 1 orange
2 tbsp cornflour
2 tbsp water
2 tbsp honey
salt and freshly ground black pepper, to taste
75 g/3 oz rice, cooked, hot

Put all the ingredients, except the cornflour, water, honey, salt, pepper and rice, in the slow cooker. Cover and cook on High for 4–6 hours. Remove the chicken and keep warm. Turn the heat to High and cook for 10 minutes. Stir in the combined cornflour, water and honey, stirring for 2–3 minutes. Season to taste with salt and pepper. Serve the chicken breasts and sauce over the rice.

Chicken Mole

The easy mole sauce is made with canned chilli beans.

SERVES 4

Mole Sauce (see right)
4 skinless chicken breast fillets, about 100 g/4 oz each
175 g/6 oz rice, cooked, hot
chopped fresh coriander, to garnish
120 ml/4 fl oz soured cream

Spoon half the Mole Sauce into the slow cooker. Top with the chicken breasts and the remaining sauce. Cover and cook on Low for 4–6 hours. Spoon over the rice. Sprinkle generously with fresh coriander and serve with soured cream.

Mole Sauce (V)

This recipe is classed as suitable for vegetarians, but do make sure you use vegetarian Worcestershire sauce (some are not) if this is important to you.

SERVES 4

400 g/14 oz can kidney beans in hot chilli sauce with their liquor
1 onion, coarsely chopped
2 garlic cloves
50 g/2 oz ready-made tomato sauce
1 tbsp Worcestershire sauce
½ tsp ground cinnamon
15 g/½ oz plain chocolate, finely chopped
25 g/1 oz flaked almonds

Process all the ingredients in a food processor until smooth.

Chicken Divan

Chicken breasts and broccoli cooked in a delicious sauce.

SERVES 6

Sauce Divan (see page 269)
6 skinless chicken breast fillets, about 100 g/4 oz each, halved
500 g/18 oz broccoli florets and sliced stems
100 g/4 oz brown rice, cooked, hot
freshly grated Parmesan cheese and paprika, to garnish

Spoon one-third of the Sauce Divan into the slow cooker. Top with the chicken and remaining sauce. Cover and cook on Low for 4–5 hours, stirring in the broccoli during the last 30 minutes. Spoon over the rice. Sprinkle with Parmesan cheese and paprika.

Sauce Divan (V)

A rich sherry-flavoured sauce.

MAKES 600 ML/1 PINT

3 tbsp butter or margarine
25 g/1 oz plain flour
600 ml/1 pint single cream or full-fat milk
50 ml/2 fl oz dry sherry
salt and freshly ground black pepper, to taste

Melt the butter or margarine in a medium pan. Stir in the flour and cook for 1–2 minutes. Whisk in the cream or milk and heat to boiling, whisking until thickened, about 1 minute. Whisk in the sherry. Season to taste with salt and pepper.

Easy Chicken Casserole

This dish can be made easily using convenient canned and frozen ingredients.

SERVES 4

300 g/11 oz can condensed cream of chicken soup
300 ml/½ pint semi-skimmed milk
250 ml/8 fl oz water
450 g/1 lb boneless skinless chicken breasts, cubed (2 cm/¾ in)
2 onions, sliced
275 g/10 oz frozen mixed vegetables, thawed
2 tbsp cornflour
50 ml/2 fl oz water
salt and freshly ground black pepper, to taste

Combine the soup, milk and water in the slow cooker. Stir in the chicken and onions. Cover and cook on Low for 5–6 hours, adding the mixed vegetables during the last 20 minutes. Turn the heat to High and cook for 10 minutes. Stir in the combined cornflour and water, stirring for 2–3 minutes. Season to taste with salt and pepper.

Red Pepper Chicken with Pepperoni

Simple and packed with flavour and colour, you can also serve this recipe by Carolyn Humphries with rice, fluffy mashed potato or couscous.

SERVES 4

2 tbsp cornflour
salt and freshly ground black pepper
4 skinless chicken breasts
2 good handfuls of frozen sliced mixed peppers, or 1 red and 1 green pepper, sliced
65 g/2½ oz ready-sliced pepperoni
400 g/14 oz can of chopped tomatoes
4 tbsp dry white wine
1 tbsp tomato purée
5 ml/1 tsp caster sugar
1.5 ml/¼ tsp crushed dried chillies, or chopped chillies from a jar
5 ml/1 tsp chopped garlic from a jar, or 1 garlic clove, chopped
2.5 ml/½ tsp dried oregano
2.5 ml/½ tsp pimènton
ribbon noodles and a green salad, to serve

Mix the cornflour with a little salt and pepper in the slow cooker. Add the chicken and turn to coat completely. Add all the remaining ingredients and stir well. Cover and cook on High for 3 hours or Low for 6 hours until the chicken is really tender. Taste and re-season if necessary. Serve spooned over ribbon noodles with a crisp green salad.

Country Chicken

This piquant casserole is beautifully warming on an autumn or winter evening.

SERVES 6

700 g/1½ lb skinless chicken breast fillets, cubed (2.5 cm/1 in)
250 ml/8 fl oz chicken stock
175 g/6 oz tomato purée
225 g/8 oz cabbage, coarsely chopped
2 onions, chopped
1 green pepper, chopped
2 large garlic cloves, crushed
1 bay leaf
1 tbsp lemon juice
1 tbsp Worcestershire sauce
1 tbsp sugar
2 tsp dried basil
2 tsp Dijon mustard
3–4 drops Tabasco sauce
salt and freshly ground black pepper, to taste
100 g/4 oz rice, cooked, hot

Combine all the ingredients, except the salt, pepper and rice, in the slow cooker. Cover and cook on Low for 6–8 hours. Discard the bay leaf. Season to taste with salt and pepper. Serve over the rice.

Chicken with Beans and Chickpeas

Canned chickpeas and baked beans combine with chicken in a chilli-spiked stew.

SERVES 8

275 g/10 oz skinless chicken breast fillets, cubed
2 x 400 g/14 oz cans baked beans or pork and beans

400 g/14 oz can chickpeas, drained and rinsed
400 g/14 oz can chopped tomatoes
1 large onion, chopped
1 red pepper, chopped
2 garlic cloves, crushed
2–3 tsp chilli powder
¾ tsp dried thyme
salt and freshly ground black pepper, to taste

Combine all the ingredients, except the salt and pepper, in the slow cooker. Cover and cook on High for 4–5 hours. Season to taste with salt and pepper.

Sweet Potato with Chicken

The casserole is also delicious made with potatoes or a combination of potatoes and sweet potatoes.

SERVES 4

450 g/1 lb skinless chicken breast fillets, cubed (2.5 cm/1 in)
375 ml/13 fl oz chicken stock
350 g/12 oz sweet potatoes, peeled and cubed (2 cm/¾ in)
1 large green pepper, sliced
2–3 tsp chilli powder
½ tsp garlic powder
2 tbsp cornflour
50 ml/2 fl oz water
salt and freshly ground black pepper, to taste

Combine all the ingredients, except the cornflour, water, salt and pepper, in the slow cooker. Cover and cook on High for 4–5 hours. Stir in the combined cornflour and water, stirring for 2–3 minutes. Season to taste with salt and pepper.

Chicken and Mashed Potato Casserole

The mounds of mashed potatoes enriched with cheese that top this hearty casserole are delicious. The potatoes can be made one day in advance and refrigerated, covered.

SERVES 4

450 g/1 lb skinless chicken breast fillets, cubed (2 cm/¾ in)
250 ml/8 fl oz chicken stock
1 onion, chopped
2 small carrots, sliced
1 celery stick
75 g/3 oz mushrooms, sliced
½ tsp dried rosemary
½ tsp dried thyme
50 g/2 oz frozen petits pois, thawed
1–2 tbsp cornflour
3–4 tbsp cold water
salt and freshly ground black pepper, to taste
½ quantity Real Mashed Potatoes (see page 264)
1 egg yolk
50 g/2 oz Cheddar cheese, grated
1–2 tbsp butter or margarine, melted

Combine the chicken, stock, onion, carrots, celery, mushrooms and herbs in the slow cooker. Cover and cook on Low for 6–8 hours. Add the peas, turn the heat to High and cook for 10 minutes. Stir in the combined cornflour and water, stirring for 2–3 minutes. Season to taste with salt and pepper.

While the casserole is cooking, make Real Mashed Potatoes, mixing in the egg yolk and cheese. Spoon the potato mixture into four mounds on a greased baking sheet and refrigerate, covered, until chilled, about 30 minutes. Drizzle the potatoes with butter or margarine. Bake at 220°C/gas 7/fan oven 200°C until browned, about 15 minutes. Top bowls of casserole with potatoes.

Slow-roast Stuffed Chicken

Carolyn Humphries suggests you pop the chicken in a very hot oven for 30 minutes at the end to brown the skin.

SERVES 4

85 g/3½ oz packet of sage and onion or sausage and thyme stuffing mix
a handful of raisins
sunflower oil, for greasing
1 oven-ready chicken, about 1.5 kg/3 lb
5 ml/1 tsp soy sauce
300 ml/½ pint boiling chicken stock
45 ml/3 tbsp plain flour
45 ml/3 tbsp water
salt and freshly ground black pepper

Make up the stuffing mix with boiling water as in the packet directions and stir in the raisins. Use some to stuff the neck end of the bird and secure the flap of skin with a skewer. Put the remaining stuffing on a piece of greased foil and fold up to form a parcel. Place a double thickness of foil in the slow cooker so it comes up the sides of the pot (to enable easy removal of the bird after cooking). Brush the foil with oil. Place the bird on the foil in the slow cooker and brush with the soy sauce. Rest the foil packet of stuffing at the leg end. Pour the boiling stock around. Cover and cook on High for 2–3 hours or Low for 4–6 hours until the bird is cooked through and the juices run clear when pierced with a skewer in the thickest part of the leg. Using the foil, lift the bird out of the pot and transfer to a roasting tin (still on the foil). Roast in a preheated oven at 230°C/gas 8/fan oven 210°C for 30 minutes to brown and crisp. Remove from the oven and leave to stand for 10 minutes before carving. Meanwhile, blend the flour with the water in a saucepan. Blend in the cooking juices from the slow cooker, bring to the boil and cook, stirring, for 2 minutes. Season to taste, if necessary. Carve the bird and serve with the gravy, stuffing and your usual accompaniments.

271

Chicken and Mushrooms

Serve this piquant casserole with warm slices of Parmesan Bread (see page 364).

SERVES 4

450 g/1 lb skinless chicken breast fillets, cubed (2 cm/¾ in)
250 ml/8 fl oz chicken stock
175 g/6 oz tomato purée
1 tbsp Worcestershire sauce
225 g/8 oz mushrooms, thickly sliced
1 large onion, chopped
2 garlic cloves, crushed
2 large carrots, coarsely grated
1 bay leaf
1 tsp dried Italian herb seasoning
¼ tsp dry mustard powder
1–2 tbsp cornflour
2–4 tbsp water
salt and freshly ground black pepper
225 g/8 oz spaghetti, cooked, hot

Combine all the ingredients, except the cornflour, water, salt, pepper and spaghetti, in the slow cooker. Cover and cook on High for 4–6 hours. Stir in the combined cornflour and water, stirring for 2–3 minutes. Discard the bay leaf. Season to taste with salt and pepper. Serve over the spaghetti.

Chicken and Wild Mushrooms

Wild, or cultivated exotic, mushrooms are seasonal but they're well worth buying, when you can get them, to make dishes such as this one.

SERVES 4

450 g/1 lb skinless chicken breast fillets, cubed
120 ml/4 fl oz chicken stock
120 ml/4 fl oz dry white wine or extra chicken stock
225 g/8 oz mixed wild mushrooms, coarsely chopped
2 spring onions, thinly sliced

1 small leek (white part only), thinly sliced
1 tbsp drained capers
1–2 tbsp cornflour
2–4 tbsp water
salt and freshly ground black pepper
75 g/3 oz brown rice, cooked, hot

Combine all the ingredients, except the capers, cornflour, water, salt, pepper and rice, in the slow cooker. Cover and cook on Low for 6–8 hours. Add the capers, turn the heat to High and cook for 10 minutes. Stir in the combined cornflour and water, stirring for 2–3 minutes. Season to taste with salt and pepper. Serve over the rice.

Lemon Chicken

Fresh lemon juice and chilli are flavour accents in this delicious dish.

SERVES 6

450 g/1 lb skinless chicken breast fillets, cubed
2 x 400 g/14 oz cans chopped tomatoes
1 jalapeño or other medium-hot chilli, finely chopped
2 garlic cloves, crushed
1 tsp instant chicken bouillon granules, or a chicken stock cube
2 tsp dried basil
350 g/12 oz broccoli florets
50–75 ml/2–2½ fl oz lemon juice
salt and freshly ground black pepper
350 g/12 oz angel hair pasta or vermicelli, cooked, hot
freshly grated Parmesan cheese, to garnish

Combine all the ingredients, except the broccoli, lemon juice, salt, pepper, pasta and cheese, in the slow cooker. Cover and cook on High for 4–5 hours, adding the broccoli during the last 20 minutes. Season to taste with lemon juice, salt and pepper. Serve over the pasta, sprinkled with Parmesan cheese.

Spinach Rice

An all-purpose rice dish that is especially good with Mediterranean dishes.

SERVES 6

½ onion, chopped
oil, for greasing
275 g/10 oz long-grain rice
600 ml/1 pint chicken stock
150 g/5 oz spinach, sliced

Sauté the onion in a lightly greased medium pan until tender, 2–3 minutes. Stir in the rice and stock and heat to boiling. Reduce the heat and simmer, covered, until the rice is tender, about 25 minutes, stirring in the spinach during the last 10 minutes.

Chicken in Cider and Cream

Carolyn Humphries' glamorous dish requires minimal effort. You can use apple juice instead or cider.

SERVES 4

450 g/1 lb frozen steamable mixed
baby vegetables such as baby
sweetcorn cobs, carrots, green beans
100 g/4 oz fresh button or frozen
sliced mushrooms
450 g/1 lb diced chicken meat
45 ml/3 tbsp cornflour
salt and freshly ground black pepper
2 tbsp dried onion flakes
150 ml/¼ pt medium-dry cider
150 ml/¼ pint boiling chicken stock
1 bouquet garni sachet
90 ml/6 tbsp double cream
buttered rice, to serve
2 tbsp chopped fresh or frozen parsley

Put all the ingredients except the cream and parsley in the slow cooker and mix together thoroughly. Cover and cook on High for 3 hours or Low for 6 hours. Discard the bouquet garni and stir in the cream. Taste and re-season, if necessary. Serve on a bed of buttered rice, garnished with the parsley.

Chicken with Spinach Rice

Spinach Rice is a flavourful accompaniment to this French-style dish.

SERVES 6

1 whole chicken, about 900 g/2 lb, cut
into pieces
250 ml/8 fl oz chicken stock
175 g/6 oz tomato purée
8 tomatoes, seeded and coarsely
chopped
1 onion, chopped
1 small red pepper, chopped
50 g/2 oz mushrooms, sliced
1 garlic clove, crushed
½ tsp dried basil
½ tsp dried tarragon
½ tsp dried oregano
a generous pinch of freshly grated
nutmeg
2 courgettes, sliced
40 g/1½ oz pitted black olives
1–2 tbsp cornflour
2–4 tbsp cold water
salt and freshly ground black pepper,
to taste
Spinach Rice (see left)

Combine all the ingredients, except the courgettes, olives, cornflour, water, salt, pepper and Spinach Rice, in the slow cooker. Cover and cook on Low for 6–8 hours, adding the courgettes and olives during the last 20 minutes. Turn the heat to High and cook for 10 minutes. Stir in the cornflour and water, stirring for 2–3 minutes. Season to taste with salt and pepper. Serve over Spinach Rice.

Orange Chicken and Vegetables

Both orange juice and the zest are used to give this casserole a refreshing citrus tang. Serve over aromatic rice.

SERVES 6

1.25 kg/2½ lb skinless chicken breast fillets
375 ml/13 fl oz orange juice
275 g/10 oz tomatoes, chopped
250 g/9 oz potatoes, unpeeled and cubed
2 onions, sliced
2 large carrots, thickly sliced
2 garlic cloves, crushed
½ tsp dried marjoram
½ tsp dried thyme
2 tsp grated orange zest
1 piece cinnamon stick (2.5 cm/1 in)
2 tbsp cornflour
50 ml/2 fl oz water
salt and freshly ground black pepper, to taste

Combine all the ingredients, except the cornflour, water, salt and pepper, in a 5.5 litre/9½ pint slow cooker. Cover and cook on Low for 6–8 hours. Turn the heat to High and cook for 10 minutes. Stir in the combined cornflour and water, stirring for 2–3 minutes. Season to taste with salt and pepper.

Ginger and Orange Chicken with Squash

Any winter squash, such as butternut or pumpkin, is appropriate for this fragrant dish.

SERVES 6

700 g/1½ lb skinless chicken breast fillets, cubed
250 ml/8 fl oz chicken stock
400 g/14 oz can chopped tomatoes
120 ml/4 fl oz orange juice
500 g/18 oz butternut or other winter squash, peeled and cubed
2 floury potatoes, peeled and cubed
2 small onions, coarsely chopped
1 small green pepper, coarsely chopped
2 garlic cloves, crushed
1 tbsp grated orange zest
½ tsp ground ginger
120 ml/4 fl oz soured cream
1 tbsp cornflour
salt and freshly ground black pepper, to taste
275 g/10 oz noodles or brown basmati rice, cooked, hot

Combine all the ingredients, except the soured cream, cornflour, salt, pepper and noodles or rice, in a 5.5 litre/9½ pint slow cooker. Cover and cook on Low for 6–8 hours. Stir in the combined soured cream and cornflour, stirring for 2–3 minutes. Season to taste with salt and pepper. Serve over the noodles or rice.

Apricot Chicken

Dijon mustard and apricot jam flavour the wine sauce in this casserole.

SERVES 6

700 g/1½ lb skinless chicken breast fillets, quartered
75 ml/2½ fl oz chicken stock
75 ml/2½ fl oz dry white wine or chicken stock
90 g/3½ oz apricot jam
1 carrot, chopped
1 celery stick, chopped
4 spring onions, sliced
2 tbsp Dijon mustard
1 tsp dried rosemary, crushed
1 tsp paprika
50 g/2 oz frozen petits pois, thawed
1–2 tbsp cornflour
2–3 tbsp water
salt and freshly ground black pepper, to taste
100 g/4 oz rice, cooked, hot

Combine all the ingredients, except the peas, cornflour, water, salt, pepper and rice, in the slow cooker. Cover and cook on High for 4–5 hours, adding the peas during the last 20 minutes. Stir in the combined cornflour and water, stirring for 2–3 minutes. Season to taste with salt and pepper. Serve over the rice.

Chicken with Dried Fruit

Prunes and dried apricots add sweetness and depth of flavour to this chicken dish. If you prefer the sauce to be a little thicker, stir in 1–2 tbsp cornflour combined with 2 to 3 tbsp water towards the end of cooking.

SERVES 4

450 g/1 lb skinless chicken breast fillets, cubed (4 cm/1½ in)
300 ml/½ pint chicken stock
2 small onions, finely chopped
1 small red pepper, finely chopped
1 garlic clove, crushed
½ tsp ground ginger
1 bay leaf
200 g/7 oz mixed raisins
175 g/6 oz stoned prunes, coarsely chopped
175 g/6 oz dried apricots, coarsely chopped
2–4 tbsp light rum (optional)
salt and freshly ground black pepper, to taste
175 g/6 oz rice, cooked, hot

Combine all the ingredients, except the dried fruit, rum, salt, pepper and rice, in the slow cooker. Cover and cook on High for 4–5 hours, adding the dried fruit and rum during the last 1½ hours. Discard the bay leaf and season to taste with salt and pepper. Serve over the rice.

Red Wine Chicken with Mushrooms

Based on the classic French dish, coq au vin, this is so easy to make. Serve with creamed potatoes or rice and green beans.

SERVES 4

a good handful of frozen diced onion, or 1 fresh onion, chopped
10 ml/2 tsp softened butter
100 g/4 oz smoked lardons
4 skinless chicken breasts
100 g/4 oz baby button mushrooms, or 1 x 300 g/11 oz can of button mushrooms, drained
300 ml/½ pint red wine
1 tbsp tomato purée
45 ml/3 tbsp cornflour
2 tbsp brandy
250 ml/8 fl oz boiling chicken stock
5 ml/1 tsp caster sugar
2.5 ml/½ tsp dried mixed herbs
salt and freshly ground black pepper
chopped fresh parsley, to garnish

Mix the onion with the butter in the slow cooker. Sprinkle the lardons over, then add the chicken and mushrooms. Blend the wine with the tomato purée and cornflour until smooth, then stir in the brandy, stock, sugar and herbs. Pour over the chicken and season with salt and pepper. Cover and cook on High for 3 hours or Low for 6 hours until the sauce is rich and the chicken is tender. Stir well. Taste and re-season, if necessary. Garnish with a little chopped parsley.

Chicken Veronique

Red and green seedless grapes add flavour and colour to this traditional dish. Serve over aromatic rice, such as jasmine or basmati.

SERVES 4

450 g/1 lb chicken breast fillets, quartered lengthways
300 ml/½ pint chicken stock
50 ml/2 fl oz dry white wine (optional)
50 g/2 oz thinly sliced leek (white part only)
4 spring onions
2 garlic cloves, crushed
¾ tsp dried tarragon
50 g/2 oz red seedless grapes, halved
50 g/2 oz green seedless grapes, halved
2 tbsp cornflour
50 ml/2 fl oz cold water
salt and freshly ground black pepper, to taste

Combine all the ingredients, except the grapes, cornflour, water, salt and pepper, in the slow cooker. Cover and cook on High for 4–5 hours, adding the grapes during the last 10 minutes. Stir in the combined cornflour and water, stirring for 2–3 minutes. Season to taste with salt and pepper.

Tarragon and Mustard Chicken

Aniseedy tarragon is often cooked with chicken, and here it is partnered with Dijon mustard for a sweet and tangy flavour.

SERVES 4

450 g/1 lb skinless chicken breast
    fillets, cubed
250 ml/8 fl oz chicken stock
2 chopped onions, sliced
1 large carrot, sliced
100 g/4 oz small Brussels sprouts,
    halved
2 small celery sticks, chopped
1–2 tbsp Dijon mustard
2 tsp dried tarragon
2 tsp brown sugar
1 tsp lemon juice
2 tbsp cornflour
50 ml/2 fl oz water
salt and freshly ground black pepper,
    to taste
75 g/3 oz rice, cooked, hot

Combine all the ingredients, except the cornflour, water, salt, pepper and rice, in the slow cooker. Cover and cook on Low for 6–8 hours. Turn the heat to High and cook for 10 minutes. Stir in the combined cornflour and water, stirring for 2–3 minutes. Season to taste with salt and pepper. Serve over the rice.

Honey and Mustard Chicken

Dijon mustard and honey are given a spicy edge, adding a hint of curry to give this chicken recipe a lift.

SERVES 4

450 g/1 lb skinless chicken breast
    fillets, cubed
375 ml/13 fl oz chicken stock
225 g/8 oz small cauliflower florets
2 onions, chopped
1 large carrot, sliced
2 tbsp honey
1 tbsp Dijon mustard
1–2 tsp curry powder
1–2 tbsp cornflour
2–4 tbsp water
salt and freshly ground black pepper,
    to taste
75 g/3 oz rice, cooked, hot

Combine all the ingredients, except the cornflour, water, salt, pepper and rice, in the slow cooker. Cover and cook on High for 4–5 hours. Stir in the combined cornflour and water, stirring for 2–3 minutes. Season to taste with salt and pepper. Serve over the rice.

Chinese Chicken, Pepper and Corn Curry

A quick and easy mild curry from Carolyn Humphries.

SERVES 4

a good handful of frozen diced onion, or 1 fresh onion, chopped
1 tbsp sunflower oil
450 g/1 lb diced chicken meat
45 ml/3 tbsp cornflour
1 large fresh pepper, sliced
100 g/4 oz fresh or frozen baby sweetcorn cobs
200 ml/7 fl oz boiling chicken stock
10 ml/2 tsp chopped garlic from a jar, or 2 garlic cloves, chopped
1 tbsp mild curry powder
10 ml/2 tsp light brown sugar
2 tbsp soy sauce
salt
rice, to serve

Mix the onion with the oil in the slow cooker. Toss the chicken in the cornflour and place in the slow cooker with any remaining cornflour. Scatter the pepper and sweetcorn cobs over. Blend the stock with all the remaining ingredients and pour over. Cover and cook on High for 3 hours or Low for 6 hours until the chicken is really tender and the sauce is thick. Stir gently, taste and re-season if necessary. Serve spooned over rice.

Sweet-and-sour Chicken with Vegetables

Chicken and vegetables are cooked in cider and seasoned with honey and vinegar for a refreshing sweet–sour flavour.

SERVES 6

450 g/1 lb skinless chicken breast fillets, cubed
120 ml/4 fl oz cider or apple juice
130 g/4½ oz canned chopped tomatoes
350 g/12 oz butternut or winter squash, peeled and cubed
175 g/6 oz floury potatoes, peeled and cubed
175 g/6 oz sweet potatoes, peeled and cubed
100 g/4 oz sweetcorn, thawed if frozen
150 g/5 oz shallots, chopped
½ red pepper, chopped
2 garlic cloves, crushed
1½ tbsp honey
1½ tbsp cider vinegar
1 bay leaf
¼ tsp freshly grated nutmeg
1 small cooking apple, peeled and sliced
salt and freshly ground black pepper, to taste
100 g/4 oz basmati rice, cooked, hot

Combine all the ingredients, except the apple, salt, pepper and rice, in the slow cooker. Cover and cook on Low for 5–6 hours, adding the apple during the last 20 minutes. Discard the bay leaf. Season to taste with salt and pepper. Serve over the rice.

Chicken with Tomatoes and Beans

Wine brings out the flavour of tomatoes in this sauce for chicken. It's great served over Polenta (see page 356) or rice.

SERVES 6

700 g/1½ lb skinless chicken breast fillets, cubed
400 g/14 oz can chopped tomatoes
400 g/14 oz can cannellini beans, drained and rinsed
250 ml/8 fl oz chicken stock
120 ml/4 fl oz dry white wine or extra chicken stock
50 ml/2 fl oz tomato purée
175 g/6 oz mushrooms, sliced
2 onions, sliced
2 garlic cloves, crushed
2 tsp lemon juice
1 bay leaf
½ tsp dried oregano
¼ tsp dried thyme
salt and freshly ground black pepper, to taste

Combine all the ingredients, except the salt and pepper, in the slow cooker. Cover and cook on Low for 6–8 hours. Discard the bay leaf. Season to taste with salt and pepper.

Chicken with Couscous

This recipe from Carolyn Humphries has a fiery sweet flavour.

SERVES 4

8 small or 4 large skinless chicken thighs
4 belly pork slices, halved
a good handful of frozen diced onion, or 1 fresh onion, chopped
2 large handfuls of frozen sliced mixed peppers, or 1 red and 1 green fresh pepper, sliced
2.5 ml/½ tsp chopped chillies from a jar or dried chilli flakes
1 tbsp light brown sugar
2.5 ml/½ tsp ground cinnamon
a good pinch of ground cloves
2.5 ml/½ tsp dried thyme
10 ml/2 tsp red wine vinegar
300 ml/½ pint boiling chicken stock
Salt and freshly ground black pepper
225 g/8 oz couscous
green salad, to serve

Put the chicken, pork, onion, peppers and chilli in the slow cooker. Blend together all the remaining ingredients except the couscous and pour over, seasoning with some salt and lots of pepper. Cover and cook on High for 4 hours or Low for 8 hours until everything is tender. Gently stir in the couscous, re-cover and leave on Low for 5 minutes while the couscous absorbs the stock. Gently fluff up the couscous with a fork and serve in bowls. Accompany with a green salad.

Chicken with Vegetables and Lentils

This healthy casserole combines chicken and lentils with a medley of vegetables. Serve in shallow bowls.

SERVES 6

1 chicken (about 1.5 kg/3 lb), cut into pieces
400 g/14 oz can chopped tomatoes
375 ml/13 fl oz chicken stock
175 g/6 oz brown or Puy lentils
1 celery stick, sliced
1 carrot, sliced
75 g/3 oz broccoli florets
1 onion, chopped
2 garlic cloves, crushed
½ tsp dried marjoram
3 bacon rashers, cooked until crisp and crumbled
salt and freshly ground black pepper, to taste

Combine all the ingredients, except the bacon, salt and pepper, in a 5.5 litre/ 9½ pint slow cooker. Cover and cook on Low for 6–8 hours. Stir in the bacon. Season to taste with salt and pepper.

Garden Chicken with Couscous

Take advantage of seasonal vegetables, either home-grown or from the market, to make this casserole, substituting whichever vegetables are in abundance.

SERVES 6

1.25 kg/2½ lb skinless chicken breast fillets, halved or quartered
375 ml/13 fl oz chicken stock
4 medium tomatoes, coarsely chopped
225 g/8 oz baby carrots, halved
225 g/8 oz sliced shiitake or button mushrooms
2 onions, thickly sliced
1 turnip, cubed

1 small jalapeño or other medium-hot chilli, finely chopped
2 courgettes, sliced
15 g/½ oz fresh coriander, chopped
salt and freshly ground black pepper, to taste
75 g/3 oz couscous, cooked, hot

Combine all the ingredients, except the courgettes, coriander, salt, pepper and couscous, in a 5.5 litre/9½ pint slow cooker. Cover and cook on Low for 6–8 hours, adding the courgettes during the last 30 minutes. Stir in the coriander and season to taste with salt and pepper. Serve over the couscous.

Chicken Fricassee

Cloves and bay leaves add a warm and slightly exotic edge to this dish. The traditional herbs of rosemary and thyme can be used instead, if you prefer.

SERVES 6

700 g/1½ lb skinless chicken breast fillets, halved or quartered
400 ml/14 fl oz chicken stock
2 onions, cut into wedges
1 large carrot, sliced
1 large celery stick, sliced
2 garlic cloves, crushed
16 whole cloves, tied in a muslin bag
2 bay leaves
2 tbsp cornflour
50 ml/2 fl oz water
1–2 tsp lemon juice
salt and freshly ground black pepper, to taste
350 g/12 oz fettuccine, cooked, hot

Combine all the ingredients, except the cornflour, water, lemon juice, salt, pepper and pasta, in the slow cooker. Cover and cook on Low for 6–8 hours. Turn the heat to High and cook for 10 minutes. Stir in the combined cornflour and water, stirring for 2–3 minutes. Discard the cloves and bay leaves. Season to taste with salt and pepper. Serve over fettuccine.

Chicken Gumbo

Garlic, peppers and okra make a delicious and easy-to-prepare gumbo.

SERVES 4

**450 g/1 lb chicken breast, cubed
(2 cm/¾ in)
400 g/14 oz can tomatoes
450 ml/¾ pint chicken stock
2 onions, chopped
½ red or green pepper, chopped
2 garlic cloves, crushed
½ tsp dried thyme
¼ tsp crushed chilli flakes
225 g/8 oz okra, trimmed and halved
salt and freshly ground black pepper,
to taste
75 g/3 oz rice, cooked, hot**

Combine all the ingredients, except the okra, salt, pepper and rice, in the slow cooker. Cover and cook on Low for 6–8 hours, adding the okra during the last 30 minutes. Season to taste with salt and pepper. Serve over the rice.

El Paso Chicken

Serve this dish chicken dish with tomatoes, sweetcorn and French beans over rice, sprinkled with tortilla chips and cheese.

SERVES 4

**450 g/1 lb skinless chicken breast
fillets, cubed
2 x 400 g/14 oz cans tomatoes
400 g/14 oz can pinto beans, drained
and rinsed
275 g/10 oz French beans, cut into
short lengths
225 g/8 oz sweetcorn
½ packet taco seasoning mix
salt and freshly ground black pepper,
to taste**

Combine all the ingredients, except the salt and pepper, in the slow cooker. Cover and cook on Low for 6–8 hours. Season to taste with salt and pepper.

Chicken and Black-eyed Pea Gumbo

Black-eyed peas, okra, sweetcorn and butter beans combine nicely in this nourishing gumbo. Serve with Spoon Bread (see page 360).

SERVES 6

**450 g/1 lb skinless chicken breast
fillets, cubed
450 ml/¾ pint chicken stock
400 g/14 oz can chopped tomatoes
400 g/14 oz can black-eyed peas,
drained and rinsed
150 g/5 oz drained canned butter
beans, rinsed
150 g/5 oz sweetcorn, thawed if frozen
1 medium ham hock (optional)
2 onions, chopped
½ celery stick, chopped
½ small red or green pepper, chopped
1 bay leaf
¼ tsp dried thyme
100 g/4 oz okra, trimmed and sliced
salt and freshly ground black pepper,
to taste**

Combine all the ingredients, except the okra, salt and pepper, in the slow cooker. Cover and cook on Low for 6–8 hours, adding the okra during the last 30 minutes. Discard the ham hock and bay leaf. Season to taste with salt and pepper.

Brunswick Chicken

Serve this homely dish with mashed potato and lightly steamed spring greens.

SERVES 4

450 g/1 lb skinless chicken breast fillets, cubed (2.5 cm/1 in)
250 ml/8 fl oz chicken stock
400 g/14 oz can butter beans, drained and rinsed
400 g/14 oz can chopped tomatoes, undrained
100 g/4 oz sweetcorn
1 onion, chopped
½ green pepper, chopped
¼ tsp crushed chilli flakes
100 g/4 oz okra, trimmed and sliced
1–2 tbsp cornflour
50 ml/2 fl oz water
salt and freshly ground black pepper, to taste

Combine all the ingredients, except the okra, cornflour, water, salt and pepper, in the slow cooker. Cover and cook on High for 4–5 hours, adding the okra during the last 30 minutes. Stir in the combined cornflour and water, stirring for 2–3 minutes. Season to taste with salt and pepper.

Green Salsa Chicken

This yummy casserole is served in shallow bowls over refried beans and rice.

SERVES 6

250 ml/8 fl oz chicken stock
450 g/1 lb mild or hot ready-made green salsa
1 small cos lettuce, leaves sliced
700 g/1½ lb skinless chicken breast fillets, halved or quartered
1 small onion, chopped
1 garlic clove, chopped
50 ml/2 fl oz soured cream
1 tbsp cornflour
15 g/½ oz fresh coriander, chopped
salt and freshly ground black pepper, to taste
400 g/14 oz can refried beans
75 g/3 oz rice, cooked, hot

Process the stock, salsa and lettuce in a food processor or blender until almost smooth. Add to the slow cooker with the chicken, onion and garlic. Cover and cook on High for 3–4 hours. Stir in the combined soured cream and cornflour, stirring for 2–3 minutes. Stir in the coriander. Season with salt and pepper. Serve over refried beans and the rice.

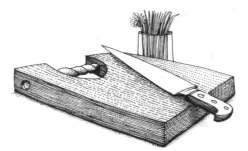

Caribbean Sweet-and-sour Chicken

Sweet-and-sour flavours team with chicken, pineapple and beans for this Caribbean-inspired dish. Serve with jasmine rice or couscous.

SERVES 6

700 g/1½ lb skinless chicken breast fillets, quartered lengthways
450 ml/¾ pint chicken stock
400 g/14 oz can black beans, drained and rinsed
2 onions, sliced
1 green pepper, sliced
1 red pepper, sliced
2 garlic cloves, crushed
2 cm/¾ in piece fresh root ginger, finely grated
2 tsp finely chopped jalapeño or other medium-hot chilli
2 tbsp light brown sugar
2 tbsp cider vinegar
2–3 tsp curry powder
550 g/1¼ lb unsweetened canned pineapple chunks, drained
2 tbsp cornflour
50 ml/2 fl oz water
salt and freshly ground black pepper, to taste

Combine all the ingredients, except the pineapple, cornflour, water, salt and pepper, in the slow cooker. Cover and cook on Low for 6–8 hours, adding the pineapple during the last 20 minutes. Turn the heat to High and cook for 10 minutes. Stir in the combined cornflour and water, stirring for 2–3 minutes. Season to taste with salt and pepper.

Curried Chicken with Banana and Cashew Nuts

Top this fruity chicken curry with sliced banana or plantain and cashew nuts.

SERVES 6

700 g/1½ lb skinless chicken breast fillets, cubed
375 ml/13 fl oz chicken stock
75 g/3 oz dried apples
75 g/3 oz dried apricots
75 g/3 oz raisins
2 spring onions, sliced
2–3 tsp curry powder
¼ tsp crushed chilli flakes
2–3 tsp lime juice
salt and freshly ground black pepper, to taste
100 g/4 oz rice, cooked, hot
1 ripe banana or plantain, sliced
25 g/1 oz cashew nuts, chopped

Combine all the ingredients, except the lime juice, salt, pepper, rice, banana or plantain and cashew nuts, in the slow cooker. Cover and cook on High for 3–4 hours. Season to taste with lime juice, salt and pepper. Serve over the rice and top with banana or plantain slices and cashew nuts.

Creole Sausages with Sweetcorn

Use any kind of sausage you like in this casserole – vegetarian sausages are delicious too. Serve over rice or cornbread to soak up the juices.

SERVES 4

**350–450 g/12 oz–1 lb spicy turkey
  sausages, sliced (2.5 cm/1 in)
2 x 400 g/14 oz cans chopped tomatoes
2 onions, chopped
100 g/4 oz sweetcorn, thawed if frozen
½ green pepper, chopped
2 garlic cloves, crushed
½ tsp dried thyme
salt and freshly ground black pepper,
  to taste
Tabasco sauce, to serve**

Combine all the ingredients, except the salt and pepper, in the slow cooker. Cover and cook on High for 4–5 hours. Season to taste with salt and pepper. Serve with Tabasco sauce.

Black Bean and Okra Gumbo

Gumbo filé is a traditional spice mix that you'll find in specialist food stores. You can substitute chilli powder. The gumbo is just right served over warm cornbread.

SERVES 8

**450 g/1 lb smoked turkey sausage,
  sliced
400 g/14 oz can tomatoes
2 x 400 g/14 oz cans black beans,
  drained and rinsed
250 ml/8 fl oz chicken stock
225 g/8 oz small mushrooms
2 onions, chopped
1 red pepper, chopped
1 green pepper, chopped
1 large carrot, sliced**

**1 tbsp chilli powder
1 tsp gumbo filé
2 cups okra, trimmed
salt and freshly ground black pepper,
  to taste**

Combine all the ingredients, except the okra, salt and pepper, in a 5.5 litre/9½ pint slow cooker. Cover and cook on Low for 6–8 hours, adding the okra during the last 30 minutes. Season to taste with salt and pepper.

Easy Chicken and Celery Cobbler

Make this easy cobbler by using bought scones. This dish can also be served over noodles or Real Mashed Potatoes (see page 264).

SERVES 6

**700 g/1½ lb skinless chicken breast
  fillets, cubed
375 ml/13 fl oz chicken stock
2 onions, chopped
3 carrots, thickly sliced
1 celery stick, sliced
¾ tsp dried sage
2 tbsp cornflour
50 ml/2 fl oz water
salt and freshly ground black pepper,
  to taste
50 g/2 oz frozen peas, thawed
3 plain scones, halved**

Combine all the ingredients, except the cornflour, water, salt, pepper, peas and scones, in the slow cooker. Cover and cook on Low for 6–8 hours. Turn the heat to High and cook for 10 minutes. Stir in the combined cornflour and water, stirring for 2–3 minutes. Season to taste with salt and pepper. Stir in the peas and put the scone halves, cut sides down, on the casserole. Cover and cook for 10 minutes.

Indonesian-style Coconut Chicken

This spicy dish is enhanced with the unique flavours of coconut milk and ginger.

SERVES 6

**700 g/1½ lb skinless chicken breast
  fillets, cubed**
250 ml/8 fl oz coconut milk
250 ml/8 fl oz chicken stock
**400 g/14 oz can red kidney beans,
  drained and rinsed**
1 onion, thinly sliced
½ large green pepper, thinly sliced
2 spring onions, sliced
1 garlic clove, crushed
**2 cm/¾ in piece fresh root ginger,
  finely grated**
1 tbsp cornflour
2 tbsp lime juice
salt and cayenne pepper, to taste
100 g/4 oz rice, cooked, hot
**finely chopped fresh coriander,
  to garnish**

Combine all the ingredients, except the cornflour, lime juice, salt, cayenne pepper and rice, in the slow cooker. Cover and cook on Low for 6–8 hours. Turn the heat to High and cook for 10 minutes. Stir in the combined cornflour and lime juice, stirring for 2–3 minutes. Season to taste with salt and cayenne pepper. Serve over the rice, sprinkled generously with coriander.

Luau Chicken in Pineapple Juice

Pineapple juice gives the chicken a moreish sweet–sour flavour.

SERVES 6

**700 g/1½ lb skinless chicken breast
  fillets, cubed**
120 ml/4 fl oz chicken stock
**120 ml/4 fl oz unsweetened pineapple
  juice**
225 g/8 oz mushrooms, sliced
2 carrots, diagonally sliced
1 small red onion, thinly sliced
1 garlic clove, crushed
2–3 tbsp rice or cider vinegar
2–3 tbsp soy sauce
**2 small tomatoes, cut into thin
  wedges**
100 g/4 oz frozen peas, thawed
1–2 tbsp cornflour
2–4 tbsp water
**salt and freshly ground black pepper,
  to taste**
100 g/4 oz rice, cooked, hot

Combine all the ingredients, except the tomatoes, peas, cornflour, water, salt, pepper and rice, in the slow cooker. Cover and cook on Low for 6–8 hours, adding the tomatoes during the last 30 minutes. Add the peas, turn the heat to High and cook for 10 minutes. Stir in the combined cornflour and water, stirring for 2–3 minutes. Season to taste with salt and pepper. Serve over the rice.

Caribbean Chicken with Black Beans

Cinnamon, cloves and rum bring this chicken and black bean dish alive.

SERVES 4

450 g/1 lb skinless chicken breast fillets, cut into thin strips
250 ml/8 fl oz chicken stock
400 g/14 oz can black beans, drained and rinsed
225 g/8 oz ready-made tomato sauce
1 onion, chopped
½ large green pepper, chopped
2 garlic cloves, crushed
½ tsp ground cinnamon
¼ tsp ground cloves
2–4 tbsp light rum (optional)
salt and cayenne pepper, to taste
75 g/3 oz rice, cooked, hot

Combine all the ingredients, except the rum, salt, cayenne pepper and rice, in the slow cooker. Cover and cook on High for 4–5 hours. Season to taste with rum, salt and cayenne pepper. Serve over the rice.

Chicken with Vermouth

Vermouth always brings a touch of elegance. At the end of cooking time, the juices can be thickened with a combined 2 tbsp cornflour and 50 ml/2 fl oz cold water, if you like.

SERVES 8

1.5 kg/3 lb skinless chicken breasts and thighs
175 ml/6 fl oz chicken stock
120 ml/4 fl oz dry vermouth or chicken stock
4 new potatoes, cubed
4 carrots, thickly sliced
100 g/4 oz button mushrooms, halved or quartered
1 large onion, thinly sliced
2 celery sticks, sliced
1 garlic clove, crushed
½ tsp dried thyme
salt and freshly ground black pepper, to taste

Combine all the ingredients, except the salt and pepper, in a 5.5 litre/9½ pint slow cooker. Cover and cook on Low for 6–8 hours. Season to taste with salt and pepper.

Chicken with Broccoli in White Wine

A yellow summer squash contrasts beautifully with the broccoli in this dish, but green courgette will work just as well. Serve with rice or Italian bread to soak up the delicious stock.

SERVES 4

450 g/1 lb skinless chicken breast fillets, cubed
120 ml/4 fl oz chicken stock
120 ml/4 fl oz dry white wine
1 onion, chopped
2 large garlic cloves, crushed
1 bay leaf
1 tsp dried oregano
1 tsp dried thyme
175 g/6 oz small broccoli florets
175 g/6 oz yellow courgette or patty pan squash, cubed
salt and freshly ground black pepper, to taste

Combine all the ingredients, except the broccoli, courgette or squash, salt and pepper, in the slow cooker. Cover and cook on High for 4–5 hours, adding the broccoli and courgette or squash during the last 20 minutes. Discard the bay leaf. Season to taste with salt and pepper.

Sherried Chicken

Mangetouts and red pepper are excellent with chicken simmered in a ginger, sherry and soy-accented stock.

SERVES 4

450 g/1 lb skinless chicken breast
   fillets, cubed
250 ml/8 fl oz chicken stock
2 onions, chopped
½ red pepper, chopped
1 garlic clove, crushed
1 cm/½ in piece fresh root ginger,
   finely grated
150 g/5 oz mangetouts, sliced
1½ tbsp cornflour
2 tbsp dry sherry (optional)
3–4 tbsp soy sauce
1–2 tsp toasted sesame oil
salt and freshly ground black pepper,
   to taste
350 g/12 oz Chinese egg noodles or
   vermicelli, cooked, hot
2 spring onions, sliced

Combine the chicken, stock, onion, pepper, garlic and ginger in the slow cooker. Cover and cook on High for 3–4 hours, adding the mangetouts during the last 20 minutes. Stir in the combined cornflour, sherry and soy sauce, stirring for 2–3 minutes. Season to taste with sesame oil, salt and pepper. Serve over the noodles, sprinkled with spring onions.

Burgundy Chicken with New Potatoes

Red wine is perfect for making a good, strong sauce for chicken and mushrooms. Serve over noodles or rice with a green salad.

SERVES 6

1 chicken, about 1.25 kg/2½ lb, cut
   into pieces
120 ml/4 fl oz chicken stock
120 ml/4 fl oz Burgundy wine
225 g/8 oz small mushrooms, halved
6 small new potatoes, scrubbed
100 g/4 oz baby onions or shallots
6 spring onions, sliced
1 garlic clove, crushed
¾ tsp dried thyme
1–2 tbsp cornflour
2–4 tbsp water
salt and freshly ground black pepper,
   to taste

Combine all the ingredients, except the cornflour, water, salt and pepper, in a 5.5 litre/9½ pint slow cooker. Cover and cook on Low for 6–8 hours. Turn the heat to High and cook for 10 minutes. Stir in the combined cornflour and water, stirring for 2–3 minutes. Season to taste with salt and pepper.

Chicken Provençal

Wine, tomatoes, lots of garlic and the French combination of herbs gives lots of flavour to tender cooked chicken.

SERVES 4

450 g/1 lb skinless chicken breast
   fillets, cubed (2 cm/¾ in)
2 x 400 g/14 oz cans chopped tomatoes
120 ml/4 fl oz dry white wine
120 ml/4 fl oz chicken stock
4 potatoes, peeled and thinly sliced
4 garlic cloves, crushed
1½–2 tsp herbs de Provence or mixed
   herbs
2 tbsp cornflour
50 ml/2 fl oz water
salt and freshly ground black pepper,
   to taste
finely chopped fresh basil, to garnish

Combine all the ingredients, except the cornflour, water, salt and pepper, in the slow cooker. Cover and cook on Low for 6–8 hours. Turn the heat to High and cook for 10 minutes. Stir in the combined cornflour and water, stirring for 2–3 minutes. Season to taste with salt and pepper. Sprinkle generously with basil.

Coq au Vin

This easy version of the French classic is perfect for the slow cooker.

SERVES 6

6 skinless chicken breast fillets, about 100 g/4 oz each, halved
120 ml/4 fl oz chicken stock
120 ml/4 fl oz Burgundy wine
4 bacon rashers, diced
3 spring onions, sliced
100 g/4 oz baby onions or shallots
225 g/8 oz small mushrooms
6 small new potatoes, halved
1 garlic clove, crushed
½ tsp dried thyme
1–2 tbsp cornflour
2–4 tbsp water
salt and freshly ground black pepper, to taste

Combine all the ingredients, except the cornflour, water, salt and pepper, in the slow cooker. Cover and cook on Low for 6–8 hours. Turn the heat to High and cook for 10 minutes. Stir in the combined cornflour and water, stirring for 2–3 minutes. Season to taste with salt and pepper.

Chicken Paprikash

Serve this dish with thick slices of warm sourdough bread.

SERVES 4

450 g/1 lb skinless chicken breast fillets, quartered lengthways
400 g/14 oz can tomatoes
120 ml/4 fl oz chicken stock
2 onions, finely chopped
2 garlic cloves, crushed
1 green pepper, chopped
75 g/3 oz mushrooms, sliced
2½–3 tsp paprika
1 tsp poppy seeds
120 ml/4 fl oz soured cream
1 tbsp cornflour
salt and freshly ground black pepper, to taste
275 g/10 oz noodles, cooked, hot

Combine all the ingredients, except the soured cream, cornflour, salt, pepper and noodles, in the slow cooker. Cover and cook on Low for 6–8 hours. Stir in the combined soured cream and cornflour, stirring for 2–3 minutes. Season to taste with salt and pepper. Serve over the noodles.

Kashmir Chicken

This hearty casserole is flavoured with sweet Middle Eastern spices and raisins.

SERVES 6

350–450 g/12 oz–1 lb skinless chicken breast fillets, cubed (2.5 cm/1 in)
2 x 400 g/14 oz cans haricot beans, drained and rinsed
400 g/14 oz can plum tomatoes
3 onions, chopped
½ large red pepper, chopped
2 tsp minced garlic
¼ tsp crushed chilli flakes
1 tsp ground cumin
1 tsp ground cinnamon
50 g/2 oz raisins
salt and freshly ground black pepper, to taste
225 g/8 oz couscous, soaked, hot

Combine all the ingredients, except the raisins, salt, pepper and couscous, in the slow cooker. Cover and cook on High for 4–5 hours, adding the raisins during the last 30 minutes. Season to taste with salt and pepper. Serve over the couscous.

Chicken Curry with Apple and Carrot

Apple and raisins bring sweetness to this tasty curry.

SERVES 4

450 g/1 lb skinless chicken breast fillets, cubed
250 ml/8 fl oz chicken stock
1 large carrot, sliced
½ onion, chopped
2 spring onions, sliced
1 garlic clove, crushed
1–2 tsp curry powder
½ tsp ground ginger
1 apple, peeled and sliced
40 g/1½ oz raisins
175 ml/6 fl oz semi-skimmed milk
1 tbsp cornflour
salt and freshly ground black pepper, to taste
75 g/3 oz rice, cooked, hot

Combine the chicken, stock, carrot, onion, garlic and spices in the slow cooker. Cover and cook on High for 4–5 hours, adding the apple and raisins during the last 30 minutes. Stir in the combined milk and cornflour, stirring for 2–3 minutes. Season to taste with salt and pepper. Serve over the rice.

Thai-spiced Chicken and Carrots

If you can't find Thai peanut sauce, 1 tbsp peanut butter and ¼–½ tsp crushed chilli flakes can be used instead.

SERVES 4

450 g/1 lb skinless chicken breast fillets, cubed
300 ml/½ pint chicken stock
4 carrots, diagonally sliced
6 spring onions, sliced
2.5 cm/1 in piece fresh root ginger, finely grated

3 large garlic cloves, crushed
1 tbsp soy sauce
1 tbsp Thai peanut sauce
1 tsp sugar
½–1 tsp toasted sesame oil
salt and freshly ground black pepper, to taste
75 g/3 oz rice, cooked, hot

Combine all the ingredients, except the sesame oil, salt, pepper and rice, in the slow cooker. Cover and cook on High for 3–4 hours. Season to taste with sesame oil, salt and pepper. Serve over the rice.

Indian Curried Chicken and Vegetables

The mixture of spices in the Curry Seasoning gives this dish a unique flavour.

SERVES 6

450 g/1 lb skinless chicken breast fillets, quartered lengthways
175 ml/6 fl oz vegetable stock
175 ml/6 fl oz coconut milk
400 g/14 oz can chopped tomatoes
175 g/6 oz tomato purée
225 g/8 oz mushrooms, coarsely chopped
175 g/6 oz potato, cubed
1 large carrot, sliced
100 g/4 oz small cauliflower florets
150 g/5 oz French beans, cut into short lengths
2 onions, finely chopped
2 tbsp white wine vinegar
2 tbsp brown sugar
1–2 tbsp Curry Seasoning (see page 290)
100 g/4 oz okra, trimmed and cut into short lengths
salt, to taste
75 g/3 oz brown rice, cooked, hot

Combine all the ingredients, except the okra, salt and rice, in a 5.5 litre/9½ pint slow cooker. Cover and cook on Low for 6–8 hours, adding the okra during the last 30 minutes. Season to taste with salt. Serve with the rice.

Curry Seasoning Ⓥ

Why use bought curry powder when you can make your own?

SERVES 6

2 tsp ground coriander
1 tsp ground turmeric
1 tsp chilli powder
½ tsp ground cumin
½ tsp dry mustard powder
½ tsp ground ginger
½ tsp black pepper

Combine all the ingredients.

Curried Chicken with Cauliflower and Potatoes

A variety of spices are combined to make the fragrant curry that seasons this dish.

SERVES 4

350–450 g/12 oz–1 lb skinless chicken breast fillets, cubed
250 ml/8 fl oz chicken stock
½ small cauliflower, cut into florets
2 potatoes, cubed
2 carrots, thickly sliced
1 large tomato, chopped
1 onion, chopped
2 garlic cloves
¾ tsp ground turmeric
½ tsp dry mustard powder
½ tsp ground cumin
½ tsp ground coriander
1–2 tbsp lemon juice
salt and cayenne pepper, to taste

Combine all the ingredients, except the lemon juice, salt and cayenne pepper, in the slow cooker. Cover and cook on Low for 5–6 hours. Season to taste with lemon juice, salt and cayenne pepper.

Curry and Ginger Chicken

This chicken dish is seasoned with a great-tasting Curry and Ginger Spice Blend.

SERVES 10

2 chickens, about 1.25 kg/2½ lb each, cut into pieces
375 ml/13 fl oz chicken stock
4 onions, chopped
200 g/7 oz tomatoes, peeled, seeded and chopped
2 garlic cloves, crushed
Curry and Ginger Spice Blend (see below)
175 g/6 oz frozen peas, thawed
15 g/½ oz fresh coriander, chopped
250 ml/8 fl oz soured cream
2 tbsp cornflour
salt and freshly ground black pepper, to taste
100 g/4 oz rice, cooked, hot

Combine the chicken, stock, onions, tomatoes, garlic and Curry and Ginger Spice Blend in a 5.5 litre/9½ pint slow cooker. Cover and cook on Low for 6–8 hours, adding the peas during the last 20 minutes. Stir in the coriander and combined soured cream and cornflour, stirring for 2–3 minutes. Season to taste with salt and pepper. Serve over the rice.

Curry and Ginger Spice Blend Ⓥ

This will keep for a few days.

SERVES 10

5 cm/2 in fresh root ginger, finely grated
1 tbsp sesame seeds
2 tsp coriander seeds
1 tsp cumin seeds
1 tsp ground turmeric
1 tsp salt
¼ tsp peppercorns
¼ tsp fennel seeds
¼ tsp crushed chilli flakes

Process all the ingredients in a spice mill or food processor until finely ground.

Curried Chicken and Apple

The flavours of apple and ginger give this chicken dish a lovely, warm sweetness. Serve with Spinach Rice (see page 273).

SERVES 6

700 g/1½ lb skinless chicken breast fillets, halved or quartered
375 ml/13 fl oz chicken stock
2 onions, chopped
2 large carrots, sliced
1 garlic clove, crushed
1½ tbsp curry powder
1 tsp ground ginger
1 small cooking apple, peeled and sliced
250 ml/8 fl oz soured cream
2 tbsp cornflour
salt and freshly ground black pepper, to taste

Combine all the ingredients, except the apple, soured cream, cornflour, salt and pepper, in the slow cooker. Cover and cook on Low for 5–6 hours, adding the apple during the last 30 minutes. Stir in the combined soured cream and cornflour, stirring for 2–3 minutes. Season to taste with salt and pepper.

Moroccan Chicken with Couscous

Tantalise your taste buds with this spicy and fruity casserole.

SERVES 4

450 g/1 lb skinless chicken breast fillets, cubed (2 cm/¾ in)
2 x 400 g/14 oz cans tomatoes
½ onion, finely chopped
2 garlic cloves, crushed
½ tsp ground cinnamon
½ tsp ground coriander
¼ tsp crushed chilli flakes
75 g/3 oz ready-to-eat dried apricots, quartered
75 g/3 oz currants
½ tsp cumin seeds, lightly crushed
salt and freshly ground black pepper, to taste
100 g/4 oz couscous, soaked, hot

Combine all the ingredients, except the salt, pepper and couscous, in the slow cooker. Cover and cook on High for 3–4 hours. Season to taste with salt and pepper. Serve over the couscous.

Moroccan Chicken and Chickpeas

This dish is great for entertaining because it serves eight and can be easily doubled for an 8 litre/14 pint slow cooker.

SERVES 8

8 skinless chicken breast fillets, about 100 g/4 oz each, halved or quartered
400 g/14 oz can chickpeas, drained and rinsed
120 ml/4 fl oz chicken stock
2 small onions, chopped
4 garlic cloves, crushed
2 tsp ground ginger
1 tsp ground turmeric
1 cinnamon stick
75 g/3 oz raisins
2–3 tbsp lemon juice
salt and freshly ground black pepper, to taste

Combine all the ingredients, except the raisins, lemon juice, salt and pepper, in a 5.5 litre/9½ pint slow cooker. Cover and cook on High for 4–5 hours, adding the raisins during the last 30 minutes. Discard the cinnamon stick. Season to taste with lemon juice, salt and pepper.

Middle Eastern-style Chicken

Chicken and chickpeas are warmly spiced with cumin, allspice and cloves and cooked with couscous and raisins.

SERVES 4

450 g/1 lb skinless chicken breast fillets, cubed (2.5 cm/1 in)
375 ml/13 fl oz chicken stock
400 g/14 oz can chickpeas, drained and rinsed
400 g/14 oz tomatoes, chopped
2 small onions, chopped
½ large green pepper, chopped
2 garlic cloves, crushed
1 bay leaf
1½ tsp dried thyme
1 tsp ground cumin
¼ tsp ground allspice
175 g/6 oz couscous
40 g/1½ oz raisins
salt and freshly ground black pepper, to taste

Combine all the ingredients, except the couscous, raisins, salt and pepper, in the slow cooker. Cover and cook on High for 4–5 hours, adding the couscous and raisins during the last 5–10 minutes. Discard the bay leaf. Season to taste with salt and pepper.

Chicken Marengo

The orange-scented tomato sauce, lightly seasoned with herbs and wine, benefits from slow cooking to meld the flavours.

SERVES 6

6 skinless chicken breast fillets, about 100 g/4 oz each, quartered
250 ml/8 fl oz chicken stock
120 ml/4 fl oz dry white wine

3 tbsp tomato purée
175 g/6 oz mushrooms, sliced
1 large carrot, sliced
1 small onion, chopped
3 garlic cloves, crushed
2 tbsp grated orange zest
1 tsp dried tarragon
1 tsp dried thyme
40 g/1½ oz frozen peas, thawed
salt and freshly ground black pepper, to taste
350 g/12 oz linguine or other flat pasta, cooked, hot

Combine all the ingredients, except the salt, pepper and pasta, in the slow cooker. Cover and cook on High for 4–5 hours. Season to taste with salt and pepper. Serve over the pasta.

Chicken with Artichokes

Serve Red Pepper Rice (see page 310) to complement this Mediterranean-inspired chicken dish.

SERVES 4

450 g/1 lb skinless chicken breast fillets, cubed (2.5 cm/1 in)
400 g/14 oz can chopped tomatoes
200 g/7 oz drained canned artichoke hearts, quartered
1 onion, chopped
1 celery stick, thinly sliced
1 tsp dried oregano
75 g/3 oz pitted black olives, halved
salt and freshly ground black pepper, to taste

Combine all the ingredients, except the olives, salt and pepper, in the slow cooker. Cover and cook on High for 4–5 hours, adding the olives during the last 30 minutes. Season to taste with salt and pepper.

Chicken with Cinnamon, Lemon and Feta

Cinnamon, lemon and feta cheese give this tomato-based casserole the signature flavours of Greece.

SERVES 4

450 g/1 lb skinless chicken breast fillets, cubed (2 cm/¾ in)
400 g/14 oz can tomatoes
120 ml/4 fl oz chicken stock
3 canned artichoke hearts, quartered
1 onion, finely chopped
1 tbsp lemon juice
2 garlic cloves, crushed
1 cinnamon stick
1 bay leaf
1–2 tbsp dry sherry (optional)
salt and freshly ground black pepper, to taste
225 g/8 oz egg noodles, cooked, hot
25 g/1 oz Feta cheese, crumbled

Combine all the ingredients, except the sherry, salt, pepper, noodles and cheese, in the slow cooker. Cover and cook on High for 4–5 hours. Discard the cinnamon stick and bay leaf. Season to taste with sherry, salt and pepper. Serve over the noodles. Sprinkle with Feta cheese.

Spanish Chicken and Rice

Saffron and sherry add flavour to this simple Spanish dish, called arroz con pollo.

SERVES 6

450 g/1 lb skinless chicken breast fillets, cubed (4 cm/1½ in)
750 ml/1¼ pints chicken stock
2 onions, chopped
½ green pepper, chopped
½ red pepper, chopped
2 garlic cloves, crushed
¼ tsp crushed saffron threads (optional)
225 g/8 oz easy-cook long-grain rice
1–2 tbsp dry sherry
100 g/4 oz frozen peas, thawed
salt and cayenne pepper, to taste

Combine all the ingredients, except the rice, sherry, peas, salt and cayenne pepper, in the slow cooker. Cover and cook on Low for 5–6 hours, adding the rice during the last 2 hours and the sherry and peas during the last 20 minutes. Season to taste with salt and cayenne pepper.

Mediterranean Chicken with Tomatoes

Balsamic vinegar adds depth to this casserole of chicken and olives. Thicken the sauce casserole with cornflour if you like. Serve over couscous or rice.

SERVES 6

700 g/1½ lb skinless chicken breast fillets, cubed (2.5 cm/1 in)
250 ml/8 fl oz chicken stock
120 ml/4 fl oz dry white wine or extra chicken stock
50 ml/2 fl oz balsamic vinegar
225 g/8 oz small mushrooms, halved
6 plum tomatoes, chopped
40 g/1½ oz Kalamata or black olives, halved
3 garlic cloves, crushed
1 tsp dried rosemary
1 tsp dried thyme
salt and freshly ground black pepper, to taste

Combine all the ingredients, except the salt and pepper, in the slow cooker. Cover and cook on High for 4–5 hours. Season to taste with salt and pepper.

293

Mediterranean Chicken with Artichokes

Serve this wine and herb-flavoured dish over Red Pepper Rice (see page 310) or Polenta (see page 356).

SERVES 4

**450 g/1 lb skinless chicken breast
  fillets, cubed (4 cm/1½ in)**
120 ml/4 fl oz chicken stock
120 ml/4 fl oz dry white wine
4 tomatoes, quartered
75 g/3 oz mushrooms, sliced
1 onion, chopped
1 garlic clove, crushed
1 tsp dried thyme
1 tsp dried rosemary
1 tsp dried tarragon
**3 drained canned artichoke hearts,
  quartered**
**40 g/1½ oz Kalamata or black olives,
  sliced**
**salt and freshly ground black pepper,
  to taste**
25 g/1 oz Feta cheese, crumbled

Combine all the ingredients, except the artichoke hearts, olives, salt, pepper and Feta cheese, in the slow cooker. Cover and cook on High for 4–5 hours, adding the artichoke hearts and olives during the last hour. Season to taste with salt and pepper. Sprinkle each serving with the Feta.

Chicken Peperonata

Cans of tomatoes with herbs are useful for quick dishes such as this Tuscan casserole. Serve over rice or your favourite pasta.

SERVES 4

**450 g/1 lb skinless chicken breast
  fillets, cubed (2.5 cm/1 in)**
**400 g/14 oz can chopped tomatoes
  with herbs**
2 onions, sliced

½ red pepper, sliced
½ green pepper, sliced
1 small garlic clove, crushed
**salt and freshly ground black pepper,
  to taste**
4 tbsp freshly grated Parmesan cheese

Combine all the ingredients, except the salt, pepper and cheese, in the slow cooker. Cover and cook on High for 4–5 hours. Season to taste with salt and pepper. Sprinkle each serving with Parmesan cheese.

Chicken and Ravioli

Red kidney beans make an unusual addition to chicken and ravioli in this garlicky casserole.

SERVES 4

**450 g/1 lb skinless chicken breast
  fillets, quartered lengthways**
**2 x 400 g/14 oz cans red kidney
  beans, drained and rinsed**
400 g/14 oz can chopped tomatoes
120 ml/4 fl oz chicken stock
2 small onions, chopped
4 garlic cloves, crushed
½ tsp dried thyme
**150 g/5 oz fresh sun-dried tomato
  ravioli, cooked, hot**
**salt and freshly ground black pepper,
  to taste**

Combine all the ingredients, except the ravioli, salt and pepper, in the slow cooker. Cover and cook on High for 4–5 hours, adding the ravioli during the last 10 minutes. Season to taste with salt and pepper.

Chicken with Vegetables and Pasta

Sun-dried tomatoes and black olives lend an earthiness to this colourful mixture.

SERVES 4

450 g/1 lb skinless chicken breast fillets, cubed (2.5 cm/1 in)
400 g/14 oz can chopped tomatoes with herbs
175 ml/6 fl oz chicken stock
1 large carrot, sliced
1 onion, chopped
½ green pepper, chopped
2 garlic cloves, crushed
2 bay leaves
1 tsp dried marjoram
3 tbsp chopped sun-dried tomatoes (not in oil)
40 g/1½ oz Kalamata or black olives, pitted and halved
2 courgettes or yellow summer squash such as patty pan, cubed
175 g/6 oz small broccoli florets
100 g/4 oz rigatoni, cooked, hot
salt and freshly ground black pepper, to taste

Combine all the ingredients, except the olives, courgettes or squash, broccoli, rigatoni, salt and pepper, in the slow cooker. Cover and cook on High for 4–5 hours, adding the courgettes or squash, broccoli and rigatoni during the last 20 minutes. Discard the bay leaves. Season to taste with salt and pepper.

Chicken Marinara

Team this dish with a crisp salad for an easy Italian meal.

SERVES 4

450 g/1 lb skinless chicken breast fillets, cubed
400 g/14 oz can chopped tomatoes
120 ml/4 fl oz chicken stock
3 onions, chopped

75 g/3 oz mushrooms, quartered
1 celery stick, finely chopped
1 carrot, finely chopped
2 garlic cloves, crushed
1 tsp dried Italian herb seasoning
1 courgette, chopped
salt and freshly ground black pepper, to taste
225 g/8 oz penne, cooked, hot

Combine all the ingredients, except the courgette, salt, pepper and pasta, in the slow cooker. Cover and cook on High for 4–5 hours, adding the courgette during the last 20 minutes. Season to taste with salt and pepper. Serve over the pasta.

Chicken, Mushroom and Tomato with Polenta

Cooking polenta in the microwave is easy and fast, but it can also be made in the slow cooker (see page 356).

SERVES 4

450 g/1 lb skinless chicken breast fillets, cubed (2.5 cm/1 in)
2 x 400 g/14 oz cans Italian plum tomatoes, coarsely chopped, with juice
225 g/8 oz ready-made tomato sauce
2 tbsp tomato purée
225 g/8 oz mushrooms, sliced
1 carrot, sliced
1 onion, chopped
2 garlic cloves, crushed
1 tsp sugar
1 tsp dried basil
1 tsp dried thyme
salt and freshly ground black pepper, to taste
Microwave Polenta (see page 296)

Combine all the ingredients, except the salt, pepper and Microwave Polenta, in the slow cooker. Cover and cook on High for 4–5 hours. Season to taste with salt and pepper. Serve over the Microwave Polenta.

Microwave Polenta Ⓥ

It's so easy to make polenta in the microwave, and very useful if your slow cooker is already being used.

SERVES 4

150 g/5 oz polenta
½ tsp salt
750 ml/1¼ pints water
250 ml/8 fl oz semi-skimmed milk
1 onion, diced

Combine all the ingredients in 2.5 litre/ 4¼ pint glass casserole. Cook, uncovered, in the microwave on High for 8–9 minutes, whisking half-way through the cooking time. Whisk until smooth. Cover and cook on High for 6–7 minutes. Remove from the microwave, whisk and leave to stand, covered, 3–4 minutes.

Chicken Cacciatore

Richly flavoured with garlic and oregano, this Italian dish was traditionally made from game brought back from the hunt.

SERVES 4

225 g/8 oz skinless chicken breast
fillet, cubed (2 cm/¾ in)
225 g/8 oz boneless chicken thighs,
cubed (2 cm/¾ in)
2 x 400 g/14 oz cans chopped
tomatoes
120 ml/4 fl oz dry red wine or water
225 g/8 oz mushrooms, quartered
2 onions, chopped
1 green pepper, chopped
6 garlic cloves, crushed
2 tsp dried oregano
½ tsp garlic powder
1 bay leaf
1–2 tbsp cornflour
2–4 tbsp water
salt and freshly ground black pepper
225 g/8 oz noodles, cooked, hot

Combine all the ingredients, except the cornflour, water, salt, pepper and noodles, in the slow cooker. Cover and

cook on Low for 6–8 hours. Turn the heat to High and cook for 10 minutes. Stir in the combined cornflour and water, stirring for 2–3 minutes. Discard the bay leaf. Season to taste with salt and pepper and serve over the noodles.

Italian-style Beans and Vegetables with Polenta

This colourful mélange can also be served over pasta or rice. Pork sausages would also work well instead of the turkey.

SERVES 6

275 g/10 oz turkey sausages, casings
removed
oil, for greasing
400 g/14 oz can chopped tomatoes
400 g/14 oz can chickpeas, rinsed and
drained
400 g/14 oz can red kidney beans,
rinsed and drained
3 onions, chopped
175 g/6 oz portabella mushrooms,
chopped
4 garlic cloves, crushed
1½ tsp dried Italian herb seasoning
¼ tsp crushed chilli flakes
350 g/12 oz broccoli florets and sliced
stems
175 g/6 oz courgette, preferably
yellow, or patty pan squash, sliced
salt and freshly ground black pepper
500 g/18 oz packet ready-made
Italian herb polenta, or 300 g/11 oz
polenta, cooked, hot

Cook the sausagemeat in a greased medium frying pan until browned, crumbling with a fork. Combine with the remaining ingredients, except the broccoli, courgette or squash, salt, pepper and polenta, in a 5.5 litre/9½ pint slow cooker. Cover and cook on Low for 6–8 hours, adding the broccoli and courgette or squash during the last 30 minutes. Season to taste with salt and pepper. Serve over the polenta.

Alfredo Chicken

The Parmesan cheese melts into the petits pois and asparagus sauce to give creaminess to the chicken.

SERVES 4

450 g/1 lb skinless chicken breast fillets, cubed (2 cm/¾ in)
450 ml/¾ pint chicken stock
2 spring onions, sliced
1 garlic clove, crushed
1 tsp dried basil
100 g/4 oz asparagus, sliced
40 g/1½ oz frozen petits pois, thawed
2 tbsp cornflour
120 ml/4 fl oz semi-skimmed milk
40 g/1½ oz freshly grated Parmesan cheese
salt and freshly ground black pepper, to taste
225 g/8 oz fettuccine or tagliatelle, cooked, hot

Combine the chicken, stock, spring onions, garlic and basil in the slow cooker. Cover and cook on High for 4–5 hours, adding the asparagus and peas during the last 20 minutes. Stir in the combined cornflour and milk, stirring for 2–3 minutes. Add the cheese, stirring until melted. Season to taste with salt and pepper. Serve over the fettuccine.

Apricot-glazed Poussins

Poussins, cooked to moist tenderness, are topped with a herb-infused apricot glaze.

SERVES 4

2 poussins, about 550 g/1¼ lb each
paprika
salt and freshly ground black pepper
75 ml/2½ fl oz chicken stock
Apricot Glaze (see page 298)
2 tbsp cornflour
50 ml/2 fl oz water

Sprinkle the poussins with paprika, salt and pepper. Put in the slow cooker and

add the stock. Cover and cook on Low until the legs move freely, 5½–6 hours, brushing with Apricot Glaze two to three times during cooking. Remove the poussins to a serving platter and cover loosely with foil. Stir any remaining Apricot Glaze into the slow cooker. Cover and cook on High for 10 minutes. Stir in the combined cornflour and water, stirring for 2–3 minutes. Spoon the sauce over the poussins.

Tuscan Chicken

Dried porcini mushrooms are a useful ingredient to keep in the cupboard to give an extra flavour dimension to your Italian cooking.

SERVES 6

250 ml/8 fl oz boiling chicken stock
25 g/1 oz dried porcini mushrooms
700 g/1½ lb skinless chicken breast fillets, cubed (2.5 cm/1 in)
400 g/14 oz can chopped tomatoes with herbs
400 g/14 oz can cannellini, haricot or butter beans, drained and rinsed
120 ml/4 fl oz dry white wine or chicken stock
2 small onions, chopped
3 garlic cloves, crushed
2 tbsp cornflour
50 ml/2 fl oz water
salt and freshly ground black pepper, to taste

Pour the stock over the mushrooms in a small bowl. Leave to stand until the mushrooms are softened, about 10 minutes. Drain the mushrooms. Strain and reserve the stock. Slice the mushrooms. Combine the mushrooms, reserved stock and the remaining ingredients, except the cornflour, water, salt and pepper, in the slow cooker. Cover and cook on High for 4–5 hours. Stir in the combined cornflour and water, stirring for 2–3 minutes. Season to taste with salt and pepper.

Apricot Glaze Ⓥ

This can be used to glaze poultry and sweet pastry desserts and also to moisten the top of a Christmas cake before covering with marzipan.

SERVES 4

200 g/7 oz apricot preserve
2 tbsp orange juice
finely grated zest from ½ orange
½ tsp dried thyme
½ tsp dried rosemary

Mix all the ingredients.

Home-style Turkey

Tenderly cooked turkey breast with root vegetables, mushrooms and peas makes a great family meal.

SERVES 4

12–450 g/1 lb turkey breast, cubed (2 cm/¾ in)
400 ml/14 fl oz chicken stock
1 large carrot, sliced
175 g/6 oz potatoes, unpeeled and cubed
2 onions, chopped
100 g/4 oz mushrooms, halved
1 tsp dried thyme
1 tsp celery seeds
100 g/4 oz frozen peas, thawed
salt and freshly ground black pepper, to taste

Combine all the ingredients, except the peas, salt and pepper, in the slow cooker. Cover and cook on Low for 6–8 hours, adding the peas during the last 20 minutes. Season to taste with salt and pepper.

Sausages with Potatoes and Peppers

Vibrantly coloured peppers give this dish an attractive appearance as well as lots of flavour. If you can't find smoked turkey sausage, smoked pork will work just as well.

SERVES 4

350 g/12 oz smoked turkey sausage, thinly sliced
175 ml/6 fl oz chicken stock
700 g/1½ lb waxy potatoes, thinly sliced
1 red pepper, thinly sliced
1 green pepper, thinly sliced
1 yellow pepper, thinly sliced
2 onions, thinly sliced
25 g/1 oz sun-dried tomatoes (not in oil), quartered
1 tsp dried thyme
1 tsp dried marjoram
1–2 tbsp cornflour
50 ml/2 fl oz water
salt and freshly ground black pepper, to taste

Combine all the ingredients, except the cornflour, water, salt and pepper, in the slow cooker. Cover and cook on High for 4–5 hours. Stir in the combined cornflour and water, stirring for 2–3 minutes. Season to taste with salt and pepper.

Turkey Ragout with White Wine

Rosemary, sage and garlic blend with white wine and tomatoes to make a tasty sauce for turkey breast. Delicious over rice or Polenta (see page 344).

SERVES 6

700 g/1½ lb turkey breast, cubed (2.5 cm/1 in)
400 g/14 oz can plum tomatoes, chopped, with juice
120 ml/4 fl oz dry white wine
225 g/8 oz mushrooms, sliced
2 onions, chopped
1 carrot, sliced
1 celery stick, sliced
2 large garlic cloves, crushed
½ tsp dried rosemary
½ tsp dried sage
1–2 tbsp cornflour
2–4 tbsp cold water
salt and freshly ground black pepper, to taste

Combine all the ingredients, except the cornflour, water, salt and pepper, in the slow cooker. Cover and cook on Low for 6–8 hours. Turn the heat to High and cook for 10 minutes. Stir in the combined cornflour and water, stirring for 2–3 minutes. Season to taste with salt and pepper.

Turkey and Wild Rice

Wild rice, which is actually a grass, has a more noticeable taste than brown rice and gives this turkey and vegetable casserole texture and flavour.

SERVES 4

450 g/1 lb turkey breast, cubed
450 ml/¾ pint chicken stock
1 onion, chopped
1 tsp dried sage
2 carrots, sliced

100 g/4 oz wild rice
250 g/9 oz small broccoli florets
salt and freshly ground black pepper, to taste

Combine the turkey, stock, onion, sage and carrots in the slow cooker. Cover and cook on Low for 6–8 hours, stirring in the rice during the last 2 hours and the broccoli during the last 30 minutes. Season to taste with salt and pepper.

Turkey with Apricots

Cumin and fresh coriander accentuate the flavour of the apricots in this fragrant dish.

SERVES 4

450 g/1 lb turkey breast, cubed (2.5 cm/1 in)
400 ml/14 fl oz chicken stock
2 onions, chopped
200 g/7 oz tomatoes, chopped
2 garlic cloves, crushed
1 tsp ground cumin
½ tsp ground allspice
10 ready-to-eat dried apricots, quartered
2 tbsp cornflour
50 ml/2 fl oz water
15 g/½ oz fresh coriander, chopped
salt and freshly ground black pepper, to taste
25 g/1 oz rice, cooked, hot

Combine all the ingredients, except the cornflour, water, coriander, salt, pepper and rice, in the slow cooker. Cook on Low for 5–6 hours. Turn the heat to High and cook for 10 minutes. Stir in the combined cornflour and water, stirring for 2–3 minutes. Stir in the coriander. Season to taste with salt and pepper. Serve over the rice.

South American Chilli Turkey

This casserole is seriously spicy! For less heat, omit the jalapeño chilli.

SERVES 6

700 g/1½ lb turkey breast, cubed (2.5 cm/1 in)
400 g/14 oz can red kidney beans in chilli sauce
400 g/14 oz can tomatoes
120 ml/4 fl oz chicken stock
½ green pepper, chopped
½ red pepper, chopped
2 small onions, chopped
1 small jalapeño or other medium-hot chilli, finely chopped
2 garlic cloves, crushed
1 tbsp chilli powder
1 tsp ground cumin
salt and freshly ground black pepper to taste

Combine all the ingredients, except the salt and pepper, in the slow cooker. Cover and cook on High for 3–4 hours. Season to taste with salt and pepper.

Turkey Meatloaf

This meatloaf can also be formed into a loaf in the slow cooker. See Simple Meatloaf on page 217 for instructions.

SERVES 8

700 g/1½ lb minced turkey breast
1 onion, finely chopped
½ red or green pepper, finely chopped
1 egg
120 ml/4 fl oz chicken stock
30 g/1¼ oz dry breadcrumbs
3 tbsp steak sauce
1 tsp dried thyme
1 tsp salt
½ tsp pepper
120 ml/4 fl oz chilli sauce

Mix all the ingredients, except the chilli sauce in a bowl. Pack the mixture into a greased 23 x 13 cm/9 x 5 in loaf tin and top with the chilli sauce. Insert a meat thermometer so that the tip is in the centre of the meatloaf. Place the tin on a rack in a 5.5 litre/9½ pint slow cooker. Cover and cook on Low until the thermometer registers 76°C, 6–7 hours.

Italian Meatball Casserole

This meatloaf has a distinctly Italian feel and will soon become a family favourite.

SERVES 6

Italian Turkey Meatballs (see page 176)
250 ml/8 fl oz beef stock
2 x 400 g/14 oz cans chopped tomatoes
3 carrots, thickly sliced
100 g/4 oz small mushrooms, halved
1 tsp dried Italian herb seasoning
2 small courgettes, sliced
50 g/2 oz frozen peas, thawed
2 tbsp cornflour
50 ml/2 fl oz water
salt and freshly ground black pepper, to taste
350 g/12 oz noodles or fettuccine, cooked, hot

Combine the Italian Turkey Meatballs, stock, tomatoes, carrots, mushrooms and herbs in a 5.5 litre/9½ pint slow cooker, making sure the meatballs are submerged. Cover and cook on Low for 6–8 hours, adding the courgettes and peas during the last 20 minutes. Turn the heat to High and cook for 10 minutes. Stir in the combined cornflour and water, stirring for 2–3 minutes. Season to taste with salt and pepper. Serve over the noodles.

Latin American Turkey and Squash

Enjoy this hearty mixture of squash, sweet potato, potato and black beans with a zip of chilli. Serve over rice.

SERVES 4

450 g/1 lb turkey breast, cubed (2 cm/¾ in)
400 g/14 oz can black beans, drained and rinsed
400 ml/14 fl oz chicken stock
225 g/8 oz tomato purée
350 g/12 oz butternut squash, peeled and cubed
175 g/6 oz sweet potato, peeled and cubed
175 g/6 oz potato, peeled and cubed
2 onions, chopped
1 jalapeño or other medium-hot chilli, finely chopped
1 tsp cumin seeds, toasted
salt and freshly ground black pepper, to taste
25 g/1 oz cashew nuts, coarsely chopped

Combine all the ingredients, except the salt, pepper and cashew nuts, in the slow cooker. Cover and cook on Low for 6–8 hours. Season to taste with salt and pepper. Sprinkle each serving with cashew nuts.

Turkey Cacciatore

Just a few ingredients can transform turkey breast into a tasty meal.

SERVES 4

450 g/1 lb turkey breast, sliced (5 cm/2 in)
400 g/14 oz can tomatoes
75 ml/2½ fl oz water
65 g/2½ oz mushrooms, sliced

¾ tsp dried oregano
2 small courgettes, cubed
salt and freshly ground black pepper, to taste
225 g/8 oz pasta, cooked, hot

Combine all the ingredients, except the courgettes, salt, pepper and pasta, in the slow cooker. Cover and cook on High for 4–5 hours, adding the courgettes during the last 30 minutes. Season to taste with salt and pepper. Serve over the pasta.

Sausage with Hot Peppers

Lots of garlic and chilli makes this a fun way to cook sausage and it works just as well with a smoked pork or vegetarian sausage, if you prefer.·

SERVES 4

12–450 g/1 lb smoked turkey sausage, sliced (2.5 cm/1 in)
400 g/14 oz can chopped tomatoes
250 ml/8 fl oz chicken stock
2 small onions, cut into thin wedges
3 large garlic cloves, crushed
½–1 small jalapeño or other medium-hot chilli, thinly sliced
1½ tsp dried Italian herb seasoning
¼ tsp crushed chilli flakes
1 courgette, halved lengthways and thickly sliced
100 g/4 oz rigatoni, cooked
salt and freshly ground black pepper, to taste
25 g/1 oz freshly grated Parmesan cheese

Combine all the ingredients, except the courgette, pasta, salt, pepper and cheese, in the slow cooker. Cover and cook on High for 4–5 hours, adding the courgette and pasta during the last 20 minutes. Season to taste with salt and pepper. Sprinkle each serving with Parmesan.

301

Turkey Sausage and Fennel Stew

Use your preference of sweet or hot sausage in this harvest stew.

SERVES 4

275 g/10 oz turkey sausage, sliced
400 g/14 oz can chopped tomatoes
250 ml/8 fl oz chicken stock
450 g/1 lb butternut squash, peeled and cubed
8 small Brussels sprouts, halved
1 onion, cut into thin wedges
2 parsnips, sliced
1 small fennel bulb, sliced
a pinch of crushed chilli flakes
1 tsp dried Italian herb seasoning
1–2 tbsp cornflour
2–4 tbsp water
salt and freshly ground black pepper, to taste

Combine all the ingredients, except the cornflour, water, salt and pepper, in the slow cooker. Cover and cook on Low for 5–6 hours. Turn the heat to High and cook for 10 minutes. Stir in the combined cornflour and water, stirring for 2–3 minutes. Season to taste with salt and pepper.

Smoky Chickpea Stew

Smoked turkey sausage gives this stew lots of flavour. The beans and vegetables make it extra-nutritious.

SERVES 6

450 g/1 lb smoked turkey sausage, sliced
2 x 400 g/14 oz cans chopped tomatoes
2 x 400 g/14 oz cans chickpeas, drained and rinsed
2 chopped onions
1 green pepper
150 g/5 oz French beans, cut into short lengths
2 garlic cloves, crushed
2 tsp dried oregano
2 courgettes, sliced
salt and freshly ground black pepper, to taste

Combine all the ingredients, except the courgettes, salt and pepper, in a 5.5 litre/9½ pint slow cooker. Cover and cook on High for 4–5 hours, adding the courgettes during the last 30 minutes. Season to taste with salt and pepper.

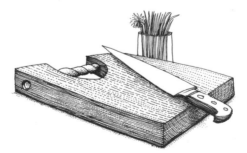

Fish and Seafood Dishes

Fish cooks quickly, even in the slow cooker, so you need to be a little more careful with your timing to avoid spoiling its delicate texture and flavour.

Tuna and Noodle Casserole

Here is comfort food at its finest, with canned soup to make an easy and tasty base. Be careful not to overook the noodles during preparation.

SERVES 6

300 g/11 oz can cream of mushroom soup
175 ml/6 fl oz semi-skimmed milk
120 ml/4 fl oz mayonnaise
100 g/4 oz cheese, grated
½ celery stick, chopped
½ small green pepper, chopped
1 small onion, finely chopped
salt and freshly ground black pepper
175 g/6 oz medium egg noodles, cooked al dente
2 x 200 g/7 oz cans tuna in water, drained
50 g/2 oz frozen peas, thawed
1–2 tbsp butter or margarine
15 g/½ oz fresh breadcrumbs
30 g/1¼ oz flaked almonds

Mix the soup, milk, mayonnaise, cheese, celery, pepper and onion in the slow cooker. Season to taste with salt and pepper. Mix in the noodles and tuna. Cover and cook on Low for 4–5 hours, adding the peas during the last 30 minutes.

Melt the butter or margarine in a small frying pan over medium heat. Mix in the breadcrumbs and almonds, cooking until browned, about 5 minutes. Sprinkle over the tuna mixture.

Poached Salmon with Lemon and Caper Sauce

Slow cooking gives the salmon extra moistness, but it's actually a very quick meal!

SERVES 4

120 ml/4 fl oz water
120 ml/4 fl oz dry white wine
1 yellow onion, thinly sliced
1 bay leaf
½ tsp salt
4 salmon steaks, about 100 g/4 oz each
Lemon and Caper Sauce (see below)

Combine all the ingredients, except the salmon and the Lemon and Caper Sauce, in the slow cooker. Cover and cook on High for 20 minutes. Add the salmon. Cover and cook on High until the salmon is tender and flakes with a fork, about 20 minutes. Serve with Lemon and Caper Sauce.

Lemon and Caper Sauce

Use vegetable stock if you want to make a vegetarian version.

SERVES 4

2–3 tbsp butter or margarine
3 tbsp flour
400 ml/14 fl oz chicken stock
2–3 tsp lemon juice
3 tbsp capers
¼ tsp salt
a pinch of white pepper

Melt the butter or margarine in a small pan. Stir in the flour and cook over medium heat for 1 minute. Whisk in the chicken stock and lemon juice. Heat to boiling, whisking until thickened, about 1 minute. Stir in the capers, salt and pepper.

303

Salmon Loaf with Cucumber Sauce

Made with canned salmon, this loaf is always a favourite and makes a perfect lunch or light dinner.

SERVES 4

200 g/7 oz can salmon, drained
50 g/2 oz fresh wholemeal breadcrumbs
2 spring onions, chopped
50 ml/2 fl oz milk
1 egg
2 tbsp lemon juice
2 tbsp capers, rinsed and drained
1 tbsp dried dill
½ tsp salt
¼ tsp pepper
Cucumber Sauce (see right)

Make foil handles (see page 10) and fit them into the slow cooker. Combine all the ingredients except the Cucumber Sauce. Form into a loaf inside the slow cooker. Cover and cook on Low for 4–5 hours. Remove the loaf, using the foil handles. Slice and serve with Cucumber Sauce.

Halibut in Lettuce Leaves

Try this attractive recipe for halibut cooked in white wine. It would also work well with cod or hake steaks.

SERVES 4

250 ml/8 fl oz dry white wine
8–12 large cos lettuce leaves
4 halibut steaks, about 100 g/4 oz each
1 tsp mixed herbs or dried tarragon
salt and freshly ground black pepper, to taste
40 g/1½ oz spinach, thinly sliced

Pour the wine into the slow cooker. Cover and cook on High for 20 minutes. Cut the large centre vein from the lettuce leaves, leaving the leaves intact. Immerse in boiling water just until the leaves are wilted, about 30 seconds. Drain well. Sprinkle the fish with the herbs, salt and pepper, and scatter the spinach over the top. Wrap the fish in the lettuce leaves, using 2 to 3 leaves for each. Place, seam sides down, in the slow cooker. Cover and cook on High until the fish is tender and flakes with a fork, about 1 hour.

Cucumber Sauce Ⓥ

A cool and refreshing sauce.

SERVES 4

120 ml/4 fl oz plain yoghurt
50 g/2 oz cucumber, chopped
½ tsp dill
salt and white pepper, to taste

Mix all the ingredients.

Red Snapper with Caramelised Garlic Sauce

The garlic sauce is equally delicious with salmon or any firm-fleshed white fish, such as halibut, cod or haddock.

SERVES 4

1 red snapper fillet, about 550 g/1¼ lb
salt and freshly ground black pepper, to taste
50–120 ml/2–4 fl oz vegetable stock
Caramelised Garlic Sauce (see page 305)

Line the slow cooker with foil or make foil handles (see page 10). Sprinkle the fish lightly with salt and pepper. Put in the slow cooker. Add the stock. Cover and cook on High until the fish is tender and flakes with a fork, about 30 minutes. Remove the fish, using the foil handles. Serve with Caramelised Garlic Sauce.

Caramelised Garlic Sauce

Use vegetable stock for a vegetarian version.

SERVES 4

12 garlic cloves, peeled
1–2 tbsp olive oil
175 ml/6 fl oz chicken stock
2 tbsp dry white wine (optional)
1 tbsp flour
1 tbsp finely chopped parsley
salt and white pepper, to taste

Cook the garlic in the oil in a medium frying pan, covered, over medium heat until tender, about 10 minutes. Cook, uncovered, low heat until the garlic cloves are golden, about 10 minutes, then mash slightly. Add the combined stock, wine and flour. Heat to boiling, stirring until thickened, about 1 minute. Stir in the parsley. Season to taste with salt and pepper.

Tuna-stuffed Spaghetti Squash

Look out for spaghetti squash in ethnic markets or from organic suppliers in the autumn. Here it is cooked with a tuna and olive stuffing, then mixed with the filling before serving. You can also cook it plain, then fluff up the strands with a fork and toss with butter and herbs.

SERVES 4

400 g/14 oz can chopped tomatoes
75 g/3 oz black olives, sliced
2 x 200 g/7 oz cans tuna in water, drained and flaked
1 tsp dried oregano
salt and freshly ground black pepper, to taste
1 small to medium spaghetti squash, about 1.25 kg/2½ lb, halved lengthways and seeded
120 ml/4 fl oz water
25 g/1 oz freshly grated Parmesan cheese

Combine the tomatoes and liquid, olives, tuna, oregano, salt and pepper. Spoon into the squash halves and place in the slow cooker. Add the water. Cover and cook until the squash is tender, 3–4 hours on High or 6–8 hours on Low. Fluff the strands of squash with a fork, combining it with the tuna mixture. Sprinkle with the Parmesan cheese.

Seafood with Herbs and Wine

Scallops, prawns and cod make a tempting combination. Serve with generous squares of warm Roasted Chilli Cornbread (see page 352).

SERVES 8

2 x 400 g/14 oz cans tomatoes
250 ml/8 fl oz water
120 ml/4 fl oz dry white wine
2 onions, finely chopped
4 garlic cloves, crushed
1 tsp dried basil
1 tsp dried oregano
½ tsp ground turmeric
2 bay leaves
450 g/1 lb cod or other white fish fillets, such as haddock or whiting, sliced (2.5 cm/1 in)
225 g/8 oz large, raw prawns, peeled and deveined, thawed if frozen
225 g/8 oz scallops, halved if large
salt and freshly ground black pepper, to taste

Combine all the ingredients, except the seafood, salt and pepper, in the slow cooker. Cover and cook on Low for 6–7 hours. Increase the temperature to High and add the seafood for a further 10–15 minutes. Discard the bay leaves. Season to taste with salt and pepper.

Fennel-scented Monkfish Casserole

Orange zest and fennel seeds complement white fish beautifully.

SERVES 8

1 litre/1¾ pints fish stock
120 ml/4 fl oz dry white wine
5 tomatoes, peeled and chopped
1 large carrot, chopped
2 onions, chopped
3 garlic cloves, crushed
1 tbsp finely grated orange zest
1 tsp fennel seeds, lightly crushed
900 g/2 lb firm fish fillets, such as monkfish, cod, red snapper or salmon, cut into pieces (4 cm/1½ in)
15 g/½ oz fresh parsley, chopped
salt and freshly ground black pepper, to taste

Combine all the ingredients, except the fish, parsley, salt and pepper, in the slow cooker. Cover and cook on Low for 6–8 hours, adding the fish during the last 15 minutes. Stir in the parsley. Season to taste with salt and pepper.

Fish Salsa Verde

You can use another variety of medium-hot chilli instead of the jalapeño chilli.

SERVES 8

1 litre/1¾ pints fish stock
120 ml/4 fl oz dry white wine
5 tomatoes, peeled and chopped
1 large carrot, chopped
2 onions, chopped
3 garlic cloves, crushed
1 small jalapeño chilli, very finely chopped
1 green pepper, finely chopped
½ tsp cumin seeds, crushed
½ tsp dried oregano

900 g/2 lb firm fish fillets, such as monkfish, cod, red snapper or salmon, cut into pieces (4 cm/1½ in)
salt and freshly ground black pepper, to taste
chopped fresh coriander, to garnish

Combine all the ingredients, except the fish, salt and pepper, in the slow cooker. Cover and cook on Low for 6–8 hours, adding the fish during the last 15 minutes. Season to taste with salt and pepper. Sprinkle each serving generously with chopped coriander.

Haddock and Sun-dried Tomatoes

Add 1 tbsp drained capers to this rich tomato-based casserole, if you like, and serve over Polenta (see page 356), pasta, or rice.

SERVES 4

250 ml/8 fl oz chicken stock
225 g/8 oz ready-made tomato sauce
400 g/14 oz tomatoes, chopped
1 large onion, chopped
½ green pepper, chopped
1 carrot, chopped
3 tbsp chopped sun-dried tomatoes (not in oil), at room temperature
1 garlic clove, crushed
1 tsp dried marjoram
½ tsp dried oregano
450 g/1 lb haddock fillet or other firm-fleshed white fish, sliced (2.5 cm/1 in)
salt and freshly ground black pepper, to taste

Combine all the ingredients, except the fish, salt and pepper, in the slow cooker. Cover and cook on Low for 6–8 hours, adding the fish during the last 10–15 minutes. Season to taste with salt and pepper.

Cioppino with Pasta

Substitute other kinds of fresh fish for this California favourite, according to availability and price.

SERVES 6

120 ml/4 fl oz fish or chicken stock
120 ml/4 fl oz dry white wine
600 g/1 lb 6 oz chopped tomatoes
1 green pepper, chopped
2 onions, chopped
75 g/3 oz button mushrooms, sliced
4 garlic cloves, crushed
1 tbsp tomato purée
2 tsp dried oregano
2 tsp dried basil
1 tsp ground turmeric
225 g/8 oz scallops, halved if large
225 g/8 oz white crabmeat, in chunks
100 g/4 oz haddock or whiting fillet,
** cubed (2.5 cm/1 in)**
12 mussels, scrubbed and beards
** removed (discard any that remain**
** open when tapped)**
salt and freshly ground black pepper,
** to taste**
350 g/12 oz fettuccine, cooked, hot

Combine all the ingredients, except the seafood, salt, pepper and fettuccine, in a 5.5 litre/9½ pint slow cooker. Cover and cook on Low for 6–8 hours, adding the seafood during the last 15 minutes. Discard any mussels that have not opened. Season to taste with salt and pepper. Serve over the fettuccine.

Smoked Haddock Kedgeree

Catherine Atkinson's subtly spiced rice dish makes an ideal supper, ready to eat in about an hour.

SERVES 4

a little softened butter, for greasing
250 ml/8 fl oz hot (not boiling)
** vegetable stock**
75 g/3 oz easy-cook long-grain rice
1 tsp curry powder
salt and freshly ground black pepper
100 g/4 oz smoked haddock fillet,
** skinned**
1 tsp lemon juice
1 tbsp fresh or frozen chopped chives,
** coriander or parsley**
1 hard-boiled egg, quartered
** (optional)**
fingers of hot buttered toast, to serve

Grease the base of the ceramic cooking pot with the butter, then pour in the stock. Add the rice and curry powder, stir well and season with a little salt and pepper. Cover with the lid and switch on the slow cooker to High. Cook for 45 minutes. Meanwhile, cut the fish into bite-sized pieces. Sprinkle the lemon juice over, then stir into the rice. Cook for a further 15–20 minutes or until the rice and fish are cooked and most of the stock has been absorbed. Stir in most of the chopped herbs and spoon on to a warm serving plate. Sprinkle with the remaining herbs and top with the egg quarters, if using. Serve with fingers of hot buttered toast.

Crab and Prawn Rarebit

You could use fresh, but I find canned crabmeat is convenient and very good.

SERVES 6

225 g/8 oz grated Cheddar cheese
225 g/8 oz soft cheese, at room temperature
250 ml/8 fl oz beer
½ tsp dry mustard powder
½ tsp Worcestershire or mushroom sauce
100 g/4 oz crabmeat, coarsely chopped
cayenne pepper, to taste
6 slices multigrain bread, toasted
12 slices tomato
18–24 cooked asparagus spears
18 large cooked prawns
chopped fresh parsley, to garnish

Combine the cheeses, beer, mustard and Worcestershire sauce in the slow cooker. Cover and cook on low until the cheeses have melted, about 2 hours, stirring twice during cooking. Stir in the crabmeat and season to taste with cayenne pepper. Put the toasted bread on serving plates. Put 2 tomato slices and 3 or 4 asparagus spears on each slice and spoon the rarebit mixture over. Top each with 3 prawns and sprinkle with parsley.

Seafood with Potatoes and Broccoli

Haddock, prawns and scallops go well with potatoes and broccoli in a well-seasoned sauce. Serve with Spinach Rice (see page 273).

SERVES 6

450 ml/¾ pint fish or chicken stock
500 g/18 oz potatoes, peeled and cubed (2 cm/¾ in)
4 onions, chopped
1 large garlic clove, crushed
1–2 tbsp dry sherry (optional)
1 bay leaf
½–¾ tsp dried thyme
½–¾ tsp dried basil
¼ tsp dry mustard powder
350 g/12 oz broccoli, in small florets
175 ml/6 fl oz semi-skimmed milk
1 tbsp cornflour
225 g/8 oz haddock or other white fish fillet, cubed (4 cm/1½ in)
225 g/8 oz cooked peeled medium prawns, thawed if frozen
225 g/8 oz scallops, halved if large
2–3 tsp lemon juice
salt and white pepper, to taste

Combine all the ingredients, except the broccoli, milk, cornflour, seafood, lemon juice, salt and pepper, in a 5.5 litre/9½ pint slow cooker. Cover and cook on High for 4–6 hours, adding the broccoli during the last 20 minutes. Stir in the combined milk and cornflour, stirring for 2–3 minutes. Add the haddock, prawns and scallops. Cover and cook for 5–10 minutes. Discard the bay leaf. Season to taste with lemon juice, salt and pepper.

Bayou Snapper

Serve this Southern-style favourite with Roasted Chilli Cornbread (see page 364). Any white fish fillets can be substituted for the red snapper.

SERVES 4

400 g/14 oz can tomatoes
250 ml/8 fl oz water
1 onion, chopped
½ green pepper, chopped
1 carrot, chopped
2 garlic cloves, crushed
2–3 tsp Worcestershire sauce
100 g/4 oz okra, trimmed and cut into pieces
450 g/1 lb red snapper fillets, cut into pieces (2.5 cm/1 in)
salt and cayenne pepper, to taste
75–175 g/3–6 oz cooked rice, hot
Tabasco sauce

Combine the tomatoes, water, vegetables, garlic and Worcestershire sauce in the slow cooker. Cover and cook on High for 4–6 hours, adding the okra during the last 30 minutes and the fish during the last 10–15 minutes. Season to taste with salt and cayenne pepper. Serve over the rice with Tabasco sauce.

Snapper Casserole

This US Gulf Coast favourite has a robust sauce with just a hint of cayenne heat. Red Pepper Rice is the perfect accompaniment.

SERVES 6

400 g/14 oz can chopped tomatoes
120 ml/4 fl oz fish or chicken stock
2–3 tbsp tomato purée
1 onion, chopped
½ green pepper, chopped
4 spring onions, sliced
1 celery stick, thinly sliced
4 garlic cloves, crushed

¾ tsp dried oregano
1 bay leaf
700 g/1½ lb red snapper fillets, cut into pieces (5 cm/2 in)
salt and Tabasco sauce, to taste
Red Pepper Rice (see page 310)

Combine all the ingredients, except the fish, salt, Tabasco sauce and Red Pepper Rice, in the slow cooker. Cover and cook on High for 4–5 hours, adding the fish during the last 15 minutes. Discard the bay leaf. Season to taste with salt and Tabasco sauce. Serve over Red Pepper Rice.

Creole Fish

Good, strong flavours make this easily prepared dish ideal for a weekday meal. You could also use cubed mixed fish for pie fillings to make an even quicker version.

SERVES 4

2 x 400 g/14 oz cans chopped tomatoes
50 ml/2 fl oz dry white wine or water
4 onions, chopped
1 green pepper, chopped
1 large celery stick, chopped
½ tsp dried thyme
¼ tsp crushed chilli flakes
2 garlic cloves, crushed
2 tbsp soy sauce
1 tbsp paprika
2 bay leaves
450 g/1 lb cod fillet, cubed
salt and freshly ground black pepper, to taste
75 g/3 oz rice, cooked, hot

Combine all the ingredients, except the cod, salt, pepper and rice, in the slow cooker. Cover and cook on High for 4–5 hours, adding the cod during the last 10–15 minutes. Discard the bay leaves. Season to taste with salt and pepper. Serve over the rice.

Red Pepper Rice ⓥ

You could substitute a fresh red pepper, simmered for a few minutes until softened, for the pepper from a jar.

SERVES 6

350 g/12 oz long-grain rice
¼ tsp ground turmeric
½ tsp paprika
1 roasted red pepper from a jar, coarsely chopped

Cook the rice according to the packet instructions, stirring the turmeric into the cooking water. Stir the paprika and roasted red pepper into the cooked rice.

Cod Creole

Try this recipe with any other firm white fish if you fancy a change.

SERVES 6

400 g/14 oz can chopped tomatoes
120 ml/4 fl oz fish or chicken stock
2–3 tbsp tomato purée
1 onion, chopped
½ green pepper, chopped
4 spring onions, sliced
1 celery stick, thinly sliced
4 garlic cloves, crushed
½ tsp dried marjoram
½ tsp thyme
½ tsp celery seeds
½ tsp ground cumin
700 g/1½ lb cod fillets, cut into pieces (5 cm/2 in)
salt and Tabasco sauce, to taste
75–175 g/3–6 oz cooked rice, hot

Combine all the ingredients, except the fish, salt, Tabasco sauce and rice, in the slow cooker. Cover and cook on High for 4–5 hours, adding the fish during the last 15 minutes. Season to taste with salt and Tabasco sauce and serve over the rice.

Caribbean Sweet-and-sour Salmon

Sweet-and-sour flavours go particularly well with oily fish such as salmon, cooked here with pineapple and beans plus the heat of chilli.

SERVES 4

400 g/14 oz can black beans, drained and rinsed
225 g/8 oz can pineapple pieces in juice, undrained
2 onions, coarsely chopped
½ red pepper, sliced
½ green pepper, sliced
4 garlic cloves, crushed
2 cm/¾ in piece fresh root ginger, finely grated
1 jalapeño or other medium-hot chilli, finely chopped
2–3 tbsp light brown sugar
2–3 tbsp cider vinegar
2–3 tsp curry powder
50 ml/2 fl oz water
1½ tbsp cornflour
450 g/1 lb salmon fillet, cubed (4 cm/1½ in)
salt and freshly ground black pepper, to taste
100 g/4 oz rice, cooked, hot

Combine all the ingredients, except the water, cornflour, salmon, salt, pepper and rice, in the slow cooker. Cover and cook on High for 4–5 hours. Stir in the combined water and cornflour, stirring for 2–3 minutes. Add the salmon. Cook for 10–15 minutes. Season to taste with salt and pepper. Serve over the rice.

Aioli Ⓥ

You can use aioli in any dishes that you would dress with mayonnaise.

SERVES 8

175 ml/6 fl oz mayonnaise
1 tsp tarragon vinegar
1 tsp lemon juice
½–1 tsp Dijon mustard
3 garlic cloves, crushed
salt and white pepper, to taste

Mix all the ingredients, seasoning to taste with salt and pepper.

Spicy Salmon Steak

This mild fish curry is wonderfully fragrant and using the creamy coconut sauce is an excellent way to cook salmon, keeping it moist and succulent.

SERVES ???

25 g/1 oz creamed coconut, roughly chopped
150 ml/¼ pint hot (not boiling) vegetable stock
4 spring onions, trimmed and finely sliced
1 tsp grated fresh root ginger or bottled ginger
10 ml/2 tsp korma or other mild curry paste
150 g/5 oz skinned salmon steak
salt and freshly ground black pepper
rice or warmed naan bread, to serve

Put the creamed coconut in the slow cooker. Pour in the stock and stir until the coconut has dissolved. Add the spring onions, ginger and curry paste and stir again until blended. Lightly season the salmon with salt and pepper. Add to the pot, cover with the lid and switch on the slow cooker to High or Low. Cook for ¾ hour on High or 1–1¼

hours on Low or until the salmon is just cooked. Carefully remove the salmon from the slow cooker and serve on a warm plate with the sauce spooned over. Accompany the salmon with boiled or steamed rice or warmed naan bread.

Salmon Bouillabaisse

This version contains salmon and shellfish, but you can also make it with white fish in the traditional way

SERVES 8

250 ml/8 fl oz fish or chicken stock
250 ml/8 fl oz dry white wine
2 x 400 g/14 oz cans chopped tomatoes
2 onions, chopped
½ fennel bulb, sliced, or 1 celery stick
2 leeks (white parts only), thinly sliced
1 garlic clove, crushed
1 bay leaf
½ tsp dried thyme
½ tsp dried rosemary
½ tsp grated orange zest
450 g/1 lb salmon fillet, cubed (4 cm/1½ in)
225 g/8 oz cooked peeled medium prawns, thawed if frozen
225 g/8 oz scallops, halved if large
12 mussels, scrubbed and beards removed (discard any that remain open when tapped)
15 g/½ oz parsley, chopped
salt and freshly ground black pepper, to taste

Combine all the ingredients, except the seafood, parsley, salt and pepper, in a 5.5 litre/9½ pint slow cooker. Cover and cook on High for 4–5 hours, adding the seafood during the last 15 minutes. Discard the bay leaf and any mussels that do not open. Stir in the parsley and season to taste with salt and pepper.

Bouillabaisse St Tropez

This version of the favourite dish includes oysters, and Aioli adds the finishing touch.

SERVES 8

2 x 400 g/14 oz cans chopped tomatoes
450 ml/¾ pint fish or chicken stock
1 onion, chopped
2 garlic cloves, crushed
½ tsp dried basil
½ tsp dried thyme
a pinch of crushed saffron threads (optional)
a pinch of fennel seeds
1 bay leaf
¼ tsp crushed chilli flakes
225 g/8 oz haddock, cod or hake fillets, cubed
225 g/8 oz lemon sole or flounder fillets, cubed
225 g/8 oz white crab or lobster meat, chopped
16 oysters, shucked
2 tbsp cornflour
50 ml/2 fl oz water
salt and freshly ground black pepper, to taste
8 slices lemon
8 slices French bread
Aioli (see page 311)

Combine all the ingredients, except the seafood, cornflour, water, salt, pepper, lemon, bread and Aioli, in the slow cooker. Cover and cook on High for 4–5 hours, adding the seafood during the last 10–15 minutes. Stir in the combined cornflour and water, stirring for 2–3 minutes. Discard the bay leaf. Season to taste with salt and pepper. Stir in the lemon slices.
Spread the bread slices with Aioli and put one in each of eight soup bowls. Ladle the casserole over the bread. Serve with the remaining Aioli.

Luxury Fish Pie

A layer of ready-made or leftover cooked mashed potato helps to seal in all the juices from the fish and prawns as they cook. The filling has the simplest of sauces, made by mixing herby cream cheese with milk.

SERVES 4

150 g/5 oz fresh or smoked haddock fillet, skinned
50 g/2 oz shelled raw prawns, halved if large
1½ tsp cornflour
25 g/1 oz frozen sweetcorn
25 g/1 oz frozen peas
50 g/2 oz full-fat plain cream cheese or cream cheese with garlic and herbs
45 ml/3 tbsp milk
salt and freshly ground black pepper
225 g/8 oz cold mashed potato or ½ x 400 g/14 oz packet of ready-made mashed potato
a mixed green salad, to serve

Cut the haddock into bite-sized pieces and place in a bowl with the prawns. Sprinkle the cornflour over and toss to coat. Add the sweetcorn and peas. Blend together the cream cheese and milk and a little salt and pepper. Pour over the fish and vegetables (this mixture will be very thick but will be diluted by the juices from the fish as it cooks) and gently mix together. Spoon into the ceramic cooking pot and switch on the slow cooker to High. Give the mashed potatoes a brief stir to soften, then spoon on top of the fish mixture in an even layer. Cover with the lid and switch on to High. Cook for 1 hour or until the fish is cooked. Serve straight away with a mixed green salad.

Haddock Marsala

Marsala adds a distinctive, appealing note to this simple Italian fish casserole.

SERVES 4

600 ml/1 pint chicken stock
150 ml/¼ pint Marsala or chicken stock
50 ml/2 fl oz tomato purée
2 onions, chopped
½ red pepper, chopped
½ green pepper, chopped
1 celery stick, chopped
1 garlic clove, crushed
1 tsp dried thyme
450 g/1 lb haddock fillet, cubed (5 cm/2 in)
100 g/4 oz pasta shells, cooked, hot
2–3 tbsp lemon juice
salt and freshly ground black pepper, to taste

Combine all the ingredients, except the fish, pasta, lemon juice, salt and pepper, in the slow cooker. Cover and cook on High for 4–5 hours, adding the fish and pasta during the last 10–15 minutes. Season to taste with lemon juice, salt and pepper.

Scallops and Prawns with Risotto Milanese

Microwave Risotto is stirred into this tomato and courgette dish for a delicious gourmet touch. Or it can be served over cooked rice.

SERVES 4

400 g/14 oz can chopped tomatoes
250 ml/8 fl oz chicken stock
1 onion, chopped
1 garlic clove, crushed
¼ tsp crushed saffron threads (optional)
1 small courgette, sliced
225 g/8 oz scallops, halved if large
225 g/8 oz cooked, peeled medium prawns, thawed if frozen
Microwave Risotto (see page 314), hot

25 g/1 oz freshly grated Parmesan cheese
salt and freshly ground black pepper, to taste

Combine the tomatoes with 120 ml/4 fl oz of the stock, the onion, garlic and saffron in the slow cooker. Cover and cook on Low for 6–7 hours, adding the courgettes during the last 30 minutes and the seafood during the last 10 minutes. Stir in the Microwave Risotto and Parmesan, adding the remaining stock, if you like. Season to taste with salt and pepper.

Prawn Risotto

Brown cap mushrooms, often called chestnut mushrooms, look very attractive in this recipe.

SERVES 4

750 ml/1¼ pints vegetable stock
1 small onion, chopped
3 garlic cloves, crushed
75 g/3 oz brown cap or button mushrooms, sliced
1 tomato, chopped
1 tsp dried thyme
350 g/12 oz arborio rice
50 g/2 oz frozen peas, thawed
225–350 g/8–12 oz cooked, peeled prawns, thawed if frozen
25 g/1 oz freshly grated Parmesan cheese
salt and freshly ground black pepper, to taste

Heat the stock to boiling in a small pan. Pour into the slow cooker. Add the remaining ingredients, except the peas, prawns, Parmesan cheese, salt and pepper. Cover and cook on High until the rice is al dente and the liquid is almost absorbed, about 1¼ hours, adding the peas and prawns during the last 15 minutes (watch carefully so that the rice does not overcook). Stir in the cheese. Season to taste with salt and pepper.

Microwave Risotto

Use vegetable stock if preferred.

SERVES 4

175 g/6 oz arborio rice
2 tsp olive oil
650 ml/22 fl oz chicken stock
½ tsp dried thyme
salt and white pepper

Combine the rice and oil in a 2.5 litre/
4¼ pint glass casserole. Microwave,
uncovered, on High for 1 minute. Stir
in the stock and thyme. Microwave,
covered, on High, for 7–8 minutes, giving
the casserole a half-turn after 4 minutes.
Stir and microwave, uncovered, on High,
for 11–13 minutes or until the stock is
absorbed. Leave to stand, covered, for
2–3 minutes. Season to taste with salt
and pepper.

Italian-style Scallops

*Scallops make an easy and healthy meal
when cooked this way.*

SERVES 4

400 g/14 oz can plum tomatoes,
**   chopped, with juice**
250 ml/8 fl oz chicken stock
1 medium onion, chopped
1 medium green pepper, chopped
1 garlic clove, crushed
1 bay leaf
1 tsp dried basil
350 g/12 oz broccoli, in small florets
350–450 g/12 oz–1 lb scallops, halved
**   if large**
2 tsp cornflour
50 ml/2 fl oz water
2–4 tbsp dry sherry (optional)
salt and freshly ground black pepper,
**   to taste**
75 g/3 oz white or brown rice,
**   cooked, hot**

Combine the tomatoes, stock, onion,
pepper, garlic and herbs in the slow
cooker. Cover and cook on High for 4–5
hours, adding the broccoli during the last
30 minutes and the scallops during the
last 5–10 minutes. Stir in the combined
cornflour and water, stirring for 2–3
minutes. Discard the bay leaf and season
to taste with sherry, salt and pepper.
Serve over the rice.

Italian-style Monkfish

*Monkfish is a firm white fish that tastes
similar to shellfish. It works well in this
well-seasoned casserole.*

SERVES 4

250 ml/8 fl oz chicken stock
120 ml/4 fl oz dry white wine or extra
**   chicken stock**
700 g/1½ lb tomatoes, peeled and
**   chopped**
65 g/2½ oz button mushrooms, halved
3 large garlic cloves, crushed
2 tsp dried Italian seasoning
¼ tsp crushed chilli flakes
450 g/1 lb monkfish fillet, sliced
25 g/1 oz fresh parsley, chopped
salt and freshly ground black pepper,
**   to taste**

Combine all the ingredients, except the
fish, parsley, salt and pepper, in the slow
cooker. Cover and cook on High for 4–5
hours, adding the fish and parsley during
the last 10 minutes. Season to taste with
salt and pepper.

Mediterranean Cod with Courgettes

Garlic goes well with fish cooked in a rich tomato sauce, flavoured here with lemon pepper.

SERVES 4

2 x 400 g/14 oz cans plum tomatoes, chopped with juice
250 ml/8 fl oz fish or chicken stock
1 large onion, chopped
1 carrot, sliced
4 garlic cloves, crushed
1 tsp dried basil
½ tsp lemon pepper
2 courgettes, cubed
450 g/1 lb cod, cubed (2.5 cm/1 in)
25 g/1 oz fresh parsley, chopped
salt and freshly ground black pepper, to taste

Combine all the ingredients, except the courgettes, cod, parsley, salt and pepper, in the slow cooker. Cover and cook on High for 4–5 hours, adding the courgettes during the last 45 minutes and the cod during the last 10 minutes. Stir in the parsley. Season to taste with salt and pepper.

Paella

This staple of Spanish cookery, was traditionally prepared with whatever seafood and ingredients the cook had on hand, so the recipe can vary.

SERVES 4

225 g/8 oz skinless chicken breast fillets, quartered lengthways
75 g/3 oz back bacon, cut into thin strips
600 ml/1 pint chicken stock
400 g/14 oz can chopped tomatoes
400 g/14 oz can artichoke hearts, drained and halved
2 onions, chopped
½ red pepper, chopped
½ green pepper, chopped
2 garlic cloves, crushed
¾ tsp dried thyme
¾ tsp dried basil
¼ tsp crushed saffron threads (optional)
275 g/10 oz easy-cook long-grain rice
225 g/8 oz cooked, peeled medium prawns, thawed if frozen
salt and cayenne pepper, to taste

Combine all the ingredients, except the rice, prawns, salt and cayenne pepper, in the slow cooker. Cover and cook on Low for 6–8 hours, adding the rice during the last 2 hours and the prawns during the last 10 minutes. Season to taste with salt and cayenne pepper.

Thai-style Prawns

Chinese chilli sauce is HOT, so use cautiously! You may be able to get it from your regular supermarket, otherwise visit your local Chinese supermarket to buy an authentic sauce.

SERVES 4

450 ml/¾ pint chicken stock
175 g/6 oz pak choi, chopped
1 red pepper, sliced
9 spring onions, sliced
50 g/2 oz beansprouts
100 g/4 oz cellophane noodles, cut into 5 cm/2 in lengths
50 ml/2 fl oz rice wine vinegar
½–1 tsp Chinese chilli and garlic sauce
450 g/1 lb cooked, peeled medium prawns, thawed if frozen
soy sauce, salt and freshly ground black pepper, to taste

Combine the stock and vegetables in the slow cooker. Cover and cook on High for 4–5 hours. While the casserole is cooking, soak the cellophane noodles in hot water until softened. Drain. Add the noodles, vinegar, chilli sauce and prawns to the slow cooker and cook for 10 minutes. Season to taste with soy sauce, salt and pepper.

Prawn and Vegetable Garden Casserole

Smoked sausage adds a hearty flavour to this easy casserole.

SERVES 4

**400 g/14 oz can chopped tomatoes
100 g/4 oz smoked sausage, thickly
    sliced
1 225 g/8 oz baby carrots, halved
100 g/4 oz small Brussels sprouts
100 g/4 oz sweetcorn
1 onion, cut into thin wedges
1 tsp chilli powder
350–450 g/12 oz–1 lb cooked, peeled
    medium prawns, thawed if frozen
salt and freshly ground black pepper,
    to taste
75 g/3 oz rice, cooked, hot**

Combine all the ingredients, except the prawns, salt, pepper and rice, in the slow cooker. Cover and cook on High for 4–5 hours, adding the prawns during the last 10–15 minutes. Season to taste with salt and pepper. Serve over the rice.

Herbed Prawns

Enjoy this herb-seasoned dish with its bounty of perfectly cooked prawns.

SERVES 4

**2 x 400 g/14 oz cans chopped
    tomatoes with garlic
250 ml/8 fl oz vegetable stock
1 medium onion, finely chopped
1 large celery stick, finely chopped
2 garlic cloves, crushed
1 tsp dried thyme
1 tsp dried basil
25 g/1 oz fresh parsley, chopped
450 g/1 lb cooked, peeled medium
    prawns, thawed if frozen
75 g/3 oz rice, cooked, hot
salt and freshly ground black pepper,
    to taste**

Combine all the ingredients, except the parsley, prawns, rice, salt and pepper, in the slow cooker. Cover and cook on Low for 6–7 hours, adding the parsley, prawns and rice during the last 10 minutes. Season to taste with salt and pepper.

Spicy Prawns and Rice

Paprika, garlic and lots of thyme flavour this prawn and vegetable dish.

SERVES 6

**450 ml/¾ pint chicken stock
400 g/14 oz can chopped tomatoes
1 large onion, chopped
1 carrot, chopped
1 celery stick, chopped
1 green pepper, chopped
2 large garlic cloves, crushed
1 bay leaf
1½ tsp dried thyme
¾ tsp paprika
75 g/3 oz rice, cooked, hot
450 g/1 lb cooked, peeled medium
    prawns, thawed if frozen
salt, cayenne and freshly ground
    black pepper, to taste**

Combine all the ingredients, except the rice, prawns, salt and pepper, in the slow cooker. Cover and cook on High for 4–5 hours, adding the rice and prawns during the last 10–15 minutes. Discard the bay leaf. Season to taste with salt, cayenne and black pepper.

Prawns with Artichokes and Peppers

Artichokes and peppers are frequent Mediterranean partners. Canned artichoke hearts are a convenient way of adding this delicately flavoured vegetable to your cooking.

SERVES 4

400 g/14 oz ready-made tomato sauce
400 g/14 oz artichoke hearts, drained and quartered
175 ml/6 fl oz chicken or vegetable stock
2 onions, thinly sliced
½ small red pepper, sliced
½ small green pepper, sliced
1 garlic clove, crushed
350 g/12 oz cooked, peeled medium prawns, thawed if frozen
1–2 tbsp dry sherry (optional)
salt and freshly ground black pepper, to taste
225 g/8 oz penne, cooked, hot

Combine all the ingredients, except the prawns, sherry, salt, pepper and penne, in the slow cooker. Cover and cook on Low for 5–6 hours, adding the prawns during the last 10 minutes. Season to taste with sherry, salt and pepper. Serve over the penne.

Prawn and Okra Casserole

This is also very good served with plain boiled rice, if you don't feel like making the Polenta.

SERVES 4

400 g/14 oz ready-made tomato sauce
225 g/8 oz okra, trimmed and cut into pieces
175 ml/6 fl oz chicken or vegetable stock
2 onions, thinly sliced
1 garlic clove, crushed

350 g/12 oz cooked, peeled medium prawns, thawed if frozen
salt and freshly ground black pepper, to taste
Polenta (see page 356)
chopped fresh parsley, to garnish

Combine all the ingredients, except the prawns, salt, pepper and Polenta, in the slow cooker. Cover and cook on Low for 5–6 hours, adding the prawns during the last 10 minutes. Season to taste with salt and pepper. Serve over Polenta and sprinkle each serving with parsley.

Scallops with Prawn and Peppers

Brightly coloured and with a hint of chilli and lemon, this seafood dish is quick to get together.

SERVES 4

375 ml/13 fl oz fish or chicken stock
1 red pepper, diced
1 green pepper, diced
½ yellow pepper, diced
2 onions, coarsely chopped
200 g/7 oz tomatoes, chopped
2 large garlic cloves, crushed
1 tsp grated lemon zest
½ tsp dried thyme
a pinch of crushed chilli flakes
225 g/8 oz cooked, peeled medium prawns, thawed if frozen
225 g/8 oz scallops, halved if large
15 g/½ oz fresh parsley, chopped
2–3 tsp lemon juice
salt and freshly ground black pepper, to taste
225 g/8 oz vermicelli, cooked, hot

Combine all the ingredients, except the seafood, parsley, lemon juice, salt, pepper and pasta, in the slow cooker. Cover and cook on High for 4–5 hours, adding the seafood and parsley during the last 10 minutes. Season to taste with lemon juice, salt and pepper. Serve over the pasta.

Creole Prawns with Ham

Crisply cooked strips of ham and dry sherry, with a shake of Tabasco, add complementary flavours to this prawn dish.

SERVES 6

100 g/4 oz lean ham, cut into thin strips
1–2 tbsp olive oil
2 x 400 g/14 oz cans chopped tomatoes
120 ml/4 fl oz water
2–3 tbsp tomato purée
1 onion, finely chopped
1 celery stick, finely chopped
½ red or green pepper, finely chopped
3 garlic cloves, crushed
700 g/1½ lb large raw prawns, peeled and deveined, thawed if frozen
2–4 tbsp dry sherry (optional)
¼–½ tsp Tabasco sauce
salt and freshly ground black pepper, to taste
100 g/4 oz rice, cooked, hot

Cook the ham in the oil in a small frying pan over medium-high heat until browned and crisp, 3–4 minutes. Remove and reserve. Combine the tomatoes, water, vegetables and garlic in the slow cooker. Cover and cook on Low for 6–7 hours, adding the reserved ham, prawns, sherry and Tabasco sauce during the last 10 minutes. Season to taste with salt and pepper. Serve over the rice.

Cajun Prawns, Sweetcorn and Beans

Red kidney beans, sweetcorn and milk make this a substantial dish, perked up with chilli. Serve over Spoon Bread (see page 360).

SERVES 4

400 g/14 oz can red kidney beans, drained and rinsed
400 g/14 oz can creamed sweetcorn
250 ml/8 fl oz fish or chicken stock
1 onion, finely chopped
1 jalapeño or other medium-hot chilli, finely chopped
2 garlic cloves, crushed
1 tsp dried thyme
½ tsp dried oregano
175 g/6 oz broccoli, in small florets
250 ml/8 fl oz full-fat milk
2 tbsp cornflour
350–450 g/12 oz–1 lb raw large prawns, peeled and deveined, thawed if frozen
salt and Tabasco sauce, to taste

Combine the beans, sweetcorn, stock, onion, chilli, garlic and herbs in the slow cooker. Cover and cook on Low for 6–7 hours, adding the broccoli during the last 20 minutes. Stir in the combined milk and cornflour, stirring for 2–3 minutes. Add the prawns. Cook for 5–10 minutes. Season to taste with salt and Tabasco sauce.

Prawn and Sausage Gumbo

Okra thickens the gumbo while giving it a characteristic Creole flavour.

SERVES 4

2 x 400 g/14 oz cans tomatoes
100 g/4 oz smoked sausage, thickly sliced
1 large red pepper, finely chopped
1 garlic clove, crushed
a pinch of crushed chilli flakes
225 g/8 oz okra, trimmed and sliced
350 g/12 oz cooked, peeled medium prawns, thawed if frozen
salt, to taste
75 g/3 oz rice, cooked, hot

Combine all the ingredients, except the okra, prawns, salt and rice, in the slow cooker. Cover and cook on Low for 6–7 hours, adding the okra during the last 30 minutes and the prawns during sthe last 10 minutes. Season to taste with salt. Serve over the rice.

Vegetarian Dishes

There's a feast of vegetarian options in this chapter, which will be enjoyed by vegetarians and non-vegetarians alike. Note that the recipes do use dairy products, so you will need to choose a vegetarian brand. Fortunately there are now many options in the supermarkets.

Pasta with Fresh Tomatoes and Herb Sauce (V)

Enjoy this dish when local or home-grown tomatoes are at their peak of ripeness.

SERVES 6

1 kg/2¼ lb tomatoes, chopped
1 onion, finely chopped
120 ml/4 fl oz dry red wine or water
2 tbsp tomato purée
6 large garlic cloves, crushed
1 tbsp sugar
2 bay leaves
2 tsp dried basil
1 tsp dried thyme
a pinch of crushed chilli flakes
salt, to taste
350 g/12 oz flat or shaped pasta, cooked, hot

Combine all the ingredients, except the salt and pasta, in the slow cooker. Cover and cook on Low for 6–7 hours. If you prefer a thicker consistency, cook uncovered, on High, during the last 30 minutes. Season to taste with salt and serve the sauce over the pasta.

Winter Vegetable Risotto (V)

Arborio rice is a short-grain rice grown in the Arborio region of Italy. It's especially suited for making risotto, as it cooks to a wonderful creaminess.

SERVES 4

750 ml/1¼ pints vegetable stock
1 small onion, chopped
3 garlic cloves, crushed
75 g/3 oz brown cap or button mushrooms, sliced
1 tsp dried rosemary
1 tsp dried thyme
350 g/12 oz arborio rice
100 g/4 oz small Brussels sprouts, halved
175 g/6 oz sweet potato, peeled and cubed
25 g/1 oz freshly grated Parmesan cheese
salt and freshly ground black pepper, to taste

Heat the stock to boiling in a small pan. Pour into the slow cooker. Add the remaining ingredients, except the Parmesan cheese, salt and pepper. Cover and cook on High until the rice is al dente and the liquid is almost absorbed, about 1¼ hours (watch carefully so that the rice does not overcook). Stir in the cheese. Season to taste with salt and pepper.

Porcini Risotto Ⓥ

Dried porcini mushrooms are such a useful storecupboard standby. They last for ages, take up very little room and quickily regain their full strength of flavour on soaking.

SERVES 4

10 g/¼ oz dried porcini or other dried mushrooms
250 ml/8 fl oz boiling water
500 ml/17 fl oz vegetable stock
1 small onion, chopped
3 garlic cloves, crushed
350 g/12 oz arborio rice
½ tsp dried sage
½ tsp dried thyme
100 g/4 oz frozen petits pois, thawed
1 small tomato, chopped
50 g/2 oz freshly grated Parmesan cheese
salt and freshly ground black pepper, to taste

Put the mushrooms in a bowl and pour the boiling water over. Leave to stand until softened, about 15 minutes. Drain, reserving the liquid. Heat the stock to boiling in a small pan. Pour into the slow cooker and add 250 ml/8 fl oz of the reserved mushroom-soaking water. Add the remaining ingredients, except the peas, tomato, Parmesan cheese and salt and pepper. Cover and cook on High until the rice is al dente and the liquid is almost absorbed, about 1¼ hours, adding the peas and tomato during the last 15 minutes (watch carefully so that the rice does not overcook). Stir in the cheese. Season to taste with salt and pepper.

Broccoli and Pine Nut Risotto Ⓥ

You can toast the pine nuts in a dry frying pan, tossing them until they are lightly browned – but do keep an eye on them as they burn easily.

SERVES 4

750 ml/1¼ pints vegetable stock
1 small onion, chopped
3 garlic cloves, crushed
350 g/12 oz arborio rice
1 tsp dried Italian herb seasoning
175 g/6 oz small broccoli florets
40 g/1½ oz raisins
25 g/1 oz toasted pine nuts
50 g/2 oz freshly grated Parmesan cheese
salt and freshly ground black pepper, to taste

Heat the stock to boiling in a small pan. Pour into the slow cooker. Add the onion, garlic, rice and herbs. Cover and cook on High until the rice is al dente and the liquid is almost absorbed, about 1¼ hours, adding the broccoli, raisins and pine nuts during the last 20 minutes (watch carefully so that the rice does not overcook). Stir in the cheese. Season to taste with salt and pepper.

Risi Bisi Ⓥ

Opinions vary as to whether Risi Bisi is a risotto or a thick soup. If you agree with the latter definition, use an additional 120–250 ml/4–8 fl oz of stock to make the mixture a thick soup consistency.

SERVES 4

750 ml/1¼ pints vegetable stock
1 small onion, chopped
3 garlic cloves, crushed
350 g/12 oz arborio rice
2 tsp dried basil
225 g/8 oz frozen petits pois, thawed
50 g/2 oz freshly grated Parmesan cheese
salt and freshly ground black pepper, to taste

Heat the stock to boiling in a small pan. Pour into the slow cooker. Add the remaining ingredients, except the peas, Parmesan cheese, salt and pepper. Cover and cook on High until the rice is al dente and the liquid is almost absorbed, about 1¼ hours, adding the peas during the last 15 minutes (watch carefully so that the rice does not overcook). Stir in the cheese. Season to taste with salt and pepper.

Summer Vegetable Risotto Ⓥ

If you have a vegetable patch, this recipe would make full use of your wonderful summer produce.

SERVES 4

750 ml/1¼ pints vegetable stock
4 spring onions, sliced
3 garlic cloves, crushed
200 g/7 oz chopped plum tomatoes
1 tsp dried rosemary
1 tsp dried thyme
350 g/12 oz arborio rice
250 g/9 oz courgettes, cubed
250 g/9 oz patty pan squash or yellow courgettes, cubed

25 g/1 oz freshly grated Parmesan cheese
salt and freshly ground black pepper, to taste

Heat the stock to boiling in a small pan. Pour into the slow cooker. Add the remaining ingredients, except the Parmesan cheese, salt and pepper. Cover and cook on High until the rice is al dente and the liquid is almost absorbed, about 1¼ hours (watch carefully so that the rice does not overcook). Stir in the cheese. Season to taste with salt and pepper.

Mushroom and Basil Egg Pie Ⓥ

Make this tasty pie, which is like crustless quiche, to serve for a light lunch or for brunch.

SERVES 4

5 eggs
25 g/1 oz plain flour
1/3 tsp baking powder
¼ tsp salt
¼ tsp pepper
225 g/8 oz grated Monterey Jack or mild Cheddar cheese
225 g/8 oz cottage cheese
75 g/3 oz mushrooms, sliced
¾ tsp dried basil
oil, for greasing

Beat the eggs in a large bowl until foamy. Mix in the combined flour, baking powder, salt and pepper. Mix in the remaining ingredients and pour into the greased slow cooker. Cover and cook on Low until set, about 4 hours. Serve from the slow cooker or remove the crock, leave to stand on a wire rack for 5 minutes and invert on to a serving plate.

Note: this dish can also be cooked in a 1 litre/1¾ pint soufflé dish or casserole. Put on the rack in a 5.5 litre/9½ pint slow cooker and cook until set, about 4½ hours.

Grilled Vegetable Bake Ⓥ

Frozen grilled vegetables – a mix of grilled red and yellow peppers, courgettes and aubergines – are Catherine Atkinson's tip for this recipe.

SERVES 4

softened butter or sunflower oil, for greasing
175 g/6 oz frozen grilled vegetables, thawed
1 egg
1.5 ml Dijon mustard
150 ml/¼ pint milk
2 tbsp ground almonds
15 ml fresh white breadcrumbs
50 g/2 oz grated Gruyère cheese
salt and freshly ground black pepper
25 g/1 oz flaked almonds
ciabatta or focaccia bread, to serve

Place an upturned saucer or a metal pastry cutter in the base of the ceramic cooking pot. Pour in about 5 cm/2 in of very hot (not boiling) water, then turn on the slow cooker to Low. Grease a 13–15 cm/5–6 in round heatproof dish with the butter or oil. Put the vegetables in the dish. Whisk together the egg and mustard, then stir in the milk, ground almonds, breadcrumbs and cheese. Season with salt and pepper, then pour carefully over the vegetables. Let the mixture settle for about a minute, then sprinkle the flaked almonds over the top. Cover the dish with clingfilm or lightly greased foil and place on top of the saucer or pastry cutter in the pot. Pour in enough boiling water to come half-way up the side of the dish. Cover with the lid and cook for 2–4 hours or until the vegetables are very tender and the mixture is lightly set (check this by pushing a thin knife or skewer into the middle – it should feel hot and there should be little liquid). Serve hot with ciabatta or focaccia bread.

Layered Lasagne Ⓥ

It's easy to make lasagne using a ready-made sauce and the oven-ready lasagne sheets that do not need to be precooked. This lasagne is delicate in texture, and rich in flavour.

SERVES 6

700 g/1½ lb ready-made tomato and basil pasta sauce
8 no-precook lasagne sheets
550 g/1¼ lb Ricotta cheese
275 g/10 oz Mozzarella cheese, grated
1 egg
1 tsp dried basil
25 g/1 oz freshly grated Parmesan cheese

Spread 75 g/3 oz of the sauce over the base of a 23 x 13 cm/9 x 5 in loaf tin. Top with a lasagne sheet and 75 g/3 oz of the Ricotta cheese and 40 g/1½ oz of the Mozzarella cheese. Repeat the layers, ending with 75 g/3 oz of the sauce on top. Sprinkle with the Parmesan cheese. Put the tin on the rack in a 5.5 litre/9½ pint slow cooker. Cover and cook on Low for 4 hours. Remove the tin and cool on a wire rack for 10 minutes. The lasagne may look sunken in the centre, but will become more even as it cools.

Pasta Salad with Aubergine Ⓥ

Balsamic vinegar and lemon juice add zing to this summer pasta dish. Serve warm or at room temperature.

SERVES 6

1 aubergine, about 450 g/1 lb
200 g/7 oz tomatoes, coarsely chopped
3 spring onions, sliced
2 tbsp balsamic or red wine vinegar
1 tbsp olive oil
1–2 tsp lemon juice
salt and freshly ground black pepper
350 g/12 oz wholemeal spaghetti, cooked, at room temperature
50 g/2 oz freshly grated Parmesan cheese

Pierce the aubergine six to eight times with a fork and put it into the slow cooker. Cover and cook on low until tender, about 4 hours. Leave to stand until cool enough to handle. Cut the aubergine in half. Scoop out the pulp and cut into 2 cm/¾ in pieces. Toss together the aubergine, tomatoes, onions, vinegar, oil and lemon juice. Season to taste with salt and pepper. Toss with the pasta and Parmesan cheese.

Spiced Veggie Pasta Ⓥ

This pasta has a wonderful Mexican flavour.

SERVES 6–8

6 x 400 g/14 oz cans chopped tomatoes
400 g/14 oz can red kidney beans, drained and rinsed
175 g/6 oz tomato purée
175 ml/6 fl oz beer or water
350 g/12 oz Quorn or beef-flavoured soya mince
2 onions, chopped

1 green pepper, chopped
2 garlic cloves, crushed
1 tbsp light brown sugar
1 tbsp cocoa powder
1–2 tbsp chilli powder
1–2 tsp ground cumin
1–2 tsp dried oregano
¼ tsp ground cloves
175 g/6 oz cooked elbow macaroni
salt and freshly ground black pepper

Combine all the ingredients, except the macaroni, salt and pepper, in a 5.5 litre/9½ pint slow cooker. Cover and cook on Low for 6–8 hours, stirring in the macaroni for the last 30 minutes. Season to taste with salt and pepper.

Welsh Rarebit Ⓥ

This piquant mix of cheeses flavoured with beer is also delicious served over sliced ham or chicken breast and asparagus on toast.

SERVES 6

225 g/8 oz grated Cheddar cheese
225 g/8 oz soft cheese, at room temperature
250 ml/8 fl oz beer
½ tsp dry mustard powder
½ tsp vegetarian Worcestershire or mushroom sauce
cayenne pepper, to taste
6 slices multigrain bread, toasted
12 slices tomato
paprika and chopped chives, to garnish

Combine the cheeses, beer, mustard and Worcestershire sauce in the slow cooker. Cover and cook on low until the cheeses have melted, about 2 hours, stirring twice during cooking. Season to taste with cayenne pepper. Put the toasted bread on serving plates. Top with the sliced tomatoes and spoon the rarebit mixture over. Sprinkle with paprika and chopped chives.

Macaroni and Tomato Casserole Ⓥ

Always popular with children, this creamy macaroni dish is yummy comfort food.

SERVES 6

225 g/8 oz small elbow macaroni, cooked
450 g/1 lb chopped tomatoes, drained
1 onion, chopped
450 ml/¾ pint evaporated milk
1 tbsp cornflour
3 eggs, lightly beaten
50 g/2 oz freshly grated Parmesan cheese
½ tsp ground cinnamon
½ tsp freshly grated nutmeg
½ tsp salt
paprika, to garnish

Combine the macaroni, tomatoes and onion in the slow cooker. Mix the remaining ingredients, except the paprika, and pour over the macaroni mixture. Cover and cook on Low until the custard is set, about 3 hours. Sprinkle with paprika.

Penne with Four Cheeses Ⓥ

Mozzarella, Cheddar, blue cheese and Parmesan make this a richly flavoursome cheese and pasta combination.

SERVES 8

750 ml/1¼ pints full-fat milk
75 g/3 oz plain flour
50 g/2 oz Mozzarella, grated
50 g/2 oz Cheddar cheese, grated
100 g/4 oz blue cheese, crumbled
50 g/2 oz freshly grated Parmesan cheese
450 g/1 lb penne, cooked al dente

Mix the milk and flour until smooth in a large bowl. Add the remaining ingredients, except 15 g/½ oz of the Parmesan cheese and the pasta. Mix in the pasta and spoon the mixture into the slow cooker. Sprinkle with the remaining Parmesan cheese. Cover and cook on Low for 3 hours.

Any-season Vegetable Casserole Ⓥ

Use any vegetables in season for this healthy veggie mixture.

SERVES 4

375 ml/13 fl oz vegetable stock
2 medium tomatoes, chopped
225 g/8 oz French beans, halved
225 g/8 oz small new potatoes, halved
2 small carrots, sliced
2 turnips, sliced
4 spring onions, sliced
½ tsp dried marjoram
¼ tsp dried thyme
4 vegetarian 'bacon' rashers, fried until crisp and crumbled
100 g/4 oz frozen peas, thawed
6 artichoke hearts, quartered
8 asparagus spears, cut into short lengths (5 cm/2 in)
2 tbsp cornflour
50 ml/2 fl oz water
salt and freshly ground black pepper, to taste
75 g/3 oz rice, cooked, hot

Combine all the ingredients, except the vegetarian rashers, peas, artichoke hearts, asparagus, cornflour, water, salt, pepper and rice, in the slow cooker. Cover and cook on Low for 6–7 hours, adding the rashers, peas, artichoke hearts and asparagus during the last 30 minutes. Stir in the combined cornflour and water, stirring for 2–3 minutes. Season to taste with salt and pepper. Serve over the rice.

Chilli with Attitude Ⓥ

In this vegetarian version of a recipe from Cincinnati, lentil chilli is flavoured with spices and cocoa, and served over spaghetti.

SERVES 6

450 ml/¾ pint vegetable stock
400 g/14 oz can chopped tomatoes
75 g/3 oz dried red lentils
1 onion, chopped
3 garlic cloves, crushed
1 tsp olive oil
½–1 tbsp chilli powder
1 tbsp cocoa powder
½ tsp ground cinnamon
¼ tsp ground allspice
salt and freshly ground black pepper, to taste
350 g/12 oz linguine, cooked, warm

toppings: kidney beans, chopped onion and pepper, grated Cheddar cheese

Combine all the ingredients, except the salt, pepper and linguine, in the slow cooker. Cover and cook on Low for 6–8 hours. If you prefer a thicker consistency, cook, uncovered, on High for the last 30 minutes. Season to taste with salt and pepper. Serve over the linguine with a choice of toppings.

Vegetable Medley with Chilli Cobbler Topping Ⓥ

This is a chilli recipe, but could be made without. Poblano chillies are fairly mild, but this recipe includes chilli powder as well, so do be careful about how much you add if you're not keen on too much chilli heat.

SERVES 6

2 x 400 g/14 oz cans chopped tomatoes
400 g/14 oz can black-eyed peas, drained and rinsed
400 g/14 oz can red kidney beans, drained and rinsed
4 onions, chopped
250 g/9 oz butternut squash or pumpkin, peeled and cubed
1–3 poblano, or mild, chillies, coarsely chopped
1 red pepper, coarsely chopped
1 yellow pepper, coarsely chopped
3 garlic cloves, crushed
1–3 tbsp chilli powder, or to taste
1½–2 tsp ground cumin
¾ tsp dried oregano
¾ tsp dried marjoram
100 g/4 oz okra, trimmed and halved
salt and freshly ground black pepper, to taste
3 large scones, halved
chilli powder
50 g/2 oz grated Cheddar cheese

Combine all the ingredients, except the okra, salt, pepper, scones, chilli powder and cheese, in a 5.5 litre/9½ pint slow cooker. Cover and cook on Low for 6–8 hours, adding the okra during the last 30 minutes. Season to taste with salt and pepper. Put the scones, cut sides down, on the mixture. Sprinkle with chilli powder and the cheese. Cover and cook on Low until the cheese has melted, about 5 minutes.

325

Vegetable Garden Casserole Ⓥ

This colourful casserole is served over healthy millet or couscous.

SERVES 4

450 ml/¾ pint vegetable stock
225 g/8 oz mushrooms, sliced
225 g/8 oz cauliflower, in florets
225 g/8 oz potatoes, cubed
2 onions, cut into wedges
2 tomatoes, cut into wedges
2 garlic cloves, crushed
1 tsp dried thyme
1 bay leaf
2 small courgettes, sliced
salt and freshly ground black pepper, to taste
175 g/6 oz millet or couscous, cooked, hot

Combine all the ingredients, except the courgettes, salt, pepper and millet or couscous, in the slow cooker. Cover and cook on Low for 6–8 hours, adding the courgettes during the last 30 minutes. Discard the bay leaf, season to taste with salt and pepper and serve over millet or couscous in shallow bowls.

Wheat Berries with Lentils Ⓥ

Wheat berries and lentils combine with potatoes and vegetables to make a wholesome and sustaining meal.

SERVES 8

750 ml/1¼ pints vegetable stock
100 g/4 oz wheat berries
75 g/3 oz dried brown or green lentils
700 g/1½ lb floury potatoes, unpeeled and cubed
2 onions, chopped
1 carrot, sliced
1 celery stick, sliced
4 garlic cloves, crushed

1 tsp dried mixed herbs
salt and freshly ground black pepper, to taste

Combine all the ingredients, except the salt and pepper, in the slow cooker. Cover and cook on Low for 6–8 hours. Season to taste with salt and pepper.

Sweet-and-sour Squash with Potatoes Ⓥ

Cider and honey, plus apple and sweet potatoes, give this homely vegetable casserole its refreshing sweet-sour flavour

SERVES 6

400 g/14 oz can chopped tomatoes
250 ml/8 fl oz cider
500 g/18 oz butternut squash, peeled and cubed
500 g/18 oz floury potatoes
350 g/12 oz sweet potatoes, peeled and cubed
2 tart green eating apples, unpeeled and sliced
175 g/6 oz sweetcorn
150 g/5 oz shallots, chopped
½ red pepper, chopped
2 garlic cloves, crushed
1½ tbsp honey
1½ tbsp cider vinegar
1 bay leaf
¼ tsp freshly grated nutmeg
2 tbsp cornflour
50 ml/2 fl oz water
salt and freshly ground black pepper, to taste
100 g/4 oz basmati or jasmine rice, cooked, hot

Combine all the ingredients, except the cornflour, water, salt, pepper and rice, in a 5.5 litre/9½ pint slow cooker. Cover and cook on Low for 6–8 hours. Turn the heat to High and cook for 10 minutes. Stir in the combined cornflour and water, stirring for 2–3 minutes. Discard the bay leaf. Season to taste with salt and pepper. Serve over the rice.

Wild Mushrooms with Cannellini

Three flavourful varieties of fresh mushrooms make this a beautifully rich dish. Dried mushrooms, softened in hot water, can be substituted for some of the fresh mushrooms to increase the richness further.

SERVES 6

3 x 400 g/14 oz cans cannellini beans, drained and rinsed
250 ml/8 fl oz vegetable stock
120 ml/4 fl oz dry white wine or vegetable stock
225 g/8 oz portabella mushrooms, chopped
175 g/6 oz shiitake mushrooms, sliced
225 g/8 oz brown cap or button mushrooms, sliced
100 g/4 oz leeks (white parts only), sliced
1 red pepper, chopped
1 onion, chopped
3 large garlic cloves, crushed
½ tsp dried rosemary
½ tsp thyme
¼ tsp crushed chilli flakes
300 g/11 oz Swiss chard or spinach, sliced
salt and freshly ground black pepper, to taste
Polenta (see page 356)

Combine all the ingredients, except the Swiss chard, salt, pepper and Polenta in a 5.5 litre/9½ pint slow cooker. Cover and cook on Low for 6–7 hours, adding the Swiss chard during the last 15 minutes. Season to taste with salt and pepper. Serve over the Polenta.

Veggie Casserole with Bulghar

Nutritious bulghar helps to thicken this lightly spicy mix of mushrooms, root vegetables and peppers. Serve with warm Parmesan Bread (see page 364).

SERVES 4

400 g/14 oz can chopped tomatoes
250 ml/8 fl oz spicy tomato juice
2 large carrots, thickly sliced
225 g/8 oz brown cap mushrooms, halved
175 g/6 oz floury potatoes, unpeeled and chopped
2 onions, chopped
1 red pepper, thickly sliced
1 green pepper, thickly sliced
2–3 garlic cloves, crushed
50 g/2 oz bulghar
1 tsp dried thyme
1 tsp dried oregano
2 courgettes, cubed
1 patty pan squash or yellow courgette, cubed
salt and freshly ground black pepper, to taste

Combine all the ingredients, except the courgettes, squash, salt and pepper, in the slow cooker. Cover and cook on High for 4–5 hours, adding the courgettes and squash during the last 30 minutes. Season to taste with salt and pepper.

Garlic Lentils with Vegetables 🅥

This lentil casserole is flavoured with chilli, ginger and lots of garlic. It's very spicy, but you can adjust the seasoning according to your taste. Remember, though, that the flavours will mellow as the casserole cooks.

SERVES 8

450 ml/¾ pint vegetable stock
8 small potatoes, cubed
6 onions, sliced
600 g/1 lb 6 oz tomatoes, chopped
225 g/8 oz carrots, chopped
225 g/8 oz French beans
75 g/3 oz dried brown or green lentils
1–4 small jalapeño, or other medium-hot, chillies, mashed into a paste or 1–2 tsp cayenne pepper
2.5 cm/1 in piece fresh root ginger, finely grated
1 cinnamon stick
10 garlic cloves
6 whole cloves
6 cardamom pods, crushed
1 tsp ground turmeric
½ tsp crushed dried mint
225 g/8 oz frozen peas, thawed
salt, to taste
100 g/4 oz soaked couscous, hot plain yoghurt, to garnish

Combine all the ingredients, except the peas, salt and couscous in a 5.5 litre/9½ pint slow cooker. Cover and cook on Low for 6–8 hours, adding the peas during the last 15 minutes. Season to taste with salt. Serve over the couscous and garnish with dollops of yoghurt.

Lentils with Spiced Couscous 🅥

Earthy brown lentils cook perfectly in the slow cooker.

SERVES 6

400 g/14 oz can chopped tomatoes
750 ml/1¼ pints vegetable stock
350 g/12 oz dried brown lentils
2 onions, chopped
1 red or green pepper, chopped
1 large celery stick, chopped
1 large carrot, chopped
1 garlic clove, crushed
1 tsp dried oregano
½ tsp ground turmeric
salt and freshly ground black pepper, to taste
Spiced Couscous (see below)

Combine all the ingredients, except the salt, pepper and couscous, in a 5.5 litre/9½ pint slow cooker. Cover and cook on Low for 6–8 hours. Season to taste with salt and pepper. Serve over Spiced Couscous.

Spiced Couscous 🅥

Couscous is also a great addition to a buffet table or a picnic.

SERVES 6

2 spring onions, sliced
1 garlic clove, crushed
¼ tsp crushed chilli flakes
½ tsp ground turmeric
1 tsp olive oil
300 ml/½ pint vegetable stock
175 g/6 oz couscous

Sauté the spring onions, garlic, chilli flakes and turmeric in the oil in a medium pan until the onions are tender, about 3 minutes. Stir in the stock. Heat to boiling. Stir in the couscous. Remove from the heat and leave to stand, covered, for 5 minutes or until the stock is absorbed.

Black Bean and Vegetable Casserole Ⓥ

Puréed haricot beans provide the perfect thickening for this dish.

SERVES 6

375 ml/13 fl oz vegetable stock
400 g/14 oz can black beans, rinsed and drained
400 g/14 oz can haricot beans, puréed
400 g/14 oz tomatoes, chopped
130 g/4½ oz mushrooms, sliced
1 courgette, sliced
1 carrot, sliced
1 onion, chopped
3 garlic cloves, crushed
2 bay leaves
¾ tsp dried thyme
¾ tsp dried oregano
100 g/4 oz frozen peas, thawed
salt and freshly ground black pepper, to taste
275 g/10 oz noodles, cooked, hot

Combine all the ingredients, except the peas, salt, pepper and noodles, in the slow cooker. Cover and cook on High for 4–5 hours, adding the peas during the last 15 minutes. Discard the bay leaves. Season to taste with salt and pepper. Serve over the noodles.

Bean and Squash Casserole Ⓥ

This dish of butter beans and red kidney beans with golden squash cooks slowly to savoury goodness. Serve with Buttermilk Bread (see page 359).

SERVES 6

2 x 400 g/14 oz cans chopped tomatoes
400 g/14 oz can red kidney beans, drained and rinsed
400 g/14 oz can butter beans, drained and rinsed
350 g/12 oz butternut squash or pumpkin, peeled and cubed
3 onions, chopped
1½ green peppers, chopped
2 garlic cloves, preferably roasted, crushed
½–¾ tsp dried Italian herb seasoning
salt and freshly ground black pepper, to taste

Combine all the ingredients, except the salt and pepper, in the slow cooker. Cover and cook on High for 4–5 hours. Season to taste with salt and pepper.

Hearty Beans and Barley with Spinach Ⓥ

Warm crusty bread would be the perfect accompaniment to this substantial chickpea and kidney bean dish.

SERVES 6

2.25 litres/4 pints vegetable stock
75 g/3 oz dried chickpeas, drained and rinsed
75 g/3 oz kidney beans, drained and rinsed
1 carrot, thinly sliced
50 g/2 oz pearl barley
175 g/6 oz potatoes, cubed
1 courgette, cubed
1 onion, sliced
2 garlic cloves, crushed
25 g/1 oz elbow macaroni, cooked
150 g/5 oz spinach, sliced
2–4 tbsp lemon juice
salt and freshly ground black pepper, to taste

Combine all the ingredients, except the macaroni, spinach, lemon juice, salt and pepper, in a 5.5 litre/9½ pint slow cooker. Cover and cook on low until the beans are tender, 6–8 hours, stirring in the macaroni and spinach during the last 20 minutes. Season to taste with lemon juice, salt and pepper.

Sweet Bean Casserole Ⓥ

Cider, sweet potatoes and raisins give this pinto bean dish sweetness, which goes well with the peppers and spices. Serve with Spoon Bread (see page 360).

SERVES 8

3 x 400 g/14 oz cans pinto beans, drained and rinsed
2 x 400 g/14 oz cans tomatoes with chilli, chopped, with juice
175 ml/6 fl oz cider
2 red or green peppers, chopped
3 onions, chopped
250 g/9 oz sweet potatoes, peeled and cubed
175 g/6 oz courgettes
2 garlic cloves, crushed,
2 tsp chilli powder
1 tsp cumin seeds, lightly crushed
½ tsp ground cinnamon
75 g/3 oz raisins
salt and freshly ground black pepper, to taste

Combine all the ingredients, except the raisins, salt and pepper, in a 5.5 litre/9½ pint slow cooker. Cover and cook on Low for 6–8 hours, adding the raisins during the last 30 minutes. Season to taste with salt and pepper.

Black Bean and Spinach Stew Ⓥ

The amount of chillies and fresh root ginger in this heartily spiced dish can be decreased if less hotness is desired.

SERVES 8

3 x 400 g/14 oz cans black beans, drained and rinsed
400 g/14 oz can chopped tomatoes
2 onions, chopped
1 red pepper, cubed
1 courgette, cubed
1–2 jalapeño or other medium-hot chillies, finely chopped
2 garlic cloves, crushed
2.5 cm/1 in piece fresh root ginger, finely grated
1–3 tsp chilli powder
1 tsp ground cumin
½ tsp cayenne pepper
225 g/8 oz spinach, sliced
salt, to taste
100 g/4 oz rice, cooked, hot

Combine all the ingredients, except the spinach, salt and rice, in the slow cooker. Cover and cook on Low for 6–7 hours, adding the spinach during the last 15 minutes. Season to taste with salt. Serve over the rice.

Sweet, Hot and Spicy Beans and Vegetables Ⓥ

Sweet spices and fiery chillies combine nicely in this filling casserole.

SERVES 6

2 x 400 g/14 oz cans chopped tomatoes
400 g/14 oz can black beans, drained and rinsed
400 g/14 oz can pinto beans, drained and rinsed
375 ml/13 fl oz vegetable stock
6 carrots, sliced
6 waxy potatoes, unpeeled and cubed
3 onions, chopped
1–3 tsp finely chopped Serrano or other hot chillies
2 garlic cloves, crushed
1½ tsp dried oregano
¾ tsp ground cinnamon
½ tsp ground cloves
1 bay leaf
1 tbsp red wine vinegar
salt and freshly ground black pepper, to taste

Combine all the ingredients, except the salt and pepper, in a 5.5 litre/9½ pint slow cooker. Cover and cook on Low for 6–8 hours. Discard the bay leaf. Season to taste with salt and pepper.

Winter Beans with Roots Ⓥ

Black beans and butter beans are cooked here with root vegetables to make a satisfying dish to serve with Healthy Garlic Bread (see page 248).

SERVES 6

400 g/14 oz can black beans, drained
  and rinsed
400 g/14 oz can butter beans, drained
  and rinsed
375 ml/13 fl oz vegetable stock
2 onions, chopped
175 g/6 oz floury potato, peeled and
  cubed
175 g/6 oz sweet potato, peeled and
  cubed
1 large tomato, cut into wedges
1 carrot, sliced
65 g/2½ oz parsnip, sliced
½ green pepper, chopped
2 garlic cloves, crushed
¾ tsp dried sage
2 tbsp cornflour
50 ml/2 fl oz water
salt and freshly ground black pepper,
  to taste

Combine all the ingredients, except the cornflour, water, salt and pepper, in the slow cooker. Cover and cook on Low for 6–7 hours. Stir in the combined cornflour and water, stirring for 2–3 minutes. Season to taste with salt and pepper.

Spiced Tofu with Vegetables Ⓥ

Cumin and thyme flavour this mix of tofu, potatoes, carrots and spinach. Tempeh also works well in this combination and, like tofu, is a healthy protein choice.

SERVES 4

1 litre/1¾ pints Rich Mushroom Stock
  (see page 29) or vegetable stock
275 g/10 oz firm tofu, cubed (1 cm/½ in)
350 g/12 oz waxy potatoes, peeled
  and sliced
2 large carrots, sliced
1 onion, sliced
1 celery stick, sliced
3 garlic cloves, crushed
1 bay leaf
1 tsp ground cumin
½ tsp dried thyme
275 g/10 oz frozen chopped spinach,
  thawed
15 g/½ oz fresh parsley, finely
  chopped
salt and freshly ground black pepper,
  to taste

Combine all the ingredients, except the spinach, parsley, salt and pepper, in the slow cooker. Cover and cook on Low for 6–7 hours, adding the spinach during the last 20 minutes. Discard the bay leaf. Season to taste with salt and pepper.

Aubergine, Pepper and Okra Casserole Ⓥ

Try this piquant selection of vegetables with Roasted Chilli Cornbread (see page 364).

SERVES 4

400 g/14 oz can chopped tomatoes
250 ml/8 fl oz vegetable stock
1 large carrot, thickly sliced
1 courgette, thickly sliced
1 small aubergine, peeled and cubed (2.5 cm/1 in)
¾ green pepper, coarsely chopped
¾ red pepper, coarsely chopped
2 spring onions, sliced
4 garlic cloves, crushed
225 g/8 oz baby onions or shallots
100 g/4 oz okra, trimmed and sliced
2–3 tsp wholegrain mustard
Tabasco sauce, salt and freshly ground black pepper, to taste

Combine all the ingredients, except the baby onions or shallots, okra, mustard, Tabasco sauce, salt and pepper, in the slow cooker. Cover and cook on Low for 6–8 hours, adding the baby onions or shallots during the last hour and the okra during the last 30 minutes. Season to taste with the mustard, Tabasco sauce, salt and pepper.

Italian Vegetables with Cheese Tortellini Ⓥ

Fresh tortellini take just a few minutes to cook, and taste great topped with peppers, mushrooms and basil in a tomato sauce.

SERVES 4

400 g/14 oz can tomatoes
400 ml/14 fl oz vegetable stock
75 g/3 oz mushrooms, sliced
1 green pepper, sliced
1 onion, finely chopped
¼ tsp allspice
1 tsp dried basil
4 small courgettes, cubed
salt and freshly ground black pepper, to taste
250 g/9 oz fresh cheese tortellini, cooked, hot

Combine all the ingredients, except the courgettes, salt, pepper and tortellini, in the slow cooker. Cover and cook on High for 4–5 hours, adding the courgettes during the last 30 minutes. Season to taste with salt and pepper. Serve over the tortellini in shallow bowls.

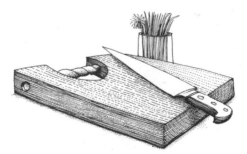

Colombian-style Chickpeas ⓥ

Sweetcorn, peas and root vegetables add to a melange of flavours, which are accentuated by fresh coriander.

SERVES 8

2 x 400 g/14 oz cans chopped
   tomatoes
400 g/14 oz can chickpeas, drained
   and rinsed
375 ml/13 fl oz vegetable stock
120 ml/4 fl oz dry white wine or
   vegetable stock
4 potatoes, peeled and cubed
4 carrots, thickly sliced
4 celery sticks, thickly sliced
2 onions, chopped
100 g/4 oz sweetcorn, thawed if frozen
4 garlic cloves, crushed
2 bay leaves
1 tsp dried cumin
¾ tsp dried oregano
1½ tbsp white wine vinegar
100 g/4 oz frozen peas, thawed
25 g/1 oz fresh coriander, chopped
salt and freshly ground black pepper,
   to taste

Combine all the ingredients, except the peas, coriander, salt and pepper, in a 5.5 litre/9½ pint slow cooker. Cover and cook on High for 4–5 hours, adding the peas during the last 15 minutes. Stir in the coriander. Discard the bay leaves. Season to taste with salt and pepper.

Argentinean Vegetables ⓥ

This vegetarian version of a traditional dish has lots of sweet-sour flavour and a lovely fruitiness from fresh peaches.

SERVES 12

2 x 400 g/14 oz cans chopped
   tomatoes
450 ml/¾ pint vegetable stock
120 ml/4 fl oz dry white wine
   (optional)
500 g/18 oz potatoes, peeled and
   cubed
500 g/18 oz sweet potatoes or
   butternut squash, peeled and cubed
4 red onions, coarsely chopped
1 large green pepper, chopped
5 garlic cloves, crushed
2 tbsp brown sugar
2 tbsp white wine vinegar
2 bay leaves
1 tsp dried oregano
6 corn cobs, each cut into 4 cm/1½ in
   pieces
450 g/1 lb courgettes, thickly sliced
6 small peaches, peeled and halved
salt and freshly ground black pepper,
   to taste

Combine all the ingredients, except the corn, courgettes, peaches, salt and pepper, in a 5.5 litre/9½ pint slow cooker. Cover and cook on Low for 6–8 hours, adding the corn, courgettes and peaches during the last 20 minutes. Discard the bay leaves. Season to taste with salt and pepper.

Bean and Macaroni Casserole Ⓥ

This traditional dish is a cross between a soup and a casserole – it's thick, rich and tasty.

SERVES 6

400 g/14 oz can cannellini beans, drained and rinsed
400 g/14 oz can Italian plum tomatoes, chopped
450 ml/¾ pint vegetable stock
1 large carrot, sliced
1 large celery stick, sliced
2 onions, chopped
1 garlic clove, crushed
½ tsp dried oregano
½ tsp dried basil
75 g/3 oz elbow macaroni, cooked
salt and freshly ground black pepper, to taste
freshly grated Parmesan cheese

Combine all the ingredients, except the macaroni, salt, pepper and cheese, in the slow cooker. Cover and cook on High for 4–5 hours, adding the macaroni during the last 15 minutes. Season to taste with salt and pepper. Pass the Parmesan cheese to sprinkle over.

Chickpeas with Roasted Peppers and Creamy Polenta Ⓥ

Use a ready-made tomato sauce and roasted red peppers from a jar to add a quick flavour punch to chickpeas. The slow-cooker Polenta can also be used in this recipe (see page 356).

SERVES 4

400 g/14 oz can chickpeas, drained and rinsed
400 g/14 oz ready-made tomato sauce
400 g/14 oz can tomatoes
200 g/7 oz roasted red peppers from a jar, drained and chopped
1 onion, chopped
1 garlic clove, crushed
1 tsp dried Italian herb seasoning
1 courgette, cubed
salt and freshly ground black pepper, to taste
25 g/1 oz freshly grated Parmesan cheese
Microwave Polenta (see page 296)

Combine all the ingredients, except the courgette, salt, pepper, cheese and Microwave Polenta, in the slow cooker. Cover and cook on High for 2–3 hours, adding the courgettes during the last 30 minutes. Season to taste with salt and pepper. Stir the Parmesan cheese into the Microwave Polenta. Serve the casserole over Microwave Polenta.

Ratatouille with Feta Aioli Ⓥ

Greek Feta cheese imparts a welcome tang to this Mediterranean casserole.

SERVES 4

2 x 400 g/14 oz cans chopped tomatoes
1 aubergine, cubed
2 onions, finely chopped
1 yellow pepper, sliced
3 garlic cloves, crushed
2 tsp dried Italian herb seasoning
2 small courgettes, halved and thinly sliced
salt and freshly ground black pepper, to taste
Feta Aioli (see page 335)

Combine all the ingredients, except the courgettes, salt, pepper and Feta Aioli, in the slow cooker. Cover and cook on High for 4–5 hours, adding the courgettes during the last 30 minutes. Season to taste with salt and pepper. Serve with Feta Aioli.

Feta Aioli ⓥ

The Feta cheese brings a delightful salty tartness to this aioli.

SERVES 4

25 g/1 oz Feta cheese, crumbled
50 ml/2 fl oz mayonnaise
2–3 garlic cloves, crushed

Process all the ingredients in a food processor or blender until smooth.

Curried Okra and Sweetcorn with Couscous ⓥ

Serve these spicy vegetables with a selection of accompaniments to provide flavour accents.

SERVES 4

250 ml/8 fl oz vegetable stock
225 g/8 oz okra, tops trimmed
100 g/4 oz sweetcorn, thawed if frozen
75 g/3 oz mushrooms, sliced
2 onions, chopped
2 carrots, sliced
2 tomatoes, chopped
1 garlic clove, crushed
1½ tsp curry powder
100 g/4 oz couscous
salt and freshly ground black pepper, to taste
accompaniments: plain yoghurt, raisins, chopped cucumber, peanuts and chopped tomato

Combine all the ingredients, except the couscous, salt and pepper, in the slow cooker. Cover and cook on High for 4–5 hours. Stir in the couscous and turn the heat off. Cover and leave to stand for 5–10 minutes. Season to taste with salt and pepper. Serve with the accompaniments.

Vegetable Tajine ⓥ

In Moroccan cuisine, tajines are traditionally cooked in earthenware pots, also called tajines, with the couscous steamed above the casserole. The slow-cooker version retains all the flavour of the vegetables. Cook the couscous separately and keep it hot, to serve.

SERVES 6

2 x 100 g/14 oz cans chopped tomatoes
400 g/14 oz can chickpeas, drained and rinsed
120 ml/4 fl oz vegetable stock or orange juice
200 g/7 oz French beans, cut into short lengths
175 g/6 oz butternut or acorn squash, chopped
150 g/5 oz turnip or swede, chopped
175 g/6 oz stoned prunes, chopped
1 onion, chopped
1 carrot, sliced
1 celery stick, sliced
1–2 cm/½–¾ in piece fresh root ginger, finely grated
1 garlic clove, crushed
1 cinnamon stick
2 tsp paprika
2 tsp ground cumin
2 tsp ground coriander
40 g/1½ oz small pitted black olives
salt and freshly ground black pepper, to taste
225 g/8 oz couscous, cooked, hot

Combine all the ingredients, except the black olives, salt, pepper and couscous, in a 5.5 litre/9½ pint slow cooker. Cover and cook on High for 4–5 hours, adding the olives during the last 30 minutes. Season to taste with salt and pepper. Serve over the couscous.

Spanish Tofu Ⓥ

A delicious dish that picks up the colours and flavours of the Mediterranean. It would also work well with Quorn.

SERVES 4

400 g/14 oz can chopped tomatoes
175 ml/6 fl oz vegetable stock
275 g/10 oz firm tofu, cubed (2.5 cm/1 in)
2 onions, chopped
1 courgette, diced
100 g/4 oz button mushrooms
1 large carrot, sliced
1 garlic clove, crushed
1 strip orange zest
½ tsp dried thyme
½ tsp dried oregano
2 tbsp cornflour
50 ml/2 fl oz water
salt and freshly ground black pepper, to taste
75 g/3 oz couscous or rice, cooked, hot

Combine all the ingredients, except the cornflour, water, salt, pepper and couscous or rice, in the slow cooker. Cover and cook on Low for 6–7 hours. Stir in the combined cornflour and water, stirring for 2–3 minutes. Season to taste with salt and pepper. Serve over the couscous or rice.

Vegetable Medley with Couscous Ⓥ

This Moroccan favourite is bursting with spicy flavours and vegetables.

SERVES 12

3 x 400 g/14 oz cans chickpeas, drained and rinsed
450–750 ml/¾–1¼ pints vegetable stock
1 small cabbage, cut into 12 wedges
1 large aubergine, cubed
225 g/8 oz carrots, sliced
225 g/8 oz small potatoes, cubed
225 g/8 oz turnips, cubed
225 g/8 oz French beans, cut into short lengths
225 g/8 oz butternut squash or pumpkin, peeled and cubed
4 tomatoes, quartered
3 onions, chopped
3 garlic cloves, crushed
2 tsp ground cinnamon
1 tsp paprika
½ tsp ground ginger
½ tsp ground turmeric
275 g/10 oz drained canned artichoke hearts, quartered
75 g/3 oz raisins
25 g/1 oz parsley, chopped
salt and cayenne pepper, to taste
450 g/1 lb couscous, cooked, hot

Combine the beans, stock, fresh vegetables, garlic and spices in a 5.5 litre/9½ pint slow cooker. Cover and cook on Low for 5–7 hours, adding the artichoke hearts, raisins and parsley during the last 30 minutes. Season to taste with salt and cayenne pepper. Serve over the couscous.

African Sweet Potato Casserole Ⓥ

A spicy garlic paste seasons this casserole of chickpeas, sweet potatoes and okra.

SERVES 6

2 x 400 g/14 oz cans chickpeas, drained and rinsed
2 x 400 g/14 oz cans chopped tomatoes
375 ml/13 fl oz vegetable stock
700 g/1½ lb sweet potatoes, peeled and cubed
2 onions, thinly sliced
Garlic Seasoning Paste (see below)
175 g/6 oz okra, trimmed and cut into short lengths
salt and freshly ground black pepper, to taste
Tabasco sauce, to taste
175 g/6 oz couscous, cooked, hot

Combine all the ingredients, except the okra, salt, pepper, Tabasco sauce and couscous, in a 5.5 litre/9½ pint slow cooker. Cover and cook on High for 4–5 hours, adding the okra during the last 45 minutes. Season to taste with salt, pepper and Tabasco sauce. Serve over the couscous.

Garlic Seasoning Paste Ⓥ

A useful paste for flavouring casseroles, especially vegetarian ones.

SERVES 6

6 garlic cloves
2 x 5 mm/¼ in slices fresh root ginger
2 tsp paprika
2 tsp cumin seeds
½ tsp ground cinnamon
1–2 tbsp olive oil

Process all the ingredients in a food processor or blender until smooth. Or crush the garlic and finely grate the ginger, then mash with the other ingredients to make a paste.

Vegetable Stroganoff Ⓥ

A warming dish for cold winter evenings. Substitute turnips, parsnips or swedes for one of the potatoes, if you like.

SERVES 6

375 ml/13 fl oz vegetable stock
225 g/8 oz mushrooms, halved
3 onions, thinly sliced
2 floury potatoes, peeled and cubed
2 sweet potatoes, peeled and cubed
1 tbsp dry mustard powder
1 tbsp sugar
100 g/4 oz frozen peas, thawed
250 ml/8 fl oz soured cream
2 tbsp cornflour
salt and freshly ground black pepper, to taste
275 g/10 oz tagliatelle, cooked, hot

Combine all the ingredients, except the peas, soured cream, cornflour, salt, pepper and noodles, in a 5.5 litre/9½ pint slow cooker. Cover and cook on Low for 6–8 hours, adding the peas during the last 30 minutes. Stir in the combined soured cream and cornflour, stirring for 2–3 minutes. Season to taste with salt and pepper. Serve over the noodles.

Cabbage Ragout with Real Mashed Potatoes Ⓥ

The pronounced aromatic highlights of fresh fennel, fresh root ginger and apple make this cabbage and aubergine casserole particularly tasty.

SERVES 6

550 g/1¼ lb aubergine, cubed (2.5 cm/1 in)
450 ml/¾ pint vegetable stock
900 g/2 lb thinly sliced cabbage
2 onions, chopped
½ fennel bulb or 1 celery stick, thinly sliced
3 large garlic cloves, crushed
2.5 cm/1 in piece fresh root ginger, finely grated
1 tsp fennel seeds, crushed
2 eating apples, peeled and coarsely chopped
250 ml/8 fl oz soured cream
2 tbsp cornflour
salt and freshly ground black pepper, to taste
Real Mashed Potatoes (see page 264)

Combine the ingredients, except the apples, soured cream, cornflour, salt, pepper and Real Mashed Potatoes, in a 5.5 litre/9½ pint slow cooker. Cover and cook on Low for 6–8 hours, adding the apples during the last 20 minutes. Turn the heat to High and cook for 10 minutes. Stir in the combined soured cream and cornflour, stirring for 2–3 minutes. Season to taste with salt and pepper. Serve over Real Mashed Potatoes in shallow bowls.

Squash and Potato Goulash Ⓥ

This goulash would also be delicious with Spinach Rice (see page 273) instead of the noodles.

SERVES 6

400 g/14 oz can tomatoes, chopped
250 ml/8 fl oz vegetable stock
120 ml/4 fl oz dry white wine or extra vegetable stock
500 g/18 oz butternut squash, peeled and cubed
500 g/18 oz floury potatoes, peeled and cubed
1½ red peppers, diced
1½ green peppers, diced
2 onions, coarsely chopped
1 garlic clove, crushed
1–2 tsp caraway seeds, lightly crushed
3 tbsp paprika
250 ml/8 fl oz soured cream
2 tbsp cornflour
salt and freshly ground black pepper, to taste
275 g/10 oz wide noodles, cooked, hot

Combine all the ingredients, except the paprika, soured cream, cornflour, salt, pepper and noodles, in a 5.5 litre/ 9½ pint slow cooker. Cover and cook on Low for 6–8 hours. Stir in the paprika and combined soured cream and cornflour, stirring for 2–3 minutes. Season to taste with salt and pepper. Serve over the noodles.

Side Dishes

This chapter contains some great dishes for breakfast, snacks and side dishes for main meals.

Maple-fruit Oatmeal Ⓥ

Let breakfast cook while you're sleeping – this is the best breakfast ever!

SERVES 4–6

100 g/4 oz pinhead oatmeal
1 litre/1¾ pints water
175 g/6 oz maple syrup,
75 g/3 oz dried fruit, chopped
20 g/¾ oz butter or margarine
½ tsp salt

Combine all the ingredients in the slow cooker. Cover and cook on Low for 6–8 hours.

Multigrain Breakfast Cereal Ⓥ

A breakfast cereal just bursting with energy-giving ingredients to set you up for the day ahead.

SERVES 4–6

50 g/2 oz pinhead oatmeal
25 g/1 oz oat groats
25 g/1 oz wheat berries
1 litre/1¾ pints water
175 g/6 oz maple syrup,
75 g/3 oz dried fruit, chopped
20 g/¾ oz butter or margarine
½ tsp salt
40 g/1½ oz millet or quinoa

Combine all the ingredients, except the millet or quinoa, in the slow cooker. Cover and cook on Low for 6–8 hours. Toast the millet or quinoa in a small frying pan over medium heat and stir into the slow cooker. Cover and cook on Low for a further 1 hour.

Chunky Apple Sauce Ⓥ

Great served warm, or chilled, as an accompaniment to meat, game or oily fish, or as a topping for pudding cakes (see pages 383–4).

SERVES 6

1.5 kg/3 lb eating apples, peeled and coarsely chopped
150 ml/¼ pint water
100 g/4 oz caster sugar
ground cinnamon

Combine all the ingredients, except the cinnamon, in the slow cooker. Cover and cook on High until the apples are very soft and form a sauce when stirred, 2–2½ hours. Sprinkle with cinnamon, then serve.

Artichokes with Mock Hollandaise Sauce Ⓥ

The Mock Hollandaise Sauce is also excellent served over asparagus spears, broccoli or cauliflower.

SERVES 4

4 whole small globe artichokes, stems removed
1 lemon, quartered
175 ml/6 fl oz water
Mock Hollandaise Sauce (see page 340)

Cut 2.5 cm/1 in from tops of the artichokes and discard. Squeeze a wedge of lemon over each artichoke and put in the slow cooker. Add 2.5 cm/1 in water to the slow cooker. Cover and cook on High until the artichokes are tender (the leaves at the base will pull out easily), 3½–4 hours. Remove the artichokes and cover with foil to keep warm. Discard the water in the slow cooker. Make the Mock Hollandaise Sauce and serve with the artichokes for dipping.

Mock Hollandaise Sauce Ⓥ

This can also be made on the hob. Cook the ingredients in a small pan over a medium-low heat, stirring until smooth.

SERVES 4

175 g/6 oz soft cheese, at room temperature
75 ml/2½ fl oz soured cream
3–4 tbsp semi-skimmed milk
1–2 tsp lemon juice
½–1 tsp Dijon mustard
a pinch of ground turmeric (optional)

Place all the ingredients in the slow cooker. Cover and cook on High until the cheese has melted and the mixture is warm, about 10 minutes, stirring once or twice to blend.

Italian-style Asparagus and White Beans Ⓥ

A substantial side dish to serve with grilled or roasted meat.

SERVES 8

400 g/14 oz can cannellini beans, drained and rinsed
175 ml/6 fl oz vegetable stock
400 g/14 oz plum tomatoes, chopped
1 large carrot, chopped
1 tsp dried rosemary
450 g/1 lb asparagus, sliced (5 cm/2 in)
salt and freshly ground black pepper
225 g/8 oz linguine or thin spaghetti, cooked, hot
25–50 g/1–2 oz freshly grated Parmesan cheese

Combine the beans, stock, tomatoes, carrot and rosemary in the slow cooker. Cover and cook on High until the carrots are tender, about 3 hours, adding the asparagus during the last 30 minutes. Season to taste with salt and pepper. Toss with the linguine and cheese.

Greek-style French Beans Ⓥ

Fresh French beans are cooked with tomatoes, herbs and garlic.

SERVES 8–10

450 g/1 lb French beans
2 x 400 g/14 oz cans chopped tomatoes
1 onion, chopped
4 garlic cloves, crushed
¾ tsp dried oregano
¾ tsp dried basil
salt and freshly ground black pepper

Combine all the ingredients, except the salt and pepper, in the slow cooker. Cover and cook on High until the beans are tender, about 4 hours. Season to taste with salt and pepper.

Oriental French Beans Ⓥ

A great dish to serve with meat or poultry.

SERVES 4

275 g/10 oz French beans, halved
½ onion, chopped
¼ red pepper, chopped
2 cm/¾ in piece fresh root ginger, finely grated
2 garlic cloves, crushed
120 ml/4 fl oz water
150 g/5 oz drained canned black or aduki beans
50 g/2 oz sliced water chestnuts
1 tbsp rice wine vinegar
1–2 tsp tamari
salt and freshly ground black pepper

Combine the French beans, onion, pepper, ginger, garlic and water in the slow cooker. Cover and cook on High until the French beans are tender, about 1½ hours. Drain. Add the remaining ingredients, except the salt and pepper. Cover and cook on High for 30 minutes. Season to taste with salt and pepper.

French Bean Casserole ⓥ

Fresh ingredients make this old favourite possible in a healthier form.

SERVES 6

**300 g/11 oz can cream of mushroom soup
120 ml/4 fl oz soured cream
50 ml/2 fl oz semi-skimmed milk
275 g/10 oz frozen sliced French beans, thawed
salt and freshly ground black pepper
½ cup canned French-fried onions**

Mix the soup, soured cream and milk in the slow cooker. Stir in the French beans. Cover and cook on Low for 4–6 hours. Season to taste with salt and pepper. Stir in the onions just before serving.

Green Beans Supreme ⓥ

A luxurious variation on the recipe above.

SERVES 6

**75 g/3 oz brown cap mushrooms, sliced
1 tbsp butter or olive oil
2 spring onions, thinly sliced
300 g/11 oz can cream of mushroom soup
120 ml/4 fl oz soured cream
50 ml/2 fl oz semi-skimmed milk
275 g/10 oz frozen sliced French beans, thawed
salt and freshly ground black pepper
4 slices crisp cooked bacon, crumbled**

Sauté the mushrooms in the butter or olive oil until tender. Mix the mushrooms, onions, soup, soured cream and milk in the slow cooker. Stir in the French beans. Cover and cook on Low for 4–6 hours. Season to taste with salt and pepper. Stir in the bacon just before serving.

Santa Fe Baked Beans ⓥ

These baked beans are hot, sweet and spicy. Modify the amounts of chillies for your preferred level of heat!

SERVES 8

**2 onions, chopped
½ small poblano or other mild chilli or green pepper, chopped
½–1 Serrano or jalapeño chilli, finely chopped
2 x 400 g/14 oz cans pinto beans, drained and rinsed
100 g/4 oz sweetcorn, thawed if frozen
6 sun-dried tomatoes (not in oil), softened and sliced
2–3 tbsp honey
½ tsp ground cumin
½ tsp dried thyme
3 bay leaves
salt and freshly ground black pepper, to taste
50 g/2 oz Feta cheese, crumbled
15 g/½ oz fresh coriander, finely chopped**

Combine all the ingredients, except the salt, pepper, cheese and coriander, in the slow cooker. Season to taste with salt and pepper. Cover and cook on Low for 5–6 hours, sprinkling with cheese and fresh coriander during the last 30 minutes.

Tuscan Bean Bake Ⓥ

Cannellini beans are lemon scented and seasoned with sun-dried tomatoes, garlic and herbs in this easy bake.

SERVES 6

3 x 400 g/14 oz cans cannellini beans
250 ml/8 fl oz vegetable stock
1 onion, chopped
½ red pepper, chopped
2 garlic cloves, crushed
1 tsp dried sage
1 tsp dried rosemary
2–3 tsp grated lemon zest
6 sun-dried tomatoes (not in oil), softened and sliced
salt and freshly ground black pepper, to taste

Combine all the ingredients, except the salt and pepper, in the slow cooker. Cover and cook on Low until the beans are thickened, 5–6 hours. Season with salt and pepper.

Brazilian Black Bean Bake Ⓥ

The festive flavours of Brazil combine in this irresistible dish.

SERVES 12

4 onions, chopped
1–2 tbsp finely chopped jalapeño or other medium-hot chilli
2.5–5 cm/1–2 in piece fresh root ginger, finely grated
4 x 400 g/14 oz cans black beans, drained and rinsed
2 x 400 g/14 oz cans chopped tomatoes
175 g/6 oz honey
100 g/4 oz light brown sugar
¾ tsp dried thyme

¾ tsp ground cumin
salt and freshly ground black pepper, to taste
½ mango, sliced
½ banana, sliced

Combine all the ingredients, except the salt, pepper, mango and banana, in the slow cooker. Season to taste with salt and pepper. Cover and cook on Low until the beans are thickened, 5–6 hours. Top with the mango and banana before serving.

Ginger Baked Beans Ⓥ

Slow baking adds goodness to this special ginger and sweet-spiced bean dish.

SERVES 2–4

3 onions, chopped
5–7.5 cm/2–3 in fresh root ginger, finely chopped
3–4 garlic cloves, crushed
4 x 400 g/14 oz cans cannellini beans, drained and rinsed
100 g/4 oz light brown sugar
175 g/6 oz ready-made tomato sauce
175 g/6 oz golden syrup
1 tsp dry mustard powder
1 tsp ground ginger
1 tsp dried thyme
¼ tsp ground cinnamon
¼ tsp ground allspice
2 bay leaves
freshly ground black pepper, to taste
50 g/2 oz gingersnap biscuits, coarsely crushed

Combine all the ingredients, except the pepper and gingersnap crumbs, in the slow cooker. Season to taste with pepper. Cover and cook on Low until thickened, about 6 hours, mixing in the gingersnap crumbs during the last hour. Discard the bay leaves.

Beetroot Dijon

Mustard goes incredibly well with the earthy flavour of beetroot. You can also try different mustards, such as horseradish mustard, wholegrain or honey mustard.

SERVES 4

450 g/1 lb beetroot, peeled and cubed (1 cm/½ in)
1 small onion, finely chopped
2 garlic cloves, crushed
75 ml/2½ fl oz soured cream
1 tbsp cornflour
2 tbsp Dijon mustard
2–3 tsp lemon juice
salt and white pepper, to taste

Combine the beetroot, onion, garlic and soured cream in the slow cooker. Cover and cook on High until the beetroot is tender, about 2 hours. Stir in the combined cornflour, mustard and lemon juice, stirring for 2–3 minutes. Season to taste with salt and pepper.

Honeyed Beetroot 🅥

Beetroot are easy to peel if cooked with their skins on – just rinse under cool water and the skins can be rubbed off. Then cook them again in a sweet-and-sour mixture with walnuts and dried fruit.

SERVES 6

700 g/1½ lb medium beetroots, unpeeled
450 ml/¾ pint hot water
½ red onion, very finely chopped
2 garlic cloves, crushed
40 g/1½ oz currants or raisins
3–4 tbsp walnuts, toasted
75 g/3 oz honey
2–3 tbsp red wine vinegar
1 tbsp butter
salt and freshly ground black pepper, to taste

Combine the beetroot and water in the slow cooker. Cover and cook on High until the beetroot is tender, 2–2½ hours. Drain. Peel the beetroot and cut into 2 cm/¾ in cubes. Combine the beetroot and the remaining ingredients, except the salt and pepper, in the slow cooker. Cover and cook on High for 20–30 minutes. Season to taste with salt and pepper.

Sugar-glazed Brussels Sprouts and Baby Onions 🅥

Small pickling onions taste good with Brussels sprouts in this simple dish. For quick peeling, first blanch the onions in boiling water for 1 minute.

SERVES 4–6

225 g/8 oz small Brussels sprouts, halved if large
225 g/8 oz baby onions
375 ml/13 fl oz hot water
15 g/½ oz butter
50 g/2 oz caster sugar
salt and white pepper, to taste

Combine the Brussels sprouts, onions and water in the slow cooker. Cover and cook on High until tender, about 2 hours. Drain. Add the butter and sugar. Cover and cook on High until glazed, about 10 minutes. Season to taste with salt and pepper.

Wine-braised Cabbage

Aromatic anise and caraway seeds, with crisply cooked bacon, add a flavour dimension to cabbage.

SERVES 4–6

1 cabbage, thinly sliced
2 small onions, chopped
½ green pepper, chopped
3 garlic cloves, crushed
½ tsp caraway seeds, crushed
½ tsp anise seeds, crushed
50 ml/2 fl oz vegetable stock
50 ml/2 fl oz dry white wine
2 bacon rashers, diced, cooked until
  crisp and drained
salt and freshly ground black pepper,
  to taste

Combine all the ingredients, except the bacon, salt and pepper, in the slow cooker. Cover and cook on High until the cabbage is tender, 3–4 hours. Stir in the bacon. Season to taste with salt and pepper.

Creamed Cabbage ⓥ

A great accompaniment to the Sunday roast, especially pork, but also vegetarian nut roasts.

SERVES 4–6

1 cabbage, thinly sliced
2 small onions, chopped
½ green pepper, chopped
3 garlic cloves, crushed
½ tsp caraway seeds, crushed
½ tsp anise seeds, crushed
50 ml/2 fl oz vegetable stock
50 ml/2 fl oz dry white wine
120 ml/4 fl oz soured cream
1 tbsp cornflour
salt and freshly ground black pepper,
  to taste

Combine all the ingredients, except the soured cream, cornflour, salt and pepper, in the slow cooker. Cover and cook on High until the cabbage is tender, 3–4 hours. Stir in the combined soured cream and cornflour. Cover and cook on Low for 5–10 minutes. Season to taste with salt and pepper.

Gingered Carrot Purée ⓥ

This traditional French vegetable purée can easily be made in the slow cooker. It has an intense flavour and a velvety texture.

SERVES 6–8

900 g/2 lb carrots, sliced
350 g/12 oz floury potatoes, peeled
  and cubed
250 ml/8 fl oz water
15–25 g/½–1 oz butter or margarine
50–120 ml/2–4 fl oz semi-skimmed
  milk, warm
½ tsp ground ginger
salt and freshly ground black pepper,
  to taste

Combine the carrots, potato and water in the slow cooker. Cover and cook on High until the vegetables are very tender, about 3 hours. Drain well. Process the carrots and potato in a food processor or blender until smooth. Return to the slow cooker. Cook on High, uncovered, until the mixture is very thick, about 30 minutes, stirring occasionally. Beat the butter or margarine and enough milk into the mixture to make a creamy consistency. Stir in the ground ginger. Season to taste with salt and pepper.

Cauliflower and Fennel Purée Ⓥ

The easiest way to prepare the cauliflower is to separate it into small florets.

SERVES 6–8

900 g/2 lb cauliflower, sliced
350 g/12 oz floury potatoes, peeled and cubed
250 ml/8 fl oz water
15–25 g/½–1 oz butter or margarine
50–120 ml/2–4 fl oz semi-skimmed milk, warm
1–1½ tsp crushed fennel or caraway seeds
salt and freshly ground black pepper, to taste

Combine the cauliflower, potato and water in the slow cooker. Cover and cook on High until the vegetables are very tender, about 3 hours. Drain well. Process the cauliflower and potato in a food processor or blender until smooth. Return to the slow cooker. Cook on High, uncovered, until the mixture is very thick, about 30 minutes, stirring occasionally. Beat the butter or margarine and enough milk into the mixture to make a creamy consistency. Stir in the fennel or caraway seeds. Season to taste with salt and pepper.

Celeriac Purée Ⓥ

Celeriac is also known as celery root.

SERVES 6–8

900 g/2 lb celeriac, sliced
350 g/12 oz floury potatoes, peeled and cubed
250 ml/8 fl oz water
15–25 g/½–1 oz butter or margarine
50–120 ml/2–4 fl oz semi-skimmed milk, warm
salt and freshly ground black pepper, to taste

Combine the celeriac, potato and water in the slow cooker. Cover and cook on High until the vegetables are very tender, about 3 hours. Drain well. Process the celeriac and potato in a food processor or blender until smooth. Return to the slow cooker. Cook on High, uncovered, until the mixture is very thick, about 30 minutes, stirring occasionally. Beat the butter or margarine and enough milk into the mixture to make a creamy consistency. Season to taste with salt and pepper.

Herbed Broccoli Purée Ⓥ

Prepare the broccoli by separating it into florets and then slicing the tougher stems into short lengths.

SERVES 6–8

900 g/2 lb broccoli, sliced
350 g/12 oz floury potatoes, peeled and cubed
250 ml/8 fl oz water
15–25 g/½–1 oz butter or margarine
50–120 ml/2–4 fl oz semi-skimmed milk, warm
½ tsp dried marjoram
½ tsp dried thyme
salt and freshly ground black pepper, to taste

Combine the broccoli, potato and water in the slow cooker. Cover and cook on High until the vegetables are very tender, about 3 hours. Drain well. Process the broccoli and potato in a food processor or blender until smooth. Return to the slow cooker. Cook on High, uncovered, until the mixture is very thick, about 30 minutes, stirring occasionally. Beat the butter or margarine and enough milk into the mixture to make a creamy consistency. Stir in the marjoram and thyme. Season to taste with salt and pepper.

Orange-glazed Baby Carrots Ⓥ

A spicy glaze for carrots makes a pleasant change. It is also delicious over sweet potatoes or beetroot.

SERVES 4

450 g/1 lb baby carrots
175 ml/6 fl oz orange juice
15 g/½ oz butter
100 g/4 oz light brown sugar
½ tsp ground cinnamon
¼ tsp ground mace
2 tbsp cornflour
50 ml/2 fl oz water
salt and white pepper, to taste

Combine all the ingredients, except the cornflour, water, salt and white pepper, in the slow cooker. Cover and cook on High until the carrots are tender, about 3 hours. Turn the heat to high and cook for 10 minutes. Stir in the combined cornflour and water, stirring for 2–3 minutes. Season to taste with salt and pepper.

Cauliflower with Creamy Cheese Sauce Ⓥ

For flavour variations, make the cheese sauce with other cheeses, such as Havarti, Gruyère or Stilton.

SERVES 6

1 cauliflower, about 450–550 g/1–1¼ lb
375 ml/13 fl oz water
Creamy Cheese Sauce (see below)
paprika, to garnish

Put the cauliflower in the slow cooker and add the water. Cover and cook on High until the cauliflower is tender, about 2 hours. Put the cauliflower on a serving plate. Spoon the Creamy Cheese Sauce over and sprinkle with paprika.

Creamy Cheese Sauce Ⓥ

You'll get perfect results with this cheese sauce, as long as you keep stirring!

SERVES 6

2 tbsp finely chopped onion
15 g/½ oz butter or margarine
2 tbsp flour
250 ml/8 fl oz semi-skimmed milk
50 g/2 oz Cheddar cheese, cubed
¼ tsp dry mustard powder
2–3 drops Tabasco sauce
salt and white pepper, to taste

Sauté the onion in the butter or margarine in a small pan for 2–3 minutes. Stir in the flour. Cook for 1 minute. Whisk in the milk and heat to boiling, stirring until thickened, about 1 minute. Reduce the heat and add the cheese, mustard and sauce, whisking until the cheese has melted. Season to taste with salt and pepper.

Easy Three-cheese Cauliflower Ⓥ

Cauliflower cheese is a popular enough dish or side dish but it's even better with a three-cheese sauce!

SERVES 6

1 cauliflower, about 450–550 g/1–1¼ lb
375 ml/13 fl oz water
50 g/2 oz Red Leicester cheese, grated
50 g/2 oz Cheddar cheese, grated
25 g/1 oz blue cheese, crumbled
paprika, to garnish

Put the cauliflower in the slow cooker and add the water. Cover and cook on High until the cauliflower is tender, about 2 hours. Drain the cauliflower and return to the slow cooker. Sprinkle with all the cheeses, cover and cook on Low until the cheese has melted, about 5 minutes. Sprinkle with paprika.

Sweetcorn Flan Ⓥ

Creamed courgette and sweetcorn are combined here in a delicate custard.

SERVES 6

250 ml/8 fl oz full-fat milk
3 eggs, lightly beaten
1 tsp sugar
400 g/14 oz can creamed courgette
275 g/10 oz frozen sweetcorn, thawed
½ tsp salt
¼ tsp pepper
oil, for greasing

Mix the milk and eggs until well blended. Mix in the remaining ingredients and pour into a greased 1.5 litre/2½ pint soufflé dish or casserole. Put the soufflé dish on the rack in a 5.5 litre/9½ pint slow cooker. Cover and cook on Low until the custard is set, about 3 hours.

Note: the recipe can be made without a soufflé dish. Pour the mixture into a greased 2.75 litre/4¾ pint slow cooker. Cover and cook on High until set and a sharp knife inserted between the centre and the edge comes out clean, 2½–3 hours.

Corn Pudding Ⓥ

A great-tasting corn pudding, spiked with chillies!

SERVES 6

275 g/10 oz frozen sweetcorn, thawed
250 ml/8 fl oz full-fat milk
3 eggs
2 tbsp flour
½ tsp ground cumin
1 tsp salt
¼ tsp pepper
oil, for greasing
225 g/8 oz Monterey Jack or Cheddar cheese, grated
¼ green pepper, finely chopped
½–1 small jalapeño or other medium-hot chilli, finely chopped

Process 75 g/3 oz of the sweetcorn with the milk, eggs, flour, cumin, salt and pepper in a food processor or blender until smooth. Pour into the greased slow cooker. Mix in the remaining sweetcorn, the cheese, pepper and chilli. Cover and cook on Low until the pudding is set, about 3 hours.

Leek Custard Ⓥ

A unique vegetable dish that will complement any main course.

SERVES 6

4 large leeks (white parts only), thinly sliced
2 tbsp finely chopped shallots or onion
2 tbsp olive oil
250 ml/8 fl oz full-fat milk
2 eggs, lightly beaten
a pinch of freshly grated nutmeg
¼ tsp salt
¼ tsp white pepper
50 g/2 oz Jarlsberg, Emmental or Gruyère cheese, grated
2 tbsp freshly grated Parmesan cheese

Sauté the leeks and shallots or onion in the oil in a small frying pan until tender, about 8 minutes. Combine the leek mixture and the remaining ingredients, except the Parmesan cheese, and pour into a 1 litre/1¾ pint soufflé dish. Put on the rack in a 5.5 litre/9½ pint slow cooker. Cover and cook on Low for 3½ hours. Sprinkle the custard with the Parmesan cheese. Cover and cook until the custard is set and a sharp knife inserted halfway between the centre and the edge comes out clean, about 30 minutes.

Savoury Stuffed Onions

Goats' cheese, sun-dried tomatoes and pine nuts combine deliciously in this stuffing for sweet onions.

SERVES 6

3 medium sweet onions
25 g/1 oz fresh Italian breadcrumbs
100 g/4 oz goats' cheese, crumbled
4 sun-dried tomato halves (not in oil), chopped
2 tbsp pine nuts
2 garlic cloves, crushed
½ tsp dried thyme
¼ tsp salt
¼ tsp pepper
1 egg white
120 ml/4 fl oz hot chicken stock

Boil the onions in water to cover for 10 minutes. Drain and cool. Cut the onions crosswise into halves and remove the centres, leaving a shell several layers thick. Reserve the centres for soup or another use. Combine the remaining ingredients, except the stock. Fill the onion halves with the mixture. Add the stock and onions to the slow cooker. Cover and cook on High until the onions are very tender but still hold their shape, about 4 hours.

Candied Sweet Potatoes Ⓥ

Golden and full of flavour, these sweet potatoes make a lively side dish to accompany a fresh stir-fry or grilled meats with steamed vegetables.

SERVES 8–10

900 g/2 lb sweet potatoes, peeled and sliced (5 mm/¼ in)
150 g/5 oz light brown sugar
salt and freshly ground black pepper, to taste
25 g/1 oz cold butter or margarine, cut into small pieces
120 ml/4 fl oz water
2 tbsp cornflour

Layer the sweet potatoes in the slow cooker, sprinkling each layer with brown sugar, salt and pepper, and dotting with butter or margarine. Combine the water and cornflour and pour over the top. Cover and cook on Low for 3 hours. Increase the heat to High and cook until the potatoes are tender, about 1 hour.

Fruit and Nut Sweet Potatoes Ⓥ

Sprinkle the top of the potatoes with 6 tbsp of miniature marshmallows during the last 5–10 minutes of cooking time, if you like.

SERVES 8–10

900 g/2 lb sweet potatoes, peeled and sliced (5 mm/¼ in)
40 g/1½ oz currants or raisins
40 g/1½ oz toasted pecan nuts
150 g/5 oz light brown sugar
salt and freshly ground black pepper, to taste
25 g/1 oz cold butter or margarine, cut into small pieces
120 ml/4 fl oz water
2 tbsp cornflour

Layer the sweet potatoes in the slow cooker, sprinkling each layer with the raisins, pecan nuts, brown sugar, salt and pepper, and dotting with butter or margarine. Combine the water and cornflour and pour over the top. Cover and cook on Low for 3 hours. Increase the heat to High and cook until the potatoes are tender, about 1 hour.

Sweet Potato Loaf with Apple and Cranberry Relish Ⓥ

This warming loaf tastes great with the accompanying relish for a winter meal.

SERVES 6

200 g/7 oz sweet potatoes, peeled and coarsely grated
1 small onion, finely chopped
½ small tart eating apple, grated
40 g/1½ oz raisins
½ tsp dried thyme
¼ tsp ground cinnamon
a pinch of freshly grated nutmeg
25 g/1 oz plain flour
50 ml/2 fl oz orange juice
salt and freshly ground black pepper, to taste
1 egg
oil, for greasing
Apple and Cranberry Relish (see below)

Mix all the ingredients, except the salt, pepper, egg and Apple and Cranberry Relish. Season to taste with salt and pepper. Mix in the egg. Pack the mixture into a greased 13 x 7.5 cm/5 x 3 in loaf tin and cover securely with foil. Put on a rack in a 5.5 litre/9½ pint slow cooker. Add 5 cm/2 in hot water. Cover and cook on High until the sweet potatoes are tender, about 3 hours. Remove from the slow cooker and leave to stand on a wire rack for 5 minutes. Invert on to a serving plate. Slice the loaf and serve with Apple and Cranberry Relish.

Apple and Cranberry Relish Ⓥ

You could substitute walnuts for the pecan nuts and lemon zest for orange, if you like.

SERVES 6

175 g/6 oz cranberry sauce
¼ tart eating apple, chopped
¼ orange, in segments without membrane, chopped
2 tbsp chopped pecan nuts
2–4 tbsp sugar
1 tbsp grated orange zest

Combine all the ingredients.

Sweet Potato Pudding Ⓥ

This comfort food has a surprise topping of marshmallows.

SERVES 6

vegetable cooking spray
4 sweet potatoes, peeled and cubed
50 ml/2 fl oz orange juice
15–25 g/½–1 oz butter or margarine
50 g/2 oz light brown sugar
1 tbsp grated orange zest
¼ tsp ground cinnamon
¼ tsp ground cloves
¼ tsp salt
3 eggs, lightly beaten
40 g/1½ oz miniature marshmallows

Spray the base and side of the slow cooker with cooking spray and add the sweet potatoes. Cover and cook on High until the potatoes are tender, about 3 hours. Remove the potatoes and mash with the remaining ingredients, except the eggs and marshmallows. Mix in the eggs. Return the potatoes to the slow cooker. Cover and cook on High for 30 minutes, sprinkling with the marshmallows during the last 5 minutes.

Sweet Autumn Pudding Ⓥ

A medly of sweet root vegetables with a dash of orange and a hint of mace.

SERVES 6

vegetable cooking spray
250 g/9 oz sweet potatoes, peeled
   and cubed
250 g/9 oz squash, peeled and cubed
2 carrots, sliced
50 ml/2 fl oz orange juice
15–25 g/½–1 oz butter or margarine
50 g/2 oz light brown sugar
1 tbsp grated orange zest
½ tsp ground mace
¼ tsp salt
3 eggs, lightly beaten

Spray the base and side of the slow cooker with cooking spray and add the sweet potato, squash and carrots. Cover and cook on High until the vegetables are tender, about 3 hours. Remove the vegetables and mash with the remaining ingredients, except the eggs. Mix in the eggs. Return to the slow cooker. Cover and cook on High for 30 minutes.

Potatoes Gratin Ⓥ

These potatoes taste beautifully rich and creamy.

SERVES 8

900 g/2 lb floury potatoes, peeled and
   sliced (5 mm/¼ in)
½ onion, thinly sliced
salt and freshly ground black pepper,
   to taste
Cheddar Cheese Sauce (see below)
freshly grated nutmeg, to taste

Layer half the potatoes and onion in the slow cooker. Sprinkle lightly with salt and pepper. Pour half the cheese sauce over. Repeat the layers. Cover and cook on High until the potatoes are tender, about 3½ hours. Sprinkle with nutmeg.

Cheddar Cheese Sauce Ⓥ

There are so many uses for a good cheese sauce and this one is really easy.

SERVES 8

25 g/1 oz butter or margarine
3 tbsp finely chopped onion
3 tbsp flour
375 ml/13 fl oz semi-skimmed milk
50 g/2 oz processed cheese, cubed
75 g/3 oz Cheddar cheese, grated
½ tsp dry mustard powder
salt and freshly ground black pepper,
   to taste

Melt the butter or margarine in a small pan. Add the onion and flour and cook for 1–2 minutes. Gradually whisk in the milk. Heat to boiling, stirring until thickened, 2–3 minutes. Reduce the heat and add the cheeses and mustard, stirring until melted. Season to taste with salt and pepper.

Easy Potato Gratin Ⓥ

This is an ideal accompaniment to many dishes but I like it best with a roasted or boiled gammon joint.

SERVES 8

900 g/2 lb floury potatoes, peeled and
   sliced (5 mm/¼ in)
½ onion, thinly sliced
75 g/3 oz Cheddar cheese, grated
salt and freshly ground black pepper,
   to taste
120 ml/4 fl oz water
freshly grated nutmeg, to taste

Layer half the potatoes, onion and cheese in the slow cooker. Sprinkle lightly with salt and pepper. Repeat the layers. Pour the water over. Cover and cook on High until the potatoes are tender, about 3½ hours. Sprinkle with nutmeg.

Scalloped Potatoes Ⓥ

If you want to make an even richer dish, substitute 150 ml/¼ pt of the milk with the same measure of double cream.

SERVES 8

900 g/2 lb floury potatoes, peeled and sliced (5 mm/¼ in)
½ onion, thinly sliced
salt and freshly ground black pepper, to taste
40 g/1½ oz butter or margarine
3 tbsp finely chopped onion
25 g/1 oz flour
450 ml/¾ pint semi-skimmed milk
freshly grated nutmeg, to taste

Layer half the potatoes and sliced onion in the slow cooker. Sprinkle lightly with salt and pepper. Melt the butter or margarine in a small pan. Add the chopped onion and flour and cook for 1–2 minutes. Gradually whisk in the milk. Heat to boiling, stirring until thickened, 2–3 minutes. Season the sauce with salt and pepper to taste. Pour half the sauce over the potatoes. Repeat the layers. Cover and cook on High until the potatoes are tender, about 3½ hours. Sprinkle with nutmeg.

Creamy Potatoes and Ham

A quick dish to make, using canned soup for lots of flavour without much effort.

SERVES 8

750 g/1¾ lb potatoes, scrubbed and cubed
350 g/12 oz smoked ham, cubed
275 g/10 oz cream of mushroom soup
250 ml/8 fl oz semi-skimmed milk
175 g/6 oz Cheddar cheese, grated
¼ tsp pepper

Combine the potatoes and ham in the slow cooker. Mix in the combined remaining ingredients. Cover and cook on Low for 6–7 hours.

Winter Vegetables Baked in Cream Ⓥ

The season's root vegetables, slow cooked in cream, are a delicious treat.

SERVES 6

4 small waxy potatoes, sliced
2 parsnips, sliced
2–3 small leeks (white parts only), sliced
1 fennel bulb, sliced
2 garlic cloves, crushed
½ tsp dried thyme
250 ml/8 fl oz vegetable stock
250 ml/8 fl oz single cream
250 ml/8 fl oz soured cream
2 tbsp cornflour
salt and freshly ground black pepper, to taste

Combine all the ingredients, except the soured cream, cornflour, salt and pepper, in the slow cooker. Cover and cook on High until the vegetables are tender, about 5 hours. Stir in the combined soured cream and cornflour, stirring for 2–3 minutes. Season to taste with salt and pepper.

Spinach Bake ⓥ

Slow cooked and delicious, this humble spinach recipe, flavoured with basil, thyme and nutmeg, makes a great side dish.

SERVES 4–6

275 g/10 oz frozen spinach, thawed
1 small onion, coarsely chopped
1 celery stick, thickly sliced
1 garlic clove
2 tbsp olive oil
½ tsp dried basil
½ tsp dried thyme
a pinch of freshly grated nutmeg
salt and freshly ground black pepper,
to taste
2 eggs
50 g/2 oz Emmental or Gruyère
cheese, grated
oil, for greasing
25 g/1 oz freshly grated Parmesan
cheese

Process the spinach, onion, celery, garlic, oil, herbs and nutmeg in a food processor or blender until very finely chopped. Season to taste with salt and pepper. Add the eggs and process until smooth. Stir in the Emmental or Gruyère cheese. Spoon the mixture into a greased 1 litre/ 1¾ pint soufflé dish and sprinkle with the Parmesan cheese. Put the soufflé dish on a rack in a 5.5 litre/9½ pint slow cooker. Cover and cook on Low until the mixture is set and a sharp knife inserted half-way between the centre and the edge comes out clean, about 4 hours.

Spaghetti Squash Parmesan ⓥ

The delicate flavour of the squash is complemented by the combination of Italian herb seasoning and Parmesan cheese.

SERVES 4

1 spaghetti squash, about 900 g/2 lb
2 spring onions, sliced
1 garlic clove, crushed
1 tbsp butter or margarine
50 ml/2 fl oz vegetable stock
1½ tsp dried Italian herb seasoning
50 g/2 oz freshly grated Parmesan
cheese
salt and freshly ground black pepper,
to taste

Cut about 2.5 cm/1 in off the ends of the squash and put the squash in the slow cooker. Cover and cook on High until just tender, 3–4 hours on High or 6–8 hours on Low. Cut the squash lengthways into halves. Scoop out and discard the seeds. Fluff the strands of squash with the tines of a fork, leaving the squash in the shells. Sauté the spring onions and garlic in the butter or margarine in a small pan until tender, 3 to 4 minutes. Stir in the stock and Italian herb seasoning and heat to boiling. Spoon half the mixture into each squash half and toss. Sprinkle with Parmesan cheese and season to taste with salt and pepper.

Courgette and Mushroom Soufflé Ⓥ

Serve the soufflé immediately it soars above the dish!

SERVES 8

4 eggs
175 ml/6 fl oz full-fat milk
25 g/1 oz plain flour
450 g/1 lb courgettes, finely chopped
100 g/4 oz mushrooms, sliced
2 tbsp snipped fresh chives or
**   chopped parsley**
1 garlic clove, crushed
½ tsp dried Italian herb seasoning
¾ tsp salt
a pinch of pepper
50 g/2 oz freshly grated Parmesan
**   cheese**
paprika

Beat the eggs, milk and flour in a bowl until smooth. Mix in the remaining ingredients, except 25 g/1 oz of the Parmesan cheese and a little paprika. Pour the mixture into a 1.5 litre/2½ pint soufflé dish or casserole. Sprinkle with the remaining Parmesan cheese and a little paprika. Put the soufflé dish on a rack in a 5.5 litre/9½ pint slow cooker. Cover and cook on High until puffed and set, about 4 hours. Serve immediately.

Courgette and Corn Timbale with Roasted Red Pepper Sauce Ⓥ

A summer treat made with fresh seasonal vegetables and served with a bright red pepper sauce.

SERVES 6

4 courgettes, coarsely grated
225 g/8 oz sweetcorn, thawed if frozen
1½ onions, chopped
15 g/½ oz fresh coriander, chopped

50 ml/2 fl oz dry white wine
5 eggs
150 ml/¼ pint evaporated milk
75 g/3 oz Cheddar cheese, grated
½ tsp salt
a pinch of pepper
Roasted Red Pepper Sauce (see page 63)

Combine all the ingredients, except the Roasted Red Pepper Sauce, in a 1 litre/1¾ pint casserole or soufflé dish. Put on a rack in a 5.5 litre/9½ pint slow cooker. Cover and cook on High until the vegetables are tender, about 4 hours. Serve with Roasted Red Pepper Sauce.

Tomato Pudding Ⓥ

Bought croûtons can be substituted for home-made if you want to make this a super-quick dish.

SERVES 6

1 celery, finely chopped
1 onion, finely chopped
½ green pepper, finely chopped
400 g/14 oz can chopped tomatoes
½ tsp celery seeds
½ tsp dried marjoram
1 tbsp light brown sugar
salt and freshly ground black pepper,
**   to taste**
1 tbsp cornflour
2 tbsp cold water
Crispy Croûtons (see page 30)

Combine all the ingredients, except the salt, pepper, cornflour, water and Crispy Croûtons, in the slow cooker. Season to taste with salt and pepper. Cover and cook on High for 2 hours. Stir in the combined cornflour and water, stirring for 2–3 minutes. Stir in the Crispy Croûtons. Cover and cook on High 15 for minutes.

Tomato Sauce

*You can't beat a home-made fresh
tomato sauce to add flavour to dishes,
or to serve with pasta and Parmesan or
Mozzarella cheese for a simple meal.
This sauce tastes particularly good
made with tomatoes when in season,
as these will have the most sweetness.
You can also make the sauce using 2½
cans of chopped plum tomatoes. The
sauce is ideal for freezing in batches
so that you can add it to slow-cooker
recipes instead of using a ready-
made sauce from a jar. Remember
to thaw it completely, and preferably
allow it to reach room temperature
before adding it to the slow cooker.*

SERVES 6

**1 kg/2¼ lb tomatoes peeled, seeded
and chopped
1 onion, chopped
1 garlic clove, crushed
120 ml/4 fl oz olive oil
2 tsp dried oregano
2 tsp dried basil
2 tsp cayenne pepper
2 tsp salt
2 tsp freshly ground black pepper
½ tsp cinnamon**

Put the tomatoes, onion, garlic and olive
oil in the slow cooker. Stir in the oregano,
basil, cayenne pepper, salt, pepper and
cinnamon. Cover and cook on Low for
10–15 hours.

Spinach and Cheese Noodle Pudding

*This is popular with all the family, so be
forewarned – everyone will want seconds!*

SERVES 8

**225 g/8 oz cottage cheese
75 g/3 oz soft cheese, at room
temperature
3 large eggs, lightly beaten
300 ml/½ pint full-fat milk
75 g/3 oz raisins
½ tsp ground cinnamon
275 g/10 oz frozen spinach, thawed
100 g/4 oz egg noodles, cooked
al dente
½ tsp salt
freshly grated Parmesan cheese
paprika, to garnish**

Combine the cottage cheese and soft
cheese. Mix in the eggs, blending well.
Mix in the remaining ingredients, except
the Parmesan cheese and paprika. Spoon
into a 1 litre/1¾ pint soufflé dish or
casserole and sprinkle with the Parmesan
cheese and a little paprika. Put the soufflé
dish on a rack in a 5.5 litre/9½ pint slow
cooker. Cover and cook on Low until set,
about 4 hours.

Note: this recipe can also be cooked in a
2.75 litre/4¾ pint slow cooker, without
using a soufflé dish. The cooking time will
be about 3½ hours.

Hungarian Noodle Pudding Ⓥ

This kugel, flavoured with raspberry preserve and almonds, can also be served as a dessert!

SERVES 10

4 eggs, separated
100 g/4 oz caster sugar
250 ml/8 fl oz soured cream
1 tbsp grated orange zest
2 tsp ground cinnamon
oil, for greasing
225 g/8 oz egg noodles or small elbow macaroni, cooked
2 tbsp butter or margarine
175 g/6 oz seedless raspberry preserve, melted
50 g/2 oz almonds, chopped

Beat the egg yolks and sugar in a small bowl until thick and lemon-coloured, about 5 minutes. Beat in the soured cream, orange zest and cinnamon. Beat the egg whites in a large clean bowl with clean beaters until stiff peaks form. Fold the yolk mixture into the egg whites. Grease the inside of the slow cooker.

Mix the noodles or macaroni, butter or margarine and egg mixture in a large bowl. Spoon half the mixture into the greased slow cooker. Spoon the preserve over the noodles and sprinkle with half the almonds. Top with the remaining noodle mixture and the remaining almonds. Cover and cook on High until set, about 1 hour. Serve from the slow cooker or invert on to a serving platter.

Cherry and Peach Dessert Kugel Ⓥ

The kugel is a staple of Jewish cuisine; the word itself is Yiddish for 'ball' and refers to the fact that the noodles were often shaped into a ball enclosing the sweet or salty filling.

SERVES 10

4 eggs, separated
100 g/4 oz caster sugar
250 ml/8 fl oz soured cream
1 tbsp grated orange zest
2 tsp ground cinnamon
oil, for greasing
225 g/8 oz egg noodles or small elbow macaroni, cooked
2 tbsp butter or margarine
225 g/8 oz cottage cheese
225 g/8 oz canned peaches, drained and chopped
50 g/2 oz dried cherries
50 g/2 oz almonds, chopped

Beat the egg yolks and sugar in a small bowl until thick and lemon-coloured, about 5 minutes. Beat in the soured cream, orange zest and cinnamon. Beat the egg whites in a large clean bowl with clean beaters, until stiff peaks form. Fold the yolk mixture into the egg whites. Grease the inside of the slow cooker.

Mix the noodles or macaroni, butter or margarine, cheese, peaches, cherries and egg mixture in a large bowl. Spoon half the mixture into the greased slow cooker and sprinkle with half the almonds. Top with the remaining noodle mixture and the remaining almonds. Cover and cook on High until set, about 1 hour. Serve from the slow cooker or invert on to a serving platter.

Mushroom Bread Pudding ⓥ

This can be cooked after assembling, but is more flavourful if refrigerated overnight.

SERVES 8

225 g/8 oz Italian or sourdough bread, cubed (2.5 cm/1 in)
olive oil cooking spray
1 tsp dried thyme
225 g/8 oz brown cap mushrooms, thinly sliced
1 celery stick, thinly sliced
2 small onions, thinly sliced
¾ green pepper, thinly sliced
1 garlic clove, crushed
1–2 tbsp olive oil, plus extra for greasing
250 ml/8 fl oz single cream
250 ml/8 fl oz full-fat milk
4 eggs, lightly beaten
½ tsp salt
a pinch of pepper
25 g/1 oz Parmesan cheese, finely grated

Spray the bread cubes lightly with cooking spray. Sprinkle with the thyme and toss. Bake on a baking sheet at 190°C/gas 5/fan oven 170°C until just beginning to brown, about 15 minutes. Sauté the mushrooms, celery, onions, pepper and garlic in the oil in a large frying pan until tender, about 8 minutes. Grease the inside of the slow cooker.

Mix the cream, milk, eggs, salt and pepper until well blended in a large bowl. Mix in the bread cubes and sautéed vegetables. Spoon into the slow cooker pot and sprinkle with the Parmesan. Refrigerate overnight. Put the crock in the slow cooker. Cover and cook on High until set, 4½ to 5 hours.

Note: the bread pudding can also be cooked in a greased 1.5 litre/2½ pint soufflé dish or casserole. Put on a rack in a 5.5 litre/9½ pint slow cooker. Cover and cook on High for 5 hours.

Savoury Oatmeal ⓥ

This is the perfect side dish for any meat, poultry or fish entrée.

SERVES 6

100 g/4 oz pinhead oatmeal
900 ml/1½ pints vegetable stock
250 ml/8 fl oz dry white wine
175 g/6 oz small chestnut mushrooms, sliced
1 leek (white part only), halved and thinly sliced
1 garlic clove, crushed
1 tsp dried basil
1 tsp dried oregano
1 tsp dried thyme
1 tsp salt
1 tsp pepper
50–75 g/2–3 oz freshly grated Parmesan cheese

Combine all the ingredients, except the cheese, in the slow cooker. Cover and cook on Low for 6–8 hours. Stir in the cheese.

Polenta ⓥ

Creamy polenta is a wonderful side dish, and this basic recipe has many possible variations.

SERVES 6

75 g/3 oz yellow polenta
450 ml/¾ pint water
2 tbsp butter or margarine
50 g/2 oz freshly grated Parmesan cheese
salt and freshly ground black pepper, to taste

Mix the polenta and water in the slow cooker. Cover and cook on High for 1½ hours, stirring once after 45 minutes. Stir in the butter or margarine and cheese. Cover and cook for 15 minutes (polenta should be soft, but should hold its shape). Season to taste with salt and pepper.

Blue Cheese Polenta (V)

There are many varieties of crumbly blue cheese to choose from and all should work well.

SERVES 6

75 g/3 oz yellow polenta
450 ml/¾ pint water
2 tbsp butter or margarine
50 g/2 oz blue cheese, crumbled
salt and freshly ground black pepper, to taste

Mix the polenta and water in the slow cooker. Cover and cook on High for 1½ hours, stirring once after 45 minutes. Stir in the butter or margarine and cheese. Cover and cook for 15 minutes (polenta should be soft, but should hold its shape). Season to taste with salt and pepper.

Goats' Cheese Polenta (V)

Goats' cheese has a characteristic, delicious tartness. Recent studies have shown that it is higher in protein than cheese made from cow's milk.

SERVES 6

75 g/3 oz yellow polenta
450 ml/¾ pint water
2 tbsp butter or margarine
25–50 g/1–2 oz goats' cheese, crumbled
salt and freshly ground black pepper, to taste

Mix the polenta and water in the slow cooker. Cover and cook on High for 1½ hours, stirring once after 45 minutes. Stir in the butter or margarine and cheese. Cover and cook for 15 minutes (polenta should be soft, but should hold its shape). Season to taste with salt and pepper.

Garlic Polenta (V)

You could sauté the garlic mixture while the polenta is cooking instead of beforehand.

SERVES 6

½ onion, finely chopped
4–6 garlic cloves, crushed
1 tbsp olive oil
75 g/3 oz yellow polenta
450 ml/¾ pint water
2 tbsp butter or margarine
salt and freshly ground black pepper

Sauté the onion and garlic in the olive oil in a small frying pan until tender, 2–3 minutes. Mix the polenta and water in the slow cooker. Cover and cook on High for 45 minutes. Stir, re-cover and cook for a further 30 minutes. Add the onion and garlic mixture, re-cover and cook for a further 15 minutes. Stir in the butter or margarine, re-cover and cook for 15 minutes (polenta should be soft, but should hold its shape). Season to taste with salt and pepper.

Roasted Pepper and Goats' Cheese Polenta (V)

Sweet red pepper perfectly complements the slight sharpness of goats' cheese.

SERVES 6

75 g/3 oz yellow polenta
450 ml/¾ pint water
2 tbsp butter or margarine
50–100 g/2–4 oz goats' cheese, crumbled
½ roasted red pepper, chopped
salt and freshly ground black pepper

Mix the polenta and water in the slow cooker. Cover and cook on High for 1½ hours, stirring once after 45 minutes. Stir in the butter or margarine, cheese and chopped pepper. Cover and cook for 15 minutes (polenta should be soft, but should hold its shape). Season to taste with salt and pepper.

357

Basil Polenta Ⓥ

*To my mind basil is the Italian herb.
You can buy it growing in small pots in
supermarkets and it's a great herb to
keep on the windowsill for countless
recipes.*

SERVES 6

3 spring onions, sliced
2 garlic cloves, crushed
1 tsp dried basil
2 tsp olive oil
75 g/3 oz yellow polenta
450 ml/¾ pint water
2 tbsp butter or margarine
**50 g/2 oz freshly grated Parmesan
  cheese**
**salt and freshly ground black pepper,
  to taste**

Sauté the spring onions, garlic and basil in
the olive oil in a large pan until tender,
about 2 minutes. Mix the polenta and
water in the slow cooker. Cover and cook
on High for 45 minutes. Stir, re-cover and
cook for a further 30 minutes. Add the
the onion mixture, re-cover and cook for
a further 15 minutes. Stir in the butter or
margarine, re-cover and cook for 15
minutes (polenta should be soft, but
should hold its shape). Season to taste
with salt and pepper.

Cheese and Rice Torta Ⓥ

*Spinach, cherry tomatoes, olives and
Mozzarella flavour this unique rice dish.*

SERVES 6

**225 g/8 oz arborio rice, cooked until
  al dente**
**275 g/10 oz frozen spinach, thawed
  and squeezed dry**
2 eggs, lightly beaten
1 onion, finely chopped
65 g/2½ oz cherry tomatoes, halved
75 g/3 oz Mozzarella cheese, grated
40 g/1½ oz black olives, sliced
½ tsp salt
a pinch of pepper
oil, for greasing

Combine the rice, spinach and eggs in a
bowl. Mix in the remaining ingredients.
Spoon into a greased 18 cm/7 in
springform cake tin. Put the tin on a rack
in a 5.5 litre/9½ pint slow cooker. Cover
and cook on Low until set, about 3 hours.
Remove the cake tin and cool on a wire
rack for 5–10 minutes. Loosen the side of
the tin and cut into wedges.

Breads and Sandwiches

Here are some more ideas for when you need delicious snacks and accompaniments.

Buttermilk Bread ⓥ

Yummy with soups and casseroles – serve warm with butter.

SERVES 8

**175 g/6 oz plain flour
2 tsp baking powder
a pinch of bicarbonate of soda
½ tsp salt
50 g/2 oz cold butter or margarine,
    cut into pieces
175 ml/6 fl oz buttermilk
1 tbsp dried parsley
oil, for greasing**

Combine the flour, baking powder, bicarbonate of soda and salt in a bowl. Cut in the butter until the mixture resembles small crumbs. Stir in the buttermilk and parsley.

Knead the dough on a floured surface for 1–2 minutes. Pat the dough into a greased 18 cm/7 in springform cake tin and put on a rack in a 5.5 litre/9½ pint slow cooker. Cover and cook on High until a cocktail stick inserted into the centre comes out clean, 2–2½ hours. Cool in the tin on a wire rack for 10 minutes. Remove the side of the tin. Break off pieces to serve.

Pepper and Herb Bread ⓥ

Originally buttermilk was the tartly flavoured liquid left behind after churning butter out of milk but nowadays you can buy cartons of cultured buttermilk from the supermarket.

SERVES 8

**175 g/6 oz plain flour
2 tsp baking powder
a pinch of bicarbonate of soda
½ tsp salt
50 g/2 oz cold butter or margarine,
    cut into pieces
175 ml/6 fl oz buttermilk
2 tsp dried chives
1 tsp coarse ground pepper
1 tsp dried dill
oil, for greasing**

Combine the flour, baking powder, bicarbonate of soda and salt in a bowl. Cut in the butter until the mixture resembles small crumbs. Stir in the buttermilk, half the chives and all the pepper and dill.

Knead the dough on a floured surface for 1–2 minutes. Pat the dough into a greased 18 cm/7 in springform cake tin and put on a rack in a 5.5 litre/9½ pint slow cooker. Cover and cook on High until a cocktail stick inserted into the centre comes out clean, 2–2½ hours. Cool in the tin on a wire rack for 10 minutes. Sprinkle the top of the bread with the remaining dried chives. Remove the side of the tin. Break off pieces to serve.

Rosemary and Raisin Bread 🅥

I have specified dried rosemary but if you are lucky enough to have it growing in your garden you could use 1 tsp of fresh leaves, chopped, instead.

SERVES 8

175 g/6 oz plain flour
2 tsp baking powder
a pinch of bicarbonate of soda
½ tsp salt
50 g/2 oz cold butter or margarine, cut into pieces
175 ml/6 fl oz buttermilk
1 tbsp dried parsley
50 g/2 oz sultanas
½ tsp dried, crushed rosemary
oil, for greasing

Combine the flour, baking powder, bicarbonate of soda and salt in a bowl. Cut in the butter or margarine until the mixture resembles small crumbs. Stir in the buttermilk, parsley, sultanas and rosemary.

Knead the dough on a floured surface for 1–2 minutes. Pat the dough into a greased 18 cm/7 in springform cake tin and put on a rack in a 5.5 litre/9½ pint slow cooker. Cover and cook on High until a cocktail stick inserted into the centre comes out clean, 2–2½ hours. Cool in the tin on a wire rack for 10 minutes. Remove the side of the tin. Break off pieces to serve.

Spoon Bread 🅥

Use a spoon to serve this bread in shallow bowls topped with casserole, or invert the bread on to a serving plate and break it into pieces.

SERVES 6–8

175 ml/6 fl oz boiling water
50 g/2 oz yellow polenta
2 tsp butter or margarine, at room temperature
2 egg yolks
75 ml/2½ fl oz buttermilk
½ tsp salt
½ tsp sugar
½ tsp baking powder
¼ tsp bicarbonate of soda
2 egg whites, whisked to stiff peaks
oil, for greasing

Stir the boiling water into the polenta in a bowl. Leave to cool until barely warm, stirring occasionally. Stir in the butter or margarine and egg yolks, blending well. Mix in the buttermilk and combined remaining ingredients, except the egg whites. Fold in the egg whites.

Pour the batter into a greased 18 cm/ 7 in springform cake tin. Put the tin on a rack in a 5.5 litre/9½ pint slow cooker. Cover and cook on High until a cocktail stick inserted into the centre of the bread comes out clean, 2½–2¾ hours. Serve immediately.

Fruited Bran Bread ⓥ

Serve this bread warm with honey or jam – fabulous!

SERVES 16

175 g/6 oz plain flour
50 g/2 oz wholemeal flour
2 tsp baking powder
½ tsp bicarbonate of soda
½ tsp salt
25 g/1 oz bran flakes
175 ml/2½ fl oz buttermilk
175 g/6 oz light brown sugar
50 g/2 oz butter or margarine, melted
1 egg
175 g/6 oz dried mixed fruit
50 g/2 oz walnuts, chopped
oil, for greasing

Combine the flours, baking powder, bicarbonate of soda, salt and bran flakes in a medium bowl. Add the buttermilk, brown sugar, butter or margarine and egg, mixing until the dry ingredients are just moistened. Gently fold in the dried fruit and walnuts.

Pour the batter into a greased and floured 23 x 13 cm/9 x 5 in loaf tin. Put the tin on a rack in a 5.5 litre/9½ pint slow cooker. Cover and cook on High until a cocktail stick inserted into the centre of the loaf comes out clean, 2–3 hours. Cool in the tin on a wire rack for 5 minutes. Remove from the tin and finish cooling on the wire rack.

Apricot and Date Bran Bread ⓥ

A tasty and nutritious bread that is moist enough to enjoy on its own but is even better sliced and buttered.

SERVES 16

175 g/6 oz plain flour
50 g/2 oz wholemeal flour
2 tsp baking powder
½ tsp bicarbonate of soda
½ tsp salt
25 g/1 oz bran flakes
175 ml/2½ fl oz buttermilk
175 g/6 oz light brown sugar
50 g/2 oz butter or margarine, melted
1 egg
40 g/1½ oz dates, chopped
40 g/1½ oz dried apricots, chopped
50 g/2 oz pecan nuts, chopped
oil, for greasing

Combine the flours, baking powder, bicarbonate of soda, salt and bran flakes in a medium bowl. Add the buttermilk, brown sugar, butter or margarine and egg, mixing until the dry ingredients are just moistened. Gently fold in the dates, apricots and nuts.

Pour the batter into a greased and floured 23 x 13 cm/9 x 5 in loaf tin. Put the tin on a rack in a 5.5 litre/9½ pint slow cooker. Cover and cook on High until a cocktail stick inserted into the centre of the loaf comes out clean, 2–3 hours. Cool in the tin on a wire rack for 5 minutes. Remove from the tin and finish cooling on the wire rack.

Pumpkin and Pecan Bread Ⓥ

Next time you cook some pumpkin or squash, make extra to use in this tasty bread.

SERVES 16

225 g/8 oz pumpkin, cooked and mashed
50 g/2 oz butter or margarine, at room temperature
100 g/4 oz caster sugar
100 g/4 oz light brown sugar
120 ml/4 fl oz semi-skimmed milk
2 eggs
225 g/8 oz plain flour
2 tsp baking powder
½ tsp bicarbonate of soda
¾ tsp salt
1½ tsp ground cinnamon
¼–½ tsp ground mace
50 g/2 oz pecan nuts, toasted and chopped
oil, for greasing

Beat the pumpkin, butter or margarine and sugars in a bowl until well blended. Mix in the milk and eggs. Mix in the combined dry ingredients. Mix in the pecan nuts.

Spoon the batter into a greased 23 x 13 cm/ 9 x 5 in loaf tin and put on a rack in a 5.5 litre/9½ pint slow cooker. Cover and cook on High until a cocktail stick inserted into the centre of the bread comes out clean, about 3½ hours. Cool in the tin on a wire rack for 5 minutes. Remove from the tin and finish cooling on the wire rack.

Brown Sugar Banana Bread Ⓥ

Apple sauce adds moistness to this banana bread with its caramel flavour from the brown sugar. Make your own apple sauce if you have time by cooking 1 peeled, cored and sliced cooking apple in a small pan with 1 tbsp water until very soft.

SERVES 16

50 g/2 oz butter or margarine, at room temperature
50 ml/2 fl oz ready-made apple sauce
2 eggs
2 tbsp semi-skimmed milk or water
175 g/6 oz light brown sugar
3 ripe bananas, mashed
200 g/7 oz plain flour
2 tsp baking powder
½ tsp bicarbonate of soda
¼ tsp salt
25 g/1 oz walnuts or pecan nuts, coarsely chopped
oil, for greasing

Beat the butter or margarine, apple sauce, eggs, milk and brown sugar in a large bowl until smooth. Add the bananas and mix at low speed. Beat at high speed for 1–2 minutes. Mix in the combined flour, baking powder, bicarbonate of soda and salt. Mix in the walnuts or pecan nuts.

Pour the batter into a greased 23 x 13 cm/ 9 x 5 in loaf tin. Put the tin on a rack in a 5.5 litre/9½ pint slow cooker. Cover and cook on High until a cocktail stick inserted into the centre of the bread comes out clean, 2–3 hours. Cool in the tin on a wire rack for 5 minutes. Remove the bread from the tin and finish cooling on the wire rack.

Apple and Pecan Nut Banana Bread

You can ring the changes with this tasty bread and use any dried fruit or nut you prefer.

SERVES 12

6 tbsp butter or margarine, at room
   temperature
100 g/4 oz caster sugar
2 eggs
3 ripe bananas, mashed
200 g/7 oz self-raising flour
½ tsp salt
10 g/¼oz dried apples, chopped
50 g/2 oz pecan nuts, chopped
oil, for greasing

Beat the butter or margarine and sugar in a large bowl until fluffy. Beat in the eggs and bananas. Mix in the flour and salt. Mix in the dried apples and pecan nuts.

Pour the batter into a greased 23 x 13 cm/ 9 x 5 in loaf tin. Put on a rack in a 5.5 litre/9½ pint slow cooker. Cover and cook on High until a wooden skewer inserted into the centre of the bread comes out clean, about 3½ hours. Cool on a wire rack for 5 minutes. Remove from the tin and finish cooling on the wire rack.

Boston Brown Bread

The dough for this moist polenta, walnut and raisin bread is steamed in two tins in the slow cooker.

MAKES 2 LOAVES, EACH SERVES 6–8

65 g/2½ oz wholemeal flour
50 g/2 oz yellow polenta
40 g/1½ oz walnuts, chopped
50 g/2 oz raisins
2 tbsp light brown sugar
¾ tsp bicarbonate of soda
½ tsp salt
150 ml/¼ pint semi-skimmed milk
75 g/3 oz golden syrup
1 tbsp lemon juice
oil, for greasing

Combine all the ingredients, except the milk, golden syrup and lemon juice, in a bowl. Add the combined milk, golden syrup and lemon juice, mixing well. Spoon the mixture into two greased and floured 450 g/1 lb tins. Cover the tops of the tins with greased foil, securing it with string.

Stand the tins in the slow cooker. Add enough boiling water to come half-way up the sides of the tins, making sure the foil does not touch the water. Cover and cook on High for 2 hours. Turn the heat to Low and cook until a wooden skewer inserted into the breads comes out clean, about 4 hours. Uncover the tins and stand on a wire rack to cool for 10 minutes. Loosen the sides of the bread by gently rolling the tins on the worktop, or remove the bases of the tins and push the breads through.

363

Roasted Chilli Cornbread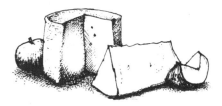

This cornbread is extra moist and chilli hot! Reduce the amount of chilli if you prefer it a bit milder.

SERVES 8

¼ small red pepper, chopped
¼ poblano or other mild chilli, chopped
¼ jalapeño or other medium-hot chilli, chopped
1 large spring onion, chopped
oil, for greasing
75 g/3 oz plain flour
25 g/1 oz yellow polenta
2 tbsp light brown sugar
1½ tsp baking powder
¼ tsp ground cumin
¼ tsp dried oregano
¼ tsp salt
1 egg, lightly beaten
120 ml/4 fl oz buttermilk
25 g/1 oz sweetcorn
2 tbsp finely chopped fresh coriander

Cook the pepper, chillies and spring onion in a lightly greased frying pan over medium heat until tender, about 5 minutes. Reserve. Combine the flour, polenta, brown sugar, baking powder, cumin, oregano and salt in a medium bowl. Add the combined egg and buttermilk, mixing until just combined. Stir in the sautéed vegetables, sweetcorn and coriander.

Pour the batter into a greased and floured 18 cm/7 in springform cake tin. Put the tin on a rack in a 5.5 litre/9½ pint slow cooker. Cover and cook on High until a cocktail stick inserted into the centre of the bread comes out clean, about 2 hours. Cool in the tin on a wire rack for 10 minutes. Serve warm.

Parmesan Bread

This melty cheese bread is a perfect accompaniment to soups and casseroles. Choose an oval or round loaf that will fit into your slow cooker.

SERVES 6–8

1 small ciabatta loaf
75 g/3 oz butter or margarine, at room temperature
25 g/1 oz freshly grated Parmesan cheese

Without cutting all the way through the base of the loaf, cut the bread into six to eight slices. Spread both sides of the bread slices with the combined butter or margarine and Parmesan cheese. Wrap the loaf securely in foil. Put in the slow cooker and cook on Low for 2 hours.

Note: the bread can also be baked at 180°C/gas 4/fan oven 160°C until warm, about 20 minutes.

Brunch Bread Pudding Ⓥ

This bread pudding is assembled in advance and refrigerated overnight before cooking. Make the pudding in a soufflé dish or cook it directly in the crock.

SERVES 6

275 g/10 oz stale French bread, cubed (1 cm/½ in)
75 g/3 oz dried apricots, chopped
50 g/2 oz flaked almonds
3 eggs
100 g/4 oz sugar
600 ml/1 pint milk
1 tsp vanilla essence
1 tsp ground cinnamon
warm maple syrup, to serve

Combine the bread cubes, apricots and almonds in a large bowl. Beat the eggs in a large bowl until thick and pale coloured, about 5 minutes. Beat in the sugar, milk, vanilla and cinnamon. Pour over the bread mixture and toss. Spoon into a 1.5 litre/2½ pint soufflé dish or casserole. Refrigerate, covered, overnight.
Put the soufflé dish on a rack in a 5.5 litre/9½ pint slow cooker. Cover and cook on High until the pudding is set, about 5 hours. Serve warm with maple syrup.

Sloppy Joes

A great sandwich for kids of all ages! Serve with lots of pickles and fresh vegetable relishes.

SERVES 6–8

450 g/1 lb lean minced beef
oil, for greasing
2 onions, chopped
1 green or red pepper, chopped
2 garlic cloves, crushed
250 ml/8 fl oz tomato ketchup
120 ml/4 fl oz water
50 g/2 oz light brown sugar
2 tbsp prepared mustard
2 tsp celery seeds
2 tsp chilli powder
salt and freshly ground black pepper, to taste
6–8 wholemeal burger buns, toasted
sliced cornichons or pickles, fresh relishes, to serve

Cook the minced beef in a lightly greased frying pan until browned, crumbling with a fork. Combine the minced beef and the remaining ingredients, except the salt, pepper and buns, in the slow cooker. Cover and cook on High for 2–3 hours. Season to taste with salt and pepper. Serve in buns with cornichons, pickles and relishes.

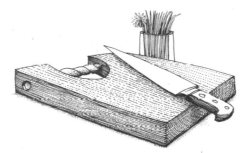

Vegetarian Joes ⓥ

A great meat-free alternative to Sloppy Joes but you don't have to be vegetarian to enjoy it!

SERVES 6–8

225 g/8 oz textured vegetable protein
100 g/4 oz mushrooms, sliced
oil, for greasing
2 onions, chopped
1 green or red pepper, chopped
2 garlic cloves, crushed
250 ml/8 fl oz tomato ketchup
375 ml/13 fl oz water
50 g/2 oz light brown sugar
2 tbsp prepared mustard
2 tsp celery seeds
2 tsp chilli powder
salt and freshly ground black pepper,
    to taste
6–8 wholemeal burger buns, toasted
sliced cornichons or pickles, fresh
    relishes, to serve

Cook the textured vegetable protein and mushrooms in a lightly greased frying pan until browned, crumbling with a fork. Combine with the remaining ingredients, except the salt, pepper and buns, in the slow cooker. Cover and cook on High for 2–3 hours. Season to taste with salt and pepper. Serve in buns with cornichons, pickles and relishes.

Cheeseburger Joes

Look out for mild American-style hot-dog mustard on supermarket shelves to use in this recipe.

SERVES 12

900 g/2 lb lean minced beef
2 small onions, chopped
1 small green pepper, chopped
225 g/8 oz mushrooms, sliced
3 large garlic cloves, crushed
100 g/4 oz bacon, cooked until crisp
    and crumbled

100 g/4 oz sweet pickle relish
120 ml/4 fl oz yellow mustard
175 ml/6 fl oz tomato ketchup
1 tbsp Worcestershire sauce
225 g/8 oz processed cheese, cubed
salt and freshly ground black pepper,
    to taste
12 burger buns, toasted

Cook the beef, onion and pepper over medium heat in a large frying pan until the beef is browned, crumbling it with a fork. Transfer to the slow cooker. Add the remaining ingredients, except the salt, pepper and buns. Cover and cook on Low for 2–3 hours. Season to taste with salt and pepper. Serve on buns.

Vino Joes

This grown-up version of the family favourite, Sloppy Joes, is flavoured with red wine, Worcestershire sauce and Dijon mustard.

SERVES 12

450 g/1 lb lean minced beef
2 small onions, chopped
1 small green pepper, chopped
2 garlic cloves, crushed
400 g/14 oz can chopped tomatoes,
    drained
120 ml/4 fl oz dry red wine
2 tbsp Worcestershire sauce
50 g/2 oz light brown sugar
2 tbsp Dijon mustard
2 tsp celery seeds
salt and freshly ground black pepper,
    to taste
12 ciabatta rolls, lightly toasted

Cook the beef, onions, pepper and garlic over medium heat in a large frying pan until the beef is browned, crumbling it with a fork. Transfer to the slow cooker. Add the remaining ingredients, except the salt, pepper and rolls. Cover and cook on High for 2–3 hours. Season to taste with salt and pepper. Serve in rolls.

Chicken Burger Buns

Chicken is cooked in a tangy sauce (which contains a surprise ingredient) until meltingly tender and then shredded before it is used to fill burger buns.

SERVES 8

450 g/1 lb skinless chicken breast fillets, quartered
350 ml/12 fl oz cola
250 ml/8 fl oz tomato ketchup
75 ml/2½ fl oz yellow mustard
50 g/2 oz light brown sugar
1 onion, chopped
1 garlic clove, crushed
2 tbsp cornflour
50 ml/2 fl oz water
salt and freshly ground black pepper, to taste
8 burger buns

Combine all the ingredients, except the cornflour, water, salt, pepper and buns, in the slow cooker. Cover and cook on Low for 6–8 hours. Turn the heat to High and cook for 10 minutes. Stir in the combined cornflour and water, stirring for 2–3 minutes. Stir to shred the chicken. Season to taste with salt and pepper. Serve in buns.

Punchy Pork Rolls

Sweet and tender pork is shredded and then added to a bun and topped with a garlicky White Barbecue Sauce.

SERVES 12

900 g/2 lb boneless pork loin
Brown Sugar Rub (see below)
120 ml/4 fl oz chicken stock
12 small rolls or scones
White Barbecue Sauce (see right)

Rub the pork loin with Brown Sugar Rub. Put in the slow cooker with the stock. Cover and cook on Low for 6–8 hours. Remove the pork and shred. Reserve

the cooking liquid for soup or another use. Spoon the meat on to the bottom halves of the rolls and top with White Barbecue Sauce and the roll tops.

Brown Sugar Rub Ⓥ

You could use ground cinnamon if you don't have cumin.

SERVES 12

50 g/2 oz light brown sugar
1 tsp garlic powder
½ tsp ground cumin
½ tsp salt
½ tsp pepper

Mix all the ingredients.

White Barbecue Sauce Ⓥ

The horseradish provides an exciting tartness but you can omit it if you're not a fan.

SERVES 12

375 ml/13 fl oz mayonnaise
50 ml/2 fl oz cider vinegar
1 tbsp sugar
1 garlic clove, crushed
2 tsp horseradish
1–2 tbsp lemon juice

Mix all the ingredients, adding the lemon juice to taste.

Curry Spice Rub Ⓥ

This rub will keep for weeks in an airtight jar.

1½ tsp curry powder
1½ tsp paprika
¾ tsp ground cinnamon
¾ tsp garlic powder
¾ tsp salt
½ tsp freshly grated nutmeg
½ tsp ground ginger

Combine all the ingredients.

Pork and Chutney Sandwiches

Rub a curry mix into pork before roasting, then serve sliced in granary bread with chutney. You can make your own Mango Chutney, if you like (see page 241).

SERVES 12

900 g/2 lb boneless pork loin
Curry Spice Rub (see below)
120 ml/4 fl oz chicken stock
48 slices granary, ciabatta or
  sourdough bread
500 g/18 oz mango chutney

Rub the pork loin with Curry Spice Rub. Insert a meat thermometer in the centre of the roast so that the tip is in the centre of the meat. Put the pork in the slow cooker and add the stock. Cover and cook on Low until the meat thermometer registers 71°C, about 3 hours. Remove the pork to a cutting board and leave to stand, loosely covered with foil, 10 minutes. Reserve the stock for soup or another use. Slice the pork and make sandwiches, spooning about 2 tbsp of chutney into each.

Beef and Provolone Sandwich

Tender beef cooked in wine, then sliced and served in a crusty roll with Provolone makes a fun change. Put the stock in a bowl for dipping.

SERVES 12

1.5 kg/3 lb braising steak, in a piece
freshly ground black pepper, to taste

450 ml/¾ pint beef stock
250 ml/8 fl oz dry red wine
1 packet onion soup mix
1 garlic clove, crushed
12 crusty rolls
175 g/6 oz sliced Provolone cheese

Sprinkle the steak lightly with pepper and put in the slow cooker. Add the remaining ingredients, except the rolls and cheese. Cover and cook on Low for 6–8 hours. Remove the steak and slice thinly. Serve the beef on crusty rolls with Provolone cheese slices. Offer the stock for dipping.

Mozzarella Steak Rolls

Sliced steak cooked with onions and peppers is served in a crusty roll with a cheese topping.

SERVES 6–8

450 g/1 lb rump steak, thinly sliced
2 onions, thinly sliced
1 green pepper, thinly sliced
250 ml/8 fl oz beef stock
1 garlic clove, crushed
1 tbsp Worcestershire sauce
salt and freshly ground black pepper,
  to taste
6–8 crusty rolls
175–225 g/6–8 oz Mozzarella cheese,
  grated

Combine all the ingredients, except the salt, pepper, rolls and cheese, in the slow cooker. Cover and cook on Low for 6–8 hours. Season to taste with salt and pepper. Top the rolls with the meat and vegetable mixture. Sprinkle with cheese. If you like, grill until the cheese has melted, 3–4 minutes.

Hot Focaccia with Salami and Ham

Piquant Olive Relish gives this meat and cheese sandwich plenty of flavour. Make sure the size of the loaf will fit into your slow cooker.

SERVES 6

Olive Relish (see below)
1 round focaccia or sourdough loaf (about 20 cm/8 in diameter), halved
100 g/4 oz thinly sliced Italian salami
100 g/4 oz smoked ham, sliced
100 g/4 oz Provolone or Fontina cheese, sliced

Spread half the Olive Relish on the bottom half of the bread. Top with salami, ham and cheese, the remaining Olive Relish and the top of the bread. Press the sandwich together firmly and wrap securely in foil. Line the base of the slow cooker with a large piece of foil. Put the sandwich in the slow cooker. Cover and cook on Low for 2 hours. Cut into wedges to serve.

Olive Relish

Omit the anchovy fillet if you want to make a vegetarian version.

SERVES 6

75 g/3 oz pitted black olives, chopped
75 g/3 oz pitted green olives, chopped
90 g/3½ oz tomatoes, chopped
15 g/½ oz fresh parsley, chopped
50 ml/2 fl oz olive oil
1 anchovy fillet, mashed (optional)
juice of ½ lemon
freshly ground black pepper, to taste

Mix all the ingredients, except the pepper. Season to taste with pepper.

Bratwurst Buns with Peppers and Onions

Cook the sausages in beer with peppers, onions and mushrooms, then serve in buns with the savoury vegetables heaped on top. The sausages can be briefly browned in a frying pan or under the grill before serving, if you like.

SERVES 6–8

6–8 fresh bratwurst sausages, about 700 g/1½ lb
2–3 x 350 ml/12 fl oz bottles beer
2 onions, chopped
1 red pepper, sliced
1 green pepper, sliced
225 g/8 oz small chestnut mushrooms, sliced
2 garlic cloves, crushed
salt and freshly ground black pepper, to taste
6–8 hot dog buns or soft rolls

Combine all the ingredients, except the salt, pepper and buns, in the slow cooker. Cover and cook on Low for 6–8 hours. Season with salt and pepper. Serve the sausages in buns with the vegetable mixture spooned over.

Polish Sausage and Sauerkraut Rolls

A lovely mixture with typical Polish flavourings.

SERVES 4–6

4–6 lean Polish sausages, about 450 g/1 lb
225–350 g/8–12 oz sauerkraut, drained and rinsed
1 onion, thinly sliced
1 small tart eating apple, peeled and thinly sliced
1 tsp fennel seeds
1 tsp caraway seeds
120 ml/4 fl oz chicken stock
freshly ground black pepper, to taste
4–6 hot dog buns or rolls
wholegrain mustard

Put the sausages in the slow cooker. Top with the combined remaining ingredients, except the pepper, buns and mustard. Cover and cook on Low for 6–8 hours. Season to taste with pepper. Serve the sausages and sauerkraut in the buns with mustard.

Italian Beef Rolls

Simple to throw together and tastily cooked to savoury goodness.

SERVES 12

1 boneless beef joint such as rump, about 1.5 kg/3 lb
750 ml/1¼ pints beef stock
4 tbsp dried Italian herb seasoning
1 bay leaf
1 tsp freshly ground black pepper
12 buns or ciabatta rolls

Combine all the ingredients, except the buns, in the slow cooker. Cover and cook on Low for 10–12 hours. Remove the meat and shred. Return to the slow cooker. Serve the meat and juices in the buns or rolls.

Aubergine Meatballs with Harlequin Sauce

Granary rolls are filled with Italian-style beef and aubergine meatballs cooked with peppers in a pasta sauce.

SERVES 6

Aubergine Meatballs (see page 215)
2 red peppers, sliced
2 green peppers, sliced
450 g/1 lb ready-made pasta sauce, hot
6 large granary or white rolls, lightly toasted on the cut side

Make the Aubergine Meatballs, shaping into 24. Combine the Aubergine Meatballs, peppers and pasta sauce in the slow cooker, covering the meatballs with sauce. Cover and cook on Low for 6–8 hours. Serve in the rolls.

Turkey Pitta Breads

Fill pittas with this zesty mix of turkey with olives, mushrooms and tomatoes.

SERVES 8–12

450 g/1 lb boneless, skinless turkey breast or thighs, cubed (5 cm/2 in)
400 g/14 oz can chopped tomatoes
175 g/6 oz ready-made tomato sauce
225 g/8 oz mushrooms, sliced
1 onion, chopped
75 g/3 oz pitted green olives, sliced
1 mild chilli, seeded and sliced
1 tbsp prepared mustard
1 tsp dried oregano
salt and freshly ground black pepper, to taste
4–8 large pitta breads, halved

Combine all the ingredients, except the salt, pepper and pitta breads, in the slow cooker. Cover and cook on Low for 6–8 hours. Season to taste with salt and pepper. Stir to shred the turkey. Serve in pitta halves.

Greek Pitta Breads

A minted cucumber and yoghurt sauce plus crumbled Feta cheese makes a perfect topping for herby lamb meatballs. Minced beef, instead of lamb, for the meatballs would also work well.

SERVES 4

450 g/1 lb lean minced lamb
40 g/1½ oz fresh breadcrumbs
1 egg
½ onion, finely chopped
1 tsp dried oregano
1 tsp dried mint
¾ tsp salt
½ tsp pepper
175 ml/6 fl oz chicken stock
2 pitta breads, halved
Cucumber and Yogurt Sauce (see below)
50 g/2 oz Feta cheese, crumbled

Combine the lamb, breadcrumbs, egg, onion, oregano, mint, salt and pepper. Shape into 16 meatballs. Put in the slow cooker with the stock. Cover and cook on Low for 4 hours. Drain and discard the juices, or save for another use. Spoon four meatballs into each pitta half. Top the meatballs in each pitta with 2 tbsp Cucumber and Yogurt sauce and a quarter of the Feta cheese.

Cucumber and Yogurt Sauce Ⓥ

A refreshing sauce that goes well with many Greek and Indian dishes.

SERVES 4

50 ml/2 fl oz yoghurt
50 g/2 oz cucumber, seeded and finely chopped
1 tsp dried mint

Mix all the ingredients.

Moo Shu Wraps

Enjoy the traditional flavours of Chinese spiced pork in a tortilla wrap.

SERVES 6

450 g/1 lb pork tenderloin
2 tsp Chinese five-spice powder
2 garlic cloves, crushed
120 ml/4 fl oz plum sauce
50 ml/2 fl oz water
1 tbsp soy sauce
2 cm/¾ in piece fresh root ginger, finely grated
40 g/1½ oz bamboo shoots, cut into thin strips
salt and freshly ground black pepper, to taste
6 x 15 cm/6 in flour tortillas, warmed
120–175 ml/4–6 fl oz hoisin sauce
6 small spring onions

Rub the pork with the Chinese five-spice powder and garlic. Leave to stand for 30 minutes. Put the pork in the slow cooker. Add the combined plum sauce, water, soy sauce and ginger. Cover and cook on Low until the pork is very tender, about 3 hours. Remove the pork and shred with two forks. Return to the slow cooker. Add the bamboo shoots. Cover and cook on Low for 30 minutes. Season to taste with salt and pepper. Spread each tortilla with 1 tbsp hoisin sauce and lay a spring onion in the centre. Divide the pork mixture between the tortillas and roll up.

Picadillo Tortillas

The tenderest cut of pork is cooked with spices and flavourings, then mixed with raisins and almonds to make a superb filling for tortillas, topped with avocado and tomato. They make ideal party food.

SERVES 6

350 g/12 oz pork tenderloin
50 ml/2 fl oz water
2 spring onions, thinly sliced
1 garlic clove, crushed,
1 tsp finely chopped jalapeño or other
**   medium-hot chilli, finely chopped**
1 tsp ground cinnamon
¼ tsp dried oregano
1–2 tsp cider vinegar
40 g/1½ oz raisins
25 g/1 oz flaked almonds
salt and freshly ground black pepper,
**   to taste**
6 x 15 cm/6 in flour tortillas, warmed
150 g/5 oz tomato, chopped
1 avocado, chopped
fresh coriander sprigs, to garnish
salsa, to serve

Combine the pork, water, spring onions, garlic, chilli, cinnamon, oregano and vinegar in the slow cooker. Cover and cook on Low for 3 hours. Remove the pork and shred with 2 forks. Return to the slow cooker. Add the raisins and almonds. Cover and cook on Low for 1 hour. Season to taste with salt and pepper. Divide the pork mixture between the tortillas. Sprinkle with 1 tbsp each of tomato and avocado, and several sprigs of coriander. Roll up and serve with salsa.

Melts

Serve melty warm rolls from the slow cooker for delicious party fare. Make a medley from the recipes below and label them for guests to choose from. A 2.75 litre/4¾ pint slow cooker will easily hold 10–12 of these small rolls; a 5.5 litre/9½ pint slow cooker will hold many more!

Ham, Cheese and Pesto Melts

SERVES 4

2–4 tbsp pesto
4 small soft or crusty rolls, halved
100 g/4 oz thinly sliced ham
50 g/2 oz thinly sliced Provolone
**   cheese**

Spread the pesto on the bottom halves of the rolls. Top with ham, cheese and the roll tops. Wrap each roll in foil. Put in the slow cooker. Cover and cook on Low for 2 hours. Serve warm.

Turkey Cranberry Melts

SERVES 4

**50 g/2 oz soft cheese, at room
  temperature
1 tbsp chopped pecan nuts or walnuts
4 small rolls, halved
100 g/4 oz thinly sliced turkey
4 tbsp cranberry sauce**

Spread the combined soft cheese and
nuts on the bottom halves of the rolls.
Top with the turkey, cranberry sauce and
roll tops. Wrap each roll in foil. Put in the
slow cooker. Cover and cook on Low for
2 hours. Serve warm.

Goats' Cheese and Salami Melts

SERVES 4

**50 g/2 oz goats' cheese, at room
  temperature
50 g/2 oz soft cheese, at room
  temperature
4 small buns or crusty rolls
2–4 tbsp sun-dried tomato pesto
2–75 g/3 oz thinly sliced salami**

Spread the combined goats' and soft
cheese on the bottom halves of the buns.
Top with the pesto, salami and bun tops.
Wrap each bun in foil. Put in the slow
cooker. Cover and cook on Low for 2
hours. Serve warm.

Reuben Melts

SERVES 4

**2–4 tbsp thousand island salad
  dressing
4 small rye rolls, halved
100 g/4 oz thinly sliced deli-cooked
  salt beef
4–6 tbsp well-drained sauerkraut
50 g/2 oz thinly sliced Emmental or
  Gruyère cheese**

Spread the salad dressing on the bottom
halves of the rolls. Top with the beef,
sauerkraut, cheese and roll tops. Wrap
each roll in foil. Put in the slow cooker.
Cover and cook on Low for 2 hours. Serve
warm.

Cucumber Cheese Melts Ⓥ

SERVES 4

**50 g/2 oz soft cheese, at room
  temperature
1 tbsp crumbled blue cheese
4 small multigrain rolls, halved
8 thin cucumber slices
2 tbsp apricot jam**

Spread the combined soft cheese and
blue cheese on the bottom halves of the
rolls. Top with the cucumber slices, jam
and roll tops. Wrap each roll in foil. Put in
the slow cooker. Cover and cook on Low
for 2 hours. Serve warm.

Blue Cheese and Pear Melts Ⓥ

SERVES 4

**50 g/2 oz Cheshire cheese, thinly
  sliced
4 small soft white or wholemeal rolls
75 g/3 oz orange marmalade
½ small pear, thinly sliced
2 tbsp crumbled blue cheese**

Put the Cheshire cheese on the bottom
halves of the rolls. Top with the
marmalade, pear, blue cheese and roll
tops. Wrap each sandwich in foil. Put in
the slow cooker. Cover and cook on Low
for 2 hours. Serve warm.

Desserts and Cakes

The slow cooker is surprisingly good at creating delicious desserts and cakes, so here are some mouth-watering recipes to get you interested. Because they cook more evenly in a cake tin inside the crock pot, you will need a larger slow cooker for many of these recipes.

Cream Cheese Frosting (V)

Spread this frosting on the cake and, if you like, decorate the top with walnut halves.

MAKES 300 G/11 OZ

50 g/2 oz soft cheese, at room temperature
1 tbsp butter or margarine, at room temperature
½ tsp vanilla essence
250 g/9 oz icing sugar
milk

Beat the cheese, butter or margarine and vanilla essence in a medium bowl until smooth. Beat in the icing sugar and enough milk to make thick topping consistency.

Chocolate Frosting (V)

Ideal for filling and topping sponge cakes.

MAKES 150 G/5 OZ

130 g/4½ oz icing sugar
2 tbsp cocoa powder
½ tsp vanilla essence
milk

Mix the icing sugar, cocoa, vanilla essence and enough milk to make a topping consistency.

Sweet Topping (V)

The butter or margarine needs to be cold, not at room temperature.

MAKES ENOUGH TO FILL ONE CAKE

20 g/¾ oz cold butter or margarine
2 tbsp flour
2 tbsp sugar

Cut the butter or margarine into the combined flour and sugar until crumbly.

Lemony Carrot Cake with Cream Cheese Frosting (V)

A carrot cake with raisins and walnuts and the zing of lemon.

SERVES 12

175 g/6 oz butter or margarine, at room temperature
175 g/6 oz light brown sugar
3 eggs
2 carrots, grated
50 g/2 oz raisins
40 g/1½ oz walnuts, coarsely chopped
grated zest of 1 lemon
175 g/6 oz self-raising flour, plus extra for dusting
1 tsp baking powder
¼ tsp salt
oil, for greasing
Cream Cheese Frosting (see left)

Beat the butter or margarine and sugar in a large bowl until fluffy. Beat in the eggs a little at a time, beating well. Mix in the carrots, raisins, walnuts and lemon zest. Fold in the combined flour, baking powder and salt. Pour into a greased and floured 18 cm/7 in springform cake tin. Put on a rack in a 5.5 litre/9½ pint slow cooker. Cover and cook on High until a cocktail stick inserted into the centre of the cake comes out clean, about 3½ hours. Cool in the tin on a wire rack for 10 minutes. Remove from the tin and allow to cool completely. Spread with Cream Cheese Frosting.

Pumpkin Ginger Cake Rounds with Warm Rum Sauce Ⓥ

Large cans make handy cake tins for baking in the slow cooker. Serve these spiced cakes for dessert, sliced into rounds and accompanied with a warm rum sauce.

MAKES 2 CAKES, EACH SERVES 4–6

100 g/4 oz pumpkin, cooked and mashed
100 g/4 oz light brown sugar
50 g/2 oz butter or margarine, at room temperature
75 g/3 oz golden syrup
1 egg
175 g/6 oz plain flour, plus extra for dusting
½ tsp baking powder
½ tsp bicarbonate of soda
½ tsp ground allspice
½ tsp ground cloves
½ tsp ground ginger
oil, for greasing
Warm Rum Sauce (see right)

Combine the pumpkin, sugar, butter or margarine, syrup and egg in a large mixer bowl. Beat vigorously until well blended. Mix in the combined flour, baking powder, bicarbonate of soda, allspice, cloves and ginger, blending gently until moistened.

Pour the batter into a two greased and floured 450 g/1 lb tins. Stand the tins in the slow cooker. Cover and cook on High until a wooden skewer inserted into the cakes comes out clean, about 2½ hours. Stand the tins on a wire rack to cool for 10 minutes. Loosen the sides of the cakes by gently rolling the tins on the worktop, or remove the bottom ends of the tins and push the cakes through. Slice and serve with Warm Rum Sauce.

Warm Rum Sauce Ⓥ

This goes well with any spicy or fruity cake.

SERVES 8–12

50 g/2 oz caster sugar
1 tbsp cornflour
300 ml/½ pint semi-skimmed milk
2 tbsp rum or ½ tsp rum essence
25 g/1 oz butter or margarine
½ tsp vanilla essence
a pinch of freshly grated nutmeg

Mix the sugar and cornflour in a small pan. Whisk in the milk and rum or rum essence. Whisk over medium heat until the mixture boils and thickens, 1–2 minutes. Remove from the heat. Stir in the butter or margarine, vanilla essence and nutmeg. Serve warm.

Vanilla Frosting Ⓥ

If you want to boost the vanilla flavour, add a teaspoonful of vanilla sugar

MAKES 200 G/7 OZ

175 g/6 oz icing sugar
1 tsp vanilla essence
6–8 tsp milk

Mix the icing sugar and vanilla essence, adding enough milk to make a thick topping consistency.

Buttercream Frosting Ⓥ

A good topping and filling for sponge cakes.

MAKES 450 G/1 LB

425 g/15 oz icing sugar
1 tbsp butter or margarine, at room temperature
½ tsp vanilla essence
1–2 tbsp milk

Mix the icing sugar, butter or margarine, vanilla essence and enough milk to make a spreading consistency.

Apple Cake with Vanilla Frosting Ⓥ

Porridge oats add to the homely goodness of this dessert. Serve warm with ice-cream or frozen yoghurt.

SERVES 12

100 g/4 oz butter or margarine, at room temperature
175 g/6 oz light brown sugar
1 egg
175 ml/6 fl oz ready-made apple sauce
1 tsp vanilla essence
100 g/4 oz plain flour, plus extra for dusting
50 g/2 oz wholemeal flour
50 g/2 oz porridge oats
2 tsp baking powder
½ tsp salt
½ tsp ground cinnamon
¼ tsp bicarbonate of soda
¼ tsp ground cloves
oil, for greasing
Vanilla Frosting (see below)

Beat the butter or margarine and sugar in a large bowl until blended. Beat in the egg, apple sauce and vanilla essence. Mix in the combined remaining ingredients, except the Vanilla Frosting, stirring until well blended.

Pour the batter into a greased and floured 1.5 litre/2½ pint fluted cake tin. Put the tin on a rack in a 5.5 litre/9½ pint slow cooker. Cover and cook on High until a cocktail stick inserted into the centre of the cake comes out clean, 2½–3 hours. Cool in the tin on a wire rack for 10 minutes. Invert on to the rack and allow to cool completely. Spread with Vanilla Frosting.

Red Velvet Cake

Also known as Waldorf Astoria Cake, this colourful red dessert is reputed to trace its origins to the famed New York hotel. Bizarre though it seems, it really does contain a whole bottle of food colouring.

SERVES 8

175 g/6 oz caster sugar
3 tbsp white vegetable fat
1 egg
1 tsp vanilla essence
25 g/1 oz red food colouring
100 g/4 oz cocoa powder
130 g/4½ oz plain flour, plus extra for dusting
1 tsp bicarbonate of soda
½ tsp salt
120 ml/4 fl oz buttermilk
1½ tsp white distilled vinegar
oil, for greasing
Buttercream Frosting (see page 375)

Beat the sugar and fat in a large bowl until well blended. Add the egg and vanilla essence, blending well. Beat in the food colouring and cocoa until well blended. Mix in the combined flour, bicarbonate of soda and salt alternately with the combined buttermilk and vinegar, beginning and ending with the dry ingredients.

Pour the batter into a greased and floured 1 litre/1¾ pint soufflé dish. Put on a rack in a 5.5 litre/9½ pint slow cooker. Cover and cook on High until a cocktail stick inserted into the centre of the cake comes out clean, 2–2¾ hours. Remove to a wire rack and cool in the tin for 10 minutes. Invert on to the rack and allow to cool completely. Spread with Buttercream Frosting.

Chocolate Chip Peanut Butter Cake Ⓥ

Chocolate and peanut butter – a comfort food combination that can't be beaten. Serve as a dessert with chocolate sauce, if you like.

SERVES 8

65 g/2½ oz butter or margarine, at room temperature
65 g/2½ oz caster sugar
65 g/2½ oz light brown sugar
2 eggs
100 g/4 oz crunchy peanut butter
120 ml/4 fl oz soured cream
190 g/6½ oz self raising flour, plus extra for dusting
¼ tsp salt
50 g/2 oz plain chocolate chips
oil, for greasing
chocolate sauce (optional)

Beat the butter or margarine and sugars in a bowl until fluffy. Beat in the eggs, blending well. Mix in the peanut butter and soured cream. Mix in the flour, salt and chocolate chips.

Pour the batter into a greased and floured 1.5 litre/2½ pint fluted cake tin. Put on a rack in a 5.5 litre/9½ pint slow cooker. Cover and cook on High until a cocktail stick inserted into the centre of the cake comes out clean, 2–2½ hours. Cool in the tin on a wire rack for 10 minutes. Invert on to the rack and allow to cool completely. Serve with chocolate sauce.

Chocolate Sauerkraut Cake Ⓥ

Vegetables are often added to cakes to make them beautifully moist. In this cake there are two unusual ingredients for a delicious cake: sauerkraut and beer.

SERVES 8

175 g/6 oz caster sugar
50 g/2 oz white vegetable fat
1 egg
1 tsp vanilla essence
25 g/1 oz cocoa powder
130 g/4½ oz plain flour, plus extra for dusting
½ tsp baking powder
½ tsp bicarbonate of soda
¼ tsp salt
120 ml/4 fl oz beer
40 g/1½ oz sauerkraut, rinsed, well-drained and finely chopped
oil, for greasing
Chocolate Frosting (see page 374)

Beat the sugar and fat in a large bowl until blended. Beat in the egg, vanilla essence and cocoa. Mix in the combined flour, baking powder, bicarbonate of soda and salt alternately with the beer, beginning and ending with the dry ingredients. Mix in the sauerkraut.

Pour the batter into a greased and floured 1.5 litre/2½ pint fluted cake tin. Put on a rack in a 5.5 litre/9½ pint slow cooker. Cover and cook on High until a cocktail stick inserted into the centre of the cake comes out clean, 2½–3 hours. Cool in the tin on a wire rack for 10 minutes. Invert on to the rack and allow to cool completely. Spread the Chocolate Frosting over.

Date and Nut Ginger Slices Ⓥ

For a really delicious treat, spread the cake slices with softened cheese and apricot preserve.

MAKES 2 CAKES, EACH SERVES 4–6

100 g/4 oz pumpkin, cooked and mashed
100 g/4 oz light brown sugar
50 g/2 oz butter or margarine, at room temperature
75 g/3 oz golden syrup
1 egg
175 g/6 oz plain flour, plus extra for dusting
½ tsp baking powder
½ tsp bicarbonate of soda
½ tsp ground allspice
½ tsp ground cloves
½ tsp ground ginger
40 g/1½ oz dates, chopped
25 g/1 oz walnuts, chopped
oil, for greasing

Combine the pumpkin, sugar, butter or margarine, syrup and egg in a large mixer bowl. Beat vigorously until well blended. Mix in the combined flour, baking powder, bicarbonate of soda, allspice, cloves and ginger, blending gently until moistened. Stir in the dates and walnuts.

Pour the batter into a two greased and floured 450 g/1 lb tins. Stand the tins in the slow cooker. Cover and cook on High until a wooden skewer inserted into the cakes comes out clean, about 2½ hours. Stand the tins on a wire rack to cool for 10 minutes. Loosen the sides of the cakes by gently rolling the tins on the worktop, or remove the bottom ends of the tins and push the cakes through. Slice and serve.

Gingerbread Cake Ⓥ

Enjoy this moist and perfectly spiced cake with its cream cheese topping.

SERVES 12

175 g/6 oz self-raising flour
50 g/2 oz plain flour
1 tsp ground cinnamon
½ tsp ground ginger
¼ tsp ground allspice
¼ tsp salt
100 g/4 oz butter or margarine, at room temperature
225 g/8 oz golden syrup
175 g/6 oz light brown sugar
1 egg, lightly beaten
120 ml/4 fl oz semi-skimmed milk
½ tsp bicarbonate of soda
oil, for greasing
Cream Cheese Frosting (see page 375)

Combine the flours, spices and salt in a large bowl. Combine the butter or margarine, syrup and sugar in a 1 litre/1¾ pint glass measuring jug. Microwave on High until the butter or margarine is melted, about 2 minutes, stirring to blend. Whisk the butter mixture into the flour mixture, blending well. Whisk in the egg. Whisk in the combined milk and bicarbonate of soda until blended.

Pour the batter into a greased and floured 18 cm/7 in springform cake tin. Put on a rack in the slow cooker. Cover and cook on High until a cocktail stick inserted into the centre of the cake comes out clean, about 5 hours. Cool in the tin on a wire rack for 10 minutes. Remove the side of the tin and allow to cool completely. Spread with Cream Cheese Frosting.

Chocolate Courgette Cake (V)

Chocolate cakes can be disappointingly dry in texture, but not when one of the ingredients is courgettes. Top this moist and spicy cake with Chocolate Frosting (see page 374), if you like.

SERVES 8

50 g/2 oz butter or margarine, at room temperature
50 ml/2 fl oz ready-made apple sauce
175 g/6 oz caster sugar
1 egg
50 ml/2 fl oz buttermilk
1 tsp vanilla essence
150 g/5 oz plain flour, plus extra for dusting
2 tbsp cocoa powder
½ tsp bicarbonate of soda
½ tsp baking powder
¼ tsp salt
¼ tsp ground cinnamon
¼ tsp ground cloves
175 g/6 oz courgettes, finely chopped or grated
25 g/1 oz plain chocolate chips
oil, for greasing
icing sugar, to decorate

Beat the butter or margarine, apple sauce and sugar in a large bowl until smooth. Mix in the egg, buttermilk and vanilla essence. Mix in the combined flour, cocoa, bicarbonate of soda, baking powder, salt and spices. Mix in the courgettes and chocolate chips.

Pour the batter into a greased and floured 1.5 litre/2½ pint fluted cake tin. Put the tin on a rack in a 5.5 litre/9½ pint slow cooker. Cover and cook on High until a cocktail stick inserted into the centre of the cake comes out clean, 3–4 hours. Cool in the tin on a wire rack for 10 minutes. Invert the cake on to the rack and allow to cool completely. Sprinkle generously with icing sugar.

Chocolate and Coffee Cake (V)

The flavours of coffee and chocolate were made in heaven! This cake can also be baked in a greased 2.75 litre/4¾ pint slow cooker. Cooking time will be about 2½ hours. Using foil handles (see page 10) will make this cake easier to remove from the slow cooker.

SERVES 12

6 tbsp butter or margarine, at room temperature
275 g/10 oz caster sugar
2 eggs
100 g/4 oz plain flour, plus extra for dusting
40 g/1½ oz cocoa powder
½ tsp bicarbonate of soda
¼ tsp baking powder
¼ tsp salt
1–2 tbsp instant or espresso coffee
1–2 tbsp boiling water
75 ml/2½ fl oz soured cream
oil, for greasing
Coffee Frosting (see page 381)

Beat the butter or margarine and sugar in a bowl until fluffy. Beat in the eggs a little at a time, beating well after each addition. Mix in the combined dry ingredients alternately with the combined coffee, boiling water and soured cream, beginning and ending with the dry ingredients. Pour the batter into a greased and floured 1.5 litre/2½ pint fluted cake tin. Put the tin on a rack in a 5.5 litre/9½ pint slow cooker. Cover and cook on High until a cocktail stick inserted into the centre of the cake comes out clean, 4–4½ hours. Cool in the tin on a wire rack for 10 minutes. Invert the cake on to the rack and allow to cool completely. Spread the cake with Coffee Frosting.

Soured-cream Cake with Cranberry Filling ⓥ

This lovely moist cake has a fruity filling made using dried cranberries.

SERVES 8

40 g/1½ oz butter or margarine, at room temperature
2 tbsp ready-made unsweetened apple sauce
65 g/2½ oz caster sugar
50 g/2 oz light brown sugar
1 egg
1 tsp vanilla essence
130 g/4½ oz plain flour
¾ tsp baking powder
¾ tsp bicarbonate of soda
½ tsp ground cinnamon
¼ tsp salt
120 ml/4 fl oz soured cream
oil, for greasing
Cranberry Filling (see page 381)
icing sugar, to decorate

Beat the butter or margarine, apple sauce and sugars until smooth. Beat in the egg and vanilla essence. Mix in the combined flour, baking powder, bicarbonate of soda, cinnamon and salt alternately with the soured cream, beginning and ending with the dry ingredients.

Spoon one-third of the batter into a greased and floured 1.5 litre/2½ pint fluted cake tin. Spoon half the Cranberry Filling over the batter. Repeat the layers, ending with the batter. Put the tin on a rack in a 5.5 litre/9½ pint slow cooker. Cover and cook on High until a cocktail stick inserted into the centre of the cake comes out clean, about 3 hours. Cool the cake on a wire rack for 10 minutes. Invert on to a serving plate. Sprinkle generously with icing sugar and serve warm.

Almond Cake ⓥ

The Sweet Topping disappears into the cake during cooking, creating a rich texture. Serve this delicious cake for brunch, or enjoy with coffee or afternoon tea.

SERVES 8

100 g/4 oz plain flour
100 g/4 oz caster sugar
1½ tsp baking powder
½ tsp salt
4 tbsp butter or margarine, at room temperature
120 ml/4 fl oz semi-skimmed milk
1 egg
½ tsp almond essence
oil, for greasing
Sweet Topping (see page 374)
50 g/2 oz icing sugar
1–2 tsp semi-skimmed milk
3 tbsp flaked almonds, toasted

Beat all the ingredients, except the Sweet Topping, icing sugar, 1–2 tsp milk and the almonds, in a bowl until blended. Beat on medium speed for 2 minutes. Pour the batter into a greased 18 cm/7 in springform cake tin. Sprinkle with Sweet Topping. Put the tin on a rack in a 5.5 litre/9½ pint slow cooker. Cover, placing three layers of kitchen paper under the lid, and cook on High until a cocktail stick inserted into the centre comes out clean, 3–3½ hours. Cool on a wire rack. Remove the side of the tin and put the cake on a serving plate.

Mix the icing sugar with the rest of the milk to make a thin glaze consistency. Drizzle the glaze over the top of the cake. Sprinkle with the almonds.

Coffee Frosting (V)

If you make this to a fairly thick consistency, you can spread the top of the cake with icing, then pipe any remaining into shells around the edge of the cake.

MAKES 150 G/5 OZ

130 g/4½ oz icing sugar
1 tbsp butter or margarine, melted
2–3 tbsp strong brewed coffee

Mix the icing sugar, butter or margarine and enough coffee to make a topping consistency.

Flourless Mocha Mousse Cake (V)

This sinfully rich cake has a light mousse-like texture. Cut with a sharp knife, wetting the knife between every slice.

SERVES 8

50 g/2 oz cocoa powder
175 g/6 oz light brown sugar
3 tbsp flour
2 tsp instant espresso coffee powder
a pinch of salt
175 ml/6 fl oz semi-skimmed milk
1 tsp vanilla essence
100 g/4 oz plain chocolate, coarsely chopped
1 egg
3 egg whites
a pinch of cream of tartar
65 g/2½ oz caster sugar
oil, for greasing
cocoa powder or icing sugar, to decorate

Combine the cocoa powder, brown sugar, flour, coffee powder and salt in a medium pan. Gradually whisk in the milk and vanilla essence to make a smooth mixture. Whisk over medium heat until the mixture is hot and the sugar has dissolved (do not boil). Remove the pan from the heat. Add the chocolate, whisking until melted. Whisk about 50 ml/2 fl oz of the chocolate mixture into the egg. Whisk the egg mixture back into the pan. Cool to room temperature.

Whisk the egg whites and cream of tartar to soft peaks. Whisk to stiff peaks, gradually adding the caster sugar. Stir about one-quarter of the egg whites into the cooled chocolate mixture. Fold the chocolate mixture into the remaining egg whites.

Pour the batter into a lightly greased 18 cm/7 in springform cake tin. Put on a rack in a 5.5 litre/9½ pint slow cooker. Cover, putting three layers of kitchen paper under the lid, and cook on High until a cocktail stick inserted 1 cm/½ in from the edge of the cake comes out clean (the cake will look moist and will be soft in the centre), 2¼–3¼ hours. Remove the tin to a wire rack and cool completely. Refrigerate, loosely covered, for 8 hours or overnight. Remove the side of the tin and put the cake on a serving plate. Sprinkle the top of the cake generously with cocoa powder or icing sugar.

Cranberry Filling (V)

If you have any dried cranberries left in the packet, they are very good and healthy for snacking!

MAKES ENOUGH TO FILL ONE CAKE

175 g/6 oz dried cranberries
175 ml/6 fl oz water
2 tbsp sugar
1 tbsp flour
a pinch of salt

Combine all the ingredients in a small pan and heat to boiling. Reduce the heat and simmer, uncovered, until the mixture is thick, 5–8 minutes. Cool.

Marble Pound Cake Ⓥ

This delicious cake can also be dusted with icing sugar instead of frosting.

SERVES 8

175 ml/6 fl oz buttermilk
1 tsp vanilla essence
½ tsp bicarbonate of soda
75 g/3 oz butter or margarine,
    at room temperature
225 g/8 oz caster sugar
1 egg
175 g/6 oz plain flour, plus extra
    for dusting
2 tbsp cornflour
a pinch of salt
40 g/1½ oz plain chocolate, melted
    in a heatproof bowl over a pan of
    gently simmering water
oil, for greasing
Chocolate Frosting (see page 374)

Mix the buttermilk, vanilla essence and bicarbonate of soda in a bowl. Leave to stand for 2–3 minutes. Beat the butter or margarine and sugar in a large bowl until fluffy. Beat in the egg, blending well. Mix in the combined flour, cornflour and salt alternately with the buttermilk mixture, beginning and ending with the flour mixture. Reserve 375 ml/13 fl oz of the batter. Stir the melted chocolate into the remaining batter.

Spoon the batters alternately into a greased and floured 23 x 13 cm/9 x 5 in loaf tin. Swirl gently with a knife. Put the tin on a rack in a 5.5 litre/9½ pint slow cooker. Cover, putting three layers of kitchen paper under the lid, and cook on High until a cocktail stick inserted into the centre of the cake comes out clean, 4–4½ hours. Remove the tin from the slow cooker and cool on a wire rack for 10 minutes. Invert the cake on to the rack and allow to cool completely. Spread with Chocolate Frosting.

Orange Pound Cake Ⓥ

This moist cake needs no filling or topping as the orange syrup seeps into it.

SERVES 8

175 ml/6 fl oz buttermilk
1 tsp orange essence
½ tsp bicarbonate of soda
75 g/3 oz butter or margarine, at
    room temperature
225 g/8 oz caster sugar
1 egg
175 g/6 oz plain flour, plus extra
    for dusting
2 tbsp cornflour
a pinch of salt
oil, for greasing
Orange Syrup (see below)

Mix the buttermilk, orange essence and bicarbonate of soda and leave to stand for 2–3 minutes. Beat the butter or margarine and sugar until fluffy. Beat in the egg. Mix in the combined flour, cornflour and salt alternately with the buttermilk mixture, beginning and ending with flour. Spoon into a greased and floured 23 x 13 cm/9 x 5 in loaf tin. Put the tin on a rack in a 5.5 litre/9½ pint slow cooker. Cover, putting three layers of kitchen paper under the lid, and cook on High until a cocktail stick inserted into the centre comes out clean, 4–4½ hours. Remove and cool on a wire rack for 10 minutes. Pierce the top of the warm cake every 2.5 cm/1 in with a long-tined fork. Spoon over Orange Syrup.

Orange Syrup Ⓥ

Make this syrup quite runny so it soaks right through the cake.

MAKES 150 G/5 OZ

130 g/4½ oz icing sugar
120 ml/4 fl oz orange juice

Heat the icing sugar and orange juice to boiling in a small pan, stirring until the sugar is dissolved. Cool slightly.

Hot Fudge Pudding Cake (V)

Part cake, part pudding – the ultimate treat! Use a springform cake tin that has a tight seal to prevent the batter from leaking. A 1 litre/1¾ pint soufflé dish that measures 18 cm/7 in in diameter can also be used. Serve the warm pudding cake with a scoop of vanilla or chocolate ice-cream and light aerosol cream or whipped cream.

SERVES 6

100 g/4 oz plain flour
100 g/4 oz light brown sugar
6 tbsp cocoa powder
1½ tsp baking powder
¼ tsp salt
120 ml/4 fl oz semi-skimmed milk
2 tbsp vegetable oil
1 tsp vanilla essence
oil, for greasing
65 g/2½ oz granulated sugar
375 ml/13 fl oz boiling water

Wrap the base of a springform cake tin in foil. Combine the flour, brown sugar, half the cocoa powder, the baking powder and salt in a medium bowl. Whisk the combined milk, oil and vanilla essence into the flour mixture, mixing well.

Spoon the batter into a greased 18 cm/ 7 in springform cake tin. Mix together the remaining cocoa powder and the granulated sugar. Sprinkle over the cake batter. Slowly pour the boiling water over the back of a large spoon or spatula over the batter. Do not stir. Put the tin on a rack in 1.5 litre/2½ pint slow cooker. Cover and cook on High until the cake springs back when touched, about 2 hours. Cool the tin on a wire rack for 10 minutes. Remove the side of the tin and serve the cake warm.

Mocha Latte Pudding Cake (V)

Try serving this warm pudding cake with a scoop of vanilla or chocolate ice-cream or whipped cream – or even both!

SERVES 6

100 g/4 oz plain flour
100 g/4 oz caster sugar
6 tbsp cocoa powder
1 tbsp instant espresso powder
½ tsp ground cinnamon
1½ tsp baking powder
¼ tsp salt
120 ml/4 fl oz semi-skimmed milk
2 tbsp vegetable oil
1 tsp vanilla essence
oil, for greasing
65 g/2½ oz granulated sugar
375 ml/13 fl oz boiling water

Wrap the base of a springform cake tin in foil. Combine the flour, caster sugar, half the cocoa powder, the espresso powder, cinnamon, baking powder and salt in a medium bowl. Whisk the combined milk, oil and vanilla essence into the flour mixture, mixing well.

Spoon the batter into a greased 18 cm/ 7 in springform cake tin. Mix together the remaining cocoa powder and the granulated sugar. Sprinkle over the cake batter. Slowly pour the boiling water over the back of a large spoon or spatula over the batter. Do not stir. Put the tin on a rack in 1.5 litre/2½ pint slow cooker. Cover and cook on High until the cake springs back when touched, about 2 hours. Cool the tin on a wire rack for 10 minutes. Remove the side of the tin and serve the cake warm.

Carrot and Pineapple Pudding Cake Ⓥ

An utterly effort-free dessert the whole family will enjoy.

SERVES 12

vegetable cooking spray
1 x 500 g/18 oz packet carrot cake mix
1 x 25 g/1 oz packet instant vanilla pudding
250 ml/8 fl oz soured cream
250 ml/8 fl oz water
175 ml/6 fl oz canola oil
1 egg
1 x 225 g/8 oz can crushed pineapple, undrained

Spray the bottom and sides of the slow cooker with vegetable spray. Combine the remaining ingredients in a bowl. Beat thoroughly with an electric mixer or by hand until combined. Pour into the slow cooker. Cover and cook on Low for 5–6 hours. The cake will rise almost to the top of the slow cooker. It will bubble slowly and is done when bubbling stops and the cake begins to pull away from the side of the slow cooker. Spoon warm cake on to plates.

Double-chocolate Pudding Cake

Serve with hot fudge sauce or chocolate syrup – which would promote it to Triple-chocolate Pudding Cake!

SERVES 12

vegetable cooking spray
1 x 500 g/18 oz packet chocolate fudge cake mix
1 x 25 g/1 oz packet instant chocolate pudding
250 ml/8 fl oz soured cream
250 ml/8 fl oz water
175 ml/6 fl oz canola oil
1 egg

Spray the bottom and sides of the slow cooker with vegetable spray. Combine the remaining ingredients in a bowl. Beat thoroughly with an electric mixer or by hand until combined. Pour into the slow cooker. Cover and cook on Low for 3½–4 hours. The cake will rise almost to the top of the slow cooker. It will bubble slowly and is done when bubbling stops and the cake begins to pull away from the side of the slow cooker. Spoon warm cake on to plates.

New York-style Cheesecake Ⓥ

This slow-cooker version of the famous cooked cheesecake will get top marks from cheesecake fans.

SERVES 8

450 g/1 lb soft cheese, at room temperature
100 g/4 oz caster sugar
2 eggs
1½ tbsp cornflour
¼ tsp salt
175 ml/6 fl oz soured cream
1 tsp vanilla essence
Biscuit Crumb Crust (see opposite)

Beat the cheese and sugar in a large bowl until light and fluffy. Beat in the eggs, cornflour and salt, blending well. Mix in the soured cream and vanilla essence. Pour into the crust in the springform cake tin.

Put the tin on a rack in a 5.5 litre/9½ pint slow cooker. Cover, putting three layers of kitchen papers under the lid, and cook on High until the cheesecake is set but still slightly soft in the centre, 2–3 hours. Turn off the heat and leave to stand, covered, in the slow cooker for 1 hour. Remove from the slow cooker and cool on a wire rack. Refrigerate, covered, for 8 hours or overnight.

Biscuit Crumb Crust ⓥ

A good base for any style of cheesecake.

MAKES ONE 18 CM/7 IN CRUST

**175 g/6 oz digestive biscuits, crushed
   into crumbs**
2 tbsp caster sugar
3 tbsp butter or margarine, melted
1–2 tbsp honey

Combine the biscuit crumbs, sugar and
butter or margarine in an 18 cm/7 in
springform cake tin. Add enough honey
so that the mixture sticks together. Pat
the mixture evenly over the base and
2.5 cm/1 in up the side of the tin.

Latte Cheesecake ⓥ

*If you don't have espresso coffee, just use
double strength instant coffee.*

SERVES 8

**450 g/1 lb soft cheese, at room
   temperature**
100 g/4 oz caster sugar
2 eggs
2 egg yolks
1½ tbsp cornflour
¼ tsp salt
175 ml/6 fl oz soured cream
1 tsp vanilla essence
75 ml/2½ fl oz espresso coffee
a pinch of freshly grated nutmeg
Biscuit Crumb Crust (see above)
**150 ml/¼ pint whipping or double
   cream, whipped**
**a little ground cinnamon and
   chocolate shavings, to decorate**

Beat the cheese and sugar in a large bowl
until light and fluffy. Beat in the eggs,
egg yolks, cornflour and salt, blending
well. Mix in the soured cream, vanilla
essence, coffee and nutmeg. Pour into
the crust in the springform cake tin.

Put the tin on a rack in a 5.5 litre/9½ pint
slow cooker. Cover, putting three layers of
kitchen papers under the lid, and cook on
High until the cheesecake is set but still
slightly soft in the centre, 2–3 hours.
Turn off the heat and leave to stand,
covered, in the slow cooker for 1 hour.
Remove from the slow cooker and cool
on a wire rack. Refrigerate, covered, for
8 hours or overnight. Spread the top of
the chilled cheesecake with the cream
and sprinkle lightly with cinnamon and
chocolate shavings.

Chocolate Chip and Pecan Cheesecake ⓥ

*This delicious cheesecake looks great
speckled with chocolate chips and nuts.*

SERVES 8

**450 g/1 lb soft cheese, at room
   temperature**
100 g/4 oz caster sugar
2 eggs
1½ tbsp cornflour
¼ tsp salt
175 ml/6 fl oz soured cream
1 tsp vanilla essence
40 g/1½ oz chocolate chips
40 g/1½ oz pecan nuts, chopped
Biscuit Crumb Crust (see left)
chocolate curls, to decorate

Beat the cheese and sugar in a large
bowl until light and fluffy. Beat in the
eggs, cornflour and salt, blending well.
Mix in the soured cream, vanilla essence,
chocolate chips and nuts. Pour into
the crust in the springform cake tin.

Put the tin on a rack in a 5.5 litre/9½ pint
slow cooker. Cover, putting three layers
of kitchen papers under the lid, and cook
on High until the cheesecake is set but
still slightly soft in the centre, 2–3 hours.
Turn off the heat and leave to stand,
covered, in the slow cooker for 1 hour.
Remove from the slow cooker and cool
on a wire rack. Refrigerate, covered, for
8 hours or overnight. Decorate the top
of the cheesecake with chocolate curls.

Pear Cheesecake Ⓥ

The Ginger Nut Crumb Crust adds a flavour contrast to the pears in this creamy cheesecake.

SERVES 8

225 g/8 oz soft cheese, at room temperature
100 g/4 oz caster sugar
2 tbsp flour
¼ tsp salt
250 ml/8 fl oz soured cream
1 egg
1 tsp vanilla essence
1 medium pear, peeled and thinly sliced
Ginger Nut Crumb Crust (see below)
chopped crystallised ginger, to decorate

Beat the cheese, sugar, flour and salt in a large bowl until smooth. Beat in the soured cream, egg and vanilla essence. Arrange the pear slices over the crust in the springform cake tin. Pour the filling over the pears. Put the tin on a rack in a 5.5 litre/9½ pint slow cooker. Cover, putting three layers of kitchen paper under the lid, and cook on High until the cheesecake is just set in the centre, 3½–4 hours. Turn off the heat and leave to stand, covered, in the slow cooker for 1 hour. Remove from the slow cooker and cool on a wire rack. Refrigerate, covered, for 8 hours or overnight. Decorate with crystallised ginger.

Ginger Nut Crumb Crust Ⓥ

If you want to make this extra-gingery, use all ginger nut biscuits.

MAKES ONE 18 CM/7 IN CRUST

50 g/2 oz digestive biscuits, crushed into crumbs
50 g/2 oz ginger nut biscuits, crushed into crumbs

2–3 tbsp melted butter or margarine
2–3 tbsp honey

Combine the biscuit crumbs and butter or margarine in an 18 cm/7 in springform cake tin. Add enough honey for the mixture to stick together. Pat the mixture evenly over the base and 2.5 cm/1 in up the side of the tin.

Raspberry Swirl Cheesecake Ⓥ

Find a good-quality raspberry preserve to get fantastic results, and top the cheesecake with fresh raspberries for an added treat, if you like.

SERVES 8

450 g/1 lb soft cheese, at room temperature
250 ml/8 fl oz sweetened condensed milk
2 eggs
1 tsp vanilla essence
¼ tsp salt
Biscuit and Pecan Crust (see page 387)
175 g/6 oz seedless raspberry preserve

Beat the cheese in a large bowl until fluffy. Beat in the sweetened condensed milk, eggs, vanilla essence and salt. Pour the mixture into the crust in the springform cake tin. Swirl in the raspberry preserve.

Put the tin on a rack in a 5.5 litre/ 9½ pint slow cooker. Cover, putting three layers of kitchen papers under the lid, and cook on High until the cheesecake is set but still slightly soft in the centre, about 3 hours. Remove from the slow cooker and cool on a wire rack. Refrigerate, covered, for 8 hours or overnight.

Biscuit and Pecan Crust (V)

Toasted hazelnuts would also work well instead of the pecan nuts.

MAKES ONE 18 CM/7 IN CRUST

100 g/4 oz malted milk biscuit crumbs
25 g/1 oz ground toasted pecan nuts
2–3 tbsp melted butter or margarine
2–3 tbsp honey

Combine the biscuit crumbs, pecan nuts and butter or margarine in an 18 cm/ 7 in springform cake tin. Add enough honey for the mixture to stick together. Pat the mixture evenly over the base and 2.5 cm/1 in up the side of the cake tin.

Blueberry Swirl Cheesecake (V)

Lightly swirl the blueberry preserve into the cheese mixture.

SERVES 8

450 g/1 lb soft cheese
250 ml/8 fl oz condensed milk
1 tbsp soft brown sugar
2 eggs
1 tsp orange essence
1 tbsp grated orange zest
¼ tsp salt
Biscuit and Pecan Crust (see above)
175 g/6 oz seedless blueberry preserve

Beat the cheese in a large bowl until fluffy. Beat in the sweetened condensed milk, sugar, eggs, orange essence, orange zest and salt. Pour the mixture into the crust in the springform cake tin. Swirl in the blueberry preserve.

Put the tin on a rack in a 5.5 litre/9½ pint slow cooker. Cover, putting three layers of kitchen papers under the lid, and cook on High until the cheesecake is set but still slightly soft in the centre, about 3 hours. Remove from the slow cooker and cool on a wire rack. Refrigerate, covered, for 8 hours or overnight.

Chocolate Cheese Pie (V)

Decorate this yummy dessert with whipped cream and chocolate curls.

SERVES 10

450 g/1 lb soft cheese, at room temperature
175 g/6 oz sugar
2 eggs
1 tsp vanilla essence
¼ tsp salt
25 g/1 oz dark chocolate, melted in a heatproof bowl over a pan of gently simmering water
25 g/1 oz cocoa powder
Chocolate Cookie Crumb Crust (see page 388)
150 ml/¼ pint whipping or double cream, whipped
chocolate curls, to decorate

Beat the cheese in a large bowl until fluffy. Beat in the sugar, eggs, vanilla essence and salt. Mix in the melted chocolate and cocoa powder. Pour the filling into the crust in the springform cake tin.

Put the tin on a rack in a 5.5 litre/9½ pint slow cooker. Cover, putting three layers of kitchen paper under the lid, and cook on High until the cheesecake is just set in the centre, 2½–3 hours. Turn off the heat and leave to stand, covered, in the slow cooker for 1 hour. Remove from the slow cooker and cool on a wire rack. Refrigerate, covered, for 8 hours or overnight. Spread the whipped cream over the cheesecake and decorate with chocolate curls.

Note: to make chocolate curls, melt some chocolate and spread it out into a thin layer on your work surface. Allow to firm up. Use a sharp flat-ended knife or metal spatula to shave off thin slices of chocolate, holding the blade at a 45° angle. The shavings will curl up as you cut.

Chocolate Cookie Crumb Crust Ⓥ

The easiest way to make biscuit crumbs is to place the biscuits in a plastic bag and crush them gently with a rolling pin.

MAKES ONE 18 CM/7 IN CRUST

150 g/5 oz chocolate chip cookie crumbs
2 tbsp sugar
3 tbsp butter or margarine, melted
1–2 tbsp honey

Combine the cookie crumbs, sugar and butter or margarine in an 18 cm/7 in springform cake tin. Add enough honey for the mixture to stick together. Pat the mixture evenly over the base and 2.5 cm/1 in up the side of the tin.

Black Forest Cheesecake Ⓥ

To make this cheesecake extra-special, serve the slices with cherry pie filling spooned over.

SERVES 10

450 g/1 lb soft cheese, at room temperature
175 g/6 oz sugar
2 eggs
2 tbsp brandy or brandy essence
¼ tsp salt
50 g/2 oz dark chocolate, melted in a heatproof bowl over a pan of gently simmering water
25 g/1 oz cocoa powder
Chocolate Cookie Crumb Crust (see above)
150 ml/¼ pint whipping or double cream, whipped
chocolate curls, to decorate

Beat the cheese in a large bowl until fluffy. Beat in the sugar, eggs, brandy or brandy essence and salt. Mix in the melted chocolate and cocoa powder. Pour the filling into the crust in the springform cake tin.

Put the tin on a rack in a 5.5 litre/9½ pint slow cooker. Cover, putting three layers of kitchen paper under the lid, and cook on High until the cheesecake is just set in the centre, 2½–3 hours. Turn off the heat and leave to stand, covered, in the slow cooker for 1 hour. Remove from the slow cooker and cool on a wire rack. Refrigerate, covered, for 8 hours or overnight. Spread the whipped cream over the cheesecake and decorate with chocolate curls.

Chocolate Chip Bars Ⓥ

Walnuts and chocolate pair well together to make these tasty biscuits.

MAKES ABOUT 16

100 g/4 oz butter or margarine, at room temperature
1 egg
1 tsp vanilla essence
50 g/2 oz caster sugar
50 g/2 oz light brown sugar
100 g/4 oz plain flour
½ tsp bicarbonate of soda
¼ tsp salt
50 g/2 oz plain chocolate chips
50 g/2 oz walnuts, coarsely chopped
oil, for greasing
vegetable cooking spray

Beat the butter or margarine, egg and vanilla essence in a bowl until fluffy. Mix in the combined sugars. Mix in the combined flour, bicarbonate of soda and salt. Mix in the chocolate chips and walnuts. Spread the dough evenly in the base of a greased 18 cm/7 in springform cake tin. Cover and cook on High until a cocktail stick inserted into the centre comes out clean, 3–3½ hours. Turn the lid askew and cook, part-covered, for 20 minutes longer. Cool in the tin on a wire rack for 5 minutes. Remove the side of the tin. Cut into bars while warm.

Coconut and Walnut Layer Bars 🕧

These bars are perfectly moist and chewy – delicious!

MAKES ABOUT 16

175 g/6 oz digestive biscuits, crushed into crumbs
1 tbsp melted butter or margarine
1 tbsp honey
65 g/2½ oz plain chocolate chips
25 g/1 oz flaked coconut
40 g/1½ oz walnuts, toasted and chopped
100 g/14 oz can sweetened condensed milk

Press the combined digestive biscuit crumbs, butter or margarine and honey in the base of an 18 cm/7 in springform cake tin. Sprinkle with the chocolate chips, coconut and walnuts. Drizzle the condensed milk over the top. Put the tin on a rack in a 5.5 litre/9½ pint slow cooker. Cover and cook on Low until the milk is absorbed and the biscuits are almost firm to the touch, 3–3½ hours. Cool on a wire rack for 5 minutes for the biscuits to firm. Remove the side of the tin. Cut into wedges or squares while still slightly warm.

Note: to toast nuts, put them in a dry pan and heat over medium heat, tossing frequently, until browned

Easy Brownies 🕧

When you're short of time, make some quick brownies from a packet with some extra ingredients to make them fudgey and rich.

MAKES ABOUT 16

550 g/1¼ lb brownie mix from a packet
50 g/2 oz butter or margarine, melted

50–100 g/2–4 oz walnuts, chopped
oil, for greasing

Make the brownie mix according to the packet instructions, adding the butter or margarine and walnuts. Pour the batter into a greased 18 cm/7 in springform cake tin and put on a rack in a 5.5 litre/9½ pint slow cooker. Cover and cook on High until a cocktail stick inserted into the centre comes out almost clean, about 6 hours. Cool on a wire rack. Remove the side of the tin and cut into squares or wedges.

Chocolate Indulgence Brownies 🕧

Dates add flavour and moisture to brownies that are simply made using biscuit crumbs.

MAKES ABOUT 24

3 eggs
175 g/6 oz light brown sugar
2 tsp vanilla essence
25 g/8 oz chocolate chip cookies, crushed into crumbs
3 tbsp cocoa powder
¼ tsp salt
100 g/4 oz dates, chopped
50 g/2 oz plain chocolate chips

Beat the eggs, sugar and vanilla essence in a large bowl until thick. Fold in the cookie crumbs, cocoa powder and salt. Fold in the dates and chocolate chips.

Pour the batter into a greased and floured 23 x 13 cm/9 x 5 in loaf tin. Put on a rack in a 5.5 litre/9½ pint slow cooker. Cover and cook on High until a cocktail stick inserted into the centre comes out almost clean, about 3 hours. Cool on a wire rack for 10 minutes. Invert on to a wire rack and cool. Cut into 2 cm/¾ in slices, then cut the slices into halves.

Warm Caramel Brownie Bars ⓥ

Another time-saving brownie recipe, this one is sprinkled with fruit and nuts and smothered with a toffee sauce.

MAKES ABOUT 16

550 g/1¼ lb brownie mix from a packet
50 g/2 oz butter or margarine, melted
oil, for greasing
toffee ice-cream sauce, warmed
chocolate-covered raisins, chopped
**   walnuts and flaked coconut,**
**   to decorate**

Make the brownie mix according to the packet instructions, adding the butter or margarine. Pour the batter into a greased 18 cm/7 in springform cake tin and put on a rack in a 5.5 litre/9½ pint slow cooker. Cover and cook on High until a cocktail stick inserted into the centre comes out almost clean, about 6 hours. Cool on a wire rack. Remove the side of the tin and cut into squares or wedges. Spoon warm toffee ice-cream sauce over the warm brownies and sprinkle with chocolate-covered raisins, chopped walnuts and flaked coconut.

Orange Glaze ⓥ

The sticky glaze will stay on top of the cake rather than seep through.

MAKES ABOUT 100 G/4 OZ

75 g/3 oz icing sugar
1 tsp grated orange zest
2–4 tsp orange juice

Mix the icing sugar, orange zest and enough orange juice give a coating consistency.

Carrot Cake Snackers ⓥ

A sticky orange glaze tops these spiced oaty bars containing raisins and nuts.

MAKES ABOUT 16

50 g/2 oz butter or margarine, at
**   room temperature**
175 g/6 oz light brown sugar
175 ml/6 fl oz semi-skimmed milk
1 egg
1 tbsp lemon juice
1 tsp vanilla essence
150 g/5 oz porridge oats
50 g/2 oz plain flour, plus extra
**   for dusting**
25 g/1 oz wholemeal flour
2 tsp baking powder
¼ tsp bicarbonate of soda
1 tsp ground cinnamon
¼ tsp salt
1 large carrot, grated
75 g/3 oz raisins
50 g/2 oz chopped pecan nuts or
**   walnuts**
oil, for greasing
Orange Glaze (see left)

Beat the butter or margarine and sugar in a large bowl until blended. Beat in the milk, egg, lemon juice and vanilla essence. Mix in the combined oats, flours, baking powder, bicarbonate of soda, cinnamon and salt. Mix in the carrots, raisins and nuts.

Pour the batter into a greased and floured 18 cm/7 in springform cake tin. Put the tin on a rack in a 5.5 litre/9½ pint slow cooker. Cover and cook on High until a cocktail stick inserted into the centre of the cake comes out clean, about 3 hours. Cool the cake in the tin on a wire rack for 10 minutes. Remove the side of the tin and cool. Drizzle with Orange Glaze. Cut into squares or wedges.

Note: be sure to use a springform cake tin that does not leak, or line the bottom of the tin with foil.

Lemon Cream-cheese Bites (V)

Make a simple cake mix into something much more exciting.

MAKES ABOUT 12

**225 g/8 oz plain sponge cake mix
1 egg
1 tbsp butter or margarine, at room temperature
oil, for greasing
50 g/2 oz soft cheese, at room temperature
50 g/2 oz sugar
½ tsp vanilla essence
1 tbsp finely grated lemon zest
1 tbsp flour
¼ tsp salt
Lemon Glaze (see below)**

Mix the cake mix, egg and butter or margarine in a bowl. Reserve about 250 ml/8 fl oz of the dough. Pat the remaining dough evenly over the base of a greased 18 cm/7 in springform cake tin. Bake at 180°C/gas 4/fan oven 160°C until lightly browned, about 10 minutes.

Beat the cheese, sugar and vanilla essence in a bowl until smooth. Mix in the combined lemon zest, flour and salt. Pour into the tin and spoon teaspoonfuls of the reserved dough over the top. Put the tin on a rack in a 5.5 litre/9½ pint slow cooker. Cover and cook on High until set, 2½–3½ hours. Cool in the tin on a wire rack. Drizzle with Lemon Glaze. Cut into squares or wedges.

Lemon Glaze (V)

Don't make this glaze too runny as you want it to stay on top of the cake.

MAKES 100 G/4 OZ

**75 g/3 oz icing sugar
2 tsp finely grated lemon zest
3–4 tsp lemon juice**

Mix the icing sugar and lemon zest, adding enough lemon juice to give a coating consistency.

Crème Caramel (V)

Golden caramel tops egg custard in this traditional and popular dessert.

SERVES 4–6

**150 g/5 oz caster sugar
600 ml/1 pint full-fat milk
3 eggs, lightly beaten
2 tsp vanilla essence**

Heat 65 g/2½ oz of the sugar in a small frying pan over medium-high heat until the sugar melts and turns golden, stirring occasionally (watch carefully, as the sugar can burn easily). Quickly pour the syrup into the base of a 1 litre/1¾ pint soufflé dish or casserole and tilt it to spread the caramel evenly. Set aside to cool.

Heat the milk and the remaining sugar until steaming and just beginning to bubble at the edges. Whisk the mixture into the eggs. Add the vanilla essence. Strain over the caramel into the soufflé dish. Put the soufflé dish on a rack in a 5.5 litre/9½ pint slow cooker. Add 2.5 cm/1 in hot water to the slow cooker and cover the dish with a plate, lid or foil. Cover and cook on Low until the custard is set and a sharp knife inserted half-way between the centre and the edge comes out clean, 1½–2 hours. Remove the soufflé dish to a wire rack, uncover and cool. Refrigerate for 8 hours or overnight.

To unmould, loosen the edge of the custard with a sharp knife. Put a rimmed serving dish over the soufflé dish and invert.

Rosemary Flan Ⓥ

If you have rosemary growing in your garden, you could use 1 tsp of the chopped fresh leaves instead of dried.

SERVES 4–6

150 g/5 oz caster sugar
600 ml/1 pint full-fat milk
1 tsp dried rosemary
3 eggs, lightly beaten
2 tsp vanilla essence

Heat 65 g/2½ oz of the sugar in a small frying pan over medium-high heat until the sugar melts and turns golden, stirring occasionally (watch carefully, as the sugar can burn easily). Quickly pour the syrup into the base of a 1 litre/1¾ pint soufflé dish or casserole and tilt it to spread the caramel evenly. Set aside to cool.

Heat the milk with the remaining sugar and the rosemary until boiling. Whisk the mixture into the eggs. Add the vanilla essence. Leave to stand for 10 minutes, then strain over the caramel into the soufflé dish. Put the soufflé dish on a rack in a 5.5 litre/9½ pint slow cooker. Add 2.5 cm/1 in hot water to the slow cooker and cover the dish with a plate, lid or foil. Cover and cook on Low until the custard is set and a sharp knife inserted half-way between the centre and the edge comes out clean, 1½–2 hours. Remove the soufflé dish to a wire rack, uncover and cool. Refrigerate for 8 hours or overnight.

To unmould, loosen the edge of the custard with a sharp knife. Put a rimmed serving dish over the soufflé dish and invert.

Steamed Marmalade Pudding Ⓥ

This is old-fashioned comfort food for a winter dessert. You can vary the flavour by choosing a different marmalade, such as grapefruit, tangerine or orange with brandy.

SERVES 8

100 g/4 oz caster sugar
65 g/2½ oz butter or margarine, at
**   room temperature**
2 eggs, lightly beaten
165 g/5½ oz plain flour
1½ tsp baking powder
2 tbsp orange juice or milk
225 g/8 oz orange marmalade
oil, for greasing
Orange Marmalade Sauce (see page
**   393)**

Beat the sugar and butter or margarine in a bowl until fluffy. Beat in the eggs. Stir in the combined flour and baking powder. Stir in the orange juice or milk. Spread the marmalade over the base of a greased 1 litre/1¾ pint bowl, soufflé dish or pudding mould and spoon the batter over. Cover tightly with foil or a lid. Put the bowl on a rack in a 5.5 litre/9½ pint slow cooker. Pour boiling water into the cooker to come about two-thirds up the side of the bowl. Cover and cook on Low until a cocktail stick inserted into the centre of the pudding comes out clean, about 1½ hours. Remove from the slow cooker. Remove the foil and cool on a wire rack for about 30 minutes. Loosen the edge of the pudding with a knife. Invert on to a serving platter. Serve warm with Orange Marmalade Sauce.

Orange Marmalade Sauce Ⓥ

Try using a different fruit marmalade, such as grapefruit, ginger or lime.

SERVES 8

225 g/8 oz orange marmalade
2 tsp cornflour
150 ml/¼ pint cold water

Heat the marmalade to boiling in a small pan over medium heat. Stir in the combined cornflour and water, stirring until thickened, about 1 minute.

Cranberry Toffee Bread Pudding with Toffee Sauce Ⓥ

Rich and fruity, this pudding could well become a winter favourite.

SERVES 6

375 ml/13 fl oz full-fat milk
2 eggs
65 g/2½ oz light brown sugar
100 g/4 oz dried cranberries
50 g/2 oz toffee, broken into small chips
100 g/4 oz day-old sourdough or
**   white farmhouse bread, cubed**
40 g/1½ oz walnuts, coarsely chopped
Toffee Sauce (see right)

Whisk the milk and eggs in a large bowl until well blended. Mix in the sugar, cranberries and toffee chips. Gently mix in the bread and walnuts. Spoon the mixture into a 23 x 13 cm/9 x 5 in loaf tin or 1 litre/1¾ pint soufflé dish. Cover securely with foil. Put the tin or dish on a rack in the slow cooker. Cover and cook on High until the pudding is set and a cocktail stick inserted into the centre comes out clean, about 2 hours. Serve warm with Toffee Sauce.

Toffee Sauce Ⓥ

You could use dark brown sugar instead of light, and rum essence in place of vanilla.

SERVES 6

100 g/4 oz light brown sugar
120 ml/4 fl oz water
2 tbsp golden syrup
½ tsp vanilla essence

Combine the sugar, water and golden syrup in a small pan. Heat to boiling, stirring until the sugar has dissolved. Reduce the heat and simmer until the sauce is a thick but pourable consistency, about 10 minutes. Stir in the vanilla essence.

Old-fashioned Raisin Bread Pudding Ⓥ

You could add 1–2 tbsp light rum or ½ tsp rum essence to the Toffee Sauce, if you like.

SERVES 6

375 ml/13 fl oz full-fat milk
2 eggs
65 g/2½ oz light brown sugar
100 g/4 oz raisins
100 g/4 oz day-old sourdough or
**   white farmhouse bread, cubed**
40 g/1½ oz walnuts, coarsely chopped
50 g/2 oz pecan nuts, coarsely chopped
¾ tsp ground cinnamon
a pinch of freshly grated nutmeg
Toffee Sauce (see above)

Whisk the milk and eggs in a large bowl until well blended. Mix in the sugar and raisins. Gently mix in the bread, walnuts, pecan nuts, cinnamon and nutmeg. Spoon the mixture into a 23 x 13 cm/9 x 5 in loaf tin or 1 litre/1¾ pint soufflé dish. Cover securely with foil. Put the tin or dish on a rack in the slow cooker. Cover and cook on High until the pudding is set and a cocktail stick inserted into the centre comes out clean, about 2 hours. Serve warm with Toffee Sauce.

Blueberry Bread Pudding with Lemon Sauce Ⓥ

Blueberries are a very good for you indeed. They contain antioxidants that may reduce inflammation and risks of some diseases, including cancer.

SERVES 6

375 ml/13 fl oz full-fat milk
2 eggs
65 g/2½ oz light brown sugar
100 g/4 oz fresh or thawed frozen blueberries
100 g/4 oz day-old sourdough or white farmhouse bread, cubed
40 g/1½ oz walnuts, coarsely chopped
Lemon Sauce (see below)

Whisk the milk and eggs in a large bowl until well blended. Mix in the sugar and blueberries. Gently mix in the bread and walnuts. Spoon the mixture into a 23 x 13 cm/9 x 5 in loaf tin or 1 litre/1¾ pint soufflé dish. Cover securely with foil. Put the tin or dish on a rack in the slow cooker. Cover and cook on High until the pudding is set and a cocktail stick inserted into the centre comes out clean, about 2 hours. Serve warm with Lemon Sauce.

Lemon Sauce Ⓥ

This is a good sauce to serve with a fruity pudding – or just spread on bread, especially a sweet loaf such as brioche.

SERVES 6

2 tbsp butter or margarine
150–225 g/5–8 oz sugar
250 ml/8 fl oz lemon juice
2 eggs, lightly beaten

Melt the butter or margarine in a small frying pan. Add the sugar and lemon juice, stirring over medium heat until the sugar is dissolved. Whisk about 120 ml/

4 fl oz of the lemon mixture into the eggs. Whisk the mixture back into the pan. Whisk over low heat until the mixture coats the back of a spoon, 2–3 minutes.

Chocolate and Mandarin Bread Pudding Ⓥ

Wholemeal bread gives this citrus and chocolate bread pudding a lovely rich and rounded flavour.

SERVES 8

350 g/12 oz day-old wholemeal bread, cubed
300 g/11 oz can mandarin oranges, drained and halved
oil, for greasing
350 g/12 oz evaporated milk
350 g/12 oz dark brown sugar
100 g/4 oz cocoa powder
1 egg

Toss the bread and mandarin oranges in the lightly greased slow cooker. Heat the evaporated milk, sugar and cocoa powder in a large pan over medium-high heat, stirring until the sugar has melted, about 5 minutes. Whisk about half the mixture into the egg. Whisk the egg mixture back into the pan. Pour the mixture over the bread, making sure the bread is covered. Cover and cook on High until the pudding is set and a cocktail stick inserted into the centre comes out clean, about 4 hours. Serve warm.

Pineapple Custard Bread Pudding (V)

Canned pineapple is a handy storecupboard ingredient to make this homely pudding. You could also use multigrain or sourdough bread – day-old bread is best.

SERVES 8

100 g/4 oz butter or margarine, at room temperature
100 g/4 oz caster sugar
100 g/4 oz light brown sugar
½ tsp ground cinnamon
2 eggs
400 g/14 oz can crushed pineapple, drained
150 g/5 oz French bread, lightly toasted and cubed
6 tbsp coarsely chopped macadamia nuts or flaked almonds

Beat the butter or margarine, sugars and cinnamon in a large bowl until fluffy. Beat in the eggs. Mix in the pineapple and bread cubes. Spoon the mixture into the slow cooker. Cover and cook on Low until the pudding is set and a sharp knife inserted into the centre comes out clean, about 3 hours. Serve warm. Sprinkle each serving with macadamia nuts or flaked almonds.

Creamy Rice Pudding (V)

For a summer treat, mix raspberries, strawberries or blueberries into this tasty rice pudding before serving.

SERVES 6

1 litre/1¾ pints full-fat milk
100 g/4 oz caster sugar
½ tsp salt
175 g/6 oz easy-cook long-grain rice, cooked
1½ tbsp cornflour
ground cinnamon, to decorate

Heat 750 ml/1¼ pints of the milk, the sugar and salt to boiling in a medium pan. Combine with the rice in the slow cooker. Stir in the combined remaining milk and the cornflour. Cover and cook on Low until the pudding is thick and creamy, about 4 hours. Serve warm or refrigerate and serve cold. Sprinkle with cinnamon.

Apple Rice Pudding (V)

A delicious and easy variation on rice pudding. Use a tasty eating apple for best results.

SERVES 6

1 litre/1¾ pints full-fat milk
100 g/4 oz muscovado sugar
½ tsp salt
175 g/6 oz easy-cook long-grain rice, cooked
1½ tbsp cornflour
1 tbsp butter
1 apple, peeled, cored and coarsely chopped
1 tsp vanilla essence

Heat 750 ml/1¼ pints of the milk, the sugar and salt to boiling in a medium pan. Combine with the rice in the slow cooker. Stir in the combined remaining milk and the cornflour. Cover and cook on Low until the pudding is thick and creamy, about 4 hours.

When almost ready to serve, heat the butter in a small frying pan and fry the apple until lightly browned. Stir into the rice pudding with the vanilla essence. Serve warm or refrigerate and serve cold.

Almond Rice Pudding Ⓥ

Anyone who likes almonds will love this sophisticated flavour.

SERVES 6

1 litre/1¾ pints full-fat milk
50 g/2 oz caster sugar
½ tsp salt
175 g/6 oz easy-cook long-grain rice, cooked
1 cinnamon stick
1½ tbsp cornflour
65 g/2½ oz finely chopped almonds, toasted
2 tsp vanilla essence
1 tsp almond essence
450 ml/¾ pint single cream

Heat 750 ml/1¼ pints of the milk, the sugar and salt to boiling in a medium pan. Combine with the rice and cinnamon stick in the slow cooker. Stir in the combined remaining milk and the cornflour. Cover and cook on Low until the pudding is thick and creamy, about 4 hours. Stir the almonds, vanilla essence and almond essence into the pudding. Fold in the cream and refrigerate until chilled.

Baked Stuffed Apples Ⓥ

The old favourite of stuffed apples still brings a smile, particularly when they are filled with spiced fruit and pecan nuts. Serve warm with ice-cream.

SERVES 4

4 cooking apples
75 g/3 oz dried mixed fruit, chopped
2–4 tbsp chopped toasted pecan nuts
3 tbsp sugar
½ tsp ground cinnamon
a pinch of freshly grated nutmeg
25–40 g/1–1½ oz cold butter, cut into pieces

Core the apples, cutting to, but not through, the base. Peel 2.5 cm/1 in of the skin from the tops. Fill the apples with the combined remaining ingredients and put in the slow cooker. Cover and cook on Low until tender, 3–4 hours.

Cranberry and Apple Tart Ⓥ

Perfect for autumn, with the combination of fruit plus a zing from citrus.

SERVES 8

500 g/18 oz frozen shortcrust pastry, thawed if frozen
flour, for dusting
175 g/6 oz sugar
2 tbsp flour
75 ml/2½ fl oz water
2 tsp grated orange zest
a pinch of freshly grated nutmeg
3 eating apples, peeled and sliced
100 g/4 oz fresh or thawed frozen cranberries
icing sugar, to decorate

Roll the pastry on a floured surface into a 25 cm/10 in round. Fit into the base and 4 cm/1½ in up the side of an 18 cm/7 in springform cake tin. Bake at 190°C/gas 5/fan oven 170°C until lightly browned, about 15 minutes.

Mix the sugar and flour in a large pan. Add the water, orange zest and nutmeg. Heat to boiling, stirring to dissolve the sugar. Add the apples and cranberries. Simmer for 10 minutes or until the cranberries pop, stirring occasionally. Spoon the fruit mixture into the crust, spreading evenly. Put the tin on a rack in a 5.5 litre/9½ pint slow cooker. Cover and cook on High for 2½ hours. Cool on a wire rack. Sprinkle with icing sugar before serving.

Pears Belle Hélène ⓥ

Tuck a shortbread biscuit beside each dish to complete this elegant offering.

SERVES 4

4 pears, peeled, with stems intact
375 ml/13 fl oz apple juice
375 ml/13 fl oz water
50 g/2 oz sugar
375 ml/13 fl oz frozen vanilla yoghurt
Dark Chocolate Sauce (see below)

Stand the pears upright in the slow cooker. Heat the apple juice, water and sugar to boiling in a small pan. Pour over the pears. Cover and cook on High until the pears are tender, 1½–2 hours. Drain and serve warm with Dark Chocolate Sauce, or cool the pears in the syrup and refrigerate until chilled. To serve, flatten a scoop of yoghurt in each of four dessert dishes. Put a pear on top and drizzle with Dark Chocolate Sauce.

Dark Chocolate Sauce ⓥ

A delicious and versatile chocolate sauce for puddings and ice-cream.

SERVES 4

40 g/1½ oz cocoa powder
50 g/2 oz sugar
75 ml/2½ fl oz semi-skimmed milk
1 tbsp butter or margarine
1 tsp vanilla essence
¼ tsp ground cinnamon

Mix the cocoa powder and sugar in a small pan. Stir in the milk and add the butter or margarine. Stir over medium heat until boiling. Reduce the heat and simmer until the sauce is smooth and slightly thickened, 3–4 minutes. Stir in the vanilla essence and cinnamon. Serve warm or at room temperature.

Poached Pears with Fruit in Rosemary Syrup ⓥ

Perfectly poached pears combine other with fresh fruit in a fragrant sugar syrup.

SERVES 4

2 large pears, peeled and cored
Rosemary Syrup (see below)
175 g/6 oz raspberries, fresh or
thawed frozen
175 g/6 oz blueberries, fresh or
thawed frozen
1 large orange, peeled and cut into
segments
mint sprigs, to decorate

Stand the pears upright in the slow cooker. Pour the Rosemary Syrup over. Cover and cook on High until the pears are tender, 1½–2 hours. Remove the pears to a shallow bowl. Strain the syrup over the pears and cool. Refrigerate until chilled, 1–2 hours. Cut the pears into halves. Arrange the pears and the remaining fruit in shallow serving bowls. Spoon the Rosemary Syrup over the fruit. Decorate with mint.

Rosemary Syrup ⓥ

If you have rosemary growing in your garden, use 2 tbsp of the chopped fresh leaves instead of dried rosemary. You can substitute apple juice for the white wine, if you wish.

MAKES ABOUT 300 ML/½ PINT

150 g/5 oz caster sugar
150 ml/¼ pint dry white wine
1 tbsp balsamic vinegar
1 tbsp dried rosemary
1 bay leaf
1 tsp grated orange or lemon zest

Heat all the ingredients to boiling in a small pan. Discard the bay leaf.

Blueberry and Pear Compôte with Cinnamon Sour Cream Ⓥ

Pears in a sweet and zesty syrup taste great with blueberries topped with a delicious cinnamon-flavoured cream in this very straightforward dish.

SERVES 4

4 pears, peeled, with stems intact
150 g/5 oz light brown sugar
120 ml/4 fl oz water
1 tbsp lemon juice
1 tsp grated lemon zest
25 g/1 oz butter or margarine
225 g/8 oz fresh or thawed frozen blueberries
Cinnamon Soured Cream (see below)

Stand the pears upright in the slow cooker. Heat the sugar, water, lemon juice, lemon zest and butter or margarine to boiling in a small pan. Pour over the pears. Cover and cook on High until the pears are tender, about 2 hours. Remove the pears to a serving dish. Turn the slow cooker to High and cook, uncovered, until the liquid is a syrup consistency, about 15 minutes. Stir the blueberries into the syrup. Spoon the warm blueberry mixture around the pears in shallow bowls. Serve with Cinnamon Soured Cream.

Cinnamon Soured Cream Ⓥ

A smooth and spicy sweet cream to use as a topping for a variety of fruit or chocolate desserts.

MAKES 120 ML/4 FL OZ

120 ml/4 fl oz soured cream
1 tbsp light brown sugar
¼ tsp ground cinnamon

Mix together all the ingredients until thoroughly blended.

Rhubarb and Strawberry Compôte Ⓥ

Fresh rhubarb has only a short season, so take advantage of it while you can, although you can also use thawed frozen fruit if you want to enjoy the dessert at other times of the year.

SERVES 6

450 g/1 lb strawberries, quartered
450 g/1 lb rhubarb, thickly sliced
100 g/4 oz caster sugar
50 ml/2 fl oz water

Combine all the ingredients in the slow cooker. Cover and cook on High until the fruit is soft, about 1½ hours. If you prefer a thicker consistency, cook, uncovered, for a further 30 minutes.

Winter Fruit Compôte Ⓥ

A useful storecupboard dessert that has lots of flavour and all the goodness that dried fruit contains. Serve over slices of Orange Pound Cake (see page 382) or scoops of ice-cream.

SERVES 6

200 g/7 oz dried mixed fruit
175 g/6 oz dried peaches or pears
½ lemon, thinly sliced
150 ml/¼ pint sweet red wine or apple juice
120 ml/4 fl oz apple juice
150 g/5 oz caster sugar
½ cinnamon stick
6 whole cloves
a pinch of salt

Combine all the ingredients in the slow cooker. Cover and cook on High for 2–3 hours, stirring after 1 hour. Serve warm or at room temperature.

Apple and Cranberry Compôte (V)

Such an easy dessert to prepare and so tasty, topped with crunchy granola.

SERVES 6

**4 eating apples, peeled, cored and
  sliced
100 g/4 oz dried cranberries
65 g/2½ oz light brown sugar
25 g/1 oz butter (optional)
1 tsp ground cinnamon
¼ tsp freshly grated nutmeg
¼ tsp salt
75 g/3 oz granola with nuts**

Combine all the ingredients, except the granola, in the slow cooker. Cover and cook on High until the apples are tender, 1½–2 hours. Sprinkle each serving with granola.

Almond Streusel (V)

Great for sprinkling over fruit or ice-cream.

SERVES 6

**75 g/3 oz plain flour
50 g/2 oz sugar
25 g/1 oz chopped almonds
50 g/2 oz butter, melted
a pinch of salt**

Mix all the ingredients with a fork until the mixture is crumbly. Using your hands, squeeze the mixture into clumps, using 2–3 tbsp for each. Put on a baking sheet. Bake at 180°C/gas 4/fan oven 160°C until lightly browned, about 10 minutes. Break into medium–large pieces with a fork.

Autumn Fruit Crisp (V)

Late-harvest peaches and cooking apples combine to capture the flavours of autumn.

SERVES 6

**10 peaches, sliced
2 small cooking apples, sliced
50 g/2 oz raisins
75 g/3 oz honey
Almond Streusel (see below)**

Combine the peaches, apples, raisins and honey in the slow cooker. Cover and cook on High until the apples are tender, about 1½ hours. Serve warm, sprinkling each serving with Almond Streusel.

Peach and Apple Cobbler (V)

Baked scones make a perfect cobbler topping. Serve with dollops of whipped cream or scoops of vanilla ice-cream.

SERVES 8

**4 cooking apples, peeled and sliced
900 g/2 lb fresh peaches, peeled and
  sliced
150 g/5 oz caster sugar
150 g/5 oz light brown sugar
2 tbsp flour
½ tsp ground cinnamon
¼ tsp freshly grated nutmeg
3 tbsp cold butter or margarine, cut
  into pieces
4 scones, halved
2 tsp butter or margarine, melted
1 tbsp cinnamon sugar**

Toss the fruit with the combined sugars, the flour and spices and spoon into the slow cooker. Cover and cook on High until the fruit is tender, about 2 hours. Arrange the scone halves, cut sides down, on the fruit during the last 30 minutes of cooking, and dot with cold butter or margarine. Brush the scones lightly with the melted butter or margarine and sprinkle with cinnamon sugar. Serve warm.

Chocolate Fondue Ⓥ

Back to the 1970s for the revival of a popular party dish. It's a must for chocaholics!

SERVES 16

900 g/2 lb dark chocolate, coarsely chopped
175–250 ml/6–8 fl oz single cream or full-fat milk
3–4 tbsp rum or brandy (optional)
dippers: whole strawberries, fruit pieces, cake

Combine the chocolate and cream or milk in a 1.5 litre/2½ pint slow cooker. Cover and cook on Low until the chocolate has melted, 30–45 minutes. Whisk in the rum or brandy. Serve with the dippers.

Chocolate and Orange Fondue Ⓥ

The classic combination with the added punch of liqueur.

SERVES 16

900 g/2 lb milk chocolate, coarsely chopped
175–250 ml/6–8 fl oz single cream or full-fat milk
3–4 tbsp orange liqueur (optional)
dippers: whole strawberries, fruit pieces, cake

Combine the chocolate and cream or milk in a 1.5 litre/2½ pint slow cooker. Cover and cook on Low until the chocolate has melted, 30–45 minutes. Whisk in the liqueur. Serve with the dippers.

Chocolate and Coconut Fondue Ⓥ

An interesting combination that gives you a South Seas flavour.

SERVES 16

450 g/1 lb dark chocolate, coarsely chopped
450 g/1 lb milk chocolate, coarsely chopped
175–250 ml/6–8 fl oz single cream or full-fat milk
400 g/14 oz can coconut milk
25 g/1 oz flaked coconut
1 tsp vanilla essence
dippers: whole strawberries, fruit pieces, cake

Combine the chocolates, cream or milk and coconut milk in a 1.5 litre/2½ pint slow cooker. Cover and cook on Low until the chocolate has melted, 30–45 minutes. Stir in the flaked coconut and vanilla essence. Serve with the dippers.

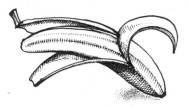

Chocolate and Cream Cheese Fondue Ⓥ

A delicious option with a cream cheese addition.

SERVES 16

450 g/1 lb dark chocolate, coarsely chopped
450 g/1 lb milk chocolate, coarsely chopped
175–250 ml/6–8 fl oz single cream or full-fat milk
450 ml/¾ pint full-fat milk
175 g/6 oz cream cheese, at room temperature

dippers: whole strawberries, fruit pieces, cake

Combine the chocolates and cream or milk in a 1.5 litre/2½ pint slow cooker. Cover and cook on Low until the chocolate has melted, 30–45 minutes. Whisk in the cream cheese. Serve with the dippers.

White Chocolate Fondue Ⓥ

For those who love rich, white chocolate.

SERVES 16

900 g/2 lb white chocolate chips
175–250 ml/6–8 fl oz single cream or full-fat milk
75 g/3 oz chopped almonds, toasted

dippers: whole strawberries, fruit pieces, cake

Combine the chocolate and cream or milk in a 1.5 litre/2½ pint slow cooker. Cover and cook on Low until the chocolate has melted, 30–45 minutes. Whisk in the almonds. Serve with the dippers.

Rum Raisin Caramel Fondue Ⓥ

Sweet and naughty! A fun fondue for party time. You can buy marshmallow fluff from specialist suppliers.

SERVES 12

600 ml/1 pint caramel or toffee ice-cream topping
100 ml/3½ fl oz marshmallow cream (marshmallow fluff)
50 g/2 oz chopped raisins
1–2 tbsp light rum or ½ tsp rum essence

dippers: vanilla wafers, pretzels, apple slices, banana pieces

Combine all the ingredients in a 1.5 litre/ 2½ pint slow cooker. Cover and cook on Low until hot, 1–1½ hours. Serve with the dippers.

Peanut Butter Caramel Fondue Ⓥ

Another sweet and fluffy fondue, but with a crunch too!

SERVES 12

600 ml/1 pint caramel or toffee ice-cream topping
100 ml/3 ½ fl oz marshmallow cream (marshmallow fluff)
100 g/4 oz peanut butter
40 g/1½ oz peanuts, coarsely chopped and toasted

dippers: vanilla wafers, pretzels, apple slices, banana pieces

Combine the ice-cream topping and marshmallow cream in a 1.5 litre/2½ pint slow cooker. Stir in the peanut butter and peanuts. Cover and cook on Low until hot, 1–1½ hours. Serve with the dippers.

Drinks

Finally, here is how you can use your slow cooker to make some delectable drinks.

Hot Mulled Cider Ⓥ

Slow cookers are great for making warm beverages and keeping them at the perfect serving temperature.

SERVES 16

2.25 litres/4 pints cider
100 g/4 oz light brown sugar
1½ tsp whole cloves
1 tsp whole allspice
2 cinnamon sticks
1 orange, unpeeled and sliced

Combine all the ingredients in the slow cooker, tying the spices in a muslin bag. Cover and cook on High for 2–3 hours (if the mixture begins to boil, turn the heat to Low). Remove the spice bag. Turn the heat to Low to keep warm for serving.

Ginger-spiced Cider Ⓥ

Ginger and cider go surprisingly well together to make a warming winter drink.

SERVES 16

2.25 litres/4 pints cider
8 x 5 mm/¼ in slices fresh root ginger

Put the cider and ginger slices in the slow cooker. Cover and cook on High for 2–3 hours (if the mixture begins to boil, turn the heat to Low). Remove the ginger with a slotted spoon. Turn the heat to Low to keep warm for serving.

Rosemary-scented Cider Ⓥ

Not a combination that might spring immediately to mind, but do try it because it's delicious.

SERVES 16

2.25 litres/4 pints cider
2 x 10 cm/4 in sprigs of fresh rosemary or 1 tbsp dried rosemary leaves

Put the cider and rosemary in the slow cooker, tying the rosemary in a muslin bag. Cover and cook on High for 2–3 hours (if the mixture begins to boil, turn the heat to Low). Remove the muslin bag. Turn the heat to Low to keep warm for serving.

Lavender-scented Cider Ⓥ

Lavender has a great many culinary uses but more often in desserts and cakes than as part of a mulled drink.

SERVES 16

2.25 litres/4 pints cider
2 x 10 cm/4 in sprigs of lavender or 1 tbsp dried lavender leaves

Put the cider and lavender in the slow cooker, tying the lavender in a muslin bag. Cover and cook on High for 2–3 hours (if the mixture begins to boil, turn the heat to Low). Remove the muslin bag. Turn the heat to Low to keep warm for serving.

Apricot and Apple Cider 🅥

You could also use any exotic fruit juice, such as mango, instead of the apricot juice.

SERVES 16

**1.2 litres/2 pints cider
1.2 litres/2 pints apricot juice
100 g/4 oz light brown sugar
1½ tsp whole cloves
1 tsp whole allspice
2 cinnamon sticks
1 orange, unpeeled and sliced
50–120 ml/2–4 fl oz apricot brandy
  (optional)**

Combine all the ingredients, except the apricot brandy, in the slow cooker, tying the spices in a muslin bag. Cover and cook on High for 2–3 hours (if the mixture begins to boil, turn the heat to Low). Remove the muslin bag. Turn the heat to Low to keep warm for serving. At the end of cooking time, stir in the apricot brandy, if using.

Fruit Wassail 🅥

A warming hot drink, made with a blend of fruit juices, spiked with rum.

SERVES 12

**450 ml/¾ pint cranberry juice
450 ml/¾ pint pineapple juice
450 ml/¾ pint orange juice
1 small orange, unpeeled and sliced
100 g/4 oz caster sugar
1 cinnamon stick
1 tsp whole allspice
50–120 ml/2–4 fl oz lemon juice
120 ml/4 fl oz light rum (optional)**

Combine all the ingredients, except the lemon juice and rum, in the slow cooker. Cover and cook on High for 2–3 hours (if the mixture begins to boil, turn the heat to Low). Season to taste with lemon juice. Stir in the rum, if using. Turn the heat to Low to keep warm for serving.

Cranberry Cider 🅥

The nutritional value and antioxidant qualities of cranberries are well-known, so you can enjoy this drink all the more as you will be doing yourself good!

SERVES 16

**1.5 litres/2½ pints cider
750 ml/1¼ pints cranberry juice
1½ tsp whole cloves
1 tsp whole allspice
2 cinnamon sticks
1 orange, unpeeled and sliced
brown sugar, to taste**

Combine all the ingredients, except the brown sugar, in the slow cooker, tying the spices in a muslin bag. Cover and cook on High for 2–3 hours (if the mixture begins to boil, turn the heat to Low). Remove the muslin bag. Sweeten to taste with brown sugar. Turn the heat to Low to keep warm for serving.

Hot Spiced Wine 🅥

What drink could be better for winter celebrations such as Halloween, Christmas and New Year?

SERVES 16

**1.8 litres/3¼ pints sweet red wine or
  sweet sherry
100 g/4 oz light brown sugar
1½ tsp whole cloves
1 tsp whole allspice
2 cinnamon sticks
1 orange, unpeeled and sliced**

Combine all the ingredients in the slow cooker, tying the spices in a muslin bag. Cover and cook on High for 2–3 hours (if the mixture begins to boil, turn the heat to Low). Remove the muslin bag. Turn the heat to Low to keep warm for serving.

Five-spice Fruit Punch (V)

Commercial Chinese five-spice mixes tend to vary but the most common combination is star anise, cloves, cinnamon, Sichuan pepper and fennek seeds, not necessarily in equal quantities.

SERVES 12

450 ml/¾ pint cider
450 ml/¾ pint pineapple juice
450 ml/¾ pint orange juice
1 small orange, unpeeled and sliced
100 g/4 oz caster sugar
1 tbsp Chinese five-spice powder

Combine all the ingredients in the slow cooker. Cover and cook on High for 2–3 hours (if the mixture begins to boil, turn the heat to Low). Turn the heat to Low to keep warm for serving.

Glogg

This hot wine punch is traditionally made with raisins and whole almonds.

SERVES 12

1 bottle (750 ml) Bordeaux
1 bottle (750 ml) port
2 tbsp grated orange zest
4 small cinnamon sticks
4 cardamom pods
4 whole cloves
100 g/4 oz blanched almonds
175 g/6 oz raisins
120–250 ml/4–8 fl oz Cognac or brandy

Combine all the ingredients, except the almonds, raisins and Cognac or brandy, in the slow cooker, tying the orange zest and spices in a muslin bag. Cover and cook on High for 2–3 hours (if the mixture begins to boil, turn the heat to Low), adding the almonds and raisins during the last hour. Remove the muslin bag and stir in the Cognac or brandy. Turn the heat to Low to keep warm for serving.

Hot Ginger Lemonade (V)

Yes, there is lemonade for every season! Enjoy this gingery version hot, or chill and serve over ice in the summer.

SERVES 12

1.2 litres/2 pints water
175 ml/6 fl oz lemon juice
175 g/6 oz sugar
5 cm/2 in piece fresh root ginger, sliced

Combine all the ingredients in the slow cooker. Cover and cook on High for 2–3 hours (if the mixture begins to boil, turn the heat to Low). Turn the heat to Low to keep warm for serving.

Hot Cranberry Mint Lemonade (V)

Slow cooking allows the flavour of even this small quantity of mint to permeate into the cranberry juice to make an intriguingly fresh, yet warm, drink.

SERVES 12

600 ml/1 pint water
600 ml/1 pint cranberry juice
175 ml/6 fl oz lemon juice
175 g/6 oz sugar
1 tbsp dried mint

Combine all the ingredients, except the mint, in the slow cooker. Cover and cook on High for 2–3 hours, adding the mint, tied in a muslin bag, for the last hour (if the mixture begins to boil, turn the heat to Low). Remove the muslin bag. Turn the heat to Low to keep warm for serving.

Sweet Cinnamon Java Ⓥ

This spiced coffee is also refreshing served chilled over crushed ice.

SERVES 12

2.25 litres/4 pints water
40 g/1½ oz dark roast regular ground coffee
100–150 g/4–5 oz light brown sugar
2 small cinnamon sticks
8 whole cloves

Combine all the ingredients in the slow cooker, tying the spices in a muslin bag. Cover and cook until hot and steaming (do not boil), about 2 hours. Remove the muslin bag. Turn the heat to Low to keep warm for serving.

Honey and Orange Coffee Ⓥ

The combination of coffee, honey, spices and orange may be unusual – but try it and you'll agree that it really does work.

SERVES 12

2.25 litres/4 pints water
40 g/1½ oz dark roast regular ground coffee
75 g/3 oz honey
2 small cinnamon sticks
8 whole cloves
grated zest from ¼ orange

Combine all the ingredients in the slow cooker, tying the spices and orange zest in a muslin bag. Cover and cook until hot and steaming (do not boil), about 2 hours. Remove the muslin bag. Turn the heat to Low to keep warm for serving.

Honey Chai Ⓥ

This aromatic spiced tea is flavoured with cinnamon, cardamom and ginger, and sweetened with honey.

SERVES 12

1.5 litres/2½ pints water
450 ml/¾ pint whole milk
2 cinnamon sticks
1 tsp ground cardamom
2.5 cm/1 in piece fresh root ginger, sliced
175 g/6 oz honey
12 black tea bags or 20g/¾oz loose black tea

Combine all the ingredients in the slow cooker. Cover and cook on High until hot and steaming (do not boil), about 2 hours. Remove the tea bags and fresh root ginger with a slotted spoon. Turn the heat to Low to keep warm for serving, strained if necessary.

Green Tea and Soya Chai Ⓥ

Green tea is believed to have many health benefits, including assisting weight loss and preventing heart disease and cancer.

SERVES 12

1.5 litres/2½ pints water
450 ml/¾ pint vanilla soya milk
2 cinnamon sticks
1 tsp ground cardamom
2.5 cm/1 in piece fresh root ginger, sliced
12 green tea bags or 20g/¾oz loose green tea
75–175 g/3–6 oz honey

Combine all the ingredients, except the honey, in the slow cooker. Cover and cook on High until hot and steaming (do not boil), about 2 hours. Remove the tea bags and fresh root ginger with a slotted spoon. Turn the heat to Low to keep warm for serving, strained if necessary. Sweeten to taste with honey.

Hot Chocolate

A favourite drink for after a swim, or in the winter – or just about anytime. Add marshmallows to each cup of Hot Chocolate, if you like.

SERVES 12

50 g/2 oz cocoa powder
100 g/4 oz sugar
½ tsp ground cinnamon
a pinch of salt
2.25 litres/4 pints whole milk
½ tsp vanilla essence

Combine the cocoa powder, sugar, cinnamon and salt in the slow cooker. Whisk in enough milk to make a smooth paste. Whisk in the remaining milk and the vanilla essence.

Cover and cook on High until hot and steaming (do not boil), about 2 hours. Turn the heat to Low to keep warm for serving.

Brazilian Mocha Ⓥ

Strong and sweet – great for serving to friends at a winter gathering.

SERVES 12

50 g/2 oz cocoa powder
100 g/4 oz sugar
a pinch of salt
1.2 litres/2 pints whole milk
750 ml/1¼ pints strong brewed coffee

Combine the cocoa powder, sugar and salt in the slow cooker. Whisk in enough milk to make a smooth paste. Whisk in the remaining milk and the coffee.

Cover and cook on High until hot and steaming (do not boil), about 2 hours. Turn the heat to Low to keep warm for serving.

Spiced White Chocolate Ⓥ

For a richer hot chocolate, substitute single cream for part of the milk.

SERVES 12

175 g/6 oz white chocolate chips
1.8 litres/3¼ pints whole milk
¼ tsp ground cinnamon
¼ tsp freshly grated nutmeg

Put the chocolate chips in the slow cooker. Cover and cook on Low until the chocolate has melted, about 30 minutes.

Gradually whisk in the milk and spices. Cover and cook on High until hot and steaming (do not boil), about 2 hours. Turn the heat to Low to keep warm for serving.

Peppermint Cocoa Ⓥ

Deliciously indulgent and great for after dinner.

SERVES 12

175 g/6 oz white chocolate chips
1.8 litres/3¼ pints whole milk
½–1 tsp peppermint essence
whipped cream and crushed
**   peppermint sweets, to decorate**

Put the chocolate chips in the slow cooker. Cover and cook on Low until the chocolate has melted, about 30 minutes.

Gradually whisk in the milk and peppermint essence. Cover and cook on High until hot and steaming (do not boil), about 2 hours. Turn the heat to Low to keep warm for serving. Serve topped with whipped cream and crushed peppermint sweets.

Index